Corporatism and Development

Corporatism and Development

The Portuguese Experience

Howard J. Wiarda

The University of Massachusetts Press
Amherst 1977

40000

Copyright © 1977 by
Howard J. Wiarda
All rights reserved
Library of Congress Catalog Card Number 76–8761
ISBN 0–87023–221–5
Printed in the United States of America
Designed by Mary Mendell
Library of Congress Cataloging in Publication
data appear on the last printed page of the book.

To Iêda
with love and many thanks
and to Jonathan
bebê português

Contents

40000

Preface

This book is both a case study of corporatism and development in modern Portugal and an exploration with broader implications in the realms of comparative political theory and sociology. It grows out of a long-term scholarly interest in the comparative processes of national development, focused particularly on Latin America.

Despite the obvious differences between a Paraguay, say, and a Peru, there are also some remarkable similarities among the several Latin American countries, particularly so as the values, assumptions, and sociopolitical underpinnings of Latin American civilization, viewed as a culture area, are contrasted with those of North America. Whereas the North American context is thoroughly liberal and Lockean in assumptions, in Latin America one is impressed by the continuity and persistence of organicist and corporatist conceptions of society and polity, of elitist, vertical, segmented, hierarchical, patrimonialist structures and practices. Not only is there little discernible trend in Latin America toward liberalism patterned on the North American model, but, contrary to our usual social-science assumptions, Latin America's own traditional institutions have shown remarkable adaptability to change and modernization.

The Latin American systems and their development patterns conform imperfectly at best to the great social science paradigms with which North American students most frequently come in contact. Moreover, a closer examination of the Latin American and Iberian literature and development experience reveals not only that the cultural and political-sociological frameworks for dealing with modernization are distinct but that there is a whole body of political theory and sociological literature "out there" with which North Americans are almost wholly unacquainted. This literature and tradition stand as the Iberic-Latin alternative to the other major paradigms in history and the social sciences with which we are more familiar. What I have termed "the corporative model" helps form the Iberic-Latin-Catholic world's response to the great twentieth-

century issues of capitalism, industrialization, alienation, and mass society. It is, furthermore, a tradition of thought and institutions with
which we must come to grips if we are to understand the nature of politics and social change in Iberia and Latin America, *and* to understand
it on their terms rather than through the biased, often ethnocentric perspectives of North American sociology and political science. Hence the
idea for a research project in Iberia to get at the historical roots of these
differences and the origins of the distinct Iberic-Latin tradition.

There are other currents and concerns running through the book. One
involves the distinction between what might be called "natural corporatism" in the Iberic-Latin tradition and monolithic totalitarianism and
fascism, as for example in Nazi Germany. Another, already hinted at,
involves the appropriateness (or inappropriateness) of so much of what
passes for "universal" social science in the study of Iberia and Latin
America. A third concerns the degree to which "liberal" North America, and perhaps other modern industrial states, may have also come to
approximate the highly centralized, bureaucratic-authoritarian, and corporatist systems of Iberia and Latin America. Fascinating also are topics
such as the role and importance of intellectuals in the Portuguese system, the question of succession in a corporatist-authoritarian polity, and
the decline-of-ideology theme as it relates to the discussion of corporatism
in Portugal. Finally, there is the possible convergence between liberal,
corporatist, and socialist systems, and the question of whether, in terms
of regime performance, "systems" matter very much at all.

These are big and important issues; they cannot all be resolved here.
The book is organized around the subject area of the theory and practice of Portuguese corporatism, and surely a study of the Portuguese
political system in its own right is long overdue. But the book's implications reach beyond Portugal to encompass parallel issues of corporatist development elsewhere in the Iberic-Latin world—and perhaps in
our own and other modern nations as well. Though the case study materials here used are drawn from Portugal, the broader theme of corporatist development seen in historical and comparative perspective is of
at least equal importance.

Having said what the book is about, we should mention what is left
out. Although, like almost everyone in Portugal, the author was fascinated and preoccupied with the Portuguese colonial situation, this subject is not dealt with in any detail except as it became intertwined with
domestic Portuguese politics and insofar as the effort was made to export the corporative system to the "overseas." Nor does the book deal
extensively with the politics of the Portuguese opposition groups during

the long Salazar-Caetano era, except as their critiques of the corporatist system had implications for this study. Finally, although the author has followed closely the Portuguese revolution since 1974 and has elsewhere written about it, in this book the revolution's chronology is not traced in detail. Instead, in keeping with the main focus of the study, the author has concentrated on showing how easy it was to dismantle the *formal apparatus* of the corporative state, yet how difficult it is to overcome or transcend the nation's historic, *natural* corporatist tradition, and how persistent corporatist forms and institutions are, even in the newer charged and revolutionary context.

This is a serious and scholarly book, but it is also likely to be a provocative one. Portugal has become a modern nation over the course of the past several decades, but it became so on the basis of frankly authoritarian and corporatist institutions. Given our frequent assumptions of unilinear development toward democracy and pluralism, that a nation can modernize on an authoritarian-corporatist basis may be surprising to some, that it can do so without having much desire for liberalism and democracy, North American style, may be more controversial. This book argues that corporatism, authoritarianism, and patrimonialism may be characteristic, even permanent features of the Portuguese and Iberic-Latin systems, not just transitory ones doomed inevitably to fade away or be superseded in the course of societal evolution. These contentions will doubtless provoke disagreement since they run contrary to popular beliefs and hopes and to many of the accepted "truths" growing out of the development literature and the great systemic models in the social sciences. They also challenge some of the prevailing interpretations of the revolution of 1974 by implicitly questioning just how "democratic" and "liberalizing" that revolution was. The book is purposely provocative in these regards: it was conceived and designed with the expectation of challenging prevailing orthodoxies, and it is hoped that the ideas presented will stimulate discussion of themes too often closed.

This study is hardly an apology for the Salazar regime, but it is not a blanket condemnation of the Estado Novo either. The book seeks to strike a balance between the contending interpretations of the Portuguese regime, to be fair and impartial in analyzing both the successes and the failures of the Portuguese corporative experiment. The corporative system of Salazar and Caetano was far more social justice oriented than it is often portrayed, and use of the "fascist" label serves more to perpetuate myths about the regime than to illuminate its actual assumptions and workings. However, those long sympathetic to the Portuguese regime will find the corporative system did not work at all in accord with the original theory; contrary to what many, especially Catholic and Latin American writers, thought in the 1930s, the future proved not to lie in Portugal.

Field work for this study was undertaken in Portugal from November 1972 until July 1973 with the aid of a research fellowship from the Foreign Area Fellowship Program, Joint Committee on Latin American Studies of the American Council of Learned Societies and the Social Science Research Council. The research in Portugal was part of an ambitious sabbatical year granted by the University of Massachusetts, which enabled us also to conduct research in the Dominican Republic and Venezuela during the spring and summer of 1972 and in Brazil during the fall, before going on to Portugal. That experience, plus the requirement that we visit Spain at least once every sixty days to get our Portuguese visas renewed, enabled us to gain a broader and renewed comparative perspective on corporative development in the Iberic-Latin world that proved invaluable in framing this book. In March/April 1974 the author returned to Portugal for further interviews and to update some of his materials; in May/June 1975 he was again in Portugal to conduct research on the revolution.

It should be noted that the first-person plural in the preceding paragraph refers not to the royal "we" but to the whole family: Dr. Iêda Siqueira Wiarda, herself an American-trained political scientist who embodies that rare combination of an understanding of the general theoretical literature plus a capacity to function in and understand Iberic-Latin society as only a native to the area can; Kristy Lynn, our *dominicanita;* Howard Elvindo, our *gringo;* and Jonathan, a *português* whose arrival greatly facilitated our acceptance into Portuguese society. I am deeply indebted also to the "luncheon crew" of Sidney Greenfield, Richard A. H. Robinson, and Douglas Wheeler, augmented from time to time by other scholars working in Portugal during this period, whose bibliographic assistance, helpful hints as to how to find certain materials, and general discussion of the workings of the Portuguese system were invaluable.

The research for this book is based chiefly on archival and library materials, participant observation in most of the agencies studied, and interviews. The author is especially grateful to Dr. Manuel Estevens, Director of the National Library, and his staff; and to Professor Antonio da Silva Leal, then Director of the Center for Social and Corporative Studies in the Ministry of Corporations and Social Assistance (now Ministry of Labor), who, without imposing any conditions on the research, put the facilities, materials, and personnel of the ministry largely at the author's disposal. Professors J. Pires Cardoso, João Pinto de Costa Leite, João Baptista Nunes Pereira Neto, and Dr. Henry H. Keith helped also in numerous ways. Interviewing was a complex, difficult, and sensitive phenomenon in authoritarian Portugal, which the author found was facilitated by preinterview assurances of anonymity (a brief Note on Methodology follows the main body of the book). Though they cannot all be thanked by name here, the numerous government officials, trade union leaders, corporations officials, and many others in various sectors of Portuguese society who granted the author access and interviews proved invaluable to the further understanding of how the Portuguese system worked (or failed to work).

Mrs. Doris Holden proved to be an excellent editor as well as the best typist ever; and Leone Stein and Malcolm L. Call, director and editor respectively of the University of Massachusetts Press, provided much useful counsel. Kenneth P. Erickson and the late Kalman H. Silvert offered long, useful critiques of the entire manuscript; Philippe C. Schmitter has helped the author see some of the broader ramifications of corporatist development.

None of these individuals or organizations is responsible for the final conclusions reached; that responsibility rests solely with the author.

Howard J. Wiarda
Norwich Hill *Quinta*
Summer 1976

Corporatism and Development

I

Introduction: Portugal and the Corporative Framework

Why Portugal?

A number of the themes mentioned in the preface demand further explanation. Some of the ideas expressed may be surprising, a few shocking. The main questions are: Why study Portugal at all, other than as a single, heretofore unimportant nation whose internal politics have suddenly become of interest to us; and what is there, if anything, that we can possibly learn from the Portuguese and, more broadly, Iberic-Latin development experience? [1]

These are good questions, and they merit serious consideration. We are used to thinking of Latin America along with the rest of the "emerging," "backward," or "developing" nations, and we think of Spain and Portugal (when we think of them at all) as the retrograde backwaters of Western Europe. It is not only our economic indices that confine Spain, Portugal, and Latin America to an inferior place, however, but our social, political, and perhaps even moral measures as well. We tend to consider these nations as twentieth-century anachronisms, countries whose authoritarian, patrimonialist, and corporative political institutions are of another, earlier era, bound inevitably to give way or be transcended under the onslaught of modernizing pressures. Some of this sentiment stems from historic prejudices held by North Americans and northern Europeans ("Europe stops at the Pyrenees"), some undoubtedly originates in racial and ethnic prejudice, and some probably comes from a certain vague hostility which the Protestant and secular nations of the North still direct toward the Catholic cultures of the South. What gives these historic prejudices the cover of academic respectability is that vast body of development literature which, despite numerous individual differences in formulation, continues to posit a unilinear path to modernization. The "developed" society is seen as open, liberal, pluralist, secular, and democratic, a society in fact "just like us," or at least as we thought of ourselves up to the mid-1960s. Viewed in terms of these ostensibly "scientific" and "value-free" but actually heavily normative developmental characteristics, the Iberian and Latin American nations clearly do not measure up.[2]

Intervention in the Dominican Republic in 1965, Vietnam, the decline of United States power and influence, reassertive nationalism in other areas of the world, the structural weaknesses of the American economy, Nixon, Watergate, the decline of many of our own institutions, the fact that other countries have surpassed us in both social services and per capita income—these things and others have disillusioned us and sapped our belief in the superiority of American institutions. They have also helped challenge our assumptions of the inevitability of progress, American style, and of the unilinear nature of the development process, with our own and perhaps a select group of Western European nations serving as the model toward which all other nations both aspired and inevitably developed. The recent crisis in American and "Western" institutions has also been influential in forcing social scientists to see more clearly what should have been perceived all along: that there are not one or two but several paths to development and that the particular North American and North European one is not only not universal or inevitable but may not even be desirable.

By this time it is likely that we do not have the will or power to impose our particular model of society, economy, and polity on the rest of the world. Nor do the models based exclusively on the North American and North-West European development experience any longer carry much credibility as universally valid phenomena. Meanwhile, our own political institutions, which derive from the time of the English Tudors, have recently been challenged as being as old-fashioned, outdated, and "underdeveloped" as are those of the "developing nations."[3] It may surprise us to know that four and a half centuries ago Spanish and Portuguese intellectuals saw the fundamental flaws in the liberal-secular model that the "death of liberalism" scholars are now again bringing to our attention. The question merits more attention than can be given here, but we raise it nonetheless: who are we, after all, to assume that the in many ways prevailing Thomistic-Suárezian-corporatist social and political institutions of Iberia and Latin America are any more dated or less developed than liberal-Lockean ones, any more corrupt or nefarious in an ethical sense, or any less functional or capable of adaptation, responsiveness, and modernization?[4]

The twentieth century, particularly the period between its two world wars, has been a time of intense interest in such "system" issues and of immense competition among contrasting ideologies. Organized Communist, Socialist, Corporatist, Fascist, and a number of other major movements have emerged. The ideas undergirding these movements had all been present before; what now gave them special importance were the mushrooming collapse of aristocratic society in Britain, Germany, and Austria, World War I and the changes it ushered in, the Russian Revolution, the world market crash, the intense political conflicts of the 1920s and 1930s, the rise of Hitler and Mussolini, and the events leading to World War II. In this context new and challenging social and political forces grew while old ones struggled to survive, and various means of combining them were attempted. To moderates and Catholics, socialism, especially as practiced in Stalin's Russia, was totally unacceptable; the depression seemed to indicate that liberalism and capitalism were no longer viable; and the totalitarian excesses of National Socialism were also repugnant. To comprehend the impact of corporatism as an alternative "great ism," particularly in the Catholic southern European and Latin American context, one must try to place oneself in the collapsing, disintegrating context of the 1930s and to understand corporatism's popularity in the light of what seemed the unacceptability of the other alternatives.

Full-fledged corporatist regimes came to power not only in Portugal, Spain, Brazil, Argentina, and a number of other Latin American countries but also in Austria, Poland, and France. Corporative institutions or "mixed" corporative systems were also established in one form or another in *all* the other Iberian and Latin American nations and in countries as diverse as Belgium, Holland, Italy, Norway, Sweden, and the United States (such institutions as the Tennessee Valley Authority, the National Labor Relations Board, and the Works Progress Administration all derived in part from corporatist inspiration). The Nazi regime incorporated some corporative aspects, but these had been shunted aside by 1936 in favor of the totalitarian behemoth. Italian fascism was closer to the Iberic-Latin (perhaps Mediterranean) model, but corporatism in Italy was consistently a dependent variable, subordinate to Mussolini's personal ambitions, the concept of the all-powerful state, and Italian great-power pretensions. Aside from these two "deviant cases," there were numerous other corporatist institutions and systems that were not only humane and socially just but also oriented toward national modernization. Our understanding of these systems, however, has been neglected and frequently obscured by our mistakenly lumping all of them together under the "fascist" label and by the common assumption that corporatism's time, historically, had already come—and passed.[5] But what did become of all those corporatist systems and institutions of the interwar period; were they viable, how were they formed, and how did they work; what are their ideological underpinnings and assumptions; how have they merged and perhaps converged with other institutions and ideologies; what are we to make of the contemporary revival of corporatist systems in Brazil, Chile, Peru, and elsewhere and of the new wave of academic interest in them; and what are the implications of corporatism as an alternative model for national development? These are some of the questions probed in this book.

The corporative tradition of the late nineteenth and especially the twentieth centuries is one of which we are almost wholly ignorant, or we are so hostile toward it that we dismiss it without further consideration. The fact is, nonetheless, that corporatist theory and organization form the foundation on which virtually all the labor laws and social security systems of the Iberian and Latin American nations are based, through which labor and industrial relations are structured, and on which the majority of the Iberic-Latin social and political systems are grounded, either *de jure* or *de facto*.[6] Corporatism and the corporatist tradition are a "natural," almost inherent part of Iberic-Latin political culture. Although the constitutional forms are often liberal and republican, patterned after British parliamentarism or United States representative democracy, the operating realities in Iberia and Latin America continue to be influenced heavily by both formal corporatist structures and, more importantly, organicist, vertical, hierarchical, and patrimonialist conceptions that lie at the heart of a broader, deeper corporatist tradition.

There is abundant literature on corporatism in French, Italian, German, Spanish, and Portuguese, but almost none in English.[7] Corporatism is a very old concept of state and society, but as a theory it never gained much importance in North American political thought. This relates to the fact that corporatism lies outside the mainstreams of the Anglo-American tradition and the liberal-Lockean ethos. John Quincy Adams and John C. Calhoun have both been claimed for corporatism, but their concepts made little dent in the prevailing individualism and liberalism of North America.[8] In the Continental systems, however, and particularly in the southern, Catholic, Latin nations of Europe and America, with their powerful hierarchical and agrarian-feudal traditions, corporatism found a fertile, lasting, and perhaps permanent breeding ground.[9]

It is important to distinguish between corporatism in the Iberic-Latin tradition and monolithic fascism as practiced in Nazi Germany. "Fascism" is one of those terms that through widespread common usage has lost almost all analytic meaning; it has become a label of disapproval rather than a precise term of analysis. Corporatism was so discredited by its sometime association with nazism that we tend to forget that Brazil, Portugal, Belgium, even Spain and Italy, practiced a form of corporatism that was fundamentally different from that of Nazi Germany. In the Iberic-Latin context the "fascist" label has served often to obscure rather than assist our understanding of these systems, especially as the term implies a blanket condemnation. Nor is it true, as the North American and northern European literature frequently emphasizes, that "the Latins just aren't up to it," that corporatism in such diverse nations as Mexico, Spain, Portugal, Argentina, Peru, or Brazil is merely a "backward" and "less developed" version of German and Italian fascism. Of course there is some overlap between the two concepts, and clearly what such classic writers as Orwell, Burnham, Hemingway, and Ortega y Gasset had to say in the 1930s regarding the looming threat of corporate-fascist-technocratic organization must weigh heavily upon us. In this book, furthermore, we shall be showing how a regime born in a corporatist tradition of concern for social justice and limited government ("corporatism of association" rather than "state corporatism") became an increasingly fascist one. But the distinction between the two forms must still be kept in mind, and there are some fundamental differences. The fact is that in Iberia and Latin America we are not dealing universally with fascist (although they may be corporatist) systems or with retrograde versions of a single "fascist" type. Rather, in the corporatist tradition we are treating a distinctive, alternative, and in many ways peculiarly Iberic-Latin way of coping with and managing the great modern issues of industrialization, mass society, and accelerated social change. This tradition deserves to be examined with care.[10]

Not only have significant development and modernization been achieved in Iberia and Latin America within the corporatist framework, but we should remember also that corporatism, like liberalism or socialism, may take a variety of forms, both as between nations and within a single nation over time. There are humane forms as well as bureaucratic-authoritarian ones, pluralistic types as well as autocratic ones. There are modern, progressive, Christian-Democratic examples as well as earlier Catholic-conservative ones. Corporatism may be fused with liberalism, as in Colombia, or it may take a more socialist or syndicalist form, as in Bosch's Dominican Republic, Goulart's Brazil, Allende's Chile, and perhaps the revolutionary regime that came to power in Portugal in 1974. Although it adds somewhat to the terminological confusion, we must recognize that corporatism may exist in diverse forms and combinations. At the least, therefore, we must examine closely the several national corporatist variations and begin to evaluate them, not through liberal lenses or the biased perspectives of North American social science, but within their own corporate contexts. We shall also be trying to show the factors that account for these variations, the evolution of corporative institutions within a single nation, the relations of corporatism and socioeconomic development, and the dynamic, societal processes by which a simple and traditionalist corporative system may become a modern and complex one.[11]

That is where the study of Portugal enters in. For Portugal was the "purest" of the Iberic-Latin corporative systems, the only one of the numerous corporative experiments of the 1920s and 1930s to have survived into the 1970s—and perhaps beyond. In Portugal a vast body of corporative literature was elaborated, and the structures and institutions of the corporative state were strongly institutionalized. For a time in the 1930s the Portuguese corporative system was *the* model to which many Latin American states looked for inspiration. Moreover, the Portuguese consciously cultivated corporatism as *the* Iberic-Latin alternative to liberalism and socialism. While they were willing to concede that liberal democracy was appropriate for the Anglo-Saxon countries, they saw their own history and institutions as attuned to a different tradition. In Argentina, Bolivia, Brazil, the Dominican Republic, Ecuador, Mexico, Panama, Spain, and elsewhere throughout Europe and the Western Hemisphere, similar sentiments often prevailed and various kinds of manifestly corporative experiments were tried. But these never became full-fledged corporative systems as Portugal did, and in the post-World War II period they exhibited increasingly mixed and overlapping patterns of corporatism, liberalism, and sometimes socialism or syndicalism. Portugal too has by now experienced the superimposition of these other philosophies onto its older corporatist tradition, and since the revolution of 1974 many of the formal corporative institutions associated with the former regime have been dismantled. But for a long time Portugal was the most complete and fully elaborated corporative system extant, and as such it remained a unique social and political laboratory for looking at the "ism" that Manoïlesco forty years ago predicted would be the dominant one of the twentieth century.[12] Moreover, given the remarkable persistence of a broader corporatist-patrimonialist political culture and tradition in Iberia and Latin America where, despite the recent overlaps of other forms and even some revolutionary restructuring, the corporative assumptions and modes may still be dominant (although now altered fundamentally by pluralist and/or syndicalist conceptions), it is instructive to look at the Portuguese experience with corporatism not only because it is interesting and significant in its own right but also because of what it tells us about the workings of other corporatist-inspired political systems.[13]

Implicit in the above discussion are two meanings of the word *corpo-*

ratism. This distinction is critical, but in common usage it is often blurred and has led to a great deal of misunderstanding regarding "the corporative model." The first meaning refers to the consciously and manifestly "corporative" ideology and institutions of the 1920s and 1930s. This is what most people have in mind when they think of corporatism. Corporatism in this sense derives from an ideology articulated in the last half of the nineteenth century, most often Catholic but sometimes secular in origin, which stressed an organicist-solidarist conception of the state and society (government is natural, not evil—it must be unified and harmonized, not checked and balanced), in which governing bodies are chosen not by the direct vote of individuals (as in liberalism) but by indirect election by professional, institutional, social, or economic groups, based on a system of functional representation. This meant the organization of all sectors of the economy, both capital and labor, into exclusive, monopolistic groups and the integration of these groups into a hierarchy of syndicates and representative bodies culminating at the top in a series of "corporations" (hence the term *corporatism*) for each of the nation's major social, political, and economic sectors (government, industry, armed forces, agriculture, religion, and so on).[14] If such structuring was carried out voluntarily and at the grass-roots level, it was called corporatism of association; carried out under government control and direction, as fairly consistently proved to be the case, it meant authoritarian "state corporatism." Within this framework a great number of distinct national corporatist systems and representational schemes were possible.

In theory at least, the various corporative plans of the 1920s and 1930s were aimed at restoring unity to strife-torn nations, providing harmony rather than class conflict, guaranteeing representation to all sectors, providing for social justice, ensuring collective bargaining, ameliorating the alienation of modern mass man, and assuring that the national public interest would be served instead of some narrower sectoral or partisan interest. In the context of the interwar period corporatism struck a tremendously responsive chord, particularly in the Latin-Catholic nations of southern Europe and America, and virtually every one established one or another corporatist-inspired agency or body (most often the labor and social assistance ministries but sometimes also legislatures and councils of state based in whole or part on corporatist functional representation), often with elaborate accompanying legislation. However, with the war, the Nazi atrocities, Nuremberg, and the discrediting of all such "integralist," "corporatist," or "fascist" experiments (the terms were used interchangeably), all these nations (with

Portugal the single exception) divested themselves of their corporatist philosophies, or at least changed the labels of the institutions operating under that name.

Here is where the second definition of corporatism enters in, however, for while in many nations the labels were changed, actual practice remained much the same. The system of corporate sectoral and functional representation, of bureaucratic-patrimonialist state authority, of hierarchy and centralization, of an elite-directed *patrón-cliente* system, of a predominantly Catholic-organicist society and political culture, of an essentially mercantilist and state capitalist economy, was often retained, in whole or in part; but, "for the English (or maybe the Americans or the world) to see," it was rebaptized under "progressive," "populist," "liberal," or "neodemocratic" ("justicialist" in Argentina) labels. Moreover, most of these same practices and institutions have a history reaching back not just to the 1920s or late nineteenth century but hundreds of years to the very origins of Iberian civil society and the state system. This tradition will not be altered overnight regardless of the labels used or the substitution of one ruling clique for another. Although other terms might also be appropriately used (the concept of the "organic state," for example), it is this dominant, historic set of values and institutions in Iberic-Latin society and polity that I have referred to by the shorthand terms "the corporative tradition" or "the corporative model." [15]

This tradition and the undergirding political culture of Catholic, patrimonialist, organicist, corporatist values and institutions remain far stronger than any ephemeral "ism." Indeed, as we shall argue, the consciously "corporative" experiments in Portugal beginning in the 1930s were not a sudden apparition but represented a logical, sequential, twentieth-century extension and elaboration of an older, deeper, "natural" corporatist tradition that had long governed the structure of political institutions and behavior and continues in important ways to do so today. This also helps explain why the corporative solution to "the social question," to the demands of an emerging labor movement, was so strongly favored throughout the Iberic-Latin world, for it was in accord both with prevailing traditions and with the preservation of elitist-patrimonialist hegemony. It also helps make Portugal an interesting case since it provides a veritable "living ideal type," to use Philippe Schmitter's phrase, for observing the overlap and fusion (as well as the later dysfunctional aspects) of the historic corporative tradition with the modern practice of "corporatism." In one form or another the effort to adapt the historic corporatist traditions to the newer institutional requisites of twentieth-century national organization, administration, public policy, and rising social demands remains perhaps the most pressing problem with which all the Iberian and Latin American nations must cope.[16]

The two meanings of *corporatism* hence come together in the study of Portugal. We shall here be concerned not only with the workings and evolution of the Portuguese corporative state from the 1930s through the revolution of 1974 (and beyond) but also with showing how these twentieth-century corporative developments related to (or eventually proved out of accord with) Portugal's historic, *natural* corporatist traditions. We shall be concerned with how the two overlap and commingle and with how the Portuguese state and society have, under corporative auspices, modernized, failed at modernization, or modernized in a skewed pattern. In tracing these developments we shall be drawing out the differences between corporative theory, the ideal-typical corporative model, presented in chapters 1 and 3, *and* the actual practice of Portuguese corporatism, chapters 4–10. This implies also that if corporatism and the Portuguese corporative system are to be criticized, such criticism must be on that model's and society's own terms and in their own context. Comparisons with other systems may also be made, but clearly Portuguese corporatism cannot be condemned (if that is our final conclusion) on the basis of some outside and foreign model bearing little relation to Portuguese culture and history, or by its "failure" to live up to liberal-democratic standards (never its intention; on the contrary, Portugal had explicitly rejected the liberal model). Rather, the Portuguese corporative system can most appropriately be evaluated by considering what preceded it in Portugal's own history, by what succeeded it, and by the realistic choices open to it in the course of the corporative state's own evolution.

These comments imply further that there are dynamics of choice and change within authoritarian-corporative systems, that bureaucratic statism does not rule out the give-and-take of politics and the interest conflict that is part and parcel of it, that the "corporative model" of Iberia and Latin America may be far more flexible and adaptable in responding to political and social pressures than we ordinarily think, and that these systems may, on their terms, be as efficient, rational, and functional in dealing with modernization as the liberal-democratic polities of the North.[17] Such statements fly in the face of our common assumptions regarding Iberia and Latin America, but such assumptions are precisely what this book aims to challenge. For as stifling bureaucracy, centralization, privilege, a certain de facto corporatism, and officially sanctioned immoralism seem to grow in our own society, we have hopefully become a bit more modest as regards our inherent moral and political superiority. These shortcomings have also served to stimulate a reexamination of the American model and of the assumption that liberal democracy U.S.-style occupies a higher, more "developed" plateau and that somehow we know what is right for the rest of the world. Is it in fact the case that the liberal-democratic or social-democratic model is appropriate for or even desired by other nations cast in a different political-cultural framework? Is it not arrogant for us to impose —as we did so often in the 1960s, justified by so much of the social science literature—a set of particularistic, liberal-Lockean and/or New Deal institutions on culture areas where they do not fit? If we are to cease being the policeman of the world, is it not time also for our social scientists to cease presuming to be its philosopher-kings? And as American society seems to be wracked by crime, conflict, crisis, and a certain national disintegration, would it not be interesting to examine a society that has undergone a parallel experience of modernization, but apparently without sacrificing the sense of community, personalism, moral values, and national purpose which we seem to have lost and whose passing we now lament?

The practice of corporatism in Portugal, as it turned out, proved inauspicious for demonstrating the effectiveness and humaneness of the distinct Iberic-Latin development process. Even Portugal had its advantages, however, and unconventional though it may seem to North Americans and northern Europeans, a case can be made that, in comparison with both the liberal and the socialist alternatives, a number of the Iberic-Latin systems, founded upon corporatist principles, come out not altogether badly on a variety of indices of participation, social justice, and the management of the twentieth-century change process. These indices would of course have to be more precisely spelled out, and doubtless some of them would differ from those social scientists have most often used to measure "development." But perhaps terms like *participation* and even *democratization* mean different things in different cultural contexts, and maybe the indices of electoral participation used by North American social scientists are themselves culture bound. Moreover, given the growing realization that the United States has not coped very well with, much less solved, its fundamental problems of poverty, racism, unemployment, alienation, inadequate human services, and the like, it may be that the Iberic-Latin model and practice of dealing with some of these same issues contain lessons from which we can learn. These comments are not meant to minimize Latin America's own problems, the poverty existent, the immense social gaps, but to say that their way of fusing traditional and modern through essentially corporative as opposed to liberal means, of accommodating to change while at the same time preserving what is considered valuable in the past, of adapting to modernization without being overwhelmed by it, may offer instruction concerning our own developmental dilemmas and institutional malaise.

These remarks lead to a related theme, the increasing convergence of the corporative and the liberal polities, and perhaps the socialist ones as well. Spain, Portugal, and the nations of Latin America have increasingly taken on the characteristics of modern systems. This means not just smog, traffic jams, and pollution but also the large-scale organizational paraphernalia of complex, highly developed states: planning offices, regulatory agencies, technical offices, elaborate social welfare systems, price and wage commissions, agencies for worker-management consultation and corepresentation, and mass associations for nearly everyone: workers, elites, professionals, women, students, farmers. They are no longer the simple "banana republics" of *New Yorker* cartoons and popular stereotypes but complex, highly differentiated and rationalized, *modern* systems. Although many of these more recent changes have come under corporative auspices, one could see in them certain "liberal," "pluralist," and, in their more advanced forms, syndicalist and socialist features. But while Iberia and Latin America have in a sense been "liberalized," we have undoubtedly been "corporatized." Many Iberian and Latin American scholars familiar with their northern neighbors and looking at the trends there toward increased centralization and bureaucratization, the incorporations of officially sanctioned and monopolistic interest groups into the administrative state apparatus, price and wage commissions with government intervenors, compulsory collective bargaining, corepresentation, and functionally representative organs at all levels, make a cogent case that, despite the liberal and social-democratic labels, the nations of North America and North Europe have since the war been practicing and evolving increasingly toward a disguised form of corporatism.[18] In the United States, although most liberals hailed the move, the regulation of wages, prices, and production administratively and from above, as in Phase 1 of Nixon's economic controls, instead of through direct bargaining from below, was unheard of previously in peacetime America. The government's setting of prices, wages, and production quotas had long been characteristic of the corporative systems of Iberia and Latin America, not of a liberal laissez-faire polity; and although his comment was an exaggeration, George Meany's cry of "Fascism!" when the Wage and Price Board was first announced was not altogether inaccurate. Canada and other modern industrial nations have experienced recently similar corporatizing trends.

If there is something to this convergence theory, if bigness, bureaucracy, and technocratic state administration of industrial and labor relations are the hallmarks of the modern systems rather than the political "isms" of the past, then we must ask ourselves whether ideology counts for much any more, whether "systems" matter, and if they do, how and in what sense. We know that there has been a certain decline of ideology in other modern nations, that liberalism and socialism may well have lost some of their appeal;[19] is there any reason to think that, as modernization goes forward in the Iberic-Latin countries, the same phenomenon will not occur as regards corporatism? Perhaps such a decline has already occurred. Or, in a related vein, is this the wrong question to ask? Is it true that the corporatist ideology and political culture determined the nature and structure of the Portuguese Estado Novo, or was it rather such structural variables as class and power that determined the direction Portuguese corporatism took? Is corporatism the dependent variable, the elite-bourgeois society and authoritarian state established by Salazar the independent ones? Or is it the case that both sets of factors were important and interrelated in shaping the direction of Portuguese corporative development? Answers to these questions are critical both for understanding the Portuguese regime and for looking at other systems similarly fashioned in the corporatist framework.[20]

Corporatism as a political tradition, ideology, and mode of sociopolitical organization must be taken seriously and examined with care. For just as we take liberalism and socialism seriously, we must also examine this other great "ism" in a serious way. Going further, it may be said that corporatism is *not just* a part of some ideological superstructure or facade, a "confidence trick" played upon the workers (as was the case with corporatism in Italy), nor was it merely a smoke screen to disguise the power ambitions of the Portuguese elites and thus an instrument of class oppression (although, as we shall see, it became that also). The corporatist ideology and political structures, this study clearly shows, had some autonomy and existence of their own; in addition, in the broader political-cultural sense in which the term is also used, corporatism may have been among the most important determinants of how the system actually worked. Portuguese businessmen and workers took corporatism seriously indeed; the same was true for a whole generation of university students and government officials. An entire national system was erected on the corporatist edifice, and much of the corporative system was alive and functioning right to the end. Certainly there were numerous gaps between theory and practice, but the same could be said for liberalism and socialism, and in any case the gaps themselves tell us much about how the system worked or failed to work. It is also the case that corporatism was only tardily and partially implemented, that the "corporative complex" was gradually shunted aside until it was no longer at the base of the entire national system, and that some of the main centers of power in Portugal lay outside the corporative system. All that is true also in varying degree of the other great "isms," and again, the reasons for this and the processes by which these developments occurred are what interest us here. Had the corporatist experiment run its course by the 1960s and, if so, why; and how did that parallel or diverge from the evolution of other types of systems? The study of the Portuguese corporative regime helps answer these questions—if at the same time we recognize that corporatism is but one part of a broader Iberic-Latin political culture and tradition and, similarly, that the corporatist institutions established in Portugal in the 1930s must be studied in the light of other institutions (secret police, armed forces, the instruments of dictatorship, state capitalism, class rule) which gained equal, perhaps greater importance as explanatory variables.[21]

There are two other themes noted in the preface that deserve brief mention. The first, not intrinsic to the main arguments of the book but intriguing nonetheless, concerns the role of intellectuals in power. Not only was the Portuguese corporative system designed by intellectuals, it was also staffed and run in large measure by them. Perhaps in few other nations have intellectuals and sheer intellectual brilliance (as long as it was within the corporatist tradition) been so rewarded in terms of high-level government posts and decision-making influence as in the *catedrátocracia* of Portugal. The fact the system was implemented by the same intellectuals who designed it makes the huge gap between theory and practice especially intriguing. It also suggests some interesting hypotheses as to why Portugal under a particular group of corporatist intellectuals remained locked into a discredited and increasingly dysfunctional form of corporatism at a time when similarly cast corporatist regimes under more pragmatic leadership (Brazil, Spain) cast off their corporatist ideological baggage, or skillfully updated and modernized their systems while staying within the broadly corporatist tradition.[22]

A test of any system and ideology, furthermore, lies in its ability to adjust, survive, and persist in a changing national context and after the demise of its first-generation leadership. Hence our concern also with the transfer of leadership following the end of the longest one-man rule of the twentieth century, with the post-Salazar regime of Marcello Caetano and his efforts to preserve and redynamize the corporative regime while at the same time loosening it somewhat and modernizing and updating it.[23] This subject takes on particular poignancy in the light of the revolution of 1974, the formal repudiation of "corporatism" as practiced by Salazar and Caetano, and the question of whether a new national "ism" will take its place or whether the corporatist tradition will be perpetuated in a new and different form.

The questions raised here for discussion are large, and they speak to some critical issues of social change, political development, and national modernization, not just in Portugal but throughout the Iberic-Latin world. By an interesting inversion of priorities, philosophies, and self-inspection in recent years, they have also come to have relevance to our own time and place.[24] The theme of the "Latin-Americanization" or "corporatization" of the United States no longer seems so farfetched.[25] But as the "purest" and most complete of corporative systems, the Portuguese experience offers abundant illustrative materials as to the special, distinctive character of corporatist development in Iberia and Latin America—and of its implications. Some of those implications may also carry lessons for us.

The Corporative Model

The nations of Iberia and Latin America have long been woefully misunderstood.[26] Although geographically a part of Europe, Spain and Portugal are culturally and politically often considered apart from it; Latin America is frequently lumped with the "non-Western areas." But in their Iberian origins these nations, including the so-called Indian countries of Bolivia, Guatemala, and Peru, are an integral part of a dominantly Western tradition, fragments of that tradition, perhaps, in Louis Hartz's terms, but still deeply and profoundly Western—and, many Iberians argue, with their powerful Roman and Christian traditions, perhaps more "Western" even than the rest of Europe and North America. Nor with their long histories as independent sovereignties do they fit the "new nations" syndrome. And despite the efforts of a few intellectuals to identify them with the cause of "Third Worldism," few Iberian or Latin American nations have very close ties with the nations of Asia and Africa, and when they do, they like to think of themselves not as equals but as leaders and teachers of the Third World in accord with their more developed condition, as bridges between it and the West.[27]

It is not only the classificatory schemes that have proved problematic, however, but the models and paradigms used for explaining Iberic-Latin development as well. The Iberic-Latin systems fail to correspond very well to the Rostovian "stages of growth" or to the Almondian developmental paradigm on the one hand or the Marxian categories on the other. Socioeconomic "modernization" and political "development" have not gone forward hand in hand, one "stage" has stubbornly refused to be replaced by another, the usual developmental correlates do not correlate very well, and the pluralism, middle-class consensus, and greater democratization that supposedly lie at the higher reaches of the development process have failed to take shape. At the same time, the Marxian paradigm has not accounted very well for either the modernizing tendencies of the traditional elites or the continued conservativeness of labor, peasants, and even students; it does not help us understand much about the "class" behavior of such institutions as the Army or the Church; nor does it explain adequately why such commonly middle-sector-dominated nations as Brazil, Peru, Mexico, Portugal or Spain should go in such distinct ideological directions. Class has not proved to be the mirror reflection of socioeconomic history, nor can the political, ideological, or organizational structures of the Iberic-Latin nations be neatly subordinated to some supposed class determinants. The fact that few of these systems correspond very well to the major categories and models used in the social sciences helps account for the many bad books written about them. For we only weakly perceive the Iberic-Latin development process, and when we have sought a better comprehension, we have usually applied to the area a model derived from our own developmental experience that fits poorly, if at all, in the Iberic-Latin ambience.[28]

This brief critique of some of the conventional "wisdom" regarding the nations of Iberia and Latin America serves as the main point of departure for this section; namely, that there are some unique aspects to the processes of sociopolitical change in the Iberic-Latin tradition. Because of their history and antecedents, the Iberic-Latin nations are subject to special imperatives of interpretation and require a model of sociopolitical change derived from the actual Iberic-Latin experience. The Iberic-Latin model, however, is one that seldom finds expression in our studies of the history of political thought or the literature of social and political change. It is one of the arguments of this book that the corporative model helps provide that needed framework, a distinctive, even *fourth* "world of development" that has not yet received the attention it merits.

The major historical influences on the Iberian mother countries of Spain and Portugal were probably the Roman system of law and governance, Christianity and the Thomistic tradition, feudalism and the medieval guild system, and the centuries-long reconquest of the peninsula from the Moors. Roman law gave Spain and Portugal their legal and political foundations; Christianity provided them not only a religious and moral base but also a lasting system of natural law and, culturally, a powerful unifying ingredient; feudalism, patrimonialism, and the guild system brought forth some characteristic forms of social and economic organization; while the crusade against the Moorish "infidels" gave religion a more militant outlook and shaped the Iberian pattern of walled-enclave cities, military orders and special privileges, and class-caste stratification that predominates today. These traditions came together and perhaps reached their apogee in the conquest of the Americas.[29]

We can better understand Iberic-Latin development if we view that culture area as founded upon traditional feudal, semifeudal, and patrimonial institutions rather than "modern" ones. In fifteenth- and sixteenth-century Spain and Portugal, and in the colonies they established in the New World, the dominant institutions were an essentially feudal-patrimonial system of land ownership, power, and lord-peasant relations; an absolutist, hierarchical, and centralizing structure of political authority; a similarly authoritarian and hierarchical Church structure that buttressed and reinforced the state concept; a social order divided vertically in terms of its various corporate units (Church, Army, nobility, universities, municipalities, and so on) and horizontally according to a rigid system of estates, rank orders, statuses, and supposedly "natural" or God-given inequalities; an economy based on monopoly, mercantilism, and privileged grants emanating from the highest authority; and an educational system and intellectual tradition based on absolute truth, deductive reasoning, and scholasticism. Forged and crystallized during and in the aftermath of the crusade against the Moors, these traditions had been firmly established in Spain and Portugal by the end of the fifteenth century, and beginning in 1492 they were transferred to the Americas, where they persisted and received a new lease on life.[30]

The isolation of Latin America from the outside world during the next four centuries, as well as the isolation of Spain and Portugal from the rest of Europe, helped to lock the Iberic-Latin nations into this historic pattern and made their development pattern distinctive. The Iberic-Latin nations were largely bypassed by the great revolutions associated with the making of the modern world. The Protestant Reformation, the rise of capitalism, the Enlightenment and the growth of science, the emergence of social pluralism and of a dominant middle class, the concept of separation of powers and of representative government, the Industrial Revolution and its many-faceted ramifications—

all of these had little effect on the nations of Iberia and Latin America. They remained cut off and isolated from these modernizing currents, at the margin of the ideological trends and sociopolitical movements emerging elsewhere in Europe, fragments of an Iberic-European tradition dating from approximately 1500 with a political culture that was two-class, authoritarian, elitist, patrimonial, hierarchical, and Catholic to its core. Moreover, it was not just an accident that the Iberic-Latin nations were formed in this pattern and experienced only weakly those secular and liberalizing forces taking place to the north; rather, it often involved a conscious, careful filtering or rejection of that route to modernization, an opting instead for a path that was slower, to be sure, but that enabled the Iberic-Latin nations to adapt to change while preserving the traditions and institutions considered valuable from the past.[31]

Given the times and circumstances, it should not be surprising that the Iberic-Latin nations should be structured on these lines. What *is* remarkable is the durability and persistence of these patterns and structures to the present. For despite the recent accelerated onslaught of modernization, the traditional political culture and institutions have proved amazingly permeable and accommodative, bending to change rather than being overwhelmed by it, absorbing what was useful in modernization but rejecting the rest, and thus in many respects retaining their traditional essence even under the pressures of social forces set loose by twentieth-century changes.[32]

In chapter 2 we shall be tracing in more detail the sociopolitical underpinnings of the Portuguese corporative system and in chapter 3 its theoretical and ideological foundations, but it is useful here to outline some of the main currents of this tradition to set it in proper perspective. For example, in the realm of political thought, while modern political analysis beginning with Machiavelli was to lead to the glorification of the accomplished fact and of political pragmatism, secularism, and materialism, Iberic-Latin culture retained at its base a sense of moral idealism, of philosophical certainty, and of a Catholic-corporate-unified-organic view of state and society. The Iberic-Latin conception derived from Cicero and Seneca, from Augustine and Aquinas, and from the traditional legal precepts of medieval times.[33]

In pursuing paths other than those of Protestant or secular thought, the great Spanish thinkers of the sixteenth century such as Suárez laid the foundations for a modern theory of the Christian state and corporative society. In contrast to the separation of politics from morality, which dates from Machiavelli and which *we* usually take to be the beginning of modern political analysis, the Iberic-Latin ideal remained the organic integration of the ethical and sociopolitical spheres. Suárez was able to fuse the older Thomistic conception and the system of juridical estates derived from Spanish feudal and customary law with the newer concept of absolute, state-building, royal authority.[34]

Iberic-Latin political culture, therefore, continued to rest on a philosophy of absolutism, of a world governed by divine authority, of a hierarchy of laws and estates, and of a distrust of popular democratic rule. Government remained feudal, aristocratic, and patrimonial, dominated by "natural" elites, and with the rights and obligations of all groups defined in elaborate charters. The prevailing view of the state and society was organic and conservative and rejected liberal individualism and the materialistic and secular conceptions that accompanied development in northern Europe. Power remained centered in the crown, around which all of national life swirled; there was no conception of separation of powers or of authority resting ultimately in the people. Rather, a unified, monistic structure was required to keep the peace and to maintain the natural order. The king could not rule as a tyrant, however, and he was obligated to respect the fundamental rights of the nation's component corporate groups. This fundamental sixteenth-century pattern remained dominant not only through the colonial and imperial periods of the seventeenth and eighteenth centuries but also, obviously restructured and updated in various ways, during the emergent republicanism of the nineteenth century and even the accelerated industrialization of the twentieth. Indeed, it is the remarkable persistence of this dominant pattern even today, now further adapted to account for contemporary pressures and requirements, that makes the Iberic-Latin development experience so distinctive.[35]

In the sociopolitical realm similar patterns prevail. A good starting point is to picture Iberic-Latin society as organized horizontally in terms of sharply defined hierarchies and a persistent and overriding two-class structure, and vertically in terms of a variety of sharply segmented corporate elites and *interesses*. The crown—and, now, the central state apparatus—controls, manages, and regulates all these sectors and components. Each corporate unit as well as each "class" in the hierarchy has its own responsibilities, status, and special privileges, corresponding to natural law and God's just ordering of the universe. Men are expected to accept their station in life; there can thus be little questioning of the system and little social mobility. The crown (or premier or president) rests at the apex of the sociopolitical pyramid, employing its near monopoly of financial affairs as well as its supreme authority to grant or withhold legal recognition to regulate the corporate group life that swirls beneath it. These units, hence, tend to relate to each other bureaucratically through the central administration, rather than through direct negotiations. The Iberic-Latin model of sociopolitical organization is essentially a patrimonialist one where the wealth of the realm and the groups and individuals that make it up are all a part of the ruler's private domain.[36]

The nineteenth century brought on a severe legitimacy crisis in the political realm, through the influx of republican ideas and the breaking of the ties between colonies and metropoles. However, few sharp changes occurred in the socioeconomic underpinnings or the dominant political culture. Indeed, in many ways the independence movements in Latin America were conservative movements, designed to preserve and perpetuate the system of corporate privilege against the democratizing currents then at work. Republicanism called for some new institutional arrangements, but in essence the hierarchical patterns of class and caste, the system of *fueros* (*foros* in Portuguese) and corporate privilege, the seignorial system of *patrón-cliente* relations, the dominant Catholic political culture, the patrimonialist political structure were in the main unchanged in their fundamentals by nineteenth-century trends.[37]

Considerable change and some modernization could and did take place within this framework; however, these changes were accompanied by only limited shifts in the basic structure of power and society. Thus, in the late nineteenth and early twentieth centuries the rising merchant and business elements were coopted into the prevailing elitist system, and the traditional *hacienda* began to give way to the capitalistic farm or plantation, but without the fundamental *patrón-clientela* relations of the *hacienda* system being very much altered. From roughly the teens on, the emerging middle sectors began to be assimilated in a similar fashion; rather than forming a distinguishable "middle class" with an ideology and consciousness of their own, however, these middle elements aped upper-class ways, subscribed to the elitists values (such as disdain for manual labor), and thus helped preserve the dominant two-class system instead of paving the way for a more pluralist and multi-class one. By the 1930s—and this is largely what the manifestly corporative experiments of that time were all about—it had become the turn of the working class. They too were absorbed into the prevailing structure through the creation of corporatist-inspired, officially sponsored and directed syndicate organizations. By the 1960s it was the peasants' turn to be assimilated, largely through "agrarian reform" programs and the extension of the labor laws of the 1930s and 1940s to the rural areas. In this fashion all the rising social forces have been integrated, in varying degrees, into the prevailing pattern; new corporate and institutional pillars have been repeatedly added onto the original structure consisting of Church, Army, nobility, university, and the like.

But with all these modifications, the basic order of society and polity has remained intact.[38]

Change in the Iberic-Latin context has thus not been "fundamental" in the Marxian or Weberian sense (that is, implying a revolutionary transformation of one class to another or the replacement of one form of authority by another) as it has been a gradual, mediating accommodation of the forms and labels of modern industrial civilization to a political tradition that is still in essence creole-feudal, patrimonialist, and Iberic-Catholic. Numerous adjustments have been made and some new social groups have been assimilated, but this has taken place under the guidance, tutelage, and containment of the older power brokers. The traditional structure of the Iberic-Latin nations, thus, far from having been rigid and impenetrable, has had sufficient flexibility for a good many of its component parts to be updated, but without a swift and radical process of "modernization." [39]

The contemporary change process is consonant with that older historic tradition. In keeping with the Catholic-Thomistic conception (although this conception has by now been largely secularized), society and the state in the Iberic-Latin context are still thought of as an organic whole with a profoundly moral purpose. Attempts are thus made, through personal and family ties, the *compadrazgo,* and personal identification with the leader, as well as an increasingly elaborate system of corporate associations, to construct various linkages so that a sense of "belonging" is engendered, alienation is reduced, and all are integrated into the prevailing structure. Branch associations and official "syndicates" now exist for all major groups in the society. The national system is, hence, conceived of in terms of the family metaphor, implying strong benevolent leadership, assigned and accepted duties, paternalism, a purpose greater than the sum of its individual parts. The state and its myriad agencies now serve as the agent of national integration, holding together the diverse groups, guilds, and *interesses* functioning in the national polity, and serving as the filter and regulator through which the legitimacy of new social and political forces is recognized and through which they are admitted into the system.[40]

Power remains concentrated in the executive, more specifically in the *person* of the president, and in the bureaucratic-patrimonialist state machinery. The president is thus viewed as the personification of the nation with a direct identification with and knowledge of the "general will" of the people. The bureaucracy serves to dispense the available favors and privileges to the deserving. The traditional *patrón-cliente* relationship remains strong, with the government and its many bureaus and local representatives replacing the *caudillos,* viceroys (literally "vice-kings," the crown's personal agents), and *hacendados* of the past.[41]

The historic hierarchical, elitist, corporative, and authoritarian system has been modified by twentieth-century changes but by no means destroyed by them.[42] Politics still centers around the old hierarchically organized and vertically compartmentalized structure of corporate interests, now expanded to include the newer social elements (middle-sector associations, trade unions, peasant leagues, and the like) but still authoritarianly controlled from the top and linked together through the governmental apparatus. The government controls and directs virtually all of associational life, holding power to grant or withhold not only recognition (the *sine qua non* for the group's very existence) but also access to official funds and favors without which no group is likely to succeed or even survive. Group "rights" or *fueros* hence have priority over individual rights; similarly, it is the "general will" and the power of the state that prevail over particular interests. The government not only regulates all associations and corporate bodies but also seeks to tie those that have earned their place in the existing system into a collaborative effort for integral, institutionalized national development. Obviously, such a system works best in a traditional context and within a framework of shared values, but what makes it so interesting is that it is not incompatible with a growing pluralism of ideologies and social forces.

In the virtually inherently corporative and patrimonial systems of Iberia and Latin America, the effort is more to ameliorate social and political conflict, to deal with it bureaucratically rather than to provoke divisiveness, class conflict, and breakdowns—hence, the strong controls imposed on capital, labor, and other types of interest associations and the loathing of competitive party politics, all of which are seen as divisive agencies subtracting from and perhaps threatening the unity and solidarity of the system. Administration supersedes politics in both theory and practice: society is represented functionally in terms of its component sectors and organized bureaucratically, with the government seeking to maintain the proper balance between the various interests and to coordinate them into the state apparatus.[43] Parties tend to be called national "movements" or "civic associations"; they are more likely to serve as patronage agencies and as mechanisms of the state apparatus than as agents of mass mobilization or electoral politics. Political issues in such a system are dealt with generally by coopting new elites into the orbit of the patrimonial state through the granting of access and favors, spoils and privileges that accrue with acceptance into the system.[44] Effective program implementation is difficult for bureaucracies in systems where this was always at best a secondary function.

In the Iberic-Latin systems, the great need is felt to be social and political solidarity. There can be little room for divided loyalties, autonomous political organizations, or challenges to the system's fundamental structure. The personnel of government may shift, new groups and ideas may be assimilated, and the elites may circulate in power.[45] But the essentials of the sociopolitical order and the base on which it rests must remain steadfast. The newer groups may be coopted and incorporated but they cannot seek to topple the system per se. Those that try will likely be crushed—unless their goal is the limited one of trying to demonstrate a power capability and the right to be admitted as a participant in the larger system. This kind of controlled and usually carefully orchestrated violence (the student demonstration, the march on the National Palace, the general strike) may be tolerated, even accepted; a movement aimed at undermining the entire system, in contrast, can expect to and will probably be suppressed.[46]

Considerable change can and does take place within a corporative system, but it usually comes from the top downward rather than as a result of grass-roots pressure from below. A culturally conditioned form of "democracy" may be established, as in Venezuela, Colombia, Costa Rica, or even Mexico, but its structure is that of a tutelary democracy directed from above. Moreover, one must be careful not to overstress the democratic aspects of these systems at the expense of their authoritarian, elitist, and corporative features. For government tends to remain dominated by elite interests and values, hierarchy and corporatism remain deeply ingrained, and the so-called democratic system is ordinarily founded on a structure of coopted and *institutionalized* popular movements, rather than on independent and genuinely pluralist ones.[47]

Whether the system is authoritarian or "democratic," the change process is dealt with in much the same way. An attempt is made to transfer the elitist values and political culture to the rising newer groups through education, cooptation, and example. First the business-commercial elements were "civilized" in this way, then the rising middle sectors, and now the lower or popular classes. This helps explain the persistent presence in the Iberic-Latin context of state-supported and controlled labor federations, peasant leagues, professional associations, and the like. Through these agencies, which like the parties often function as bureaucratic appendages of the state, the prevailing systems have sought to institutionalize and thus contain the rising social forces. Middle- and lower-class elements have been given certain benefits and a place in the system as a means of defusing discontent and of subordinating them to the bureaucratic-paternalistic direction of the state. Labor legislation and more recently agrarian reform have been used as instruments more of social control than of social change. In this way the dominant elites and the patrimonialist structure have managed the historic unfolding of the development process, channeling it in acceptable directions and either coopting in or snuffing out new challenges to their power and way of life.[48] Through adaptation the traditional order, instead of being overwhelmed or discarded as development has gone forward, has profited, proving to be remarkably resilient and even strengthening itself in the process.

It is the duty of the state and its *lider* to organize public opinion and maintain the delicate equilibrium through the manipulation and balancing of these interests. Decisions are ordinarily made by a coterie of elite group representatives, linked by formal and informal ties to the administrative hierarchy and centering, ideally, in a single individual who personifies the national values, "knows" the general will, and is the most qualified leader. In much of Latin America during the 1960s (but not in Portugal), the United States ambassador and the various U.S. mission heads were at times also included in the decision-making machinery. Traditionally, patronage, status, favors, and special access to the centers of wealth and influence have served as the chief political currency, with privileges, even whole programs and agencies, being doled out by the state to groups and individuals who might otherwise attempt organized opposition. These benefits are distributed in return for loyal support and/or acquiescence to official policies. It is worth noting the reverse side of this coin also, that opposition to the regime in power in the Iberic-Latin context is not usually for the ideological and partisan reasons that American headlines often suggest but is simply a means by which the opposing group or individual will also in some fashion be included in the spoils system. Government thus becomes a kind of vast social security system, a haven for friends, relatives, clientele of various sorts, dissident oppositionists, and even for a large part of the middle class and now, increasingly, the peasant and labor leaders who are, in effect, "bought off" by being placed on the public payroll.[49]

The corporative system thus helps maintain the traditional structure while concurrently providing for change through the incorporation of new social and political units into the state administration. Corporate structures reinforced by a political culture grounded on hierarchy, status, and patronage are what enable the prevailing system to hang on so tenaciously. The status quo is thus preserved, while provision is also made for the incremental accommodation to newer currents. The corporative system may thus respond to modernization and adopt those aspects that are useful and can be controlled; but in seeking to preserve stability and continuity, it may reject many of the social and political concomitants that accompanied development elsewhere. It should be reiterated that the corporative structures and values outlined here are not just a creation of the 1930s but have deep roots in the entire Iberic-Latin tradition. They have been reformulated, adjusted, and updated numerous times, but the fundamental nature of the corporative-patrimonial system has endured.[50]

In the Iberic-Latin political systems new social and political forces, new ideas and institutional arrangements may be added on in a continuous fusion-absorption process; but owing to the absence of genuinely revolutionary transformations in that tradition, old ones are seldom discarded.[51] Only in Mexico, Cuba, and perhaps (and incompletely) Bolivia, Peru, Chile, and now Portugal have there been sharp breaks with the past which destroyed the power of the traditional elites. In the other countries, traditional structures remain strong. Furthermore, even in those nations that have had revolutions (and one thinks particularly of Mexico, Bolivia, Peru, Portugal, and Chile in this regard, although Cuba may also qualify), the corporative-syndicalist-patrimonialist mentality and political culture remain exceedingly powerful, perhaps still predominant, even though the formal "corporatist" institutions established in the 1930s may have disappeared. The longevity and persistence of these traditional aspects, however updated to meet twentieth-century contingencies, remind one of Anderson's "living museum" idea.[52] Organizational forms and societal forces that have died off or been discarded elsewhere in the West continue in the Iberic-Latin context to exhibit a remarkable durability and viability; instead of being swept away, they have proceeded to adapt, persisting and continuing to coexist with and even absorb the newer currents spawned by industrialization and modernization.

As a result of the tenacity of these traditional sociopolitical institutions, there has been limited "development" in the Iberic-Latin nations in either a Marxian or an Almondian sense. The Iberic-Latin political process has involved not so much the transcendence of one "class" or "stage" over another, but the combination of diverse elements, rooted in distinct historical epochs, in a tentative working arrangement. The question has been not so much one of "development" or "modernization" as of reconciling the features of the older patrimonialist order with the imperatives of a twentieth-century urban and industrial one. The traditional order in these societies has not been so rigid as is usually pictured, but flexible, permeable, and capable of absorbing a variety of newer currents, without being undermined in the process. It has assimilated those features of modernity that were necessary and could be absorbed, but it has rejected the rest.

As the newer elites and social forces have been absorbed into the prevailing system, therefore, the number of participants and of institutionalized corporate groups has increased, but the system itself has changed little. Hence, in virtually all the Iberic-Latin nations there has grown up a series of layers of distinct social and political forms and world views, each superimposed upon the other, with new elements continuously being appended and adapted to an older tradition but without that older tradition being sloughed off or even undergoing many fundamental transformations. These distinct but overlapping layers originate in historical eras that range over the centuries from "feudal" to "modern," combined and blended in the Iberic-Latin tradition. It is the genius and ongoing challenge of politics and politicians in these nations that they have been able to function and accomplish anything at all of a developmental sort, given the tentative, heterogeneous, frequently crazy-quilt political systems in which they must work.[53]

In seeking to explain these aspects of the Iberic-Latin change process, Richard N. Adams has fashioned a theory of what he calls "secondary development." [54] This refers to the course development takes when it enters an area previously isolated from the modern world. Hence, development in Iberia and Latin America does not *follow* the developmental patterns of northern Europe and North America but involves the *adaptation* of the newer forces to an older order. This is a process of assimilation and reorganization, not of innovation; it involves not the replacement of an already established sociopolitical order by a newer, more modern one but the adaptation of the newer wines to the older bottles.

In Anderson's terms, the key dilemma in the politics of these nations is to find a formula for reaching agreement among the various corporate groups and "power contenders," made difficult because their power is unequal and because their interests and world views are almost totally incompatible. Characteristically, the political process involves manipulation and constant negotiations among these several power contenders, since elections are tentative and but one legitimate means to power and do not carry the definitiveness of elections in the Anglo-American context.[55] The shuffling and reshuffling of the delicate power balance, the management of a diverse coalition, are necessary, almost everyday preoccupations. Anderson emphasizes that while new power contenders may be accommodated and admitted to the system, if they accept and conform to its rules, old ones are not eliminated. However, because the several elites and *interesses,* including the Army, the Church, the oligarchy, the university, labor, the peasants, and so forth, emerged from distinct historical time periods with distinct expectations and uneven bases for their power and legitimacy, the attempt to fashion an accommodation among them is exceedingly difficult. The job of the president, who must juggle and reconcile these contending forces and maintain a working balance between them, is complex and uncertain.

Multiple currents of sociopolitical evolution may thus be operating within the framework of a given nation, institution, or even individual. Politics, Anderson says, involves the capacity to combine these heterogeneous and incompatible power contenders and capabilities in a conditional, continuously shifting arrangement. Frequently, these efforts involve what to North Americans appear to be incredible marriages of convenience—alliances that defy not only all "reason" but also our conception of ideological consistency—or the stretching or reinterpretation (or frequent rewriting) of the law and constitution so as to render them all but meaningless. Yet it is precisely these features—the application of a little "grease" here or a little "cement" there, a delicate compromise, accommodation, or favor—that help account for the distinctive flavor of the development process in these countries and that give them their dynamism and capacity to respond. Furthermore, if we wish to understand the Iberic-Latin development process, the focus of scholarly inquiry ought also to be in this direction. We must study, for example, how traditional institutions have been remolded and modified to meet the exigencies of modern times, as well as how such "modernizing" groups as trade unions have frequently used the traditional structure to further their own ends and have been incorporated into the classic system of hierarchy, corporatism, and authority.[56] These mechanisms, which lie at the heart of the Iberic-Latin change and development process, often bear little correspondence to the systems paradigms with which we are more familiar.

The late Kalman Silvert's analysis of what he termed the "Mediterranean ethos" or "syndicalism" closely parallels what is here called the "corporative framework." [57] This ethos is founded upon a value system and political culture dedicated to hierarchy, order, and absolutes. The urge toward corporatism is a powerful manifestation of this ethos, since the organization of men by functions is in accord with the historic tradition and actualizes the love of order and hierarchy, serves to contain divisive class conflict, and avoids the hated liberal and materialistic values. It also provides for the slow and at least partial adaptation of traditional, patrimonial society to urbanization, industrialization, and modernization. An effort is made through the prevailing system to bring into harmonious coexistence those characteristics venerated from the past and those considered valuable in modernity. The good society is still pictured as one in which each individual is rooted and secure in his life station, where representation is determined by function and status and not as the result of mere citizenship, where decision making is centered in the hands of corporate, sectoral elites who are harmonized and coordinated into an organic whole, and where the state exercises firm but benevolent authority over the entire system. The City of God still takes precedence in many respects over the City of Man, but since a modern society can no longer exist on this simple biinstitutional basis, the Iberic-Latin response has been to erect new institutional pillars to accommodate the changes taking place. Each vertical pillar or corporative sector in this hierarchical arrangement remains highly striated by social class with recruitment into the upper levels still largely a function of social position. As Silvert concludes, the major social purpose of the syndicalist or corporatist approach is to find a way of subsuming the new class complications of modernization to hierarchy and the ancient order, preserving the principle of authority, leaving inviolate the privileges and power of the traditional while at the same time adapting to the newer currents and thus achieving development while escaping the secularization and, to Latin eyes, immorality of the modern era.

It is clear from the above that the Iberic-Latin model here termed "corporatist" conforms to neither the liberal-pluralist nor the "fascist" or totalitarian model.[58] There is no evidence that the Iberic-Latin nations are moving inevitably or unilinearly in a liberal-pluralist direction or that they have much desire to do so. With their strong natural-law traditions, the concepts of countervailing corporate group life, the competition of rival power contenders for power, and in the absence of any intense racial or ethnic persecution or of an all-powerful state or single party, the Iberic-Latin systems clearly do not fit fascist and totalitarian molds either. Authoritarian in certain respects, yes; but totalitarian, no.[59] Moreover, it bears reiterating that the "corporative system" provides for considerable change and modernization. The Iberic-Latin nations are not all wholly static and vegetative (Portugal almost became so) but have shown an almost incredible capacity to change, coopt, and adapt, even within an authoritarian-corporatist context. They have accommodated themselves to the changed circumstances and the new social forces to which industrialization and modernization gave rise, but they have done so in a way that has enabled them to maintain many of their historic values and institutions. Fitting neither the liberal framework nor the fascist-totalitarian one, far more dynamic and change-oriented than is often thought, the Iberic-Latin model is a distinct type, with its own philosophic traditions, characteristics, and culturally conditioned behavior patterns and institutions. The Iberic-Latin tradition of corporatism merits examination on its own terms as "the other great ism." [60]

This is what the present book seeks to do. We shall be looking at the Portuguese system in terms of those historic traditions and institutions that have shaped its development. More importantly, we shall try to show how the manifestly "corporative state" that grew up in the 1930s to deal with the newer phenomena of industrialization, rapid social change, and mass man was a reflection and modern-day extension of that earlier corporative tradition. We shall be tracing the evolution of the Portuguese corporative system and seeking to assess its capacity to cope and deal with the same great twentieth-century issues for which liberalism and socialism represent alternative responses. Finally, we shall be seeking to weigh the capabilities of the corporative system to continue to function and survive, its various alternative futures, and the implications of the overthrow of the system in April 1974.

In many ways the corporative systems of Iberia and Latin America are now undergoing pressures never before experienced. The ancient fabric of natural law has been challenged from both within and without, some of the older power bases are in decline, new social forces have emerged organized around different principles than those previously considered the only right or legitimate ones, class-based and issue-oriented politics have grown up alongside the ancient patrimonialist system, the pace of change has accelerated and the number of interests to be satisfied has grown, the older solidarity has been challenged, and a framework of change has increasingly replaced the older one of order and stability. Throughout the Iberic-Latin world these and other currents have posed an increasing challenge to the older tradition, raising the question of whether the corporative scheme will one day be submerged or swept away, or whether its contours will be so altered as to constitute a significant structural transformation. Or will the traditional order be able to weather and survive the contemporary challenge and crisis as it has weathered so many others in the past? These questions came to a dramatic head in the Portugal of 1974. It is toward the exploration and analysis of this corporative framework—using Portugal as the main focus but with the implications extending to other Iberic-Latin systems and perhaps to our own society as well—that the present study is directed.

II

Portuguese Background and Political Culture

From the time Portugal emerged as the first unified nation-state in Europe in the twelfth century, it was cast in the Catholic-authoritarian-corporatist-patrimonialist mold. This dominant tradition in Portuguese history, society, and political culture has been obscured because the history books which discuss the country and with which we are most familiar have been in the main written by English and American historians who share the common Anglo-American liberal biases and whose studies are often directed toward looking for a *cortes* that never played (and was never intended to play!) the role of the British Parliament, institutions of popular, representative, self-government that in Portugal never existed, and a liberal and democratic tradition that never received majority support. Of necessity, these accounts have branded Portuguese history a "failure," for it has not lived up to the ideals the Anglo-American writers ethnocentrically assumed to be common to all men. And in explaining the causes of this "failure," the historians have consistently painted the presumed foes of democracy, such as the Church, the monarchy, strong government, Pombal, *caciquismo,* the Estado Novo, and much of Portuguese political culture in the vilest of terms, instead of examining them in an unbiased manner and in terms of their role or position in the Portuguese context. The works in English on Portuguese history are rather consistently condescending, written from the point of view of a "superior" political culture, and aimed at discovering in Portugal a liberal-democratic tradition that at best exists as a distinct minority viewpoint.[1]

This chapter tries to look at Portuguese history and the development of its society and political culture on their own terms rather than through an Anglo-American frame of reference. It seeks to understand that history in the light of Portuguese political institutions, values, and traditions, rather than branding it a "failure." This effort must perforce be incomplete, because of the inadequacies of the historical record and the limitations of space. And yet this way of looking at Portuguese history must be attempted if we are to escape the prejudices of our Anglo-American interpretations and if we are to understand the workings of the modern Portuguese system. There is a dominant tradition in Portuguese history, but that tradition (or at least its major historical current) was and is hardly democratic and it is misleading and self-defeating to try to assert that it is or that it should be so.

The Portuguese Background

Although Portugal emerged as a distinct national entity in the twelfth century, its characteristic political culture and form of political organization had begun to emerge long before that time.[2]

We know relatively little about the primitive peoples who first inhabited Lusitania. As was the case with other areas on the Iberian coast, it was visited by the Phoenicians and probably the ancient Greeks, and in the third century B.C. its southern region came under the domination of the Carthaginians. But it was not until Roman times, beginning in the first century B.C., that the region of Lusitania was stamped with a dominant and lasting imprint and its characteristic form of political organization and culture began to take shape.

The Romans built numerous bridges, highways, aqueducts, and buildings. The bridges and road network, to say nothing of the establishment of a central administration, helped link Lusitania's diverse and distant regions and provided a sense of unity they had lacked before. Unity and a certain cultural coherence were also forged gradually through a common language and law and eventually through Christianity. Roman law, administration, and politico-military (the two were inseparable) organization were imposed and indelibly imprinted on the area, in a form which would later reach definitive shape in terms of the growth of an administrative or bureaucratic state apparatus. In addition, the Romans gave to Portugal its particular conception of citizenship, its stoic conception of rights and obligations, its juridical structure of group rights and charters, its sense of hierarchy and class, and indeed much of its characteristic sociopolitical organization. And if later corporative theorists are correct, in its structuring of military orders, the religious caste, and a hierarchy of professional associations, Rome also laid the basis for the future establishment of a corporative state and society.[3]

During the five centuries of Roman rule, the foundations were laid on which future Iberian civilization would develop. Spain and Portugal remain products of Rome in a way they are not of earlier or subsequent cultures.[4] The collapse of the empire paved the way for a Visigothic conquest, which resulted in more of an overlay on the earlier Roman tradition than a submerging of it. From the fifth to the seventh century A.D. the Visigoths helped spread Christianity and Catholic culture through the institutionalization of a state church. Visigothic rule also led to a certain hardening of absolutism and of authoritarian, centralized rule. Moorish rule, always softer and less complete in Lusitania than in Spain, was similarly an overlay on the dominant Roman tradition, since the Moors ruled as overlords and did not impose their culture and religion on the native Iberians. The centuries-long Moorish domination beginning in 714–16 left its influence on the language, in architecture, and—some historians would have us believe—in terms of the inferior status of women in peninsular society. But the Moorish influence never reached as far and as deep into society, polity, and culture as did the Roman, and when the Moors were eventually driven from the peninsula, it was the Roman tradition that remained dominant.

The disorder and intermittent warfare occasioned by the long-drawn-out reconquest of the peninsula from the Moors retarded the growth of feudalism in Iberia, in contrast, to its development in France. Nevertheless, some further characteristic forms of social and political organization were now grafted onto the Roman base. During the reconquest the Church became more than ever an arm of the civil authority. And as the reconquest proceeded, the power of the nobility and of the fighting lords became territorial as well as political and military, usually as a result of grants to them of the lands and peoples they had helped reconquer. Each lord was sovereign in his own territory, and an elaborate network of vassalage and of *patrón*-dependent relations began eventually to grow up. The system of special *foros,* or "rights" and obligations, which defined the relationship of the citizen individually and of the community collectively to its overlord, who could be the monarch, noble, Church, military order, or even municipality, thus became the means by which society and polity were defined. The forms of authority were organized hierarchically and in a traditional fashion in which the wealth and lands of the area, as well as the persons living in it, were considered a part of the overlord's private preserve. No separation existed between the public and the private domains. A strongly institutionalized patrimonialist social and political structure emerged, which only later took on its agrarian-feudal aspects.[5]

Present-day Portugal emerged out of the north or Trás-os-Montes area, an isolated, mountainous, obscure territory where the Spanish provinces of León and Galicia meet and still overlap in language, trade, and culture with the provinces of Portugal beyond the Rio Douro. Early in the twelfth century a separate kingdom of Portugal began to develop, independent of León, although it was not until 1139 with the victory of Afonso Henriques over the Moors near Santarém that a separate Portuguese national unit was founded. During the next three centuries, as the Portuguese conquered south, wresting more and more territory from the Moors, while also fending off León and Spain to the east, the consolidation of Portugal as a separate nation went forward and its distinct characteristics began to emerge.

The traditions and institutions developed during the period of nation building and consolidation from the twelfth to the fourteenth centuries are crucial for understanding latter-day developments, for they were the foundation on which the modern Portuguese state was built.[6] Their origins lay in the Roman system of civil law, politics, and administration, in the spreading Thomistic philosophy of hierarchy and natural law, and in the emerging semifeudal pattern of land and conquest as the basis of wealth with payment in goods, services, and loyalty. The barons, the nobility, and the new landed aristocrats—*o senhor territorial* —derived their positions from the king, surrounding him like a "college of influentials," owing allegiance to him, and receiving in turn his favors. The Church, the military, and the advisers of the king all became a part of the same centralizing, bureaucratic, state apparatus. Governance came to be exercised through a number of consulting organs or councils and directly through the king's ministers who served as his personal agents. The system was one of rule from above, of elite protection of those below them in the hierarchy in return for fealty and service. This was a reciprocal arrangement between "the *povo*" and their "betters" in a classic patrimonialist structure.[7]

These arrangements were rationalized and reinforced in the Thomistic conceptions of the proper ordering of state and society. For the Catholic Church was intimately involved in the founding and historic development of the Portuguese state and society. Catholicism helped provide the cultural, social, and religious base on which the nation was grounded. Society was organized hierarchically, on Christian principles, in accordance with natural law and God's just ordering of the universe. The "natural" inequalities among men meant that one was bound to accept the station in life to which he had been born. The social order was viewed as fixed and immutable. The state conception was similarly hierarchical, authoritarian and governed by natural law. Political authority flowed from God and was absolute in character; dissent and the right to rebellion were extremely circumscribed. Society and the state were viewed as "natural" rather than as originating in a contract between government and governed, and this organic conception was (and remains) almost inherently traditionalist and absolutist. In terms of the philosophical foundations of political authority and civil society grounded in Catholic theology, the establishment of Catholicism as the official state religion, the close harmony and overlap between the civil and the religious hierarchies, the foundation of art and education in Catholic teachings and ceremony, and in a host of other ways, the Portuguese Church and the Portuguese state were one and indivisible. The Church, like the fighting barons and nobility, was more than a mere "interest group" in the American sense; it was the backbone, indispensable prop, and very essence of the state itself.[8]

Among the corporate groups, military orders, and municipalities existent in the emerging Portuguese system by the end of the fourteenth century, the monarchy and the central state apparatus had become overwhelmingly preeminent, regulating both social structure and economic life. The privileges and monopolies granted by the crown to favored groups and individuals helped develop and unify Portugal. It was a system based on status, hierarchy, and royal favor. No group or individual could challenge or reject the "proper" place in society to which it or he had been assigned. Eventually, a commercial elite would grow up in Portugal alongside its barons and landed oligarchy—and it was the commercial elements who, with royal support and under royal auspices, in the fifteenth century launched the conquest of the vast Portuguese overseas empire. Despite this gradual change from feudalism to mercantilism, however, it was the patrimonialist state apparatus that remained constant, continuing to regulate the entire economy and to strengthen itself in the process.

Thus, as a class system began to emerge in Portugal in the early modern period, the structure of state patrimonialism continued to coexist along with it. Commerce, war, exploration, and colonization were all a part of the same extension of royal authority, at a time when the system of agrarian feudalism was also being consolidated under royal patronage. Further, in the promotion of trade and colonization, Portugal never developed a full-fledged system of capitalism. State capitalism or mercantilism, yes, but individual entrepreneurship and *laissez faire,* no. Hence, while commercialism and capitalism of a sort grew up parallel to the feudal landholding system, the former never replaced the latter but instead was fused with it. Meanwhile, the one constant remained the patrimonialist state apparatus and a social and political structure depending on and deriving its legitimacy from royal favors and patronage. As Herminio Martins, one of Portugal's leading political sociologists, has written: "Portuguese social stability stems in part from the circumstance that the formation of the state and the definition of national identity took place centuries ago, long before the social crises brought on by industrialization, urbanization, and other phases of modernization." [9]

Because this tradition is so strong and so omnipresent, it merits further elaboration. One can say, thus, that the Portuguese state was modeled after that of the imperial Roman Caesars, now updated and given a Christian base. It was absolutist and administrative. The king exercised power in the name of the general interest, the *res publica*. He required all powers and prerogatives for his superior mission of governance. Society remained dominated by the idea and presence of the state. The land of the kingdom and its individual members belonged to the monarch as part of his private domain. And the kings could name their own successors. [10]

The crown might grant part of its patrimony to certain individuals, sometimes in perpetuity, in return for their support and service. The concessions of land, favors, or a special monopoly were alienated in return for a formal oath of loyalty, a *juramento a fidelidade*. The system was highly personal and paternal. A vassal might abandon his contract with the king only if he received injury from him—and vice versa. The relations of lord or king to vassal, or to a corporate body, were thus not wholly one-way but were governed by reciprocal relations, in a classic *patrão-cliente* pattern. [11]

The crown was limited in other ways. Natural and divine law provided a set of guidelines beyond which the crown could go only at the risk of provoking rebellion. The crown was limited also by the traditional rights of the emerging orders and municipalities. Further, during the thirteenth and fourteenth centuries the first corporations of *artes e oficios* were founded; the Casa de Vinte e Quatro (a corporately organized assembly of notables based on functional representation) was born, and certain other corporations and some artisans' groups came to be recognized by the king. These bodies too served as a check on royal absolutism. When the king overstepped his authority, he was likely to face a revolt on the part of the nobility, whose bloody uprisings continued throughout this period. [12] Custom, tradition, and the family also served as constraints on royal prerogatives.

The king had the supreme "fiscalizing" power to regulate and pass on all contracts and agreements. He also exercised his sovereignty by *confirming* the acts of the *senhor*—for example, his military service, his land and vassals, or his right to a place in the *cortes*. Thus, the king was not only theoretically supreme but his effective power was enhanced by his ability almost literally to handpick those who sat in his parliament. The same individual who received a grant of land or monopoly from the crown would frequently serve as the king's royal agent in that territory.

The political evolution of Portugal during this period served as a means to reconstitute and unify the state and establish national sovereignty through the leadership of the king.[13]

The rediscovery of Roman law had given special impetus to these trends. The *corpus juris civis* provided a model of a powerful state, hierarchical and authoritarian in character, in which a strong central administration assured order and justice. The Roman law favored the consolidation of the state by the crown against feudal rights, excesses, and violence. It contributed to the growth of royal power and also made it absolutist. The monarch became the focus of the *direito positivo*. He assumed the position of defender of "the public interest" in return for which the nation granted him virtually all power. This tradition evolved as the Iberic concept of popular sovereignty, and it found powerful echoes in the rule of Salazar.[14]

The development of royal power resulted in the weakening of the legislative power, in the growth of general as opposed to localized taxes, in limits on seignorial power, in the affirmation gradually of secular power over the Church, in the development of central administrative organs, in the fiscalization and intervention of the crown in political and economic life, and in the delegation of certain powers and privileges in return for fealty. Eventually, the doctrine of the illegality of usurping royal authority emerged, the idea that the king was not only superior in relation to other authorities but that he or his delegated agents had a true monopoly. The doctrine asserted that the "rights" (*foros*) of the various societal and corporate units came only through concessions from the king and not through any inherent or natural rights. In the sixteenth century the extension of this idea and the full consolidation of the crown's power led to royal absolutism.[15]

In opposition to the emerging absolutist doctrines and practices, the nobles continued to assert the crown's obligation to defend their traditional rights, to guard good customs, and to protect the rights of the people. This gave rise to the idea that the relations between the crown and "the classes" were governed by a kind of pact and maintained by mutual accords. The inviolability of these *foros* was always invoked in conflicts with the king. The various "colleges," orders, brotherhoods, *guilds,* municipalities, and corporations all claimed to be governed by these norms. At the same time the king reserved the right not to respect these privileges when he had just cause.[16] Throughout Portuguese history, indeed, this conflict between the centralizing, absolutist forces and tendencies, on the one hand, and the defenders of corporate privilege and group rights, on the other, remained dominant. At no time in this long history of conflict between the crown and the various component units of the nation, even up to the present, was there a strong force arguing for genuine popular sovereignty and democratization in the Anglo-American mold.

Implied in the above is the fact that the Portuguese *cortes* would never become an effective agent for popular representation. The cortes originated in the royal curia or council of the king. Its chief functions were consultative and administrative; it did not legislate. Although the cortes at several points accumulated some modicum of authority, no real separation of powers emerged, and it existed largely at the king's pleasure. Represented in it were the nobles and *homens bons,* generally those allied with the king or owing him fealty; the Church was also represented along with the masters of the major military orders, the heads of the major corporative bodies, and the *procuradores* of the principal cities. The cortes could only be called into session by the king, and its members were required to heed this call as an obligation of their vassalage.[17]

The ordinary curia, or royal council, remained an administrative arm of the king; however, the extraordinary curia, comprising the greater nobles and Church prelates, gradually devolved greater economic and legislative functions and was involved in some of the great political questions of the thirteenth and fourteenth centuries. But as the *cortes* sought to expand its powers, it was called less and less frequently. The three chief estates—clerical, noble, and military—were all represented, as were the municipalities, the heads of the major corporative bodies, and some persons of elevated position. But the franchise was always severely limited: the people were represented by their "betters"; municipalities also tended to choose local notables who *andam no governo*— "went along with the governmental team." What vote existed was ordinarily for an assigned list of the "better" people, and the king would often suggest for whom one should vote—those who enjoyed his *confiança.*[18]

The cortes met, irregularly and briefly, by separate functional estates, each jealous of its own privileges. It nonetheless gradually acquired some power over the purse, was sometimes consulted by the king in the event of war, gained some limited power over lawmaking, and could exercise some choice in the succession in cases where the dynasty had died out. It remained limited, however, never employing the supremacist doctrine that some few of its members occasionally voiced, and the king most often legislated without the cortes through decree-law. The power of the people thus remained nil, and the crown reserved the right to revoke the *foros* and liberties even of the major corporate groups and privileged elites. It was the popular sectors, day laborers and

peasants, beginning to emerge in the fifteenth century though with nowhere near the power of the nobility or clergy, who probably had the
most interest in the meeting of the cortes, but they were the weakest of
society's sectors and had virtually no representation. Only the elites
enjoyed representation, and they had no more interest in genuinely popular and democratic government than the king. Hence, in the great conflicts between royal authority and the nobles of the realm, whose relative
power varied over time depending on the force of each and the vicissitudes of politics, the *povo* never had any voice at all.[19]

Was the cortes ever representative of society or of the nation? Em-
phatically not, at least in the modern Anglo-American sense of popular
representation. In the Portuguese sense the cortes *was* representative,
however, for when a Spaniard or Portuguese speaks of society or the
nation he tends to think of it in terms of its component units: the religious institutions, the municipalities, the *gremios* and *sindicatos,* the
entrepreneurial interests, military orders, grand foundations, and the
like—in other words, the major social and corporate groups. Not included in this conception is the general public or public opinion. Hence,
the cortes was at best occasionally an imperfect representative only of
"the classes." Its membership was limited to certain privileged clergy,
nobles, cities, military orders, *homens bons,* and so forth, and it was
their rights that were protected. The general public was not represented,
and individual rights were protected only insofar as they corresponded
to those of the major *interesses.* However, the cortes did represent at
least the major elites and corporate bodies and, more than that, it sometimes presumed to speak in defense of the common interests. But the
king also claimed that power, and eventually he won out. The cortes
met less and less frequently, the last time (at least in the pre-Republican
period) in 1696–98. Then divine-right monarchy triumphed absolutely,
and the cortes came to be replaced by nonelective secretaries of state
and superior tribunals. The cortes never acquired the power of the
British Parliament; the idea of popular sovereignty (and all its accompanying paraphernalia—elections, party government, separation of powers, popular rights, and so on) was never secured nor did it become
even a principle of public law.[20]

The themes developed above are important for several reasons. First,
it is clear that the evolution of the Portuguese system up to this point
has shown a close correspondence to the model of corporative society
and of the patrimonialist political order outlined in chapter 1. Second,
this structure served as the base on which the *modern* Portuguese state
system was erected from the fifteenth century on. These ideas were

probably most clearly articulated by the Infante Dom Pedro, brother of Henry the Navigator and a shrewd political analyst and royal adviser; by Alvaro Pais, the Franciscan bishop of Elvas; and later by Francisco Suárez, the great Spanish jurist (who also taught at Coimbra), who laid the basis for the modern Iberic conception of the Christian (Thomistic) state and authority. In their rationalizations of the emerging power relationships, political power derived from God and was both natural and immutable. The king was obliged to exercise power for the common good; he was a tutor whose power must be used to promote the general well-being of his people. The true king was thus distinguished from a tyrant in that his authority rested on a popular base through his knowledge of the general will. Power stemmed, therefore, not only from God but also through a pact of subjection by which the people agreed to submit to the authority of the prince and he in turn was obligated to rule justly. The king thus governed as a king, not as a tyrant, and in so doing he was obligated to take the corporate *interesses* into account. In Suárez (though not in Dom Pedro) this contract was viewed as superior to the king himself, so that if the king acted as a tyrant, the contract could be revoked. In Portugal, especially with the election of the new Avis dynasty in 1385, this doctrine had particular significance, and it was also used to justify the ending of Spain's sixty-year domination of Portugal in 1640. With the era of Louis XIV, the doctrine of limited, tutelary monarchy disappeared and that of divine right triumphed, but until then—and indeed virtually continuously in the Portuguese tradition —it was the conception of royal authority governing in an enlightened way and respecting the traditional *foros* that predominated. It was Dom Pedro who put all this political theory together, who showed the king how to grasp and exercise all the levers of power and patronage, and who erected an artfully fashioned model of the national patrimonialist state and society. It is no accident that the king he instructed, João II, is recognized by virtually all historians as the best ruler Portugal ever had.[21]

Third, one cannot help but be impressed with the parallels between this fifteenth-century conception and the Estado Novo of Salazar and Caetano. In terms of the authoritarian but tutelary role of the state, the limited role of the assembly (actually referred to as the "general cortes of the regime"), the treatment of opposition, the respect for the traditional interests, the concept of social structure as fixed and immutable, the erection of a corporative system of social and political organization, functional representation, the low place of public opinion and popular sovereignty, the emphasis on group *foros* rather than individual rights, the patrimonialist state apparatus, and so on, the parallels are remarkable. In part, of course, this is so because Salazar consciously tried to resurrect in his corporate state a model patterned in some respects on the older tradition. But one suspects it also represents the continuity of a dominant historical pattern and tradition, the logical extension in twentieth-century form of a historic form and order always characteristic of Portuguese society and polity.

The patrimonialist state apparatus, put together so painstakingly and with so much struggle from the twelfth to the fifteenth century, remained the dominant form of Portuguese political organization. Portugal's early consolidation as a nation and the development of its political institutions help explain the incredible, almost inconceivable Portuguese world explorations and conquests—in Africa, Asia, and Latin America —during the fifteenth and sixteenth centuries. This far-flung empire may be viewed as a worldwide extension of continental Portugal itself, a bureaucratic empire reflecting the dominant institutions of the metropole and carried over to the new worlds. It was not an empire of separate units but rather was integrated as a whole into the patrimonialist state apparatus and reflected the sociopolitical structure of the homeland.[22]

The sixteenth century saw the further elaboration and refinement of the prevailing system. Spanish and Portuguese jurists and political philosophers, especially Suárez, helped rationalize the emerging system, reconciled the older Thomistic and feudal order with the newer requirements of centralized, expansionist, state-building royal rule, and fashioned a system of power and society that proved remarkably durable.[23] The bureaucratic structure grew, chiefly through the creation of a variety of royal councils to help govern the newly acquired empire and through the grant of land and authority (*donatários*) to Portuguese colonists, especially in Brazil. Through the *ordenações* and other imperial institutions, the colonies were similarly organized in a hierarchical and patrimonialist fashion, coming to represent smaller-scale extensions of society and polity in the mother country. The Church, the military, the civil administration, and so on, were all a part of the bureaucratic state apparatus with all the lines, however tenuously and ambiguously at times, reaching back to the crown.[24]

Politics and economic life, in the mother country and in her colonies, remained intimately linked. For the Portuguese patrimonialist state, from ancient times, was formed in the conception that the king would be not only the ultimate political authority but also the major merchant, landholder, and industrialist. Hence, the preoccupation with securing economic monopolies as well as political ones, with the minute regulation of the economy and the various economic interests, and with the extraction of a royal percentage from virtually all economic transactions. One cannot but be impressed, for example, with the remarkable consistency with which the monarch was able to collect his royal due and revenue from all those who owed to him their grants of lands, mines, monopolies, and other favors. In this connection also, it should be emphasized that the Portuguese state and empire were organized not so much on a capitalistic basis, at least as capitalism came to be known in northern Europe, but rather on a monopolistic, tributary, mercantilist basis. The roots of this system lay more in the Roman and feudal patterns of allegiance, tribute, and vassalage than in the entrepreneurial, laissez-faire or capitalist, order. The *estamento burocrático* meant not free enterprise a la Adam Smith, but an economy of privileges and special favors derived from the king.[25]

Not only had Portugal rejected, and in a sense been bypassed by, the philosophy of laissez-faire capitalism and thus never experienced until much later its own form of industrial revolution, but it also remained marginal to the other great social and political currents that we associate with the making of the modern world. In part this was due to conscious choices, in part to the force of circumstances. Portugal never experienced the Protestant Reformation; indeed, it repudiated Protestantism and took vigorous steps to root it out. Retaining its intensely Catholic culture and identity, Portugal was thus never challenged by the pluralism of beliefs and value systems to which the Reformation helped give rise, nor did the this-worldly concerns that linked Protestantism to the growth of capitalism gain widespread acceptance. In part because its industrialization was postponed, Portugal's middle class grew but slowly, and society remained fixed in the two-class pattern of lord and vassal, patron and client, elite and mass.

Education and intellectual life likewise remained dominated by the Church. At the base of its art and method of reasoning continued a Christian tradition of moral certainty, and Portugal thus rejected, or only weakly received, the influences of the Renaissance, the scientific revolution of Newton and Galileo, and the Enlightenment. Nor did Portugal experience, or want much to do with, the trend toward limited, representative government, as in England. Instead Portugal developed by the end of the sixteenth century in an even more absolutist direction. When there was political dispute at all, it revolved around the issue of this new absolutist conception as opposed to the efforts of other interests of the realm to retain or restore their traditional *foros*. The issue was never one of popular or democratic government; instead, the political process focused almost entirely on competing elites and their relations with the crown or central state apparatus.

As in the reconquest, the Church, the nobility, the king, and the cavalry remained at the center of state power. The patrimonialist state continued, molded into a more efficient form of mercantilism. Elitist rule was perpetuated, exercised through the imperial state apparatus by means of royal patronage and military and Church control. In this way the state remained largely autonomous, exercising control over the social classes and regulating through them the entire nation. Under the system of absolute monarchy, the king exercised unlimited authority and the traditional *foros* were submerged. The prince and the state became one; the *res publica* became identified with the will of the monarch. There was no participation of the nation in the government. The king could still grant privileges, but they were no longer inviolate; he had "free administration" over all. This seventeenth- and eighteenth-century concept of an "organic monarchy" represented a further elaboration and more absolutist form of the earlier model. The authoritarian, hierarchical, corporate, patrimonialist state and society fashioned by the fifteenth and sixteenth centuries remained the operating reality, and even in the era of Portugal's decline in succeeding periods, it was this older and historic model that the Portuguese harked back to and sought to resurrect, not a more democratic one.[26]

From its high point in the early sixteenth century, the Portuguese empire went into a centuries-long process of decay and eventual fragmentation. Portugal was a small country and lacked the resources to manage such a far-flung empire in competition with the more powerful Dutch, British, and French. Moreover, as the royal family degenerated, its kings lost the skills necessary for the management of this complex, worldwide patrimonialist order. In retrospect, what seems important is not so much the Portuguese decline of the seventeenth and eighteenth centuries but the fact that such a small nation was able to explore, conquer, and hold as much as it did for as long as it did. In no small part, this was due to the strength and viability of the political institutions Portugal had developed, which, however, as we have repeatedly stressed, remained fundamentally different from those emerging in England and elsewhere in northern Europe.

The era of Pombal's reforms, 1750–77, is important to this discussion in two major ways. First, Pombal curtailed sharply the influence of some of the major corporate units in Portugal, the Church (especially the Order of Jesus) and the guilds. This was not so much the end of "feudalism" in Portugal and the ushering in of a new Enlightenment, however, as it was an effort to reassert the power of the centralizing authority, in the classic fashion, against the newest decentralizing tendencies that had been underway for some decades under a succession of weak and incompetent monarchs. Pombal's efforts at reform were aimed not so much at bringing Portugal abreast of the rest of Europe as at expanding the ruling elite loyal to absolutism. In terms of this historic struggle between the central authority on the one hand, and the influence of the nobility and the powers and *foros* of special interests on the other, this was really not a step toward "modernization" but, in fact, the reassertion of the classic Portuguese political struggle going back for hundreds of years. The second aspect of the Pombalian era that requires comment is the question of whether or not Pombal was a dictator. History provides a clue, for in essence what Pombal did, in an era of crisis comparable to that in Portugal in the 1920s, was to gather more of the strings of power in his hands than any ruler of Portugal in roughly two and a half centuries. Pombal was in a sense a precursor of the modern-day dictatorship of Salazar, but he was also a particularly adept manipulator of the patrimonialist state apparatus, a late eighteenth-century practitioner of an ancient system which was and remained the dominant form of exercising political authority.[27] In this sense, too, there are parallels with Salazar and Caetano.

Following Pombal's demise, Portugal floundered again. The threads holding together society and polity unraveled further. The monarchy was again ineffectual. The unraveling reached the point of almost complete disintegration under the onslaught of French revolutionary ideas, the Napoleonic occupation, the popular uprising and expulsion of Napoleon's forces, and finally the loss of Brazil. In the meantime a fledgling middle class had grown up, principally in Porto and Lisbon, liberal and rationalist ideas had become fashionable among some urban elements, and Masonic and other movements had challenged the hegemony of Church and crown.

Previously, the operational code of the Portuguese system had always been that while elite rule was necessary and that the dominant institutions would be perpetuated, the bases of elite rule could be broadened through patronage, sinecures, and accommodation to new social groups. Now, however, with the ruling elites failing to accommodate themselves to this code, the aspiring liberal republican forces had no choice but to go outside the system and seek to overthrow it. This occurred in the liberal revolutions of 1820 and 1836; it would occur again in the republican revolts of 1891 and 1910, and in the revolution of 1974.

The old order cracked, but it did not crumble. Although the constitution of 1822 and the abolition of the guilds in 1834 represented liberal triumphs, the ancient system of privilege and aristocratic rule survived. The new elites aped and adopted the old aristocratic ways. The laws changed and the persons in power changed, but the system endured. The landholding pattern remained intact, and the Church maintained its near monopoly on educational and cultural life. Nor was the political structure altered very much in its operating realities. Indeed, in the person of the crown, now limited somewhat by "constitutional" restrictions, and in the administrative machinery, much of the structure of the patrimonialist state also remained intact.[28]

The theory of absolute monarchy of the seventeenth and eighteenth centuries had not been notably popular in Portugal because of the Portuguese tradition of countervailing corporate privilege and group *foros;* in the early nineteenth century the traditional ties with and admiration for Great Britain, the newer rationalist writings and liberal philosophy, and the growing popularity of French revolutionary doctrines made the old absolutism even less acceptable. Monarchy remained the ideal, but in the Portuguese tradition this would be a *monarquia temperada* ("tempered monarchy"). The monarch would still hold the reins, but more loosely, and he would be restricted in his powers. This ideal, however, was now combined in a confused way with only half-digested Enlightenment ideas, with the model of the French Revolution, and with British parliamentarianism, party politics, and loyal opposition, which the Portuguese never fully comprehended and which were at variance with their own history and national values. Legal theorist and *político* Ribeiro dos Santos, for example, was a staunch admirer of the British ideas of contract between ruler and ruled, supremacy of laws, inviolable rights, popular sovereignty, and all the classic nineteenth-century liberal values. At the formal and constitutional level, indeed, these ideas triumphed in the nineteenth century, as reflected in the imitation of British institutional forms. In the idea of a constitutional monarchy in 1808, the liberal constitution of 1822, and finally the establishment of a republic in 1910, one sees the effort to solve Portugal's manifest and centuries-long problems through the imitation of a foreign, especially British, model.[29]

Though the forms were constitutional and republican, the operating realities were quite different. It proved impossible to establish a system of self-government in a country where such traditions were wholly absent. The two "parties" that emerged, Regenerators and Progressives, were in fact coteries of politicians and local notables without solid backing from the people.[30] Elections were chiefly efforts by these two rival factions to buy the votes of the public. As in Spain, *caciquismo* flourished, with local and regional notables and "bosses" delivering the vote in their areas in return for certain favors and patronage. Rather than implying much genuine "democratization," politics became the way for the new urban bourgeoisie to rise to positions of power and wealth.[31] It was a means of expanding the elite somewhat to accommodate to nineteenth-century pressures, while maintaining the elitist system intact.

No one, neither elites nor bourgeoisie, took the ideas of popular sovereignty and participation seriously. And though the remnants of feudal privilege had been legally abolished, the power of the Church, the oligarchy, and other historic corporate groups remained intact. These sectors, and the *homens bons,* continued to dominate Portuguese society and politics as they had always done in the past. Moreover, in the more authoritarian constitution of 1824, which became the rallying cry of conservative elements opposed to the liberal document of 1822, the old ideas remained powerful, and the concept of the traditional monarchy with representation in the cortes by the three traditional estates was resurrected. Indeed, these competing ideas and forces, the struggles and frequent civil wars between those who defended unequivocally the traditional authority structures of the *ancien régime* and those who would modify them somewhat to provide for the admission of several new elites to the system, furnish the background for much of nineteenth-century Portuguese history. Real democracy, however, was out of the question; indeed, it was seldom mentioned.

It is tempting to dismiss the entire century of Portuguese "liberalism" and "republicanism" from 1822 until 1926 as an aberration, a temporary break in what was a far longer and stronger authoritarian tradition, a set of institutions solely "for the English to see" and without basis in Portuguese history. This is what the New State propagandists attempted to do in their repudiation of the republican and liberal ideologies, painting this era in the vilest of terms, emphasizing its negative attributes and downgrading its accomplishments. While this interpretation is certainly too strong, the opposite and liberal one is certainly wrong as well. As exemplified especially in the writings of the liberal historian A. H. de Oliveira Marques,[32] the nineteenth century is pictured as a period of great progress, characterized by the gradual opening and democratization of the political system and hence demonstrating an *inevitable evolution* toward liberalism and republicanism, which culminated in the final overthrow of the monarchy and the establishment of the Republic in 1910. This interpretation is not only overstated and hence inaccurate as regards nineteenth-century Portuguese history but also biases our perspective of the twentieth by lending support to the myth that the military revolution of 1926 that brought Salazar to power and the corporatist regime were of necessity unpopular and reactionary developments, a turning back from what had seemed the inevitable progression of liberalism and pluralism.

First, it should be said that Oliveira Marques is himself a liberal and thus has a strong interest in marshaling the facts that support his interpretation. Second, it is clear that he has overstressed the "liberalizing" and "democratizing" influences of this period, for we have already seen that Portugal in the nineteenth century was still an elitist and patrimonialist system with only weakly articulated notions of genuine popular rule and where the historic corporatist and authoritarian patterns remained dominant despite the facade of constitutionalism and parliamentarism. The elites were expanded, to be sure, and some new elements managed to circulate in power, but the historic *system* remained.[33]

Third, the progress of the "liberal" period can easily be exaggerated. True, Portugal began a modest economic takeoff in the nineteenth century and some other of her institutions were reformed, but one can also argue that, given the times, economic progress was virtually inevitable no matter who was in power and in fact would have been far greater had the country not been plagued by the partisan conflict and civil strife that passed for "democracy" during this period. Fourth, it is significant that even the so-called republican regimes and institutions in Portugal exhibit authoritarian, elitist, and patrimonialist features and in reality are not altogether different from those regimes and institutions that were manifestly authoritarian. One need only look, for example, at the so-called Magna Charta of Portuguese associational life, the decree-law of May 9, 1891, governing the organization of class associations, to see that even in this "liberal" document group and associational life was about as carefully regulated and controlled from above as it had been under absolutism and would continue to be under the Estado Novo. The so-called republican era in Portugal was, in fact, far less republican and liberal and far more authoritarian and elitist than its proponents would admit. Indeed, as Oliveira Marques's own research has shown, the only time that the parliamentary regime functioned at all effectively was when it was least parliamentary—namely, when it was governed by a strong monarch.[34]

Having said all this, it must also be admitted that some new currents and social forces had emerged in Portugal during the nineteenth century, that alongside the traditional pyramid of power and only partially integrated with it there had, as in Spain, grown up a new and parallel structure, a "second Portugal," nascently liberal in character and challenging the traditional assumptions and institutions. Although it remained a minority strain, still secondary to the dominant elitist, authoritarian, and patrimonialist tradition, it was strong enough that it could not be dismissed out of hand. When Salazar later made an attempt to put it down, he found that to do so would require a full-fledged dictatorship and widespread repression—all ingredients, as we shall see, in the ultimate failure of his corporative experiments. This liberal and democratizing current culminated in the establishment of a Republic from 1910 to 1926;[35] it would later reemerge in the 1974 revolt.

The first Portuguese Republic, initiated in 1910, was characterized by disorder, chaos, and a long-term trend toward fragmentation, polarization, and anarchy. The litany of the Portuguese Republic is the oft-repeated history of a futile effort to erect an inorganic, liberal parliamentary system in a country where organicism, centralism, and unity had always been the dominant characteristics. Its parties were personalistic and so fractionalized that no one of them was able to command anywhere near a majority. The country and its politicians lacked previous experience with effective self-government; excesses abounded and the usual machinery of government tended to break down. Radical reforms were initiated but seldom implemented; they nevertheless served to provoke the hostility of the traditional forces. A rising middle class in the cities was eager to inherit the wealth and privileges previously reserved for the elites, and a nascent trade union movement was similarly organizing to challenge the traditional order. But the newer social and political forces were still inchoate and disorganized. During the sixteen years of the Republic, Portugal experienced twenty-one revolutions and forty-four cabinet reorganizations. There were numerous assassinations, strikes, and bombings. The web of traditional society began to become unraveled; the historic way of managing change seemed to be getting out of hand.[36]

There were continuities as well. Patronage and spoils continued to serve as the grease that kept the wheels moving, only now the rewards and support system were managed in new ways and for the benefit of a somewhat expanded constituency. Even at the height of this Republican period, Portugal remained an oligarchic system governed by the *homens bons*. The system remained authoritarian, tutelary, and paternalistic; government programs were carried out occasionally for the benefit of the popular classes, but these programs emanated from the top and in no sense did the lower classes *participate* in their formulation or implementation. The administrative state continued to stand, though it was now manned by a new political elite which created new public positions and sinecures filled by its own friends and supporters. All in all, the Republic did not represent such a sharp break with the past as is often imagined. Moreover, under the dictatorship of Sidonio Pais in 1917/18, judged by many historians to be the best government Portugal had during this so-called republican period, some of the earliest experimentation with a revived structure of corporatist state organization and interest representation went forward.

To the political problems of the republic were added the economic crises of 1918/19, the bank-note scandal of 1924/25,[37] and a virtually continuous history of economic mismanagement and corruption. Meanwhile, right-wing and traditionalist forces of both integralist and monarchist orientation launched a number of abortive coups which came close to toppling the government on at least three occasions.[38] The Army was also restless. It had come out of World War I discredited; poorly trained and equipped, its recruits became to their humiliation the "trench diggers of Europe." Following the war the Army was more and more determined to restore both its own and the nation's prestige.[39]

Public sentiment began to swing away from the Republic. Significantly, this shift encompassed both the university students and the trade union leaders, as well as the bulk of the middle class who were made increasingly impatient by the disorder and accelerating chaos.[40] A whole generation of young intellectuals had grown up convinced of the bankruptcy of liberal parliamentarianism and of the unacceptability of socialism. To them, a third alternative, corporatism, seemed the wave of the future. Other integralist and Catholic political movements, Integralismo Lusitano and the Centro Académico de Democracia Cristã, were similarly gaining strength.[41] In the Army, too, the same corporative, integralist, and nationalist ideas were widespread. Although the details had not been worked out, as early as 1922 it was clear that there would soon be a military solution and that the solution would be corporatist, authoritarian, and nationalist in character.[42]

The coup that toppled the Republic in 1926 was thus not just the response of a handful of military officers and reactionaries but a reflection of widespread public dissatisfaction and general erosion of support for republican ideas. Certainly no one rose up to defend the Republic; there were few laments for its passing and many cheers. Nor was the coup of 1926 the entirely reactionary movement often pictured. It was not the most right-wing Integralists, Monarchists, and Fascists who came to power but the more moderate elements, who sought to restore a system of order and social peace. Nor did they want necessarily to roll back the reforms that had occurred under Republican rule. In keeping with its nationalist character, the new regime sought to restore Portugal to its previous national prestige. It sought to create indigenous institutions to replace the British imports that in the Portuguese context had proved inappropriate. In other words, the new government sought not to turn the clock back but to ratify the social and political changes that had taken place (the emergence of new elites and bourgeoisie and of an urban labor movement) and to do so within a framework of order, discipline, and authority.

Other than these vague general ideas, however, characteristic of so many military coups in the Iberic-Latin context, the generals who seized power in 1926 lacked a concrete program. Hence, the government muddled along through 1927 and 1928, when Salazar first became finance minister, and even until 1930, by which time he had more strongly consolidated his influence.[43] For Salazar and his supporters *did* have a specific plan and program, a "third way" that called for the corporatization of the entire Portuguese system. It is toward the explication and analysis of the theory *and* practice of Portuguese corporatism, and its implications, that this book is dedicated.

Portuguese Political Culture: An Overview of Social and Economic Structures

In 1926 Portugal remained, as it does today, at the outer margins of Europe, a distant country far from the centers of "civilization," as measured not only in kilometers but also in time. Portugal was *in* Europe geographically but not *of* Europe socially, politically, or psychologically, an ambiguity that is as true now, as Portugal debates its entry into the Common Market while still seeking to maintain its separate identity, as it was in the fifteenth and sixteenth centuries when the modern Portuguese nation emerged.[44]

Continental Portugal lies at the westernmost point of Europe, bounded on the west and south by the Atlantic Ocean and on the north and east by Spain. It is shaped somewhat like an upright rectangle running approximately 350 miles from the northern border with Spanish Galicia along the Minho River to the southern coast of the Algarve on the Gulf of Cadiz. Across, it is approximately 140 miles from the Atlantic to the Spanish border. Including the Azores and Madeira islands, Portugal contains about 35,000 square miles, roughly the size of the state of Indiana.

Geographically, mainland Portugal is divided into three distinct regions.[45] The North is hilly and mountainous, characterized by small plots and farms carved out of the valleys and hillsides. The land is harsh and cruel, the temperatures extreme, and for six months of the year (October through March) there is no rainfall. One need only look at this rocky countryside to understand why Portugal was never able to develop the agricultural surplus on which a more advanced economy might have been based. Over the centuries strong, resilient smallholders, through backbreaking hand labor, have cut steps into this mountainous terrain and carefully conserved and tilled the meager soil, and it is in the weather-beaten but enduring faces of these people that many Portuguese still see the true virtues and original character, Catholic and conservative, of their people and their nation.

Southern Portugal, the Alentejo, is flat and gently rolling, dominated by large estates and a lord-peasant pattern that, until recently, had not changed greatly since feudal times. The land here is also generally infertile, suitable for grazing but probably not for intensive agriculture. That Portugal could solve its rural and agricultural problems by dividing up these estates and giving the land to the peasants, a recurrent theme in reformist and revolutionary programs, may be no more than a panacea. The issue is a charged one politically, but economically it is clear that land redistribution by itself will not be sufficient to make the Alentejo prosperous and viable.

Central Portugal is more varied, in terms of the size of the landholdings, social relations, and economic conditions. There are numerous medium-sized and family farms, something of a rural middle class, and agriculture oriented toward internal consumption. This area includes the country's major city, Lisbon, most of the industry, and hence an urban-industrial class system as well as a rural-agricultural one. The three regions of Portugal thus support quite different life styles, and their social structures often reflect their varied patterns of man-to-land and man-to-man relations. To integrate these diverse regions, to link them by roads and other grids, and to centralize authority in a diverse and difficult land have been among the historic tasks of all Portuguese governments.

The population of continental Portugal is just under nine million, and in recent decades it has been declining. This is due both to falling birth rates and to heavy emigration, chiefly to the other Western European nations where wages are higher. Emigration, the drafting of a generation of young men to fight in Africa, plus the steady flow of rural elements to the big cities like Porto and Lisbon, have drained the farm areas of their ablest workers, while at the same time adding to the slums and concomitant social problems of the cities. Reflecting its agricultural and traditional character and the incipient nature of its industry, Portugal remains 30 to 40 percent rural, but the rural/urban ratio is changing rapidly. Porto now has a population of approximately 350,000 while that of Lisbon is around 900,000; numerous smaller towns and provincial capitals have populations ranging from 20,000 to 100,000.[46]

Socially, Portugal retained, even in modern times, a hierarchical and rigidly stratified system with immense gaps between classes.[47] Its elites, we have seen, had been expanded somewhat, but the system was still an elitist one, and the elites themselves constituted no more than 1 or 2 percent of the total population. While these elites were often exceedingly wealthy and influential, the urban and rural masses remained powerless and shockingly poor by European standards, while the middle class was comparatively small, constituting perhaps 15 to 20 percent of the population. Illiteracy was officially given at about 20 percent of the population, but in terms of actual and functional illiteracy the percentage was surely far higher. In the areas of housing, medical care, social services, and the like, Portugal also lagged far behind the rest of Europe. Family, neighborhood, kinship, and patronal ties remained exceedingly important at all levels of society, often more important than the impersonal ties of professional associations, political organizations, and government social programs.

Since Portugal had never had a full-scale social revolution, its ancient ruling classes remained largely intact. The nobility and the older aristocratic families were still powerful, and there remained a strong monarchist movement. The elite was not monolithic, however; its members could be found in a number of political movements. The elite's wealth to a considerable extent was concentrated in land and agriculture and in the picturesque *quintas* and *latifundia* that dot the Portuguese countryside. But in recent decades commerce, industry, shipping, banking, and manufacturing had grown immensely. There emerged not one but several elites, both old rich and new rich, though often intermarried and interrelated, an older rural aristocracy and several newer urban ones. Well-connected, wealthy, arrogant, and socially "superior," closely bound up with the state and its various political and economic activities, able generally to protect its interests no matter which faction controlled the government, the power of these elite elements was all-pervasive, though they were not always of a single mind.

The growing middle sector developed little consciousness as a class, tending to ape upper-class ways. Although this group is expanding in numbers there is no such thing as a "middle-class society" emerging in Portugal in the Anglo-American mold. The line between those who work with their hands and those who do not has remained a rigid, almost impenetrable, barrier, perpetuating the fundamental two-class nature of society. Social mobility existed for some lower-class elements, but only up to a certain point, when the ascriptive criteria of wealth, family, prestige, social background, and the right access and connections became all-important.[48]

The Portuguese lower classes are diverse, but they are all exceedingly deprived by any one of a host of social and economic measures. The ranks of the "popular" classes include the smallholders and tenant farmers of the North, the day laborers and peasant farmers of the Alentejo, the flood of recent arrivals in the cities' teeming shantytowns, the slightly better-off industrial workers and low-level government employees. Except for the latter groups, the bulk of the lower classes had received few benefits from recent government social programs and had not yet begun to share in the new affluence of modern Europe. It is among these elements that illiteracy, malnutrition, and malnutrition-related diseases were most pronounced; frustration and despair were also widespread. Largely disfranchised, uninvolved in national social and political life, without any say in the government programs that affect them most intimately, the Portuguese lower classes, who constitute the overwhelming majority of the population, remained only marginally a part of the nation; they constituted the "clients" of the upper- and upper-middle-class "patrons," third- and fourth-class citizens looked down upon and kept in place by the other two.

Class lines in Portugal were, if anything, even more tightly drawn than in Latin America. Portugal was not only a Latin society organized in the historic hierarchical fashion but also decidedly Old World— and Old World in a pre-World War I sense.[49] It is as though a whole half century (or more) had passed Portugal by, and in a sense it had. There were probably few societies left in the world—and certainly not in Europe—where breeding, dress, family, speech, bearing, and the proper credentials remained as important in determining where an individual fit in the social order. The sense of place, status, and hierarchy was all-important. The system provided for little social mobility across class lines, except perhaps through education and through government itself (a theme particularly important for our study since Salazar, Caetano, and many others of the Estado Novo were of comparatively humble, middle-class origins and earned their elevated positions in the society through intellectual brilliance and achievement and then through government service). One's turn in line, how and when one gets waited on by service people, access to government officials or to the *patrão,* when one's papers are processed, the treatment one receives in a store, business, or governmental agency—all of these are determined by where one fits in the system, what rank one holds.

Historically, Portugal has been a poor country, the poorest in Western Europe, an economic "embarrassment" to the West, just as Albania is to the East. Portuguese workers are the lowest paid in Western Europe, and in the rural areas the bulk of the population ekes out a meager subsistence. More recently, however, Portugal, too, (particularly her upper and middle classes) has begun to benefit from the new economic affluence which characterizes so much of Western Europe. GNP has increased in recent years at a steady rate of 5 to 6 percent per year, and since the 1940s per capita income has doubled, tripled, and is now close to $1,000 per person per year. Although one still is shocked at the poverty, wretched living conditions, and disease endemic in both rural and urban slums, it is clear that Portugal has begun to "take off" economically to the extent that it is difficult any longer to classify Portugal with the rest of the underdeveloped world. Though the economy is still often weak, the income curve skewed, and the standard of living low by the standards of the rest of Western Europe, Portugal has clearly passed an economic threshold; its society has accelerated the process toward modernity and even a certain "embourgeoisement." All this has important implications for our study of corporative ideology and institutions and their relation to Portuguese development.[50]

Until the 1930s Portugal remained overwhelmingly an agricultural economy and country, and even today in outlying areas and villages social and economic arrangements are still largely tied to the ownership of land and the traditional relations of *patrão* and peasant.[51] At present, agriculture contributes only about 15 percent of GNP, but it still employs some 30 percent of the labor force in arrangements generally hampered by a lack of modern production techniques. Since the 1930s, manufacturing and industry have constituted a steadily increasing share of GNP (now up to 35 percent), creating a large urban work force, raising living standards and expectations, and hence hastening the flood of migrants to the cities. Tourism has also become a major Portuguese industry in recent years, with both its positive and negative consequences. Portugal is moderately rich in mineral resources, with significant deposits of wolfram (especially profitable during World War II), tin, iron ore, coal, and copper. The fishing industry is of special importance, tied as it is to Portugal's historic preoccupation with the sea. Principal exports include wine and other alcoholic beverages, wood and wood products, textiles, chemical products, both common and precious metals, and electrical equipment. Imports include chiefly the mineral and vegetable products which Portugal does not produce, chemical products, clothing, machinery, trucks, and transport equipment.

There are three further points about the Portuguese economy that should be emphasized. First, although Portugal was in a sense a capitalist system, it remained dominated in so many ways by a historic tradition of monopoly, mercantilism, and state ownership that some distinct interpretations of political economy are required to understand how the system worked.[52] The Portuguese were not so much Schumpeterian entrepreneurs but rather a nation of small merchants, family enterprises, and established or aspiring burghers, tied together at the top by class, family, and political relationships and dependent on government for contracts, access, and special privileges. It is more an etatist system, or system of state capitalism, than one of laissez-faire and free enterprise.

The second point that needs emphasis is the close relationship between the state-capitalist economy of metropolitan Portugal and that of her former overseas possessions, principally Angola and Mozambique. The two were bound together through a powerful conglomerate of banks, shipping companies, import-export concerns, landholding and mining interests, and so forth—to say nothing of the governmental structure of a bureaucratic empire.[53] And, third, we should mention the increasing importance of Portugal's economic relations with Europe and the Common Market with its implications for Portuguese trade, internal industrial development, and international alignments.[54]

In the first part of this chapter we have emphasized the pervasive influences of elites and elitism in Portuguese history, of authoritarian-corporatist social and political structures, and of the expanding patrimonialist state apparatus in the Portuguese system. These structures and behavior patterns encompass not only the civil bureaucracy but also the Army, the Church (although in present-day Portugal Church and state are officially separated and the Catholic Church seems less important as a political force), and virtually all groups and institutions. Elitist, authoritarian, corporatist, and patrimonialist social and political patterns are so strongly a part of the Portuguese political culture that they remained intact even in the face of significant economic growth, industrialization, and accelerated social change. Indeed, the persistence of these traditional institutions, the way they have adapted to modernization, is one of the main themes of this study.

One cannot but be struck by the historic conservative and traditionalist character of the entire Portuguese nation, socially, politically, economically, and psychologically. The importance of history, place, tradition, formality, hierarchy, and the past is the main theme running through the travel accounts as well as the more scholarly literature.[55] Portugal remained a nation of melancholy, frequently of lethargy and social stagnation. Its people were peaceful, patient, acquiescent, and conservative. Theirs was a culture and character molded by detachment from the outside world, by centuries of struggle against sea and infertile hillside, by resignation, by hard labor and few opportunities for advancement. Although their condition was improving and most Portuguese by the early 1970s had come to feel more optimistic about the future, life had always been difficult for them. Even in an era of rising economic prosperity, they continued to cling to the older and simpler values and to reject the untried, the uncertain, and the new. In many respects, therefore, theirs remained a *subject* political culture rather than a *participatory* one.[56] Clearly the Portuguese revolution will force a reinterpretation of some of these stereotypes, but just what has changed and how much Portugal remains the same in the wake of the revolution is still an open question.

In short, Portugal had, at least until the 1974 revolution and perhaps beyond, *both* a *corporate state,* formally instituted in the 1930s, *and* a *corporate society, culture, and tradition.* The emphasis throughout Portuguese history, reaching back to the origins of Lusitania, in virtually all areas of national life and among all social sectors, had been on hierarchy, authority, patrimonialism, and a kind of inherent, ingrained, almost *natural* corporatism. The following chapters will explore how this historic corporative form and system have dealt with twentieth-century change and modernization, the capacity of the system to continue to adapt to newer pressures, and the implications for Portugal of its particular form of corporatist development, as well as the at least partial demise and eclipse of corporatism following the revolution of 1974.

III

Corporative Theory and Ideology

Portuguese corporatism has been widely seen as not only anachronistic, a product of the interwar period whose time had clearly passed, but also irrelevant, a smoke screen erected by wealthy elements to disguise their self-seeking motives. Corporatist theory and ideology have thus been frequently dismissed as mere rationalization, an unimportant part of the political-ideological facade which had little to do with the real locus of power in the Portuguese system. This interpretation in part grows out of a similar assessment of Mussolini's corporatist experiments as post hoc rationalizations or, worse, a "confidence trick." Because the regime failed to live up to its ideological promises, the temptation has been strong to dismiss the ideology as a hoax or as mere window dressing of only symbolic importance.[1]

This contemptuous judgment, as Philippe C. Schmitter has pointed out, is probably both premature and naive. Corporatist ideology and institutions are clearly not anachronistic, as demonstrated both by their continued strength throughout the Iberic-Latin culture world and by their recent resurgence in such diversely modernizing nations as Peru, Spain, Chile, Mexico, Argentina, and Brazil.[2] In many respects, indeed, corporatism remains the dominant form of sociopolitical organization throughout the Iberic-Latin world and is still at the base of its political culture and history.

Nor should Portuguese corporatism be dismissed as an irrelevant smoke screen, for while it was not what its erstwhile proponents claimed, its functions were many and diverse. It not only served to organize and rationalize the regime's actions from the 1930s on but also helped explain broader Portuguese political behavior. Corporatism and the corporatist institutions have served as agencies of controlled social change, with the emphasis on *both* the *control* and the *change*. Corporatism was thus both a means of positively channeling some progressive changes in certain preferred, corporatist directions and a means of negatively preventing that change from getting out of hand. In addition, in its wider political-cultural meaning, corporatism serves as an Iberic-Latin counterpart to the great isms of liberalism and socialism, a Latin and southern European response and alternative, we have said, to the same issues of emerging capitalism, anomie, alienation, and mass society that also shook the roots of society in northern Europe and North America. Surely, if we take liberalism and socialism seriously, if we find ideas of worth in the writings of Marx, Lenin, Locke, or Jefferson, then we must also look at "the other great ism," corporatism, and its major intellectual and programmatic forebears in the same light.

In Portugal the argument for the importance of corporatist ideology in shaping the regime's actions for over forty years carries special weight. For in Portugal we are looking not at post hoc rationalizations a la Mussolini but at a set of ideas and institutions formulated far in advance of their actual implementation, supported by a strong mass movement, and enjoying at the beginning the support of majority public opinion. In terms of the legalistic, bureaucratic, patrimonialist nature of the Portuguese political culture, furthermore, one could make a strong case that, particularly in the 1930s, corporatism was strongly in accord with that dominant political culture. Finally, a crucial point for understanding the Portuguese system is that the men who wrote the influential books and speeches on corporatism frequently became—largely on the strength of these intellectual activities—the ministers and agency heads charged with carrying out the corporative programs. Unlike the situation in Mussolini's Italy and Franco's Spain, where practical politicians and men of affairs remained dominant and not the corporative ideologues, in Portugal men like Salazar, Caetano, Teotonio Pereira, Costa Leite, Castro Fernandes, Fernando Campos, Augusto da Costa, Costa Pinto, Cid Proença, Gonçalves Proença, and others were not only the chief intellectual architects of the corporative system but also its chief builders, developers, and administrators. This gave Portuguese corporatism a continuing importance that it lacked in Spain, for example, where Franco quickly shunted the corporatist ideas of the Falange to one side and ruled more as a pragmatic *caudillo* than as a Falangist ideologue.[3]

In addition, the fact that the Portuguese leadership was so strongly committed to the corporatist ideology of the 1930s also served to retard the country's postwar development. For while in Spain a realistic leadership was able quickly to reorient itself in the changed circumstances and to strike out in new economic and social-development directions,[4] in Portugal the ruling element remained locked into the corporative mentality of the 1930s (or even earlier) and failed adequately to modernize and update itself (despite Caetano's notable efforts in this direction) even within its own corporatist ideological context. In all these respects it is clear that corporatist theory and ideology have had a sustained and even continuing impact whose importance should not be underestimated.

The Historic Tradition of Corporatism:
Origins and Antecedents

Corporative theorists trace the roots of their ideology back to ancient times, not only to Greece and Rome but to the very origins of civil society in family, clan, and tribe. It is in Greek philosophy and social organization, however, that corporatists see the antecedents of later, more complex forms: some of the earliest of professional organizations, the first theoretical considerations of the importance of organic unity in state and society, the role of the family and of other "natural" associations, the concepts of solidarity and of social grouping, and the bases of the state in the "natural" associations of the society.[5]

In the Roman system these links and continuities become stronger. Corporatists see in the Roman system of *colegios* and in its structure of family, professional, military, and religious institutions the precursors of both the medieval and their own corporative associations. Both the *colegios publicos* (government officials) and the *colegios privados* (professionals) had their own legal status and charters; moreover, none could exist without the prior authorization of the state. The monistic (unitary) and absolutist conceptions of the Roman state were also influential in shaping the thinking of later corporatists, as was its elitist and hierarchical structure. The impact of Roman law and of Christianity was similarly important in the later corporative concept, for it brought moral monism, reinforced the Roman ideas of order and hierarchy, and emphasized the importance of the common (as opposed to the individual) good. Indeed, while recognizing the danger of historical parallels and analogies, Mihaïl Manoïlesco, one of the foremost corporative theorists of the 1930s, saw in the Portuguese *Estado Novo* a direct extension and reflection of the Roman system: the important role of the state and of moral authority, the new-forged unity between the state and the nation, the monism of state and religion, the concepts of equilibrium and balance, the organization of the state on the basis of "natural" social organisms, the system of representation by "class" and corporate group, the party and the corporations as the needed links between the state and the people, the organic conception, the stress on moral regeneration, the tutelary and "civilizing" role of the state, the hierarchical order, the Christian conception, and so forth. It is no accident that, in its theoretical as well as its sociopolitical foundations, the Roman impact on Portugal and Portuguese corporatism remains considerable.[6]

From Augustine, Thomas Aquinas, and their own national religious traditions, the corporatists derived a Christian-hierarchical and compartmentalized concept of society, the stewardship concept of property, the idea that property had a social use and should redound to the good of society, and also the theory of just price based upon both objective value and a fair wage, as set presumably by the state. Purchaser and seller, employer and employee, should reap mutual advantages from their transactions; these were to be governed by harmony rather than conflict in a regime of social peace. From Aquinas also the latter-day corporativists took the concept of natural law and of the "common good." In Saint Thomas they saw a reinforcement in Christian terms of the Roman and Augustinian concepts of virtue, hierarchy, authority, and estates. In fact, it is Manoïlesco's contention that the Roman and the Christian influences were most important in shaping the corporative tradition; even further, he argues that it is how these two were balanced and blended that largely determined the variations in the pattern of development of the several Latin states.[7]

Perhaps more than any other aspect of medieval life and thought, it was the institution of the guild that influenced twentieth-century corporatists.[8] The guilds helped provide an acceptable answer to Catholic disapproval of commercial enterprise, for they were closed, monopolistic associations with strict rules for admittance and mechanisms available for regulating prices, wages, and production for (in the corporatists' later, romanticized view) the "common good." The first guilds, or *gremios,* in Portugal go back to the thirteenth and fourteenth centuries, precisely the time the Portuguese state was being consolidated and its basic characteristics defined. Also important in shaping the corporatist conception was the emerging system of feudal contracts, governing not only the relation of vassal to lord and lord to king but also the relations of such institutions as the municipalities, the university, and various societal groups to the central authority. But it was the guilds that commanded most attention, particularly as class conflict and economic breakdown accelerated in Portugal after World War I. For the guilds implied close cooperation between masters and workmen, not conflict as in the Marxian tradition, and the ability to choose one's own "class" representatives in the guild council. Membership in the guilds was compulsory, since the guild enjoyed a monopoly of the local trade or business in its specialized product. The members were classified hierarchically—master, journeyman, apprentice—and mutual rights and duties governed the relations between the several hierarchical levels. Looking back from the chaos setting in all about them, twentieth-century corporatists saw in the guilds a model (however idealized) of peaceful, harmonious, orderly socioeconomic relations. They sought to imitate the system of compulsory membership of both employers and employees in the same corporation, participating equally and without class rancor in decision making, and advocated a hierarchical yet integrated organization similar to that of the guild system.[9]

Many of the functions performed by the guilds were resurrected in the designs for a modern corporative system. The guilds set prices, fixed production quotas, regulated wages and hours, settled conflicts among members, and lessened competition. They administered a form of social security for the sick and unemployed, gave pensions to retired members, and often provided funeral expenses. These services were sustained out of a guild fund or "patrimony" raised through donations, dues, and fines and frequently supplemented by the state. In the Estado Novo the corporative agencies and the government took on many of these same functions, and recent corporatists also adopted the concepts of "patrimony" and the "right to work." [10]

According to much medieval political philosophy, the guild, together with such other "natural" associations or "corporations" as the family, the local community, and the Church, would serve to limit the power of the state and help prevent tyranny and absolutism. The guilds would also function as the representatives of their trades or "classes" in their relations with the state. Hence, their concern would be not just with the private profit of their members but with the "common good." Some latter-day corporatists argued that the corporations, harmonized and integrated in this fashion, would become *the* fundamental political unit, ruling out the need for political parties, rival interest groups, and class organizations, as in the liberal-pluralist model. This was an extension of the medieval practice of giving guild officials representation in the cortes or in other areas of decision making and of providing them important positions in the municipal government in return for political loyalty and service.[11]

At another level, meanwhile, Portuguese (and Spanish) political theory remained consonant with this same corporatist-patrimonialist tradition and supportive of it. For while "modern" political thought beginning with Machiavelli in the sixteenth century would elsewhere in Europe lead eventually to concepts based on secularism, materialism, equality, and pragmatism, in the Latin countries of Spain and Portugal the focus continued to be Christian, moral idealism, philosophic certainty, and a unified, organic, hierarchical, corporative view of the proper ordering of state and society. The foundations for these systems lie in what Richard Morse has called the "Thomistic-Aristotelian notion of functional social hierarchy," [12] and they find their major expression in the political thought of Spain's Golden Century.

Vitoria, Soto, Suárez, Molina, and Mariana were the chief intellectual architects of the modern sixteenth-century Spanish (and Portuguese) patrimonialist state apparatus. Their conception rested on Christian rather than secular assumptions. Empirical facts had to show the credentials of logic, rightness, and relation to abstract (Christian) justice. Rather than separating moral and ethical precepts from the pragmatic needs of the state or prince, as in Machiavelli, the ideal of the Spanish-Portuguese theorists remained the fusion of the moral and the political. From the "modern," secular viewpoint, this "traditionalist," "scholastic" approach locked Spain and Portugal into the sixteenth-century pattern and removed them and their colonies from the "mainstream" of modern history. But perceived from another, less utilitarian perspective, this political-philosophic tradition also gave Spanish and Portuguese life its firm moral and natural-law base, its standards of behavior and dominant political culture, and its distinct pattern of national development.[13]

Vitoria and Suárez stand as the great system builders on whose foundations the Spanish-Portuguese empires and Iberic-Latin society were constructed. Their genius lay in fusing the Roman system of law and governance, the Thomistic-Catholic tradition, and the system of juridical estates and "classes" derived from customary law into a unified concept of state-building royal authority. The common assumptions of all these early writers included an ordered and God-directed universe, the Thomistic hierarchy of laws, and a Christian state and society. All shared a certain disdain for the common man; what they meant by "popular" government was feudal and aristocratic, based on a structure of privilege and special *foros,* the power of the traditional estates, hierarchy, and "natural" elites.[14] Their view of the state was the organic one, that government was natural, necessary, and ordained by God for achieving harmony among men. This conception, Guenter Lewy has argued, is an almost inherently conservative one and accords with our previous comments regarding the generally conservative nature of Portuguese political culture. For in contrast to contract theory which, except in Hobbes, tends to be individualistic, liberal, and democratic, organic theory subordinates human law to natural and divine law, is more tolerant of authority, slights the individual in favor of group "rights" or a superior "common good," accepts and justifies the status quo, reserves extensive powers for traditional vested interests, and leans inherently toward some form of corporate order that subordinates man to some allegedly higher purpose.[15]

In comprehending the Iberic-Latin systems, one must think, thus, in terms of a hierarchically and vertically segmented structure of class and caste stratifications, of social rank orders, functional corporations, estates, municipalities, guilds, and *interesses,* all fairly well defined in law and in terms of where they fit in this functional, hierarchical order. It is a rigid and yet adaptable system whose component parts are tied to and derive legitimacy from the authority of the patrimonialist state apparatus or its leader. There is, of course, a secular version of this bureaucratic-authoritarian-patrimonialist structure of state and society, but in the Iberic-Latin tradition at this point and on into the twentieth century its bases lay chiefly in Thomistic and neo-Thomistic thought. The best form of government is, therefore, an enlightened monarchy, or strong but just executive; there is little room for "separation of powers" or "checks and balances" on the Anglo-American model. Rather, a monistic structure is required to keep the peace and maintain the "natural" order. Extensive power is also reserved for such corporate entities as the Army, the Church, the *gremios* (and eventually *sindicatos*), and other interests. Organic-corporatist theory hence rejects liberal individualism and, in the Iberic-Latin tradition, also the materialistic, secularizing conceptions that accompanied development elsewhere in Europe. Although this repudiation does not *necessarily* follow from the organic, Catholic, and scholastic premises, it certainly has a powerful basis in them. And when bolstered by a similar, parallel, and reinforcing sociopolitical history and cultural tradition going back to the root origins of Iberic society, this "corporative model" takes on even greater importance.[16]

Although the sixteenth-century state structure was subsequently refined, modified, expanded, and further institutionalized, it continued to serve as the foundation on which Spain, Portugal, and their New World colonies were based. Indeed, given the absence in the Iberic-Latin world of any of those profound social revolutions that took place elsewhere in Europe, the basic institutional and behavioral features of the Spanish-Portuguese systems remained largely unchanged until the onslaught of liberalism in the nineteenth century. Pombal had threatened certain vested interests and abolished some of their feudal privileges, but he also authorized the creation of new merchant, artist, and other associations, and in the end he simply rotated some of the elites rather than destroy the old system of feudal privilege once and for all. Both the "organic monarchy" of the seventeenth and eighteenth centuries and the Pombalian regime were essentially extensions of the sixteenth-century model rather than repudiations of it. The corporatist-patrimonialist state, given modern form by Suárez, Dom Pedro, and others, thus remained the operative form to the end of the eighteenth century.

The Three Great Isms: Liberalism, Socialism, and Corporatism

The French Revolution of 1789 had as one of its chief goals the abolition of feudal rights and privileges. The guilds of the Old Regime were swept away, their demise made final by the law of March 2, 1791. The revolutionary concepts of liberty and equality served to undermine the ancient structure of privilege and hierarchy, and these concepts also had their effect on Portugal. We have already traced in chapter 2 the evolution of Portuguese liberalism and republicanism in the early nineteenth century and its eventual "triumph" in the liberal constitution of 1822 and the decree of 1834 which legally abolished the guilds and all forms of corporate privilege. Unlike the situation in France, however, in Portugal this decree was not accompanied by social revolution, which meant that even under the "liberal" regime of the nineteenth century Portuguese elites remained dominant and the de facto system of corporatism and special privilege largely intact.

For some Portuguese traditionalists, however, even the limited liberalism that did exist was too much. In his *Dissertation in Favor of Monarchy* (1799) the Marques de Penalva sought to counter the spreading "subversive" doctrines of the encyclopedists. Joaquim de Santo Agostinho Brito França Galvão sought to combat the "false doctrines" of Rousseau. The archbishop of Evora authored various pastorals on the unity of the spiritual and temporal authorities and on the Catholic basis of the Portuguese nation, while the bishop of Viseu, Francisco Alexandre Lobo (1763–1844), urged the restoration of royal authority limited only by the traditional estates of Church and nobility. In his *Novo Principe,* José da Gama e Castro, another monarchist, invoked the glory of the sixteenth-century model. Such thinkers as Antonio Ribeiro Saraiva, Antonio de Almeida, Faustino José da Madre de Deus, and Antonio Joaquim de Gouveia Pinto expressed similar monarchist ideas, defended the rights of the Church and of the traditional estates, and helped lead the struggle against early nineteenth-century liberalism and constitutionalism.[17]

This tradition of Portuguese thought, parallel to traditions in early- to mid-nineteenth-century France and Spain, was clearly reactionary in character. It set itself against the currents of the French Revolution and was unalterably opposed to the concepts of liberty, equality, and democracy then beginning to emerge. It sought to correct the agnostic, individualistic, atomistic, and laissez-faire tendencies of the nineteenth century. It sought to resurrect the status quo ante, a system of monarchy and of estates which favored the privileged few. A number of these thinkers, anticipating later solutions, would have been willing to expand the corporate elites somewhat to encompass the new urban bourgeoisie beginning to develop in Portugal, but in general—and by their own admission—we can characterize this current as almost wholly traditionalist and reactionary in character.

These brief comments on the liberal and traditionalist currents in Iberia help place in perspective the corporatist current, which purported to offer a middle way and thus help resolve the almost continuous civil strife between the other two warring factions. For if, as the traditionalists argued, liberalism was guilty of ignoring seven and more centuries of Iberic history, the traditionalists were guilty of ignoring the changes and realities of their own century. In the 1860s and 1870s, therefore, there began to be articulated in the Iberic-Latin nations a new body of ideas and developmental ideology, not only uniquely attuned to their own traditions but also seeking to face up to modern problems in a positive and even progressive way. Spain and Portugal were also beginning to be affected by the new pressures of capitalism, industrialization, urbanization, and accelerated social change. The trend in ideas hence began to turn away from reaction and medievalism and toward the serious study of these contemporary problems. French, Spanish, and Portuguese theorists began to wrestle with the same fundamental questions that concerned Marx, Weber, Tönnies, and others and to develop a framework of thought and action consistent with their past but also looking toward the future, an Iberic-Latin counterpart to the modernizing ideologies of liberalism and socialism. This body of thought came to be called "corporatism," and it is this tradition that is almost wholly ignored in our intellectual and social histories but which is crucial for an understanding of Iberic-Latin development.

The corporatists drew upon many of the same ideas as did liberals and socialists: utopian socialism, the works of Proudhon and a variety of early nineteenth-century social reformers, and positivism. But they also relied heavily on the newer and reformist ideas of many Catholic thinkers—such as La Farelle and Saint-Simon who elaborated guild schemes adapted more to their own generation than to the medieval system—and also on their own updated structure of authority and hierarchy. In this way, as Matthew Elbow notes, the Old Regime was not entirely obliterated (and it never entirely disappeared) but was merely placed in the background while new elements appeared in the foreground.[18] The ancient structure of corporate elites was not wiped out but was expanded to incorporate the rising social forces. The older theory was not repudiated; it was overlaid with new ideas. Still within the corporate-organic mold, for instance, French, Spanish, and Portuguese thinkers sought to fuse the traditional regard for order and hierarchy with the newer requirements of change and modernization. They attempted to deal with the new phenomena of mass man by erecting structures that provided for class harmony rather than conflict, structured participation rather than rootlessness and alienation. The corporate system was extended to encompass the rising middle sectors and the working class rather than, as in the past, simply putting these new class movements down through police repression and lockouts.

It was the crisis of "the social question" in mid-nineteenth century Europe that gave rise to the revival of corporate thought. What could be done about the new power of organized labor? The corporatist answer was that representation would be controlled and determined by functions (business, labor, agriculture, and the like) rather than through the anarchic laissez-faire and disruptive individualism (one man, one vote) of liberalism. The state would be given the power to regulate the process by which new groups would be admitted to the system and given a chance to share in its benefits. Rather than repudiating change, as did the early nineteenth-century reactionaries, the new philosophy called for accommodation to it. But this change would be carefully regulated to allow for the gradual, evolutionary process of modernization, in contrast to the hated system of liberalism where, according to the corporatists, the "rights" (still a feudal, group concept rather than an individual one) of all classes had been repudiated and the workers, hence, had no guarantee or protection in law. In this way, the Iberic-Latin nations sought to face up to modern realities without sacrificing the organic-corporate structure of the past.

One looks in vain in the standard works on political theory for more than passing mention of this dominant Iberic-Latin tradition. For once in the "modern" era, attention turns away from Spain and Portugal and toward the northern and presumably more dynamic "developing" nations of Europe: Locke and the Anglo-American experience, Rousseau and the Revolution, the Germans Kant and Hegel. By the nineteenth century our focus has become even more circumscribed: English utilitarianism, pragmatism, and Manchester liberalism, socialist thought, and the ideological concomitants of rising nationalism and industrialization —again confined chiefly to the northern European tradition. Later, our books and courses may trace the evolution of democratic and pluralist thought, the varieties of socialism, and the ideological underpinnings of totalitarianism in Nazi Germany or Stalinist Russia. The Iberian and corporatist strains of thought are ignored. Part of the bias and ethnocentrism that pervades the development literature, it would seem, stems from this prevailing view of the evolution of political thought in "the West" and from our selectivity as to which themes and movements are worthy of attention and celebration and which are not. But in structuring thinking along these lines we miss an important current of thought that remains dominant in the Iberic-Latin nations, that lies at the heart of their national histories and development processes, and that, because we ignore or reject it out of hand, continues to cloud our comprehension of that area. As Richard Morse suggests, ours has been a Protestant and is now a pluralist nation, and our academic disciplines have been of an increasingly secular and "scientific" orientation, with the result that both as Americans and as social scientists we are often insensitive and vaguely hostile to the sociological, psychological, and religio-theoretical foundations of Catholic society.[19]

Although we cannot here survey the entire history of the corporative revival, some of its chief figures and ideas may be mentioned. From the 1820s on, more and more Catholic writers had begun to become aware of the problems posed by the rise of capitalism and of "the social question"; they discussed it, defined its dimensions, took some initial positions, and even began to perceive the need for a more progressive stand on social matters. By the 1860s and 1870s, at the same time Marx was writing his major studies, these ideas had been crystallized into an emerging social doctrine. Wilhelm Ketteler, the bishop of Mainz, later a parliamentary deputy and a long-time leader in the German Catholic social movement, was perhaps the first to articulate these views into a unified statement of position. In his *Freiheit, Autoritat, und Kirch* [Liberty, authority, and church], 1862, and his *Die Arbeiterfrage und das Christendum* [Christianity and the worker question], 1864, Ketteler began to speak of the evil effects of unlimited competition, of the danger of an atomized society, and of the need to limit the power of the state. He talked of the social responsibility of property, the need for a wide distribution of society's goods, and the need for nations to concentrate on social as well as political issues. In supporting the new workers' associations then growing up and in calling for social reforms in the areas of wages, hours, and profit sharing, Bishop Ketteler was looking beyond the paternalistic charity efforts of the past. He viewed the labor question as essentially one of subsistence and proposed a regenerated guild regime as a solution. His influence on two generations of Catholic social thinkers, young priests, and trade union leaders was considerable.[20]

Also important was the French corporatist school of the Marques La

Tour du Pin, Albert de Mun, and Leon Harmel. They in turn had been influenced strongly by the writings of such earlier social Christians as Frédéric Le Play, Charles Périn, and Emile Keller, who in the decade prior to 1870 had begun to formulate ideas for an organization combining employers and employees to regulate each industry, trade, or profession; the family and other "natural" associations as the basis of society; the evils of liberalism and laissez-faire; an organic concept of the state; a just wage and a just price, and other ideas that went into the corporate scheme. However, it was not until the 1870s that the term *corporate regime* came into general usage and that a body of corporative doctrine, weaving together these diverse ideas, developed. Acting on these ideas, La Tour du Pin and de Mun in 1871 organized a network of Catholic Workingmen's Circles, which had grown to approximately 50,000 members in 400 circles by 1884. The circles were directed *by* its elite leadership *for* the benefit of its working-class members. Their aim was not to promote independent action on the part of workers but to place them in Christian corporations along with employers under the tutelage of directive committees recruited from the "better" classes. La Tour du Pin, the guiding force behind the organization and the author of its doctrine, was a vigorous opponent of liberalism and insisted on the corporative reorganization of society. He remained an aristocrat and a monarchist, but de Mun came eventually to see the need for a strong, *independent* workers' association within the corporative framework, and Harmel shocked his industrialist friends by advocating profit sharing and encouraging the workers to organize independently within his own factory.[21]

In the meantime, other Catholic social movements, workers' associations, and agricultural associations were springing up throughout France. Similar corporatist ideas were being articulated by Baron Karl von Vogelsgang in Austria, Manning and Gibbons in England, Decurtino in Switzerland, and a number of others in Germany, Italy, Spain, and Portugal. A body of corporative doctrine began to emerge that purported to provide the answer to the ills of capitalism. Nor were the Church and Leo XIII strangers to these doctrines.[22] The Church too was starting new efforts at Catholic revival based upon a system of social solidarity and Christian associations. In 1884 La Tour du Pin met with Leo XIII, and there is no doubt that the pope was strongly influenced by the corporatist ideas. A considerable body of writings on corporatism had grown up by the 1880s, along with a number of fledgling movements on the local, provincial, and even national levels. There remained the job of bringing unified coherence to these still vague ideas and of forging a movement transcending national boundaries.

In 1881 the pope charged a commission of theologians and Catholic social thinkers to study social and economic questions in relation to Catholic dogma. These leaders met at Freiburg in 1884 and helped provide the growing corporatist movements with needed unity and direction. Corporatism was now clearly defined for the first time as a "system of social organization that has at its base the grouping of men according to the community of their natural interests and their social functions, and as true and proper organs and institutions of the state, they direct and coordinate labor and capital in matters of common interest." The Freiburg meeting brought corporatist leaders, philosophers, and organizers from different countries together for the first time, gave their movement a coherence and legitimacy it had lacked before, and served as an impetus to the growth of the corporatist and Catholic social movements in the various countries represented. The theses adopted at Freiburg also had a strong impact on the Vatican's representatives and served as a precursor to many of the statements contained in the justly famous *Rerum Novarum*. Another conference of Catholic leaders, held in Berlin in 1890 under papal auspices to discuss improving working-class living conditions, adopted a similar corporative program on the eve of the promulgation of Leo XIII's "workingman's encyclical." [23]

It should be emphasized that by today's standards the corporatist movements of the 1870s and 1880s were by no means radical and revolutionary, although in the context of that time and in terms of the institutions (for example, the Church) and nations represented (Bismarckian Germany, Victorian England, Restorationist Spain, and so on) they did represent some fundamental shifts from past positions. A good illustration of the "conservative" (by present standards) and aristocratic nature of the movement is found in the makeup of the subcommittee that drafted the Freiburg Theses: among the ten members were two barons, five counts, and a duke. And men like Tour du Pin, for example, continued to speak of a "natural" ruling class who expected the deference due them as a result of their hereditary status. The Catholic workers' movements were still led by upper and middle class elements often with the desire to provide paternalistic protection or to use these agencies to combat socialism.[24]

And yet, as Michael Fogarty's research makes clear, the 1880s marked a real watershed in the history of the Catholic social movements. Aristocratic attitudes toward "the social question" were gradually changing, and a positive conception of the place of trade unions began to be substituted for the earlier negative and repressive one. The first workingmen's clubs had attracted the pious and the weak, not the militants; now, however, real *working-class* movements began to be organized, run by the workers themselves. Over and over, it had been demonstrated that paternalism did not work, that this was not the way to mobilize an intelligent and effective social movement. Thus, while collaboration and harmony between the classes remained the ideal, it was recognized that this could be achieved only if both capital and labor were strong enough to stand on their own feet. The paternalistic conception was being replaced by one in which a strong workers' organization was required, one that would defend its own interests and the dignity of its members. The workers could achieve their just demands, the newer argument ran, only through collective action and the free choice of their own leadership. Independent action could also include a strike, if conditions of a "just grievance" prevailed. In all these reformulations, one can still hear strong echoes of the older Thomistic conceptions, but these conceptions were now updated to meet the needs of a modern-day mass organization and of a progressive social reform movement capable of competing on even terms with liberalism and socialism for the loyalty of the emerging working class.[25]

The promulgation of *Rerum Novarum* in 1891 provided a special impetus to the entire Catholic social movement. It was, in a sense, a revolutionary document and sweeping in its implications for both Catholic Europe and Latin America. *Rerum Novarum* argued that, like the family, labor associations were a part of the natural order. The rights of men to organize into trade unions and to engage in labor activities were thus inherent; these rights could not be denied by employers or the state. Property and capital were obligated to have social functions, and the rights of workers were considered coequal with those of employers. Not only were these pronouncements quite radical in the context of those times but, perhaps more important, *Rerum Novarum* gave the Catholic and other workers' movements a legitimacy they had never enjoyed before. In a political culture where juridical recognition by the state provides the *sine qua non* for any group's existence, *Rerum Novarum* elevated the workers to a place of status, where the legitimacy of the workers' association was recognized and where the growing labor movements could take their place alongside the other legitimated pillars of the corporative regime. Although the implications of this statement were often tardy in development, until reiterated in even stronger and more urgent terms in *Quadragesimo Anno* (1931), *Rerum Novarum* nonetheless served as an inspiration for the entire Christian Democratic movement as well as for a host of parallel Catholic social and workers movements throughout Europe and Latin America.[26]

The corporatist ideas were given added appeal during this period by the rejection of liberal, contractual, and democratic conceptions of state and society in the writings of such prominent theorists as Gumplowicz, Mosca, Pareto, Michels, and Sorel. Particularly in the Latin countries and in southern Europe from roughly 1890 to 1914, antiparliamentary and antiliberal sentiments were strong and widespread. Gumplowicz, Mosca, and Pareto marshaled powerful arguments against the democratic and egalitarian ideologies and urged recognition of the inherent inequalities in society and its inevitable rule by elites. Michels pointed to the "iron law of oligarchy" present in even the most democratic of organizations, while Sorel exposed the social myths on which bourgeois and laissez-faire society rested. All these writers saw society in terms of the rulers and the ruled, in terms of various theories of elites, as pyramidal and hierarchical in character. Like the Catholic corporatists, they were organicist in their conceptions of state and society; they emphasized group rights over individual rights; they posited a strong role for the state as a moral leader and the need for authoritarian allocation of society's goods and services; they were "integralists" and "solidarists" in their conceptions of the unifying and coordinating functions of the state. In Mosca and Pareto the conception of the "circulation of elites" gained prominence, and the idea that it was the responsibility of the state to supervise change. The old ruling class would be transformed, and change would go forward not by revolution but by the ruling elites assimilating those elements of the subordinate classes that agree to accept the prevailing system and its rules. These were, of course, all secular conceptions, and of their influence on Mussolini's thought and Italian fascism there can be no doubt.[27] But many of these ideas dovetailed also with the Catholic-corporatist conception and were absorbed by Catholic social philosophers. It is no accident that the Portuguese Labor Statute of 1933, one of the fundamental documents of the corporatist order, represented a blend of both the secular conceptions of Mussolini's *Carta del lavoro* and the Catholic ideas of *Rerum Novarum* and *Quadragesimo Anno.* It is perhaps no accident either that this conception of how a state- and elite-directed political society manages change sounds remarkably similar to the model of the Iberic-Latin political process as elaborated by Charles W. Anderson and others.[28]

Beginning in the 1890s, and now with the impetus and legitimacy provided by the Church and *Rerum Novarum,* as well as the growing volume of antiliberal, antiparliamentary sentiment, a great variety of Catholic-inspired social and political movements began springing up and rapidly expanding all over Europe. We cannot here discuss the histories of the various national corporatist movements. Our purpose is rather to show the context in which Portuguese corporatism took root and grew and also to demonstrate how widespread these movements and currents of thought were. For by the turn of the century corporatist labor and workingmen's organizations, mutual benefit associations, social movements, and study groups where corporatist ideas were discussed had grown up throughout the Continent. In 1895 in Germany the first national Catholic trade union federation had been founded, and by the first decade of the twentieth century such federations had been established in virtually every country. Christian Democratic and Catholic-corporatist parties and movements of various shades of ideology rose up to become major contenders for political office. There was a great and lively debate on the strategies to be employed, the social programs to be adopted, and the routes that social mobilization should take. Associations for youth, women, university students, professionals, and others were founded, in addition to the associations for workers and employers. New concepts of social security and working conditions were articulated, and the Catholic social movement began to come to the forefront in promoting social change. Of course, in most of these movements heavy stress was still placed on the family and religion, and the social benefits and services provided were often of the charitable sort. But this was still a far cry from the aristocratic paternalism of the 1870s and represented a major adjustment as compared with the reactionary stance the Church and most Catholic social thinkers had assumed since 1789. By 1900 we see an increasingly modern and progressive series of movements wrestling with the complex modern issues of mass man, alienation, class conflict, and the like, and seeking to do so in a way that preserved intact those institutions considered valuable from the past (religion, family, hierarchy, authority, and the like) while also providing for adaptation and accommodation to modern, twentieth-century life. It is in this context that we turn to an examination of emerging corporatism in Portugal.[29]

The Catholic Social Movement in Portugal:
The Emerging Corporatist Ideology

Although the corporatist revival of the later part of the nineteenth century had begun chiefly as a Catholic response to the issues of modernization, by the first decades of the twentieth century it had veered off in several directions and was represented by several distinct schools of thought. Philippe C. Schmitter has identified four such schools of corporatist thought, and by this time in actual practice there are undoubtedly several more. Schmitter[30] distinguishes among (1) a social-Christian form as exemplified by Albert de Mun, Tour du Pin, and Joaquín Azpiazu, many of whose ideas found expression in the encyclicals *Rerum Novarum* of Leo XIII and *Quadragesimo Anno* of Pius XI, and also in a variety of Catholic and Christian Democratic movements;[31] (2) an authoritarian, bureaucratic, nationalist, secular, modernizing school whose ideologists included Spann, Manoïlesco, Gentile, Mussolini, and others of the Italian corporatist school;[32] (3) a radical (in the French sense) parliamentary, bourgeois, "solidarist" tradition as exemplified by Léon Bourgeois, Charles Gide, and perhaps Emile Durkheim;[33] and (4) a leftist, socialist, "syndicalist" line of thought whose spokesmen would include Saint-Simon, Sorel, the Guild Socialists, and, according to Trotsky, Joseph Stalin.[34] For illustrative purposes and to show the wide variety of regimes falling under this broad corporative umbrella, we can say that Allende in Chile, Bosch in the Dominican Republic, and perhaps Goulart in Brazil represent approximations of categories 3 and 4. Although she never developed a strong Christian Democratic movement nor was she ever so secular and Fascist as the Italian regime, Portugal was closer to categories 1 and 2.[35] Indeed, it was frequently the conflict between the Christian social-justice aspiration, on the one hand, and its secular authoritarian practices, on the other, that accounted for the internal dynamics of the Portuguese corporative regime and for the controversy that has swirled about it.

In Portugal and in the other Catholic countries of southern Europe, far more so than in the northern countries, the corporative ideas had a powerful impact. For it was there that the newer corporative currents fitted most comfortably with the historical and political cultural patterns of corporatism, authority, paternalism, and patrimonialism. As with other European influences over the centuries, however, it took some time for the corporative theories and organizations to reach Portugal.

The corporative resurgence in Portugal was closely tied to the Catholic revival beginning in the last third of the nineteenth century,[36] which, in turn, owed much to the reappearance of the Jesuits and other orders from about the 1850s on. By the 1890s there had been an important increase in the number of religious institutions, including almshouses, orphanages, colleges, hospitals, missionary bodies, convents, and the like. That same decade saw the establishment of a few of the first Catholic Workingmen's Clubs, inspired by *Rerum Novarum,* and of the Portuguese version of the French *Semaines Sociales,* week-long Catholic study groups.

Other Catholic-inspired organizations were formed in Portugal around the turn of the century that were especially important in providing a base for the later formation of a strong corporatist political movement. A Catholic *Centro Nacional,* modeled on similar political organizations in Germany and Belgium, had been formed in the 1890s, but it was not until 1903, as Richard A. H. Robinson puts it, that the desire to propagate papal doctrines and re-Christianize public life led to the definite creation of a Catholic Nationalist party.[37] With the slogan "Country and Religion," the Nationalists attempted to inspire all Catholics to political action within the framework of the existing (monarchist-parliamentary) regime. The party's patrons were the bishops, although its leader, Jacinto da Silva, insisted it was nonconfessional. Most of its proponents, however, as well as its foes, thought of it as an avowedly Catholic party, indeed as *the* Catholic party. Its purpose was to strengthen national institutions and reinvigorate social and economic life through an adherence to the papal encyclicals. Significantly, it preferred to think of itself as a Christian civic association rather than as a political party, perhaps foreshadowing the Salazar *União Nacional.* Equally significant for our purposes was its advocacy of a strong program of social justice for peasants and workers, demonstrating that it was not cast in the early nineteenth-century reactionary Catholic mold but in the newer and more progressive framework of *Rerum Novarum.* The Nationalists' program was incorporated in the integralist and nationalist movement of May 28, 1926.

Another major organization was the *Centro Académico de Democracia Cristã* (CADC), a Catholic study group founded at Coimbra in 1903 by Professor Sousa Gomes. As Robinson states, the Centro's founding inspired the bourgeois intellectual elites with a newer, more combative Catholic spirit and marked the beginning of their reconquest from their previous flirtations with humanism, anarchism, and republicanism.[38] The Centro, which also established a strong Lisbon branch took its program from the democratic reformism of Leo XIII; it sought to organize Catholic students, to propagate papal social teachings, and to support the Catholic workingmen's clubs then being formed. Through its periodical, *Estudos sociais,* it sought to make the university and high-school educated classes aware of the European-wide Catholic-Thomistic revival and of the new, emerging, corporative models of social and political organization. The CADC was especially important as the "school" from which a whole generation of Portuguese corporatist intellectuals emerged, including Salazar, Caetano, corporate organizer Teotonio Pereira, Cardinal Patriarch Manuel Cerejeira, writer and cabinet minister Costa Leite, and many others who would be leaders of the New State.[39]

The Catholic social movement in Portugal gained ground rapidly in the first decade of this century. The network of Catholic Workingmen's Circles (*Círculos Operários*) spread to most major cities and provincial capitals and to the mushrooming workers' neighborhoods (*bairros*) of Lisbon. The number of Catholic study groups, social centers, and charitable and other institutions multiplied. In 1906 the first national Christian Democratic congress met, bringing together *mutualistas* from all over the country. As the name implies, these organizations were still often cast in the traditional and paternalistic mold. They consisted chiefly of mutual benefit societies oriented toward Christian charity and social work, as distinct from the more class-based Catholic trade unions then emerging in France.

What gave particular impetus to these movements, and provided them with political purpose, was the establishment of the liberal, secular Portuguese Republic in 1910. This obviously is not to say that all Catholics were anti-Republican; they were not. But more and more Portuguese came to be opposed to the particular direction that republicanism took in their country. The separation of Church and state and the anticlerical and anti-Church measures taken by the Republic galvanized the bishops into action. More important was the sheer anarchy, chaos, and corruption for which the Republic came to stand. Opposition to the Republican regime served as the unifying banner around which virtually all the dissident elements could rally. Moreover, for the corporatist ideologues, the dismal performance of the Republic provided endless evidence for their contention, arrived at long before, that liberalism and parliamentarism were total failures. The Republican period seemed to confirm the corporatists' arguments regarding the pettiness and corruption of liberal politicians; the dysfunctionality of inorganic individualistic democracy; the divisiveness of a multiparty system; the bankruptcy of elections and the one man, one vote concept; the economic ruination brought on by laissez-faire capitalism; and the inappropriateness of foreign (in this case, British) institutions. It also appeared to demonstrate the need for strong, centralized direction; for the reestablishment of authority, national prestige, and social justice; of the Church and of a Catholic political culture. It underlined the necessity of a system of representation that would guarantee a voice to all groups, the need for order and discipline, and for a corporatist restructuring. These, of course, were precisely the planks in the Catholic-corporatist program. By playing on the growing disillusionment with the Republic, the Nationalist, Catholic, and Integralist opposition garnered large mass support. Because of this, the coup of 1926 was warmly welcomed by virtually all sectors of the population.

Thus, by the teens and early twenties, Republican sentiment was on the wane and Nationalist, corporatist, and Integralist ideas clearly ascendent. The question was no longer *if* an integralist, nationalist, and corporatist movement would topple the Republic but when and what precise form it would take. The number of small newspapers and opposition splinter groups was mushrooming. Though all these groups and factions differed somewhat in their programmatic prescriptions, they showed a common hostility to the Republic and to the liberal and individualistic ideas that undergirded it. In the large-circulation Catholic newspapers like *A epoca* and *Novidades,* liberalism and republicanism were, with considerable reason in the Portuguese context, scornfully attacked. A stream of flyers and pronouncements came from such study groups as the CADC. One must almost have lived during this period to comprehend the bitterness and scathing critiques of the anti-Republican opposition; moreover, one must measure republicanism not by its accomplishments in the Anglo-American tradition but by its almost total failure in the Portuguese context. For liberalism and republicanism had not begun to resolve any of Portugal's pressing problems; under the parliamentary regime, in fact, the old problems of divisionism, favoritism, conflict, and corruption had been exacerbated. The gaps between rich and poor had continued to widen, the social services were nonexistent, the economy was in a shambles, the polity had disintegrated. The Portuguese poured out their cumulated frustrations against the Republic and heaped venom upon it. To the strong intellectual movements already discussed, there was now added a new factor: powerful political movements that would soon succeed in toppling the entire Republican structure.[40]

Among these political organizations were the Monarchists, known in Portugal historically as the *miguelistas* after the exiled crown prince of the House of Bragança. The Monarchists were made up largely of aristocratic families, although the roots of their support reached into many sectors of Portuguese society. In terms of their social bases, ideological position, and historic origins, the Portuguese Monarchists were comparable to the Carlists in Spain.[41] What makes them interesting for our purposes is that they shared the beliefs and values of an authoritarian, antiparliamentary, ultramontane, and corporatist society. Though it may be difficult for most Americans to grasp, the Monarchists were still a powerful force in Portugal, nearly toppling the Republic on several occasions and contributing strongly to its demise in 1926. Although they initially supported the Nationalist regime that took power that year, they became disillusioned with its failure to restore the monarchy, and in 1931 a Monarchist demonstration against the government was suppressed only with difficulty. The following year the death of the exiled Prince Manuel deprived the Monarchists of their unifying symbol. Salazar, by then firmly ensconced in power, had the body brought back to Portugal for a lavish state funeral, thereby appeasing this powerful faction without bowing to its demands. Although the Monarchists were corporatist in ideology and a key force in the anti-Republican coalition, they did not produce the leaders who would design and administer the Estado Novo.

Far more important was Integralismo Lusitano, which some have termed the Portuguese version of fascism.[42] The actual situation was more complex than this, though there can be no doubt of the important influence of the Integralists in the Portuguese *Estado Novo*. Founded in 1914 by Antonio Sardinha as an intellectual study group chiefly inspired by the ideas of Sorel, Charles Maurras, and *Action française,* Integralismo Lusitano within five years had achieved the status of a major movement. Like the Monarchists, the *integralistas* were strongly anti-Republic and led several unsuccessful revolts against it—until the final *putsch* in 1926. The Integralist ideology, also authoritarian, nationalist, and corporatist in character, strongly influenced the military leaders who seized power with the overthrow of the Republic. Integralismo Lusitano was important, however, not just because of the corporatist ideology it expounded but also because some of its young leaders, men like Marcello Caetano and Teotonio Pereira, were among the chief architects of Salazar's corporatist system.

It is instructive to read now what the young leaders of Integralismo Lusitano were writing back in the teens and twenties. Their review, *Ordem nova* [New order], of which Caetano was a founding editor, proclaimed itself antiliberal, antidemocratic, antibourgeois, and anti-Bolshevik, intolerant, intransigent, apostolic, Roman, and monarchical.[43] It lamented the disappearance of good manners, chivalry, and honor. It was against indiscipline, materialism, dissolution of the family, government impotence, the French Revolution, the Portuguese Republic and all it stood for. The Integralists fulminated against secularism, against equality, against the sovereignty of the people, and against parliamentary democracy. Some Integralists were also strongly anti-Semitic and anti-Protestant, though this part of their thinking was cast in a nationalist and cultural mold rather than a racial one. That is, to the extent that Protestants, Jews, or any other religious elements detracted from the unity and integrity of the dominant Catholic-corporate tradition and heritage, the Integralists were opposed to them; but never in Portugal did this take the form, as in Nazi Germany and to some extent in Fascist Italy, of intense racial or religious persecution. In the religious and cultural as well as the political spheres, the Integralists were antiliberal and antipluralist; nor did they ever pretend to be otherwise.[44]

The Integralists called for a "new order" and a "new state." They wanted leadership, authority, and rule by a new elite in finance, bureaucracy, and government. They wanted *good* government (in the Thomistic, natural-law sense) under monarchical rule. The monarch would have "concentrated authority," but he would not be a tyrant; he would be surrounded by various elites, assisted by technical councils, counseled by a general cortes, inspired by Catholic and nationalist principles. The Integralists called for a restoration of the Catholic religion and culture and also of such traditional corporative institutions as the family, the *municipio*, the *gremios*, and the Casa de Vinte e Quatro, all of these to be based on principles of Christian morality.

The Integralists wanted an organic monarchy but a limited one; the coordinating and moderating authority of the crown but also genuine representation through the nation's historic corporate interests; a regime of vigor and unity which royal authority could provide, but held in check by countervailing elites. The Integralist regime, as one of their ideologues put it, would be "nationalist in principle, corporatist in means, monarchist in conclusion." They demanded that the National Assembly be reorganized on the basis of functional representation and that the "rights" and privileges of the Church and other traditional groups be restored. They called for a "spiritual nation"—a regime which would give protection to the Church and agree to a concordat with Rome. The Integralists called for a national resurgence, urged a repudiation of class strife, and demanded a system based upon the corporative principles and in accord with Portugal's Latin and Christian tradition.[45] "And don't tell us that systems don't matter," the Integralist journal *Politica* warned:

Reason, history, and contemporary events convince us that political institutions, in their form and above all in their essence, condition the realization of national aspirations in all their multiple manifestations, being good only insofar as they help the nation to progress and develop in both a moral and a material sense. Upon the nature of the political system also depend the peace and collective security of the individuals who make it up. There are good and there are bad political principles. From bad principles we arrive at political institutions that are nefarious in their essence and in their application; in contrast, from the political principles that experience proves to be in accord with the history and cultural milieu of the people come sound political institutions. It is *tradition* that teaches us what that system will be. And it is in this sense that Herculano, with his vision as a historian, argues that we need to develop the institutions that are most harmonious, most in accord with the traditions and temper of the Portuguese family.[46]

In keeping with the need to develop a political system based on indigenous traditions and not those imported from the outside, Teotonio Pereira wrote, "We must reject English parliamentarism and our status as a de facto British colony. Southern Europe is different from northern Anglo-Saxon Europe," he said; "our tradition is more spiritual than material. Ours is a special and distinct tradition, and we must stop aping the ways of the rest of Europe. We must seek to modernize and regenerate our structures but in accord with our own traditions. We must restore Portugal to its true nature and its legitimate power through the erection of a corporate system in accord with our own history and culture." [47]

Although the Integralists shared many of the ideas of the CADC, relations between them were not always harmonious. Integralismo Lusitano was militant, intolerant, and politically activist. The CADC was less extreme, more explicitly Catholic and intellectual. The CADC wished to establish an ordered and Catholic society in accord with Papal teachings, but it was neither so monolithic nor so "fascistic" as the Integralists.[48] In contrast to the CADC, Integralismo Lusitano used street demonstrations and other subversive tactics to undermine the Republic. And whereas the CADC derived its chief principles from the encyclicals, the Integralists were often open admirers of Mussolini. Integralismo succeeded in capturing important segments of a generation of university students and became an important political movement. Some of its leaders were in the forefront of an emerging national syndicalist movement, admired Sorel and the use of structured violence, and urged a far more extensive "fascistization" of Portugal than in fact its Catholic-corporatist leaders ever contemplated.

Eventually known as the "Jacobins of the Right," Integralist strength lay mainly with young students and military officers. Along with the Monarchists they participated in virtually every uprising and military conspiracy against the Republic from 1917 on. They supported the short-lived corporatist regime of Sidonio Pais in 1917/18, whose rule as a precursor of the Estado Novo in Portugal was in some ways similar to that of Primo de Rivera as a precursor of Nationalist Spain. But when Pais was assassinated in December 1918, they resumed their campaign of subversion. Between 1918 and 1926, though weakened by various schisms, the Integralists (and a separate organization Acção Realista) waged a two-pronged campaign against both the Republic and what they termed the democratic-liberal principles of the constitutional monarchists. They helped discredit and destroy the Republic and warmly welcomed the military dictatorship under Generals Gomes da Costa and Carmona initiated in May 1926.[49] Given the fact that that military movement was "integralist" and "nationalist" in character, it appeared as though Integralismo Lusitano, or at least its principles, had come to power.

Such an interpretation is not entirely accurate, nor is the one that sees Salazar's Estado Novo as a mere extension of the "fascism" of the Integralist movement. For one thing Integralismo Lusitano's intellectual and chief driving force, Sardinha, died in 1925; and the following year the papal condemnation of Maurras's writings encouraged many Catholics to leave the movement in favor of more moderate groups. Not only was Integralismo Lusitano never quite so strong after these two events, but there is considerable doubt that Sardinha, had he lived, would have even supported the Estado Novo. In fact, almost the entire Integralist "Old Guard" continued to press for a monarchical restoration and, when this failed to transpire, went into opposition against Salazar. Hence, it was the Integralist "New Guard," Caetano and Pereira, less militant and extremist, more humane, and more committed to social justice than the "Old Guard," who were assimilated into the Salazar regime. *Quadragesimo Anno* and Manoïlesco would come to serve as their guides, not Hitler, Maurras, or Mussolini.[50]

Although close to the Integralists on some points and ambivalent on others, Salazar and the young intellectuals around him never accepted the Integralists' violent tactics. Nor did they accept their monarchist design or their "fascism." Corporatism and authoritarianism, yes, in keeping with both Salazar's ideas and those of the military he initially served, but monarchism and fascism, no. Indeed, one of the cleverest strategies pursued by Salazar after 1926 was his acceptance of the Integralist principles of corporatism and nationalism (ideas Salazar himself firmly believed in) while at the same time elevating the military to the role of *poder moderador* rather than the monarch, thus in one deft sweep securing the loyalty of the Army, appeasing the more moderate Integralists, and securing even greater independent authority for himself. The conservatives and Catholics in Portugal had sometimes sided with the fascist Integralists to discredit, undermine, and help overthrow the Republic that they all hated, but once this common purpose had been accomplished the Salazar regime suppressed the more radical of the Integralists, domesticated others, and in the process expanded its own support while isolating the more extreme opposition.[51]

To say that the Estado Novo was an extension of Integralismo Lusitano and thus "fascist" is to distort the facts and avoid the complexity and diversity involved. There were Integralists who were openly pro-Nazi right through World War II, but they were never dominant in the Salazar regime and many bitterly opposed his policies. Nor did the regime, once it had consolidated itself, take very seriously those Integralists who urged the formation of a militant mass movement, an armed militia, or any of the other trappings of the fascist systems. The Blueshirts had been disbanded by 1934, the youth organizations took on functions comparable to the Boy Scouts, the official party played a demobilizing role, and anti-Semitism never became official policy. The *real* fascists (and there were some in Portugal in the 1920s and 1930s) were jailed or exiled by the Salazar regime, or absorbed into the official União Nacional where they quickly adopted the ideas of Salazar. It is chiefly in such younger New State advocates as Caetano and Pereira that *integralismo* was represented in the regime, but these leaders' views were so moderated by time and their official responsibilities that they ceased to be Integralists in any real sense. The ideological themes of corporatism and authoritarianism were common to a large number of political groups in the teens and 1920s and these, along with some of their advocates, were used in the service of the Estado Novo. But beyond this the evidence does not support the notion that the Salazar system was Integralist and, hence, fascist in character.

Probably the strongest single intellectual and political movement in shaping Salazar's thought and, hence, the ideology of his regime was the Centro Católico Português (ccp).[52] It was far more moderate than the Monarchists, Integralists, and other radical rightist groups. The ccp called itself an autonomous, centrist, nonparty pressure group, but it was tied closely to the Church hierarchy, and its goal was to organize Catholics for the re-Christianization of public life through *legal means* and *in obedience to the legitimate (Republican) authorities.*

The ccp was often vague in its program since it sought to serve as a broad umbrella organization for all Catholic political groups to defend and promote their common goals. Unlike the Integralists, it was willing to work through the existing system to achieve its goals. It urged an organic and corporative state structure and was critical of liberalism. But it welcomed also the papal condemnation of the Maurrassian doctrines in 1926 and declared itself, in obvious reference to the Integralists, against sedition and rebellion. The ccp, like many Portuguese centrist groups, welcomed and accepted the military coup of that year but was not instrumental in leading it. It was more ascetic and intellectual than the other movements analyzed here, a direct descendent in the political sphere of the university-oriented cadc from which Salazar sprang. Indeed, Salazar himself was one of the ccp's key leaders and in 1921 had even been elected to parliament (an experience that helped shape his view of the slowness, chaos, and disorganization of parliamentary regimes) on the ccp slate.

The Centro, as Richard Robinson's research makes clear, served essentially as a political training center for a solid core of intellectuals and politicians emanating from the CADC. This same group, Catholic and corporatist but moderate within those traditions, was successful in fighting off an attempted takeover by the extremist Integralists in the mid-1920s. It was thus the CADC and later the CCP and their programs, not the Integralists, that laid the foundations for the establishment of the New State. Although it is perhaps more dramatic to trace the origins of the Salazar system to *integralismo,* that influence was only one among many; and the fact is that it was the less dramatic Coimbra-CADC-CCP-shaped vision of Salazar himself that was overwhelmingly preponderant in determining the direction of Portuguese corporatism.

Even this last statement must be further qualified, however, for while Salazar was undoubtedly influenced by the encyclicals and the Catholic social movement and was a leading member of both the CADC and the CCP, it is doubtful that these influences, by themselves, are sufficient to explain the shape and direction of his regime. In formulating his own corporatist system Salazar was eclectic, borrowing from diverse intellectual currents and political movements as well as building upon Portugal's own history and traditions. He borrowed from Leo XIII, Maurras, Mosca, Pareto, the Integralists, Manoïlesco, and others, but his system was not an exact imitation of any of them.[53] Labels like "fascist" or "clerical-fascist," hence, do not capture the complex, eclectic, and changing character of his regime and its underlying ideology. Indeed, there is some doubt as to whether Salazar was influenced by ideological arguments at all. For though his own thinking and background were strongly Catholic, corporatist, and authoritarian, as a politician, particularly in the early decades, Salazar was an enormously shrewd pragmatist who sought and wielded power with consummate skill. In essence, what he did was to synthesize a body of ideas already widely held and weave together the diverse threads of some varied political movements. By doing so he was able to coopt and assimilate the entire broad Center and moderate Right of the Portuguese political spectrum, isolate both the Left and the extreme Right, and meanwhile build his own base of support. For example, Salazar's acceptance of the major planks of the Integralist platform—except for restoring the monarchy—enabled him to bring into his regime the moderates in that movement while at the same time providing a means for himself and the army to enhance their positions. His insistence on order and discipline but without the Integralists' "blood and thunder" also appealed to many Portuguese who were fed up with the chaos of the Republic but did not want fascist totalitarianism either. In the aftermath of Prince Manuel's death and the

Salazar-staged state funeral, most Monarchists had no alternative but to accept his regime. His background and program also made it possible for Salazar to capture the support of all the Catholic movements and factions, but that did not prevent him from keeping the hierarchy in its place, maintaining the separation of Church and state, and ruling unfettered by clerical interference. These are the tactics of an eminently practical politician, not the corporatist ideologue that is often pictured. Salazar thus appears as a politician in whom power and not ideology was the guiding principle.

Salazar put the corporatist revolution into effect and gave it body and substance. He, of course, had been in the forefront in articulating these ideas, but it should be remembered that the corporative-authoritarian-nationalist ideas and programs he advanced were also the guiding ideas of the dominant military and civilian elites. In contrast to the often prevailing view which sees the regime as maintained chiefly by force, Salazar, like any effective politician, operated close to the mainstream of political sentiment in his country—at least initially.[54] It was in the postwar period that the regime began to lose touch with the mainstream, and it is no accident that it was then that the regime did become a full-fledged dictatorship. Indeed, a key theme of this book is the constant tension that existed between the theory of the Estado Novo and its practice, between implementing the corporatist system and bowing to practical political contingencies. For it is in the interconnections and divergences between the ideological currents and the practical political ones that the dynamics of the regime lie, and also the fate of the entire corporatist experiment.

The Vision of the Corporatist State and Society

Most of the voluminous books, essays, speeches, and pronouncements of the 1920s and 1930s outlining the main themes of Portuguese corporatism[55] begin with a repudiation of the alternative systems, liberalism and socialism. Socialism is rejected for its bloody and violent past, its totalitarian impulses under the Bolsheviks and Stalin, its emphasis on man's material nature to the exclusion of all else, its rejection of and threat to religion, its labor theory of value, its stress on class strife rather than solidarity, its dialectical reasoning, its historical determinism, its conclusions regarding the inevitability of class warfare and of socialism, its ethic of conflict instead of cooperation, and a variety of other reasons. Liberalism is rejected for its excessively individualistic character, its philosophical assumptions regarding the inorganic state of nature out of which compacts of government arise, its representative nature based on

one man, one vote, its assumptions of equality in a real world of hierarchy and inequality, its failure to pay attention to national goals (the
summum bonum), its excessive emphasis on the procedural aspects of
democracy rather than the common good, its divisive, anarchic, chaotic
"pluralistic" tendencies which serve to fragment and polarize the nation rather than unify it. It is especially significant that this critique was
always based upon the unhappy *Portuguese* experience with liberalism
and parliamentarism from the nineteenth century through 1926 and did
not imply a rejection of all national forms of liberalism. If liberalism
worked in Great Britain and the United States, then so be it. What the
Portuguese were arguing was that in their own nation, where the tradition and political culture were distinct, liberalism was inappropriate, a
set of foreign (in this case, British) institutions imposed on a society
and polity where they simply did not fit.[56]

Along with the rejection of liberalism went a repudiation of liberalism's various institutional accoutrements. The need for unity and authority in the state ruled out checks and balances and an independent,
coequal parliament. Divisive political parties and factions would also be
eliminated in favor of a single, national movement. In a system where
society's interests would be represented through the corporative structure and where the common good would become known through other
channels, competitive elections could be sacrificed and more plebiscitary
ratifications used instead. Civil liberties would be respected, but they
would be limited for the higher end and purpose of the common good.
While these changes would serve to increase the power of the central
state, the creation of the corporate intermediary structure and the revitalization of society's natural associations (family, community, guilds,
and so on) would allow a certain degree of decentralization, constituting
a limit on the state.[57]

The New State was *nationalist* in two interrelated ways. On the one
hand, it rejected the British and other foreign institutions and influences
which had been implanted in the country in ways that were exploitive
and contrary to Portugal's own traditions. In modern parlance, the New
State implied a rejection of Portugal's historic dependency: economically, intellectually, politically. While repudiating foreign influences,
however, the Portuguese were searching diligently for what was useful
and viable in their own tradition, on which a new, *nationalist* sociopolitical order could be based. In trying to erect a new national myth to
replace the discredited Republican one, the Portuguese went back to
the glorious days of Rome and of incipient nationhood in the twelfth
and thirteenth centuries, and above all to that model of state and so-

ciety of the fifteenth and sixteenth centuries when Portugal achieved its greatest power and prestige as a nation. In rediscovering the *casas do povo, casas dos pescadores, gremios,* and other historic institutions upon which the political structure of Portuguese corporatism would be built, they romanticized the past. But that is perhaps a natural tendency in a political regime trying to build a new political order upon the ruins of the old. In this sense the Portuguese experience of the 1920s and 1930s was similar to that of today's newer nations: rejecting the foreign British, American or colonialist models of the past and seeking to discover in their own histories an indigenous framework for national development.

Repudiating liberal individualism, the Portuguese sought to reconstruct state and society on the organicist mold characteristic of their own tradition. Attempts to fashion an *inorganic* form of parliamentary government, they argued, had resulted in recurrent chaos, breakdowns, and civil wars between 1822 and 1926. In contrast to contract theory, the Portuguese corporatists saw government as both natural and necessary, ordained by God and required for man's social and individual betterment. This natural-law conception implied that society should be based on such "natural" associations as the family, the municipality, the Church, and other corporate units and not on such "unnatural," ephemeral entities as political parties or class-based associations. In the corporatist vision each man would be rooted and secure in his natural station in life—peasant, urban worker, cleric, or professional—and representation would be based on these natural groupings. Group membership would guarantee representation to all elements in society, as well as enabling them to qualify for the rights and privileges due them as members of an officially sanctioned body.

Under the Thomistic natural-law assumptions, authority, which was also "natural," would be required in both social affairs and the governmental structure. The so-called black-box concept of liberalism, under which government is merely the neutral filter through which competing groups channel their interests, was rejected.[58] The role of the state is to govern, the corporatists argued, not just to administer. The state would be not just a traffic policeman of the separate interests but a moral leader. Parliamentarism had subjected Portugal to the tyranny of a political assembly largely conditioned by irresponsible, divisive, selfish aims. The corporative regime, however, would assure that the state would be both *authoritative* in providing for the independence, security, and continuity of its rulers and *unified,* in the sense that the assembly would be an advisory and consulting agency rather than an independent legislative one. Instead of the classic separation of powers, which the Portuguese saw as divisive and impotent, authority would be concentrated, centralized, and monistic.[59]

Authoritarianism, however, should not be confused with totalitarianism.[60] This is where Salazar's outside critics often had the most difficulty in comprehending the regime, for in their secular conception it seemed inconceivable that a state which was not limited in its power by constitutional checks and balances and pluralistic interest groups would not become totalitarian. In the corporatist system, however, the power of the executive was to be checked by a law that was independent of and superior to the will of either the executive or the people: the Natural Law. The constitution of the Portuguese New State provided that the power of the state was limited by morality and right. Salazar himself had explained this rather imprecise phrasing in his declaration that "the power of the State stops at the limits imposed on it by the moral law." By moral law he meant not the vague conventions of pragmatism, utilitarianism, or situational ethics but what the Catholic theologians and philosophers meant by it, namely the Natural Law which is immortal, a reflection of God's Eternal Law which lays down immutable norms for human conduct, tells men how they *ought* to act, and puts *limits* on the exercise of authority.

For those whose politics and morality are cast in a more secular and pragmatic mold, these words sound strange and old-fashioned. In Catholic Portugal, however, and especially given the Catholic-Thomistic background of the New State's principal leaders, the Natural Law tradition remained as a severe restraint on unlimited power. There were bounds beyond which neither men nor government could go. The state was thus an instrument, not an end in itself as in the totalitarian systems. It recognized moral and spiritual values of a validity and permanence outreaching its own. Repeatedly throughout the history of the New State, these constraints continued to operate. Even during the period when the dictatorship was strongest, the self-imposed restraints of the Natural Law, rather than any institutional checks and balances, were what prevented the emergence of full-fledged totalitarianism.[61]

In the corporative scheme the state would accept responsibility for the rational ordering of the national political and economic life, but without assuming full control over that life. As the Portuguese saw it, the laissez-faire state had failed; yet, neither could they countenance, as in the socialist and totalitarian systems, the state's taking monopoly power in every area of the economy. Hence, it would be the role of the state to stimulate, encourage, coordinate, and regulate the economy but not totally direct it. The state could intervene in the economy, but it could not completely control it. It was the state's obligation to help stimulate production, encourage cooperation between all economic sectors for the common good, approve and validate the collective contracts signed between capital and labor, and veto exploitive economic practices as applied to groups who could not defend themselves. In this way, as corporatist ideologue Augusto da Costa saw it, labor would be dignified and property would be harmonized with the needs of society.[62]

The state was thus given broad regulative powers, but there were some limits placed upon it. These broad powers, together with the patrimonialist tradition, help account for the curious circumstance that the Portuguese economy, which we identify as a capitalistic system, had such a large public sector. The answer to this riddle lies in the fact that in Iberia and Latin America we are essentially talking of updated mercantilist models, or perhaps models of state capitalism, and not so much of private enterprise or laissez-faire capitalism.[63] This also helps account for the heavy role of the state in virtually all interest-group bargaining. Indeed, the conflict between the rather idealized *corporatisme d'association,* as pictured by the corporatist visionaries, and the almost inevitable tendency toward *corporatisme d'état* helps explain much of the dynamics of corporatist development in the 1930s—and ultimately, as Salazar moved increasingly toward state corporatism, the widespread disillusionment with that scheme.

The Portuguese corporatists sought to speak not just to man's economic needs, however, but to his moral, spiritual, cultural, and social needs as well. This clearly was an extension of the corporatists' critique of Marxism as well as, interestingly, of liberal capitalism. The corporatists recognized the alienation of the workers in modern industrial society, but they saw economic deprivation as only one aspect of the problem. The Estado Novo would not only seek to raise wages, therefore, but would also organize working-class clubs and social centers, build libraries and retreats, encourage education and cultural activities, provide for religious instruction and spiritual guidance, stage dances and sporting events, and so on—all as a way of integrating the lower classes back into society, of reforging the links between state and nation, government and people. The corporative agencies would thus perform a tutelary function, educating and civilizing the various social forces and incorporating them into the prevailing norms and values.[64]

The individual would have his place in Portuguese society as a member of such "natural" groups as the family, the guild, the corporation, the municipality, and so on. The concrete rights (*foros*) and privileges due him (as well as his obligations and responsibilities) would come via membership in these organic, natural groupings, however, not through mere citizenship or any abstract notion of individual rights. In the Portuguese corporatist conception, man could realize his true nature only through such natural group solidarities.

The state was obligated to respect these rights, and this obligation, along with the Natural Law, served as a further major constraint on unlimited authority. Although it adds somewhat to the confusion of terms, the rights and autonomous existence of these groups enabled the Portuguese to call theirs a genuinely pluralist system. By this they did not mean the free-wheeling, laissez-faire pluralism of the American system, but rather a more feudal construct in which, again, the "rights" or *foros* of each group are defined in law and the group enjoys a certain contractually defined independence from the state. A state was pluralist in the Portuguese conception if and insofar as it allowed and safeguarded within itself centers or agencies of power other than itself: autonomous units, religious, regional, municipal, cultural, educational, professional, philanthropic, designed to promote the rights and interests of their individual members and to protect them against encroachment on the part of the state or of other groups or interests. Some of these autonomous units, such as the Church or the family, were viewed as prior to the state, in theory at least, in terms of both natural law and history. The rights of the municipalities, the university, the Army, and other corporate units were guaranteed through law and contractual arrangement. It would be one of the primary goals of the Estado Novo, in responding to the emerging "social question," to extend these rights to the rising labor class and, eventually, to rural workers and domestic servants.[65]

These same groups formed the base on which the Portuguese corporative system would be grounded. At the grass-roots level would be the basic, organizational units: the family, the municipality, the *casas do povo,* the *casas dos pescadores,* the *sindicatos,* and the *gremios.* These entities were not only "natural" (in contrast to the more recent "artificial" units, such as political parties), but they also had deep roots in Portuguese history and tradition. At the regional and provincial level, as elaborated in the corporative legislation of the 1930s, would stand various *uniões* and *federações,* encompassing the smaller local or municipal agencies. At the "cupola" of the system would stand the *corporações* themselves, national organizations representing all those units below them in the hierarchy. The corporations would be organized in accord with the chief productive sectors: agriculture, commerce, fishing, industry, transportation, and the like. Such noneconomic corporations as the Army, the Church, and the university would also be guaranteed their legitimate, rightful place in the system. All these groups would be represented functionally in a Chamber of Corporations and in the smaller Corporative Council and, through them, at the very pinnacle of the entire state apparatus. The corporative agencies were to be not mere agents of their private members but "institutions of public interest integrated into the state." In this way each group would be institutionalized and guaranteed its rightful place in the system; its voice would be heard in national decision making, without the corrupting effects of interest-group lobbying as in the American system. The entire structure would serve to link the government with the governed in a way that had not existed under liberalism. At the same time, the fact that the corporative structure was to be autonomous, a "corporatism of association" rather than a "corporatism of the state," would guarantee against a dictatorship, as in Italian fascism.[66]

What made this corporative structure especially interesting, and also provided its link with the papal encyclicals, was its provision that within each corporation capital and labor were to coexist in harmony and equality. This provision, of course, came directly out of *Rerum Novarum,* once referred to by Caetano as the Magna Charta of Portuguese corporatism. *Rerum Novarum* analyzed the causes of the crisis between capital and labor, recommended workers' corporations, and advocated that the state assist them, provide for social assistance and security, and serve to conciliate between capital and labor for the common good. Workers and employers might still have differences, but these were to be ameliorated through mutual trust and compromise, not conflict. Hence, the strike and the lockout would no longer be necessary. The rights of workers and those of employers would be respected equally, and each would be guaranteed equal representation in the highest administrative organs of the system. Therefore, it was theorized (wrongly, as it turned out in practice), no one class could or would control or profit from the nation's resources at the expense of any other. Rather, all classes were to be subordinated to the higher national interest of service to the common good.[67]

As thus seen, Portuguese corporatism, at least as originally conceived, was not necessarily "fascistic." Corporatism in Portugal had a long and independent history of its own. It reflected both the Portuguese Roman and Christian background, as well as the traditions of order, authority, and natural corporatism solidly grounded in the Portuguese national political experience. It drew upon some parallel currents in Italy, Germany, France, and Spain but was not a copy of any of them. Its origins lay also in the guild assumption of the fundamental unity of purpose of master workmen and journeymen, and in the historic pattern of rights and mutual obligations between the crown and the *interesses* and among the various corporate units themselves. Portuguese corporatism, its advocates liked to say, repudiated liberty without authority as in the anarchic liberal model, *and* authority without liberty as in the fascist and totalitarian systems.[68]

In Portugal the corporative agencies were to be given a juridical personality of their own, in contrast to Italy where they had been subordinated to the state. The Portuguese corporative organizations were supposed to be allowed to develop "naturally"; membership would not be compulsory. The Portuguese thus recognized the limitations of the corporatist guild system as well as its advantages, for while they repudiated its monopolistic and sometimes arbitrary features, they lauded the sense of social solidarity it had engendered. They argued that the French Revolution had succeeded in abolishing not only the bad aspects of corporatism and the guilds but the good ones too, not only the abuses of the ancient principles but the principles themselves. The Portuguese corporativists remained in favor of freedom of association and other basic rights, but they clearly felt that men could best realize their freedom through their corporative capacities. Hence the ideal remained an open, autonomous *corporatisme d'association*.

Underlying all these conceptions was a powerful social-justice motive. The men who came to power in the Estado Novo were genuinely concerned with the poverty and backwardness of their nation, with divorcing themselves from foreign influences and developing a new indigenous model, and with alleviating the miserable living conditions of both the urban and the rural poor.[69] They proposed to carry out these changes, however, without revolution and without restructuring the social order. Whether the one could be carried out without the other was a question to which they did not address themselves. Probably they actually believed that they could do both at the same time: that is, carry out reforms while preserving the existing social arrangements intact. But others suggested the bitter lessons of history—that a gain for one class necessarily implied sacrifices by the other, sacrifices that the emerging Portuguese commercial and business interests were not about to make peacefully and that they would use all their numerous resources to prevent.

The corporatist system was therefore not just a means, as its enemies have alleged, of preserving the elites in power or of stifling the just aspirations of the lower classes. Although that is the way the system came to work in actual practice, the Portuguese corporatists' intentions were, in the main, noble ones, at least initially. Whether they were practical and realistic given the existing class and power structure is another matter. One might well question some of the assumptions on which the corporative system was built, the realism or perhaps contradictory nature of its goals, its proposed end product, the means to get there, and the implications of corporative rule—all themes which lie at the heart of the present analysis. It is clear also that some non-regime figures saw from the beginning what the corporatist system implied and how private and class advantage could be reaped from it. But at least in theory, ideology, and intentions, and also in terms of the class background of those who led it, the corporative system was by no means necessarily reactionary, and it was not dominated by Portugal's historic ruling elite. Its powerful motivation to bring about social justice, to deal with the great issues of alienation and modern mass man in ways that were more humane, less divisive, and more equitable than in the other great isms, cannot be ignored. The conflicts and contradictions in its implementation and actual functioning are what concern us in succeeding chapters.

The body of corporative theory and ideology presented here, first formulated at approximately the same time Marx and Weber, Durkheim and Comte, Tönnies and the Manchester liberals were writing their major works, serves as the Catholic and Iberic-Latin world's response to the same great questions of capitalism, industrialization, and modernization. This is a tradition of social and political thought that is almost wholly neglected in our political theory and sociology literature, but it is crucial if we are to understand the modern Iberic-Latin nations. The corporatist ideology summarized here shows a close correspondence to both the general corporative model outlined in chapter 1 and to the main traditions of Portuguese history and political culture traced in chapter 2. In what follows we shall be dealing with the elaboration and implementation of corporatist theory and ideology, the establishment of a corporative institutional system in the 1930s, and then the growing gaps and eventual chasm between theory and practice as the corporative experiment unfolded.

IV

Establishing the Corporative System

Portugal in the 1920s was a nation in turmoil. While it would be wrong to ascribe total bankruptcy to the existing Republican regime, there can be no doubt that socially, politically, economically, and psychologically the Portuguese nation was in the throes of a profoundly wrenching crisis. Its military forces had suffered humiliation in World War I and were the laughingstock of Europe. Its frequent revolutions, assassinations, cabinet shuffles, and corruption under Republican rule made Portugal the butt of the cruelest of European jokes. The treasury was empty and the national economy near collapse. The traditional elitist system had been proved bankrupt, while new social forces were beginning to clamor for admission into the system and a greater share in its benefits. The war and the spiraling crises of the 1920s thus aggravated Portugal's historic problems and added a host of new ones. As Dudley Heathcote, an English observer writing in 1927, stated, there was "no country so rife or people so supremely conscious of the need of doing away with existing institutions, if they would save themselves from ruin." [1]

The Estado Novo promised a solution to these dilemmas, a salvation from the ruins of republicanism. The corporative experiment of the 1930s aimed at the restoration of internal order and unity, the defense of the *escudo* and the reestablishment of economic solvency and probity, and the revival of such historic Portuguese institutions as family, Church, and community. The new regime would be a nationalist regime, a government of order and authority, oriented toward social justice and establishing a new national equilibrium, a regime that would bring back into harmony the government, the people, and their historic traditions. To accomplish this required a complete reorganization of the country. As Pedro Teotonio Pereira, one of the New State's prime architects stated, the situation before this time had been characterized by a state without functions or services, disconnected from the needs of the country, improvising in the absence of clear goals, failing to resolve its problems, with an undeveloped private sector, a disorganized public sector, a confusion of the public and private domains, and an almost total absence of political institutionalization.[2] By 1933, corresponding with the consolidation of Salazar's power, the regime had moved to fill this organizational and ideological void.

The corporative regime was a conscious reaction against the political chaos and the economic mismanagement of the previous system. But more than that, it represented a new direction for Portugal, a positive way of dealing with the great conflicts that were tearing Portugal apart rather than merely a negative reaction to them. As Caetano explained, the corporative structure erected in the 1930s represented an effort to translate the doctrinaire corporative principles that had evolved in the preceding sixty years into an organic, realistic formula.[3] The major principle, as Caetano stated it, was the active collaboration of different social and economic interests for the common good; the formula for achieving this would be the corporative system. In fact, as we shall see, while Portugal became a corporative state in law and in principle, the implementation of this new system was subject to all the vagaries accompanying the carrying out of any "revolutionary" restructuring. Some, principally oppositionists, would argue indeed that the corporative principles so loftily proclaimed were *never* implemented (and never intended to be implemented), remaining on the drawing boards and serving as a mere smoke screen to disguise the enrichment of wealthy interests and the excesses of the Salazar dictatorship—a cruel hoax upon the workers and upon the Portuguese nation. While such an entirely negative interpretation is no more accurate than an unreserved glorification of the New State, it does provide a focus for examining the actual functioning of the corporative system, the gap between theory and practice and its implications for Portuguese society and development.

The Revolution of 1926

The accelerating political and economic crises of the post-World War I period had brought the parliamentary system in Portugal to such a state of disorder and *desconfiança* that when it was overthrown virtually no one rose up to defend it or even lamented its passing. The military uprising of May 28, 1926, against the "corruption" and "degradation" of the Republic marked one of the few instances since the beginning of the nineteenth century when the officer corps was completely united. Although some of the officers had different ideas as to what would follow (there were Monarchists, Integralists, Nationalists,

Catholics, as well as Republicans in their ranks), on the need for a coup to overthrow the discredited Old Republic, they were virtually unanimous. The coup was also widely popular among the civilian classes, not only within the elite and aristocratic elements but, as Oliveira Marques' research makes clear, among the middle and lower sectors as well.[4] Indeed, among all classes there was widespread disillusionment with republicanism and with the uncertainties, instability, corruption, and national embarrassment associated with the parliamentary regime. The coup evoked a sense of popular relief.

The coup was led by Army General Gomes da Costa but included representatives from all the services and from all levels of the officer corps. Admiral Joaquim Mendes Cabeçadas was initially chosen as president of the new junta, but within days he was ejected and Gomes da Costa himself became president. Within another six weeks Gomes da Costa was similarly "rotated" out of office and replaced by General Oscar Carmona. Under Carmona the military regime consolidated its position, and Carmona himself remained president of the junta and, after 1933, constitutional president until his death in 1951.[5]

The armed forces had come to power in Portugal with no clear program. Like many others in Iberia and Latin America, the military regime stood for the restoration of order, authority, and national unity and dignity. But it did not have many concrete plans for the solution of Portugal's ills. It was against the disorder of republicanism, and within the first year of its rule, again in the classic pattern, it dissolved many of the old political parties, exiled or jailed a number of oppositionists, and broke up the political organizations and factions associated with the former regime. The military was strongly "nationalist," and many of its officers (though probably not a majority) were broadly "integralist" and "corporatist" in sympathies. They were not sympathetic to the chief plank in the Integralist platform, however—restoration of the monarchy—and at best they only vaguely comprehended the philosophical doctrines proclaimed by Sardinha. They justified their intervention in 1926 and continued rule into the 1930s on three principal grounds: the latent civil war existing in the country between Republicans and Monarchists, which demanded that the military exercise a "moderating" role; the inadequacy of parliamentary rule in Portugal and, hence, the need for a transitional "caretaker" government until a new regime could be established that *was* in accord with Portuguese traditions; and finally, the weakness of public opinion as a base for government, which the military junta saw as too inchoate to be substituted for firm authority.[6]

Although the May 28 movement was welcomed by virtually all the political parties (from Conservatives to Socialists), the precise meaning of the coup was never quite clear.[7] Some saw it simply as a cleansing process, an opportunity to rid the country of the graft and corruption of the previous regime. The young civilian Integralists saw it as an opportunity to implant their ideology. Self-aggrandizement and prestige were the motives for a number of the military officers. And professional politicians saw it as a chance to break the political dominance of the Democratic party, which had ruled during most of the sixteen years of the Republic, and thus gain control of the governmental patronage machinery for themselves.

The other parties had little opportunity to benefit from the change, however, as the military determined to stay in power and rule without any political parties. Without access to governmental favors and support, these small factions began to wither away, helped along by governmental sanctions and deportations. The small anarchist, anarcho-syndicalist, and Communist factions initially remained fairly neutral as regards the regime, refusing to associate themselves with "bourgeois political quarrels." The working-class organizations and trade union confederation also adopted a wait-and-see attitude. Their power was gradually reduced by attrition, administrative regulations, and some outright repression, however, and by 1932 both the old parties and the old labor organizations had largely ceased existence as legal entities.

The military regime itself was still on somewhat shaky ground. A major but unsuccessful counter-coup was attempted in 1927 by left-leaning students in Porto, and subsequent plots and conspiracies both outside of and within the military continued to plague the regime. The old Monarchist vs. Republican issue also constituted a threat to military unity, and this was one reason why the moderate Catholic Carmona was elevated to the leadership of the junta. He gave out cabinet positions to both Monarchists and conservative Republicans and generally proved able to conciliate the rival factions.

The military government was more efficient, less dilatory, and less corrupt than the Republican regime, but for several years it floundered without a clear purpose. It vowed to do away with the anarchy and petty rivalries of the professional politicians, but once it had done so it had little in the way of a positive substitute. The politico-administrative apparatus was purged and civilian officials replaced by military officers. Party politics was largely eliminated in favor of an administrative, professional regime, with five or six technical commissioners, appointed by the military and their ministers and acting under their supervision, administering the day-to-day running of the country. The new regime also began a program of road repair, of valorization of the *escudo,* of reform of the Army and Navy, of administrative "cleaning house," of austerity and administrative reorganization. But it remained a government without a program, a regime (in Salazar's words) "in search of a formula." [8]

It was precisely at this point that Salazar entered the government, for what would prove to be an unprecedented stay. Although he had briefly been a deputy in 1921 and had served, also briefly, as finance minister in 1926, he came back to government on a permanent basis in 1928. Given carte blanche by the military as a virtual economic czar, he began putting Portuguese finances in shape, restoring order to the national accounts, balancing the budget, red-penciling waste, enforcing austerity, and actually producing a budgetary surplus for the first time within anyone's memory. Salazar's financial accomplishments during this period are by now the stuff of legend rather than hard fact; suffice it to say that he managed the national books the way a diligent clerk might pore over his figures. And as his capacity for economic management waxed, Salazar's prestige and political power also expanded until in 1932 he was named prime minister as well as finance minister.[9]

Between 1928 and 1932, as Martins puts it, a curious process of interaction took place between the government and its constituency whereby the new political order was gradually defined. Various options were discussed: the indefinite continuation of the military dictatorship with civilians exercising technical and administrative roles but not serving as political power holders, perhaps with a plebiscite to legitimize the regime; a return to "constitutional normalcy," which meant a restoration of democratic rule, but perhaps in a presidential rather than parliamentary form; or an integralist-Catholic-corporatist solution. All three alternatives had supporters within the military regime, and the military factions all had their counterparts among civilian groups. Although it was the corporatist alternative that emerged as the dominant one, this was accomplished not by the repudiation of the other options but by their fusion into a single all-encompassing formula. Corporatism triumphed but in a form overlaid with democratic paraphernalia (regular elections and the like) and under such strong executive leadership that it resembled a presidential system. Moreover (and this was a political masterstroke), while the corporatist system was being implemented, General Carmona continued as formal president and the military itself was elevated to a position of preeminence as the "balance wheel," defender, and ultimate arbiter of national politics. By combining these alternatives rather than rejecting any one of them, Salazar was able to broaden and secure his base of support while at the same time proceeding with his corporative reforms.[10]

The period 1926–33—especially the crucial years of 1928–32—is one of the major unstudied periods in Portuguese history. By this time we have some good studies of the Republican period, 1910–26, and we are beginning to have some worthwhile research on the Estado Novo initiated in 1933. It is that vague period in between, however, about which we know very little but which is crucially important for an understanding of later Portuguese developments.[11] The obvious question is this: How was it possible for a regime which came to power with at best a vague political purpose to suddenly achieve such definitive direction? How did it happen that a generally "law-and-order" but non-ideological military government could be literally taken over by a small, unarmed, civilian group which then imposed its corporatist ideology and program on the rest of the nation? Was this a master conspiracy, an accidental happenstance, or some combination?

Given the paucity of research on this period, it is difficult to give definitive answers to these questions. Until the historical record is clearer, however, a number of tentative answers may be offered for which we have some, although not yet definitive, evidence and which help account for the consolidation and triumph of the corporativists. First, it is likely that the military regime that came to power in 1926 was, however vaguely, considerably more ideologically committed to (or in Linz's terms, had more of a "mentality" for) a corporatist or integralist solution than we have surmised—or at least it had become so by 1929/30/31. As early as 1926 a majority of the officers were known to be not only strongly nationalist but also in favor of a single representative body, a form of functional representation, and strong, authoritarian centralization of power and control. Many also were diligent Catholics (especially Carmona) and had been influenced in varying degrees by the Catholic social and political philosophies then current. The military was thus sympathetic to the nationalist, corporatist, and integralist position on all points except the restoration of monarchy,[12] and that issue Salazar and the regime had neatly finessed by raising the military itself, and specifically General Carmona, into the constitutional role of "the moderating power," a role traditionally reserved for the monarch. This solution, as we have noted previously, satisfied all but the far-right Integralists, solidified and enhanced the military's own position, and ensconced Salazar and the corporatists in power with a program and plan of action that was extremely close to that of the Catholic CADC and CCP of ten years earlier.

Second, there is the personality and character of Salazar himself. A strong leader and dogmatist, certain of his own program while others were vague and imprecise, he provided the direction, the ideology, and the concrete strategies that the military either lacked or were timid in pursuing. In 1928 Salazar gave a speech in which he said that "for years we have been looking for a formula for equilibrium without finding one." [13] But such a formula was precisely what Salazar had formulated in the CADC at Coimbra and in the *Centro Católico* and what he now, corresponding with his own elevation in power and prestige, began to put forth publicly as an official ideology for the regime. The corporatist formula provided the answers the military lacked, and in Salazar it had a dynamic, forceful spokesman. Nor can one forget that Salazar's competence and programs as a professional economist corresponded nicely with the administrative-technocratic aims and orientation of the military. His capabilities as a shrewd political maneuverer cannot be underestimated either. By 1929/30 Salazar was emerging as the "indispensable" strong man of the regime who by force of personality was increasingly able to secure acceptance for his program.

Third, the world market crash of 1929/30, coming at precisely the same time as Salazar's own increase in power, provided a further stimulus. Caetano tells us that the crash made it absolutely mandatory that the existing organizational vacuum be filled and that the regime move quickly toward emergency controls and to set up institutions to avoid both overproduction and catastrophic unemployment[14]—and also, though left unstated, to head off the possibility for more radical solutions. Decree-law 20,342 of September 24, 1931, promulgated two full years before the corporative constitution and Labor Statute of 1933, was aimed at regulating and controlling closely both the economy and the activities of professional and associational groups. The decree gave the state broad powers to regulate all economic and group activity in the public interest, thus vastly increasing the government's authority while at the same time serving as a precursor to the more elaborate corporative decrees published later.[15]

Fourth, one must look outside Portugal, to the general climate of the time and to the solutions being advanced in other countries during this period to solve similar political and economic problems. Corporatist solutions were by now being advocated in various nations of Europe; within the next half-dozen years, corporatist regimes in one form or another would come to power in a score of countries. There was an explosion of corporatist literature in Spain, France, Germany, Italy, Austria, Belgium, and elsewhere which young ideologues like Caetano (who would serve as the author of much of the 1933 legislation) kept rigorously abreast of; in addition, they followed closely the corporatist political movements this ideology helped spawn. In the 1920s the regime of Primo de Rivera in next-door Spain experimented with corporatist structures and programs. Of course, the Italian experience was also watched closely, and Mussolini's *Carta del lavoro,* published in 1927, strongly influenced Salazar and Caetano.[16] The publication of the encyclical *Quadragesimo Anno* in 1931 provided still another outside stimulus, updating the earlier *Rerum Novarum* on which a whole generation of Catholic intellectuals like Salazar had been nourished. *Quadragesimo Anno* provided a blueprint for the erection of a corporatist system (which followed in Portugal only two years later) and gave added legitimacy, in this Catholic country and among the strongly Catholic officer corps, to the new formula.[17]

Finally, there was the politics of the corporative solution. We have already remarked how the political formula proposed by Salazar of adopting a corporatist-integralist solution but with the military rather than a monarch serving as the *poder moderador* served to secure the loyalty of the armed forces and all but the most fervent of the Monarchists and Integralists. The Salazar formula isolated the extremes on both Right and Left, however, by preempting the Republican and liberal programs for social justice while promising to prevent a more radical (namely, socialist) upheaval. Moderate reformers, Republicans, and many liberals favored the corporatist solution initially, and so did conservative and business interests. The Catholics were already in the fold. The corporatist solution also served as an attractive way out of the continuing Monarchist-Republican struggle by incorporating some facets of both philosophies (the Constitution of 1933 proclaimed Portugal a corporative *and* a republican nation) and by serving as the basis for a broad middle solution. In addition, the death in 1932 of the Monarchist pretender, Dom Manuel, proved fortuitous for the corporatists by eliminating one powerful alternative solution (it is probably impossible to convey to American readers how strong Monarchist sentiment remained in Portugal in the twentieth century; suffice it to say that it was one of the three or four leading political currents in the country) and leaving the field now all but completely open to the corporatist formula. By honoring Dom Manuel in death and effusively praising him, Salazar cleverly gained the favor of many Monarchists without giving way to a Monarchist solution. In a system where power has traditionally rested on the Right more than on the Left, Salazar built his coalition and was able to coopt the broad middle of the political spectrum, which in the Portuguese system came to be represented by corporatism.

By 1929 Salazar had begun to articulate his philosophy for the New State in a series of public utterances that received widespread attention. In 1929 he delivered an address in which he provided some of the first hints of what might be contained in a new constitution. He advocated a state system founded on solidarity, conciliation, and authority, a regime based upon the nation's "natural" associations: the family, the *freguesia* (parish), the *municipio,* the moral and economic corporative bodies.[18] In an even more important speech on July 30, 1930, he spelled out nearly all the major principles he hoped to see incorporated in the state structure. This speech contained the now-familiar critique of liberalism and parliamentarism, pointed to a new regime of peace, hope, and prosperity, and spelled out the bases of the proposed constitutional changes in considerable detail: nationalism, consolidation of the state, strengthening of the executive power, social reorganization, representation by functions, economic and social progress, reintegration of the society with the state, a social and a corporative state. In a famous passage he proclaimed: "We *have* a doctrine and we *are* in fact a strong force." [19]

In the meantime, a number of early corporatist experiments were already underway. In 1931/32, corresponding with the dissolution of the General Confederation of Labor (CGT), several new decrees were promulgated to more closely control trade union activity and to begin restructuring the unions along corporatist lines. Responding to the world market crash, the regime also issued a series of emergency decree-laws aimed at regulating the economy. In 1931 legal authorization was given for the establishment of a network of municipal *gremios,* and at the same time the Superior Council of the National Economy was organized with subsections on agriculture, industry, commerce, labor, and colonies. Plans were issued to make membership in the *ordem* (order) of medical doctors obligatory, and a series of articles entitled "A Corporative Syndicate Regime" in the journal *Cadernos corporativos* presaged virtually all the provisions that would find their way into the Labor Statute of 1933.[20] The União Nacional had also been formed by this time to absorb the old political factions and to garner support for the regime. By 1931/32, thus, the regime was already beginning to move in the direction of a corporatively organized state and society. The flood of charters and decree-laws of 1933 served to rationalize and legitimize a corporative system already coming into existence de facto and to provide a further impetus to its development.

Toward the end of 1931, following closely upon the publication of *Quadragesimo Anno,* a group of lawyers, leading businessmen, university professors, and clerics began a series of meetings with a view to drawing up the future constitution. Salazar was the leading spirit in this undertaking (Caetano also played a major role), and the constitution that emerged in draft form in the spring of 1932 closely reflected his views. By this point, Salazar had been named prime minister and had largely consolidated his power. Portugal in 1932 was undisturbed by revolt or *pronunciamento,* and the extremists had either been isolated, banished, or held at bay while administrative reorganization was beginning to go forward. The budget was balanced for the fourth year in a row, and another surplus had been produced. In this lull, Salazar asked the Army and the nation to examine and discuss the draft of the new basic law. The rest of the year was spent in refining the constitutional structures and formulations and in preparing measures to apply them in stages. These stages would be elaborated the following year in a rash of constitutional and legislative innovations that, if anything, surpassed the flurry of Roosevelt's first "Ninety Days." [21]

The Corporative Structure

The year 1933 marked a watershed in Portuguese history; in a sense, it could almost be called a revolution. The changes ushered in were massive, implying a fundamental reorganization of the state and society. The laws enacted that year gave a certain legitimacy to the regime that had come to power in 1926, but more than that they signified an effort to restructure Portugal on a corporative basis. The basic charters of 1933 and their accompanying legislation, Teotonio Pereira wrote in 1972, constituted perhaps the high point of the corporative era and of his generation.[22]

Pereira had helped design the system and draft this legislation, and he was also the first administrator of the corporative structure in the early to mid-1930s. His statement that 1933 marked the high point is thus especially significant since it implies that in the succeeding years the implementation of the corporative system never again reached the high plateau of the original grand design. The slowness of implementation, in fact, tells us a great deal about how the Portuguese system worked. Furthermore, while 1933 marked a major restructuring of the Portuguese state system, we must question just how "revolutionary" this was, whether it signaled any change in the social basis of power. The corporative system, as we shall see, remained a mixed system, never completely implemented and still exhibiting many continuities with the antecedent system. Portuguese corporatism was thus never a "pure" form in the Manoïlesco sense but represented more the grafting of another administrative and organizational layer to an older corporative-patrimonialist system. Just how much change, "revolution," or continuity was involved in this shift remains the subject of much controversy.

THE CONSTITUTION OF 1933   The Constitution of 1933 was actually drafted in 1932, ratified by popular plebiscite in 1933, and put into effect in 1934. In the plebiscite where, in keeping with the Portuguese corporative conception, the franchise was limited to heads of families, some 60 percent voted approval, less than 10 percent voted no, and 30 percent abstained. The abstentions were later counted along with the other affirmative votes, thus raising the percentage of approvals, at least in the regime's own eyes, to 90 percent.

The Constitution proclaimed Portugal to be a republican *and* a corporative state.[23] Moreover, it contained many lengthy articles spelling out the structure and mechanics of government as well as the normative and philosophical assumptions and ideology on which the New State was built. Both these aspects command our attention.

Consciously reversing the power arrangements of the Republican regime, the new basic law gave supreme authority to the executive and only limited functions to the parliament. Reflecting the de facto dual structural relationships that had grown up since 1926, the Constitution provided for both a president and a prime minister, or president of the Council of Ministers. The president would be elected by popular vote for a period of seven years. Although he had the one important power to appoint and dismiss the prime minister, the president's chief functions were ceremonial. He was, in effect, head of state rather than head of government, though he sometimes also played the role of conciliator, appeaser, and moderator in the councils of government. The president's position could have been a more important one (as the opposition demonstrated in 1958 when General Delgado ran for the presidency and promised, if elected, to dismiss Salazar), but in fact his functions were generally limited to ceremonial ribbon snippings, charitable endeavors, public appearances, the reception of foreign dignitaries, and the like. The stature of the presidency remained high and on some issues and on some occasions his influence could be considerable, but the real centers of power lay elsewhere in the system.

That "elsewhere" was chiefly in the person of Salazar, who occupied the post of prime minister, or president of the Council of Ministers, from 1932 until his incapacitation in 1968. Constitutionally, this position was charged with such extensive power that the prime minister was virtually a constitutional dictator. While the president dealt largely in ceremonial functions, the prime minister had charge of the day-to-day management of government. He was given extensive appointive powers, the authority to issue decree-laws without parliamentary approval, and broad administrative responsibilities. This position was powerful not just because of the responsibilities given it in the Constitution, however, but also because of the character and strength of Salazar: domineering, absolutist, forceful, ambitious, hard working, and brilliant. Marcello Caetano characterized the system as one of "presidentialism of the prime minister";[24] another student drew significant parallels between the structure of power in the Portuguese system and the "Bonapartism" of de Gaulle's Fifth Republic.[25]

The provisions for strong executive power were accompanied by statements regarding the immobilism and paralysis of the parliamentary regime, the need for a government that could *rule* and make authoritative decisions, and the necessity of strong, central authority to remedy the earlier dispersion and, hence, virtual absence of state power. Not only did these comments reflect the realities of governance under the post-1926 regime; they also had a strong base in corporative theory and in the Portuguese historic tradition.

The legislative branch was consciously given a subordinate role as a consultant and adviser on legislation but not an initiator of it. It was always difficult for the Portuguese opposition to criticize the regime for not giving any more power to the parliament when in fact this was never the role the parliament was designed to play. The new Constitution made no concessions to popular or parliamentary sovereignty whatever. Rather, the legislature functioned much as did the historic cortes: meeting for brief sessions, serving as adviser and consultant to the government, providing a "safe" haven for local notables as well as aspiring (and over-the-hill) politicians, having a limited representative function for the nation's major interests, and helping to funnel and administer programs emanating from the executive. The legislature was never intended to be a separate and coequal branch; instead, it was closely integrated with the executive and subservient to it in a regime not of separation of powers but of "organic unity."

The legislature, which met for the first time under the new Constitution in 1935, was bicameral. It consisted of the ninety-member (later the number of seats was raised) National Assembly, half of whose members were chosen by popular election and half (initially) by the other "house," and the Corporative Chamber. The Assembly was designed to give at least some voice, however weak, to public opinion. It was empowered to advise and consent to (and occasionally to modify) laws emanating from the executive. Under Salazar, however, even these limited representational and legislative functions were extremely circumscribed. Portugal evolved into a one-party state with largely meaningless elections, and in fact the entire slate of official regime candidates for the Assembly was ordinarily hand picked by Salazar personally and ran unopposed.

The other body, the Corporative Chamber, was more interesting for our purposes. It enshrined the principle of corporate functional representation. The Chamber consisted of representatives chosen by the major functional and corporate interests (agriculture, commerce, industry, and the like) as well as by local institutions, the Army, the various ministries, the Church, the *ordens,* and the fishermen's and people's centers (these institutions are discussed more fully later in this chapter). Each group could articulate its interests through its representatives in the Corporative Chamber. The system was not unlike the sectoral representation of the Mexican official party, though in the Portuguese case *all* the diverse groups making up the nation were to be represented, interacting through the Corporative Chamber. The Chamber also generally conducted its business by specialized sections organized similarly by corporate function, rather than in meetings of the whole Chamber (the complete representational structure of the Corporative Chamber is given in appendix A). There were twenty-four such sections, one for each major social and economic area of activity, as well as for the nation's principal moral, spiritual, and cultural categories. The sections ranged from cereals and livestock to finance, from journalism and printing to transportation and religion, from fishing and mining to national defense, wines, and forests. In keeping with corporative principles, in each of these sections, and their even more specialized subsections, capital and labor were to be equally represented, along with various "technical experts."

Hearings were to be held on issues that concerned these particular sectors of the society or economy; the viewpoints of each interested party would be presented by advocates (*procuradores*), usually lawyers with some prestige or access to the channels of influence. Ideally, once both labor and employers (or other interests) had been heard on any particular issue, then the appropriate section of the Corporative Chamber would prepare an advisory opinion (*parecer*) for use by the Assembly in its deliberations, or by the government in its considerations of new programs. The system "guaranteed" that all interests would be represented and that all voices would be heard; it also served (again ideally) to remove interest-group lobbying and influence peddling from the dark cloakrooms by institutionalizing all interests openly and legally within the political system. As we shall see later in more detail, the system functioned at best imperfectly, and most legislation came in the form of decree-laws emanating from Salazar rather than as a result of much input from the major *interesses*. That the Corporative Chamber functioned at all, however, and that it continued to serve an important, if limited, advisory function make this experiment with corporatist functional representation worthy of further study.[26]

The judicial power of the corporate state, again not a separate and coequal branch but, like the legislature, integrated into an organic whole, was vested in both ordinary and special courts. The court system functioned much as it had previously and, except as the judiciary was represented through its own section of the Corporative Chamber, was largely unaffected by the corporative reorganization.

The cabinet consisted of the Council of Ministers and its president (Salazar, later Caetano). Council ministers were appointed by the head of state upon the recommendation of the president of the Council; this meant that ordinarily they were men of Salazar's choosing. Council members' responsibilities included the countersigning of official acts, the preparation of decree-laws, the supervision of public administration in general, and the administration specifically of the ministry each Council member was appointed to head up. The Council seldom met as a unit since Salazar preferred to work with his ministers on an individual basis. As an institution, therefore, the Council collectively had limited authority, although its individual members sometimes had important responsibilities. Moreover, a Council appointment carried with it considerable prestige and administrative authority, even though the plans and general direction of policy ordinarily came from Salazar. We shall have more to say regarding Salazar's relations with his ministers; at present, what needs to be said is that the Council of Ministers always remained subordinate to its president, though for the individual minister his post often served as a symbol of status and some power and frequently a stepping-stone to other positions, prestige, and wealth.

A distinct feature of the Portuguese Constitution was the establishment of a special Council of State, comparable to previous bodies going back to 1569, that was to serve as a high-level consultative organ to the president (just as its forerunners had served a succession of monarchs). Its responsibilities as originally conceived included a number of emergency and extraordinary tasks: to verify the impossibility of having the electoral college meet to elect the chief of state; to verify the impossibility of holding legislative elections; to assist the chief of state in various critical areas, such as advising the National Assembly on constitutional revision, convoking extraordinary sessions of the Assembly, and dissolving the Assembly when that was "in the superior interest of the nation." The Council of State was to consist of the president of the Council of Ministers (Salazar), the president of the National Assembly, the president of the Corporative Council, the president of the Supreme

Court, and ten "public men of superior ability" named by the president of the Republic. Although the Council was at least in part a corporatively organized body and though its membership included some of the nation's most prominent figures (Salazar, Caetano, Pereira, Américo Thomaz, Supico Pinto, Santos Costa, Albino dos Reis, Costa Leite), it seldom functioned as a formal institution and remained largely an honorary body. It was never called into session during the various emergencies of the Salazar regime, and indeed the only time it was ever convoked was in 1968 when Salazar himself was incapacitated and the consultation began over his successor.[27]

Local government institutions received considerable attention in the Portuguese constitutional structure because these constituted part of the base of the corporative hierarchy. The family was of course the primary organizational unit, but next to it came local government. The territory of mainland Portugal was divided into *conselhos* (municipalities), made up of *freguesias* (parishes) and grouped into districts and provinces. The *conselhos* of the major cities, Lisbon and Porto, were subdivided into *bairros* (wards) and these in turn into *freguesias*. The freguesias were administered by a junta (board) of three members chosen by the heads of families of that parish. The government of the conselho would be administered by the *conselho municipal* (municipal council), the *camara municipal* (municipal assembly), and the president. Organized corporatively, the *conselho municipal* consisted of the president of the cámara (simultaneously president of the conselho), representatives of the parish boards, a representative of the local Catholic charity organization (*misericórdia*), a representative of the professions, two syndicate representatives, two representatives of the local people's centers (*casas do povo*) or fishermen's centers (*casas dos pescadores*), and three representatives of the guilds. At the provincial level there was a higher but parallel junta and conselho, also organized corporatively. Freguesias and conselhos could join together to form regional unions or federations. As we shall see later on, the unions and federations constituted the "intermediary agencies" of the corporative structure, and they were also guaranteed representation in the Corporative Chamber.

The entire structural chain from national to local level included other agencies and more specialized units, but this is not a book about Portuguese local government.[28] What is important for our purposes is to see how the local agencies were integrated into the organic structure of the corporate state: from the family, to the various agencies at the ward, parish, municipal, district, and provincial levels, up to the highest organs of the central state. Their functions included the election of aldermen (*vereadores*), communication with the central government on official matters, issuance of an annual report, review of the municipal budget and recommendations regarding taxes, and regulation of medical and social services within the municipality. In practice many of these functions were carried out sporadically and often not at all. In addition, the most important local officials were ordinarily appointed by the central government, there was much central state intervention in local affairs, the municipal governments enjoyed little independence and autonomy, and etatist influences were strong[29] Nonetheless, given the model of centralized local government existent in Portugal, the historic centralizing tendencies going back over centuries, and the realities of the Salazar dictatorship, the fact that the local systems had any functions at all and maintained even a measure of autonomy is significant.[30]

A final governmental structure with which we must be concerned is the Corporative Council. Under the decree-law (24,362) establishing the Council, it was to be the highest-level coordinating agency of the corporative system. It was charged with coordinating the corporative activities of the various ministries (a theme we shall return to later), studying and suggesting programs to the state in relation to the corporative structure, and guaranteeing unity of corporative action. Initially, its membership was to consist of the president of the Council of Ministers (Salazar) as chairman; the ministers of justice, public works and communications, and agriculture; the subsecretary of state of labor and social welfare; the two professors at the universities of Coimbra and Lisbon who taught the courses in corporative law; and others named by the president of the Council. As of 1938, however, reflecting some of the early vicissitudes of corporative implementation, the Council had not yet begun to exercise any important activity or to function at all.[31]

As interesting as the various corporative institutions set up under the 1933 Constitution were the normative and ideological statements contained within it.[32] In keeping with the corporative ideological tradition outlined in the previous chapter, the Constitution elevated the state to a position of moral leadership and gave it responsibility for directing the social and economic life of the nation. It was the state's duty to provide for national unity, to work for the harmony of all interests, to guide society and economy for the common good. The state was to be not just a reflection of economic interests but a leader of them. It had a *duty* to promote and secure the moral and material betterment of all groups. And although what the Portuguese had in mind bore little relation to the goals of the present-day women's liberation movement, the state was also obligated to protect and guarantee the rights of women.

The state was further obliged to guarantee the rights of "primary groups" such as the family, the freguesia, and other "natural" corporative institutions. The family was elevated to a position constitutionally as the basis of the state. Under Article 14 the state was bound to defend and promote family life, and it was through the family that participation in public life would occur (hence, the suffrage was to be exercised only by heads of families). The family was to be the model and metaphor on which the nation was to be based, implying strong but paternalistic authority, acceptance by all members of both rights and responsibilities, a purpose greater than the sum of its individual parts. The organic, corporatist, hierarchical, "familial" conception of society and the state was thus extended to the constitutional sphere.[33]

The state was to encourage religious worship and practice, but the separation of Church and state was to be maintained and there would be no official Church or religion. (It was largely for this reason, echoed in the Concordat of 1940, that Salazar was opposed by some ultrarightist Integralist, Monarchist, and Catholic elements.) A long list of individual rights (press, speech, assembly, and so on) was also included in the Constitution, but the government was explicitly given the right to limit these for "the common good." The vote, rather than implying choice among rival factions, was to be on a plebiscitary basis. Public opinion was viewed as important but the government was obligated to "protect," "guarantee," and "perfect" it. Thus, the classic freedoms were present but subject to a "higher morality." Similarly, from the constitutional conception of the state as a moral and ethical agency, it followed that the state was also empowered to keep out contrary notions. As we shall see in later chapters, these provisions for the "higher end and duty" of the state would help provide the justification for the growth of an etatist system and an authoritarian dictatorship.

Although the Portuguese state and especially the executive were given wide authority in the social, economic, and political spheres, this power remained limited rather than absolute. The goal of the Constitution was to reestablish the proper balance between authority and liberty. The state was empowered to "regulate," "coordinate," and "intervene" in social and economic matters; it was not designed to *control* social and economic interests in a totalitarian fashion. In the classic paternal way, the state was to "guide" and "harmonize" the old anarchy of contradictory interests rather than impose its will on them. In contrast with Mussolini's Italy, the Portuguese system was explicitly to be a "corporatism of free association" and not a "corporatism of the state." That is, the Portuguese version of the corporative state would reflect spontaneous grass-roots growth instead of, as in Italy, being imposed artificially by the state. It will be important to see how this worked out in practice.

THE LABOR STATUTE OF 1933   The Labor Statute of 1933 accompanied the Constitution of that same year and was an extension of it. Containing language that was almost a direct translation of Mussolini's *Carta del lavoro* and borrowing also from the papal encyclicals, the Labor Statute was nonetheless a distinctly Portuguese document. In far more detail than the Constitution, it spelled out the state's obligations in the social and economic spheres and contained elaborate provisions governing the relations between labor and capital. Along with the Constitution, the Labor Statute served as one of the fundamental charters of the corporative system.[34]

As in the Constitution, procedural and normative-ideological provisions went hand in hand. The statute proclaimed that the nation represented a higher interest than the groups or individuals composing it and that the state had the right *and* obligation to regulate national social and economic life in the common interest. Property, capital, and labor were all viewed as having a social function. The relations between them were to be governed by principles of cooperation and solidarity. The state was obligated to assist private economic initiative; at the same time, the patronal groups and private economic associations were compelled to cooperate with the state. The right to work was similarly guaranteed by the state, while the labor organizations were required to subordinate their interests to the common good. The work of women and children outside the home was for the first time to be regulated by the state. Concurrently, the state was obliged to provide social assistance and security to the workers, and it was made incumbent upon both employers and the corporative agencies to provide funds for these purposes. The statute sought to assist all, both workers and employers, in working for a new Portugal.

The Labor Statute sought to institutionalize the collaborative arrangements between capital and labor as proclaimed in corporative doctrine. Class conflict was to give way to class harmony. Strikes by workers and lockouts by owners were both expressly forbidden. Disputes would be settled by collective contract rather than violence and strife. A system of labor courts was to be established, and government intervenors were to step in to assure class peace if direct negotiations between workers and employers threatened to break down. Elaborate provisions spelled out the nature of the negotiation-collective-contract process, guaranteeing (in law at least) that workers and employers would have an equal voice. At the same time, workers and employers were guaranteed equal representation in the corporative structure and at hearings affecting their interests in such agencies as the Corporative Chamber. The Labor Statute formally put into law the rights and coequal status of labor and employers that *Quadragesimo Anno* and a long line of corporative thinkers before it had been urging.[35]

The government was obligated to "protect" the workers and guarantee them a just wage. The bureaucracy was "juridically obligated" to serve the welfare of all citizens and of the common good, rather than functioning for the benefit of private interests. Judges in the various labor tribunals were also to be independent and to interfere in the collective bargaining process only under special circumstances. The state's role was thus supposed to be limited: to regulate social and economic life for the common good, to establish equilibrium between labor and capital, to strengthen (but not direct) the national economy, to guarantee the highest wages compatible with production, to encourage private efforts for the good of all, to help develop the country and her people.

The Labor Statute reflected the corporative assumptions on which the entire national system was to be based. It proclaimed a *hierarchy* of goods and values: the good of the individual was below that of the social group, and that of the social group below that of the common, or national, good. Wealth was to have primarily a social function and was to be subordinate to the good of all. The statute reflected the organic conception of state and society. It proclaimed "self-direction" for the economy at the same time that the state was given the authority to coordinate society and economy for the *bem comum*. It proclaimed the "interdependence" of the forces of production, the "equilibrium" of production and consumption, mutual understanding between capital and labor, and the supremacy of the collective labor contract. It also contained provisions spelling out the length of the work week and day, providing for health and security in work and for paid vacations, regulating the labor of women and minors, and also regulating labor in the home. In many areas the Labor Statute of 1933 institutionalized rights that had never before enjoyed the status of official law.

The Labor Statute was called by its drafters the Magna Charta of the Portuguese working class. Given the vicissitudes of its implementation over the years, that phrase is clearly too optimistic. Nevertheless, the Labor Statute did mark a change from the past and was a pathbreaking document. The statute institutionalized for the first time the right of labor to be a participant member in the political society. It signaled the legitimacy of labor's claim to be accepted as a major "power contender," in accord with the model presented in chapter 1. It marked a significant step in Portuguese development and the extension of corporate group rights to a new social sector. Now, in contrast to the older system under which labor had no legal rights, the trade unions were granted juridical standing and a guarantee that their voice would be heard and their interests recognized. At the same time, the strong social-justice motivations underlying the promulgation of the Labor Statute were considerable. This was an effort *not just* to keep labor in its place, as the antiregime propaganda often stressed, but to *secure* to it certain rights and privileges, a just wage, and decent living standards. The degree to which these provisions were implemented, however, remains another story.[36]

THE SUBSECRETARIAT OF STATE OF CORPORATIONS AND SOCIAL WELFARE
The Subsecretariat of State of Corporations and Social Welfare was a new subministry (later elevated to ministry level) established in 1933 to help organize and coordinate the corporative system and to initiate a comprehensive social welfare program. The subsecretariat was thought of as a crucial post by many of the young civilian integralists and corporatists who now came to power, since it was to give concrete form to the corporative regime and implement the Constitution and the Labor Statute. The subsecretariat was charged with overseeing the process of negotiating collective labor contracts, with supporting the growth of corporative agencies and "associativeness," and with establishing a nationwide system of Caixas de Previdência (social assistance agencies). The Instituto Nacional do Trabalho e Previdência (INTP), a special institute set up within the subsecretariat, was also given broad powers to study and promulgate new labor and social security laws, to forge links between various governmental agencies and the new social programs, to help administer the labor tribunals and grass-roots corporative organizations, to ensure execution of the labor and social welfare laws, to coordinate all these activities, and to regulate production in accord with the spirit of the New State. Headed by Pedro Teotonio Pereira, who, along with Caetano, had been one of the principal leaders of the Integralist youth movement, the subsecretariat seemed to enjoy the special favor of, and direct access to, Salazar.[37]

From the beginning the organization of the subsecretariat was a matter of controversy. Pereira sought to have it located within the office of the presidency of the Council of Ministers, which would have given his agency better access to Salazar and presumably more influence in the governmental system as a whole.[38] Others wanted it to be a full ministry equivalent in status to other ministries, while some argued that it should be a superministry, superior to these others. Their reasoning was that since Portugal's Constitution proclaimed it a corporate state, the agency charged with establishing the corporative system should be above all others and able to impose a corporative mentality and system of organization on the other ministries and, indeed, on the entire national structure.

Still other advocates, whose chief spokesman at this time was Caetano, argued that there was no need for any kind of special corporative agency, that the corporative mentality should be allowed to grow spontaneously and naturally, and that eventually the whole system would be infused with corporative consciousness and organized in a corporative fashion without the need for a separate ministry or subsecretariat of corporations.[39] The same arguments were repeated in the late 1940s and early 1950s when the regime *did* move to create a separate ministry of corporations. At this stage, however, Salazar chose a middle solution, creating the subsecretariat and giving it broad functions but not endowing it with the power to impose itself on other ministries. This solution in turn gave rise to the question (posed by Manoïlesco) of whether Portuguese corporatism was "pure" (genuinely pluralist, free, and self-regulating), "mixed" (corporative forms comingled with liberal ones), or "subordinate" (corporate agencies subordinated to the state). To outsiders, such questions seemed overly formal-legalistic, scholastic, and often irrelevant; to the Portuguese and especially to the young corporatists, however, they mattered a great deal, for they served frequently as indicators of the basic direction of the regime.[40]

THE CORPORATIVE GRASS-ROOTS ORGANIZATION   That same fateful day, September 23, 1933, that saw the enactment of the Labor Statute was also the day when five other major decree-laws were promulgated, establishing a web of corporative grass-roots organizations encompassing every major social and economic sector of the population.[41]

Decree-law 23,049 established a national system of *gremios,* or guilds. The gremios were associations of employers and patronal interests in the business, commercial, or industrial areas. They were established according to the several branches of production (wine, cereals, fishing, and so on) and were originally conceived as being monopolistic in character, that is, in any one part of the country there would be only one wine producers' gremio, for example, with the power to speak for that entire branch of production. The law establishing the system stated that the gremios would be subordinate to the state and to the common good; they were further obliged to repudiate both class warfare and plutocracies. The state reserved the right to recognize a new gremio and to grant it juridical personality. In certain instances also the gremios were to be organized by the state; since in some branches of production there was no assurance the gremios would be organized voluntarily, this had to be accomplished from the top down. The gremios were obligated to "cooperate" with the workers' organizations. Their functions were to help resolve problems in their particular sector of the economy, to represent patronal interests in the Corporative Chamber and in other agencies of the state, and to negotiate collective labor contracts with the corresponding unions for their economic sector.

Replacing the liberal "charter of associability" of 1891, decree-law 23,050 established a national system of *sindicatos,* or trade unions, paralleling the structure of the gremios. The sindicatos were to be organized by districts, a measure which served to isolate and fragment the unions and prevent them from unifying on a strong national basis. Further, a sindicato required a minimum of 100 members, which served as a further impediment to unionization; because of the small size and family ownership of most Portuguese firms, this restriction kept the unions from organizing in all but the largest industries and commercial concerns. The state would give "direction" to an aspiring sindicato in the drafting of its charter, which then had to be approved in final form by the government before the sindicato could be legally sanctioned. Like the gremios, the sindicatos were made subordinate to the state and to "the common good." They were further prohibited from affiliating with international labor organizations without governmental approval. The functions of the sindicatos were also parallel to that of the gremios: to represent the interests of the workers in the Corporative Chamber and in other official agencies, to provide for the social, moral, and educational advancement of their members, and to negotiate collective contracts with the gremios (using the intermediary of the government if needed). The sindicatos, like the gremios, could join together at the provincial or regional level to form *uniões* or *federações.* Paralleling the gremios in another way, the sindicatos were monopolistic, with only one *sindicato nacional* authorized to speak for and represent each particular job category. In this last respect, the sindicatos differed slightly from the gremios, for while the gremios were organized according to the various branches of production, the sindicatos were organized more strictly according to job classification (bank workers, metallurgical workers, and so on).

The same decree that created the sindicatos authorized the creation of *ordens,* or orders. The orders were separate agencies for members of the liberal professions, of which four were eventually organized: lawyers, doctors, engineers, and agronomists. The orders also received their recognition from the state, and like the other grass-roots corporative agencies they too were monopolistic. The orders, however, were more concerned with professional matters than with "class" representation, though this last function was not neglected entirely. These professions were often connected with basic public functions such as health care, public works, and the administration of justice, so that their role in disciplining and regulating their professions and maintaining their codes of professional ethics was especially important.

Decree-law 23,051, also of September 23, 1933, established a nation-wide system of *casas do povo,* or people's community centers. The *casas* were authorized in all parishes of the country and were designed as or-ganizations of rural social cooperation. One casa could be created in each parish by either local officials or interested persons; the govern-ment was further authorized to create them by decree where appro-priate. The casas were given independent juridical personality, but the state would pass on their recognition. Nor could the casas function con-trary to the state or to national interests. Although they were designed primarily for peasants and small farmers, two classes of members were allowed: *effective members,* consisting of the heads of families and males over eighteen years of age, and *protective members,* consisting of all the parish's landowners. In practice, this meant that it was the large landowners and oligarchic interests who dominated the *casas,* not the humbler elements for whom, according to the rhetoric, they were de-signed. In fact, this implied the perpetuation of the existing two-class status quo in the countryside and of the structure of peasant dependence on the paternalistic favors of the landlord.[42]

The casas have been cited as one of the distinctive Portuguese con-tributions to corporative theory and organization. They were built upon the rather romantic notion of the stable, cooperative village community, an institution that had already begun to disappear in the Portugal of the 1930s. The casas were designed as mutual benefit associations; they gave out social assistance, provided some health and dental care, staged social activities, provided some educational services, and even helped subsidize funerals for the indigent. They aimed to stimulate local prog-ress through social cooperation at the basic rural community level. Their funds came in part from the membership, but the contributions of the state and of local benefactors (principally large landowners) were far more important. In 1933 the chief purposes of the casas were listed as social assistance, instruction, and local progress; in 1940 they were given the added political function of representing rural elements in the corporative agencies and in collective labor contract negotiations. It is significant that the casas began, at least in theory, as a means of over-coming the predominantly patriarchal and patron-dependent system in the countryside; they evolved in a fashion that made the government the largest *patrão,* eventually overshadowing even the individual landowners.[43] Meanwhile, the condition of the life of the rural poor remained just that: poor.

Recognizing eventually the inherent difficulties of grouping landowners and rural laborers in a single associational structure, the regime moved in 1937 to separate them. Separate *gremios da lavoura,* or agricultural guilds, distinct from the *casas do povo,* were created for the landowning elements.[44] These gremios came under the same system of government regulations and control as did the other corporative groups, and their functions were also parallel. Their aim was to promote rural development, represent landed interests in the Corporative Chamber and in other state agencies, and help negotiate collective contracts governing the work of rural workers. This development corresponded with several changes in the laws governing the *casas do povo* so as to permit the organization of regional federations and to give the *casas* political representation and the right to enter into collective contract negotiations with employers. The pattern of sindicato-gremio relations established in the urban, industrial areas thus now had its parallel in the countryside. Critics of these changes, including a number within the regime, were quick to point out that a system supposedly based upon the harmonization of classes had now been structured in both urban and rural areas on an adversary pattern that was not very different from the old system of class conflict.[45]

Rounding out the grass-roots corporative structure were the *casas dos pescadores,* or fishermen's centers. Like the *casas do povo,* the *casas dos pescadores* had strong roots in the Portuguese past, going back to the twelfth century; they too represented a unique Portuguese contribution to corporative organization. They were based on the historic (and again somewhat romanticized) interdependence and cooperation of the fishermen, in this traditionally most important of Portuguese industries, in the face of the grave dangers from the sea and from distant ventures into unknown waters. The fishermen's centers were also aimed at providing welfare and assistance to fishermen and their families, at raising their educational and cultural levels, and at guaranteeing them representation in government councils. Like the early *casas do povo,* however, the fishermen's centers also included such patronal interests as representatives from the big fishing companies, shipowners and masters, and the harbor master (who was also by law designated president of the local fishermen's center). In practice, this often meant that employer interests dominated and the interests of the employees were submerged. Eventually, however, the *casas dos pescadores* evolved as federations of independent bargaining agents in the same way some other grass-roots corporative agencies did, negotiating work contracts with fleet owners and the several gremios concerned with the fish industry. But unlike some of these other grass-roots and neighborhood associations, which often existed largely in the romantic notions of a few corporative ideologues, the *casas dos pescadores* had a strong basis in the Portuguese tradition and reflected a genuine sense of local and "class" solidarity. They were among the most successful and enduring of the various corporative structures. Today in many fishing centers, they still enjoy a comparatively vigorous existence.[46]

THE CORPORATIONS   The nominal capstone of the entire corporative system was, of course, the corporations themselves. In terms of the organizational pyramid that corporative officials used, the structure may be pictured as follows:

Highest organizations:	Corporations
	╱ ╲
Intermediary organizations:	Unions Federations
	╱ ╲
Primary organizations:	Casas do povo, Gremios, Ordens, Sindicatos, Casas dos pescadores

To this structure, at an even higher level, were sometimes added the hierarchy of governmental organizations: the Council of State, the Corporative Council, the Chamber of Corporations, and the Subsecretariat (Ministry) of Corporations and Social Welfare. This governmental structure was not often pictured in the organizational charts, however, for that would imply a degree of control ("state corporatism") that the regime liked not to admit.[47]

The corporations were to represent the supreme agencies through which the lower-level corporative units were supposed to come together. In a system based on the assumption of class harmony rather than conflict (which we have already intimated existed more in theory than in fact and was *not* structured into the system of grass-roots corporative associations and collective contract negotiations), the corporations were the one organization where representatives of the sindicatos and gremios, the casas do povo and the gremios da lavoura, the casas dos pescadores and the gremios of the fishing industry were supposed to meet, sit together across a bargaining table, work out their differences, and arrive at the harmony of interests on which the entire scheme was posited. The corporations were to integrate all grass-roots and intermediate-level corporate agencies, develop the corporative idea of national solidarity, coordinate the functions of the corporative organisms in accord with the National Labor Statute, provide technical and advisory opinions to the government, and promote collective labor contracts and social security. Moreover, the corporations were to be autonomous, independent of both government and domination by any single class. The corporations were to be the pinnacles of the system, the focal point around which the entire corporative structure revolved. In theory at least, they were to represent the culmination of the corporative revolution.[48]

But the corporations did not come into existence. It was not until 1956, some twenty-three years later, that the decree-laws governing the organization of the first corporations were finally handed down. Publicly, the rationale offered for the delay was that the Portuguese wanted to avoid creation of the corporations from the top (again the contrast with the etatist system), that it was first necessary to build corporative consciousness in the mass of the people so that the corporations could grow naturally, organically, from below. There were two other reasons, the first involving the crises of the 1930s and 1940s—the depression, the Spanish civil war, and World War II—which kept postponing the promulgation of the corporative plans that were, in fact, drawn up. The second involved the reluctance of the regime's chief architect and guiding force, Salazar himself, to move ahead with corporative development. The reasons for Salazar's hesitancy, which may seem curious given his prior ideological commitment, included both his own aversion to giving up any power and the fears of his supporters of what might happen if any real authority were devolved upon these "unknown" institutions (themes discussed in more detail in the following chapter). In any case Portugal became, as its critics were fond of pointing out, a corporative system without corporations. Although this criticism was somewhat unfair considering the plethora of lower-level corporative agencies already created and functioning, the fact is that at the highest level of the corporative pyramid the corporations themselves remained nonexistent all through the formative and institutionalizing phases of the Portuguese corporative experiment. The role and functions reserved for the corporations were actually given to a variety of new Organizations of Economic Coordination, a development which had most important implications for the evolution of the regime.[49]

THE ORGANIZATIONS OF ECONOMIC COORDINATION   Since the creation of a national corporative consciousness and hence of the corporations themselves would require some time, the regime began to feel the need to establish some other set of agencies to act as coordinators of the national economy and of the many grass-roots corporative units beginning to come into existence. The continuing economic crisis of the early to mid-1930s served as a particularly strong impetus for creating regulatory and control mechanisms that could help govern production, imports, exports, wages, working conditions, and the like. Hence, in 1936, by decree-law 26,757, the government authorized the structuring of a series of Organizations of Economic Coordination that would serve as economic regulatory agencies and as intermediaries between the government, on the one hand, and the lower-level corporative groups, on the other. These organizations were established as provisional units; their functions were eventually to be taken over by the corporations.[50]

There were three types of Organizations of Economic Coordination. The Regulatory Commissions were established to govern the importation of wheat, commercial items, and the like. The National Juntas were designed to foment and regulate exports; among the first created were the Junta Nacional do Vinho (wine), the Junta Nacional de Azeite (olive oil), and the Junta Nacional de Frutas (fruits). The Institutes, set up to guarantee the quality of Portuguese products, included an Institute for Canned Fish, an Institute for Port Wine, and an Institute for Bread.[51]

The Organizations of Economic Coordination served as a means by which the Portuguese state extended its control over virtually all sectors of the economy. In the classic Portuguese fashion, they functioned as the agents for the regulation, bureaucratization, and hence state control of social and economic life, for the growing etatism of an increasingly authoritarian regime. Although the Portuguese leadership continued to claim that theirs was a system of corporatism of association, in fact with the decree creating the Organizations of Economic Coordination it became a system of state corporatism, regulated, guided, and directed from above as in the historic bureaucratic-patrimonial structure. Later, when the Ministry of Corporations and then the corporations themselves were finally created, a number of corporative intellectuals argued that there was no longer any need for the Organizations of Economic Coordination, that in accord with the original law their functions should be taken over by the corporations.[52] But by that time the controls were too tight and the entire system too institutionalized to revert to the freer, more open society implied in the corporatism-of-association concept. The system of state corporatism and authoritarianism remained in effect, and the corporations were never allowed to develop the broad functions that corporative ideology had defined for them. Portugal became a full-fledged, centrally directed, tightly regulated bureaucratic state, which was quite at variance with the original corporative conception.[53]

COLLABORATIVE AGENCIES   Along with the grass-roots corporative units
and the official government organs, the regime moved in the 1930s to
incorporate various other organizations and associations into the corporative structure. These were designated "collaborative agencies" and
included the official party, the União Nacional; the Fundação Nacional
para a Alegria no Trabalho (the National Foundation for Joy at Work);
the Sociedade para a Defesa da Familia (the Society for the Defense of
the Family); the Obra das Mães pela Educação Nacional (the Work
of the Mothers for National Education); the Mocidade Portuguesa (Portuguese Youth); and the Legião Portuguesa (Portuguese Legion).

The most important of these was probably the União Nacional (UN).
Although the UN had its origins in Salazar's speech of 1930 calling for
a strong state that would be nationalist in character, it was not until
1932 that the organization was formally chartered. The UN was proclaimed an association without partisan character and independent of
the state, a movement more than a party. In this respect it was not
unlike other "apolitical" associations so frequent in the Iberic-Latin tradition. In fact, it was founded as a reaction against the anarchy of partisan politics and of party factions of the Republican era.[54]

The UN was to serve as the agency to help implement corporative
ideology at the mass level. It was proclaimed an "entity for the common
good" whose interests were to harmonize class and political differences,
to unify the nation rather than divide it. Its goal was national consolidation; it claimed to represent *all* public opinion, to be the agent for
the reintegration of state and nation which had been so long separated
during the Republic. Its first function was "the formation of national
consciousness"; its other duties included "combating" the party idea,
providing moral unity, eliminating dissent, forming a corporative mentality, "guaranteeing" the work and continuity of the government, and
integrating the life of the state. The UN was charged with generating
publicity and support for the regime, issuing studies, instilling patriotism, defending corporative principles, assisting the state, and collabo-
rating with other corporative organizations. The UN was thus not just
the agency for the creation of a single-party system but also an effort
to stamp out party spirit and all partisan activity.[55]

The União Nacional was founded upon the principles of discipline
and hierarchy. Its organization was pyramidal, hierarchical, closely parallel to the structure of the Portuguese sociopolitical and governmental
hierarchy. It had regional, provincial, local, and parish structures, and
at the top was the Central Commission whose president and chief guiding spirit was, from the beginning, Salazar. It also established a Center
for Corporative Studies, which issued a variety of books and pamphlets,

particularly during the first fifteen years. The UN was proclaimed open to all Portuguese who, regardless of previous political allegiances, accepted the work of national renovation. Although at the grass-roots level the UN never became a full-fledged mass movement, it did serve as an umbrella for a variety of political factions: Catholics, moderates, Monarchists, labor leaders, Integralists, Nationalists, some Republicans, some Fascists, supporters of the May 28 movement, and so forth.

The Portuguese União Nacional was *sui generis*. It was not the agent for the imposition of a single-party dictatorship, nor did Portugal ever become a "party state" in the fascist or totalitarian sense. Nor was this ever the regime's intention. Rather, the UN served as a political instrument of the government, as a means to garner and secure support and restore "organic unity" in place of the divisive partisan politics of the recent past. In a nation where party politics in the Anglo-American sense had never been very firmly rooted, the Portuguese UN was an attempt to restore solidarity, to link the government with the organized units of society, to serve as an intermediary between state and nation. This implies that we must take seriously at least some of the functions enumerated in the organization's statutes, for in many ways they corresponded closely to what the UN actually did do. It is perhaps unfair to criticize it for being undemocratic or for not having as its primary function the holding of elections, for that was never its purpose or function. Nor is it to be denigrated as an underdeveloped version of the European single-party totalitarian states, for that was never its aspiration either. Rather, it was a typically *Portuguese* movement, subordinate to those in power and serving them in various ways, not very ideological, not concerned with mass mobilization, a civic action association aimed at restoring a measure of national unity to replace the anarchy of the past.

The UN was not a militant party after the Italian or German examples.[56] Its roots were more in the nineteenth-century tradition of *caciquismo* and in the historic pattern of "royal" patronage agencies. It was not a disciplined elite resting on a large mass base but a loose collection of notables centering especially in Salazar. As a *national* union representing the liquidation of the old partyism, it came to enjoy a legal near monopoly of political action. These activities were not partisan in our sense, however, but had to do with patronage functions and the UN's role as a political appendage to the regime. It was never at the center of the state but was rather a bureaucratic mechanism of it. It was another of several administrative organizations tied in closely with the government and inseparable from it, a further extension of the classic patrimonialist structure and of an administrative state.

The UN served to dispense favors and patronage at the local level; it gave jobs and positions to local notables and government bureaucrats; it served as the eyes and ears of the regime to sound out local needs and opinions. It performed the upward, transmission-belt function of weakly communicating to those in power what the grass roots were thinking and the downward function of helping carry out certain government programs and policies. For example, it helped dispense milk to school children, handed out sewing machines to widows, and the like. Only incidentally did it participate in elections, with the candidates selected from an approved list. It was not a mass movement; rather, its membership consisted chiefly of government workers and bureaucrats. The names which it put up for elections to the National Assembly were usually important persons in their localities and adherents of the regime. They were ordinarily selected by Salazar beforehand. The UN's ethic was, therefore, the ethic of Salazar, and the organization was hence a highly personalistic one whose members gave loyalty and service to him in return for certain favors and status. The UN was thus not a passionate movement either; since Salazar, as the incarnation of the Catholic-corporate spirit, was dedicated to morality, asceticism, hierarchy, and authority, so too, by and large, was the UN. It remained closely intertwined with the bureaucratic framework of the corporative state but never dominated it. We shall have more to say regarding this important "collaborative agency" later in our discussion.

Among other collaborative agencies, the National Foundation for Joy at Work served to organize social and recreational activities for the lower classes. This too was in the Catholic-corporate conception of speaking to the needs of the whole man rather than just to his material wants. Working through the Subsecretariat of Corporations and Social Welfare the foundation organized sporting events, developed working-class recreational centers, and promoted other social and recreational events in an effort to alleviate the isolation and alienation of modern mass man.

The Society for the Defense of the Family was a conservative Catholic group, consisting often of the wives of government officials, aimed at preserving the integrity of the family as an institution, at praising motherhood, and at providing charity. The Work of the Mothers for National Education was also directed toward school and family, a kind of weak, paternalistic, and charity-oriented version of the PTA.

More important were the Mocidade and the Legião. The Mocidade, created on May 19, 1936, was a product of both the Fascist currents of the time and of the threatening (to the Portuguese) events in next-door Spain; it represented an effort to develop a militant youth organization for the defense of the regime.[57] It was aimed at building "the Portuguese man of tomorrow": physically, mentally, religiously, and politically. The Mocidade was to encompass all Portuguese youth, those in school and those outside, and was designed to stimulate, in the organization's own words, the integral development of youths' physical capacity, the formation of their character, and their devotion to the nation. The Mocidade was organized into the Lusitos (ages 7–10) and the Infantes (ages 10–14), obligatory for all Portuguese youth, followed by the Vanguardistas (ages 14–17) and the Cadetes (ages 17–21, except for university students, who were eligible to age 26). Both the Vanguardistas and the Cadetes were voluntary, though during the period of the Spanish civil war and World War II many were obligated to join.

The Mocidade in its early years provided civic and moral education, physical and premilitary training, and Christian-corporative education. It was proclaimed a national, premilitary organization and had its own emblems, uniforms, and symbols. It was to be a "movement for the national formation of the youth," not a party or a child assistance agency. Its basic unit was the cell. It was headed by a National Commissariat, whose director in these early days was Marcello Caetano, and it was linked to the Ministry of Education through this Commissariat. At the cadet level its members were organized into militia units, and it was obligated to coordinate with the paramilitary Legião.[58]

Though the Mocidade sounded both fierce and Fascist, in fact it never became either of these. It was a product of the 1930s and reflected the symbols, rhetoric, and organizational forms then current, but its actual operations were always far more limited. With the potential threat to Portugal posed by the Spanish conflict and World War II, it did engage in some paramilitary activities and did serve as a preparatory school for military training. But few Portuguese youth took the ideological baggage and the militancy very seriously, viewing these chiefly as a pain and a nuisance akin to attendance at catechism classes. After World War II especially the youth looked upon it with bemusement, and the Mocidade itself became more the Portuguese version of the Boy Scouts than a militant, corporatist youth movement. The African wars of the 1960s served to revive some of its para- and premilitary training aspects, but this turned out to be largely wishful thinking on the part of the 1930s generation of older regime militants and was not reflected in much actual practice or in the thinking of the youth themselves.[59]

The Legião in the 1930s was the paramilitary complement to the Mocidade and one of the few more or less spontaneous movements to emerge during this period. After the outbreak of the Spanish civil war, the pressure from volunteers to participate in the "anti-Bolshevik struggle" was such that an ad hoc militia was formed to carry the fight to Spain.[60] In September of 1936, the Legião was formally recognized. Initially it consisted of 20,000 men, growing to 30,000 during World War II.

The Legião was incorporated as another complementary structure of the New State. It was proclaimed an "organic organization" like the Army; "the Legion is integrated into the concept of an armed nation." It was a disciplined armed group, stressing the military virtues. It proclaimed itself anti-Communist, with both military and political functions. It was to serve as a standing armed force and a military reserve for urgent mobilization. Its political functions included the defense of the nation *and* the social order, the upholding of corporative principles, the repudiation of class war, anarchy, and anticlericalism. It stood for faith, family, nation, Christianity, and moral authority.[61]

The Legião was headed by a Junta Central; it had a general command, naval and air brigades, and district commands which were separate from but integrated with the regular military command structure. The Junta constituted its highest authority, with five members named by the government, two of whom were required to be active military officers. The Legião was also trained by reserve officers, and in 1942 its duties were greatly expanded when it was given the task of organizing national civil defense. Leaders of the Legião were usually important political and military persons, whose positions in this agency were often important steps toward even more influential posts.[62]

The Legião was probably the closest Portugal came to a full-fledged Fascist organization. During the war period, membership was more or less compulsory for most government employees, though later this was no longer the case. The Legião also shed most of its Fascist trappings. Originally it had sometimes served as an agent for the repression and occasional terrorization of opponents of the regime; in the postwar period, however, these functions were taken over by other agencies. Nevertheless, it remained an important organization performing a variety of military, paramilitary, and political functions related to defense, intelligence, training, propaganda, and the like. Again, the African wars beginning in the 1960s served to revive it, so that the Legião not only constituted an important reserve force and paramilitary element but was also active in domestic politics. Its alumni formed a strong pressure group, tied up closely with other powerful veterans' associations.[63]

ANCILLARY ORGANIZATIONS Presumably in a corporative state, as the Portuguese Constitution and the official rhetoric proclaimed it to be, all subnational organizations would be organized corporatively and would be included within the corporative structure. No organizations are any more corporative in character by history and tradition than the Army or the Church, for example, or the university and the civil service. Yet none of these agencies was ever fully incorporated in the corporative structure or subordinated to the discipline and hierarchy of the corporative order. As we shall see in the next chapter, the issue of whether powerful business, landed, and economic interests were ever subordinated to the corporative structure remains an open one as well.

It is one thing, after all, to proclaim Portugal a corporative state, but it is quite another to implement that proclamation fully or to subordinate powerful associations such as the Army or the Church, with their own long independent histories and special status, to an abstract principle. During the 1920s the debate waxed long and arduous as to exactly how and where to fit these agencies into the corporative order, and among corporative ideologues like Pires Cardoso this discussion has continued up to recent times.[64] For the more practical men of power like Salazar, however, who had to deal with these influential interests on an everyday basis, the abstractions of corporative ideology soon ran head-on into the realities of institutional self-interest. Some powerful interests refused to sacrifice or subordinate their already established positions in the Portuguese system, interests on whom the regime was dependent for its very survival and with whom it hence refused to tamper for fear that the regime and the entire corporative edifice might come tumbling down. The result was a series of compromises that enabled the New State to survive but that undermined many of its claims of corporative purity and intentions and may imply that it was not a full-fledged corporative state at all.

The Army provides the best illustration. By tradition it was a corporative agency par excellence[65] and was duly assigned a number of seats in the Corporative Chamber. But the Army was, of course, more than merely one corporative agency among several; it was the backbone of the regime, the instrument through which Salazar came to power and by whose suffrance the regime continued, the fundamental pillar of the entire system. The Army would obviously not be content to be represented but meagerly in the Corporative Chamber or to be subordinated to the corporative structure at all. This was recognized by Salazar, as well as by the military chiefs, with the result that the military received its customary special treatment. Its budget steadily rose; military perquisites were lavishly endowed; the presidency of the country was consistently given to military men; the services were well equipped and provided for; and the military's separate but elevated place in the society was guaranteed.

No civilian corporatist minister or bureaucrat ever exercised sway over the military's special domains, and the military itself remained the ultimate arbiter of national affairs. Against the urgings of his more ideological colleagues, the pragmatic Salazar did not attempt to subordinate the military to the corporative structure. In fact, the military remained above and beyond the corporative structure, with its lines of influence and control going directly to Salazar and other high authorities instead of being channeled through corporative intermediaries. Its existence was distinct and separate from the corporative structure, parallel to it, and in certain respects overlapping, but still segregated from it and in many ways superior. The Army constituted a government within the government, as it had historically in Portugal, and was never reorganized to bring it into accord with corporative organizational principles. That would have been too risky, and Salazar consistently backed away from any such plan. That is why also, after a due consideration of the corporative system, a separate chapter is required in this book to discuss how the Portuguese system really works.[66]

The same problem in a sense applied to the Church. The Church was similarly a corporative agency par excellence[67] and was duly given its seats in the Corporative Chamber. But it was again clear that the Church was not about to subordinate its interests to the structure of the corporative order. This was ironic in a way since it was from the Catholic encyclicals, after all, that the corporativists had received their major inspiration. Again, the problem was solved pragmatically rather than ideologically. Some Church and Church-related agencies, such as the misericórdias (alms houses) and the Instituto de Serviço Social, a charitable social service organization, were incorporated within the corporative system of social assistance.[68] But the Church proper and its hierarchy remained independent, with the Church's special rights and status defined through the 1940 Concordat rather than through corporative decree-law. Although the influence of the Church in Portugal and of the hierarchy on Salazar was undoubtedly less than is usually presumed, the Church retained its privileged position in the country, and its special access was guaranteed in ways that had nothing to do with the corporative structure. Finally, after one of those long, Thomistic, scholastic debates to which the corporative order so often gave rise, the entire issue was resolved by proclaiming that the Church was a corporative agency but "of international character." That solution enabled the Church to preserve its independence, which was never seriously in doubt, while at the same time enabling corporatists to preserve the purity of their doctrine.[69]

The university was another, though parallel, problem. Again we have a historic corporative institution of long and hallowed tradition which was given its share of seats in the Corporative Chamber but which was never subordinated to the corporative structure. Here the reason was not so much independent might (the problem with the Army) or the international and separate character of the institution (the Church) as the sheer volatility, confusion, and chaos that often reigned in the universities. The regime had intended to corporatize the university system, and various rectors (including Caetano) had proclaimed that as their goal; but postponement followed postponement, and in the end nothing was ever done to corporatize the university except to endow a chair of corporative law and to set up a corporative studies center. The first obstacles were the crises of the 1930s and World War II as well as the technical confusion inherent in attempting to corporatize such a changing, complex institution; later, the volatility of the student bodies, the political opposition of senior faculty and students, and sheer inertia were primarily responsible. In any case, another prime, "naturally" corporative body was never fully integrated into the formal corporative structure of the New State.[70]

Finally, the public service—here again we have an entity with a long corporative tradition and one whose various components were duly given representation in the Corporative Chamber. But this hardly describes the place or role of the bureaucratic structure within the Portuguese system, which was far more important than a handful of seats in the Chamber. Like the Army and the Church, the bureaucracy helped form the backbone of the regime—more than one mere pressure group among many, it constituted one of the primary supports of the entire system, the heart of this "administrative regime." We have already discussed the argument of some corporative ideologues that there was no need for a separate corporations ministry since presumably in a corporative system *all* ministries and governmental agencies would be corporatized. But as that never occurred, each ministry continued to function in a separate fashion, albeit with some bows to corporate coordination, while the Corporations Subsecretariat (later, ministry) exercised a series of functions segregated and quite distinct from these others. Although most government officials were obligated to join the União Nacional and to swear loyalty to the corporate regime, that was often the limit of their involvement in the *corporative* aspects of the regime. Like the Army, the Church, and the universities, the public service was never fully subordinated to the corporative structure; it remained, instead, separate and sometimes above and beyond that structure, a parallel organization whose position, channels, and performance bases were not tied directly to the corporative system. These institutions all had ways of making their influence felt other than through the corporative hierarchy. Hence, one can say that while Portugal was a corporate state in theory and in law, there were whole areas of the state structure that were not corporatized and that require not only separate treatment but a wholly different model for understanding.

Here is where our earlier theoretical discussion of the Iberic-Latin political tradition is useful, however, for while such agencies as the bureaucracy were never completely "corporatized" in the 1920s and 1930s sense of that term, they were nonetheless an integral part of the more general corporatist-statist-patrimonialist system that we have identified with the tradition of Iberic-Latin development. One thinks particularly in this connection of the administrative state model developed by Merêa, Faoro, and more recently Graham.[71] What makes that model particularly useful in terms of the discussion here is that in the Iberian and Latin American systems the Army, the Church, and the bureaucracy are all considered part of the same administrative state apparatus, not autonomous or separated from it. Thus, while these agencies were not incorporated into the *formal* corporative structures erected in the 1930s, they were a part of a far older corporatist-organicist-etatist tradition and political culture. We shall return to this theme in chapter 10 and in the conclusion.

The Structure of the Corporative State:
A Preliminary Assessment

The corporative structure established in the 1930s was a highly rationalized, highly complex system, with agencies created to encompass virtually all social groups and nearly all areas of national life.[72] Begun in 1932/33, virtually the entire structure was in place by 1936/37, with the creation of the Organizations of Economic Coordination and the *gremios da lavoura*. Moreover, the corporative reorganization represented a thoroughgoing change-over in the structure and power of the state apparatus; in a sense it may even be considered a revolutionary change-over, designed to adapt Portugal to the pressures of modern, industrial, twentieth-century life and to the realities of new social forces. It did not imply, as we shall see in the next chapter, a fundamental or revolutionary alteration in the social bases of power, but it did signal a major adjustment to changed social conditions and in the further institutionalization of the national system. At the same time, the new corporative state exhibited many continuities with the past and was not out of accord with a longer, historic, dominant Portuguese tradition. Finally, though it proclaimed itself authoritarian and hierarchical, the powerful concern for social justice that underlay the corporativist conception must also be emphasized. This concern was not just a concession to foreign fads or a mere "confidence trick" but represented a genuine effort to come to grips with the problems of poverty, alienation, and mass man in a positive albeit particularly Portuguese and corporatist fashion.

The Portuguese system was avowedly a mélange, a mixture of foreign and domestic inspirations, of old and new. Borrowing liberally from Vatican, French, and, to a considerable extent, Italian sources, the corporatists sought to adapt them to the unique requirements of the Portuguese situation. What further distinguished Portuguese corporatism was that its base structures reflected so closely the institutions of Portuguese society and some of its more distinguishing characteristics: the casas do povo, casas dos pescadores, gremios, sindicatos, municipal associations, parish organizations, and the like.[73] Even opposition historians like Oliveira Marques are forced to admit some of the accomplishments of the regime, its administrative and organizational advances, and its early bases in popular support.[74] The corporative restructuring, we have argued, was also in accord with a longer Portuguese tradition of authority and patrimonialism.

At the same time, the seeds of difficulty were already present at the beginning and almost inherent, given the way the system was structured. Some powerful interests remained completely outside the corporative structure, refusing to sacrifice their special place within the Portuguese system. The possibility for special treatment rather than equal treatment, for imbalance and conflict among the several power contenders instead of equilibrium and class harmony, was thus present right at the start. Further, though it proclaimed itself a system of *corporatisme d'association,* the vast powers given the state implied a *corporatisme d'état.* Salazar once justified this by arguing that in the absence of a strong corporative consciousness, the state had to assume the control of the economy and of social groups "as the representative and custodian of the people's interests." [75] The fact was that, with the exception of certain guilds (and even that was quickly changed), the entire corporative structure was to be regulated and brought into existence by governmental action. The corporations themselves were not designed to be entirely state dominated in this way, but they did not come into existence for a long time; and the Organizations of Economic Coordination that took over the functions originally conceived for the corporations were manifestly agencies of state intervention in economic and social life. Thus the corporative institutions established in the 1930s contained within them the seeds for future conflict, the possibility for favoritism and political expediency, and the ever-present potential for authoritarian state control of the entire system rather than the free associability envisioned by corporatism's ideological proponents.[76]

V

The Corporative Experiment en Marche

The military-nationalist-corporatist regime that came to power in the late 1920s and early 1930s had three priorities. In descending order of criticality these were: (1) To reestablish political order and stability after the chaos of the Republic; naturally, this implied as a first-order matter of importance the new regime's own continuance in power. (2) To reestablish economic order, fiscal solvency, and a balanced budget and to provide for economic recuperation and recovery. (3) To carry out and implement the corporatist reorganization of society.[1]

It goes without saying that these requirements were interrelated; yet, like so many things Portuguese, the priorities were ranked hierarchically. Although some young corporatist ideologues like Marcello Caetano and Teotonio Pereira argued that the corporatist restructuring should come first and that from such a restructuring both political and economic order would follow,[2] those who occupied the highest positions of power, Salazar and the Army, saw things differently. In their view the reestablishment of political order and stability had to come first; economic recovery could only occur once political order had been reestablished; and the corporative restructuring depended on the prior achievement of the other two. The corporative restructuring was not viewed as a mere luxury, however, and plainly Salazar saw the constitution and laws of 1933 as a way of institutionalizing the political and economic stability achieved after 1926. Nevertheless, it is clear that for both the prime minister and his chief advisers the need for political and economic stability took precedence over the implementation of the corporatist ideology.[3] This ranking of priorities would largely determine the success, or lack thereof, of the corporative revolution.

The Corporative Restructuring Begins

Pedro Teotonio Pereira, a young Integralist leader of good family, took up his post as the first subsecretary in the newly created Subsecretariat of State of Corporations and Social Welfare on April 14, 1933. By this point the political situation had stabilized somewhat, and so had the government's finances. The opposition to the regime had largely faded away through both cooptation and repression, while austerity and balanced budgets had halted the galloping inflation and depreciating currency of the mid-1920s. With the regime's two first-order priorities now more or less accomplished, it could turn to its third priority, the implementation of the corporatist program.

Repeatedly during the 1930s, however, new political threats to the regime or the fear that corporatist reorganization might upset the economic stability so recently and painfully achieved forced corporative implementation back to a lower-order priority. Thus, even though sufficient political and economic order had been achieved by 1932/33 to begin the corporatist restructuring, the danger continued to exist that the fragile stability on which the regime rested might again collapse. The result was that even in 1933 the corporatist reforms the government undertook were piecemeal, uneven, often exceedingly slow and cautious, frequently contradictory, and never of a sort that might upset the delicate political or economic balance.

The very creation of the new corporations agency as a "subsecretariat" offered one of the first clues as to where corporatist implementation lay in the regime's list of priorities. Pereira and the young Integralists he brought with him to office, we have already seen, had argued for the integration of the corporations administration directly under the office of the president of the Council of Ministers (Salazar's office). But instead the organization charged with implementing the corporative revolution was established as a mere subsecretariat, outside the prime minister's office, with neither direct access to Salazar nor the authority necessary to force other ministries to reorganize along corporative lines.[4]

The first thing Pereira did in his new post was to receive the congratulations of his friends and supporters. By his own account, this went on for days and days. He also reports being inundated by job seekers. Among those recruited for the corporative team were Augusto da Costa, a journalist and fellow Integralist whose writings in the late 1920s and early 1930s presaged much of the corporative legislation of 1933, and Pedro Botelho Neves, Pereira's deputy and the first director of the Instituto Nacional do Trabalho e Previdência (National Institute of Labor and Welfare). Other young Integralists, leaders of the Catholic social movement, and university students volunteered to assist. The press gave the new agency widespread publicity. All the euphoria of a new social venture in its early phases was present.[5]

On June 5, 1933, the subsecretariat launched its campaign with a big meeting in the luxurious Teatro São Carlos off the Chiado in downtown Lisbon. Salazar, his ministers, the armed forces chiefs, and other notables were in attendance. Pereira spoke on the subject of "Corporations and Social Assistance." [6] The meeting was designed to show the workers that the corporative revolution was *en marche,* but few workers attended, probably even fewer understood what corporatism was all about, and virtually none had thus far been affected by the corporatist reforms. Indeed, the changes that had occurred to this point had largely been negative: austerity and wage freezes, the illegalization of a number of fledgling socialist and Communist labor groups, and the breakup of the CGT (General Confederation of Labor).

In the meantime, the subsecretariat had begun work on the large body of labor and social legislation that was perhaps among the most significant of the corporative regime's accomplishments. It was this agency that prepared the Labor Statute of 1933 and also the series of decree-laws promulgated on September 23, 1933, that resulted in a nationwide system of sindicatos, gremios, casas do povo, and the like. A variety of new laws dealing with social security, wages, hours, working conditions, and so forth was also prepared; additional legislation set up a nationwide structure of labor tribunals, provided the machinery and administrative apparatus for collective contract agreements, and in other areas established the legal framework for the implementation of the Labor Statute. The comprehensiveness of the corporative legislation promulgated in Portugal in 1933 was remarkable. [7]

The reorganization and corporatization of the trade union movement went forward rapidly. In November 1933 the first three corporative sindicato organizations received their charters: the bank workers, the clerks, and the insurance workers. Within two years the number of sindicatos recognized by the government had increased to 191. Thereafter, the growth rate was reduced somewhat, but the number of sindicatos still increased substantially, reaching 308 in 1945 (and then tapering off drastically, a trend whose reasons and implications will be explored more fully in subsequent chapters). [8] Although the rapidity of implementation of the corporative legislation in the labor sector is impressive, these developments did not take place in an associational vacuum. The corporatists already had a variety of mutual benefit societies, Catholic trade unions, and other charitable agencies on which to build. In addition, many of the new sindicatos now registering with the Corporations Subsecretariat were merely the old trade unions rebaptized. The dissolution of the old CGT had left them in an organization lacuna that was quickly filled by the official syndicate system. With no place else to go, the old unions simply accepted the new charters written for them in the Corporations Subsecretariat and became registered as corporative sindicatos. The accomplishment of the regime in restructuring the union movement during these early years is still significant, but it is not as though it was accomplished without an organizational base on which to build.

Because the labor movement constituted the most immediate problem for (or threat to) the regime, the corporatization of the workers proceeded most speedily; but other sectors were not so far behind. The first ordens were soon organized for professionals, and the first gremios for commercial and business interests. In January 1934, on a cold, blustery day, the first casa do povo was inaugurated in the town of Barbacena. Salazar gave the inaugural speech, saying that the casas symbolized the rebirth of an atrophied rural life. The casas proliferated almost as fast as the sindicatos, with 141 already organized by 1935 and a total of 506 a decade later. Unlike the sindicatos, however, which had some bases in existing organizations, many of the casas were created simply by government fiat and continued to exist only in the pages of the *Diario do governo*.[9] Later, there was a great deal of criticism of the largely nonexistent casas do povo national structure.

In considering the reasons for the rapid corporatization of the Portuguese lower classes, Philippe C. Schmitter offers some intriguing suggestions. He argues, first, that the corporatization of the trade unions was designed not only to deprive this class of the instruments of collective struggle but also to provide governmental authorities with a complex of new institutions to capture information on worker dissatisfaction, to channel selective welfare benefits to "worthy" sectors, to coopt emerging and potentially challenging labor leaders, to restrict wages and salaries in the name of austerity and balanced budgets, and above all to fill a certain "occupational space," thereby preventing the eventual emergence of competing, potentially threatening (Socialist, anarchist, Communist) labor associations. Second, says Schmitter, the corporative system was an instrument of class rule. It was aimed at disarming and rendering dependent upon state-supported paternalism those groups (primarily labor) whose demands might have hindered the development of national entrepreneurial capital and hampered the consolidation of the political hegemony of a national bourgeoisie.[10]

The Schmitter arguments regarding the biases and distortions of the system, which begin also to get at the differences between the theory of corporatism and its actual practice in Portugal, are valid in their essentials, although there are other perspectives to be considered and a number of qualifiers must be introduced. The argument neglects, for instance, the fact that corporatism was as strongly anticapitalist as it was anti-socialist and that the corporatization of the working class was accompanied by almost equally stringent legislation regulating business and commercial elements. While this legislation was not evenly applied to both sectors, to emphasize the one and neglect the other gives a misleading picture. In fact, the corporative system came eventually to be as despised by businessmen as it was by labor. The actual situation, therefore, was not so one-sided as the above arguments imply.[11]

Second, while the Schmitter argument correctly stresses the control aspects of the corporative system, its other functions, including the strong inclination of the New State's founders to institutionalize a system of social justice, have been ignored. Though it is true that the workers' organizations were subordinated to state control through the corporative apparatus, they also were afforded a legitimacy in the system they had never enjoyed before and were the beneficiaries of a variety of new social programs. One can still question the adequacy of these new programs, but on any balance sheet of the regime's performance they must at least be taken into account.

The inference that there was a single set of hidden purposes behind the corporatist reorganization of Portuguese society is also inaccurate. Such an interpretation masks the finer differences that existed and glosses over the facts that there were distinct corporatist and other factions vying for influence and that the actual situation was more complex than is implied in such a single-cause explanation. The argument that the corporative system was designed to assist the political control of a national bourgeoisie, for example, while accurate to a considerable degree, obscures some subtler complexities, namely, the disdain Salazar and many of his lower-middle-class colleagues felt for the high bourgeoisie, the strategies used by the regime to control and limit the power and wealth of the elite, the inability of even an authoritarian regime to impose fully its restrictive controls on certain labor sectors, the fact that even the wealthiest and most powerful of social and economic forces sometimes had but limited influence on Salazar (like de Gaulle, he often simply would not listen), and the fact that politics in Portugal, as elsewhere, was never quite so mechanistic, nor was it ever such an exact mirror of socioeconomic structure, as is implicit in the explanation given above.

Where this interpretation is perhaps most misleading is in its post hoc (and without any evidence presented) attribution of certain malign, preconceived motives to the corporatist regime. The fact is there was a diversity of motives, ideas, and persons in the New State with no one of them enjoying an absolute monopoly. There *were* some who saw the corporative regime purely as a means to control the workers for the benefit of a new capitalist class, but that was certainly not the dominant conception of Salazar or his closest collaborators. To argue from the other single-cause and exclusively class-based explanation ignores the differences within the regime and its internal dynamics and political realities. It sounds like a plausible, if oversimplified, conspiracy theory, and thus it often found favor especially among Portuguese exiles and others opposed to the regime on ideological grounds. It is more a political argument than it is based on sound scholarship, and it hence is accepted among those with an interest in seeing the regime branded as simply a narrowly based elite who achieved power through stealth and conspiracy, wholly reactionary and "Fascist" in character, without popular support, and with the basest of political and class motives.

It is true of course that the corporative system did come to function as an agency favoring the new bourgeoisie (or at least some parts of it), and it did operate as a device to control (among others) the working class. There were biases and gross distortions in the way corporatism functioned in Portugal, and as it evolved the regime undoubtedly began to employ its restrictive control mechanisms more and more and to relegate its programs of social justice to a lower priority. But that had to do more with the realities of power and influence within the Portuguese system, with the requirements of practical politics and economics, with the priorities the regime had set for itself, and with the constant crises that it faced, both internal and external, than with some hidden, conspiratorial design of the corporatist regime's leaders or with corporatism as a system. To assert otherwise certainly runs contrary to the evidence collected in this research. The Schmitter argument, in short, provides a valuable corrective to some of the laudatory accounts of the Portuguese corporative system, but in making the contrary case it also oversimplifies and overstates it and thereby leads to a number of misinterpretations. In seeking to arrive at a balanced assessment, let us continue the discussion of early developments under the corporatist regime.

The corporatist reorganization ushered in in 1933 continued to go forward on a variety of fronts. Early in 1934 Pereira began meeting twice a week with labor leaders to, as he put it, exchange ideas and to get to know them. Meanwhile, the Instituto Nacional do Trabalho e Previdência (INTP) began functioning, named its sindicato delegates and, again to use Pereira's words, began gaining the confidence of the workers. The promulgation of a large body of new social legislation providing for social security, medical assistance, pension plans, paid vacations, and so forth, went forward; and to help implement it the Serviço de Acção Social was created within the Corporations Subsecretariat. The Serviço began channeling social assistance, medical care, clothing, and so forth, to the workers, as well as publicizing the new legislation governing hours, working conditions, pensions, child labor, and the like. As Pereira wrote, all this was designed to function with a minimum of bureaucracy and governmental intervention;[12] in fact, the corporative reforms were soon overwhelmed by *papelada* and stifling bureaucracy.

In the meantime, the corporative changes and reforms proceeded in many other areas of national life. In 1934/35, Marcello Caetano taught the first course in corporative law (which replaced the course in social economy) at the University of Lisbon and wrote a book based on his course;[13] a similar chair in corporative law was established at Coimbra. New sindicatos and casas do povo continued to receive recognition from the government, and the first casas dos pescadores were organized. The newly created Fundo das Casas Económicas began building low-cost workers' housing in Belém and other areas in and around Lisbon— small houses, but well built and always with a small garden. The Center for Corporative Studies of the União Nacional began functioning, and the first agencies of what would soon become a nationwide system of Caixas de Previdência (Social Assistance Funds) were established to help provide low-interest loans.

Pereira met repeatedly during this period with other ministers and agency heads seeking to coordinate their activities with the new corporative institutions. He also enlisted the collaboration of certain private agencies, for example, the Instituto de Serviço Social, a Catholic charitable organization that was now incorporated into the structure of the corporative social assistance program.[14] Pereira and his aides traveled through the country opening new rural casas, presiding at the inaugural ceremonies of a variety of new corporative bodies and social assistance agencies, and trying to stir support for the corporative reforms. The first workers' retreats and recreational centers were opened (one of the largest, along the four-lane Marginal that runs along the beach front from Lisbon to Cascais, was later named for Pereira). At the same time the local freguesias were given the authority to administer, although still on a modest level, a number of the social assistance programs drawn up in the Corporations Subsecretariat.[15]

In November 1934, the first collective contract was signed under the corporative Labor Statute. The event was celebrated enthusiastically by the regime's officials. It was a three-way contract involving the Gremio of Wine Exporters of Porto, the Gremio of Commerce for the Export of Wine, and the National Sindicato of Coopers. The signing was a festive occasion, particularly significant from the regime's point of view since the port wine industry was one of the nation's oldest and most traditional. In accord with corporative doctrine, the contract was seen as a "great work of collaboration between workers and employers," and it stimulated a host of new collective contracts during 1935 and 1936. In virtually all the negotiations leading to these contracts, the presence of Corporations Subsecretariat officials was conspicuous, as conciliators, arbitrators, and, in some cases, final judges. It is clear from these early negotiations that *corporatisme d'association* was already giving way to *corporatisme d'état*—not so much by design as through default. In a country with a weak and sometimes virtually nonexistent collective bargaining tradition, a strong role for the state as both the initiator and the ultimate arbiter of labor-employer disputes was inevitable. Although the new collective contracts regularized wages and working conditions in many industries for the first time, in almost all cases to the advantage of the workers in terms of at least modest salary increases and benefits, the strong role of the state in all these matters carried strong implications for the future of the corporative system.[16]

Other corporative institutions were soon organized. In October 1934, the Corporative Council was convened for the first time. By November of 1934 elections were set for the following year for the National Assembly, and the laws governing the organization of the Corporative Chamber were promulgated. The regime felt that there were now sufficient corporative organizations in existence (casas, gremios, sindicatos, and the like) to justify the Chamber's functioning and the naming of each sector's representatives. The Corporative Chamber's original representational scheme listed twenty-four sections and eighty-two representatives, one for virtually every economic sector and corporative interest in the country (see appendix A). Although the announcement of the creation of these corporative representational bodies came with great fanfare, the fact is that Salazar himself, in the name of national unity, prepared the list of the ninety Assembly candidates to be presented by the União Nacional, the country's only remaining political organization. And the representatives selected for the Corporative Chamber were, in the vast majority of cases, government officials or prominent persons loyal to the regime. Again, the strong hand of the state was everywhere present.[17]

A third general area of strong statist influence in the corporative system in its early years was through the Organizations of Economic Coordination. A number of these organizations had been established in preliminary and experimental form as early as 1931 and 1932 to help regulate production, prices, and so on, in certain key industries such as wine and cereals, activities made especially imperative by the devastating effects of the world depression. By 1935/36, with severe economic difficulties still plaguing the country and with the newer corporative agencies still weak or nonexistent, more of these agencies for "coordination" were created and their functions vastly increased. As noted in the previous chapter, they were supposed to disappear as the grass-roots corporative units gathered strength and as the corporations themselves were created. But that development failed to occur, and in fact the Organizations of Economic Coordination increasingly served as the means for the extension of centralized state authority into virtually all areas of Portuguese social and economic life. It was they and not the corporative agencies who, in the name of the "common good," determined prices, wages, working conditions, production levels, and so on, and all this was done without any significant input from the grass roots, as in the original corporatist conception. Moreover, the persons who staffed these agencies at the highest decision-making levels were often the same persons who had always governed Portugal, whatever the nature of the political regime: the elite, the educated, those with good family name or connections, the wealthy or rising upper-middle elements, notables and would-be notables, those with strong financial and business interests or those, particularly from the new middle classes, who aspired to the wealth and position that the elites enjoyed. It was this last group that seemed to emerge as the dominant one within the corporatist regime. Thus the Organizations of Economic Coordination came not only to serve as agencies of increasing *corporatisme d'état* rather than *corporatisme d'association* but also to function increasingly as agencies of upward striving and mobility and, ultimately, of class rule, contrary to all the corporatist conceptions of equality of representation for all social and economic groups. Such a development was probably inevitable given the Portuguese political-cultural tradition, the unwillingness of the regime to tamper with the existing structure of class relations, and Salazar's own priorities that placed economic stability above corporative implementation.[18]

In the meantime, however, the corporative system continued to grow. In March 1935 the legislation for the creation of the Institutions of Social Security was approved; the decree-laws governing the Workers' Depositories were promulgated the following year. The Fundação Nacional para a Alegria no Trabalho (National Foundation for Joy at Work) was also created in 1935, and the newly elected National Assembly met that same year. In 1936 the decree-laws regulating (and expanding) the activities of the Organizations of Economic Coordination were handed down. Meanwhile the Subsecretariat of Corporations continued to approve the charters of still more sindicatos, gremios, and casas do povo; the National Institute of Labor and Social Security (INTP) continued to promulgate new laws governing working hours, minimum wages, responsibility for labor accidents, child labor, women's labor, pensions, health care, family assistance, social security, and a host of others; and the Corporative Chamber began issuing its first *pareceres* (advisory opinions) based on its hearings and investigations of pending legislation. By 1937 the casas dos pescadores were also functioning; that same year saw the promulgation of the decree-laws creating the gremios da lavoura, gremios especially created for farmers and landholding interests. All of these *regulamentos, decretos,* and *pareceres* were lengthy documents, often with several chapters and detailed articles spelling out the aims, methods, functions, obligations, resources, titles, symbols, and so on, of every law and organization. This was often constitutional and legal engineering at its best (or worst)—beautiful laws and decrees, all harmonious, neat, parallel, covering all contingencies, but frequently with uncertain grounding in Portuguese social and political realities.[19]

Within a four- or five-year period, virtually the entire corporative structure (except the corporations themselves) was in place and actively functioning. The speed and thoroughness with which this was accomplished, as Schmitter notes, was little short of remarkable.[20] One must examine the voluminous literature written during this period and the vast body of legislation published in the monthly *Boletim do INTP* to appreciate the comprehensiveness of these changes. The Portuguese had literally legislated a revolution; as compared with the almost total vacuum that had existed in the areas of social security, workers' rights, and economic regulations, the changes made were phenomenal.

Of course, the implementation of all these decrees was sporadic, uneven, and, as we shall see, often biased in favor of certain groups. Given the Portuguese tradition and social structure, however, the fact that any of this legislation was implemented at all is astounding. For despite the abuse and wrong directions, the legislation of the 1930s laid the basis for some fundamental changes—piecemeal, evolutionary, paternalistic to be sure, in the classic Iberic-Latin pattern, but significant nonetheless. Essentially, the corporative revolution legitimized, under different auspices and leadership, many of the labor and social assistance reforms attempted without notable success by the Republic; it also signaled the definite shift to middle-class, bourgeois, and new-rich rule from the aristocratic politics of the period up to 1910. That the workers ultimately gained but modest benefits from this shift is hardly surprising; that they benefited at all, given previous history, is what commands our attention. The 1930s shift in the bases of power in Portugal under corporative auspices was thus not entirely unlike that undertaken in many Latin American countries at approximately the same time, implying gradual but limited changes, the accommodation of some new social forces but through nonrevolutionary means, and laying the bases for future adaptations to modernization. How this worked out in practice, and why Portugal eventually came to lag farther behind its sister countries in Iberia and Latin America, forms the subject matter of the rest of this and succeeding chapters.

The Biases of Corporatism[21]

Right from the beginning, conflicts and difficulties in implementing the corporative system had arisen, and these related directly to the order of the regime's priorities. That is, the maintenance of political order and economic stability was consistently placed above the implementation of the corporative reforms; more, where these latter held the potential for upsetting or shaking the political and economic order, they were quietly shelved or ignored. Given the fact that Portugal was in a state of almost permanent crisis all during this period—political challenges to the regime, depressed economic conditions, then the Spanish civil war, and following that World War II—it is not surprising that much of the corporative legislation was at best only incompletely implemented and that the corporative regime took some directions never foreseen by corporative theorists.

The first problem that had to be dealt with was that few Portuguese understood or were inclined to accept the corporatist solutions. For them it was an abstract and intellectual scheme whose origins and chief ideas were at best obscure. While the government and the Corporations Subsecretariat were staffed at the upper levels by writers, journalists, intellectuals, and university professors, many of whom had earlier been the chief CADC and corporative ideologues, the rest of the population was only vaguely aware of what corporatism was or implied. The Portuguese may have been "natural" corporatists, in the political cultural sense, but the formal ideology and program of "corporatism" as a movement remained largely unknown. The lack of understanding was as widespread among businessmen as among workers, among professionals as well as farm workers,[22] but the corporative scheme was applied differently to these distinct groups.

The unions were the first to feel the brunt of the corporative reorganization. The regime had earlier broken up many of the Communist, Socialist, and other radical unions, and in 1931 the CGT had been dissolved. By 1933 the labor organizations left in the country were weak and without an effective power base. Nevertheless, they greeted the promulgation of the corporative Labor Statute in September of that year and the subsequent regulatory legislation designed to implement it with one of the most massive attempts at a general strike the country had ever seen. Prompt and drastic measures on the part of the government kept the strikers from literally closing down the country (or at least Lisbon, which is the governmental-administrative center and the focus of the nation). Thousands of police, *guarda,* and Army troops were called out to guard railroad lines, arsenals, and all the larger factories, thus preventing disorder. Nearly all the strike leaders were arrested; the government said most of them were "Communists." As a result of this quick and repressive action, no public services were interrupted and complete order was quickly reestablished. This would prove to be the last major labor demonstration for the next thirteen years.[23]

Beginning in 1934, then, the labor movement was completely reorganized along the lines set forth in the corporative plans. The more radical labor leaders were kept in jail, exiled, or forbidden to take part in trade union activities. New leaders were found who were more favorable to the government; their loyalty was often secured, in the classic fashion, by putting them on the public payroll. Only those unions who accepted the corporatist rules (including its control mechanisms) were recognized by the government, a condition that was absolutely mandatory if the sindicato was to function at all. The government used its broad "intervention" powers to oversee trade union elections, to present its own list of candidates for sindicato leadership, and to ensure that the unions conformed to the new rules and accepted what the government gave them (including pay raises in certain industries). Although much of this sounds coercive and repressive (and it was in many instances), the fact is that, with the exception of a few radical and political-action-oriented unions, most sindicato leaders and the workers themselves saw which way the winds were blowing and simply went along. They accepted the new conditions, made their accommodations with the regime (they had few other choices: jail, exile), and in general sought to further their ends *within* the prevailing system. As this recognition grew in 1934/35, the number of officially sanctioned sindicatos also increased dramatically.[24]

Among professionals the reaction was largely the same. Once they had grasped the implications of the corporative reorganization, their initial reaction was strongly negative. Unlike the union leaders, however, the professional element was well connected, articulate, and able to make its influence felt. As a result, it was able to water down many of the control devices of the corporative regulations and to establish the right to regulate and police its own membership. Only four professional *ordens* were created under corporative auspices, the ordem of lawyers, the ordem of doctors, the ordem of engineers, and the ordem of agronomists; and by and large, their activities were not greatly changed by the corporative restructuring.[25]

The clearest case of favoritism, and one of the prime reasons the corporative revolution never succeeded, involves the business and commercial interests. As with other groups, the rising Portuguese business and commercial class had little understanding of the intellectual origins of corporatism or what it meant. Once they saw how the corporative reforms would affect them, however, they too reacted powerfully against the new legislation. For the Labor Statute and its ancillary legislation, the laws governing gremio organization and activities, and the Organizations of Economic Coordination implied as much state control over business activities as over labor. The difference was, however, that like the professionals the business elites were well connected and could make their arguments and influence felt. The more prescient among them soon realized that, while the corporative system was inconvenient, it could be gotten around and, even more importantly, could be used to control the workers, enforce labor peace, and thus serve the long-term interests of the business community. The result was a sell-out of the corporative ideal and the undermining of the basic corporative principle of the equality of treatment and representation of both workers and employers.

The original corporative decree-laws of 1933 had called for the *obligatory* organization of business-commercial interests into gremios, parallel to the sindicato structure. This legislation, however, provided businessmen with an "out" by allowing the continued existence of private commercial associations alongside the gremio system, provided their statutes were approved by the state and they conformed to general policy. The unions, of course, had no such "out." The result was that the merchants' and commercial associations of Lisbon and Porto continued largely as private associations rather than, as in the corporative scheme, "agencies of public utility." Even in 1973, after forty years of the corporative system, the strength and importance of some of these private associations were greater and the offices plusher and more strategically located than all but a few of the corporative gremios.

At the time, the *Associação Comercial de Lisboa,* the *Associação Comercial de Lojistas de Lisboa,* the *Associação Comercial de Porto,* and the *Associação dos Comerciantes do Porto* were considered "intermediaries" between the old class associations and the newer corporative gremios. But the question inevitably arose as to why the businessmen were allowed to maintain their private, "uncorporatized" class associations and the unions were not. Pereira's weak answer was that the private associations were merely transitional, that all should have faith in the government, that the existence of a corporative regime did not preclude other kinds of associations under certain circumstances, and that the corporative principles must at times be subordinated to the need for economic efficiency and growth. The state wanted to cooperate with the business groups, he said, not simply absorb them as in the Italian system.[26] This response was small comfort to the workers who already saw themselves having to bear the brunt of the government's new austerity measures. Eventually, a number of these private associations were also forced to reorganize under corporative lines, but this was nowhere near so complete or so thoroughly enforced as was the case with the workers' organizations.[27]

In those branches of production and commerce that were not already represented by a strong private association, the organization of the gremio system went forward rapidly, largely under state auspices. In response, strong protests were raised by business-commercial elements in late 1933/early 1934, not only to the obligatory nature of the gremios but also to the strict regulation of business activities by the mushrooming Organizations of Economic Coordination. These regulations were not only burdensome to the business elements, involving the clearing of endless papers, stamps, approvals, and so on, but they were also costly, involving fines, dues, and new taxes. Some of the old class associations actually passed motions stating their refusal to reformulate their statutes in accord with corporative requirements.[28] Other business and commercial interests reacted equally strongly. Not only were these interests able to make their private objections felt, but they also made the more general argument that such strict regulation of their activities would damage the economy and undermine production and stability, thus speaking directly to one of the regime's higher-order priorities. The emergency situation of the economy and the continued depression helped give these groups added bargaining power. The whole controversy raised the question of just how much control the government had over the business interests and if they could continue to operate independently of it. Eventually, over the objections of the corporative "purists," Salazar yielded to business pressure and ordered certain gremios made voluntary rather than obligatory. This, of course, had the practical effect of giving businessmen more independence and a far freer hand than other groups in the system.[29]

The new decree-law, promulgated early in 1934, caused a great deal of controversy. Corporative idealists saw it as a sell-out of their principles. Labor leaders questioned the uneven, preferential treatment of the business interests (one of the primary reasons for the attempted general strike of that year). Smaller businessmen and shopkeepers who were still locked into the obligatory gremios also were critical. Various meetings took place. Pereira was forced to give a number of speeches attempting to justify the change, and other Corporations Subsecretariat officials followed suit. Almost from the beginning of the corporative regime, therefore, it had already become clear that the corporative reforms would not involve parallel and coequal treatment of labor and business, as the doctrine proclaimed, but preferential treatment and favoritism for certain groups. The business interests were particularly skillful in manipulating the economic stability argument to their advantage and in getting Salazar, whose great accomplishment had been the restoration of economic solvency, to side with them. That summer, in response to a series of questions posed by the newspaper *Diario de Noticias,* Salazar spoke publicly to this issue, arguing that the business interests were harder to organize than the sindicatos because they did not conform to a single formula and he did not want to force business interests into an unnatural strait jacket that would also have the effect of strangling the economy.[30] This reasoning and the decision it led to, while plausible on pragmatic grounds, all but wrecked the noble intentions of the corporative experiment.

Government regulations of economic activity did not cease with the decision to allow voluntary gremios, however. Only the bigger business concerns were allowed to regulate themselves; the rest came under strict government control, both through the gremio structure and through the Organizations of Economic Coordination. Through the gremios the government regulated small businesses in much the same way it controlled the sindicatos: it "approved" their charters, "regulated" their elections, "fiscalized" their activities, and controlled their political participation. Some gremios, it was revealed in numerous *paraceres* of the Corporative Chamber, were fixing prices in a monopolitistic way, and the government moved against them. Through the Organizations of Economic Coordination, the government regulated whole branches of the economy: wheat, wine, fishing, import-export, canning, mining, cork, and so on. The effort to control some of these economic sectors and private satrapies, such as the wine industry, was a long and difficult process, but eventually this and other industries were brought under the hegemony of the state, and its power to regulate their affairs was slowly extended. By 1936/37 the Organizations of Economic Coordination were regulating virtually all national economic activity; corporatism of the state had clearly and definitely replaced corporatism of association.[31]

The decree-law of 1934 thus left the larger industries and some private entrepreneurs with a free hand, but not too free. The government lent money to firms when they needed it and if they qualified under the government's requirements. The decision to lend them money or not gave the state enormous power over the major private concerns, and the threat, usually implied, that the state might enforce the restrictive legislation now at its disposal gave it an added lever in controlling wealthy families and the bigger firms. State power increased in other ways. A state tobacco company and a state oil company were formed; the state railroads were leased to private developers, not sold. Cartels were formed for the exportation of fruit and fish, but always under a government decree and always working within the regulations set by the government. Similarly, monopolies and oligopolies were established in a great variety of other industries, all closely regulated by the regime. With a stroke of the pen, Salazar and the web of Organizations of Economic Coordination he created could raise or lower import duties, fix prices, set wages, and regulate production. This was thus not so much capitalism in the private, laissez-faire sense as a system of state capitalism in which the government took it upon itself not only to start and stimulate businesses and to accumulate capital for investment but also to create a kind of officially sanctioned entrepreneurial class in a country where none had existed before. A system of capitalism was thus created by the government, often over the violent objections and reluctance of the "capitalist class" itself. Business and labor were thus both actually "created" and controlled by the state, but in such a way as to benefit the business and commercial elites disproportionately. The price was acquiescence on the part of these groups to the regime and to the corporative system. The policy of granting monopolies and special privileges to certain favored elements in return for loyalty and service to the regime was hardly new in the Portuguese tradition; the corporative regime, under a different label, had updated and expanded this classic form.[32]

Favoritism to the business and commercial elements was one thing, but the next step involved no less than the take-over of virtually all the Organizations of Economic Coordination by those same business and commercial elites. In retrospect, given the structure of power and society in the Portuguese system, this development should perhaps have been expected, but it was not foreseen by corporative planners. For in theory at least the Organizations of Economic Coordination were set up on the same principle of coequal representation of workers and employers as the other corporative agencies. In fact, it was again those with status, wealth, education, family name, and the right connections—or those on their way to such rank—who dominated the regulatory agencies right from the beginning. Lower-class elements who lacked the education and proper connections were not included. Moreover, the very same wealthy and established interests who dominated these agencies were also the recipients of government favors and franchises. The Portuguese business elites went back and forth between private business and the public regulatory agencies routinely and on a scale that makes the American habit of military officers "retiring" into the ranks of the big defense contractors and ex-regulatory commission members going back into the businesses their agencies regulated pale into insignificance. This became in fact the expected mode of behavior: in a patrimonialist system such as the Portuguese, where the line between private gain and public service is virtually nonexistent, it was *expected* that the young lawyer or university graduate would first obtain a position in a ministry or agency, then move into private business where he could put his knowledge of "the system" to use, then perhaps move back into government at a higher decision-making level, then move back to become a member of the board of a major bank or import-export firm, and so on. In many cases it was possible for an individual to be *both* a high-ranking government official *and* the director of several private corporations deriving direct benefits and advantage from his governmental connections. Thus, as in the American system—and far predating the critiques of Ralph Nader and Theodore Lowi—the Portuguese regulatory agencies were literally "captured" and virtually monopolized by those same powerful business and commercial elements they were originally designed to regulate. It is in this sense that we spoke of the biases of corporatism as remarkably parallel to the biases of liberalism.[33]

The cooptation and take-over by the business and industrial elites of the government's regulatory agencies was not an overnight event. Rather it was a gradual process, which began with the 1934/35 exemptions and special favors granted businessmen but culminated only in the postwar period, by which time the government agencies were increasingly being used, openly and flagrantly, at the service of the commercial class. And it took seemingly even longer for the bulk of the population to recognize these biases in the system. It was not until the 1960s that scholarly works began emphasizing the emerging capitalistic structure of this supposedly anticapitalistic corporative system and that mass public opinion began increasingly to perceive that some elements were getting enormously wealthy through their dominance of government agencies while the rest of the population lagged behind. Here again the parallel with the American system may be useful: according to many recent interpretations, the Roosevelt New Deal reforms, adopted during the same period, had a similar effect of saving and revitalizing capitalism rather than destroying it; the agencies Roosevelt established were similarly dominated in the postwar period by moneyed and business interests; and it took until the 1960s for the critiques of "liberalism" to become popularized and widely accepted. Was Portuguese corporatism, therefore, a "confidence trick," a cruel hoax on the workers? The answer at this stage (and we return to the question later) is both yes and no. Yes, in that the workers were clearly victimized in the long run, and yes, in that a few elements in Portugal saw that clearly and planned it right from the beginning. But no, in that Salazar himself and his government were not tied to the business elite, dependent on, or subservient to it. Nor was corporatism itself designed or inevitably fated to produce the result it did. Could this outcome then have been predicted, given the Portuguese class and power structure? Perhaps, but far more clearly after the fact than before it. The same applies, of course, to Roosevelt's liberalism: its "biases" were similarly clear—after the fact. Could it be said then that corporatism was no more or no less a "confidence trick" than liberalism—or perhaps than socialism, given its biases, bureaucratization, and privileged "new class"? That dispute will not be resolved here, but it is raised for purposes of stimulating our thinking and challenging our assumptions.

Much the same thing as had happened with Portuguese business and commercial elements was occurring out in the countryside. The casas do povo had been designed initially as local community centers for tenants and small farmers. Allowance had also been made, however, for larger landholders to become members. Inevitably, since they were richer and of higher social status, and given the strong Portuguese lower-class sense of deference to one's "superiors," these larger landholders dominated, holding virtually all important offices. Or else it would be the local government official, himself ordinarily a notable, who would at the same time be the head of the local casa do povo. Later, when the casas were given political functions as the spokesmen for tenant and small farmers and the gremios da lavoura were created to represent larger farmers, landowners "representing" rural workers, as Schmitter acidly remarks, were called on to "bargain" with landowners representing landowners.[34] A parallel situation existed as regards the casas dos pescadores: they were by law headed by the local harbor master, and their boards and directorates were invariably dominated by the fleet owners, the fish processors and canners, and the large export firms.

The problems of the corporative system soon multiplied. Pereira had originally established the Corporations Subsecretariat with a minimum of personnel and bureaucracy. But as the new decrees continued to be handed down and as the complexity of the legislation and services grew, so inevitably did administration. The corporative agencies soon became swamped with requirements for approvals, coordination, fiscalization, overseeing, and paper shuffling. The *papelada* and legal regulations multiplied so as to become virtually overwhelming (and downright discouraging).[35] Furthermore, this served as handy justification for more and more sinecures, with the result that an initial dedicated group of reformers soon found itself surrounded by a mushrooming bureaucracy of incompetents, political appointees, and the friends and relatives of important persons. Instead of efficiently overseeing the entire corporative restructuring, therefore, the Corporations Subsecretariat itself became increasingly an agency through which those with wealth, influence, and friends or relatives in high places received special consideration or access to knowledge of pending legislation affecting their interests. Moreover, the very existence of so much *papelada* and regulation served to benefit those who already knew how to work within that system or go above or around it, and to put at a disadvantage—again the poor and the less wellborn—those who did not.[36]

Discrimination persisted and got worse. The winter of 1935 was especially severe; food was scarce and prices kept rising. People began murmuring, "Prices are going up because of the gremios." And indeed it was true that gremio members were making large profits from the special treatment given them by the price-setting mechanism (which they largely controlled), while wages were kept at a stationary level. It was the workers who carried the burden, then as later, of the government's antiinflationary measures.[37]

Meanwhile, the Corporations Subsecretariat was notably unsuccessful in corporatizing other areas of Portuguese public life. Although Pereira met repeatedly with other ministers and agency heads, these ministries did not really comprehend how corporatism applied to them. They had their own *clientela* to serve and did not always see how their best interests would be favored by paying more than lip service to the corporative principles. Though there were some exceptions (notably Duarte Pacheco, minister of public works, who frequently collaborated with Pereira) and though some gremios were incorporated as consulting bodies to various ministries (for example, the fruit producers' gremio served as a consultant to the Ministry of Agriculture, the gremio of insurers to the Ministry of Finance, various gremios to the Ministry of Commerce and Industry), the fact is that the entire Portuguese state was far from becoming completely corporatized. Corporative organization had thus far been confined to some of the major socioeconomic groups, especially the unions, and only weakly affected other areas of national life. Even the regime's administrators admitted that the corporatization of the society had gone forward far faster and more successfully than had the corporatization of the economy.[38] And, although this remained a sore point with many corporative ideologues, such "natural" corporations as the Church or the Army were never really brought into the corporative scheme at all. Especially in the Army's case, such tampering with its basic structures by a group of civilian reformers would likely have proved fatal to the regime, and neither Salazar nor the Army permitted this to happen.

Indeed, what comes through most clearly from an examination of the literature of this period and from interviews with a number of the key participants is that the real pusher for continued corporative innovation was not Salazar but Pereira and some of the other young ideologues. This puts in question not whether Salazar was a corporatist (he was and remained so) but whether he too was not motivated more by the desire for personal power and the wish to continue in office than by corporative ideology. Consistently in the 1930s it was Pereira who pushed for corporative "purity" and further implementation and Salazar who put the brakes on, who worked out the compromises with the business interests, who refused to let the young "gung-ho" corporatists upset the economy or tamper with the Army, who, in short, emerged as a preeminent political pragmatist and not the corporatist ideologue he is often pictured.[39] Pereira continued to see the corporative reorganization as the main goal of the regime and of its "revolution," the cutting edge on which economic and political stability could be based. Salazar, as head of government and with broader responsibilities, wanted economic and political stability to be secured first; only then could the corporative revolution proceed. Salazar repeatedly sided with business interests to slow down the corporative reforms, since he feared the economic (and maybe political) consequences that might follow if the corporative reorganization went too far or too fast. In Pereira's own account, he was repeatedly frustrated by his inability to persuade Salazar to make the definitive commitments to corporative implementation that Pereira felt were required, although he was too much a loyal servant of the regime to make this a public protest. In addition, once the grand design for the corporative system had been fashioned and the machinery set in place, Salazar soon turned to other great national and international issues and left the everyday administration of the corporative plans to subordinates. Bothered and eventually disillusioned by the indifference and lack of high-level support, Pereira moved on to another post while the corporative system continued to struggle along only incompletely (by Salazar's choice) implemented. Clearly there was much more politics in the Estado Novo, and political perspicacity on the part of Salazar, than we have usually acknowledged.

As early as 1934, thus, the limits of the corporative restructuring were already apparent. This was acknowledged by Salazar in a major speech that same year, in which for the first time he enumerated the problems of the corporative system:[40]

1. The diversity of concepts present and the newness of the corporative legislation
2. The need for state leadership and coordination
3. The indifference, impatience, and general malaise of the times
4. The limits to corporative implementation posed by the poverty of Portugal itself
5. Rapacious monopolies, on the one hand, and impatient workers, on the other
6. Business uncertainty
7. The absence of corporative spirit

Others quickly chimed in with their own criticisms. Caetano pointed to the absence of trained leaders to man the various corporative agencies, the general absence of understanding as to what corporatism was or what it was designed to accomplish, and the lack of mutual understanding among Portuguese to make the new system of harmonized social relations work.[41] Other observers noted that the casas do povo were not functioning as intended and that the gremio and sindicato structures were both weak and undeveloped.[42] Still others complained of bureaucratic difficulties and of inefficiencies of operations. For an authoritarian regime, there was remarkably ample freedom of expression in these criticisms, although all such criticism took place within a framework of acceptance of the basic corporative structure; public rejection of the system itself was not allowed.

Indeed, it was largely in response to these problems of implementation, and not because of some preconceived plan or conspiracy, that the regime was forced to make some of the changes we have just discussed. It was the absence of any understanding of what corporatism meant and of any historic sense of associability in the countryside that made it imperative that the *government* create the casas do povo. It was the absence of much middle-level leadership that made it incumbent that the *state* help structure the gremios and sindicatos, write their charters, and supervise their activities. It was the absence of self-regulating mechanisms in the business sector that forced the *government* to so closely regulate the gremios and to create the Organizations of Economic Co-ordination. Business interests continued to enjoy a specially privileged position because of the requirements for a stable economy, not because Salazar had great sympathy for them. And it was really the dynamics of the situation, the vacuum of leadership, the lack of community, the in-grained atomization and disunity of Portuguese social life, the exag-gerated individualism, that shaped the trend toward extensive state con-trol, not any hidden intentions of corporatism's planners.[43] This having been said, however, it must be added that these policies also served the interest of the Salazar regime in maintaining itself in power. Further, it is clear that the government did not fall unaware into this regulative role. Many corporatist planners had explicitly called for such a role by the state. But a corporatism of free associability still remained the ideal, and it was more by force of circumstance than design that a full-fledged system of state corporatism emerged.

Throughout the early years of the corporative era, thus, the govern-ment continued to intervene strongly and authoritatively in the economy and in associational life, but it did so in a prejudicial manner. The workers were forced to carry the burden of the wage freezes which the depression years mandated, while the fear that tampering with their activities would cause severe economic dislocations enabled patronal and business interests to continue their activities largely as before. As late as 1937 the Organizations of Economic Coordination, now thor-oughly dominated by the business interests, had applied the minimum-wage law adopted with so much celebration several years before in only a single industry; wages and social assistance for the workers also lagged increasingly behind. The forced corporatization and regulation of the working class proceeded far faster and more completely than did the corporatization of the business and commercial groups. In many re-spects, indeed, the business groups were never completely corporatized, while the controls and restrictions on labor activity remained severe. Right from the beginning, therefore, a fundamental asymmetry was in-troduced into the corporative scheme that undermined the fundamental premise of equality on which it rested.

At the same time the state's role increased in all areas. The govern-ment, however, repudiated any desire to absorb the whole national eco-nomic life. There was rather a dynamic tension right from the start: for the corporative system to work at all according to plan, not just state coordination but also state initiative, leadership, and control were neces-sary, and that meant increased authoritarianism. Loose control and more freedom (*corporatisme d'association*) meant not only that the corporative system failed to work but that the whole society and its various component parts tended toward a centrifugal falling apart. Salazar recognized and was caught on the horns of this dilemma. Increasingly during the 1930s, he began taking the authoritarian way out; doubtless, he believed he had no alternative. But, as we shall see in the following chapter, increased authoritarianism led eventually to full-fledged dictatorship.

The corporative state, in other words, soon took on the familiar role of national *patrão*. Despite the rhetoric of a freer, open corporatism of association, the traditional centralizing role of the authoritarian state apparatus quickly reasserted itself. The corporatists recognized the increasing encroachments of the state into a variety of areas not foreseen in the original plans, and they tried to rationalize it in various ways.[44] Some saw it as a merely temporary phenomenon, arguing that the heavy hand of the state would wither away as corporative consciousness grew and when the corporations themselves were created. Others argued that the state was simply carrying out its prescribed functions as the ultimate arbiter of national social and economic affairs but that a great deal of private activity and initiative continued to exist. Finally, incoming Corporations Subsecretary João Pinto da Costa Leite, who would soon replace Pereira but only on a temporary basis, reemphasized the "guiding role of the state" and the "just equilibrium" that only the state could provide. But he also pointed to the flexibility of the Portuguese system in contrast to the rigidities of the Italian one, the avoidance of artificial uniformities and the respect for differences of opinion and in the way groups could be organized, and finally the adaptability and responsiveness of the Portuguese system in reacting to the viewpoints of different internal interests. All this was true, to a certain extent, but it had little to do with the way the system was already evolving at the time Costa Leite wrote.

Completing the Corporative System: Establishing the Corporations

Despite the problems, most of which were recognized by the regime's leadership, the corporative reorganization continued to go forward in the middle and late 1930s. The difficulties encountered were viewed as temporary ones, which would surely resolve themselves as the corporative system became more firmly institutionalized and as corporative consciousness grew. In the meantime, new sindicatos continued to have their charters recognized, new casas do povo were organized, more gremios were restructured along corporative lines, and the other corporative institutions and agencies continued to expand in both numbers and activities.

By 1937 virtually the entire structure of the corporative state had been established, and the regime turned its attention to the implementation of the existing institutions rather than to more bold innovations, as in the 1933/34 period. By this point the Labor Statute's often vague articles had been fleshed out with a detailed, specific body of supplementary legislation, and the statute was being applied and developed systematically. The old labor organizations had been replaced by a new system of national labor syndicates with a claimed membership of over 100,000. After encountering a variety of early difficulties, several dozen casas do povo were now functioning. More gremios had been organized, and Pereira emphasized that they were now "well disciplined." Through the Organizations of Economic Coordination the government had firmly secured its control over the economy and was carefully regulating production, prices, wages, imports, exports, and so on. The labor tribunals were functioning, and they and the Corporations Subsecretariat provided a base for the new system of collective contracts. The law of social security was being implemented and the first *caixas sindicais* (workers' "savings and loan" associations) were in actual operation. Pereira's summing up of his own accomplishments admitted to a host of problems, specified that the results were uneven, and noted that there were still many areas of social, economic, and political life where the corporative reforms had not yet penetrated. But he argued that it *was* a functioning system, that the basic directions had been indicated, and that now it was necessary to maintain the thrust of the reforms already acomplished.[45]

With the main institutions of the corporative system already in place and operating, there were fewer corporative decree-laws, and the heavy volume of corporative legislation dropped off sharply. Attention began shifting in 1935/36 to the operational aspects and toward the completion of certain prior omissions, in terms of both the groups covered and the social services provided. The *Boletim do INTP* was from this time on filled more with the texts of the collective contracts being signed and with the occasional *pareceres* emanating from the Corporative Chamber than with any dramatic, innovative plans for social or corporative restructuring. In 1936 a new Corporative Technical Council of Commerce and Industry was created in the Ministry of Commerce and Industry (Pereira's new post) to help give a corporative character to all business and industry. Headed by Dr. Luis Supico Pinto, who would later become president of the Corporative Chamber, the new council established a corps of "negotiators" to deal with the complex issues of trade and commerce during the difficult pre-World War II period. In effect, these "negotiators" were really high-level *intendants* whose function was to extend further the government's regulation of and control over the economy. Other institutional changes of the period included the establishment of the gremios da lavoura in 1937 and the corresponding extension of certain representational and bargaining rights to the casas do povo.[46] But these were really modifications of the existing system rather than major innovations. The chief innovation of the period was to be the creation of the corporations.

It may be recalled that in the original design the corporations were to be located at the apex of the entire system. They were to serve as *the* focal points of workers' and employers' bargaining and class harmonization. The corporations had not been created initially along with the other lower-level corporative structures because, the regime argued, it was first necessary for corporative consciousness to grow so that when the corporations came into existence they would reflect "spontaneous," "natural" corporative sentiment. In fact, there was much uncertainty as to how to structure the corporations, who exactly would be encompassed in them, and what their precise functions would be. By the late 1930s, however, the grumbling was already being heard, both at home and abroad, that Portugal was a "corporative state without corporations."

The Organizations of Economic Coordination were supposed to serve as the nuclei for the future corporations. That is one reason they were given such broad responsibilities. They were officially labeled "precorporative organizations" and were, in the original plan, supposed to evolve into truly representative corporative structures. In 1938, through decree-laws 29,110 and 29,111, the government laid the basis for the conversion of the Organizations of Economic Coordination into true corporations. The government proclaimed that with the corporative reforms now firmly underway such strict governmental control over the economy was no longer necessary. Not only had the goal of economic stability been more or less accomplished, but in 1936 and 1937 some of the last political opposition had been put down as well. Hence, the regime probably believed that it could now go ahead with the creation of the corporations. The corporations were designed to serve a coordinating role in social and economic affairs and were to "collaborate" with the government. But the government said it wanted to remove itself from strict economic management, to give this power to the corporations, and to restore self-direction to the economy through the corporations. The tone of these pronouncements seemed to indicate that creation of the corporations was imminent.

The plans for this fundamental restructuring called for three principal steps. First, the corporations themselves would be organized, one for each major sector of production—agriculture, fishing, commerce, industry, transport, and the like. The second part of the plan involved the turning over to the new corporations of all the powers then held by the Organizations of Economic Coordination (and by the numerous offices, juntas, and commissions that had by then grown up), and the gradual disappearance of these agencies. Third, the representational system of the Corporative Chamber was to be reorganized in accord with the new structures—that is, the representatives of each corporation were to be incorporated into the several specialized sections and subsections of the Chamber.[47]

The debate over the new proposals waxed. The Corporative Chamber held hearings and prepared its recommendations. In the National Assembly few argued against the creation of the corporations, although there was strong sentiment for keeping the Organizations of Economic Coordination in existence as a means of retaining the government's ultimate control over the economy. In early 1939 an obviously pleased Pereira, no longer corporations subsecretary but still close to Salazar and with a strong continuing interest in the corporative reforms he had ushered in, made a pronouncement that the corporative system was now complete, that within a few weeks the corporations themselves would be created. In July of 1939 Corporations Subsecretary Rebelo de Andrade confirmed that the drafting of the legislation for the creation of the corporations was all but finished, that they would surely be in existence before the First Congress of Portuguese Corporatism scheduled for May 1940, and that in keeping with tradition the new legislation would most likely be officially promulgated on September 23, 1939, the anniversary of the great wave of corporative decree-laws of 1933.[48]

But that very month World War II broke out on the Continent. The storm clouds that had been gathering for so long coalesced in a torrent of hate, bitterness, and blood. The First Congress of Portuguese Corporatism never met. The decree-laws already drafted setting up the corporations were never promulgated—until seventeen years later, by which time the prospect for an open corporatism of free association had already long been lost. War postponed indefinitely the undertaking of any new social and structural experimentation. It ruled out altogether the possibility that the government could relax its control over the economy and return to a system of self-regulation. Once again the higher-order priorities of political and economic stability took precedence over the implementation of the corporative system. The war and, hence, the postponement of these new corporative reforms finished forever the ideal which many corporatists still held of a *corporatisme d'association* rather than a *corporatisme d'état,* of a system that would live up to the idealistic promises of its early visionaries. It also accelerated the tendency toward authoritarianism and a full-fledged dictatorship.

A Summing Up

The first decade of modern Portuguese corporatism, to paraphrase Schmitter's early conclusion, was a period of extraordinary activity. The changes ushered in by the corporative regime were so broad and so sweeping as to constitute a fundamental, even revolutionary, reordering of Portuguese institutional life. This period saw the promulgation of the new political Constitution, of the Labor Statute, and of a great number of decree-laws affecting virtually every area of Portuguese social, political, and economic life. Almost every article of the Labor Statute had by the end of the 1930s been supplemented by additional decrees; a vast body of corporative law had grown up to regulate the economy, the corporative agencies, collective contracts, industrial accords, and labor-employer relations. A great variety of new grass-roots organizations were also created; at the intermediary level new associations, federations, and unions had been formed; and at the top the pattern of representation, structural and bureaucratic decision making, and management and administration had been fundamentally altered. This system, as Schmitter rightly remarks, had been skewed to reflect the realities and asymmetry of the Portuguese system more generally, and had evolved in a way that benefited certain groups and class interests at the expense of others.[49] However, by 1937/38 all these interests, including most business groups, had been subordinated to the control and regulation of the central state apparatus. Already corporatism of association had clearly been superseded by corporatism of the state.

Interwoven with this set of corporative agencies and most often superordinate to them was a battery of "higher" governmental institutions with greatly expanded powers and responsibilities. These included the Subsecretariat of State of Corporations, the National Institute of Labor and Social Welfare, the National Foundation for Joy at Work, the *caixas sindicais* and of *previdência,* the national labor tribunals system, a large number of roving *intendants* who carried with them the authority of the central state, and a whole array of commissions, inspectorates, juntas, offices, and agencies for regulating virtually every area of national social and economic life. Along with this "corporative complex" was created a battery of parallel or complementary organizations: the União Nacional, the Mocidade, and the Legião.[50]

Despite this vast array of new agencies and decrees, Portugal remained at the end of this decade only a partially corporative system rather than a fully corporative one. There were still many areas of national life, and not just the Army and the Church, that remained all but untouched by the corporative revolution, and there were many groups that had only been partially corporatized. Caetano argued that such a cautious execution of the corporative experiment was the best guarantee against harmful mistakes. But he also recognized realistically that many of the corporative agencies continued to exist more on paper than in actual fact and that others were functioning not at all in accord with the original corporative design. He pronounced it a corporative system in intention more than in fact and said that it was still in its early, rudimentary stages, although he held out the hope for further institutional development and argued that the corporative bodies were by no means "artificial creations" without any real functions.[51] The corporative reforms, he said, were being implemented.

Nevertheless, it is important to recognize that even in these early, enthusiastic years the corporative agencies were never at the center of the Portuguese system of power and politics and that, contrary to both popular belief and the expectations of its true believers, corporatism never was at the base of the entire system. Rather, corporatism was largely confined to the system of labor relations and social security; the corporative system thus performed only one set of functions among many. The real centers of power in Portugal continued to be Salazar's office, the Army, the bureaucratic structure of the central state apparatus, and certain powerful social and economic groups—as was the situation before (one is tempted to say "always"). It was here that most of the fundamental decisions affecting Portuguese policy and the nation's social and economic life were made, not in the corporative agencies. Although these agencies were important in certain areas of national life, their role remained circumscribed and did not encompass a wide gamut of other political and policy arenas. Almost from the beginning, moreover, these agencies had been manipulated and coopted by the larger and more powerful economic interests. It could be said indeed that in this sense the formal corporatist structure established in the 1930s was more a dependent than an independent variable and that if we wish to understand how the Portuguese system functioned, we shall have to look beyond the corporative structure.

VI

The Spanish Crisis, the War, and the "Fascistization" of the Regime

The early accomplishments of the Salazar regime, often ignored by recent commentators, had been considerable. The 1930s saw a stable political system established in Portugal for the first time in decades, perhaps even since the onset of liberalism and republicanism in the early nineteenth century. The economy had also begun to prosper, the budget had been balanced for the first time in many years, the national accounts were managed honestly and efficiently. The Constitution of 1933 sought to reorganize Portuguese government and reinstitutionalize its historic traditions, while the Labor Statute offered the promise of protection for the worker no less than the employer.

Improvements were also effected in the public services. A country which had been all but inaccessible except by mule or ox cart had by this point developed a network of good motor roads. General improvements in rail, telegraphic, and telephonic communications, in harbor works, housing, and education had been achieved. The Navy was modernized and the Army, previously the laughingstock of Europe, rearmed and modernized. A general program of reconstruction had been launched and the social services greatly expanded. Of course, numerous problems and inequalities remained, and in comparison with the other Western European countries, Portugal continued to lag behind. These reservations, however, must be balanced against the historic conditions of poverty and backwardness in Portugal, the lack of resources on which the new nation-building projects could be developed, and the requirement of time for the returns on the new programs to accrue and for the improvements to reach all strata of society. Despite the problems and the continued poverty of many sectors, the consensus among historians and economists is that the 1930s brought some remarkable developments in the economic sphere, public works, the social services, and in terms of governmental honesty, efficiency, and stability.[1]

These accomplishments are stressed so as to lend perspective to the discussion of the corporative restructuring traced in this and the preceding chapter. Corporative implementation, we have already seen, had lagged behind; moreover, some fundamental biases had early been introduced into the corporative order which favored some groups above others and which adversely affected the corporative system's future development. The corporative restructuring was only one aspect of a many-sided reform movement, however, and while the limitations and prejudices of the corporative reforms serve as the focus of this part of our study, the changes and improvements carried out in other areas of Portuguese national life cannot be forgotten. Nor should the accomplishments of the corporative system itself be entirely neglected: corporatism provided Portugal with a new national mythos and ordering principle, badly needed after the chaos of the Republic; it served to extend certain rights to the working classes; it provided a set of agencies for the extension of social services and the rationalization of the economy; it helped fill the political and organizational vacuum that had always plagued Portugal; and it provided the framework and administrative machinery for the regularization of labor-employer relations and collective contracts. Nevertheless, the carrying out of the corporative reordering was a lower-order priority than some other programs we have discussed, and inevitably its implementation continued to lag. This was particularly true after the outbreak of civil war in Spain in 1936, continuing through World War II, and on into the postwar period. Corporative implementation now fell to an even lower-order priority, and the corporative pillars, instead of being *the* foundations of the Estado Novo, now became only one (perhaps minor) set of pillars among many. This chapter traces these developments, shows how, in line with the trends observed in the preceding chapter, the corporative structures were in considerable measure shunted aside and superseded, and analyzes the emergence of an increasingly authoritarian regime and police-state apparatus alongside of and eventually superior to a floundering corporative order.

For concomitant with the decline and eventual supplanting of the corporative order in the late 1930s—and to some extent even preceding that date—there began to emerge in Portugal the machinery of full-fledged dictatorship. Dictatorial practices had been employed before by the regime that came to power in 1926: the dissolution of the old Republican political parties, the exile of opposition leaders, the on-again-off-again press censorship, the breakup of the CGT, and so on. But from 1926 to 1935, as Herminio Martins emphasizes, political repression had taken place largely on an ad hoc and extralegal basis.[2] Up to this point the regime had sought as much as possible to coopt the center

opposition rather than repress it, it had not purged the senior civil service, and its treatment of political foes, in the time-honored fashion,
was generally quite mild, usually involving deportation to the colonies.
Though the control mechanisms of the Estado Novo had grown, it was
not yet a full-fledged dictatorial regime. And though the corporative
structure itself had already become more a system of *corporatisme d'état*
than *corporatisme d'association,* this could hardly be equated with totalitarianism.

Beginning in 1935/36, however, the regime began to move beyond
corporate authoritarianism, which had always been the expressed part
of its program, to a more systematic and thoroughgoing repressive apparatus. The emergence of this police-state apparatus was directly
related to the difficulties of implementing the corporative revolution
and to the unexpected (to the regime) resistance to corporatism by
many Portuguese after 1936. In short, as the attraction of corporatism
faded in the late 1930s as the solution to Portugal's problems, as the
lack of viability in the corporative system to regulate all social, economic, and political affairs was recognized, other structures and institutions rose up parallel to and eventually subordinating it. One of those
structures helping to fill the institutional void was the machinery of full-
fledged dictatorship, a development, however, that was as much a response to external events as to internal ones.

Internal Crises and External Threats:
The Period of the Spanish Civil War

After the initial enthusiasm and flurry of corporative activity from 1933
through 1935, interest began to die down and implementation flagged.
All the indices (see appendix B) show a remarkable growth in the
number of corporative agencies and institutions during the first few
years, a marked slowdown from 1936 to 1945, and a virtual halting of
corporate growth (until the "corporate revival" of the 1950s) in the
postwar period.[3] Moreover, once the initial institutional machinery had
been set up, there were few corporative innovations after 1935 and
practically none at all after 1937. The reasons for this are various.

A key factor was the departure, in January 1936, of Pedro Teotonio
Pereira as corporations subsecretary. Although his memoirs make clear
his growing impatience with the slow speed of corporative implementation, his powerlessness in convincing other ministries to corporatize
more completely, and his inability to get Salazar to speed up the corporative revolution or to establish it as first among the regime's priorities, Pereira nonetheless remained a faithful, energetic servant of the

regime and kept the corporative faith. In his new post as minister of commerce and industry, he was able to implement some of the inter-ministerial corporatization he was unable to carry out as corporations subsecretary, and it was Pereira who was responsible for the creation of the Corporative Technical Council of Commerce and Industry within the ministry. Pereira also brought in the gremios as officially sanctioned consulting agencies to the ministry and was instrumental in helping expand the functions of the "precorporative" Organizations of Economic Coordination, by now encompassing virtually every sector of the economy. With Pereira's departure for Spain on a special mission later in 1936, however, and his appointment in 1937 as ambassador to the Franco forces, the chief driving force and much of the spark went out of the corporative experiment. In choosing able, Coimbra-educated Costa Leite as Pereira's successor, the regime showed its continued commitment to corporative implementation, but Costa Leite's appointment was an interim one, and when he too was appointed to another post in 1936 the Corporations Subsecretariat suffered a double loss. Costa Leite was succeeded by labor court judge Manuel Rebelo de Andrade who served during the course of the Spanish civil war and who, in Pereira's bitter comment, was given the post *purposely* to slow down the corporative revolution in accord with Salazar's own wishes.[4]

The Spanish civil war was another decisive factor in accounting for the stagnation of the corporative system. It led also to the rise of a more repressive police-state apparatus. The radical swing to the Left in 1935/36 in Spain and then the civil war commencing in 1936 were viewed as a distinct threat in Portugal, which has always viewed a change of regime in its large neighbor with apprehension as a possible prelude to the reannexation by Spain of its "lost province." In this case the threat seemed particularly severe because of what were viewed as the "Bolshevik tendencies" of the later Republican regime and because of Republican propaganda and subversion directed against Portugal itself. A revolt in the Portuguese Navy, inspired by the events in Spain, shook Lisbon in 1936; a number of conspiracies were unmasked which aimed at assassinating Salazar himself; and one bomb attempt barely missed. These events served to harden the regime's controls, gave rise to new and expanded police-security agencies, provoked a strong anti-Communist campaign, increased the repression, and inspired the creation of such paramilitary agencies as the Mocidade and the Legião— the "fascistization" of the regime. It also nearly finished the prospects for a successful corporative reorganization.

In talking about the fascistization of the regime, however, care must be taken, for (1) the repressive tactics employed by Salazar never reached anywhere near the level of those used in Nazi Germany, Mussolini's Italy, or even Franco's Spain; and (2) it is still difficult to determine whether the new controls were due to real threats to national security (and, therefore, presumably justified) or were chiefly employed to eliminate the remaining opposition and proceed to the construction of an even more authoritarian state. The answer to this latter issue is, a bit of both.

There can be no doubt of the political volatility and the perceived threat to Portugal during this period. The threat was both internal and external. Internally, the regime had had to face a Monarchist revolt in 1935, a threatened leftist coup in 1936, and a whole flock of minor plots, conspiracies, and assassination attempts in 1936 and 1937. At the same time Spanish Republican agents were active in Lisbon, Spanish armies were parked on Portugal's long and undefended border, and the threat to Portuguese sovereignty seemed severe. The dangers were real, they were immediate, and, if one accepts the proposition that any government can and has the right to defend itself, they justified emergency measures.

The case is not so simple, however. For there can be no doubt that the internal and external threats also served as a way of, and excuse for, rooting out the last of the opposition to the regime and of justifying the most extreme of repressive measures. This period saw the almost total elimination of the remaining labor and democratic movements still existing from the Republican period. New internal security and secret police units were created that eliminated with swift and often brutal efficiency not only all "subversives" but virtually all dissent as well. Moreover, once the crisis period of the Spanish war and of World War II had passed, the emergency controls imposed during that period were not revoked; rather, they remained in effect and contributed to the emergence of even stronger police-state controls in the postwar period.

Whatever the final resolution of this argument over which came first, the threats or the repression, the repression or the threats, it is clear that the Spanish civil war period saw a considerable extension of the system of state controls and of repression of political foes. The Spanish conflict led to a strong "anti-Communist crusade" in Portugal which served to root out not only the real Communists, anarchists, Trotskyites, and so on, in the country but the democratic opposition as well. This was the period when the Portuguese Legion was founded (although the informal nuclei for such a paramilitary organization had been present before), the compulsory youth organization, the Mocidade, and other "fascist" trappings. The censorship was severely tightened, and beginning also in 1936 loyalty oaths were required of all members of the civil service, the teaching profession, the corporative apparatus, and so forth. Every government functionary was required to declare that he adhered to the social order established by the Constitution of 1933 and that he repudiated communism and all revolutionary doctrines. Given the immense size of the public sector in a bureaucratic state like the Portuguese, these measures automatically brought roughly half the employed population under the regime's more rigid controls. Soon loyalty oaths were required of employees in the larger private enterprises as well. The Spanish civil war, as Martins ironically remarks, returned the regime to a form of political patronage system it had claimed to have repudiated—namely, the exchange of government employment in return for political loyalty and support, with direct coercion and almost permanent political monopoly built in.[5]

Besides continuing to serve as prime minister, during the Spanish crisis Salazar took up additional portfolios as minister of war and minister of foreign affairs, thus concentrating even more power in his hands. He also retained under his own direction the Ministry of Finance. At this point also the regime's security apparatus was greatly beefed up: in addition to the Legião, the Mocidade, and the regular armed forces, the Guarda Nacional Republicana helped maintain order in the countryside, the Policia de Segurança Publica were involved in a variety of activities to maintain public security, and later the Policia Internacional e de Defesa do Estado, the dreaded PIDE, was created for political surveillance, internal security, and intelligence operations. Through these agencies repression and even terror, which before had been practiced sporadically and unsystematically, now became efficient and systematic. At the same time Salazar's personal interference in virtually every field of administration was greatly extended, down to the choice of books and pageantry for national celebrations and the minute regulation of everyday affairs. He became, in historian Oliveira Marques's words, more and more of a dictator, more and more inclined to deify himself and to trust others less.[6] As a result, his concessions of independent authority to his fellow ministers were greatly reduced, hence his ability to attract able collaborators declined, and he came even more to rely upon favorites and the use of repression. These characteristics were also carried over to the postwar period, long after the emergency justifications of the great depression, the Spanish crisis, and World War II had passed.

All these developments inevitably had their impact on the corporative system. We have already remarked on the slowed rate of growth of the corporate grass-roots organizations after 1935, the lack of many corporative innovations in the late 1930s, the indefinite postponement of the creation of the "cupola" of the entire system, the corporations themselves, and the phenomenal growth in the power and centralizing state authority of the Organizations of Economic Coordination, often at the expense of the other corporative units. At the same time collective contracts came to be more and more imposed by government intervenors and the Comissões Corporativas (appointed by the Corporations Subsecretariat), rather than through bargaining and compromise between workers and employers. Nor were the corporative social reforms proceeding as fast as expected. A new system of obligatory sindicato contributions or dues was imposed upon the workers in 1939, but these funds were channeled to sindicato functions that seemed less and less to serve the interests of the workers themselves and were often diverted to serve purposes that had nothing whatever to do with the welfare of labor.[7]

These facts and trends were recognized by the regime. In a speech of February 1939, Salazar admitted the limited gains achieved by the workers in the areas of salaries, social assistance, minimum wages, housing, employment, purchasing power, and collective contracts.[8] But he said that at this stage of the corporative revolution, and with the existing emergency conditions, higher salaries and greater benefits could not be granted. Similarly, in an essay written just as Europe was convulsed in war, Marcello Caetano pointed to the defects and limited gains of the system, and especially to the danger of absorption by the state of functions that ought to be reserved for the corporative structure.[9] As a committed corporatist who, as he put it, was joyful in the system's triumphs and sad in its defeats, Caetano inveighed against bureaucratization and excessive state power, arguing that the state had its appropriate role but that it could not serve as a substitute for individual and lower-level corporative efforts. Caetano's essay was clearly the work of a young corporatist ideologue not yet fully disillusioned, but it is equally clear that events had already far outstripped his plaintive lament.

More important perhaps than the statistics regarding the corporative system's slow growth was what was happening to its spirit. The years of depression, austerity, and crises had repeatedly forced the postponement of wage increases, social security benefits, and other reforms. Salazar repeatedly urged patience on his people promising brighter days ahead, but in a system still waiting for corporative consciousness to grow spontaneously, it was clear that such consciousness would not grow very fast if the regime continued indefinitely to postpone raises and benefits. Moral incentives (national regeneration, purification, and the like) could serve for a time, but concrete goods, salaries, and services were what the people demanded. Already considerable public and popular disillusionment with the corporative system had set in.[10]

Perhaps most disturbing from the point of view of corporatism's future was the fact that Salazar and other key decision-making agencies had already relegated it to an even lower place on the regime's list of priorities. This was probably the chief reason for the slowdown of corporative implementation after 1935. Salazar, we have seen, remained a corporatist, but he had consistently during the 1930s subordinated corporative implementation to what he saw as higher-order political and economic requirements. His conflicts with Pereira over the slow pace of corporative implementation and his fear of the implications of turning over any real economic and political power to the corporative agencies were symptomatic. The changes in the later 1930s, however, implied not only the continued low priority of corporatist implementation but its increased shunting aside in favor of other institutional pillars. These included the powerful Organizations of Economic Coordination, the increasingly authoritarian set of controls and decision-making centered in Salazar himself and his office, and the powerful police-state apparatus tending increasingly toward autonomy. By the end of 1937 almost the entire corporative structure (except the corporations) had been put in place, but all this machinery remained subordinate and powerless before Salazar and other important centers of authority. As the struggling corporatist structure was relegated to only one—and often not very important—set of institutions among many, it became questionable whether Portugal could any longer be called, as its Constitution proclaimed, a corporative state, or whether another and more appropriate label would have to be found. These debilitating trends in the corporative system, as we shall see, were accelerated during the World War II years and on into the postwar period. Given the weakness of the system in its early years, its capture by the economic elites dating from about 1935/36, and its shunting aside from the late 1930s on, we may properly question whether Portugal was *ever* a corporative system.

Wartime Controls and the Perversion of the Corporative System

The Spanish civil war had slowed drastically the rate of corporative implementation and, at the same time, dramatically increased the organization and powers of the various repressive control mechanisms. World War II, as Schmitter notes, had a more lasting and almost fatal effect on the corporative system's structure and practices.[11] For now the corporative agencies were directed away from their original functions and toward the implementation of a broad range of wartime controls which perverted their purposes and cast them in an increasingly unpopular light. They were called upon to fix prices, enforce wage freezes, allocate quotas, administer austerity, regulate production, levy fines, and administer the wartime rationing—all functions guaranteed to arouse criticism and resentment. Severe restrictions were placed upon consumption, trade, commerce, movement, salaries, and business activities. Of course, the nucleus for such strict controls had already been set in the 1930s, through the Organizations of Economic Coordination and the expanding state security apparatus. But during the war these controls were greatly expanded and tightly enforced. And once established they were never revoked, even after the crisis of the war years had passed.

Along with the controls came an even greater array of new state agencies, juntas, and commissions. Within the grass-roots corporative agencies too, the sindicatos, gremios, casas do povo, and casas dos pescadores, whatever autonomy had existed before the war was now lost. Elections were suspended, all leaders were appointed and removed from above, and the corporative agencies became purely bureaucratic appendages of the state to enforce the regime's unpopular controls. The creation of new corporative agencies was virtually halted, except where these were artificially established by the government to regulate further another industry or profession. In the name of the wartime emergencies, as Schmitter concludes, the corporative units were converted into direct agents of the regime acting only at its command and convenience. The more subtle and indirect system of corporate manipulation as practiced in the 1930s was now set aside in favor of a direct and heavy-handed system of outright governmental controls.[12]

In the regime's defense it should be said that the controls imposed in Portugal were not altogether different from those established during the war in other nations. During these years the Portuguese corporative agencies served as the agents of state intervention in the economy, just as did the Federal Trade Commission and other regulatory agencies in the United States. In interviews with cabinet-level officials of that period, the argument was presented that these controls did not mean that Salazar had lost interest in the corporative ideal, but that as a pragmatist he did what he had to do in a crisis. Moreover, the use of the corporative agencies to administer and enforce the emergency measures was justified on the grounds that there were no other grass-roots organizations in the country capable of doing so. Portugal at the time remained a poor, undeveloped, and uninstitutionalized country; and in the absence of any other institutions organized nationally and equipped to manage and enforce these necessary controls, the regime turned to the only institutional structure it had. The costs were enormous in terms of the unpopular role the corporative agencies had to play, but from the government's point of view in a period of threatened national survival, there was no other choice.[13]

Legal sanction for these controls and for stricter state regulation of the economy was provided in decrees 30,002 and 30,003 of October 29, 1939—scarcely a month after the date set for the establishment of the corporations, by now indefinitely postponed because of the war. The rationale for the expanded state role was that the corporative organizations by themselves had "insufficient structure to confront the economic emergencies created by the war." Hence, the Ministry of Commerce and Industry was given extraordinary powers to regulate *all* areas of national economic life, using the corporative structure to help carry out these policies. The need was expressed for a *comando único,* a single, strong government agency at the ministerial level to "fiscalize" and oversee the entire economy and to guarantee coherence and efficiency of action. A number of new regulatory commissions—for chemicals and pharmaceutical products, for food and vegetable oils, for metals—were now also created; at the same time some of the older institutes—for bread, wheat, and other products—were given greatly expanded regulatory powers. The *relatorios* accompanying these decrees all pointed directly to the war, and the need to control and guarantee the products affected, as the reason for the creation of these new agencies and for their increased powers.[14]

Along with the new, more powerful regulatory commissions came a number of changes in the corporative structure itself, all adding up to greater centralized direction on the part of the state. New *Regulamentos económicos dos gremios facultativos* issued in June 1940 provided for the government's formal assumption of the regulatory and control functions previously held by the "voluntary gremios." The *parecer* accompanying this decree argued for the extension of the "moderating" power of the government to "discipline" prices and production—all this after reaffirming the "self-direction" of the system! In August the government formally assumed full control of the entire casas do povo structure, making membership obligatory, fixing and standardizing dues, and tightening control over organization and social welfare. That same month, tough, hard-nosed Trigo de Negreiros was brought in as corporations subsecretary to administer the wartime controls, replacing Rebelo de Andrade who had served throughout the period of the Spanish civil war.[15]

The casas dos pescadores also came under more centralized control and direction. The state labor tribunals were similarly reorganized by decree in November 1940, giving them greatly expanded powers and the authority to set wages arbitrarily rather than this being done through the more cumbersome consultative machinery of the corporative agencies. The sindicatos were required to extract additional dues from their memberships. The National Federation for Joy at Work was further centralized under the principle of the need for unity of command; strict centralization and control went forward in various areas of production, especially agriculture, as well.[16]

In early 1940, with the war now convulsing Europe, Salazar appealed to the Portuguese people to maintain the maximum possible stability for prices and the costs of production. He appealed also for salaries to remain stable. If they did not, Salazar argued, political and economic stability would also break down.[17]

A little later, as the war crisis deepened, Salazar gave another public address in which he regretted that the government had not prepared the public adequately for the difficulties and sacrifices required. The Portuguese, he said, were unwilling to bear the hardships. Salazar said he was in sympathy with those persons who needed a little more coal or olive oil but tired of complaints from those who wanted unessentials. He noted that, though Portugal was not involved in the actual fighting, it was nonetheless in the war and suffering many of its hardships. In conclusion he urged patience, denounced the complainers and profiteers, and told his listeners to endure their suffering with equanimity.[18]

The World War II period in Portugal has been little studied. The censorship, the isolation of the country, the fact that it was removed from the main theaters of fighting, and the lack of any monographic studies have all prevented a sympathetic understanding of the horrible conditions that existed. Portugal remained neutral in the war, chiefly because of the threat of German armies poised at the Pyrenees and ready to invade the Iberian peninsula; Germany had assured Portugal that she would respect her territorial integrity and that of her overseas colonies only as long as Portugal remained neutral. Neutrality did not much help Portugal's internal situation, however, as the country was dependent on trade and imports to feed its population and to bring in all manner of raw materials and manufactured items, and this vital lifeline was all but completely severed by both German U-boats and the Allied blockade. The result, in a country as poor and underdeveloped as Portugal, was a severe shortage of food, clothing, medicines, and fuel oil, a strictly enforced rationing system whose incidence fell mostly on the shoulders of the poor, incredible hardships, and in the countryside mass hunger and deprivation.[19]

As early as 1940,[20] Salazar had warned the population that the economic repercussions of the war would be severe but that the extent of the hardship would depend on the degree to which those who controlled the sea permitted the neutral countries to be provisioned. As the war dragged on, it became clear that "degree" was exceedingly small. For Portuguese and foreigners with money, there were still many things available, but few Portuguese had money. And while Portugal also profited from the export of raw materials, chiefly wolfram, to both sides in the conflict, practically none of the profit trickled down. Food and other goods were strictly rationed, and a decree was issued prohibiting hoarding. Black market activities, smuggling, and the erection of illegal slaughterhouses were stamped out by the government. Industrial wages were frozen in a time of rapid inflation. The peasant was forced to pull in his belt more and more; in 1942, for example, he could earn thirty-five *escudos* (slightly over $1.00) per day during the harvest, while in 1943 the government fixed a maximum of sixteen *escudos* a day even though prices were up. The miserable condition of the poor was made worse by severe drought during the worst of the war years, by the reappearance of the Colorado beetle which attacked the crops, and by generally poor harvests.[21]

The depressed conditions prompted even stricter state regulation. Decree-law 32,749 of April 15, 1943, gave the legal right to the government to regulate *all* salaries and conditions of work; the power to enforce these provisions was vested in the Subsecretariat of State of Corporations, thus giving the onus of those further unhappy measures to that agency. Article 1 of this decree said that the Corporations Subsecretariat could limit salaries and stipends "in accord with the limits imposed by the higher interests of the economy and of social justice." Parallel to this was the emergence of more and more arbitration commissions, created as arms of the state to enforce price and wage controls during wartime but continued in the postwar period.

Up to this point, we have concentrated on the hardships on the poor occasioned by the war, but the same period also saw even stricter state control over business and the gremios. The state was by now intervening in all economic activities relating to production and the shipment and distribution of products, and it was the obligatory gremios that were given the responsibility of day-to-day regulation and administration of these activities. The voluntary gremios and the independent commercial associations that had maintained some measure of autonomy before the war were now also brought more tightly under state control. The gremios were charged with the "disciplining of prices," from the producer to the final consumer. Questions soon arose as to whether the gremios were competent and equipped to do this. Again, the weakness of the corporative structure is attested to by the regime's conclusion that they were not. Hence, the government responded by creating still another bureaucratic layer, various administrative commissions, whose function it was to regulate the gremios (who in turn regulated the . . . ad infinitum) in accord with government mandates. The administrators of both the commissions and the gremios were now selected exclusively by the government (even the pretense of democratic elections in the gremios was abandoned); in fact, this entire area of regulation and policing became strictly a government activity, passed off on the corporative agencies and serving further to discredit them. One cannot help wondering, of course, if it would not have been better if the government had itself undertaken these onerous activities and even if it (or some elements in it) might not have purposely been trying to discredit the corporative system. Again, the response is that there was no choice, that the gremios were the only instruments available to the government to carry out these needed, if unpopular, actions. The result, in any case, was the growth of an immense bureaucratic-gremio machinery for the further minute regulation of all economic activities, a broad expansion of the panoply of state controls, the elevation of some gremios to the status of monopolistic cartels (often highly profitable), and a series of policies being carried out by the gremios that often had little to do with the interests of their clients.[22] Another result was growing doubt about the future of the corporative organizations.

During the war, João Pinto da Costa Leite, Pereira's immediate successor as corporations subsecretary, served as minister of commerce and industry. It was his job to oversee the gremio structure and its system of regulations and controls, just as Trigo de Negreiros was doing with the other corporative agencies. The gremios served as the agents for state intervention, institutionalizing the system of government price controls, payments, production levels, taxes, and so on. On the other end, the sindicatos and the Corporations Subsecretariat were controlling wages. The casas do povo continued to function on paper but hardly at all in actual practice. In essence, the countryside largely ran itself during this period, as it always had, on the basis of traditionalism, paternalism, and the controlling influence of the landowners. Although the rural areas suffered as much or more from the wartime shortages, it was in the cities that the state system of control was most stringent.[23]

Despite the strict censorship and tightened state security of the period, we do have some accounts of the reactions these policies provoked among the Portuguese population. In mid-July 1942, a group of sindicato representatives, "knowing the great difficulties facing those who earn their daily bread caused by the repercussions of the War and the enemies of the national economy," presented a petition to Salazar, who promised that he would study their case and issue a reply. In their petition the workers' representatives drew attention to increasing hardship, the lack of social justice, and the sabotage of the corporative doctrine. They asserted that most employers' associations had no notion of their social justice obligations but worked only for their own selfish interests. Among four million workers, the petition said, only a few thousand were covered by collective contracts and programs for the relief of the aged and the infirm—a condition due to the inability of employers to recognize their obligations. Some concerns were making huge profits while the workers received few benefits. The cost of living had meanwhile gone up 44 percent with no equivalent rise in salaries.[24]

In his reply Dr. Salazar said that the government would work (1) to develop greater corporative consciousness, (2) to organize a revision of the salary scale, (3) to increase working hours to offset the increased wages, and (4) to organize a family allowance schedule. Salazar admitted that wages were low but argued that to raise them would intolerably increase the costs of production. He emphasized the benefits of Portuguese economic organization, its internal social and economic development, and public tranquillity. He pointed out that during the Estado Novo wages had increased rapidly, except for the recent war period. The weakness of the system, he said, was due largely to selfishness of *both* employers and employees. That is why such strict state control was necessary. People must bear the burden and the effects of the war, he concluded, and the only solution for now was to work more in order to earn more.[25]

This statement was hardly reassuring to the workers, and grumbling, slowdowns, discontent, and eventually full-scale strikes spread. Many began blaming the corporative agencies for the ills that affected them. The grumbling was directed particularly at the gremios, whom many blamed for the rationing and shortages and who were widely suspected of reaping large profits while the population starved. The regime responded with even stronger security measures and the promulgation in February 1943 of a wartime emergency law giving the government full powers of mobilization. Under this decree, "in the event of war being declared or being imminent, or in case of serious emergency," the government was empowered to mobilize under military control all essential services, industries, and enterprises; to impose postal, telegraphic, or telephonic censorship or to suspend any of these communications; to mobilize all workers under military auspices for work in, and the defense of, any service or industry; and to issue the mobilization order at any moment the government saw fit, using as intermediary the Portuguese Legion.[26]

Yet the discontent continued. Hunger marches were organized. After some early disturbances in the spring and summer of 1943 in the North, by July strikes in Lisbon and the industrial belt around it brought thousands of workers into the streets. The strikes were dealt with by severe police and military measures. Some strikers were shot, many were imprisoned. A governmental communiqué published at the time said the strikes had occurred among the better-paid workers and that their timing gave the impression they had been deliberately planned beforehand. Under the 1933 Labor Statute, of course, strikes and lockouts were illegal, and hence, all factories where work had stopped were ordered to close immediately and to dismiss all workers, offering employment only to those who had not engaged in violence and were willing to begin work immediately. All strikers who had not been arrested—and the figures ran to several hundred in one day—and who were not ready to return to work at once would be mobilized (under the emergency mobilization decree recently enacted) in labor battalions for heavy manual work under strict military discipline. The official statement emphasized the strikes had no political significance but were "due to the inevitable scarcity of food which the government was earnestly trying to resolve." The population was urged again to face the shortages calmly and patiently. Meanwhile, Lisbon was heavily patrolled by police and military forces, especially in the dockside and riverfront areas where the major disturbances had occurred.[27]

But conditions only worsened. The people continued to go hungry; shortages multiplied; illegal strikes persisted. The arrests also continued, and when the prisons in the Lisbon area were filled the bullrings there and in Vila Franca de Xira were pressed into service. Even the threat of exporting the strikers to forced labor camps in Africa failed to deter the demonstrations. In the meantime, speculation by moneyed interests continued, and so did the profiteering by big commercial and banking interests who turned the cartel system established by the gremios to their private profit. There was a scarcity of essential foodstuffs. Salaries were kept at prewar subsistence levels (and in some areas actually reduced) while the cost of living trebled.[28]

The effects of all this on the corporative structure were disastrous. Many casas do povo had died or their activities had been suspended during the war; those that survived vegetated or provided only the most limited of services. The casas dos pescadores fared a little better, but the sindicatos had been completely subordinated to the control mechanisms of the state. The gremios had emerged as perhaps the most discredited of all, through the perversion of their original functions and their role in carrying out the unpopular wartime regulations. But more than this, the entire corporative idea had been discredited and perverted by the functions the corporative agencies had been called upon to carry out during the war.[29] If "corporative consciousness" had grown but exceedingly slowly in the past, it would face even more severe obstacles now. The Portuguese did not easily forget, and this is a key reason why the regime did not move more quickly in the postwar period to rejuvenate its corporative institutions.

Toward the end of the war the abuses of the corporative system were acknowledged by the regime, and speculation began as to how to proceed. In a 1945 article entitled "The Destiny of Corporatism" that received widespread attention, Teixeira Ribeiro, one of the country's most distinguished constitutional lawyers and a leading architect of much of the corporative legislation of the 1930s, concluded, after a long discussion and critique, that Portuguese corporatism had clearly evolved into "corporatism of the state" and not "corporatism of association."[30] He urged a cleansing of corporatism's pernicious practices and a return to the noble purposes of its original conception. In an anonymous essay signed "Lusitano" but widely attributed to Marcello Caetano, the same theme was struck: namely, the abuses and perversion of corporatism during the war and the need now to revive the system and resurrect the social peace and social justice functions the corporative order was originally established to perform.[31] Among regime spokesmen at this time, however, there was still little public questioning of the corporative system's ultimate efficacy and viability. Some of the opposition, to be sure, was beginning to urge its abolition, but no indication has been found that Salazar himself ever seriously entertained the idea of formally setting it aside.

Probably the most serious study of corporatism during this period—and the strongest criticism of it—came from corporatist intellectual Castro Fernandes. He proposed to examine the corporative system's performance ten years after its inception according to eight principles or criteria: (1) whether the corporative organization was universal, (2) whether capital and labor were actually parallel and coequal, (3) whether the principle of organic specialization was functioning, (4) whether the principle of the superior coordination of interests was operating, (5) whether the principle of exclusivity of the corporative agencies (that is, the exclusive monopolistic representation of all interests in a given economic sector by a single recognized interest) was correct, (6) whether the principle of freedom of association was observed, (7) whether the principle of economic intervention had been legally followed, and (8) whether the principle of self-direction of the economy was working. To every one of these basic questions of principle Castro Fernandes answered a resounding "No!"[32]

In answer to the first question, whether the corporative system of organization was universal within Portugal, Castro Fernandes pointed to the limited organizational gains, the fact that the local organizations and the Church operated at the margins of the system, the fact that the Corporative Chamber performed do-nothing functions, the continued existence of private business associations outside of the corporative structure, and the "associative indolence" of the entire system. He showed (2) that rather than treating capital and labor equally, the system as then organized perpetuated class antagonisms and favored employers at the expense of employees. As for the third criterion, Castro Fernandes said all workers and all employers were not being brought together under a single organization reflecting one branch of industry, but that the system was fragmented and was being applied irregularly. The fourth principle, "superior coordination," was as yet incomplete and could not be carried out by ad hoc, sporadic, yet constant state intervention in the economy. Castro Fernandes pronounced the principle of exclusivity (5) to be contrary to the freedom of association guaranteed by both the International Labor Organization *and* the Church! The principle of freedom of association (6) had also not been lived up to, he said; rather, what Portugal had was a corporative system organized by the state and subordinated to it. Castro Fernandes also strongly criticized (7) the vast extension of state power in the economic sphere, which he saw as authorized by neither the Constitution nor the Labor Statute. Finally, as regards the principle of self-direction, Castro Fernandes said this was not the Portuguese situation, that in fact the business and commercial associations had been completely subordinated to the controls and regulations of the state.

One would have thought that after this devastating critique, and given the nature of the police-state apparatus that had by now emerged, Castro Fernandes would surely have been arrested, exiled, and bundled off to Mozambique—or maybe Timor. Instead, largely on the strength of this slim volume, he was made corporations subsecretary. For he, too, like Ribeiro, Caetano, and others remained a committed corporatist; his book concluded with a recommendation, not for scrapping the corporative system, but for its internal reform and redirection. His was, in this sense, a positive criticism and not a wholly negative one. Castro Fernandes was thus awarded the job of reorganizing the corporative order that he had had the courage to roundly criticize. He was instructed to proceed slowly, given the hostility toward corporatism that the war had engendered, to stimulate internal criticism, and to refurbish and resurrect the corporative revolution.[33]

This in fact became the dominant theme as the war ended: not to destroy the corporative system and thus repudiate all the principles on which the regime had come to power but to reconstruct and remodel it, to return it to its original conception. In 1944 Salazar himself gave a speech focusing on the problems of the corporative system—the war, the disorder in the world, the mixture and confused overlap of corporatism's social and economic functions, the deformation of the corporative spirit during the war, and even the abuses of his own regime.[34] But he also remained true to the corporative ideal (clearly by this time more in spirit than in actual practice) and vowed that Portugal would not abandon the corporative system. "We hope," he said in May 1945, "that cleansed of some abuses and excesses, it will return to the purity of the principles from which to some extent, through wartime circumstances, it has departed." [35]

The Postwar Period: The Corporative Nadir and the Rise of the Dictatorship

The victory of the allies in the war, the Nuremberg trials, and the international discrediting of all such "corporatist" and "integralist" solutions helped produce a climate in the postwar period that seemed to spell the end for Manoïlesco's vision of "the century of corporatism." Abroad in liberal and democratic circles and in the new United Nations, the sentiment was widespread that since Portugal was "corporatist," it was also "fascist" in the German and Italian sense, that with the defeat of the Axis powers, Franco and Salazar would surely be the next to fall.

Within Portugal itself the functions performed by the corporative agencies during the war had led to their discrediting, and Portuguese democrats also began to clamor for the abandonment of the corporative system. It is to be emphasized that this criticism was fundamentally different from the in-house critiques noted earlier. The in-house discussions often involved strong criticism and admitted the need for major reforms, but at the same time those who argued this position accepted the fundamental assumptions and premises of the corporative order. The opposition critiques, in contrast, implied a wholesale rejection of *the system* per se, a position which the government could not tolerate and which led during the late 1940s to the growth of an even more repressive authoritarian apparatus. As the government insisted on maintaining a structure that was increasingly discredited at home and abroad, it was forced to employ ever stronger dictatorial measures. The result was the further perversion and discrediting of the corporative idea, the freezing and stagnation of social and economic relations more generally, and the increased use of repressive measures to support a structure and particular corporative form whose time had clearly come—and gone!

For by this point, as Schmitter emphasizes,[36] a mockery had been made of some of the fundamental principles on which the corporative system was based. These principles included the ideas that society could be organized on the basis of its "natural" associations, that labor and capital could be balanced and harmonized on a coequal basis, and that decision making could be devolved upon self-governing corporations. The actual situation in Portugal, however, was quite different: it was the state that controlled and monopolized all associations from above, the business and commercial class had taken advantage of and profited immensely from the corporative system while the workers had borne the brunt of the austerity and wartime control measures, and the corporations existed as yet only in minds of a dwindling number of corporatist intellectuals. Nor did the regime, with the war now over, make any effort to correct these abuses or proceed with further corporative implementation. As Caetano has written:

> The corporative organization was intended . . . as a process designed to remove in the future many of the functions of the state . . . through self-discipline. . . . Due to the War there came a hardening of structures, characterized by a greater centralization of powers which corresponded to a weakening of the autonomy of the Organizations of Economic Coordination and the institutions of corporatism themselves, and to a reinforcing of authoritarianism, leaving the private sector without the participation and collaboration which has been intended. . . . The end of the War did not permit an immediate economic demobilization; neither did the administration show itself very disposed to renounce so easily the preponderance it had acquired. [37]

The reasons for the postwar slowing and virtual halting of the corporative restructuring were various. They had to do not only with corporatism's discrediting on both the national and international levels but also with a new series of crises that forced further postponement. These included both the international Communist threat, at least as perceived by the regime (and bolstered by references to Communist insurgency in Italy and Greece and by the march of Russian armies into Eastern Europe), and the challenge posed by a growing internal opposition. By now, however, after the successive crises of the Great Depression, the Spanish civil war, and World War II, the "crises" theme as a reason for further postponing corporative implementation was wearing rather thin. It was not any perceived "crises" that once again retarded corporative growth after World War II; by now it was clearly the preference of the Salazar regime and of its strong man himself.

Salazar's preoccupation had always been with the great issues of internal affairs and with the grand vision of Portugal's exalted place in the world. He was not so much concerned with everyday administration, nor was he ever as complete a corporatist ideologue as some of his followers. Even in the early enthusiastic years of the corporative reorganization, it will be recalled, Pereira had been the main pusher behind the movement, not Salazar. After the war the corporative system had fallen into disrepute and Salazar, as a pragmatist, set it aside for a time. He remained a corporatist, never repudiated its assumptions and structures, and later, when the time seemed more propitious, finally moved to create the corporations and resurrect the system. But for a time at least in the mid-to-late 1940s Salazar operated as though the corporative system was not there. In making decisions he largely ignored this rusting grass-roots organization and came increasingly to rely on other instruments of rule.[38] Indeed, it was the very absence or weakness of any other institutional structures in the country that helped make the mushrooming police-state agencies so powerful.

This was not, then, a headlong or entirely purposeful rush toward dictatorship. Salazar was undoubtedly supportive of some of the repressive tactics used by his security agencies, but in other areas they, in collaboration with the Army, operated independently and outside of his control. This is clearly not a case of the man who created them becoming a prisoner of his own repressive instruments, but it is to say that the real situation was considerably more complicated than the frequent oppositionist picture of a monolithic regime moving relentlessly and purposely to "fascistize" Portugal. Actually Salazar had advocated rather consistently, in his writings and speeches, a return to the principle of a self-directed economy, a withdrawal of the state from its preeminent role in economic affairs, a reduction in the role of the regulatory commissions, the restoration of a regime of human liberty, a return to a concept of more limited government, and a reorganization of the system on the bases of its original corporative principles.[39] After the war, in fact, Salazar coined the term "organic democracy" to describe the system he had previously defined as "antidemocratic," the Portuguese Legion lost much of its swagger and fascist trappings, the censorship was relaxed, and there were even promises of free elections. These gestures were not just in deference to the times and to placate international opinion. However, while proclaiming himself publicly as supportive of all these trends toward "self-direction," privately Salazar always feared the consequences of allowing greater freedom, and he consistently ended by pursuing both authoritarian and decentralizing courses at once, a posture where his naturally authoritarian outlook usually predominated. One suspects also that a haunting private suspicion that in the last analysis it would not work may have been another reason why Salazar never fully tested the corporative scheme.[40]

Although repressive tactics had grown during the 1930s and the intelligence agencies had been greatly expanded during the war, it was not until the postwar period, when corporatism was discredited, when the corporative organization was no longer viable, and when Salazar could see or admit to no other alternative, that dictatorship and the whole gamut of dictatorial controls became even more firmly cemented in place. The postwar period was a difficult time for Portugal. In addition to the international pressures to democratize and to Salazar's growing phobia regarding "the Communist threat," the fact of India's recent independence augured ill for Portugal's colonies on the subcontinent (Goa, Diu, and Damão) and ultimately for Portugal's holdings elsewhere. Portugal was isolated internationally, denied Marshall Plan aid, looked down on abroad, and refused entrance into both the United Nations and the European community. Internally a new generation of oppositionists had emerged, imbued with social-democratic ideas, and able to capitalize politically on the widespread popular impatience with wartime controls and austerity and for a share in the expected postwar affluence. It was toward the control of this opposition that the most repressive tactics were directed.[41]

The corporative system did not fare very well either. The war period had at least seen a considerable increase in the number of corporative agencies (casas, gremios, sindicatos) even though their services were often minimal and their functions perverted; the postwar period saw an end to both services and growth. Practically no new corporative agencies or branches were created. None of the end-of-the-war calls to reform of the corporative system was ever implemented. The government continued to set virtually all prices and production quotas, while wages were determined not through bargaining between sindicatos and gremios but by government labor tribunals. Repeated calls for a relaxation of the wartime controls went unheeded. Austerity continued; wages remained abysmally low; the social services were virtually nonexistent; businessmen and small merchants were hamstrung by a now incredibly bureaucratized and complex network of required licenses, stamps, permits, and approvals. The controls were continued in force through 1946 and then through 1947, 1948, 1949, and on into the 1950s. Other than the creation of a handful of new casas and sindicatos and the signing of a

very few collective contracts, these years saw no corporative innovations, virtually no activity in the corporative structure at all. The author's field notes for 1948, based upon a close examination of every
issue of the Corporations Subsecretariat's own bulletins and other publications, state, "The corporative revolution appears dead"; for the
year 1949, amassing a total of two lines of notes from these same
sources, the notes read, "This is a new low point—there is no corporative activity at all." [42]

In this period of general stagnation, not just of the corporative agencies but of the entire national system, the opposition grew. The old
Republican coalition began to come back together. A new Movement
for Democratic Unity was organized; thousands joined. Strikes multiplied in 1946 and 1947, and they were ruthlessly and often brutally
put down by the police. A new alliance seemed to be forming between
the middle-class opposition and the more militant trade unions. That
spelled a serious challenge to the regime. Many leading oppositionists
were jailed and some were tortured; opposition meetings were broken
up by the police and the Army. Informers and undercover agents multiplied. Although Salazar had initially promised in 1945 to allow full
freedom to the country and to ensure free and unbiased elections the
following year, the repressive tactics eventually forced the opposition to
withdraw from the campaign. The government and Salazar's União
Nacional rolled up some 60 percent of the vote in the 1946 elections for
the National Assembly, but the number of abstentions was large and
clearly the regime realized it was facing the most widespread opposition
it had as yet encountered. In 1949 it had to face another strong challenge in the person of Norton de Matos who ran against Carmona for
the presidency and promised, if elected, to root out the corporative
order and return to the political principles of Republican rule. The election campaign was thus based not just on the question of which person
would become president and hence chief of state but on the issue of the
destruction or survival of the regime itself. This was a challenge that
could not be taken lightly and again the opposition was severely hamstrung, harassed, and persecuted. Eventually de Matos was forced to
withdraw. Implied in all the countermeasures to control this new, widespread opposition was the use of stronger and more widespread repressive tactics. [43]

This period also saw the first strong doctrinal and practical critique
of the corporatist order by the opposition, a full repudiation of it, and
repeated calls for its scrapping. This too was a position the regime
could not tolerate. The critique began with a statement of the paradox

of corporatism: that a system aimed at replacing capitalism had in fact laid the basis for its great—and monopolistic—expansion, particularly during the war with the accumulation of vast reserves from the sale of wolfram and other commodities. The corporative system was condemned as another form of Italian fascism, now discredited and deserving of abandonment. The sindicatos were seen as paper organizations unable to defend the interests of the workers, while the gremios were exposed as agencies of wartime profiteering. The Corporations Subsecretariat was accused of siding with business and monopolistic interests and of being indifferent to the problems of the poor; the collective contracts and labor tribunals were seen as instruments of government control over the workers. The corporative scheme was beginning to be viewed as an instrument of class dominance, aided by an increasingly authoritarian regime that by now, according to its foes, had abandoned all pretense to upholding the original corporative ideals.[44]

These were strong and sweeping criticisms, and coming at the same time as the surge of postwar discontent and rising social-democratic opposition, they demanded an equally strong response. That response was an ever stronger tightening of the controls. The overwhelming desire of the regime to maintain order at all costs in the face of widespread discontent and a growing opposition led not to change or reform of the system but to full-fledged dictatorship. The web of controls over the press, the bureaucracy, and other agencies was strengthened. Opposition meetings were repeatedly broken up; the opposition's leaders were arrested and harassed; the number of political prisoners multiplied. A number of internal security laws were enacted and enforced, and the regime made frequent use of them to suspend the political rights of hundreds of oppositionists. Along with and parallel to the Army, several other intelligence and secret police units, particularly the dreaded PIDE, grew up and became virtually a separate government within the government. The number of spies, informers, and thugs on the government payroll increased. Beating and torture became commonly used techniques, and though the figures are often grossly inflated, the list of political murders lengthened. Salazar condoned the use of increasingly repressive and authoritarian tactics and he, of course, must bear the responsibility for them. But he had also become more aloof and isolated from events; he chose to believe the accounts of many of these atrocities as reported to him not by the victims but by his security officials. In addition, he could not entirely control the activities of the very agencies he had set up. The PIDE went its own way regardless, with only general authority over it being exercised by the president of the

Council of Ministers, and many brutalities and excesses were committed. If ever the regime could be called fascist or totalitarian, this was probably the time.[45]

The corporative system was also perceived increasingly as a part of this system of controls. The earlier social-justice motives had been in large measure abandoned; the system had been only partially implemented; and the corporations themselves remained, in Ralph Bowen's words, "vague projects to be realized in some distant future." Intended as machinery for modern social and economic self-government, in actual fact the corporative agencies became passive instruments for carrying out policies dictated from above by an absolute central authority, Salazar himself. Rather than serving as agencies of representation, participation, and assistance, the corporative agencies had been used to repress conflicts between labor and management, to restrict wages, and to regulate carefully national industry, commerce, and trade. As a Council of Europe report put it, "the rights of individuals and of groups are seriously limited by the corporative system and by government decrees, enforced by the political police." [46]

Salazar was, of course, aware of all these charges and of the perversion of the corporative system. For a time after the war, he appeared to lose interest in corporatism, and a number of his colleagues in the government concluded that, while he would not repudiate the system per se (too many commitments had been made and too many powerful interests were affected for that), most likely it would be allowed to wither away quietly. However, while the corporative structure was ignored, and in the absence of any other institutional and associational intermediaries in Portugal, the secret-police network inevitably grew, filling the vacuum and becoming one of the most important institutional pillars of the regime, a fact which Salazar saw and which disturbed him (but apparently not enough to force a change in his policies or practices). At the same time the vigorous doctrinaire critiques by the opposition of the entire corporative idea, an idea to which Salazar's whole life from Coimbra forward had been committed, strengthened his resolve to see it through, resurrect the system, and make it work. As compared with his more committed early collaborators, Salazar had been a pragmatist rather than an ideologue; yet, he too was convinced of the rightness of the corporative vision, and he was a stubborn, obstinate man. An attack on the corporative scheme was an attack on him personally, on the "rightness" of his ideas, indeed on his entire life's work; and it could not go unanswered. Rather than withering away, then, the corporative system had to be revived, but at a time when even the regime's strongest supporters had come to believe that corporatism's time had arrived—and already passed—in Portugal. This attempt to resurrect artificially a discredited scheme which most observers were content to have fade away would, as we shall see in the next chapter, involve the use of further repressive controls and retard still more Portugal's development.[47]

What was perhaps most disturbing about the immediate postwar period in Portugal, in addition to the police-state repression, was thus the immobility of the entire national system. Corporatism had been discredited; yet Salazar could see no other alternative. Moreover, his commitment to the older corporatist conception had been so strong and his intellectual vanity so powerful that he could not admit the advantages of other systems or even contemplate moving in newer, more developmentalist, populist-corporatist directions, as other Iberic-Latin nations were doing. In this uncertain period between 1945 and the early 1950s, therefore, the government floundered and vacillated and time stood still. The economy stagnated; there were no new ideas or programs; the political structure was frozen—at a time when Portuguese society itself was beginning to undergo some profound transformations. Salazar had increasing trouble attracting able ministers, and government performance suffered. Numerous programs and services came almost to a standstill.

Countless visitors of the time expressed shock at the depressed living conditions in postwar Portugal, the absence of social programs, the dreadful poverty, the woefully inadequate educational facilities, housing, and medical care, and, worse than that, the seeming inability or unwillingness of the government to do anything to solve the problems. The years of austerity had meant that benefits and higher wages had been repeatedly postponed. Portugal had, of course, always impressed travelers as a nineteenth-century country lagging far behind its European neighbors on virtually all indices of social and economic growth. But now these gaps vastly increased as Portugal vegetated and was bypassed by the twentieth century. At a time of recovery and rising affluence in the rest of Europe, Portugal remained locked into its prewar pattern, stagnant, isolated, immobile, unable to respond to pressing demands for decisions, looking backward rather than ahead. Its similarly stagnant, dysfunctional corporative structure and ideology were clearly among the important causes of the national malaise. In the postwar period both Portugal and Portuguese corporatism reached their nadir.[48]

And yet, even in its most repressive phase, the Portuguese system never became fully totalitarian, and the limits and restraints within which the dictatorship operated were considerable. Salazar himself, for example, was often bothered by the excesses of his underlings and the secret police and repeatedly put barriers in the way of their assuming total power. Nor did the regime ever go the route of mass persecution or even indoctrination. A single party enjoyed a monopoly on legal status, but it functioned more as a vast patronage machine than as a totalitarian party. There was censorship, but it was periodically relaxed and an impressive array of techniques was developed to get around or through it. The opposition was severely constrained in its activities, but the fact that it was allowed to exist at all made Portugal quite different from the totalitarian systems. Authoritarian controls were employed, but a kind of limited pluralism also existed. And throughout, the limits imposed on the central authority by the natural-law tradition, and the fundamental and inalienable rights which many groups enjoyed before the law (some more than others, obviously), continued to operate. Virtually every journalist and writer who went to Portugal was constrained to write that it was a "limited dictatorship," a "reluctant dictatorship," a "mild dictatorship," an "authoritarian but not totalitarian regime," a regime with "an economy of terror," a "paternalistic" and even a "benevolent dictatorship." Clearly in his personal life and rule, Salazar remained austere and unobtrusive, a stern teacher and moralist, but not a psychopathic totalitarian.[49] Even in the regime's most dictatorial and repressive phases, the limits imposed by tradition, history, group rights, and the natural law continued in effect.

Moreover, even in the depths to which the system had fallen the seeds had already been planted for a corporate revival. However imperfectly, the system continued to renegotiate and update collective contracts, to administer and even slightly expand social assistance, to reform and rewrite the corporative legislation, and even to create a few new corporative entities. The corporative system was stagnant but it was by no means yet totally dead.

In the meantime, and spurred on by the criticism of the opposition, an in-house reexamination of the corporative system was already underway by 1946/47 and the plans being laid for its revival. The sense was virtually universal that something would have to be done, and soon, to get the nation moving again; but the changes contemplated were still conceived as occurring within the corporative framework, not outside of it. Led by corporate intellectuals like Marcello Caetano, J. Pires Cardoso, and others, and aided by administrators and bureaucrats of the corporative agencies who knew firsthand how the system operated and failed to operate, the entire corporative idea and structure were subjected to a scrutiny they had never had when the system was first set up in the 1930s. The internal criticism was frequently devastating, but out of this reexamination came the corporate revival of the 1950s and 1960s and the argument for the continued viability of the system, as well as the more recent, interesting observation by Portuguese, Spanish, and other scholars of the existence of corporate structures and modes of behavior in systems, including our own, that call themselves by other labels.

VII

The Corporative Revival

Although the effort had been made to keep the corporative system functioning in the postwar period and even to reform it in certain particulars, the late 1940s had been characterized by stagnation and immobility in Portuguese corporatism that was reflected in the society as a whole. In terms of her social programs and progress, Portugal lagged farther and farther behind the other nations of Western Europe, and despite the economic accomplishments of the Salazar regime, her per capita income of less than $200.00 per year, very inequitably distributed besides, ranked Portugal with the underdeveloped countries and not the developed ones. Years of economic and political crises, depression, and threat of war had led to the repeated postponement of social reforms and wage increases. Now the discontent had begun to spill over into impatience, strikes, and a growing opposition that challenged the regime's basic principles.

The immobility and stagnation of the postwar period reflected the uncertainty among Portugal's leaders, especially Salazar, as to which direction the country should follow. Corporatism seemed to have been discredited, yet liberalism and socialism remained unacceptable alternatives. For a time after the war, we have noted, Salazar used the term *organic democracy* to refer to his hybrid regime, but Salazar was hardly a democrat, the regime changed not at all in its essentials, and the term was soon dropped. While the country drifted, however, and Salazar brooded over the great issues of the national destiny, events moved along inexorably. The opposition's challenge had to be met, and in the absence of any alternatives, the authority structures of the central state and especially its secret police emerged to fill the vacuum. As Portuguese corporatism reached its nadir in the late 1940s, the dictatorship reached its peak in severity.

Many high government officials, including Salazar himself, became alarmed at these developments and saw the need to reach some basic decisions and to restore order and rationality to national political affairs.

There ensued a considerable internal debate in 1947/48, and the view that Portugal should liberalize received a strong and vigorous airing in the highest councils of government. Within a regime so strongly committed to corporatist authoritarianism, however, liberalism was not a permissible alternative, and the real question was never really the abandonment of corporatism and authoritarianism in favor of democracy, but rather how to update the existing system and reconcile it to postwar realities. The result was a revival of corporatism but never any abandonment of the police state and authoritarian controls that had grown up over the preceding years. Rather, the two continued to exist side by side, the corporatist system, on the one hand, and an authoritarian dictatorship, on the other, as parallel pillars of the regime. Eventually, as we shall see in this and succeeding chapters, other "pillars" and structures emerged, and corporatism was confined still further to a relatively narrow area of administrative responsibilities. The corporative "revival," thus, was always more apparent than real, a lot of sound and words that sometimes obscured other, more important developments of the 1950s and 1960s—the gradual economic quickening, the rise of powerful business and entrepreneurial groups, the emergence of a middle class, the slow modernization of Portugal, and eventually the life-and-death struggle in Africa. The "revival" began, curiously, with a devastating in-house doctrinal critique of the entire corporative system.[1]

The In-House Critique

Two doctrinal critiques of the corporative system emerged in the postwar period. One, stemming from the growing social-democratic and underground Communist opposition, was usually Marxist in approach, often strident in tone, and, though insightful in revealing the Estado Novo's class biases, frequently far divorced from Portuguese realities and the actual workings of the corporative system. The second, the in-house critique, came in part as a response to the opposition criticism but represented in addition a coming to grips on the part of the government's own spokesmen with the genuine difficulties experienced by the corporative structure, which were apparent even to the regime itself. It reflected also, despite the Estado Novo's manifest authoritarianism, a long history of in-house criticism aimed at "perfecting" the system. Of the two emerging bodies of criticism, the in-house critique had a stronger and more immediate impact since it came from some of the corporative system's foremost architects, intellectuals, and government officials.

Some of the earliest strong critiques in the postwar period came from

Corporations Subsecretariat officials themselves, disillusioned and bitter about the role the corporative agencies had been forced to play during the war. Most recognized that Salazar probably had no choice but to call on the corporative agencies to perform the unpopular functions of price and wage controls, rationing, and the like. But now, led by Corporations Subsecretary Castro Fernandes, the young lawyers and bureaucrats still committed to the corporative vision began calling for a return to corporatism's original principles, the abandonment of the wartime controls, and the restoration of an "authentic corporatism" in accord with the great and noble purposes expressed in the 1933 Constitution, the Labor Statute, and the early corporative legislation. They lobbied for a return to corporatism of association rather than the prevailing corporatism of the state, for a regime of greater social justice, for the further extension of the corporative agencies to reach the 90 percent of the population still not encompassed in the system, and in general for a purer form of corporatism, unsullied by the perversions and inequalities practiced up to that time.[2]

The criticism soon became stronger. At the end of the war, Teixeira Ribeiro had weighed in with his strong statement that the Portuguese system had become one of state corporatism. In an interview published in November 1945, regime spokesman Antonio Ferro admitted the widespread dissatisfaction with the corporative system, which he ascribed to favoritism and to the fact that in many areas "private selfish interests had prevailed over the public good." [3] A special Parliamentary Investigatory Commission was established to explore the functioning of the corporative system, and the population was invited, through press and other advertisements, to convey their grievances to the commission. Many responded and the complaints, growing chiefly out of the wartime experience and directed chiefly at the gremios, were numerous. The commission compiled all these horror stories and published a report, which was so devastating that the government refused to give it any official attention and it had little public impact. It did much, however, to dissuade Salazar from going ahead with any further corporative implementation.[4]

Although the regime ignored and sought to denigrate the Parliamentary Investigatory Commission's report, its findings were widely discussed among government officials and soon became public knowledge in the small, face-to-face Portuguese system, serving further to discredit and hence postpone the institutional development of the corporative system. Other of the commission's findings later found their way into several self-criticisms published by the Corporations Subsecretariat (later, ministry) but were no less devastating for having gone this indirect route. Such was the case with Castro Fernandes's own study of the casas do povo, for example, which documented how many casas had died or suspended their activities during the war. He showed how others had vegetated or degenerated into a "dull routine," how those that remained led a "precarious existence," how a few were still providing limited social assistance but performing no educational or aggregating functions, and how others had good intentions but no money. Castro Fernandes went on to discuss sociologically the fragmented, isolated, atomized nature of Portuguese rural life, the fact that the casas encompassed more diverse kinds of workers than the urban sindicatos and that there was therefore less community of interest among rural workers. His analysis concluded with a plea for flexibility in structuring the casas to reflect the diversity of landholding and agricultural patterns in the countryside and, in keeping with the rule for in-house criticism, with a series of recommendations for "perfecting" the system.[5]

Other critiques followed. Also employing data from the Parliamentary Investigatory Commission, Carlos Hermenegildo de Sousa began by referring to the discrediting and general *má vontade* ("ill will") toward the corporative system and proposed to analyze it according to three criteria: the administration of the corporative system and its costs to the nation, the influence of the corporative organizations on the national economy, and the influence of the corporative system on society. As regards the first, Sousa said the corporative system was recent, had been hurt by the war, was directed often by men without experience, and operated in an often hostile or indifferent environment. He claimed the functions of the system were still not defined, that it had not established equilibrium between workers and employers, that during the war the corporative structure had been used to camouflage large-scale, private profiteering, that it had taken in large receipts (Esc. 236,000$00 in 1945 alone) but had paid out only meager amounts (156,000$00) in assistance, that the system had no efficient way of absorbing or administering all these funds. He charged that the corporative agencies had grown to a vast bureaucracy of 11,400 employees and even more regulations, that this bureaucracy was inefficient, bloated, and top-heavy, and that the system's administrative costs had soared far higher than its benefits. As regards corporatism and the economy, Sousa pointed to numerous improvements carried out in the 1930s but then erased by the war, the system's unfortunate administration of the unpopular austerity and rationing programs, and the fact that both businessmen and the common people had become disillusioned with the corporative experiment. As for corporatism's influence on society, Sousa limited himself to saying that during the war there was little opportunity to expand social services even though the number of corporative agencies continued to increase. His devastating conclusion was that corporatism was not succeeding in any of these three major areas, and that was why the corporative system "was characterized by an almost total lack of prestige." [6]

Others soon weighed in with equally devastating criticisms. Xavier Pintado, an official of the Corporations Subsecretariat, called for government action that would be "specifically corporative" (thereby implying that most government activity took place outside the corporative system).[7] Corporatist intellectual J. Pires Cardoso repeatedly called for an "autonomous corporatism," one that would be independent from the state and would serve to restrain absolute state power.[8] Luis Quartin Graça published an article arguing that corporatism did not fit the agricultural sector, that there was too much variety in rural life to be crammed into a single juridical mold, and that the system had shown favoritism to landowners.[9] Casas do povo administrator F. Cid Proença also argued that the euphoria of the early triumphs had since turned to disillusionment, that the primary principles on which the casas structure had been based were false, that it was not possible to create a single organization for all rural elements in line with the original theory, that each group followed its own private interests instead of the common good, that the realities of rural life were contrary to abstract logic, and that in the countryside the old traditions of paternal autocracy still reigned.[10]

In a full-length review of the entire system Emilio A. Ferreira showed how, from the corporative conception of the state as a moral and ethical agency, it could easily follow that the state could also keep out all contrary notions and thus justify almost unlimited dictatorship.[11] José Augusto Corrêa de Barros, another Corporations Subsecretariat official, demonstrated how the corporative agencies had been used to squeeze the workers by holding down wages and called for a return to "corporative normalcy." [12] F. Cid Proença came back with another critique of corporative paternalism, spoke not only of the absence of corporative consciousness but of a definitely anticorporative spirit, and argued that mere structural tinkering would not alleviate such sentiment.[13] And in a devastating and broad-ranging criticism Fezas Vital showed how various sectors of Portuguese society had lost faith in the corporative system, how the gremios were particularly hated, how the idea of "the common good" had become a smoke screen for self-serving interests, how the Organizations of Economic Coordination, which were noncorporative institutions, had achieved power far greater than that of the corporative agencies themselves. Vital was careful to say that his criticism was not of the essential corporative principles but only of the abuses carried out by certain corporative units. Because of these abuses, he said, the corporative institutions provoked a great deal of criticism and were held in low esteem. The actions of the state and especially of the gremios and Organizations of Economic Coordination had made the further development of the corporative system very difficult. In conclusion, Vital also urged a return to a freer corporatism of association and to the original corporative conceptions.[14] But as we have already seen, the web of state mechanisms and controls was already firmly established, and Salazar could not or would not let go.

These and other criticisms of corporatism's shortcomings were damaging and even devastating. But they were largely piecemeal criticisms aimed at showing how one or another aspect of the system was not working. Beginning in the early 1950s, however, criticism of a more systematic sort began to appear, which not only examined the workings (or lack thereof) of the whole corporative complex but also began to question, usually by implication, the fundamental assumptions of the entire system—and sometimes the Salazar regime itself.

Marcello Caetano's was the first and most important of these critiques. His slim volume on the "Present Situation of Portuguese Corporatism," which was initially presented as a lecture on March 23, 1950, and which was reproduced in all the newspapers, had immense repercussions throughout the country.[15] This was so not only because Caetano was an articulate critic, a widely respected intellectual, and probably the country's foremost constitutional lawyer and political scientist but also because he had been one of the original designers of the corporative schemes of the 1930s, because he had occupied various high government posts, and because he was already being touted as the heir apparent to Salazar.

Caetano began his critique by stating how close he was to the corporative ideas and, therefore, how difficult it was for him to write about them. Corporatism, he said, had begun as a great vision but it had been implemented somewhat differently. It was an abstract vision, constructed by intellectuals, but life is not such a neat system. In practice the corporative ideals were altered and transformed; there was a great distance between the doctrinaire theory and the existing political regime. The corporative principle, according to Caetano, involved the active collaboration of different interests for the common good, using the corporations as agents. As yet, however, there were no corporations and very little collaboration. Caetano thus commented that Portugal was a corporative state in intention but not in fact. "All we can say is that we have a state with a corporative base or tendency." But this was not to say the system was invalid, he hastened to add; rather, after seventeen years of existence, it now required evaluation.

Caetano then proceeded to his discussion and critique. He pointed to the absence of people to implement the corporative ideas. The Instituto de Estudos Corporativos of the União Nacional had tried to train leaders, but there were too few. The directors of the various corporative agencies, therefore, had to improvise, and the corporative ideas failed to reach the masses. The leaders of the several corporative units were often ignorant of corporative principles, furthermore, and there was little popular confidence in their leadership. The Conselho Técnico Corporativo of the Ministry of Commerce and Industry had, therefore, been created by Pereira to help coordinate, orient, and transform the system, but by now it too had been changed by force of circumstances into an administrative agency for foreign trade.

Caetano went on to argue that the creation of a special Subsecretariat of Corporations was itself an admission of the system's failure, since in theory corporatism implied the corporatization of the entire national system and not just one part of it. He too stressed the damaging impact of the war on corporatism's growth, saying the gremios and other corporative agencies were forced to take on functions for which they were ill prepared and which led to their discrediting. The war period also saw the growth of an immense corporative bureaucracy and a vast web of unpopular controls and regulations. The idea of a self-directed economy was put aside in favor of state direction, while the free interplay of all groups gave way to discipline and the threat of sanctions. The Organizations of Economic Coordination, he said, had become the executors of the government's political economy.

Caetano also pointed to the "difficult" living conditions of the workers. The corporative agencies had been forced to freeze wages at a time of rising prices. Whereas initially the Corporations Subsecretariat had had a strong interest in siding with the workers, now it appeared as the agent of their miseries. While continuing to laud the considerable accomplishments of the system, Caetano also stressed that the sindicatos now seemed impotent, that the collective contracts were frequently viewed by the government as obstacles to price and wage controls and were hence ignored, and that the system often simply failed to function. The Communists have been able to exploit these ills, Caetano warned, provoking waves of strikes in the postwar period which the government then had to put down by force. Rather than collaboration and harmony between classes, Caetano stressed, the corporative system had intensified class hatred.

The question Caetano raised was: "After all this, does the corporative spirit still exist?" He said there was an excess of regulation and bureaucracy. The complex legislation of instructions, norms, regulations, paperwork, resolutions, offices, and so on, was excessive, hindering the movements of businessmen and workers. There are areas of life, Caetano said, where one cannot take a step without violating the law. This enormous bureaucracy was no longer at the service of corporatism but only of itself. Decisions were reached (or not reached) by the endless shuffling of papers across numerous counters, through "obscure corridors," only to be recorded on some useless file card. The process was debilitating and discouraging to initiative. Economic activity was all under state control, he said; public agencies and the Organizations of Economic Coordination determine all transactions: how much and when to buy and sell, prices, profits, working conditions. These agencies can punish or reward at will. Authorization, approval, a license or permit is required for everything. It is the bureaucrat who rules, said Caetano; he has nothing to lose if he makes a mistake since he is protected by a "superior hierarchy." The sense of mobility, opportunity, and self-help has been totally lost. The state dominates all in a system where the Christian and corporative base was supposed to avoid the total submission of the individual to the state.

What to do? Caeteano discussed how corporatism was discredited by the Nazi and Fascist regimes and at Nuremberg. The Communists had exploited this by making it seem *corporatism* itself was discredited at Nuremberg, not just the Nazi and Fascist atrocities. He noted that the Christian and Iberic conception of corporatism was distinct from the Nazi and Fascist types. The corporative organizations were supposed to collaborate with the state, not be used and abused by it. Corporatism was supposed to protect civil liberties, he said, not ride roughshod over them. Yet corporatism in Caetano's view remained still the only great ism that could reconcile all the diverse currents of modern times. We must avoid both centralizing and factionalizing tendencies, he said; at present the main state institutions are bypassing the corporative representational bodies with nefarious results. He called, therefore, for a revitalization of the existing corporative agencies. We need to apply more intelligence than in the past to corporative implementation, Caetano said; we can still fulfill the goals and ideals of the corporative revolution. On this hopeful and uplifting note, he finished his discussion.

Caetano's thoughtful and balanced statement had enormous repercussions throughout the country but apparently did nothing to harm his political career and may have even furthered it.[16] Equally strong critiques had also begun coming from other quarters. Among these, we have already seen, was the *Revista do gabinete de estudos corporativos,* which had published a number of articles of a critical sort, although its orientation was still that of "positive criticism." Now, however, a young sociologist associated with the *Revista,* Adérito Sedas Nunes, published a full-length critique on philosophical grounds that was almost as devastating as Caetano's discussion of the actual workings of the system.[17]

Sedas Nunes's book was also presented as a work of "constructive criticism" and as part of "the work of corporative reexamination." His concern was the usefulness and relevance of the corporative principles to the problems of our times. "What has happened to Manoïlesco's 'Century of Corporatism?' " Sedas Nunes asked rhetorically, and answered that it had been forgotten and had disappeared all over Europe and Latin America. "After a brilliant doctrinal and theoretical flowering for some thirty years until the 1940s," he wrote, "corporatism has lost almost all the terrain it had conquered." Corporatism was severely discredited in the war, yet in Portugal it continued to hang on, indifferent to these criticisms and to the need for new ideas. Now it must be revived, wrote Sedas Nunes (one suspects, only partially convinced himself); it must be invigorated and strengthened. But to do this it would first be necessary to examine the philosophical and sociological bases of the system.

Sedas Nunes focused on the errors or deficiencies of the major corporative principles. He began by emphasizing the diversity of the national corporative experiences, the impossibility of reducing the corporative tradition to a single set of abstract principles to which all states must conform. He therefore rejected the Manoïlesco model of "pure corporatism," arguing that corporatism may take different forms in different nations at different times and that what Portugal required was an updating of its corporative forms to reflect the sociological realities of the postwar world. Second, he said, there is no simple "unity of order" in the modern state, there is no one way of ordering the modern complex nation. Corporatism oversimplified, he stated, by positing a single set of criteria for the state structure; in fact, the state is more complex and society more diversified than the corporatist writers had implied.

Third and more interesting, Sedas Nunes asked whether the corporative idea of social group or class was in line with modern sociological analysis. Portugal answered "Yes," but Sedas Nunes questioned if there was really much solidarity among workers in the same industry or between workers and employers. Do men with some common economic considerations necessarily form a unit in the corporative sense? And even given some common interests, why should this necessarily lead to the formation of a corporation? The questions posed were difficult ones, and to them Sedas Nunes added the comment that the very growth of the sindicatos, on the one hand, and of the gremios, on the other, was in itself a denial of one of the primary corporative principles—namely, the solidarity and commonality of interests between workers and employers. Sedas Nunes argued that the growth of these class associations in corporative Portugal, which was a sociological fact that could not be denied, represented a repudiation of the "class harmony" thesis of corporatism. This and other corporative ideas, he said, were grounded on a theoretical conception formulated by university professors that had little basis in sociological reality.

Corporatism is by definition a system of capitalist organization, Sedas Nunes went on to say, anticipating a later line of thought. By proclaiming itself in favor of peaceful change, by ruling out violence and conflict and thereby helping preserve the societal status quo, corporatism necessarily implied a form of development that would be capitalistic and conservative in character. Further, through the granting even originally of broad "orienting," "fiscalizing," and "directing" functions to the state, it was assured that the Portuguese pattern would be one of state corporatism rather than corporatism of free association. The absence of autonomy for the corporative agencies and the series of crises of the 1930s and 1940s made it impossible to develop a truly independent corporatism. Corporatism is statism, Sedas Nunes declared, providing a variety of agencies for the state to interfere in all areas of national life and to rule out all possibilities for opposition. Statism and capitalism add up to a system of authoritarian state capitalism, which Sedas Nunes was implying was inherent within the corporatist conception and which represented another repudiation of some of the most cherished of corporative principles.[18]

The in-house criticism and disillusionment with the corporative system were widespread and not limited just to intellectuals. The *Revista do Gabinete de Estudos Corporativos* continued to publish strong criticism, while all the time proclaiming its faith in corporatism and calling for its revitalization.[19] More and more sindicato leaders had been disillusioned, and businessmen certainly favored no further extension of the stifling system of controls, regulations, licenses, and permits. Rural peasants and smallholders saw that corporatism made little difference in their lives and viewed it with the stoic indifference they had usually afforded new policies emanating from Lisbon. Larger landholders, of course, continued to rule their estates with the classic authority of the traditional *patrão,* whether the particular form of rule was called "corporatism" or not.[20]

The Army had always resisted the corporatization of that institution, and in the postwar period, recognizing the discrediting of all such corporative schemes, it tended to resist the further extension of the corporative system even to nonmilitary spheres. Big business and the rising industrialist class, the banks, and the major import-export firms also tended to see corporatism as a national embarrassment and a hindrance to their activities; and politicians in the Assembly, the Chamber, and the União Nacional (often representing these same interests) were more and more reluctant to move forward with new corporative innovations.[21] Salazar and some of the men close to him kept the corporative faith, but even Salazar was forced to admit the corporative idea had not taken hold as expected, that corporatism had benefited some more than others, and that the corporative revolution was supposed to consist of more than mere state intervention in the economy.[22] There was so little support for the corporative system, indeed, that some were led to think the corporative complex might be allowed to wither away and possibly even be replaced gradually by a free and competitive system of associability. But this was not to be the case.[23]

The Corporative Revival

Given the range of forces arrayed against it, the international climate of opinion as regards corporatism, and the powerful disillusionment among a variety of groups within Portugal, it seems incredible that the regime should nonetheless go forward in the 1950s with a corporate revival and further extension of the system. Yet that is precisely what happened, with the promulgation in 1956, after several years of controversy, of two new decree-laws, the first establishing the corporations and the second involving an elaborate plan for social and corporative training and indoctrination. These decrees marked the first innovations in the system since the establishment of the original corporative structures in the 1930s.

Leading the campaign for corporative revival was J. Pires Cardoso and his *Revista do gabinete de estudos corporativos,* supported ultimately by Salazar, Caetano, Pereira (now back in the country after almost two decades as Portuguese ambassador in various capitals), and a handful of other corporatist intellectuals and government officials. The reasons for the revival at this time were various, and not all of them are as yet known. Salazar himself said that the war had retarded and set back corporatism's growth and progress; and in the postwar period misery, fear, lack of confidence, insidious opposition campaigns, the threat of subversion, and the prolongation of a "bellicose climate" had forced a further postponement.[24] By the 1950s this "bellicosity" had abated somewhat—and so had the economic crisis of the postwar period. The new stimulus to the economy in the 1950s, after years of hardship, austerity, and stagnation, made the regime feel it could now afford to proceed with further corporatist implementation in a way that it could not previously, when severe shortages of funds persistently forced postponement of the social-justice ideals envisioned in the original corporatist design.[25] The new prosperity also enabled the regime to relax the dictatorship somewhat, and increased prosperity plus relaxed controls, in turn, took some of the steam out of the opposition's appeals. Finally, one cannot lose sight of the fact that there were many conservatives and centrists in Portugal, often themselves sympathetic to the corporatist vision, such as Caetano and Pires Cardoso, who were appalled at the police-state controls of Salazar and of his perversion of the corporatist system. They saw the revival and extension of corporatism not only as a good in its own right but also as a means of restoring the regime to its original intentions and of checking the abusive power of both police and economic monopolists. The debate over corporatism (which in Portugal provided about the only permissible grounds for any kind of open political debate) was part of the ongoing factional struggle within the regime between those who wished to retain authoritarianism and a strict dictatorship and those who saw the need to relax the controls and open up the system somewhat.

These changes in the national mood and in the interplay of political forces within the regime helped make the climate propitious for corporative revival, but it was, of course, Salazar's personal leadership that made the campaign succeed. In 1949, after an agonizing four postwar years of seeking to decide in which direction the regime should go, Salazar had opted to go ahead with the corporative scheme, although by now confining it to a narrow range of activities. In a public statement of January 1949, Salazar had affirmed that "the regime has no intention of being destroyed, it intends to complete its evolution." [26] Shortly thereafter, he issued his oft-quoted statement: "It is time to relight the fire and continue the journey." [27] These statements provided enormous encouragement to the old corporatist ideologues, such as those in the newly formed Gabinete de Estudos Corporativos, and encouraged them to new activities. What these public statements masked, however, was the fact that Salazar had already determined that the real centers of power and decision making would continue to be located elsewhere in the system, that the corporative idea and agencies could be retained and even revived, but that their role and functions in the larger system would be carefully circumscribed.

The Gabinete de Estudos Corporativos and its *Revista* were founded in 1949 as part of the program for corporate revival. The Gabinete

(Cabinet) was located in the Centro Universitario da Mocidade Portuguesa at the University of Lisbon. The Mocidade was different then —even in the late 1940s it still retained some of its militancy and beliefs from the earlier days of the 1930s. (As the Mocidade later became oriented more toward sports interests and boy scouting, it made no sense to locate a serious study group and journal in its center, and the Gabinete was eventually transferred to the Instituto Superior de Economia e Finanças.) J. Pires Cardoso, who was then professor of corporative law at the Instituto Superior, was named director of the Cabinet, and he gathered around him a group of young lawyers, students, and budding sociologists (there was no sociology department or even any sociologists per se in Portugal at the time; even today there are only a handful, and their training is still strongly legalistic) who formed the nucleus of the Gabinete.

In these early days, neither the Gabinete nor the *Revista* had any direct assistance from the regime, financially or otherwise, except, of course, as the entire Mocidade and the Instituto Superior were budgeted by the national government. Salazar never discussed corporative developments with the Gabinete, nor did the regime interfere in its affairs. "We were totally independent," Gabinete officials stated; "we defended our point of view." Salazar, these officials maintained, was aloof and inaccessible as a person; "he never talked with us or we with him about our *Revista* or about corporative themes." Gabinete officials say they were able to make their criticisms of the corporative system (Sedas Nunes, who wrote one of the strongest critiques, was one of the young lawyer-sociologists associated with the Gabinete) without government interference. Never was an article censored, nor did any of the Gabinete's collaborators get into political trouble because of published critiques of the system. To be sure, theirs was in-house criticism, but, they claim, free discussion was always allowed. Moreover, despite his lack of direct contact with the *Revista,* its former directors maintain, "we knew we had Salazar's support and moral encouragement." For Salazar remained a corporatist to his dying days; contrary to the common belief, he never lost interest in the corporative solution as a "third way." [28]

The Gabinete de Estudos Corporativos took the lead in lobbying and propagandizing for the reform and extension of the corporative system, and also in instructing a whole new generation of lawyers and government workers trained in corporative law and organization. The opening editorial of volume 1, number 1, of the *Revista,* for example, written by Pires Cardoso, said that the Gabinete would be concerned with the formation of corporative consciousness, with training new leaders, and with completing the corporative structure. The editorial sounded the alarm over the recent stagnation and lack of innovation in terms of either corporative ideas or institutions. The purpose of the Gabinete, it said, would be not only the study and investigation of corporatism but also positive actions. Its concern would be both scholarly *and* programmatic. Meetings, lectures, courses, and a complete corporative program of study were established. The Gabinete would be concerned with examining the problems of corporative organization; while seeking to extend the corporative system, however, the group would not abstain from criticism. The quarterly *Revista* would serve as the vehicle for reconciling corporatism with modern social science.[29]

In keeping with these purposes the *Revista,* over the years, published a series of scholarly and semischolarly articles that reached into virtually every area of Portuguese (and non-Portuguese) corporatism. Pires Cardoso probed and prodded with an extended editorial in virtually every issue; a book review section was introduced; another section summarized the chief corporative developments of the preceding quarter. The thrust of the articles was toward getting the corporative agencies out of wage and price controls and returning to "corporative normalcy." They inveighed against an arbitrary state (though seldom calling Portugal that by name) and called for the reform and salvaging of the system. In this new climate, some articles began to talk about a more pluralist corporatist conception, others about the extension of the corporative system and its social legislation to the overseas colonies. Editorials urged that, since the wartime and postwar corporative phobia had passed, it was now time for a revival; other editorials attacked the "absurd confusion" of equating corporatism with fascism.[30]

A number of articles urged the extension of the corporative system to the universities. Others raised again the ancient taboo of corporatizing the Church and the armed forces. Some issued a call for a "democratic corporatism," while others analyzed the situation in the grassroots agencies and urged a more participatory corporative form. The Corporative Chamber was analyzed and the recommendation made that it be given political and deliberative functions as well as consultative ones. Sedas Nunes anticipated his later book with a series of articles dissecting corporatist ideology, and Cid Proença also published a number of critical essays. Other articles analyzed the finances of the system, the Organizations of Economic Coordination, the concept of corporative profit sharing, various social reforms, and the need, finally, to complete the structure by creating its "cupola," the corporations themselves. Lobbying for the actual creation of the corporations was one of the themes that ran consistently through the *Revista,* a cause that Pires Cardoso personally championed. The discussion in the review of these and other issues was vigorous, lively, articulate. Frequently, it involved what to North Amercians would seem some incredible hairsplitting and abstract, scholastic debate, but given the strongly legalistic and Thomistic political culture, that should not be surprising. What is most interesting for our purposes is the powerful impact this group and its *Revista* had, for out of this intellectual ferment and activism the corporative system *was* revived and restructured, the corporations were created at last, and a large number of future corporative civil servants were trained.

The dynamism stirring in the Gabinete de Estudos Corporativos was paralleled by a new ferment elsewhere in the system. In 1951 another Gabinete de Estudos Corporativos was created at the University of Coimbra. Although the Coimbra group was not so persistent or activist as Pires Cardoso's Lisbon nucleus, it did spawn in corporative lawyer J. M. Cortez Pinto a set of ideas regarding the corporative structure and its functions that, as we shall see shortly, became the dominant conception throughout the rest of the Salazar regime—and beyond! The União Nacional also revived its Center for Social and Political Studies and began reconsideration of the corporatist ideas.

Perhaps the most important single event of this period was the creation by decree-law 37,909 of August 1, 1950, of a new Ministry of Corporations and Social Welfare to replace the older subsecretariat. The elevation of this office to a ministry was a symbolic act designed to show the important place of corporatism and the corporatist structures within the system. The ministry provided a home for a myriad of offices and agencies now functioning, or about to be created, under the corporatist umbrella. It also gave corporative officials equivalent rank with their counterparts in other ministries and lent added prestige and power to the whole corporatist system. The creation of a separate Corporations Ministry was not without its critics, and there was considerable debate and discussion both in the press and in the National Assembly, but in the end, of course, Salazar prevailed and corporatists like Pires Cardoso applauded.[31]

The creation of the Corporations Ministry served as a stimulus to the invigoration, within certain carefully prescribed limits, of the entire corporative system. Beginning in 1950 the Fundação Nacional para a Alegria no Trabalho, the Instituto Nacional do Trabalho e Previdência, the Tribunais do Trabalho, and the Junta Central das Casas dos Pescadores received a new infusion of life. Strong hints were dropped that the creation of the new Corporations Ministry was a prelude to the creation of the corporations themselves. Some of the gremio, sindicato, and casas do povo structures began also to be revived, and the Ministry of Corporations commenced to flesh out its various agencies, bureaus, and offices. New concepts of social security and medical service were articulated within the ministry, and a number of new social assistance programs were begun or the coverage of the old programs extended. The family assistance program was expanded in 1954 to cover both civilian and military employees of the state, and new *caixas econômicas* were created as interest-paying depositories for workers' savings. In 1955 new requirements were promulgated governing industrial working conditions, hygiene, and safety on the job. That same year saw the further increase and extension of social security benefits and assistance, and also some renewed labor and bargaining activity among the sindicatos after some six or so years of quiescence. These innovations, although on quite a modest scale, served to revive the corporative structures somewhat and to awaken them from the postwar lethargy. These changes, in turn, were related to the relatively peaceful political situation of the early-to-mid-1950s and to the comparative economic prosperity of that decade (growth rates of GNP of 4 percent per year on the average), enabling the regime to afford an increase in social benefits, which in the 1940s it felt it could not.[32]

Despite the new corporative activities of the early 1950s, there is strong evidence that the so-called "revival" was more apparent than real. For example, the October 1950 creation of a special Commission of Economic Coordination, replacing the old Conselho Técnico Corporativo originally created by Pereira, took even greater influence over economic decision making out of the hands of the corporative structures and agencies and centralized it still further in the hands of the non-corporative economic ministries and agencies and of Salazar himself and the state. Decree-law 38,540 of November 24, 1951, provided that in cases of the suspension or dissolution of any casa do povo, its interests would henceforth be represented by the INTP (government) delegate for that district. Similar decrees emasculated further the social and economic functions of the corporative agencies, and no additional political authority was given to the Corporations Ministry or its subunits. It becomes clear, thus, that while Salazar was willing to expand somewhat the social assistance activities of the state and to use the corporative grass-roots organizations for that purpose, he had no intention whatsoever of dismantling the by-now elaborate control mechanisms of his authoritarian state. All during this period, therefore, while a number of social programs were being created or expanded, the censorship remained in effect, the secret police continued active, the opposition was held in check, and there was little real relaxation of the dictatorship. Interviews with corporative officials indeed reveal that, while Salazar gave the go-ahead to the creation of the Corporations Ministry, he also explicitly instructed the first minister, Soares da Fonseca, not to proceed with any further corporative growth, to expand the social services but not to give the corporative agencies any real power.[33]

Meanwhile, in keeping with these realities, a new conception of the role of corporatism and its utility had been growing among a number of post-1930s intellectuals and university professors. This conception was formulated, significantly, not at the more dynamic and strongly pro-corporatist Gabinete de Estudos Corporativos in Lisbon, but by João Manuel Cortez Pinto and his associates at the University of Coimbra. Cortez Pinto began his two-volume study of the structure and functions of corporatism by pointing elliptically to the absence of studies of corporatism in the postwar period. The corporative structure and conception, he said, had not been modified to meet the new economic contingencies. Before 1939 the corporative system was "insufficiently institutionalized" to create the pinnacles of the system, the corporations themselves; after the war there was a "certain hesitation and general disorientation," with the result that the enthusiasm for going ahead with corporative development was almost extinguished.

Cortez Pinto hence called for a more realistic corporatism, for a corporative structure that would be efficient and competent. Perhaps most important, in Cortez Pinto's conception the corporative structure, and specifically the corporations, should have a limited role. Gone was the conception that corporatism and the corporations should serve as *the* basis for the entire national system, as a means of national representation, and as the foundation on which social and economic life would be grounded. Instead the corporations were to be assigned primarily social assistance functions and were to have a limited role as advisory or consultative agencies in economic matters. This conception of a very circumscribed set of functions for the corporative agencies, primarily in the social welfare area and to a far lesser extent in economic affairs, was strongly in keeping with Salazar's own evolving idea and provided a rationale for his decision to continue with corporatism but not to give corporatism's agencies any real decision-making influence. The Cortez Pinto conception also reflected closely, thus, the realities of power and of the corporative system's functions as they already existed.[34]

The Creation of the Corporations:
The "Cupola" of the System

The early-to-mid-1950s may be viewed as an era of rethinking and of reconsolidation of the corporative system. A number of early mistakes were corrected (although some fundamental ones were not), the system of social assistance was expanded and reorganized, numerous collective contracts were renegotiated with the trend in wages definitely upward, new federations and gremios were created, the *caixas* were expanded, some reorientation and restructuring took place, and, in the words of the *Boletim* of the Instituto Nacional do Trabalho e Previdência, "some bad suggestions were resisted." [35] The new minister of corporations promised to fulfill Salazar's vow "to relight the old fires," to develop and progress, to fashion new programs for rural workers, to study both old and new activities of the corporative system, and to organize the corporative cupolas based on the work of such "organs of advanced study" as those of Pires Cardoso and Cortez Pinto.

For years the Portuguese regime had been criticized and mocked, both inside and outside Portugal, as "a corporative system without corporations." Now, however, with Cortez Pinto's new conception of corporatism's limited functions harmonizing neatly with the authoritarian de facto structure of the Estado Novo, the further development and consolidation of the system could go forward—with Salazar's blessing. In late 1954 Pires Cardoso began writing numerous editorials in the *Revista* of his corporative study group urging the creation of the corporations. He delivered the same message in testimony before the Corporative Chamber. The National Assembly also began to discuss the issue of the creation of the corporations, and in 1955 Pires Cardoso began marshaling his arguments for a book-length *parecer* that would serve as the intellectual basis for the entire creation.[36]

Pires Cardoso's parecer provided the rationalizations for a decision already taken in the highest ranks of the government—that is, by Salazar himself. Pires Cardoso used all the old arguments going back to the Catholic-corporatist debates of the nineteenth century. He showed the defects of both liberalism and socialism. He presented corporatism as an acceptable "third way." He analyzed in detail both the Portuguese and foreign experiences with corporatism. He brought out again all the old historical traditions and parallels. Pires Cardoso then proceeded in part 2 of his *Parecer* to explain why the structure should be completed, why the corporations should now be created. He marshaled legal and political arguments. He discussed the social and economic functions of the corporations, their coordinating role, their autonomous position (as he saw it), the criteria for their creation, the means of integrating the corporations in the broader national system, how they would be organized, even the possibility for corporative organization in the Portuguese overseas provinces.

Pires Cardoso was, of course, a lawyer, and his impressive and detailed parecer was in effect a legal brief submitted in support of pending legislation to create the corporations. Actually there was no opposition in the Assembly to establishing the corporations (with only two or three exceptions) since it was well known that Salazar had already made the decision. Mostly, what was expressed in the Assembly was uncertainty as to what the creation of the corporations meant and what the implications of this step would be. Salazar thus helped revive corporatism when others, chiefly the opposition but some important civilian and military elites as well, had already pronounced it dead. He pushed the legislation through, and given the general discrediting of the system and its weak and precarious position even then, it was only because he wanted them that the corporations were finally created at all.[37]

While the vocal opposition to establishing the corporations was virtually nil, there was considerable debate on the best way to structure them. As usual, this debate involved some fine hairsplitting that as often as not served as a smoke screen for powerful political and economic interests. Pires Cardoso's parecer favored a form of "horizontal" corporative organization, as opposed to the "vertical" scheme that was eventually adopted. That is, Pires Cardoso wanted all the participants in the entire productive cycle of a single industry—let us say, the wine industry—grouped together in a single corporation. This would include the growers, day laborers, harvesters, landowners, shippers, boatsmen, processors, import-exporters, bar owners, and so on. In other words, all those involved in the production of a certain product, from its birth through its manufacture to its commercialization, including both workers and employers, would be integrated "horizontally" into a single corporation. Pires Cardoso envisioned a variety of such corporations, one for each major industry, tied together by an elaborate network of lines of responsibility, coordination, accountability, and subordination.[38]

There was a "hidden agenda" in the Pires Cardoso design, however, disguised in part by the elaborate arguments over the proper corporative form, and that involved its author's advocacy of returning to a system of economic self-regulation, of limited state rule, and of *corporatisme d'association*. This, of course, was unacceptable in terms of the strong etatist conception of Salazar *and* from the point of view of big business, commercial, and banking interests, who had prospered under the system of state protection and monopoly and who, as we have seen in previous chapters, had learned to manipulate the corporative structure to their private advantage. Caetano, then minister of the presidency, close to Salazar, and a man of greater stature and prestige than Pires Cardoso, favored a scheme of "vertical" integration of the corporations, and it was his system that, with Salazar's and the business elite's blessing, was eventually adopted. Instead of the horizontal pattern of grouping together all elements in the production process of one particular industry into a single corporation, the vertical scheme called for their grouping according to the major "arms of production"—agriculture, transport, commerce, fishing, industry, and the like. The vertical system was considered easier and more viable, and least upsetting of already established business practices. Although the Pires Cardoso horizontal scheme was accepted in the Corporative Chamber, it was rejected in the National Assembly and the vertical one adopted instead. Once more, those who favored a freer, more open *corporatisme d'association* had lost out to the advocates of a strong state apparatus.[39]

Once the decision to create the corporations had been made and their form decided upon, the regime moved quickly toward implementation. In March 1956 Salazar submitted to the Assembly the bill authorizing the establishment of the corporations.[40] The Assembly modified the government's proposals in a few particulars, and by August the legislation had been promulgated. The actual decree creating the corporations was dated September 23, 1957, the twenty-fourth anniversary of the first wave of corporative decrees. Under the legislation introduced by Salazar, the corporations were to absorb and serve as umbrella organizations for the numerous guilds, sindicatos, casas, and so forth, already existing. The first six corporations, organized around the major economic activities, were those of agriculture, industry, commerce, credit and insurance, fishing and canning industry, and transport and tourism. Two new corporations were added in 1959: the Corporation for Press and Printing and the Corporation for Entertainment. In 1966 three others were added: the Corporation for Welfare; the Corporation for Science, Letters, and the Arts; and the Corporation for Physical Education and Sports. Since there was little prospect for the creation of a Corporation of the Armed Forces or of the Church, this new wave of legislation was widely recognized as representing the final step in the completion of the Portuguese corporative experiment.[41]

As formally structured, each corporation was to consist of an equal number of representatives from both workers' and employers' organizations. The corporative principles of parity, of equality of representation of capital and labor, and of the harmonization of classes were thus supposed to be encompassed within the actual structure of the corporations. In fact, as we shall see in more detail in the following chapter, the leadership of the corporations was dominated from the beginning by employer interests. Similarly, the functions that the new corporations took on in the 1960s—marketing surveys, technical studies, economic reports, and the like—were also largely at the service of business groups. Organizationally, the corporations were supposed to serve as intermediaries (instead of divisive political parties and class interest associations) between government and governed, but in actual practice they seldom fulfilled this function. In law at least the corporations were given fairly wide power: politically, they would serve to represent their constituent interests; they were given the task of defending the common interests of their respective branches vis-à-vis the government; they were to assist in the negotiation of collective contracts; they would develop social services and insurance and assistance programs; and they were to lay down disciplinary rules for the self-regulation of their respective branches. Despite this broad authority in law, in actual practice the corporations always exercised but very limited functions and most of these were of interest to employers rather than workers.[42]

At a press conference the new minister of corporations and social assistance, Dr. Veiga de Macedo, stated that the corporations would play an increasingly important role in the national life, that they would have the juridical status of "collective persons," and that they would have complete autonomy in representing the interests of their members. Their principal organs were to be a new, revived Corporative Council, as well as various sectional councils, a directorate, and a disciplinary court. Emphasizing that the Portuguese corporate state bore no resemblance to the prewar Italian Fascist system, the minister said that, whereas the Italian corporations had been controlled by the state, the Portuguese corporations would be independent bodies possessing powers limiting state action. At the same time, however, Veiga de Macedo noted that representatives of the government would be attached to each corporation with the task of "defending the common interests of the community and the consumers" and with the power to suspend any resolutions considered detrimental to the higher interests of the nation, pending a final decision by the Corporative Council.[43] As in the 1930s, thus, the regime was going ahead with the creation of a more elaborate corporative structure, but it remained wary of allowing too much power to devolve upon the corporations and it always reserved the right to veto any corporative action of which it disapproved.

Along with the decree establishing the corporations went another containing elaborate plans for the further dissemination of corporative ideas and for the training of new leaders to administer the system. The Plan for Social and Corporative Formation emerged from a realistic recognition of the weaknesses and limitations of the corporative system, of the absence some twenty-four years after the corporative restructuring of 1933 of very much in the way of corporative consciousness, of the suspicion and hostility toward the corporative agencies on the part of both employers and employees, and of the absence of a cadre of organizers and administrators capable of sympathetically and effectively managing the system. The Plan for Social and Corporative Formation was aimed at correcting precisely those faults that numerous in-house critics of the system had been expounding since World War II.

Under the plan a Junta da Acção Social was established within the Corporations Ministry which began a program of publication and dissemination of corporatist literature and information. A training program began in Lisbon aimed at creating a corps of well-informed organizers and administrators for the by-now numerous corporative agencies, and a series of seminars and meetings was also held at various locations throughout the country to spread the word of the benefits and assistance available under the corporative structure. The old corporative studies center of the União Nacional was revived, and it too began to hold short courses and run training programs for the spread of the corporative idea. The Plan for Social and Corporative Formation served as a spur for the spread of corporative consciousness among the general population, the absence of which had continuously frustrated the university-educated corporatist ideologues from the 1930s on and was a key reason why the creation of the corporations was so long postponed. The plan aimed also at providing the leadership cadres, whose absence had similarly retarded and perverted corporatism's growth.[44]

With the creation of the corporations and the Plan for Social and Corporative Formation, a new stimulus was given to the entire corporative apparatus. Replacing Soares da Fonseca as minister of corporations in 1955, Veiga de Macedo embarked on a real stump campaign, speaking throughout the country on behalf of the corporative order. A far more dynamic (and politically ambitious) man than his predecessor, Veiga de Macedo also came to office armed with instructions from Salazar to revive the corporative structure, especially in keeping with the new social assistance focus. Veiga de Macedo gave more speeches and held more meetings than any corporations administrator since Pereira, promising a more active part for the sindicatos in the life of the nation, new programs of social security, better working and living conditions, a new round of revised collective contracts, even action against employers who refused to live up to the corporative social and labor legislation.[45]

The old corporative machinery was similarly resuscitated and a number of significant innovations introduced. The representational structure of the Corporative Chamber was reorganized to reflect the new realities of the corporations. The old Corporative Council was resurrected to oversee the functioning of the entire corporative system. New sindicatos and casas do povo were created, largely by government decree rather than as a result of much grass-roots enthusiasm, to serve as the agencies to administer the new social programs. New uniões and federações also came into existence. Innovative pareceres were issued dealing with "Cooperatives and Corporative Organization," "Professional Classification and Corporative Organization," and the like. The membership of the various corporative units began to grow once again, and the social assistance laws were extended to cover previously marginal sectors of the population. Early in 1957 a proposal from the Ministry of Corporations suggested the creation of Federations of Casas do Povo to give them greater bargaining power; at the same time the labor tribunals were reformed and reinvigorated. Another 1957 proposal was issued to promote cooperation between the caixas de previdência and the casas do povo in the construction of low-cost housing; the Serviço Social do Trabalho was also created as a special agency of the ministry. Other new programs dealt with expanded medical care for workers, adult education, the protection of women, salaries, labor conditions, and so on. Meanwhile, Veiga de Macedo continued to crisscross the countryside giving speeches, initiating new activities, revving up the old apparatus, sparking enthusiasm, and invigorating not only the corporative order but also the whole regime. The years 1955–57 were years of great stir within the corporative system, of considerable efforts to revive and dynamize the whole structure, of seeking to revitalize a lethargic and creaky system as a reflection of the new vigor and prosperity in the nation as a whole. Within the limits already noted, it appeared that, in what had been a discredited corporative system whose time, many felt, had already passed, the revival had begun to strike a spark.[46]

Corporative Revival—and Corporative Decline

The 1950s marked a rather significant revival in Portuguese corporatism. As compared with the immediate postwar period, renewed attention was given to corporatist theory and ideology and a spate of new books, studies, and articles appeared dealing with corporatist themes. The Ministry of Corporations and Social Welfare was created and its activities expanded, particularly in the area of social security. The new stir in the corporative structure culminated in 1956 with the creation, finally, of the corporations themselves—and unlike an earlier (1939) decree authorizing their creation which, because of the war, remained only a paper document, the regime now proceeded rapidly toward implementation. Along with the establishment of the corporations came an ambitious plan for social and corporative "formation," a new, dynamic minister of corporations, and a new sense of movement and dynamism pervading the entire corporative structure.

If one probes beneath the surface appearances of renewed dynamism and change, however, one finds that the basic structures of the emerging authoritarian state apparatus continued unaltered in any of its essentials. Salaries were raised somewhat, but the sindicatos remained impotent and could not function as effective, independent bargaining agents. Salazar persisted in his policy of safeguarding national economic integrity and thus employed even stricter etatist controls rather than the principle of self-direction. The public security apparatus of the state was strengthened, and the machinery of the dictatorship continued to function. Rather than a truly corporatist system based on the equal representation of employers and employees, Portugal remained essentially a capitalist oligarchy, with incredibly low living standards for the bulk of the population and immense opportunities for enrichment for the few of wealth and good connections who had learned to manipulate and reap advantages from "the system." The oligarchic structure, in turn, was supported and preserved by an elaborate police state system of controls.

The corporative reforms of the 1950s, in short, failed to affect any of the basic structures of the regime. The newly created corporations of industry and of commerce, for example, although authorized by decree in 1956, were not actually established until several years later so as to give big business and commercial interests time to make the adjustments necessary, so that the economy would not be disturbed and so that the major economic groups could work out ways to coopt or get around the new corporative entities. Many of the newly created casas do povo and sindicatos continued to exist only on paper, and it took years before any of the new social assistance programs began to have much effect on those they were intended to benefit. Under the Plan for Social and Corporative Formation, the Corporations Ministry was able to train some new leaders and administrators; but there is no evidence that the publicity and propaganda had any effect whatsoever at the grass roots. Lower-class Portuguese treated the new corporative reforms as they had always treated bold initiatives from political leaders in the capital: with suspicion and profound indifference. Most had by this time stopped listening to Salazar and had turned cynical and indifferent; often rejecting his basic principles as an effort to resurrect ideas buried in the Middle Ages, they called his a regime of *discursos,* a "regime of speeches." The "corporative consciousness" for which the intellectuals of the regime had been looking for decades thus failed to emerge despite some considerable efforts, and the Portuguese man in the street (or in the fields) showed no more interest in this, to him, abstract scheme than he ever had.[47] Despite all the new flurry of corporative activity, therefore, little change occurred; the corporative revival ended as a dull plop and a soft whisper.

By 1958 the corporative revival was already in decline. Veiga de Macedo continued to travel and speak on behalf of the corporative reforms, but clearly the steam had gone out of the campaign. There were few corporative innovations, and implementation of the new programs and decrees was already lagging.[48] The divisive election campaign of 1958 was also on, in which General Humberto Delgado ran as an opposition candidate for president and threw down a gauntlet to the regime, which forced still another postponement of the reform program. The strikes of the time were dealt with harshly; so was the opposition. Salazar again became preoccupied with the great questions of the national destiny and the emerging conflict with India over Goa, Diu, and Damão, and with the grand international issue of Portugal's place in the world. Pires Cardoso, intellectual and spiritual author of so many of the new corporative reforms and whom everyone expected to be named minister of corporations, instead was named minister of interior during that difficult year of 1958, suffered a nervous breakdown after only a few months in office, and subsequently lost interest as an active participant in the corporative movement. His journal, which had focused on corporative issues, was soon absorbed by another academic review and its corporative focus completely abandoned.[49] A number of in-house critiques began again to be published, and in 1960 a colloquium sponsored by the Corporations Ministry itself was so critical of the entire corporative structure that much of it might as well have ceased to function.[50]

That in fact is precisely what did occur. For once the excitement of the mid-1950s had passed, once the corporations, the cupolas of the system, had been created and still nothing happened, the system reverted to its traditional lethargy and indifference. Salazar himself, by now old and tired, increasingly lost interest, and the younger postwar generation was hardly enthused by a system they saw as discredited and a product of a prewar period that had little relevance to present-day Portuguese needs. Their interests turned to the new national development plans first initiated in 1953, to the requirements for economic progress, toward Europe, and to the desire for greater social justice. That too is the direction in which national attention began to turn— the new *técnicos* and university students, government officials, and ultimately Salazar himself and the Portuguese people. What existed in the corporative sphere, therefore, especially from the point of view of its by-now numerous critics, was an old and tired bureaucracy stifling progress more often than furthering it, a stagnant and largely ineffectual system that could no longer generate enthusiasm, conditions of incredible backwardness and poverty among the lower classes, a frozen, outdated system of social relations unable to accommodate itself to the change and dynamism of mid-twentieth-century life, and an old leadership that was no longer certain in which direction to take the country and that hung onto power through a combination of inertia and ever tighter dictatorial controls.[51]

VIII

Corporatist Decline and Institutional Crisis: How the Corporatist System Functioned (or Failed to Function) in the 1960s

By the 1960s Portugal was no longer quite the sleepy, traditional, backward nation of rural peasants and small villages that it had been in the 1930s. To be sure, Portugal was less developed than its European neighbors and the Portuguese countryside as pictured in the travel ads—peaceful, pastoral, whitewashed, and beautiful—remained much the same. But that picture had begun to be superseded by another—urban, materialistic, change oriented. From the 1930s on, Portuguese industry had grown up and new sources of wealth had become available. Economic growth in the 1950s and 1960s forged ahead, not at the "miracle" pace of West Germany and Japan, but steadily at rates of 3–4–5 percent per year. Per capita income in 1964 was $400.00, nearly 50 percent higher than a decade before. The growth was accelerated by state-supported investment policies, the new national development plans begun in 1953, the long-term condition of enforced stability (both in the political and economic spheres), and the fact of virtually zero population growth. The new wealth helped give rise to a far larger middle class than had ever existed before, an ever-expanding urban working class, and a far more differentiated and complex social system than was present in the 1930s. New opportunities for enrichment helped stimulate urbanization; cities like Lisbon and Porto became big, modern metropolises, and the older provincial capitals began to overflow their ancient medieval walls for the first time since they were built six and seven centuries before. Meanwhile, the rural areas themselves were left depleted and underpopulated.[1]

Portugal, in short, had begun to experience the throes of modernization—under authoritarian auspices, to be sure, but modernization nonetheless. These changes in turn sparked widespread demands from the rising labor and middle classes for new and improved services and economic benefits and, among some sectors at least, for democratization and a greater degree of popular participation in national political life. Uncertainly and unevenly, the "revolution of rising expectations" had come to Portugal.

While in the social and economic spheres the country was modernizing, its political structures failed to develop in a parallel fashion. Portugal continued to be governed by one man; moreover, as he got older, that one man became more and more impervious to advice, set in his ways, dogmatic and doctrinaire, and, according to much popular lore, at least partly senile. Rather than broadening the base of his regime to reflect the new social changes, Salazar narrowed it, freezing the elite, relying on a decreasing circle of advisers, locking the political system into a 1930s mold that no longer applied. Increasingly, Salazar had difficulty recruiting able cabinet ministers and administrators, with the result that the quality of the services provided declined at precisely the time of greatly expanded popular demands. More and more isolated from European, world, even his own nation's realities, Salazar became less and less sure of himself; indecisive, he allowed the nation to drift. The shutting off by police-state methods of virtually all opposition following the 1958 election campaign served to rule out even further the possibilities for institutionalizing change. Meanwhile, as the walls of Portuguese isolation from the outside world began to crack, student and labor opposition mounted, the liberal and social-democratic elements grew in size, the Communists gained a foothold in the trade union movement, and even a Christian-democratic opposition was organized in this most Catholic-corporatist of states. The pervasive isolation heretofore also helps explain the tremendous shock and disbelief expressed by the Portuguese governing element as the revolt in her African colonies began in 1961 and as rebellion and independence sentiment spread. By the mid-to-late 1960s the Portuguese political structure had become paralyzed and fossilized, a fact that was reflected in the corporative structure as well.[2]

Corporative Changes

In the decades prior to 1960 Portuguese peasants and workers had repeatedly been urged by the regime to weigh the advantages of their present way of life against the uncertainties, disorder, and lack of development of the pre-Salazar era. For a long time, and in a situation of national isolation, this argument served the regime well. By the 1960s, however, it was no longer convincing. A new generation had grown up that no longer remembered the chaos of the Republic or even the terrible poverty of the 1920s and 1930s, the traditional isolation was breaking down, and the flight of Portuguese labor to other, more prosperous European countries had begun. Now the comparisons began to be made not with a distant Portuguese past but with the rest of Europe at present, and here Portugal appeared in a bad light. The Portuguese worker began to be aware that, next to the proverbially poor Albanian, he was the worst off in Europe.

In 1960 the average earned income, although rising, was still only $350.00 per person per year, which meant Portugal was not yet even close to passing the threshold (arbitrarily put at $500.00 per person per year) that separated the developed nations from the underdeveloped ones. Moreover, the income curve was heavily skewed in favor of the wealthy and the middle class; the distribution of income was the most uneven in Western Europe. A skilled electrician in 1960 could earn about 50 cents an hour and a bricklayer about 40 cents. A policeman's salary was pegged at about $7.50 per week, while a farm laborer made about $1.20 per day—on the relatively few days per year when he had any work at all. A seamstress earned about half what the farm laborer made, a maid even less than that. At the same time, roughly 20–30 percent of the population was unemployed; and countless poor families were almost wholly outside the money economy, earning little, selling little, buying little.

As late as the 1950s, in addition, Portugal had virtually no social security. Social services for workers existed on a limited scale (again the lowest in Europe) but benefited only that small percentage, chiefly skilled laborers, organized through the official sindicato system. Each major sindicato had its own *caixa de previdência* which, in return for a small weekly contribution (supplemented by limited government funds), took care of the worker's doctor bills, entitled him to 60 percent of his wages during sick leaves, and covered the costs of his medical prescriptions and one-third of those of his family. But these benefits too were limited to the "elite" of the working class, while the bulk of the population had no social security coverage at all. With the abundance of unskilled laborers in Portugal, unemployment compensation remained virtually nonexistent. And for the large army of unskilled workers themselves, both rural and urban, the majority of whom remained outside the corporate system, sickness or adversity implied dependence on relatives or Catholic charities, which frequently meant no or woefully insufficient assistance. By the 1960s some elements within the Portuguese government were awakening to the fact that such endemic poverty, backwardness, and absence of social programs might pose a menace to the regime itself.[3]

It was toward the remedying of these conditions that the thrust of corporative developments in the 1960s was directed. The intellectual basis for a new social security-social assistance orientation for the corporative system, it will be recalled, had been elaborated in the corporative literature of the 1950s and lay behind many of the recent rationalizations for corporative revival and the creation of the actual corporations themselves. Minister of Corporations Veiga de Macedo had employed his energy and considerable political skills to dynamize the moribund corporative agencies and reorient them in a social assistance direction. Now, with the appointment in May 1961 of José João Gonçalves de Proença as corporations minister, and with the blessing of Salazar, the social assistance mission went through a complete renovation. Indeed, the corporative restructuring and social assistance reorientation begun in the 1960s served as the basis for the *Estado Social*—the reforms leading to a "social state"—as envisioned later by Salazar's successor, Marcello Catetano.[4]

Like his predecessor in the Corporations Ministry, Gonçalves Proença was a dynamic, skillful, ambitious administrator and politician. He too stumped the country giving numerous speeches, explaining the new corporative emphasis, hosting innumerable conferences, and presiding at various opening ceremonies.[5] He was always careful to pay lip service to and never repudiate the older corporative doctrines of the 1930s. But the thrust was clearly now toward the social security-social assistance end of things. In every speech he gave (about every two weeks) and in every issue of the *Boletim do INTP*, the emphasis was clearly upon the social assistance mission of the corporative complex. Gone completely was the emphasis on the representational functions of the corporative agencies, their role in directing the economy, their special place as the basis for the entire national system. There are even those who suggest that the large semiannual colloquia Proença hosted, which so devastatingly showed the inadequacies of the traditional corporative functions, were designed purposely by the regime to diminish the importance of and undermine those functions and to promote the new social assistance conception.[6]

During the 1960s, thus, a great variety of new services and agencies came into existence—at least on paper and to some extent in actual fact. The new legislation and the corporative reforms were designed by no means solely to benefit the Portuguese population but also to present a favorable impression to the outside world—not so much "for the British to see," as was true of many other Portuguese institutions, but increasingly for the European community, with whom Portugal was now seeking closer ties. Among the newer agencies created were those dealing with pensions, family allowances, and housing; a *Gabinete* of

Insurance and Hygiene was created; also a National Employment Service (to provide vocational guidance, free employment placement, and facilities for emigrants to Portugal's African territories); an Institute of Accelerated Professional Training; and the Fund for the Development of Hand-Labor Skills. New requirements were promulgated for health and safety in manufacturing firms, a service was established to foment the development of cooperatives, medical services were extended, laws protecting women and children were passed, a maternity fund was begun. The new Serviço Social do Trabalho was established within the Corporations Ministry; so were the new Missions of Social Action and the *Caixa Nacional* for Insurance and Work-Related Injuries. In addition, there was a new Centro de Estudos Sociais e Corporativos which began publishing a journal in 1962, the Institute for Social and Corporative Formation, an Institute of Social Studies, a Conselho Superior de Previdência, and a Conselho Superior de Agricultura (the conselho for industry had been created earlier). The host of new agencies, bureaus, programs, institutes, and so on, represented an attempt on the part of the Portuguese both to catch up with the rest of Europe in the social security-social assistance area *and* to begin to appease their own population.[7]

The activities of the Corporations Ministry reflected this considerable new stir. Some of these activities were exciting and innovative, while others seem ludicrous from this vantage point. But all reflected the new sense of "movement" within the corporative system that had been reduced almost to the vanishing point during the 1940s. For example, beginning in 1960 the Missions of Social Action, parallel to the Cultural Missions launched by the Education Ministry to help raise literacy, were sent out with the avowed purpose of "humanizing" the corporative laws and institutions, "dignifying" employer-employee relations, and building a climate of peace and mutual confidence. The mission representatives were to be specialists in social action; and the campaign waxed enthusiastically for a time, then it waned. Also in 1960 a new Medal of Corporative Merit was created! That same year, on September 23, the date that so many earlier corporative innovations had been launched, the government announced that it would be constructing a new building to house the expanding Corporations Ministry, a building that would be the tallest in Lisbon (until it was recently surpassed by the Sheraton-Hilton).

Meanwhile, the ministry began underwriting the construction of numerous low-cost housing projects, and a new round of collective-contract negotiations commenced. A number of "Workers' Cinemas" were opened; a decree was promulgated calling for the establishment of libraries in the casas do povo and in the syndicate offices. The number of casas and sindicatos also showed a significant increase for the first time in fifteen years. The period 1960/61 was, as measured by the activities underway, another one of those "highs" in the evolution of Portuguese corporatism when it appeared some of the original promise of the system might finally be fulfilled.[8] The whole formal structure was now just about completed, there was a new vigor in the system absent since the 1930s, vast activities were underway, and the country itself was finally becoming prosperous enough to raise salaries and provide new social services. Then another wholly unexpected event occurred, which for a small nation like Portugal was comparable to World War II in its disastrous consequences: the revolt in Angola. The revolt marked the end of the Portuguese dream and myth that it, along with its colonies, was or could be a major force among the nations of the world. The nation was shocked at the Africans' rejection of what it had always genuinely thought of as a special relationship, a uniquely Portuguese way of building multiracial societies, a relationship that was different than that of other colonialist nations. The revolt meant still another in the long line of wrenching national crises, renewed isolation, continued austerity. It also provoked a further crisis in the corporative system comparable to that of the 1940s and led once more to the slowing or postponing of the recently completed plans for corporative renewal and, through the corporative system, improved living standards.

After 1961 corporative reform again went forward, but at a greatly reduced pace. A new *caixa,* or fund, was established in 1962 which provided insurance for injuries sustained in the course of work. But little of the recently passed corporative legislation was implemented very effectively now; and while there were always more speeches, these tended to be celebrations rather than indications of corporative development. The pace of reform slowed so much that, in a speech to the Corporation of Industry in early 1963, Proença felt called upon to say that, contrary to what many believed, the corporative agencies *were* alive and functioning and that the definitive structuring of the system was about to be reached.[9] The fact was that now as much as ever, once a new item of corporative legislation was passed, implementation consistently lagged far behind.

By 1963 there was more and more attention to social issues—and virtually no talk of corporatism. Pensions, holidays, work breaks, vacations, social justice—these were the concerns, not corporatist ideology or organization. Another new insurance plan was announced, covering injury, disability, unemployment, hospitalization, and death. A new Caixa Nacional de Pensões (pensions) was established, along with more regional caixas. The *Instituto de Estudos Sociais* was founded within the Corporations Ministry, with its focus on *man* and its emphasis on the study of social laws. "It doesn't matter what the system's called," said one official document accompanying the creation of the institute, "or what form it takes (ours happens to be called 'corporatism'); the important element is our focus and purpose, which is to treat social problems."[10] This comment was illustrative of the trend in the 1960s away from corporatism in the older 1930s sense and toward an emphasis on social problems—even in the Corporations Ministry!

During the rest of the 1960s the social security-social assistance emphasis continued. The infrastructure was put in place, through the corporative complex, for the implementation of a great variety of new social programs comparable to those developed in other modern systems. The year 1964 saw the launching of a new program for employment, another for the training of hand labor, still another for increased salaries. The labor legislation was revised, professional training was stepped up, the Corporative Commissions for Rural Labor were established, and the labor legislation of the 1930s began in a limited fashion to be extended to the countryside. A new *Código de processo do trabalho* was promulgated, and the period 1964/65 saw a great deal of new legislation relative to labor contracts and the renegotiation of those contracts. The new code incorporated modern concepts of juridical sociology as applied to women and minors. New caixas for assistance were organized, a family assistance program was launched, and the National Employment Service got underway. Each new casa do povo implied the extension of the social assistance programs to one more rural *freguesia*.

In 1965 came a new program for hospital care. A National Pensions Plan was also created, replacing the programs administered by individual sindicatos and patronal organizations. Meanwhile, the body of regulatory law governing virtually all areas of the country's economic and associational life continued to grow. In the midst of the African rebellions, a prolonged debate began on the possibilities for the extension of the corporative system to the overseas colonies. Corporations Minister Proença continued to stump the country, giving speeches, publicizing and drumming up support for the new programs. In 1966 three new corporations were authorized; that same year the new Corporations Ministry skyscraper was opened with much fanfare. The expansion of the social services and the refinement of the corporative structures so as to administer them continued to go forward.[11]

Another round of legislation followed, aimed at improving living conditions and thus reducing the flow of workers abroad (which reached 80,000 in 1965, at least half of them illegal). Minimum annual vacations of from six to eighteen days were announced, depending on the years of service. Workers released without cause were to be guaranteed indemnities; workers forced to work on holidays would receive extra pay and be assured of another day off. Women were to be guaranteed equal pay for equal work; also, discrimination between workers classified as employees or wage earners was to end, with all eligible for the same benefits. The chief source of funds for the new programs would be entertainment and luxury taxes: 5 percent on movies; 3 percent on sports events and bullfights; 10 percent on casinos, dance halls, and luxury cafes; 10 percent on wine and spirits; 100 percent on "luxury" dog licenses! Commenting on the new legislation, Minister Proença noted that, while it gave considerable benefits to urban sindicato workers, agriculture workers (who constituted 42 percent of the labor force), seamen, and domestic help were specifically excluded. Ironically, it was among agriculture workers, where production had lagged and yet where increases in wages had been disallowed, that the flow of illegal emigrants was the greatest.[12]

The new social assistance mission of the corporative complex and the newer concerns of the 1960s were also reflected in the Corporations Ministry's new theoretical journal, *Estudos sociais e corporativos*. Beginning in 1962 *Estudos sociais e corporativos* served as the intellectual vehicle and outlet for the new social assistance emphasis of the Corporations Ministry; indeed, its emphasis was almost exclusively on the *social* aspects and only marginally on the *corporative*. Further, there was a rather neat timetable involved: it generally took about two years from the time an article appeared in *Estudos sociais e corporativos* (let us say, dealing with the responsibility of the company in labor accidents) until the idea was formally incorporated into Portuguese labor and social security law. In fact, virtually every one of the social and corporative reforms of the 1960s discussed in the preceding paragraphs was explored first in the Centro de Estudos Sociais e Corporativos of the Junta da Acção Social and then discussed in published form in the center's journal.[13]

Estudos sociais e corporativos thus served as a sounding board for new ideas, and its personnel as the advance guard of the new form of *social* corporatism.[14] In many of its issues, indeed, which discussed national priorities and the new direction the country should take, the social preoccupation was listed as paramount and the corporative aspects either never mentioned or only in passing as part of the hallowed ritual. *Estudos sociais e corporativos* published numerous studies dealing with the more advanced social assistance programs of the other Western European nations and their application to Portugal: social security, right-to-work laws, health care systems, pension plans, even profit sharing. Moreover, as Portugal began gradually in the late 1960s to turn away from Africa and toward Europe, attention in this scholarly journal turned in parallel fashion toward questions of economic integration, the Common Market, and Portugal's place in the broader European community. *Estudos sociais e corporativos* also began to deal with some potentially revolutionary themes: the reconciliation of corporatism with a more pluralist conception of society, the implications of Marxism and class analyses for corporatist society, the Catholic social reformism ushered in with John XXIII,[15] workers' participation in company management, the need for a new dialogue on national goals, the inappropriateness of transferring essentially European-Catholic-corporatist institutions to an African context where they would not fit, and other similarly "heretical" themes. In addition, *Estudos sociais e corporativos* published some strong (and, one would think, dangerous for their authors) criticisms of the corporatist system, articles that showed the system was deficient or not working in many areas, that accused the state of employing totalitarian controls, that called for freedom for the unions, and that began to demonstrate that corporatism, rather than providing a structure of coequal representation of capital and labor, in fact served to bolster and perpetuate a system of state capitalism, resulting in enormous profits for those privileged elements who could take advantage of the system and in continued poverty and exploitation for the workers.[16]

All these changes, reforms, and new ideas were part of the general ferment beginning to stir in the Portugal of the 1960s, which would result in wholesale discontent by the 1970s. Unfortunately, little of this new movement, change, and activity had any effect on Salazar or on the way the country and the corporatist system continued to be run. More and more isolated from the events around him, Salazar either did not hear or paid no attention to the growing clamor for change. As a result, most of the innovations introduced in the corporative complex to modernize it and convert it into a genuine social assistance system remained paper documents, impressive to the uninitiated outsider but seldom implemented. The paper structure for a reformed and modernized corporatism was put in place, but little of it became operational.[17] The elaborate social assistance programs still reached only a small percentage of the population while the majority continued to live in abysmal poverty. The social security system put large numbers of bureaucrats, lawyers, and social workers on the public payroll, and perhaps it made the well-to-do feel they were fulfilling their "Christian" obligations to the poor; but it never functioned very effectively. Employers continued to exploit their employees as they had been able to do ever since the corporative experiment began in the 1930s. The expanded *caixas de previdência,* rather than providing many new benefits and expanded assistance to the poor, instead served often as a vast reserve for corrupt officials to tap and a financially strapped government to draw upon.[18] Meanwhile, to contain the growing restiveness, the secret police remained active (General Delgado was killed during this period), the censorship continued, independent political associations and activities were still prohibited, the control mechanisms (wages, price fixing, regulation, and so on) of the corporative system continued in effect, and the wars in Africa (now spread to Guinea and Mozambique) began to be increasingly felt as a severe drain on Portuguese resources.

Corporative Institutions in the 1960s:
How the System Worked

In chapter 4, we described the whole gamut of corporative institutions that came into existence in the 1930s—the Corporative Council, the Corporative Chamber, Organizations of Economic Coordination, gremios, sindicatos, ordens, casas do povo, casas dos pescadores, and so on. In subsequent chapters we traced the changes in the philosophy, functions, and role of this corporative complex and related them to broader social and political changes and pressures operating in the Portuguese system as a whole. Now it is time, from the vantage point of the 1960s, to bore into the system more deeply to see how the corporative institutions had evolved, how much (or how little) they conformed to the original conception, what functions they carried out, and, perhaps most critical, what importance (if any) they had in the broader context of Portuguese national development.

It is appropriate to ask these questions here because by this point (1966) the entire corporative complex had finally come into existence. Before, it had always been argued that lack of success in achieving some of corporatism's chief goals (class harmony, equality of capital and labor, economic self-direction, greater associability, social justice, and the like) was due to the incompleteness of the system, which itself was due to the series of "crises" through which the country had gone. Now, however, with the corporative revival of the 1950s, the program for raising social and corporative consciousness, the vast expansion of the agencies in and services provided through the Corporations Ministry, and finally the creation of the corporations themselves, the entire system seemed to have been revived and dynamized. We have already seen that much of this revival was more appearance than reality, but that does not negate the fact, as Schmitter put it, that "the system's bluff was being called."

After thirty-odd years the entire system was now in place and, except for the revolts in Africa, the regime had about run out of "crises" to explain why the lofty corporatist goals had not been realized. The excuse for rigid state authoritarianism had also been long since exhausted, and with rising gross national product, so had the one for continued abysmal poverty and social services existent largely on paper.[19] The acid test could now be applied.

The impression of a flourishing, rejuvenated system, the formal creation of the "cupolas" of the corporative system, the new training schools and publications, and the rise in the number of corporative agencies and activities, however, gave more the appearance of dynamism to the Portuguese regime than was the case in actuality. As Schmitter concluded,[20] there is little evidence that much decision-making authority was being transferred from the powerful state agencies to the corporations or to other corporative agencies, that there was any rise in "corporative consciousness" (indeed, quite the opposite), or even that many of the new agencies involved were actually performing the social assistance functions as prescribed by law. Nor is there much evidence to support the claims that the economy was becoming more self-regulating, the political system more pluralistic and decentralized, and the structure of class relations more just and harmonious. Again, by the 1960s, quite the opposite was fast becoming the case, with a flurry of new strikes and rising mass discontent. "In short," Schmitter writes, "while comparatively speaking, Portugal may be the most corporative state in existence, it has yet to become corporative in terms of the values and goals set by its own doctrine."

If we ask, therefore, what the influence of the corporative complex in general was on the decision-making process, what effect the corporations, sindicatos, gremios, and so on, had in the policy-making arena, the answer is clearly, *very little*.[21] The corporative complex, of course, did serve as an important control mechanism; it sometimes exercised a certain power to modify various acts; it performed, as we shall see in more detail in the conclusion, various preventive, cooptive, and preemptive functions; and it did carry out some important social services and labor activities. But its role in the policy- and decision-making areas was severely circumscribed. One must of course here keep in mind the other meaning of corporatism discussed in this book, the *natural* corporatist tradition to which the Estado Novo continued largely to conform. Nevertheless, the conclusion drawn from both the documentary evidence and from widespread interviews of both the Portuguese governing elite and knowledgeable foreign observers is clear: the corporative complex, that set of manifestly "corporative" agencies and institutions established in the 1930s, was, when it functioned at all, simply not very important in the critical political and policy-making arenas. With further qualifications, this conclusion would probably be valid in fact for the entire period of the corporative state from the 1930s on, but it was particularly true in the 1960s during the later years of Salazar.

Let us look then at how the various agencies of the corporative system had evolved over time and what their actual functions had become.[22] Later (in chapter 10), we shall be looking more closely at the relations of this corporative complex to the broader national system.

CORPORATIVE THEORY AND IDEOLOGY   By the 1960s reference to corporatist theory and ideology, in contrast to the "revival" years of the 1950s, had almost entirely disappeared from the speeches made by Salazar or his cabinet ministers, from official declarations, and from scholarly tomes. It was as though the official rhetoric and ideology of the 1930s, while never explicitly rejected, had been conveniently set aside and all but forgotten. About the only agency which still evoked some of the old slogans was the Corporations Ministry itself, and even here the meaning and substance had been radically altered.

In a 1960 study, for example, published by the Corporations Ministry and entitled "The Problem of the Fundamentals of Corporatism," [23] Antonio José de Brito wrote that he was no longer sure what corporatism was, arguing that it was not a complete political theory or a way of managing the economy. Corporatism was closest, he said, to being a concept of society and its ends; more than that, it was a normative social system based on the ideas of unity, order, and hierarchy which in the Portugal of the 1960s, Brito stated, were no longer relevant. This was a strong critique, not only examining carefully the philosophical basis of corporatism but examining it in a new light, in a changed society from that "sleepier" version of the 1930s, and with new questions being asked from distinct philosophical approaches. The Brito critique was part of a larger reexamination of the corporatist system, but it also was reflective of something more than that: an entirely new generation had by now arisen with none of the corporatist faith and assumptions that Salazar's had and no longer inclined to view the corporatist system with equanimity.

The same and other themes were expressed in the Corporations Ministry's professional journal, *Estudos sociais e corporativos*. In keeping with the social assistance focus of the ministry itself, the journal seldom dealt with corporatism per se and concentrated, we have seen, almost exclusively on the new social concerns. The lead editorial in volume 1, number 2 (1962), for example, which sought to identify the current national priorities, listed them as social assistance, improved living standards, education, and national unity, but never once mentioned corporatism or corporative implementation.[24] In a later article the argument was advanced that all of Portuguese social action could not be handled through the corporative agencies, that labor issues had been subordinated to the state's priorities, that the corporative complex had been largely bypassed in virtually all policy decisions, and even that corporatism might no longer be applicable to the more complex, urban, middle-class, and otherwise more differentiated society of the 1960s.[25] Other articles expressed similar skepticism, and in private their authors were often inclined to state their criticisms even more strongly.[26]

Corporations ministers Veiga de Macedo (late 1950s) and Gonçalves Proença (1960s) usually managed to remain true to the older corporative faith in their public statements, but in private they too were skeptical. They were ambitious, rising politicians who employed the usual corporatist slogans as a matter more of form than conviction, and even in their public statements they had so reinterpreted corporatism as to make it all but unrecognizable to the older generation of Salazaristas. Gonçalves Proença especially stressed the social service functions to the exclusion of almost all else, arguing that the functions of political representation had never been given to the corporative agencies and that in the economic sphere "the corporative system has been practically circumscribed." To compensate somewhat for these diminished functions, he also devised a plan for the extension of the corporative scheme to the colonies. It was the social assistance function and orientation, however, that the minister most strongly stressed during his decade in office and in his numerous excursions and speeches throughout the country. But even these activities, one suspects, were used more to build, through favors and patronage, a political base for Gonçalves Proença himself rather than out of any deep ideological conviction.[27]

By the 1960s, therefore, corporatist theory and ideology were being largely neglected and/or superseded. Significantly, the corporatist ideas were rejected by both labor *and* business elements.[28] In addition, the repudiation or loss of faith in corporatism crossed the generations: the youth and university students rejected it as outdated, old-fashioned, discredited, and elitist; middle-aged professionals, businessmen, and politicians like Gonçalves Proença could still evoke the old slogans when they had to, though they no longer conveyed much conviction; and perhaps most surprising, even old-line corporatists like Salazar, Caetano, Pires Cardoso, and Costa Leite no longer viewed corporatism as the driving force and ideological underpinning for their action it once was.[29] Even though no one could say so publicly, corporatism as an ideology of the regime and of the Portuguese people had been largely abandoned all across the board.

THE CORPORATIVE COUNCIL   The Corporative Council had been established in 1934 (see chapter 4) as the highest coordinating agency of the corporative system. Early on, during Teotonio Pereira's period as Corporations Subsecretary, various efforts were made at interministerial coordination and cooperation and, especially, at infusing *all* ministries with the corporative consciousness and way of doing things. Few of these efforts had much payoff, and in any case they were not carried out by the Corporative Council, which as of 1938, in Marcello Caetano's words, had not begun to carry out any important function. That situation of inactivity continued until the corporative revival of the mid-1950s when the Council's membership and functions were revised.[30] The Council was henceforth to consist of the minister of the presidency, the minister of the overseas, the minister of economy, and the minister of corporations. The fact that the ministries were specified and that there were few included reflected the limited role perceived for the corporative complex by this period and the abandonment of the Pereira idea that the entire system, including *all* ministries, needed to be corporatized. The Council's new functions were to suggest reforms, resolve disputes in the application of corporative law, approve the charters of the new corporations, and designate the *procuradores* for the Corporative Chamber. In fact, the agency functioned after this reform about as it did before, and that means not at all. There is no indication from the literature, the interview data, or the field research that the Corporative Council *ever* performed any useful or important functions.

THE CHAMBER OF CORPORATIONS   The Corporative Chamber was established in the 1930s as an advisory body based on an elaborate system of corporatist or functional representation. Unlike the Corporative Council, the Chamber functioned more or less throughout the entire era of the New State, but the functions and roles it carried out were often considerably at variance with those envisioned by its early designers.

The Chamber's chief function by law and constitution was to issue advisory opinions (*pareceres*) on pending legislation, especially in technical areas where its members had particular competence. The debate on such legislation (such as in the case of Pires Cardoso's famous parecer on the need to establish the corporations) was often sharp, on a high level, and with at least some impact on policy. Although the Chamber's opinions were strictly advisory, the government could ignore them often only at considerable risk and embarrassment. Many times, however, the government did choose to accept such temporary embarrassment, and the pareceres of the Corporative Chamber were then ignored or reversed by either the president or the National Assembly. In addition, since in virtually all critical policy areas the government operated largely by means of decree-law without consultation with either legislative body, the range of issues on which the Chamber had any impact was always severely circumscribed. Despite these limitations, however, the opinions issued by the Chamber did have an impact on many technical policy areas, increasingly so in the 1960s as Salazar withdrew more and more from the daily administration of government and especially after Caetano came to power. The committee work of its various sections and subsections, all structured in terms of the corporate interests represented, constituted a significant input particularly as regards routine, "everyday" legislation. Normally, in those policy areas where the Chamber or its members had special knowledge—and which did not impinge upon Salazar's power or that of the Army and implied modest and noncontroversial changes—the government was often inclined to accept the Chamber's recommendations.[31]

As a body of "political notables," however, the Chamber's influence may have been even greater. Philippe C. Schmitter's careful analysis of the social and occupational background of the Corporations Chamber's members throws further light on this.[32] For the fact is that the Chamber was not so much an agency for the representation of various corporate groups as a "home" for administrative officials of the regime and local notables beholden to it. The overwhelming bulk of its membership (about two-thirds) was appointed directly by the government from the ranks of the municipal councils and the state administration. Only about one-third were appointed by the corporate agencies, and before 1960 and the creation of the corporations even these were usually selected by the government from a list of "acceptables" submitted to it. In short, as Schmitter says, the Corporative Chamber was not quite a body representative of organized corporate interests and responsible to them but a kind of "national honor society" or functional-administrative-intellectual "college of cardinals" appointed for their usefulness to and status in the state.

Schmitter found from his background study that the Chamber had an urban and metropolitan bias, that unskilled and manual workers, however, were almost totally unrepresented, that peasants, tenant farmers, and other marginal elements had no spokesmen at all. The military profession was consistently well represented (more so in the Assembly), professors and engineers always constituted a considerable bloc, and local notables such as lawyers and physicians were prominent. Agrarian and landed interests constituted roughly 7–10 percent of the total, a relatively modest percentage, though it should be noted that many of the lawyers, physicians, and military officials also owned land. Industrialists and merchants (also often landowners) constituted some 15–20 percent of the total, with the percentage rising by the 1960s. Perhaps the key to understanding the Corporative Chamber, however, lay in the high number of ex-ministers, high-level civil servants, prominent politicians, administrators, university rectors, local notables, and middle to higher level bureaucrats among its members. Roughly half or more of the total membership came from these ranks. The Chamber was thus dominated by agents of the state and by those closely attached to the regime. It served as a sinecure for out-of-office politicians and administrators whom the regime kept loyal by retaining them on the government payroll, as a resting place for "in-transit" bureaucrats, and as a training ground for new politicians and young lawyers and professors whom the regime wanted to bring along. The position of *procurador* (spokesman for one or another corporate interest) was often given to young, beginning lawyer-politicians learning the ropes of the Portuguese regime. It is clear that the Chamber represented not so much the corporative associational life of the country as it did those interests and individuals whom the regime wished to reward, whose loyalty it could count on, or whom it wished to coopt. The mechanisms of representational selection, as Schmitter concludes, lay firmly in the hands of the regime and not in any grass-roots organizations.[33]

As a policy-making or influencing body, therefore, particularly on the important issues, the Corporative Chamber did not play a critical role. As a convenient body of regime loyalists, it occasionally could modify and amend government initiatives, but it was hardly an independent body (it was never meant to be) nor was it really representative of the nation's corporate interests (which it *was* meant to be). It was a body of local notables, influentials, administrators, and the like, hardly representative of the nation but only of its elite or ruling classes. Even the few skilled workers whose sindicato organizations were accorded a place in the Chamber's corporate organizational scheme were most often represented by lawyers and bureaucrats rather than by their own members. The peasants and workers themselves, Corporative Chamber officials and representatives reported in interviews, not used to speaking in such a public forum, either had nothing to say when invited to state their views, or else—for instance in the hearings on agrarian reform—agreed wholeheartedly with their *patrões* in full support of the existing landholding system. In the Corporative Chamber, as elsewhere in Portugal, the entire system was biased in favor of the governing class, the *homens bons,* who by wealth, status, and tradition "knew what was best" for their humble workers. The Chamber was thus an interesting and in some respects even important body, but it was not a major channel through which the various entities of the corporative complex had any strong impact in national decision making.[34]

THE CORPORATIONS   The 1933 Constitution had declared Portugal to be a unitary *and* a corporative republic. This implied that Portugal was an "organic whole" but made up of men differing in their various roles and functions who were "marshaled together in their different ranks." The nation was to be above the tumult associated with class or party warfare; but since man was a social animal he must have some form of association (not necessarily political or class based) by which to express his interests. Hence, the idea of the corporations, in which men engaged in the same or kindred activities could be represented.[35]

Each corporation was to be, at least in theory, the capstone or cupola of an arch, the two pillars of which would be constituted by organizations of employers and employees, respectively. At the bottom of the employees' pillar were the sindicatos and casas, regionally based and grouped into federations and unions. On the employers' side were the gremios, similarly based. From the sindicato and gremio base, building up through the unions and federations, the corporations, forming the arch or link between the two, were erected. The corporations, in turn, were to be represented in the Corporative Chamber and so on up to the pinnacles of the system.

Of course, in practice the structure never developed this way, for reasons we already know. For twenty-three years Portugal was a corporative state without corporations, and even when the first corporations were finally authorized, they were still very slow in getting started. Thus, although the decree-law authorizing the corporations was issued in 1956, it was not until two years later that the first one actually came into existence. Business groups especially were wary and suspicious and reacted with hostility to the plan to create the corporations. They met with Salazar, issued the usual protest that the changes would be upsetting to the economy, and sought through a variety of ways to subvert this new corporative reform. Hence, the organization of the Corporations of Commerce and of Industry was postponed until the early 1960s, purposely so as to give businessmen and industrialists time to adjust to, or gain control of, these new bureaucratic entities.[36]

The early corporations began with no funds or contributions. They were forced to secure loans from their member gremios (thus making them dependent on and beholden to the gremios) and from the government institute or junta responsible for that particular branch of production. The gremios were not eager to put their own financial resources into the corporations and only did so when forced to by the government representative assigned to them. Later, the corporations began receiving regular funds from the appropriate government ministry (commerce, industry, and so forth), but as late as 1966 most of them were still seeking to liquidate the earlier loans. Corporations officials claimed their precarious financial standing prevented them from doing anything of major importance.[37]

The corporations faced numerous other problems. They were insufficiently institutionalized and became just another rather unpretentious part of a large bureaucratic labyrinth. There was still little corporative consciousness and the corporations were not at all integrated into the national system. There were even now few gremios and sindicatos, and many grumbled that even after twenty-three years the creation of the corporations was premature, that it was foolish to erect the arch before the base had genuinely come into existence. Others argued that it was now too late, that the corporations should have been created earlier or not at all.

In an especially searching criticism sponsored and published by the Corporation of Industry, a young lawyer named Joaquim Paulo Dias da Silva Pinto, who would later serve as Minister of Corporations and would be seen as a possible successor to Marcello Caetano, asked why there were six corporations initially; why these particular six; why not other groupings; why was there no logic to the system? Why was agriculture not divided into several corporations reflecting the diverse products raised and the sociological reality of the country? Silva Pinto also questioned the way the corporations would be represented in the Corporative Chamber and raised the troubling issue of whether the corporations would now replace the government's Organizations of Economic Coordination. Silva Pinto asked other disturbing questions and concluded that the entire scheme was overly rigid, provided little flexibility, and was being unevenly implemented. He complained of the few functions assigned to the corporations; that the corporations had not yet been able to have their representatives seated, as required by the law, on any of the government's policy-making bodies; that the new corporations were occasionally consulted on pending matters but had no say in the final decisions. While these issues were being raised by business-industrial spokesmen at the public level, these same elements were meeting with Salazar and other high government officials privately to ensure that the new corporations would not entail any upsetting of the economy, which meant, of course, that they should not interfere with private profit making.[38]

Even with some of the early problems straightened around, therefore, the newly constituted corporations were only weakly established and never performed or lived up to the vast range of functions assigned to them in law and theory. Each corporation had a president, a governing council, directors and councils for its various sections, a disciplinary junta, a planning staff, study sections, and so on. Within each section and in the governing council, workers and employers were supposed to be equally represented. The corporation itself was supposed to be self-governing. But in fact, (1) *never* (until 1973, just before the coup) was there a single corporation president who came from the employee side; invariably presidents were selected who were gremio or business leaders.[39] (2) The governing councils were overwhelmingly dominated by business and bureaucratic elites. (3) The state representative in the corporation was listed right below its president and had the power to override him; representatives of the state regulatory commissions and institutes also held veto power in the supposedly self-governing corporations; the corporations were subject to the fiscalization of the Corporations Ministry, required ministerial sanction to begin operating, and could be dissolved by the government if they acted "contrary to corporative principles." (4) The "corporate" subsections were also dominated by business interests or governmental representatives, with employees again having little say. (5) The planning groups and work-study sections were never adequately staffed. (6) The corporations were never really "fleshed out" institutionally, nor did they ever become focal centers or important decision-making agencies. Their offices remained small (often a single floor or apartment in a modest building), their staffs were small (fifteen to forty full-time employees), they were located on unpretentious side streets and far from the centers of power, and the activities at the offices were minimal. The corporations lacked *movimento* and dynamism. Frequently, their constituent gremios were far more impressive and powerful organizations than the parent corporations. The private chambers of commerce, merchants' and industrialists' associations were also often far stronger than the corporations in this supposedly corporatist system. Physically and institutionally, the corporations never really got off the ground.[40]

In terms of the functions performed much of the same applies, along with a special twist reflecting the already established biases of the entire system. As conceived in corporative theory, the corporations were to represent, coordinate, and defend the interests of those integrated into them. And in the organic laws for the corporations promulgated subsequent to the 1956 decree, the corporations were charged with fomenting corporative organization and consciousness, preparing *pareceres,* promoting the interests of the membership, advising the government on matters affecting them, coordinating prices and production, and resolving wage and labor disputes. In actuality, there is no evidence that the government ever seriously attempted turning over such important functions to the corporations. It was the state, not the corporations, that continued to determine wages, prices, production, and so on, that through its Organizations of Economic Coordination regulated all aspects of the economy, and that made all important decisions. The corporations could occasionally offer technical advice and give consent, but they could not effectively dissent. On most issues, however, they were not consulted at all, and the body through which their interests were supposed to be represented, the Corporative Chamber, had only limited influence. They were supposed also to be represented on the various juntas, commissions, and institutes through which the regime ran the economy; and again on some issues—development planning, imports and exports, some areas of production, technical matters—the corporations were actually consulted. But they never performed any of the central representational, coordinating, or decision-making functions that corporative ideologues like Pires Cardoso advocated. The state reserved all those powers to itself.[41]

The limited functions the corporations *did* perform were in keeping with the nature of the whole corporative system as it had evolved from the 1930s on. That is, they tended to favor large business and wealthy interests at the expense of laboring elements. The market studies the corporations carried out, the explorations into various sectors of the economy, the published volumes issued by the corporations, were all of more interest to businessmen than to workers. The weighing of Portugal's entry into the Common Market, the compiling of trade and commercial statistics, the representation at international economic conferences—these were hardly functions that benefited the lower classes. In short, just as they had since the 1930s, the business groups first resisted and effectively toned down the new corporative plans, and then they simply took over and coopted them. The scenario outlined repeatedly by Ralph Nader, Theodore Lowi, Grant McConnell, and others in American society—namely, the take-over of the regulatory commissions by those they were designed to regulate—has some remarkable parallels in the Portuguese corporatist context.[42]

In addition to the six original corporations (Agriculture, Commerce, Industry, Fishing and Canning, Credit and Insurance, and Transport and Tourism), two more had been created in 1959 (Press and Graphic Arts, Entertainment [*Espectáculos*]), and the three final noneconomic ones in 1966 (Assistance; Science, Letters, and Arts; and Physical Education and Sports). Salazar took a great deal of pride in the creation of these final additions to the system, and in 1966 he said, "In our century, we are the only corporative revolution that triumphed." However, the most recent corporations were implemented slowly, irregularly, and no more effectively than had been the earlier ones, and the Corporation of Science, Letters, and Arts never did really begin to function, largely because of the opposition of the university community and of the sheer difficulty of organizing such an inherently individualistic sector. Rather than force a confrontation, the regime simply did not implement the new corporation's enabling act and allowed matters to run largely according to tradition and on a laissez-faire basis.[43] There were no plans during Caetano's rule for the creation of any additional corporations.

The corporations never became the focal points or even the "cupolas" of the Portuguese system, and their functions remained limited. There is considerable evidence, in fact, aside from corporatist rhetoric, that that is how the system was purposely designed.[44] That is, although Salazar wanted to complete the formal edifice of the corporative structure for reasons of both personal and national pride, he never intended to give the corporations any real power. Even with these limitations, however, the corporations did come to perform some useful services, chiefly in the areas of consultations with various government agencies, coordination of certain economic issues, and representation through the Corporative Chamber. In this sense, the corporations helped institutionalize what in the United States remains still largely informal and unregulated, namely, the triangular consultation between interest groups, legislative committees, and executive agencies, as outlined by J. Lieper Freeman and others.[45] In Portugal this structure was often weak and ineffective; nevertheless, the corporations were functioning organizations, with offices and staffs, with various branches and bureaucratic interests, with a variety of functions (however secondary) to perform.[46] An institutionalized system had grown up which could not simply be swept away without the effects being felt or new agencies created to replace them. Given the general weakness of Portuguese associational life, that would likely prove a difficult task.

THE MINISTRY OF CORPORATIONS   In the corporative system the entire economically engaged population was supposed to be organized in sindicatos, gremios, casas, ordens, and the like and, through these entities, plugged into the corporations, each of which was pledged in law and theory to represent the collective interest of its particular trade or profession. In practice, however, the membership was never given any degree of participation or democratic control and the corporations were run, like virtually every other entity in the corporative complex, as agencies of the state administered by officials approved by the Ministry of Corporations. These appointments were based primarily on political loyalty to the regime, on personal influence and patronage, and to some extent on administrative skills or technical expertise, but generally with little attention to overall merit or the views of the membership.[47]

Membership in the appropriate sindicato or gremio, including the payment of dues, was compulsory for all those engaged in a similar area of activity or trade. While the funds thus collected were supposed, particularly in the 1960s, to cover expanded social services, unemployment insurance, and the like, most of the money actually went for administrative overhead, chiefly in the form of salaries for an inflated corporate bureaucracy. The Ministry of Corporations had developed over the years into a vast sinecure agency, a place of seemingly endless opportunities to pad the government payroll or to siphon off funds into private pockets, a haven for the friends, cronies, and relatives of those in power, a kind of vast, inadvertent "social security" agency on top of and overlapping with the real social assistance functions performed by the ministry. The annual cost of this huge and often cumbersome apparatus, which at every level paralleled the regular government administration, grew voraciously during the 1950s and 1960s with the creation of a host of new programs, until the totals reached approximately one-third of the national budget.[48]

Under the corporate system, all branches of production and economic activity, from farming and handicrafts to foreign trade, were snugly divided into rigid, almost watertight compartments. The local gremio, acting under the regulations and guidelines handed down by the appropriate junta, commission, or institute (for wheat, wine, fruits, rice, fish, manufacturing, or whatever), would tell the producer what and how much he could produce, to whom he should sell, and at what price. Neither buyers nor producers were free to trade in an open market but had to deal where they were told to deal by the state agency, selling or buying prescribed quotas at fixed prices. No wholesaler handling wheat, for instance, could exceed his purchase quota unless he could find an unfulfilled quota that might be turned over to him for a commission.[49]

The antisocial, sometimes disastrous effects of the corporative system were perhaps most striking in agriculture, building in such legal and bureaucratic rigidities as to retard the adoption of improved farming methods, stifle initiative, and force severe drops in production.[50] Although the system consciously and purposely hobbled free enterprise, it provided almost unlimited opportunities for private enrichment through graft and favors to persons with the right connections. The red tape, bureaucracy, and paper work involved in acquiring an official stamp of approval were stupendous and were again consciously used by the regime to extend its control, particularly over the business community. The consequence was not only to debilitate substantially the incentives for efficiency and improvement but also to overwhelm Portugal (far more so even than most Latin countries) in legalisms and *papelada,* to institutionalize graft and favoritism at the highest levels (not Salazar himself, but at cabinet and agency levels), to elevate the state bureaucrat with the power to grant or withhold such approvals to a position of great power, and inevitably to favor those with connections and contacts in this vast labyrinth.[51] Those few with such connections had always been the chief beneficiaries of the corporative system, but they still chafed mightily at all the restrictions involved. At the heart of this entire bureaucratic structure, of course, lay the Corporations Ministry.

The corporations establishment had mushroomed since its first small and personal beginnings as a subsecretariat under Teotonio Pereira. With its conversion into a full-fledged ministry in 1951 and, particularly in the late 1950s and 1960s, with the organization of a whole gamut of social assistance programs, it grew into a large, complex bureaucracy with a wide range of interests and activities. The 1960s particularly was a period when much of the corporative and social security infrastructure came into existence, when the number of agencies, offices, and services being rendered multiplied. The Corporations Ministry came to be involved in a wide range of activities, including social security, labor relations, professional training, insurance, unemployment, housing, medical care, education, social assistance, research, health and hygiene, collective bargaining, the overseas provinces, leadership training, vocational training, pensions, and a dozen more.[52] What was called a labor or social assistance ministry in other countries was called the Corporations Ministry in Portugal. Though the labels were different, the range of services was essentially the same. Tradition, continuity, and a certain national pride were the reasons pointed to by the Portuguese in the late 1960s and early 1970s for retaining the corporative title—not any longer any deep commitment to the corporative ideology.[53]

Perhaps the high point came on September 23, 1966, when President Thomaz dedicated the new Corporations Palace, the twenty-one-story skyscraper that at the time was Lisbon's tallest building and that served as the Ministry of Corporations' new home. The dedication came on the thirty-third anniversary of the promulgation of the Portuguese Labor Statute. The building contained 370 offices, and the move into the new quarters enabled the regime to centralize a variety of services previously scattered around the city. There were some 4,000 employees working in the ministry, an agency whose various functions had become highly rationalized, specialized, bureaucratized, and complex.[54] Soon the ministry's operations had expanded beyond the capacity of even the new building to house them all, and many offices were relocated in annexes and buildings again scattered around the city. Apropos of the comments made in the preceding paragraph, of the twenty-one floors in the Corporations Ministry, only one of them by the 1970s was devoted to corporative activity. That is another indication of the changing functions of the corporative system and of the gradual shift away from manifestly corporative concerns and toward other functions.

Three areas especially deserve our attention here: the corporative activities of the ministry, its role in the area of labor relations, and its social security and assistance programs. The manifestly corporative aspects of the ministry were rather limited, consisting chiefly of the training of new corporative leaders and organizers, efforts to instill corporative consciousness, and the publication of materials dealing with corporative themes. Under the 1956 Plan for Corporative Formation several hundred young leaders were trained over the years to help fill the gap in low and middle-level administrative leadership that had been so painfully apparent in the corporative system over the years. But for the rest, little occurred. There is no evidence to point to a rise in corporative consciousness during the 1960s; in fact, we know the contrary was true. The volume of publications also dropped off, and even those few that were issued frequently had little to do with corporatism. This author's own experience doing research, interviewing, and observing in the Corporations Ministry led him to conclude impressionistically that the vast majority of its employees had no conception whatsoever of what corporatism meant—nor did they even care, nor did their not caring matter in terms of their own jobs and responsibilities. Only a handful of men in decision-making positions had any conception of the background and philosophical and social bases of corporatism, and even they were of a persuasion and conception no longer in keeping with Salazar's and a traditional, backward-looking 1930s concept.[55]

The role of the Corporations Ministry in labor relations was critical, principally through the Instituto Nacional do Trabalho e Previdência (INTP). Through its labor tribunals, the special corporative commissions appointed by the INTP (numbering over 600 by the 1960s), its supervision of union elections, and its general overseeing of all labor relations, to say nothing of the dictatorial controls enforced by other agencies of the regime, the control of the Corporations Ministry and of the state over all aspects of trade union and collective bargaining affairs was well-nigh complete. Government funds were critical for the day-to-day functioning of the sindicatos, government agents and intervenors were assigned to every sindicato and gremio, sindicato elections were carefully supervised by the state with the leadership usually "selected" from a government-approved slate, wages were set by government boards, and so on. These rules meant that the elaborate ideology and legislation providing for "self-government," coequal representation of employers and employees, negotiated collective contracts, and so forth, were largely meaningless.[56]

It is to be emphasized that these were political decisions reflecting the structure of Portuguese society and power within the regime and were not necessarily inherent within the corporative system. The fact is that the existing corporative structure could just as easily have favored workers (which it increasingly did under Caetano); instead, under Salazar, "the system" was on the side of employers, austerity, and the status quo, while the corporative and labor laws that proclaimed equality of representation were rendered inoperative. The sindicatos, for example, as provided for in the law, would periodically present their requests to the gremios for a renegotiation of their collective contracts, and the gremios would conveniently ignore them. The law further stipulated that, if one of the parties to a collective contract failed to respond to the legal request of the other within sixty days, then the Corporations Ministry could apply sanctions and an arbitration commission would be assigned to negotiate the differences. The fact is that sanctions were never applied against the gremios (they *were* against the sindicatos), and the government simply refused to enforce its own corporative laws, thus in effect supporting the illegal actions of the gremios in refusing to respond and perpetrating low wage rates in a time of rising inflation.

When the Corporations Ministry *did* step in and appoint an arbitration commission, moreover, the arbiters invariably enforced the government's austerity and wage control programs, also prejudicial against workers with fixed incomes. In part, this posture was due to the increasingly capitalistic nature of the Portuguese system and the need for a low-paid work force during a time of accelerating industrialization; in part, it was aimed at protecting Portugal's small, inefficient, family-based enterprises (and the traditional social order which this implied) which by this time even in such traditional industries as textiles, fishing, agriculture, and agricultural processing were no longer competitive; in part, also, it was due to the power motives of Salazar and the whole web of authoritarian controls now in effect; and finally, it had to do with the sheer paralysis of the regime in the 1960s. In any case, during this period the corporative system seldom functioned, and when it did, it functioned in a way that favored business and industrial interests at the expense of their workers.[57]

The major shift in the Corporations Ministry in the 1960s was the trend toward social services. As the ministry took on more and more social service functions, the older paternalism of the landlord and the *patrão* began increasingly to be superseded by the paternalism of the state. The ministry itself was rebaptized as the Ministry of Corporations *and* Social Welfare (Previdência), and the long-term trend during the last two decades was toward a social security and assistance focus and away from corporative activities. Along with this shift in focus came the creation of a great variety of new social assistance agencies and offices and the hiring of great numbers of technicians specializing in these areas but with almost no acquaintance with corporative law, theory, or ideology. Of course, many of the new social assistance programs existed more on paper than in actual implementation, but still a start on some of them was made and the infrastructure fashioned for a greater emphasis on social programs under Salazar's successor. Indeed, by the end of the decade an appropriate name for the ministry, reflecting its chief functions, would have been "Ministry of Labor Relations and Social Assistance." Its manifestly corporative activities were by then so minimal that, other than for sentimental reasons and some nationalistic and political ones, the name "Corporatism" could just as well have been dropped. Corporative activities were no longer a major part of the Corporations Ministry's activities.

The Corporations Ministry had thus grown to be a large bureaucratic organization, with all the numerous functions, divisions, sections, subsections, and so on, that are a part of a major ministry in any modern state. Its functions lay chiefly in the labor relations and social assistance areas and were comparable to the functions of labor and social assistance ministries in other avowedly noncorporative systems. Under Salazar, many of the ministry's functions had been abused or neglected, but these reflected more the preferences and structural conditions of the Salazar regime than any inherent prejudices in the corporatist principles. The institutional basis had thus been laid for a system of labor relations based on genuine collective bargaining and for far vaster social assistance-social security programs; and under Caetano the system came to function more and more in favor of the workers. The vast social services of the ministry implied also that, while the corporative label could be abolished, the social services performed by that ministry would have to be continued in some fashion. If not, then the Portuguese masses would be in even worse condition than they were under Salazar.

THE ORGANIZATIONS OF ECONOMIC COORDINATION   The Organizations of Economic Coordination had been established in 1936 as "precorporative" intermediary organizations between the state and the still nascent corporative complex. The numerous commissions, juntas, and institutes served as a means for the further extension of state power and control over virtually all areas of the national economy. As the economy developed and became more complex, the strength and influence of these agencies grew correspondingly, particularly since the corporative agencies themselves were kept weak and little power was ever turned over to them. It was the Organizations of Economic Coordination, and not the corporative entities, that set wages, fixed prices, and regulated production, and that served also as the instruments for the growth of etatism and state corporatism, rather than the freer *corporatisme d'association* as envisioned in the early doctrine.[58]

The Organizations of Economic Coordination served as the Portuguese equivalent for the plethora of regulatory agencies, bureaus, and so on, that have grown up in other modern systems for the regulation and coordination of national economic life. Even after the wartime emergency in Portugal, these agencies continued to regulate tightly the economic life of the country. Prices, wages, quotas, and so forth, were set, not through any free market mechanisms or through negotiations between employers and employees, but by the agencies of economic coordination. The sindicatos were, of course, powerless to resist, and even the strong gremios were eventually subordinated to the power of these agencies. Should a gremio have some plans for its sector of the economy which were not in accord with the government's overall policy, a clash was sure to occur, with the government agency almost always prevailing. In 1958 a clash between a gremio and the agency of economic coordination charged with regulating olive oil prices and production led to the disappearance of that product from the market for a time. Although frequently an accommodation was reached with the gremio in such cases, the overall result was a further extension of state power. The existence and power of these agencies, which functioned outside the corporative scheme of things, were often seen as evidence the corporative system itself was not working.[59]

The assumption had been that these "precorporative" agencies would disappear once the corporative bodies were strong enough to perform the regulating and coordinating functions on their own. Hence, with the actual creation of the corporations beginning in 1956, the argument was renewed for the abolition of the Organizations of Economic Coordination. This was not just an ideological argument between corporative "purists" and the defenders of absolute state power but, in the usual elliptical way that political debate had to be carried on under the dictatorship, involved some real interests and issues. Those who defended the role of the Organizations of Economic Coordination were also defending the Salazar regime and the directions it had taken. Those arguing for the abolition of these agencies and the devolution of their power upon the corporations were often liberals and social democrats urging a relaxation of state controls, indirectly criticizing the dictatorship and its excessive power, and doing all this under the guise of a debate on corporative principles. The smoke screen was, of course, recognized on both sides, and the results also were predictable: the corporations were created, but little power and authority in economic matters were ever given to them, and meanwhile the government continued to regulate virtually all areas of economic life through the Organizations of Economic Coordination.[60]

Although the Organizations of Economic Coordination remained the chief instruments for coordinating, regulating, and "disciplining" the economy and its component sectors (which helps explain why the corporations had so little to do), some concessions were made to corporatist representation. By law the various corporate units were allowed a permanently designated representative on the appropriate *junta,* commission, or institute. It is here that the corporate system perhaps most significantly "plugged into" the decision-making apparatus. Of course, these representatives were also often selected by the government, and there is again no doubt that, in this as other centers of the system, gremio, moneyed, and status quo-oriented interests had far stronger representation than the sindicatos or those who advocated change. Further, it must be remembered that the broad guidelines of macroeconomic policy were set not in these agencies but elsewhere in the system, still chiefly by Salazar. Nevertheless, in the day-to-day running of the Portuguese economy, in the setting of quotas, the fixing of prices and wages, the allocation of subsidies, the determination of the location and type of capital investment, the regulation of production, and so on, the Organizations of Economic Coordination, and through them particularly the gremios, played an important role. Although, as Schmitter emphasizes, their influence was generally confined to the modification and implementation of policy established elsewhere, that influence was frequently considerable and afforded those with the right connections opportunities to make their voices heard, to shape certain areas of policy, and to profit from the system. Like the Corporative Chamber, the Organizations of Economic Coordination provided a means for institutionalizing certain strong interests, again particularly the gremios, into the system. They helped provide another point of access and interchange, especially for business and commercial interests, allowing them to be "in" on decisions, to gain experience and knowledge of how this cumbersome bureaucratic apparatus worked, and, in classic patrimonialist fashion, to blur the private and public domains. The web of Organizations of Economic Coordination was probably the primary decision-making arena in which the corporatist bodies could make their influence felt.[61]

THE GRASS-ROOTS CORPORATIVE AGENCIES Proceeding from top to bottom in the Portuguese corporative hierarchy, we turn now to such grass-roots agencies as the sindicatos, gremios, ordens, casas do povo, casas dos pescadores, and the various uniões and federations of these agencies.

As the name implies, these grass-roots associations were to form the base of the corporative state, the foundation upon which the entire system would rest. The official myth was that the sindicatos, gremios, casas, and the like were to arise spontaneously and naturally, in Fryer and McGowan-Pinheiro's words, as a kind of social contract entered into by the people concerned.[62] The fact is, of course, they did not arise spontaneously at all but came into existence largely through government fiat. They never served as the "base" of the system; indeed, genuine grass-roots participation was specifically ruled out by the regime. The role, functions, strength, activities of all these agencies remained severely circumscribed, in fact, throughout the entire history of the Estado Novo, to some extent by design and also because of other requirements of the system. Let us look in more detail at these "grass-roots corporative agencies" as they existed in the 1960s.

The first thing to emphasize about the sindicato organizations (usually translated as "trade unions," although that is not entirely accurate) is just how weak they were. *Never*, in fact, had the regime permitted the sindicatos to develop any strong *and* independent bargaining power. Thanks to an exceedingly careful study by two young Portuguese sociologists, who based their conclusions on the government's own statistics, we have some very solid information on this score.[63] First of all, this analysis points out, the fact that the sindicatos were organized by professional category and by district made them of necessity very small in numbers. Second, the small size, geographically and in terms of membership, had given them a role in the system that had been "of little relevance." In the entire country as of 1969 (roughly corresponding with the end of Salazar's rule) there were a total of only 325 sindicatos (not all of them actually functioning), encompassing some 841,818 members, or slightly over 10 percent of the total population.[64] The average size of the sindicatos was 2,590 members; only eight had a membership over 20,000, and 3.6 percent contained 36 percent of the number of syndicalized workers. The rest tended toward very small size, reinforced by the purely local base of their organization. The result, in the eyes of this study, was the "atomization" (*pulverização*) of the sindicatos and of the working class more generally.

The study of the two sociologists went on to show that for the majority of job categories encompassed, there was only one local sindicato. The only local sindicatos that had any influence were those located in the capital city. Moreover, the only sindicatos organized on a national basis were precisely those that were the smallest and weakest. The study also examined the financial situation of the sindicatos, finding it woefully inadequate and contributing to their overall weakness. There were simply insufficient funds to engage in *any* kind of activities or even to pay the officers. At the regional união and federation level, the study found, the situation was no better. According to the 1969 figures, there were twenty-three federations and six uniões in the country, encompassing 199 of the sindicatos. The study found, however, that the uniões and federations existed more on paper than in reality and that they had few funds available, inadequate staff, and sometimes even no permanent office. In conclusion, the study reiterated the atomization and weakness (*fraqueza*) of the entire sindicato structure, its organizational and financial feebleness (*debilidade*), its fragmented, localized basis, the small percentage of the total work force encompassed within sindicato ranks, and hence the inability of the sindicatos to make their voice heard in national affairs. The report concluded with a call for the "necessary restructuring" of the entire system.

The second aspect to note about the sindicato system was the degree of government control over it, made easier, of course, by the sindicatos' small size and localized basis. In a devastating report criticizing Portugal for violating both the spirit and the letter of the International Labor Organization's conventions regarding the rights of labor organizations and of labor freedom, the International Committee for Free Trade Unions (CISL) listed no fewer than eleven areas in which Portugal was acting contrary to accepted principles.[65] Given our earlier analysis of the controls exercised during the Estado Novo over trade union activity, it is sufficient here merely to list the areas of violation, whose combined effect implied virtually no independence and freedom for the sindicatos at all:

1. Only one sindicato was allowed for each category of workers (limited labor freedom to choose).
2. All statutes of each sindicato had to be approved by the Ministry of Corporations.
3. The sindicatos were obligated to subordinate their interests to the common interest, which was defined by the state.
4. Any changes in sindicato statutes required the approval of the Ministry of Corporations.
5. Elections of sindicato officers had to be approved by the state; the state could also annul elections.
6. The state could suspend the charter of any sindicato temporarily or permanently.
7. The sindicatos were forbidden to affiliate with any international labor organization.
8. The state could impose obligatory assessments on the sindicatos.
9. All collective contracts had to be approved by the Ministry of Corporations.
10. The right to strike was not permitted.
11. Although the sindicato legislation was extended to the overseas, it encompassed only those of Portuguese origins or those Africans legally classified as "assimilated"; all others were specifically excluded.

The conclusion was obvious: *no* labor freedom existed in Portugal or its colonies. Instead, the entire sindicato system was subordinate to the state.

The third aspect to consider concerning the sindicatos is the uses to which they were actually put. Rather than an effective and independent bargaining agent for workers, they, in fact, served as instruments by which the government extended its control over them. The sindicato structure was another bureaucratic appendage of the regime, little different in that respect from the party or the Army. Its leaders were generally government functionaries owing their positions and loyalties to the state and not to the workers. No strikes or even independent bargaining activity were permitted; rather, the sindicatos served to carry out and enforce decree-laws emanating from the regime. It was not collective bargaining between workers and employers that was the critical arena; instead, it was the sindicatos' function to implement wage rates, legal requirements, austerity programs, and so on, determined at a higher governmental level. Occasionally, of course, a strike or work stoppage would be carried out anyway, and there were some unions (principally the bank workers, the clerks, the metallurgical workers, perhaps two or three others) that gained a degree of independent power. But as a rule the unions were feeble and powerless; they were a part of the bureaucratic apparatus of an authoritarian-patrimonialist state apparatus and not the agents of free and independent workers. Their function was also to serve the regime, not necessarily the interests of their members. Small wonder the rank and file so despised their own sindicatos that, when the revolution came in 1974, the sindicatos were among the first to be overturned.

Let us look a bit more closely at the biases built into the system and the obstacles to the representation of workers' interests. The fact is, of course, that the sindicatos under Salazar did not fulfill the principal function of a modern trade union, which is to bargain with employers. Strikes remained illegal and labor discipline was severe, with infractions usually punishable by dismissal. In a country where unemployed labor was plentiful and the per capita income the lowest in Western Europe, the threat of dismissal was usually sufficient to squelch almost all labor protests. Workers' demands, we have seen, could be ignored with impunity by the gremios, with the government frequently failing to enforce the law requiring periodic renegotiation of collective contracts. In addition, the arbitration commissions appointed by the government almost invariably sided with employer interests or, in accord with instructions from on high, were obligated to enforce the government's wage freezes and other antiinflationary policies.

The labor tribunals similarly functioned as agents to enforce government policies. In cases before the tribunals (let us say one involving the dismissal of a worker without just cause), employer interests and their gremio would be represented by legal counsel of their own choice, while the worker was represented by a public prosecutor, whose obligations were necessarily first to serve the government (his employer, after all) and only secondarily the interests of the worker. If the worker had an injury, it was also the public prosecutor who had to present his case in court against the employer and his insurance company (usually well connected within or a part of the state-bureaucratic structure). Even in those rare instances where (1) the worker was willing to bring his case to court, and (2) he won, the amount of indemnity was so small as to be almost canceled out by the cost of the monthly transportation to collect it. It was not just in collective contract disputes that the weight of the all-powerful government was on the side of employers; the entire system—labor courts, arbitration commissions, the Corporations Ministry, labor laws, the Organizations of Economic Coordination, and so on

—was rigged in favor of employers and especially of the government itself, and against the interests of the laboring classes.[66]

The result of these controls and manipulation was a growing resentment and hostility toward the regime on the part of the working class, manifested in a new wave of illegal strikes in the 1960s, work stoppages and slowdowns, sabotage, and a profound sullenness combined with apathy. As industrialization and economic development accelerated, the peasants and marginal rural elements migrated toward the cities, especially Lisbon, in search of work. But the jobs were few; unemployment and underemployment mushroomed. Life in the poor urban ghettos was harsh; the large pool of unskilled laborers kept wages low; government services were woefully inadequate or nonexistent. Neither Salazar nor his ministers had much understanding of the plight of the urban poor and of their misery and rising alienation. Salazar was, of course, for the workers in the abstract, but in actuality he preferred to keep his distance, bringing about certain improvements in working conditions but not at the cost of breaking down class hierarchy, which he saw as essential to the maintenance of good customs and the social order. The elite, both financial and governmental, still believed they could (and, of course, *should*) speak *for* the people; they believed in assistance and benevolence, meted out paternalistically so as not to upset the established structures. They continued to think of the urban poor and laboring classes in terms of the humble, deferential rural and servant class with whom they were acquainted in their own homes. They failed to recognize that a new class had emerged, clearly not yet in possession of power but beginning to put pressure on those who did hold it and growing enormously resentful when those pressures were crushed or brushed aside. The explosion was virtually inevitable.[67]

Curiously, the resentments against the corporative system were almost as strong on the part of employers as they were on the part of workers. Such sentiments seem "curious" since we have already seen that the chief beneficiaries of the corporate system were the nation's business, commercial, and industrial elites, precisely those whom the gremios were established to represent. Yet businessmen still resented the gremios, largely because the red tape, bureaucracy, rules, and regulations imposed barriers to unrestricted private profiteering. In a study of the Portuguese industrial elite carried out in the mid-1960s, sociologist Harry Makler found many businessmen resented their gremios, criticized the leadership (often government appointed) for being unaware of the problems confronting their particular economic sector, saw the gremios as ineffectively representing their interests, complained of slowness and lack of organization, and generally considered the gremios a waste of time. As Makler concluded, the propertied classes were grumbling about the corporative system and particularly about the gremios; they saw both as rapidly becoming "dinosauric." [68]

In 1933 the regime had promulgated a decree (23,049) making membership in the gremios obligatory for business and propertied interests. Under the decree the state could create the gremios at its own initiative, require all those in a particular economic sector to join and pay dues, and continue to regulate the internal affairs of the gremio as well as making its decisions binding on all members. A year later, faced with massive protests from business leaders, a new decree provided for voluntary rather than compulsory gremios and gave the business elites more time to adjust. The voluntary gremios could come into existence when 50 percent of the businesses in a given economic sector agreed to join; such gremios, whose charters, like those of the sindicatos, had to be approved by the Corporations Subsecretariat (later Ministry), were granted the same representational monopoly as the compulsory gremios, as well as formal access to positions on various governmental agencies and boards. Even with this major modification in the direction of voluntarism, however, the resentment continued and the gremios grew slowly. Some sectors of business and the economy were never corporatized at all. In addition, the government allowed such private class associations as the Chambers of Commerce and the Industrial Associations of Lisbon and Porto to continue in existence, and their offices were often more sumptuous and their influence greater than that of the corporative entities. The system was thus never so completely or so thoroughly corporatized on the employer side as on the worker. [69]

Despite its initial retreat in 1934, the state did use the gremio legislation to "take on" certain economic sectors and subordinate them also to governmental control. There were numerous instances in the 1930s and afterward of the state forcing the gremio structure on a reluctant business group, thereby subordinating that sector to state regulation. Many of the obligatory gremios thus became not voluntary associations of producers but direct dependents of the ministries of commerce or industry, or of the various regulatory agencies, commissions, or juntas. [70] In addition, the incentives were strong (access to government funds and favors) for the creation of more "voluntary" gremios. Hence, the number of gremios grew rapidly from the mid-1930s on, reaching a total of 495 by 1954. By 1967, corresponding approximately to the end of the Salazar era and with the impetus of the corporate revival of the late 1950s, the number had risen to 559 (as compared with 324 sindicatos), of which 91 were obligatory and 467 voluntary. It should not be forgotten, of course, that, in addition to the gremio system as a means to regulate and control the business sector, the regime as early as 1936 had moved to create a web of regulatory agencies (the Organizations of Economic Coordination) by which it could *directly* administer virtually all sectors of the economy. Very little power was ever devolved upon the corporations or the gremios by these agencies; rather, decisional authority continued to rest in the state and its bureaucratic apparatus, to which the gremios as well as all other corporate units were subordinated.[71] The gremios functioned as a part of the bureaucratic apparatus to dispense some goods and services and to carry out and implement decisions made higher up in the system. Seldom were real issues of importance discussed or decided, and later when they were obligated to meet on a monthly basis, the gremios became, according to one source, merely *grupos de chá* (tea-drinking societies).[72]

Despite the state control and the institutionalized indifference, the functions and influence of at least some of the stronger gremios were considerable, far greater than the sindicatos, for instance, and often greater than their assumed parent organizations, the corporations themselves. This was due, however, more to the smallness, compactness, and interpersonal connections within the elite and the business community, as compared with the diffuse laboring class, than to the functioning of the corporative system per se. In addition, while the businessmen frequently grumbled about the bureaucracy and red tape, this was a far cry from the revolutionary challenge of the workers. For their "loyalty" and services to the regime, the business, commercial, industrial, and landed elites (the last organized through special *gremios da lavoura*) were amply rewarded. In contrast, the "loyalty" of the peasants and workers was either taken for granted or forcibly exacted, punishable by loss of job or other sanctions if not forthcoming.

In general, therefore, whatever their small gripes, the gremios and their members learned to cope with and take advantage of the corporative system, an advantage that the sindicatos seldom enjoyed. The gremios were usually able to gain access or articulate their point of view to the regulatory agencies; often they were directly represented. They had a hand in economic planning, setting import and export quotas, international trade, fixing prices and production levels, and so on, to a far greater degree than the sindicatos. Their voice was usually dominant in wage negotiations, and they were at least consulted on most major economic decisions. At the local level, gremio leaders were often both men of wealth and municipal authorities. None of this could be said for the sindicatos. Despite their complaints about the inconvenience, cumbersome stamps, approvals, and so forth, the gremios were a part of the system while the sindicatos existed largely outside of it. It was not the discontent of the gremios and the business community that eventually brought the system down; quite the contrary, for in the long run they profited most from the system of protection and oligopoly that the regime provided.[73]

The gremios, like the corporations, were thus closely tied up with the regime and its various arms. One of the more interesting findings of the Makler study already referred to was the degree to which these private and public agencies and their personnel overlapped. Almost half (46 percent) of the industrial elite members interviewed held some public or corporative office simultaneously. Corporate leadership was found to be a "haven for those from upper socioeconomic class business and landowning origins, inheritors of family fortunes." From a C. Wright Millsian perspective, Makler's findings indicate a strong interlocking between the polity and the economy, between the elite of wealth and the elite of political influence. Frequently the meeting place for this interlocking system was in the corporative structure, either corporations or gremios, positions which often served as stepping-stones to great wealth. Makler found the gremio executives to be young heirs, owner-managers, from upper socioeconomic origins, who had used their own or family connections to gain their positions. Once educated in the intricacies and nuances of corporative law and administrative procedures, their career patterns usually meant movement back into the family business so as to best take advantage of the knowledge learned and connections made.[74] Again, the line between the public and the private domains was a very fine one—and frequently invisible. But the system rewarded only those who had the proper credentials and connections; the rest were too often left to fend for themselves.

The gremios, in the final analysis, provide an interesting illustration of how the Portuguese system worked—and failed to work. Like the other grass-roots or "base" associations, they never provided the solid foundation on which the corporative system was supposed to rest. Although they performed some useful and significant services, they were not the agencies through which most businessmen articulated their interests or organized group pressure on the regime. Most business and commercial elements circumvented the gremio structure and either went directly to the appropriate government officials or ignored the corporative system's rules entirely. At the same time the government was also insensitive to and ignored the gremios, feeling they were too cumbersome to serve as effective intermediaries. At best they served as a kind of buffer or placating agency. The business elites constituted a group to whom the regime was beholden but whom it wanted to keep at a distance. The gremios thus became an agency for the further extension of state power, but this did not go so far as to antagonize those wealthy elements whose support the regime needed. Through the compartmentalization of business and all other groups, the regime attempted both to maintain the existing class structure and to extend its control over all classes. By the 1960s, however, the gremio structure itself had been reduced to a largely formal facade and, in Makler's words, had become an object of unofficial "benign neglect" on the part of both government and businessmen.[75]

The liberal professions in Portugal were organized into orders (*ordens*), of which four were formally organized: those for lawyers, doctors, engineers, and agronomists. Each of these associations, unlike the sindicatos or gremios, covered all the territory of continental Portugal; they were *national* organizations. Their functions included the moral and intellectual improvement of their members and the setting of standards for their respective professions. The ordens were, of course, political associations in the broad sense also, but their role as representational or control agencies was nowhere near so important as in the case of the sindicatos or gremios. As with most professional associations, membership was largely a matter of form, a thing that one did in the normal course of things, and did not necessarily imply any strict adherence to corporative principles. Membership often carried with it the opportunity to supplement one's income by holding a government job as well as a private practice, the possibility of receiving government contracts, or the chance to take advantage of new government programs (the government-financed health care system was often a boon to doctors who qualified).

The leadership of the ordens was usually selected by the regime—or a single slate of prior-approved candidates was presented. Sometimes there would be disputes with the leadership, often involving manifestly political differences. Or, different factions within the associations would disagree as to what ought to be the official position of the association— for example, the debates among medical doctors over health insurance, family planning, and national health care services. The ordens were directly represented in the Corporative Chamber and on various Organizations of Economic Coordination, and they would sometimes be consulted by the government on matters directly pertaining to their technical or professional expertise. All these activities were political in nature, to one degree or another, and in addition to their strictly professional functions, there is no doubt the *ordens* also served as a means of tying middle-class professionals to the regime, buying their loyalty, and keeping them under control. Yet the number of persons encompassed was small, their importance not all that disproportionate, and their strategic influence limited. Certainly in the political dynamics of the system, the ordens, as organizations, counted for relatively little and were never in a position to make or break the regime, as was the case with both sindicatos and gremios.[76]

In the countryside the undifferentiated nature of production and, in the government's words, the "special psychological makeup of the country-dweller" called for the creation of special bodies, distinct from trade unions—the casas do povo, or people's centers. Situated in rural parishes, they include among their members both agricultural laborers *and* large landowners. The original casa structure was created in 1933; in 1934 a new decree gave the government the power to create casas by fiat; in 1938 they were declared the representational bodies of rural workers; in 1940 another decree made them the agents of social assistance in the countryside; and in 1945 a Junta Central of Casas do Povo was created ostensibly to give the casas greater bargaining power. In addition to occupational representation, therefore, the casas were supposed to play an important part in the administration of welfare and social security, and in the cultural and educational improvement of their members and their families.[77]

The existence and functions of the casas were problematic from the start. Laborers and smallholders were suspicious and hostile, regarding the *casas* as agencies of government control (as, of course, they were). As would be expected, large landholders dominated them from the beginning, monopolizing almost all offices and using the casas for their own advantage rather than that of the poor day laborers and tenants. Other than the grandiose oratory regarding corporative social cooperation, there was no specific instruction as to what activities the *casas* should have, nor were there any trained organizers at the local level who knew much about either corporatism or community development. No differentiation was made among different types of rural communities and their different needs; the *casa* structure was the same for all, whether in the North where the peasants had their own small plots of land (and hence little need for the casas) or in the Alentejo where the peasants had no land at all. The casa system, in fact, was almost exclusively the idea of urban, middle-class intellectuals, men who heavily romanticized the traditional countryside and the peasants' strength and self-reliance but who knew little about the realities of peasant life. In creating this vast superstructure out of thin air, they had never bothered to consult the peasants themselves or to investigate the real needs of the agricultural sector.[78]

The casas hence led a precarious existence. During World War II many of them died or fell into disuse. In the postwar period they continued to be neglected and performed few services and functions. They were subject to numerous investigations, prompting new tinkering with the system. The corporate revival of the 1950s restimulated interest, but it was not until the 1960s and the new emphasis upon the social security and assistance mission of corporatism that many new initiatives were taken. At this point, the government began a vigorous campaign to create new casas, but many of these, perhaps the majority, remained paper organizations with no participation at the grass roots. Some casas listed on the official rolls never actually came into existence; some served purely the interests of the local landowners; others were so small that the total membership counted only half a dozen.[79] The extension of the system's labor and social security legislation to the countryside had at long last given the casas something concrete to administer, but even in the early 1960s only about 20 percent of the rural parishes were covered, and the administration of the new programs, when it existed at all, always remained in the hands of the state and its agencies.

The functioning of the casas (or the lack thereof) was the subject of perhaps more in-house investigations than any other aspect of the corporative system. In 1947 Castro Fernandes, drawing upon his experience as corporations subsecretary, published his study pointing to the precarious existence of so many casas, their dependence on government, on the one hand, and landowners, on the other, and the inherent difficulties of organizing the diverse, fragmented, atomized rural sector of the population.[80] During the 1950s the *Revista do Gabinete de Estudos Corporativos* published a number of studies lamenting the weakness of the casas and calling for their strengthening; within the Corporations Ministry F. Cid Proença and others were analyzing the same weaknesses.[81] In 1961 Fryer and McGowan-Pinheiro in their study of the Salazar regime concluded that *on paper* the casas do povo were supposed to receive contributions from their members and, supplemented by government assistance, to pay benefits in return, but that in practice these "glorified benevolent societies" did not work well and that in most places they hardly existed at all.[82]

Finally, there is the Corporations Ministry's own investigation of the functions of the casas do povo. In one of the few attempts ever made by the Portuguese regime to study its own corporative grass-roots organizations, to tap systematically public opinion and find out what the felt needs of the people were, a 1967 *Inquérito* found that of the 3,573 parishes in the country 30 percent were now covered by casas; that of the 597 casas formally in existence, 89.9 percent were actually operating; that the total membership had reached over 400,000 (out of a rural population of approximately five million); that the financial condition and the activities of the casas were often precarious; and that of the existing casas most provided some form of assistance and recreation, roughly half had organized sports activities and an educational program, and only a handful of the wealthiest and most active had agricultural cooperative institutes or community development activities.[83] The conclusion of this inquiry listed no fewer than nineteen areas where reform was needed, including greater finances, new organizational efforts, leadership training, greater participation of the membership, new services, higher dues, greater flexibility in the structure of the casas corresponding to local needs. These findings served as the bases for the expansion of the casa structure and social services during the succeeding Estado Social of Marcello Caetano.[84]

Not only are there more within-the-system surveys of the casas than of other institutions in the corporative structure, but the casas have also been the subject of some of the only scholarly studies conducted by outside researchers during the Salazar era, mainly in the form of community studies. Joyce Riegelhaupt, José Cutileiro, and a number of students of João Pereira Neto have all done careful studies of small local communities which come to essentially the same conclusions about the casas: their limited roles, their subordination to the state, their dominance by landholding interests, their precarious existence, and their lack of essential functions. In Riegelhaupt's study,[85] the conclusion was clear: the government had taken all initiative out of the popular arena and instead instituted administrative decrees which local bodies merely enforced; the parishes were only monuments to state autarchy; and the corporate state reinforced and perpetuated the peasants' powerlessness. In Cutileiro,[86] one saw the peasants' hostility and suspicion toward the casas, their domination by *latifundistas,* and their essentially charitable *and* tax-collecting functions. He showed how the structure and functions of the casas reflected the status quo supported by the landowners, and how all local institutions, including the casa do povo, the gremio da lavoura, the *junta de freguesia,* and the *câmara municipal,* were all (1) extremely limited in their functions, (2) subordinated to the central state apparatus, and (3) dominated by the same landed and wealthy sectors. Finally, the studies supervised by Pereira Neto, emphasized the ineffectiveness of the casas do povo to the point where Pereira Neto himself denied they existed in practice or had any reality.[87]

Portugal's rural structure in the 1960s thus remained dominated by a traditional and patriarchal system that had little to do with corporatism or corporatist reforms.[88] If anything, the Estado Novo had used the corporative system to buttress the existing social hierarchy in the countryside, with a few large landholders, particularly in the central and southern areas, remaining incredibly rich, while the large mass of peasants, day laborers, tenant farmers, and smallholders continued to eke out a meager subsistence on Portugal's bare, infertile hillsides. The countryside remained backward, poor, unmechanized, and illiterate. Conditions became so bad that hundreds of thousands literally voted with their feet (there was no other way) and migrated abroad, leaving many rural villages, especially in the North, virtually abandoned and helping to make Portugal one of the few nations in the world which in the last two decades actually experienced a population decline. As a result of this and other factors, Portuguese agriculture stagnated, production dropped, and, next to Africa, the "crisis of agriculture" became one of the country's most debated national problems.[89] The corporative revolution had thus only barely touched the countryside, and where it did it tended to reinforce a status quo pointing increasingly toward disaster.

The casas dos pescadores fared somewhat better than the casas do povo. The "fisherfolk's centers" rested upon a natural community of interests often lacking in the countryside, and on a natural, functional interdependence that was not so apparent in the casas do povo. The fishermen had a long history of cooperation and association going back to the fourteenth century, whereas in the campo the history was one of diffusion, atomization, and the absence of associative agencies. Among the corporative experiments, the casas dos pescadores come nearest to representing a success.

One should not overdo the successes, however. The casas dos pescadores had been launched in 1937 and had grown slowly. By 1960 there were twenty-three casas in continental Portugal, with a total of 46,000 effective members. The casas dos pescadores, like other agencies in the system, remained completely under state control, with the local chefe do pôrto (harbor master), also a government bureaucrat, appointed president of the casa. In addition, the casas dos pescadores were frequently subordinated to gremio interests and to state regulation through the Organizations of Economic Coordination dealing with the fishing industry, which themselves were dominated by the large canners, fleet owners, and shippers. Despite these controls and the now-familiar biases within the system, the casas dos pescadores were far more aggressive in the defense of their members' interests and in carrying out activities than other, comparable corporative units. Through their Junta Central, the fishermen embarked on thirty-four housing projects resulting in the building of 2,452 individual homes; they constructed eighteen primary schools; they also built thirty-six casas for the teaching of skilled crafts. They established a special school for fishermen, provided moral and religious instruction, administered their own caixa and pension plan, and worked out a series of collective contracts that significantly improved wages. The centers were actually functioning institutions with real programs and activities. As compared with the sindicatos or casas do povo, the casas dos pescadores were veritable bright spots on an otherwise bleak corporative panorama. That is still not saying much, and it may in addition have more to do with the history and solidarity of the fishing communities themselves than with the corporative system.[90]

COLLABORATIVE AGENCIES   We may dispose of the other corporative units, the so-called collaborative agencies, with dispatch. The Fundação Nacional para a Alegria no Trabalho was formally institutionalized within the Corporations Ministry, where it continued to carry on limited recreational activities. The Mocidade became more than ever a boy-scout organization; virtually all its corporative trappings were abandoned. The Legião Portuguesa similarly lost its earlier "fascist" connections; it continued as a special paramilitary unit but with such limited strength as to be almost negligible. The União Nacional largely abandoned its corporatist ideology also and became simply a giant political and patronage apparatus at the service of the regime; we shall have more to say about the Estado Novo's "official party" in chapter 10. The Army, the Church, the university, the bureaucracy, and other "natural" corporative bodies, we have seen, were never "corporatized" in the 1930s sense of that term.

What this discussion leads to clearly is a conclusion that in the 1960s, some thirty and more years after the initiation of the corporative "revolution," the entire corporative structure remained exceedingly weak and was only feebly institutionalized. Like all grand designs, corporatism led to far fewer accomplishments in actual practice than it had promised in theory. Some parts of the system functioned more or less according to plan; the rest functioned inadequately, if at all. For all the corporative theory and superstructure, it was apparent that little of this elaborate system came into existence or, if it did, it seldom functioned as the ideology stated. Salazar remained the hub of the system, not the corporative agencies;[91] moreover, by the 1960s it was clear that power had devolved not so much on the corporative bodies as upon other groups and sectors: the banking sector, import-export concerns, certain large business and industrial interests, the Army, the secret police, the political-bureaucratic elite. We shall have more to say on these groups in chapter 10, "How the Portuguese System Really Works"; suffice it here to suggest that one key reason corporatism failed in Portugal, in this the "purest" and most complete "corporate state" in the world in a formal-legal sense, was because it was never tried.

In the meantime, Portugal itself had changed greatly in the two decades following World War II. The chief causes of the change were industrialization, migration and emigration, tourism, the mobilization forced by the African uprisings, the decline of agriculture, accelerating social change, and the increased diffusion of education and information.[92] By the mid-1960s a new urban middle class had grown up that did not fit the corporative scheme and that was impatient with its delays and cumbersomeness. The working class was restless, impatient with low pay and the worst living conditions in Europe, while the elites were increasingly divided on the direction the country should take. Salazar was old and increasingly out of touch with national realities, and neither the middle-aged nor the younger generation had any further use for the corporative scheme. The opposition was growing, and one of its demands was the abolition of the entire corporative system.[93]

Even within the government there was a new questioning of corporatism.[94] Everyone recognized that corporatism had been superseded, that that was not where power lay; and they proceeded to act almost as if the corporative structure did not exist. The issues too had changed: development planning, economic integration, growth, consumerism, the European community, and so forth—these were the Portuguese concerns, not the stale ideological battles of the interwar period. Portuguese corporatism was no longer dynamic and oriented toward change and social justice, as it had been in the 1930s; it had become old, bureaucratized, stagnant, and out of date. The Portuguese social and economic structure had changed greatly since the establishment of the corporative system some three decades back, but the system had not changed or kept pace with the new conditions. The corporative structure had been frozen in midpassage; but now it was not just the corporative complex, but rather the entire national fossilized system, personified by the aging Salazar, that had become lethargic, immobilized, holding back change rather than providing for it.[95]

By this point the questions had become: Could a rejuvenated, dynamic form of corporatism succeed in salvaging the system, and for how long; or would the entire corporatist structure be swept away in favor of other, alternative forms of a liberal and/or socialist form? Those were the questions the succeeding Caetano regime faced; and it is around the dynamics of meeting and answering those questions that politics in post-Salazar Portugal revolved—until finally, in April 1974, the revolution did away with the corporative system, at least in its more formal Salazarista aspects. Whether the country could as easily free itself from that longer and stronger Portuguese political-cultural tradition of "natural corporatism," however, may be a far more difficult question to resolve.

IX

Corporative Succession: The Caetano Regime
and the Attempt to Revitalize the System[1]

On September 6, 1968, Dr. Antonio de Oliveira Salazar, aged seventy-nine, prime minister of Portugal since 1932 and thus the longest in office of all premiers in modern history, underwent an operation for the removal of a blood clot near his brain. The operation followed an accident several weeks earlier when a deck chair in his summer residence at Estoril had collapsed and Salazar's head had been injured in the fall. At the time the injury had not been considered serious, and the premier had continued his normal routine. Later, suffering from headaches and vision problems, he had entered the Cruz Vermelha Hospital for surgery. He had seemed to be recovering from his operation when on September 16 he suffered a cerebral thrombosis and hemorrhage and was placed in an oxygen tent in critical condition. He lapsed into a coma and was pronounced "gravely ill." A medical bulletin issued on September 25 described his condition as "stationary," but by then he was semiparalyzed, barely conscious, and kept alive by an oxygenator. According to medical opinion, he would never recover the full use of his faculties, although he might be able to live for a long time. That same day, September 25, the four surgeons who had been attending the prime minister called on President Américo Thomaz to give their report.[2]

The incapacity of the prime minister brought to the fore institutions that had been almost wholly neglected during Salazar's forty years of strong, one-man rule. Constitutionally, it will be recalled, it was the president who had the power to appoint and remove premiers; and while it was simply unthinkable for long decades that Salazar himself might be removed by the president, now that power assumed new dimensions. Thomaz, a seventy-four-year-old retired admiral who had always stayed discreetly in the background and was perhaps best known for his keen interest in soccer, was a conservative, even reactionary figure with strong ties to equally reactionary military officials and Salazaristas. In accord with the Constitution, on September 17, the day after Salazar's hemorrhage, Thomaz had met with the Council of State, that body of thirteen influentials designed as a superior governmental coordinating agency but seldom (if ever) convoked previously. In keeping with its emergency and consultative role, the council had been summoned to consider what steps should be taken, since the Constitution specified that a new prime minister could be appointed only after the death or dismissal of his predecessor but did not say what should be done in cases of incapacitation. Thomaz met during this period with important military chieftains, cabinet officials, and other powerful men connected with the Salazar regime, and it was plain that a number of alternatives were being considered. On September 26, the day after the formal delivery of the doctors' report, Thomaz announced publicly that Salazar had been in a coma for ten days and that for the good of the country it was no longer possible to defer a decision. He said that after wide consultation with military and civilian leaders it had been decided that he, the president, should use his constitutional prerogative to release Dr. Salazar from his post. At the same time he appointed Professor Marcello Caetano as prime minister to succeed Salazar and asked him to form a government.[3]

The Caetano Regime

Dr. Marcello José das Neves Caetano, aged sixty-four, the son of a primary school teacher and, like Salazar, of middle-class social origins, graduated in law from the University of Lisbon. Along with Pereira, he had been a student leader of the Integralist and Catholic social movements and an editor and author of numerous essays in student Integralist reviews. Like many young Catholics of his generation, Caetano had been imbued with the Church's social ideology, particularly as embodied in the corporatist movement and the encyclicals *Rerum Novarum* and *Quadragesimo Anno*. In 1929, at the age of twenty-five, he was appointed judicial auditor to the Ministry of Finance, which had come under Salazar's direction the previous year. Strongly influenced by Sardinha and the Integralists in his student days while watching the collapse of the Portuguese Republic, Caetano modified his views somewhat under Salazar's influence to bring them closer in line with Salazar's own and those of the more moderate Catholic Centro Académico de Democracia Cristã (CADC). Caetano, along with Salazar, was probably the chief intellectual force behind and author of the wave of basic laws promulgated in 1933: the Constitution, the Labor Statute, and the series of corporative decrees. That same year he was appointed to the chair of constitutional and administrative law at the University of Lisbon. He quickly became Portugal's leading constitutional lawyer and was the author of some of the most thorough studies of Portuguese law, administration, and politics published in the next forty years.[4]

Caetano was seldom far from government service. Though holding no formal public office during the 1930s, he continued to draft legislation, was the author of a significant essay on Portuguese corporative development, and served as an adviser and assistant to Salazar and in the Corporations Subsecretariat. He also devoted himself to youth affairs and became leader of the Mocidade in 1940. In 1944 he was appointed minister for the colonies, in which capacity he drafted a new Organic Law providing that the overseas territories were in fact "provinces," no different in juridical status from the provinces of metropolitan Portugal. In 1944 he left the cabinet (but not the regime) to become president of the União Nacional, the country's sole legitimate political organization, and to guide the movement through the difficult postwar period (including the elections of 1946 and 1949) and help reform it internally. Later Caetano was elected president of the Corporative Chamber, and in 1955 at the commencement of the corporative revival of that period, he became deputy prime minister. In this capacity he helped draft the decrees creating the new corporations and was instrumental in seeing to their adoption; recall that it was the Caetano plan for "vertical," centralized integration of the corporations that was adopted rather than the looser Pires Cardoso "horizontal" scheme.

But in August 1958, just as it was becoming apparent that the so-called corporate revival was more apparent than real, Caetano abruptly left the government. He began putting some distance between himself and the regime. He was subsequently appointed rector of the University of Lisbon during a period of student unrest, a post he resigned in 1962 in protest against the entry of the police onto the university grounds without his permission. It is from this series of events that Caetano earned his reputation as a "liberal," or at least one who was more open to contemporary ideas and movements than Salazar. He remained, however, a professor of law, became a highly successful company lawyer with positions on the boards of directors of several major concerns, and was also named a member of the Council of State, that body whose first important function would be to help pick Caetano as successor to Salazar. It should also be noted that, while Salazar was a bachelor, Dr. Caetano was married and a family man with four children.

Caetano was the obvious choice to succeed Salazar, not so much because he was one of the intellectual fountains of the corporative system but because he was a practical politician, an able and proven administrator, and a man with obviously long experience in almost all civilian areas of the Portuguese system. There were other aspirants to the throne —conservative Foreign Minister Franco Nogueira, former Justice Minister João de Matos Atunes, young dynamic (and a former Caetano student) Adriano Moreira, conservative General Inacio Deslandes, far-rightist General Fernando Santos Costa, vigorous and ambitious General Kaula de Arriaga—and some of the elements of a beginning power struggle.[5] But the range of choice represented by all these elements was not wide, with each emphasizing continuity with the Salazar regime rather than any significant departures. Among these persons Caetano stood head and shoulders above the rest, but more as a pragmatic choice than an ideological one. His function would be to maintain the continuity of the system (including, at the insistence of the military and as a condition of his taking office, a hard-line position in Africa), while at the same time adapting it to the newer contingencies. Caetano sought to adjust and accommodate to the requirements of the 1960s and 1970s but to preserve the essence of the corporatist system intact. As one prominent businessman-politician said at the time, "It will be the best tribute to Salazar if his long personal rule is followed by an orderly turning to the institutions and forms that he introduced." [6]

Caetano inherited a government that, as one news account put it, was sluggish to the point of torpor. Government had all but come to a standstill during the last years of the Salazar regime, and it would be Caetano's job to invigorate, activate, and rejuvenate it, to evolve from "the dinosaur." Note that nowhere in this list of purposes do the words *liberalize* or *democratize* appear. That is where so many foreign interpretations of the immediate post-Salazar period of Portuguese politics have gone wrong. Concentration on the supposed liberalizing or democratizing tendencies (and reversals) of the Caetano era represents more wishful thinking and downright imagination on the part of outside journalists and reporters than it does the actual realities of Caetano's policies and government. For Caetano's intentions were never to democratize or liberalize Portugal, and it is inappropriate to fault him for failing to do what he never intended to do. Caetano aimed at broadening the ruling elite somewhat but by no means at providing for genuine democratization; he tried to widen the appeal and base of the official party but not to provide for real choice as between parties; he sought to curb somewhat the power of the secret police but not by sacrificing authoritarian control; he aimed at better implementation of the corporative system, but he did not intend to turn to liberalism. His goal was to adjust the regime to the new realities, make the required accommodations, restore confidence in the economy and the public service, wake up and invigorate a political structure and nation that had gone to sleep under Salazar, and revive a slumbering, almost stagnant set of corporative institutions long neglected through disuse. The evidence is overwhelming that Caetano remained a corporatist and an authoritarian, and it is within that context that his rule must be judged and not within the context of any supposed thrusts toward liberalism. He aimed at preserving, strengthening, reinvigorating, and institutionalizing the corporative system that had become moribund under Salazar, not at substituting some other system for it. Change would hence be neither swift nor spectacular.[7]

While preserving, updating, and modernizing the main pillars of corporative rule, Caetano also changed its style. He was more friendly and outgoing than the cold, austere Salazar. He went out on public occasions, toured the countryside, mingled with the people, exchanged *abraços* and actually seemed to enjoy it. Caetano smiled a lot, took pains to listen, appeared open to all points of view, and ran a much more *public* government than his predecessor. Early in his rule he began a series of televised "fireside chats" (*conversas em familia*) to explain government programs and policies to the people, something that the aloof Salazar hardly ever did and then only in a lecturing manner.[8] Through these methods the dinosauric image of the old regime was erased somewhat, and though the controls—censorship, secret police, and so on—remained in place, Caetano's regime was far more open, relaxed, free, almost friendly. As a rural peasant woman was reported to have remarked after shaking the prime minister's hand on one of his whirlwind tours, "I like this Salazar better than the old one."[9]

The policies pursued by Caetano, however, were consistently tentative, ambiguous, weak, uncertain, and, most often, reversible. He behaved as a politician whose position was always tenuous and precarious —and probably it was. Caetano was by no means the strong, dogmatic, autocratic personality that Salazar had been; although he was given the reins of government, Caetano seemed to hold those reins loosely. He did not steer the country in very many clear directions—and on most issues the pressures on him were such that he could not. He attempted some decompression from the monolithic authoritarianism of the Salazar era, but the steps he took were small and limited, and he was always careful to maintain his links with the major power centers of the old regime. Caetano recognized the growing influence of the Left, Communist, social-democratic, and Christian-democratic opposition, yet he was also surrounded by rightist, Salazarista, *situacionista* forces who appeared to hem in his every move and to constitute a constant menace to his day-to-day survival. Caetano himself in his politics was similarly conservative and authoritarian, though he saw that in order to preserve the system some change and reform were necessary. Rather than standing pat or stonewalling all attempts at change, Caetano sought to blend his form of modern conservatism with a cautious commitment to coopt the energies for change rather than being overwhelmed by them.

In seeking to blend and balance these diverse tendencies, however, Caetano often remained cautious to the point of indecisiveness, refusing or failing to grasp more firmly the levers of power or to take the decisive actions called for when the opportune moments came. Trying to juggle a variety of balls in the air on a political base that was always weak to begin with, Caetano eventually started losing control of his own juggling act, the balls started falling, and one of them finally, in April 1974, hit him on the head. But rather than coming from the Right, which had always been Caetano's preoccupation, the April coup came from the Left and resulted not only in the ouster of Caetano but also in the sweeping away of the entire corporative edifice.

Caetano's first moves as prime minister demonstrated both the tenuousness of his position and the ambiguity of his policies. In his inaugural address on September 27, 1968, for instance, Caetano both affirmed the policies of the Salazar regime and hinted at reform. He vowed to maintain continuity but declared that this implied a "notion of movement, sequence, adaptation." He stressed the nation's debt to its great teacher, Salazar, but emphasized that good pupils must do more than simply repeat what their instructors had said. He suggested that there would be greater communication between the government and the nation, but he did not say such communication would be a two-way affair or that press freedom would be restored. He emphasized the "constancy of the major outlines of Portuguese policy" but noted that Dr. Salazar had made mistakes and corrected them and that his government too would carry out whatever changes were necessary. Nowhere, however, did Caetano specify what mistakes had been made or what changes were being contemplated. His proposals for "greater communication" and other reforms were so vague that conservative Portuguese found the speech reassuring while liberals, if they wished to, could also find in it cause for hope. The speech was characteristic of the Caetano period: facing in two directions at once, never going very forcefully in either, meanwhile vacillating and stalling for time—until, of course, events themselves overtook whatever plans or intentions had existed.

Caetano had opened the door a crack to change, but he also stood ready to slam it shut again. Early in his rule he allowed exiled Socialist leader Mario Soares to return to Portugal to prepare for the scheduled 1969 elections and gave assurances of free elections to other opposition elements, but he refused to allow opposition political parties to form or campaign unhindered. He did, however, allow opposition election "campaign committees," but he banned any new ones again some two months before the voting day. Under rightist pressure he also clamped down on the small Communist groups and promised undefined "security measures" for any oppositionists advocating subversive policies. The opposition was not allowed broadcast or television time, their forays into the interior were consistently hamstrung by police and *Guarda* machinations, and censorship in the press was relaxed somewhat only in the thirty days preceding the election. Despite these restrictions, the opposition went forward with its campaign and selection of candidates, thus giving Caetano the "democratic" facade and legitimacy he wanted but without the regime sacrificing any of its monopoly of power. On election day, after what was conceded to be the most open campaign since the fall of the Republic in 1926, which is obviously not saying a great deal, the official União Nacional garnered 89 percent of the vote and the opposition only 11 percent. As was said at the time, the opposition had had the campaign it wanted, but the government had had its election!

In the meantime Caetano had more quietly gone forward with the restructuring of the official "party." Under Salazar the União Nacional had been kept weak, a loose collection of notables rather than a disciplined party machine. The changes introduced by Caetano were aimed again not so much at "liberalization" as they were at building up a strong political organization of men loyal to him personally, while at the same time jettisoning (often to the Corporative Chamber) the old line Salazaristas who had dominated the UN and whose pressures continued to make Caetano's life difficult. Franco Nogueira, for example, had consistently set himself against any real contest between the government and the opposition, arguing that dialogue would lead only to anarchy and breakdown (events in 1974 may have proved him correct) and that strong methods were necessary to enforce the law. In an effort to counterbalance Nogueira's and other rightist influence, Caetano had brought in one of his own followers to head the UN and had personally handpicked many of its candidates for National Assembly seats. Seeking to find his own basis of moderate support, he introduced many new faces as candidates, a few as "liberal" as any opposition candidates.

Later, after the elections, Caetano changed the UN's name to the Aliança Nacional Popular and continued with the restructuring. The name change represented a further attempt on Caetano's part to establish his own base of support and to use it to overcome powerful rightist resistance to his policies. In this way Caetano sought to make the regime over in his own image, while leaving its basic structure intact. But in this as in other matters Caetano vacillated, and the new ANP remained a delicate balance of older and newer political forces. The elections held in 1969, therefore, were only a part of a larger internal process whose final outcome was not determined or even very strongly influenced by the highly restricted nature of the campaigning or even the percentages and election results. There were matters other than this at stake.[10]

Along with the new faces in the official party, Caetano brought some new faces into the government. And like the shift from the UN to the ANP, this shift similarly required some time since it again involved a fundamental transfer of power from those associated with the old regime to Caetano loyalists. Hence, in January 1970 a fundamental cabinet shuffle took place, with power passing to a new "liberal" and "technocratic" group. Actually, this group was no more nonpolitical or technocratic than the outgoing one, and its "liberalism" remained doubtful. It involved more fundamentally a bringing in of some new and younger faces who owed their positions and loyalty to Caetano. In the shuffle the number of ministries was reduced from fourteen to nine. The ministries of defense and army were merged, as were those of health and corporations (more on that later) under Caetano loyalist Rebelo de Sousa. Public works and communications were also joined under the prime minister's nephew, Rui Sanches. The Foreign Ministry was given to Caetano protégé (and godson) Rui Patricio and the Ministry of Education to dynamic, Cambridge-educated Veiga Simão. The "liberal" technocrats included João Salgueiro as undersecretary of state for planning, Rogerio Martins as minister of industry, and Xavier Pintado as minister of commerce.

It should not be surprising that the so-called liberals were also the first to be ousted. Salgueiro was allowed to resign his post and became head of the genuinely nonpolitical National Board of Scientific Research. Martins and Pintado had taken some preliminary steps toward reforming the economy and returning to the hallowed corporative goal of "self-regulation" by easing price controls, streamlining the bureaucracy, and reducing the profits of the monopolies and oligopolies, which had grown immensely rich and powerful under Salazar, through a lowering of protectionist trade barriers and the opening up of Portuguese industry and commerce to broader European competition. These changes had made many enemies within the economic establishment (inseparable from the Salazarista political establishment), and Martins and Pintado had to go.[11]

In other policy areas the results were the same. Rui Patricio helped usher in new plans for greater autonomy for the Portuguese overseas provinces, by now becoming a major drain on the economy, but Caetano maintained Salazar's pledge to hang onto the colonies at all costs.

Though hoping privately for some form of commonwealth status in twenty to thirty years, Caetano seemed to have no real plan for the colonies, buying time, carrying out policy on a day-to-day basis, hoping for the best, and failing to seize any initiatives. But policy does not develop in a vacuum and by 1973/74, with the spread of the guerrilla movements and their use of larger and more sophisticated weapons, and with defense expenditures reaching upward of 45 percent of the total national budget, thus depriving the country of much-needed funds for promoting economic and social development, events had again outstripped Caetano's capacity to control them. Portugal's position deteriorated, and the Caetano strategy appeared hopelessly anachronistic and unrealistic. At that time the Portuguese began turning to the one man who *did* have a policy, General António de Spínola.

Many of the Caetano changes, so warmly welcomed as demonstrating a "liberalizing" trend, turned out to be changes in name only. "You can always tell Caetano's car in the Lisbon traffic," as one popular joke had it; "it signals left but it turns right." A new press law was promulgated which ended the censorship, but the same controls were kept on the journalists' association and a new system of "prior examination" was begun which, both reporters and editors agreed, amounted to the same thing as censorship. The notorious Salazar political police, the PIDE, was reorganized as the General Department of Security (DGS), but Caetano kept the old, hard-line, Salazarista minister of interior, the basic overhaul of the organization was never undertaken, the terror and repression continued, and the police remained, as they had been under Salazar, virtually a state within a state, an "uncontrollable force" over which the prime minister himself often had little authority. Arbitrary arrests hence continued, both with Caetano's knowledge and blessing and without it, student and opposition elements were harassed, basic freedoms were ignored. Mario Soares was sent into exile again, open discussion was curtailed, most of the clamps were reimposed. Even so, Portugal was a quite different and more open society than it had been under Salazar (Caetano himself repeated that joke about signaling left and turning right in one of his "fireside chats"—Salazar would never have done so, or even seen the humor!), but *liberalization* and *democratization* are not really the most appropriate terms to describe the changes taking place.

Even the regime's most "progressive," ongoing programs, such as those in the educational field, must be looked at not so much in terms of the supposed "democratic" opportunities they opened up but in the more limited light of regime attempts to loosen the Salazar rigidities and expand the loyal elite. Educational reform, the careful assessment of Henry H. Keith showed, and the economic development plans proposed at the same time were all part of a strategy designed by the government to widen its base of support somewhat, to gain new adherents for the official party, and to garner overwhelming majorities in the elections so as to provide Caetano with a firmer popular base. Educational reform was not designed to genuinely democratize Portugal or to make its population a politically active and participatory citizenry but, on the model of other technocratically authoritarian regimes such as Spain and Brazil, to spread educational benefits to the lower middle and middle classes while retaining strong control over potential student, faculty, even popular dissidence. Indeed, in examining the Portuguese historical experience, we find that that is the way most "development" has taken place: institutional modifications are made that help perpetuate the political system, while at the same time providing for the incorporation of new political elites or the broadening of the existing elites. The educational and other reforms initiated by Caetano were not so much indications of a general "thaw" from the "deep freeze" of the Salazar period or of a "liberalization" of social and political institutions along more democratic lines. Rather, the Caetano government moved on a variety of political, social, and economic policy fronts to widen the governing elite and those loyal to the regime, all the while carefully cultivating popularity (as a Caetano counterbalance to the situacionistas and the force of the Right) by stimulating economic development and extending social and medical benefits to larger numbers of the population. As Keith concludes, the goal was not to change the fundamental institutions of government but to create and recruit an enlarged elite, owing allegiance to the regime in general and to Caetano in particular.[12]

For the purposes of this study, the arena of labor relations and of government-employer-employee interactions is, of course, critical, and here again the same Caetano patterns were followed: first, a tenuous opening up, then a crackdown, followed by uncertainty, vacillation, new openings, renewed indecision, and an ultimately disastrous temporizing. The breakthrough for labor came in June 1969 in a decree issued by the government giving the sindicatos the right to select their own leadership without government approval.[13] Under Salazar, the labor leadership had ordinarily been preselected by the regime. Another decree provided that, on the three-man arbitration commissions used for settling wage disputes, one member would be chosen by the sindicato, one by the gremio, and the third by the other two. Under the old system the third member had been selected by the Corporations Ministry and under Salazar had almost invariably sided with employers in enforcing government austerity and wage controls. Another provision shortened the time limits given the gremios to respond to sindicato demands, making it impossible for the gremios to simply ignore the demands or throw them in the wastebasket.[14]

Within months the Portuguese sindicatos, which for decades had been trade unions in name only, began to be transformed from amorphous government agencies into genuine instruments of the workers. For the first time opposition groups, including Communists in the case of some sindicatos, swept union elections, *and the elections were allowed to stand.*[15] Under the old regime, whenever an oppositionist had somehow managed to win a union election, the election was immediately canceled and new leaders more amenable to government direction were found. At the same time, the new arbitration commissions were in numerous cases voting in favor of labor's demands. As the trade unions began to gather strength and independent bargaining power, the government for the first time began enforcing the corporative laws forcing the gremios to respond and calling for coequal bargaining power between workers and employers. Strikes, slowdowns, and protest demonstrations, although banned by law, began to multiply, with government acquiescence. A number of new collective bargaining agreements were signed in 1969, 1970, and 1971 that provided for major wage increases. With government approval, the sindicatos finally had begun to acquire some teeth.

The workers' new militancy, as Marvine Howe's 1971 account correctly emphasizes, was due not just to the government's loosening of restrictions but to broader social and political developments. By the 1960s and 1970s, expanded industrialization in such centers as Lisbon, Porto, and Setúbal had created a far larger urban work force and a real laboring *class,* as distinct from the "sleepier," earlier "servant" element. Large-scale emigration and declining population had produced some severe labor shortages, thereby strengthening the sindicatos' bargaining position. Increased tourism and contact with the outside world helped break down the traditional isolation and spread the understanding of labor conditions in other countries, and many Portuguese emigrant workers in France or Germany came home with new ideas about the unions they saw and their potential. The 1969 legislative elections also provided an impetus, stimulating the opposition (Socialists, Communists, progressive Catholics) to renewed activity and greater efforts at organizing worker support.

Then came the clamp-down. In the fall of 1970 the metallurgists, one of the most politically conscious groups, had rejected an offered labor contract, demanded higher wages, and called a meeting in a soccer stadium to rally their supporters. The government, which ordinarily did

not permit outdoor meetings, banned the rally and accused the metallurgists of "fomenting class struggle." Meanwhile, other unions had begun following the metallurgists' lead. Employers appealed to the government to do something to halt the ferment, and strong pressures were
brought to bear on the minister of corporations. The ministry responded
with two new decrees: the first gave the right to appoint the third member of the arbitration commissions back to the government, and the
second restored the government's right to suspend elected sindicato officials for activities "contrary to social discipline." The decrees opened
the way to renewed official control of the sindicatos, and armed with
this power the government summarily removed the metallurgists' leaders
on the grounds they were "trying to provoke an atmosphere of indiscipline and revolt."

These actions failed to restore labor peace. Once the door had been
opened, it proved difficult to slam it shut again. Other unions increased
their demands. Unpublicized strikes and slowdowns spread. Since strikes
were outlawed in corporative Portugal, it was left to the government
to decide whether a work "slowdown" or "stoppage" was really a strike
or not. The government vacilated, sometimes saying yes and sometimes
no. It broke up with police brutality a demonstration of the shop clerks,
but it acceded to the demands of others. It disallowed any steps toward
the creation of a strong and independent central labor confederation,
but it tolerated an interunion group representing some fifteen of the
largest sindicatos and an estimated 200,000 workers which had precisely that goal in mind and which protested strongly against the brutal
treatment of the clerks.

The government continued to speak softly but to carry a big stick and
use it when necessary. New restrictions were enforced. The government
gave local authorities the right to approve candidates for sindicato elections and, according to local labor leaders, "these petty bureaucrats use
their powers unmercifully." Candidates for union elections had to meet
endless qualifications, and local authorities—if they wished—could always find one that would disqualify a particular candidate. Whether the
laws and restrictions were enforced or not depended on whim and the
pressures of the moment. One week the government would approve an
important wage increase for one sector, the next it would reject it for
another. A whole new politics grew up around the question of when a
strike was not a strike and when a union election candidate qualified or
when he did not. The sindicatos were bitter about the indecision and
uncertainty, but they kept up the pressures. In many cases, in keeping
with its broader goals, the government allowed significant wage raises
as a means of (hopefully) increasing its popularity, but it seldom gave

the unions much independent bargaining power. In this way, too, it sought to preserve the essential paternalistic and authoritarian structure of the system while at the same time staving off discontent. Later, it forced the interunion group (*Intersindical*) back underground; hence, unsanctioned workers' committees began growing up parallel to, but outside of, the official sindicato system and these factory "unity committees" organized clandestine strikes. In turn, the unions were purged, and the secret police helped break up disputes and arrest strike leaders. But the strikes grew bigger and more determined; how long the government could continue to manage these conflicting currents began to be a serious question.

Early in his term of office, thus, Caetano had demonstrated that his style and some of his policies would be different from Salazar's. Still within the authoritarian and corporatist mold, he sought to pull the center of gravity of Portuguese politics more toward the Center and away from immobilism and the extreme Right. His actions, however, in a country which had no broad Center were denounced by the leftist opposition as farcical ("Salazarism without Salazar") and resented by the Right and the old Salazaristas as potentially undermining the entire sociopolitical base of their power. Though Caetano was able to place his own men in some critical position in the ANP, the cabinet, and as civil governors of Portugal's provinces, the Right remained exceedingly powerful while the opposition Left continued to grow. Caetano never established a sufficiently strong independent power base to become a completely free agent; he had to proceed cautiously, his friends argued, because too swift an evolution would invite a coup that would thrust the country back into the rigid, unyielding Salazarista straitjacket. In this context of increasing pressures, division, and fragmentation, the Army remained, as it had been since the early nineteenth century, the ultimate arbiter of national politics. Recognizing this, and fearing that the threat on his Right was far greater than that on his Left, Caetano had begun to reverse himself by 1970 and 1971, to close many of the doors he had opened, to clamp down again on the press, the opposition, the unions, the students, and to realign himself with conservative elements, both civilian and military.[16]

By late 1972/73 and up until the revolt of April 1974, some of these conservative and stand-pat tendencies had again been altered. The essential structures of the authoritarian state apparatus remained in place, but a considerable amount of relaxation of the controls had also occurred. Censorship remained in effect, but clever journalists and editors had devised ingenious ways to say elliptically what they could not say directly. Long essays about democracy and elections in France or Chile, for instance, were not really about France or Chile; they were about Portugal. The opposition remained under restraints; but it was still able to hold important meetings such as the Aveiro Congress, which brought together Socialists, Christian-democrats, liberals, and even some Communists from all over the country. The opposition was also allowed to publish its journals and reviews (again including Communist and Maoist magazines) and to gain publicity for its cause. A new round of elections that again brought oppositionists to positions of leadership in the sindicatos was allowed to stand, and in May/June 1973 a series of collective contracts, the result of tough hard bargaining, brought major pay increases to some 200,000 workers in the nation's largest unions.

Meanwhile, the Right also remained highly active, continuing to put enormous pressure on Caetano. Through its veterans' and active officer associations, the Army made certain its presence was felt, especially on African questions; powerful rightist politicians like Franco Nogueira issued statements that forced the government to alter its course or to clamp down on students and other dissidents; and wealthy banking and industrial interests were able, as usual, to gain direct access to the centers of governmental political-economic decision making and "to put the screws on" some of the Caetano policies. Some real power struggles took place, and the elements of politics and political competition began to come back, after being submerged so long in Salazar's bureaucratic-administrative state.

In all these conflicts Caetano himself remained an enigma. An enormously intelligent and articulate man, scholarly and professorial, he continued to be regarded as *the* great hope for the "liberalization" of the Portuguese regime. His popular image was that of a man whose heart was in all the right places, yet who was continuously frustrated in his efforts to bring change by exceedingly strong rightist and military elements. While this was the public image, there is precious little evidence that Caetano was much less authoritarian than his predecessor or that he was really the frustrated liberal of the press accounts. In retrospect what probably emerges most clearly about Caetano is his essential weakness as a leader, his vacillation, his failure to seize opportunities when they presented themselves, his inability to wield his power when he had it. There was a time, for example, when he could probably have rid himself of President Thomaz, a perpetual thorn in Caetano's side, a powerful link to rightist forces, who never let Caetano forget he was still on probation and that the president had the constitutional authority to dismiss the prime minister. He could also at one point have dissolved the Legião, another source of rightist pressure, but he had temporized and the chance slipped by. There were initiatives that Caetano failed to seize in dealing with the African situation, and other opportunities when he could have used his own personal following and the popular support he was rallying to put the rightists in place, establish his own supporters in key military positions, reform the economy, and get the old-line Salazaristas off his back—if he wished. It will remain for future historians to decide if Caetano was really as much an authoritarian as Salazar at heart, if he was instead a frustrated liberal, or if he was simply weak and indecisive.[17]

While Caetano vacillated, the country continued to drift. The economy was in trouble, unemployment increased, and inflation, always held under control by Salazar, now soared to 20 percent. Wage increases frequently failed to match the inflation, and grumbling, discontent, and popular disaffection grew. Both the political and the economic clouds looked uncertain, and oppositionists on both Left and Right began increasingly to test and challenge the regime, to see how far they could go and how much they could get away with, and eventually, in the tentative and uncertain world of Portuguese politics, to launch their own political trial balloons. Meanwhile, the debilitating wars in Africa continued, with the Portuguese position growing steadily worse, the nation more and more isolated internationally, and the drain not only on the Portuguese economy but also on her soul becoming unbearable. It is in this context that the various movements were launched culminating in the revolt of April 1974.

The regime of Marcello Caetano thus remained a profoundly conservative one in the face of mounting pressures for change. Caetano could be considered an enlightened conservative, however, probably not far from the then center of Portuguese politics. His style of leadership, like that of Salazar, was based on the fact that he saw himself as the *chefe de familia* responsible for the welfare of all Portuguese; he was conservative in wanting to preserve what he saw as the best of Portuguese traditions, including the corporate system. He was determined to reform, strengthen, and refurbish the institutions that existed rather than change the fundamental structures themselves. His orientation was toward working within the authoritarian and corporate system that he, after all, had helped design. As both designer and product of the regime, Caetano could thus be counted on to revitalize rather than eliminate it.

But Caetano also appreciated the need to modernize the regime and to provide for greater economic and social development, and he saw that reaction and traditionalism alone were inadequate. Hence, his emphasis on social reforms, on giving the unions greater bargaining power, on curbing the profiteering of the wealthy. Above all, however, he seemed determined to avoid anything that would threaten the unity and

continuity of the regime or jeopardize its order and tranquillity, as exemplified by the mottoes that adorned Lisbon telephone poles or the
titles of Caetano's volumes of collected speeches: "Progresso sem desi-
quilibrio" ("progress without disequilibrium"), "Renovação na continuidade" ("renovation in continuity"). Steering something of a middle
course, he found eventually that Portugal had precious little middle
ground; avoiding confrontation, he found himself confronted; a moderate, he was overwhelmed by powerful extremes; walking a narrow tight-
rope with the Left clamoring for a wholesale remodeling of the system,
on the one side, and the Right, on the other, determined to block any
changes, he eventually lost his ability to balance and reconcile the contending pressures and to hold them together. He seemed increasingly
out of touch. On April 25, 1974, he was ousted in a coup that came
not from the Right, as he and his supporters had always feared, but
from the Left.[18]

Corporative Developments

Under Salazar in the 1960s, the corporative system had been ignored
and rendered almost impotent. It hardly functioned at all. Minister of
Corporations Gonçalves Proença made many fine speeches and a good
deal of new social legislation was enacted, but little of this became
actual operating reality. The gremios were able to ignore with official
impunity the requests by the sindicatos for collective contract negotiations, the workers bore the brunt of austerity and of inflation's heavy
weight, social security benefits remained the lowest by far in Western
Europe—and the situation was getting comparatively worse. Corporations officials were frank to admit that under Salazar the system functioned as an essentially capitalist and exploitive system, benefiting those
with wealth and property but not at all living up to its promises of equality between employers and employees and social justice for all. The
system existed in law and on paper, but it seldom functioned in actual
practice—at least in accord with its original principles.

It would be Caetano's purpose to make the system function for the
first time—in practice as well as in theory. Caetano gave an impetus to
the corporative laws and decrees and began to implement and use what
had been an inoperative system. Creaky, rusty institutions that had
hardly functioned for decades were now revitalized, new corporative
decrees and reforms poured forth, the realm of social assistance and
sindicato activity was vastly expanded. Perhaps most important, Caetano began the transition from an essentially capitalistic-monopolistic
economic system profiting only a few to an *Estado Social* benefiting the

many. He aimed to expand the social security and assistance programs, give greater wage increases and equality of representation to workers, reduce the wide gaps between social classes, and create a society more in accord with the social-services-oriented nations of Western Europe. For all his indecision, false starts, backpedaling, and vacillation in other areas, this change, and its accompanying changes in the area of labor relations, amounted to a veritable revolution in the Portuguese context.

There can be no doubt that Caetano remained a corporatist, though like his predecessor he was aware of the changed context of the postwar period, recognized realistically the growth of other, newer institutional arrangements, and had consigned corporatism to only one or two spheres of activity. Nevertheless Caetano maintained his commitment to the corporatist plan and program and was, at the least, immensely proud of this abstract system he had been instrumental in fashioning. Within two weeks of his inauguration as premier, in October 1968 Caetano received the chairmen of the various corporative agencies. In his prepared remarks he emphasized how closely his public life had been connected with corporative doctrine and spirit. The work of constructing the corporative complex has been completed, he said; it is an extensive network that is one of the vital organs of the nation. He stressed the gradual growth, from scratch, of the workers' and employers' associations accompanying the industrial growth of the nation, the reign of social peace accomplished, and the benefits achieved for employees. Without class war or ruin, Caetano said, the Portuguese workers have obtained all the just benefits that in other systems cost the working class and the national economies immense sacrifices. The corporative agencies have accomplished much, he stated; they have served to ameliorate the tensions inherent in an industrializing society, they have helped articulate group interests, they have served as the institutions for activating and implementing a vast web of labor and social legislation, and they have been the instruments for collaboration with the government for the common good. "Gentlemen," he said in closing, "you, as chairmen of the corporative agencies, are sufficient guarantee that the corporative spirit lives and is practiced. . . . The Government, in remaining faithful to the Political Constitution, of necessity remains faithful to the corporative ideals." [19]

Caetano returned to these themes only three weeks later in an important symbolic visit to the Corporations Ministry. He repeated what he had only briefly alluded to in the earlier speech, that the corporative structure would be responsible for carrying out his ambitious social programs. He emphasized the revolutionary nature of the corporative reorganization since the 1930s as changing the bases of the society.

As contrasted with the old system, he said, where the workers had no protection and class strife was predominant, now the fruits are visible. Corporatism has provided harmony and equilibrium, maintained discipline, and promoted progress. But the job is not done, he continued, the spirit had declined, time had helped wear it down, the routine remained but not the original idealism. The Corporations Ministry had made noble progress in the past ten years, but to be viable corporatism must be lived by the whole nation. In issuing his clarion call for social justice (an *Estado Social*) as the new focus for corporative activity, however, he was careful to emphasize practical solutions: increased labor benefits must arise from greater productivity, economic progress must be the precondition for greater social security, programs to benefit one sector of the population cannot be divorced from the general interest. And clearly it would still be the state that would regulate and determine these priorities. Caetano concluded by urging "fealty to the propositions that thirty years before constituted the great promise of social reform as formulated in the corporative legislation." [20]

While Caetano was reiterating his faith in corporative principles and articulating his new conception of the Estado Social, he was also careful to hedge his commitments. And as usual his policies were ambiguous and two sided. Though issuing glowing eulogies to the corporatist faith, Caetano made it plain he intended to confine corporatism to a limited sphere of activities. Corporatism was no longer at the center of the Portuguese system but was only one (and perhaps small) part of it. He saw an important but limited role for the corporative agencies—beyond which he did not expect them to go. His frequent remarks to corporative officials, while encouraging of their work, were seldom very enthusiastic. He referred to the future of the corporative system more often than its past, its potential rather than its concrete benefits. Only two weeks after his statement at the Corporations Ministry, he made another very pragmatic speech to the National Assembly outlining the policies of his government but never once mentioning corporatist ideology or organizations. Thus, while Caetano and his government, "in remaining faithful to the Political Constitution, of necessity also remained faithful to corporative ideals," the real focus and centers of power and decision making in the system, as under Salazar, continued to lie elsewhere.

The ambiguous place, position, and functions of the corporative system in Caetano's mind were even more apparent in the minds of his corporate subordinates. When Caetano spoke of the "corporative structure," he usually meant just the corporations and the Corporative Chamber, not the ministry. For him the ministry became more and more an agency of social assistance and social welfare; the corporative label had become largely symbolic. In their public utterances Corporations Ministry officials also went through the motions of expressing adherence to corporative principles, but it was clear they knew little of corporative philosophy and ideology and said what they said as a matter of form rather than of conviction. By the 1970s the Corporations Ministry (in capitals) was a corporations ministry (lower case) in name only; most foreigners referred to it in translation as the "Ministry of Labor and Social Assistance" rather than the "Ministry of Corporations." The latter was too confusing to those who knew nothing of the earlier history, and by now it had little to do with what that ministry did. Labor relations and social assistance—these were the two chief functions of the Ministry of Corporations, while the manifestly corporative aspects were all but forgotten—except perhaps by a few old corporatist ideologues like Caetano himself. And even in Caetano's present conception, the role and functions of the "corporative complex" were far removed from his vision as articulated in the 1920s and 1930s.[21]

The actual functions of the Corporations Ministry and the other corporative agencies during Caetano's rule thus represented an effort to steer the entire system in a new social services direction. This orientation too had started earlier but had begun to flower and be implemented only under Caetano. His aim was to provide protection to the workers and social promotion to the humble, and despite the implied paternalism, there can be no doubt that Caetano's sense of social responsibility was genuine and sincere. The range and variety of the new programs were little short of phenomenal. One could almost say that the corporative reforms and revolutions begun in the 1930s were now, *for the first time,* beginning to be carried out.

From the start Caetano had personally taken a far more active role in the running of the corporative system. This was due both to his own commitments and to the growing scandal concerning the alleged embezzlement activities of the minister of corporations. Caetano made a point of being physically present at numerous activities related to the corporative system, he was the guiding force behind the rewriting of the sindicatos' Organic Law giving greater freedom to the unions, and it was on his initiative that important steps were taken beginning in 1969 to open up the system to genuine collective bargaining. By early 1970, in keeping with his strong social assistance orientation, Caetano had determined to consolidate the Corporations Ministry with that of health. The consolidation provided the rationalization for "pensioning off" the old minister, Gonçalves Proença (who became director of the Institute of Advanced Economic and Financial Sciences, a deputy in the National

Assembly, and secretary general of the Bank of Angola), and for bringing in the younger, dynamic Baltasar Leite Rebelo de Sousa, ex-
governor-general of Mozambique and one of Caetano's protégés. Rebelo
de Sousa knew nothing of corporative theory and ideology, but he was
an able administrator who could carry out on a day-to-day basis general
policies made, as always, in the prime minister's office.[22]

A new flurry of corporative activity ensued, comparable only to the
period of initiation in the 1930s and the revival of the 1950s. In the
light of criticisms that had been made for at least twenty-five years, the
casas do povo structure was revised, chiefly to convert them into local
agencies for the administration of Caetano's new social assistance programs.[23] By the end of 1973 over 80 percent of the nation's parishes
contained (on paper at least) an administrative agency, called a casa
do povo, for the dispensing of social services. At the same time, the
labor legislation built up over the preceding thirty-five years was progressively extended to the rural areas, as well as to domestic workers.
New accords were signed between the national casa do povo organization and the caixas de previdência to provide expanded health
care, family allowances, social security, and the like. New regulations
were promulgated to strengthen the intermediary corporative agencies
(uniões and federações), and the casas dos pescadores were given expanded social security coverage. Efforts were even made to force businessmen and industrialists to work through their representative gremio
organizations and to devolve upon the corporations some broader responsibilities in the areas of planning, collective contract negotiations,
economic policy making, and consultation. At the end of 1973 the first
corporations president ever to come from sindicato ranks was elected,
a symbolic gesture, of course, but not, therefore, without major importance.[24]

We have discussed labor's ups and downs in the preceding section.
The trend was decidedly toward more ups than downs. In addition to
the greater freedom to choose their own leaders and to bargain collectively, a new set of regulations governing collective contracts was promulgated in August 1969. Collective contracts were now made obligatory for workers and employers in most major industries, and the
government absented itself more and more from these negotiations. The
old idea of class collaboration gave way to one where differences of
interest were recognized as inevitable and where direct negotiations and
arbitration between the contending parties were made mandatory. Only
in exceptional cases was the government to step in.[25] Table 1 indicates
the degree to which collective bargaining and the labor contract in-

creasingly replaced the *via administrativa* (wages set by government, the prevailing pattern under Salazar).

The sindicatos additionally were made eligible for greater financial support from the government. They were allowed to organize on a basis larger than that of the locality or the single industry, a restriction which had kept them severely fragmented and atomized in the past. New regulations were also made for the Organizations of Economic Coordination, both to put them on a more permanent basis and to integrate them more rationally into the corporative system.[26] A new statute was published regulating the *tribunais do trabalho* (labor tribunals), still another for the reform of the arbitration commissions. The Corporative Chamber was called upon to give more attention to government policy proposals and to issue more *pareceres;* at the same time, a permanent section of auditors and technicians was created to assist the Chamber and the individual *procuradores* in the fulfillment of these tasks.

The Corporations Ministry itself was reorganized as new services and departments were created. The task of integrating the health and medical services with the corporative and social assistance agencies, and of coordinating, harmonizing, and expanding the services provided, required all the administrative skills of the new minister. The ministry was also decentralized somewhat and its various sections given greater autonomy. Under Caetano's leadership, thus, the entire corporative structure, as well as the rest of the governmental system, began to come out of the deep freeze of the Salazar period, to come alive again, to

Table 1   Collective Contracts vs. Government Edicts as the Means for Resolving Labor Disputes

	Collective Labor Contracts				Government Edicts (via administrativa)		
Year	Direct Negotiations	Conciliation	Arbitrated Decision	Total	State Regulations Governing	Enlargement of the Scope of Regulations	Total
1970	60	5	2	67	6	54	60
1971	84	37	25	146	19	56	75
1972	58	24	20	102	11	63	74
1973*	18	7	1	26	6	9	15
Total	220	73	48	341	42	182	224

Source: Ministerio das Corporações.   *First trimester only.

begin functioning after years of neglect. There was even a new sense of pride, absent for decades, in the corporative system and the uniqueness of the Portuguese institutions. In early 1974 the pride spilled over into a challenge to France in a contest, of all things, of corporative *futebol,* or soccer.

These changes in the structures and functions of the corporative system were also marred by the shifts and reversals, the false starts and vacillations, that had come to characterize Caetano's rule. While some of this was undoubtedly due to the prime minister's weaknesses and ambivalence in the use of power, it also had to do with the rightist pressures upon him and the tactic of taking one step backward in order to move two ahead. Further, the cumulative effect of this whole series of openings was significant, and by 1973/74 Portugal was a far different, more open, freer—yes, even more pluralist and democratic (Caetano himself began using these terms, instead of referring to it as *corporatist*) —than it had been in 1968. It may well be (and it is certainly in accord with the interpretations of the causes of other major revolutions) that Caetano was overthrown in April 1974, not when Portugal was so badly off but when it was in fact becoming better off, not when the economy and living standards were dropping but in fact when they were rising. These improvements, gradual and incremental to be sure but no less real for being so, have been obscured by the more dramatic overturn during 1974 and by the popular, *post hoc ergo prompter hoc* interpretation of the Caetano regime as wholly reactionary and backward-looking. Such an interpretation, we have seen, not only misrepresents the nature of the Caetano government and the changes it had initiated but also leads to a misinterpretation of the April revolution. Revolutions occur, Crane Brinton and a host of other scholars have shown us, not when a society falls to rock bottom (as Portugal had perhaps done in the last few years of Salazar) but when conditions are improving, albeit not fast enough to satisfy the new expectations that have been raised.[27]

In the area of new policies and social programs similar gains were also registered. Some of these innovations, as before, got little farther than the pages of the *Diario do governo;* however, many of them, including those promulgated years before by Salazar, now began to be implemented for the first time. It was not phantom programs that so frightened the Right and goaded wealthy interests into opposition to Caetano but *real* programs that threatened potentially to undermine their wealth and elevated positions. The great variety of programs, old and new, can be grouped under eight major categories: the social aspects of planning, salary policy, hand-labor training, the reorganization of the Corporations Ministry, new studies of social security and labor laws, development of labor organization and corporative agencies, employment and professional formation, and social security.[28]

In terms of the social aspects of planning, the newly created Gabinete de Planejamento of the Corporations Ministry was called upon in 1973 to prepare diverse chapters dealing with social goals and programs to be included in the Fourth National Development Plan—the first time that such goals were included in the Plan and that the Corporations Ministry was asked to contribute. As regards salary policy, the ministry continued, as already indicated, to move ahead both in authorizing significant salary increases for workers in a wide variety of industries (wages in 1973 were more than double those of a decade earlier) and in devolving the power to negotiate collective contracts directly upon the interested parties, workers and employers, rather than always having these set in the ministry itself. As for hand-labor training, the ministry commissioned a number of studies and began some educational and technical training programs, but they hardly even made a dent in the problems of the rural poor or their high rates of un- and underemployment. The reorganizations in the Corporations Ministry largely involved the closer integration of the health and social assistance programs into the corporative structure, the organization of regional and local offices for the administration of the social services, and the setting up of new specialized agencies within the ministry to administer the expanded or new programs.

The Centro de Estudos meanwhile was carrying out new studies chiefly in the social security fields: the implications of a company's closing for its former employees; the limits on the power to discipline workers; benefits and pension programs; an examination of the tendencies in the collective regulation of labor. As for the corporative organizations, numerous new sindicatos and gremios came into existence, efforts were made to strengthen the old ones, some more-or-less important functions were found for the corporations to become engaged in, and other corporate units, unused for so long, now became the centers of some, albeit limited, activities. As regards employment and professional formation, the ministry began serving as a clearinghouse for employment opportunities and publishing daily lists of available jobs in the local press. New provisions also made emigrant laborers eligible for the benefits of social security for the first time and legalized their status, while the Division of Professional Formation helped train handicapped workers, found jobs for them, and opened a number of technical schools and training programs. Finally, in the area of social security and assistance, the ministry initiated a number (never adequate, but at least something was being done) of low-cost housing projects, extended social security coverage to new categories of workers, expanded the benefits to those already covered, and created new and decentralizd caixas de previdência.

Even with all these changes, the Portuguese worker still remained the lowest paid in Western Europe, and his social security benefits were by far the most meager. But Portugal was still a poor country, with few resources and finite bounds on the percent of GNP it could spend on social programs. Certainly by European standards its position was low (that had always been the case historically and would probably continue to be the case regardless of any change of regimes); as compared with the austerity and hardship forced on them by Salazar, however, there is no doubt the Portuguese people, including the lower classes, were better off under Caetano's interim rule than they had ever been before.

Even the above list hardly does justice to the variety of programs underway within the corporative structure or to its new dynamism and activity.[29] The family allowance schedule was increased to approximately $2.80 per month for the first child and $2.40 for each additional child. A new program (again quite limited) of rural medicine was introduced. New hospitals were built (never enough) and "systemic," comprehensive health care services provided to those workers eligible under the corporative system. The government subsidized pharmacies to provide drugs to workers at half the regular price; new attention was given to the underprivileged and to the retraining of those injured in the course of work. Pension and life insurance benefits were increased, the family allowance was extended to rural workers, and at least some of the advantages of coverage under the labor laws were extended to the overseas provinces.[30] Increasingly, furthermore, these reforms were carried out quietly and efficiently, not with any great ideological fanfare but in a no-nonsense and responsible fashion under the administrative leadership of Minister Rebelo de Sousa. That is perhaps one of the most striking aspects of the Caetano-inspired reforms: the new programs were no longer just *para inglês ver* but were instead carried through unobtrusively and without great publicity, resulting in real wage increases and genuinely improved living standards rather than being merely "great promises" or purely paper documents.

And yet, despite these reforms, the corporative system was still widely resented, rejected, or treated with indifference by the Portuguese. Among the population at large, who were not very political and who indeed since Salazar had been depoliticized, indifference and apathy generally reigned. On the part of the gremios, whose members were being increasingly called upon to shoulder the burden of the wage increases and who continued to be weighed down with seemingly endless new rules and regulations, the resentments were stronger. Feelings were perhaps strongest among labor leaders who had to cope regularly with what remained an essentially paternalistic and elitist system, but here again one must differentiate between those labor "politicians" tied in with the regime and those who rejected it out of hand. Among the former, the *pelegos trabalhistas,* who were often both labor leaders and government bureaucrats at the same time, it was relatively easy to work out a compromise, to accommodate some demands, to make "the system" work. Such collaborators were most often not very ideological, able to get along with virtually any government that might come to power, and able to get benefits for their workers as long as these were confined to reasonable bounds and they themselves remained loyal to the regime.

Among the more ideological labor leadership, however, the Communists and militant Socialists, the situation was often different. They rejected the system per se. Of course, among many of these such rejection and a militant stance represented mere posturing, a way of using radical rhetoric to strike a pose, to get publicity and force the government to listen, a kind of game distinct from that of the *pelegos,* which sounded revolutionary but which in fact (as both the militants and the government recognized) had somewhat more limited goals.

The militants rejected the system as "fascistic" and derived from the Italian pattern.[31] They pointed out that, while corporatist ideology was both anticapitalist and antisocialist, in fact under Salazar Portugal became the most capitalist of nations, backed by an authoritarian state, existing at the expense of the workers. They denounced the corporative agencies as artificial creations subservient to the government, and the system of collective contracts as a means by which the state carried out its antiinflationary policies. From 1933 on, one opposition report said, collective labor negotiations had oscillated between the paternalistic intervention of the Corporations Ministry and the "good will" of employers. The corporations were castigated as agencies without any public utility, and the Portuguese regime was said to be an instrument of patronal interests. The unions had remained "pulverized," and no agency of government, it was said, was genuinely concerned with the welfare of the workers. The opposition program hence called for a restoration of the democratic order and the liquidation of the corporative system:

1. The corporations were to be abolished, to be replaced by institutions (undefined) of a "democratic nature."

2. The various other sectors and institutions of the corporative structure were to be dissolved, transformed, or integrated into the new democratic order.
3. The Organizations of Economic Coordination were to be integrated into the normal services of public administration.
4. Recognizing the importance of class associations in the social and political realm, the government would liberate the casas, ordens, and sindicatos connected with the corporate structure and give complete sovereignty to their general assemblies.
5. The gremios would be converted into class associations whose leaders would be elected by the membership.
6. The casas do povo and casas dos pescadores might continue as reorganized corporative agencies, without prejudice against the rights of labor associations also to organize their members.[32]

Although the opposition critique sounds strident in places and was frequently far removed from the everyday realities and actual workings of the Portuguese corporative system, it should not be thought that such criticisms were confined only to radical and Marxist groups. Social democrats, liberals, progressive Christians, and other moderates echoed many of the same criticisms. The liberal, social-democratic weekly *Expresso*, for example, served as one major forum where the weaknesses of the sindicatos and of the entire corporative structure were regularly discussed. *Expresso* too called for a democratic system based on free rather than government-controlled associability; it began in 1973 to refer directly to the "superfluousness" of the system and the evolution toward a "postcorporative state." [33] The liberal reviews *Seara nova* and *Vida mundial* also favored the abolition of the corporatist system, and so did, almost universally, the student generation. Young Catholics and even some clergy, brought up on Vatican II rather than *Rerum Novarum* and *Quadragesimo Anno,* similarly urged a democratic solution. Among labor leaders, although many had learned to work within the system, the sentiment was also almost universal that the corporative system constituted a set of controls and regulations that frustrated trade union activities and that the entire system was prejudicial against the working class.[34]

Nor were officials of the various corporative agencies entirely divorced from the discontent. Lawyers working for the Corporations Ministry or who had dealings with it were often so frustrated by the complex and frequently contradictory jungle of corporative legislation, decree-laws, and so on, that had grown up over some forty years that they urged a rewriting and streamlining of the entire system. Some wanted to abolish it completely. Labor officials connected with the INTP recognized the grievances of the workers, but since all major decisions regarding salary increases, benefits, and so forth, still came from on high, they felt powerless to do very much about them. Officials of the ministry, the corporations, and the Corporative Chamber recognized further that often the sindicatos were incapable of competing with the gremios on an even basis, that the gremios were not only stronger organizationally with full-time staffs and considerable resources but also well connected both in the Corporations Ministry and throughout the government. Gremio leaders could contact the other ministries and regulatory agencies directly without going through the corporative bureaucracy and the jungle of regulations: "When the gremios have a grievance," said one ministry official, "they simply call us up; the sindicatos do not because they are not used to operating in that ambience."

Albeit without the same intensity of feeling as those directly affected, corporative officials were frequently sympathetic to the problems the sindicato leaders articulated: the poverty of the workers, their essential powerlessness, the capitalistic biases of the system, rural problems and poverty, inadequacy of health and medical care and of social security benefits, the often ineffective bargaining strength of the sindicatos. To a man, however, these officials were convinced that, while the pace of change was slow, conditions were infinitely better than under Salazar, the corporative program was really being implemented for the first time, the system *was* becoming responsive, and the ministry itself was inclined more and more to side with workers in contract negotiations, instead of with employer and patronal interests as in the past. Admitting the functions of the system were quite different than in the 1930s and that the "corporative" name was at times unfortunate, these officials quashed the rumors sometimes heard elsewhere that the government might be contemplating abolishing the corporative system. "Despite the faults and limitations which we recognize," they said, "we cannot see how Portugal would function short of chaos if the institutions, procedures, and services built up and performed by the corporative complex over the years were to be suddenly abolished." [35]

On balance, then, the corporative system under Caetano had become a functioning system, albeit a seriously flawed and severely restrictive one. There can be no doubt that Caetano gave a strong impetus to the corporative laws and decrees and had begun to implement a system that had been largely unused and inoperative before. Caetano, thus, in this as in other areas, was hardly the "liberal" portrayed in the early press accounts; rather, his reform efforts can be looked at as an attempt to dynamize the existing corporative forms and institutions. It is within a corporative-authoritarian context and not a liberal-democratic one that his regime must be evaluated.

Under Salazar during the 1960s, both the corporative structure and indeed virtually the entire Portuguese system had all but ground to a halt. In terms that are now familiar, his regime especially in its later years represented a freezing of society, of the elite, of the whole governmental process. More than this, under Salazar the corporative system had become an essentially state-protected capitalist structure acting not on the basis of parity between workers and employers but in favor of the latter at the expense of the former. Caetano sought to correct these imbalances and to instigate some progressive reforms, while still operating within the context of the corporative order. His policies helped strengthen the sindicatos, to the point that some of them (clerks, bank workers, metallurgical workers, textile workers) became even stronger than the gremios of which they were counterparts. The Corporations Ministry, at the prime minister's instructions, was consciously trying to reduce the differences between the low level of the workers and the privileged place of the patrões, to make income scales more equitable, to reduce the social gaps. The forms of the corporative system existed under Salazar, but they had evolved in a way that corrupted corporatism's original goals and converted Portugal into a bastion of capitalism and special privilege. Under Caetano, however, the labor sector was strengthened and a nascent pluralist system began to come into existence. Under Salazar there were no strikes and the instruments of control fashioned by the dictatorship enforced labor "peace." Caetano allowed (within the limits imposed by his corporative conception and the realities of Portuguese politics) the first real trade union activity to take place in forty years and some tough, hard bargaining and confrontations. From the one-man monolith of the Salazar years, the regime had evolved toward some genuine (albeit limited and still controlled) interest, class, and issue oriented politics. Portugal began to change from the autocratic, closed, capitalistic structure of Salazar to an Estado Social that was both more open and more socially just. For Portugal such changes could almost be called revolutionary.[36]

It is precisely because they were genuine changes, not merely paper ones, and with potentially revolutionary implications, that the Right and those who had profited so much from the Salazar policies objected so strenuously. As we shall see in the following chapter, the real threat to Caetano's rule had always come not from the Left but from the Right. It was on the Right—in the Army, the economic oligarchy, the Salazarista bureaucracy and political organization—that the preponderance of power lay, which helps explain why Caetano's reforms were so hesitant, so gradual, and so frequently reversed. Nevertheless, the long-term trends by 1973/74 were clearly in the direction of changing the system, of reforming it, of unfreezing the elite and providing new opportunities. One need only look at the numerous reforms and changes in the corporative system—here only highlighted—to gain a sense of the sweeping transformations underway.[37] Some of these ended, of course, as only paper changes, if not any longer for the English to see, then certainly for the EEC. But the vast majority were real changes, aimed not at impressing foreigners but at improving the Portuguese standard of living. True also, the changes were piecemeal, gradual, evolutionary, often capricious, carried out under authoritarian auspices and still within the corporative structure; but their cumulative effects were immense— and all this in keeping with the model of the Iberic-Latin change process as outlined in chapter 1.

The corporative system was at last becoming a functioning system, a part of the whole national structure, one of the givens, a system that was being administered, and where the day-to-day work went on not altogether differently than it does, under different labels, in other systems. It was called a corporative system in Portugal, but the functions performed were by this time not really very different from those performed by labor and social assistance or social security ministries in other nations. The corporative structure had thus found its place; it was no longer at the base of the system, but it was performing numerous useful services in the areas of labor relations, social welfare, and, to some extent, interest representation. The corporative system had even acquired finally a degree of popular acceptance. Its faults and problems as well as the inequalities inherent within the system were recognized, but slow progress was being made toward resolving some of the most glaring defects. Perhaps no more or no less could be said for other "systems," liberal or socialist, whose chief difference from the Portuguese was coming to be more the labels used to describe them than the actual policies being pursued. It is significant that it was precisely at the time of the major modernization of the Portuguese corporative system— and at a time when that system was becoming more and more like the disguised corporate, semiliberal, and similarly state-capitalist and bureaucratic-authoritarian systems of Western Europe and North America[38]—that the revolution came.

X

Does Corporatism Matter? Or, How the Portuguese System Really Worked

Repeatedly in the course of this book we have alluded to the fact, or been led to conclude from the analysis, that power in Portugal did not lie within the corporative complex, that the real centers of decision making continued to be concentrated elsewhere within the Portuguese system. For although the Constitution of 1933 proclaimed Portugal a corporative state and though in the ideology of the regime—at least in the 1930s—corporatism was to lie at the base of the nation's associational life and to infuse all social relations and governmental structures, the fact is that little real authority was ever devolved upon the corporative agencies and "corporative consciousness" remained, at best, latent and undeveloped. But if power did not lie within the corporative structure, where *did* it lie, what were the strongest and most potent centers of influence, how did the decision-making process operate? This chapter begins to answer the question of how the Portuguese system *really* worked (or at least did work before the April 1974 coup, and perhaps, with numerous qualifiers, still does work) and also starts to assess from this more general perspective the actual role of corporatism and the corporatist structure in the broader national system.[1]

The first fact to note is that, for all its corporatist theory, law, ideology, and structures, the Portuguese system under Salazar was always an intensely personalist regime as much as it was a corporatist one. It was Salazar who managed and ran the Portuguese governmental system, not any impersonal agencies or institutions, be they "corporate" or any other kind. His was a Bonapartist and autocratic regime, with a rather delicate balance of classes and political forces in which an individual dictator, by skill and force of personality, to say nothing of a broad gamut of authoritarian controls, found ample room for maneuver and manipulation.

The Portugal of Salazar was a modern, more complex, authoritarian extension of nineteenth-century *caciquismo*—updated and renovated, to be sure, and under civilian, professorial leadership (a *catedrátocracia,* or "government of dons," as it was sometimes called) rather than military (although, as in all *cacique* regimes, it continued to exist at the suffrance of the military, of which Salazar was a master manipulator). Or, if one prefers, one can see the Salazar regime as an extension of nineteenth-century monarchy, with Salazar playing the traditional "moderating" role that the king had played up to 1910, balancing and reconciling the contending forces, while himself remaining aloof and above the everyday struggle of party politics (outlawed by Salazar, as under the monarchy) and interest group conflict (submerged within the corporative system). There is no doubt that, for all the corporate agencies and obscure philosophies, and for all the authoritarian structures in other areas, the entire Portuguese system still revolved around Salazar personally. He was at the center and apex of the system, almost a one-man government, the focus of a regime that may have been at least as much autocratic as it was authoritarian.[2]

If Salazar's own personal stature and position were so critical, it behooves us to know far more about the man and the style of his rule than we do. Henrique Galvão, the romantic oppositionist who gained fleeting notoriety when he hijacked the cruise liner *Santa Maria,* explained Salazar's rule in terms of his inordinate love for power.[3] There can be no doubt that, despite his own statements to the contrary, such a power drive was strong in Salazar, that he was jealous of his power, guarded it carefully, was fascinated by the uses of power and its manipulation, and was loathe to share it or give it up—although by all accounts Salazar was not particularly interested in the perquisites that usually go with power: money, mansions, opportunities for private self-enrichment. Power for its own sake—hoarded, monopolized, held absolutely—plus the stature, prestige, authority, and dominance that its exercise gave him, these seem to be the ends and purposes of Salazar's drives. Such a personal power drive was not incompatible with Salazar's undoubtedly sincere sense of self-sacrifice and dedicated service to the nation.

We have other images of Salazar. One is the Salazar of the Catholic preparatory school, the seminary student and roommate of Cardinal Cerejeira, the CADC founder and activist at Coimbra, the young man fascinated by the Catholic encyclicals and Catholic politics in the teens and twenties, and finally, by extension, the Salazar of what some scholars have called a "clerico-fascist regime." [4] Another image we have, not unrelated to the first, is that of the Coimbra economics professor and penny-pinching finance minister, the man of "superior" knowledge, stern and Victorian, disdainful of the common people, yet presuming to know what was best for them, the autocratic man of ideas who had grasped truth now and forever and brooked no criticism or challenge to those ancient lecture notes from either students or the man in the street. In Thomistic philosophy with its emphasis on rank, hierarchy, and immutable truths, and also in the encyclicals that claimed to present a modern-day Catholic response to the rise of capitalism and "the social question," Salazar had found his absolutes and he seldom deviated from them. These influences were powerful not only in shaping the nature of his corporatist-authoritarian system but also in explaining why it remained so fixed, immutable, frozen, and eventually dinosauric.

Then, there are the class interpretations. Salazar was petit bourgeois, small-town, and lower middle class to the core. When he took office, he based his regime on the discontent of the middle class with the old Republic and its longing for a government—any government—that could restore order and probity. He gave "social peace" to the small businessmen and merchants, better pay to the civil servants, new arms and prestige to the officer corps, a boost to Catholic teaching and missions, freedom from strikes to the commercial and industrial elements, and hefty wage increases to skilled workers. For diverse reasons, all middle-sector groups saw their champions in Salazar and the Army, and when they first came to power in the late 1920s, they enjoyed widespread "popular" (middle-sector) support.[5]

But Salazar was not only himself of the petit bourgeoisie and his regime based on middle-class support, but the entire corporatist idea and structure were, in a sense, reflective of this same middle-sector base. Representing a repudiation of both the traditionalism and aristocratic rule advocated by the wealthy elites *and* of confrontation and class war waged by the workers, Salazar's original idea was that the country should be governed by the petit bourgeoisie, or at least its most responsible members (like himself or Caetano), in the name of order, hierarchy, religion, and the family. Everyone would be disciplined and enlightened and would accept his place in the corporate hierarchy, tradition would be preserved, the country would advance, both the public interest and the welfare of its members would be enhanced, and the nation would avoid political upheaval and class rancor. As Fryer and McGowan-Pinheiro put it, this was Salazar's vision, the Philistine pedestrian vision of a plodding accountant who worked hard, counted each *tostão,* wanted everyone to spend only 90 percent of his income and squirrel away the rest of it—and who believed the national accounts should be balanced along the same lines.[6]

In the parallelogram of social forces that Salazar had concocted in the corporate scheme, he had left himself a great deal of room for personal maneuver and manipulation. He was not himself of the old elite (in fact, he despised the pompous aristocrats whose only accomplishment had been to inherit wealth and family name), and it would be a mistake to identify his regime wholly with elitism and reaction. But at the same time, Salazar would come to be manipulated by the most powerful of the emergent social classes, the new capitalistic and large, moneyed interests, which in the 1930s were not yet strong enough to openly impose their will on society. They needed Salazar to mediate between them and the growing middle sectors of society, meanwhile imposing strong controls on the working class. The business and industrial elements, never sharing Salazar's vision of a petit bourgeois corporatist society, had aims of their own; and by the mid-1930s, while continuing to see a usefulness in Salazar's rule, they had learned to manipulate him as well. What began as an authoritarian-corporatist and autocratic regime, albeit with a strong and genuine desire to carry out social justice, was thus converted into an agent of class rule, upper bourgeois, elitist, and capitalistic, chiefly through state protection for and benefits to the largest industrial and commercial enterprises.[7]

Although Salazar's (and eventually Caetano's) middle-class support was far less solid in the 1960s and early 1970s than it had been in the 1920s and 1930s, much of that support had remained—at least up to 1973—and had provided an indispensable prop for continued authoritarian rule. The wealthy economic elites recognized this support and the predominantly middle-class direction of Portuguese politics at least since 1910, and from their point of view Salazar and the corporative ideology provided a useful facade to shield their profit making and to serve as a buffer between them and the middle class. It is this latent, potential conflict that gave Salazar his independent power and some room to tack, at times squeezing still more sacrifices out of the lower and middle classes, at others taking cracks at the oligarchy. And it was the freezing of class relations in this pattern—a 1930s (or earlier) pattern modeled on Salazar's remembrances of Santa Comba Dão, the small provincial town where he grew up, with its rural, peaceful, static, hierarchical, mutually interdependent, unchanging social order—as well as the general lack of dynamism and opportunity for mobility during the entire, long Salazar era, that largely account for the stagnant and immobilist nature of Portuguese social and political life, its timeless and seemingly "feudal" characteristics. Salazar's corporate state and a conservative, deferential political culture mutually supported each other to maintain "good customs" and the social status quo.

In seeking thus to assess the influence of corporatism per se (in the 1930s sense) on public policy making in Portugal, to show how the

corporative structure fitted into a larger system of authoritarian, autocratic, *and* class rule, and to weigh the impact of the corporative agencies in the political process, we need to have a better knowledge of that
broader Portuguese *sistema* of which the corporative complex was but
one part. We have already stated the answer to the question of what the
overall role of the corporative system was in Portugal: limited and often
marginal. Philippe C. Schmitter's analysis[8] of how the general policy-
making process in Portugal shifted over time, however, sheds further
light on how this corporative complex was integrated into the larger
framework. Until the 1960's, he argues, the Portuguese system could
be described as heavily authoritarian and autocratic, with few well-
organized interests, and centering essentially in one man. It was a
strongly personalistic, executive-centered coalition, or "court" system,
in which Salazar surrounded himself with a set of trusted individuals,
each of whom represented separate functional hierarchies: the Army,
the Church, industry, the universities, finance, landowning, the bureaucracy, the party, and so on. The power and status of these representatives did not depend necessarily on any formal position they might have
held in the corporate hierarchy (although some of them did hold such
positions), or even on a formal ministerial or governmental post, but on
the more informal basis of loyalty to Salazar, service to the regime, and
personal trust and confidence. In this context the corporative structure
was used by Salazar, coopted into his system of personalist-autocratic
rule, manipulated by him to secure that rule, and never allowed to
achieve strong, independent power.

In the latter years of Salazar's rule and especially under Caetano,
many of these aging "cronies" were replaced by younger men, better
trained as managers and administrators, "technocrats" in the popular
parlance. The newer men were also attached directly to the president
of the council, and personal loyalty and service to him (a la the Nixon
staff) continued to be the overriding necessity. But by this time, in the
more complex Portuguese system of the 1960s and 1970s, intersectorial
and interministerial planning commissions, boards, and work groups,
and some major interest groups, had also become important sources for
policy initiatives, replacing to some extent the friends and old cronies
of the man in power. By now, in addition, the *sistema* was largely bypassing or ignoring the manifestly corporative structures, instead of
manipulating or coopting them as in the past.

But note that in *neither* model of the Portuguese system, neither the
"personalist" nor the "technocratic," had a major policy-making role
been given to the corporative agencies. In the former case this could be
explained in part by the relative newness of the corporative institutions

and the slowness in developing corporative consciousness; but in the latter case, as the bureaucracy and the planning and policy-making boards dealt directly with the firms, the major producers, and the big industrial, banking, and import-export concerns, and even occasionally the trade unions, the corporative agencies that had come into existence were largely ignored and disregarded in favor of more direct bureaucratic and interpersonal contacts. The corporative agencies were certainly not at the center of decision making, or, if they were, it was due to the personal influence and prestige of the individual holding a corporative position (such as Pereira in the early days, or Caetano) and not to the corporative position he might have held.

There are in the last sentences of the preceding paragraph hints of two additional cornerstones of the Portuguese edifice that, in addition to those already mentioned, help provide some critical understandings of how the entire system operated. The first refers to the formal-legalistic, but also informal and intensely personalistic, nature of the Portuguese system; the second concerns the crucial importance of the central state and of the state bureaucracy and administrative apparatus (including its control mechanisms and the apparatus of the dictatorship) in the larger picture of the Portuguese regime.

Portugal is (was?) undoubtedly among the more highly structured, formalistic, legalistic, hierarchically organized, and authoritarian of Western nations. Portugal in the 1960s and even on into the early 1970s could most appropriately be compared to pre-World War I Europe, with all the built-in rigidities, class consciousness, stiffness, and sense of place that that implies.[9] If a personal note can be interjected, I am used to operating in the often formalistic and legalistic *ambiente* of the Latin American nations, but nowhere in the New World are the old rules and regulations so strictly enforced as they were in Portugal. Credentials in Portugal are critical; without the proper dress, letters, connections, and introduction, one remains a nobody, not worth bothering with. Foreigners are somewhat outside of this hierarchical arrangement, but for the Portuguese one's place in the system is decidedly fixed.

It is interesting to observe interpersonal relations in this light, for virtually everything is dependent on dress (each class has its distinct "uniform"), speech, family, degree of education, bearing, status, and the other fellow's assessment of where one fits in the hierarchy. There is a pervasive sense of place and position; class roles and trappings are exceedingly important; society is described and behavior defined in terms of distinct, rigid types: worker, cleric, entrepreneur, servant, clerk, peasant, military officer, and so on. There is one mode of behavior and even tone of voice for dealing with equals, another for "superiors," still a third for "inferiors." Moreover, within this stratified pattern there is little possibility for advancement, which helps make the system even more rigid and unyielding. Other than through education (the Salazar and Caetano route), there is little mobility; unlike most Latin American countries, neither the Army nor competitive party politics nor any periodic changes of regimes (Portugal had none in nearly half a century) provided avenues for more than very limited upward mobility. Hence, one's turn in a waiting line or one's treatment in a store, business, or government agency are all dependent on where one fits in the system, what rank one holds. The structure of hierarchy and place is most pronounced in the countryside, but it also persists in the big cities such as Porto and Lisbon. Lisbon especially likes to think of itself as a big city, but in fact (and this is meant in an analytic, not a pejorative, sense) it is an overgrown town, quaint in its sights and customs (which makes it attractive to visitors), and still feudal and pertaining almost to the *ancien régime* in its preoccupations with rank and social position. Hierarchy, formality, legality, strict status and class consciousness— these are not only Old World characteristics but they are characteristics of an old world that largely died in 1914 in the rest of Europe but continued to live on in corporatist Portugal.[10]

It is important to emphasize these aspects of the Portuguese political culture because they also serve as control mechanisms in the broader political system. All the legalisms and formalisms, the rigidities and the hierarchies, serve—consciously so—as a means to keep the Portuguese in their place, to hold the lower and middle classes in check, to structure their participation carefully, cautiously, and under authoritarian state auspices, to erect mountains of legalistic barriers and bureaucratic procedures. It is a classic bureaucratic (in the derogatory, Kafkaesque sense) system, bureaucratic with a vengeance: pass a paper in, show identification, pay a fee, get another paper back, with nothing thereby accomplished and much time wasted. Then on to the next stage in the endless labyrinth: another paper, more identification, another fee, more papers back. It may take months and even years to extract a final authorization from the dark corridors of this bureaucratic maze.

The vast web of legalisms and bureaucratic requirements, of which those governing labor relations and the entire corporative system are the most elaborate and complex, serve as effective checks on individual and group activities and as barriers to unstructured pressures or encounters. Everything must be arranged and the appropriate responses worked out in advance. With society thought of as a set of stock characters and with each group or "class" expected to behave in accord with fixed rules, no free or open discussion can be permitted, and unexpected or unregulated contingencies are ruled out. Bureaucracy, paper work, administrative regulations—all serve as effective means to lock the faceless masses in place, freeze society, and permit only those changes of which the state approves.

On the other hand, for those with access and wide connections, chiefly among the economic and political elites, the mountains of papers and restrictions can be surmounted with no difficulty at all. On small matters like fixing the car, running errands, sending and receiving packages, and the like, the elites can send their *empregados,* whose time is not valuable and who can afford the endless hours in line which even modest transactions entail. On big things, those with wealth or good connections can simply pick up the phone, talk to a friend or relative who has access to a highly placed person in the right ministry or agency, perhaps even get that person to carry the request personally to the highest levels (Salazar's or Caetano's office) and get things done without all the legalisms and bureaucratic procedures. *Personalismo* and personal connections remain at least as important as group influence; the personalistic nature of the system also helps explain why there is such seemingly inordinate attention to cabinet remodeling, who is in or out, personal rivalries and interconnections. It is through such small and frequently subtle shifts, after all, that the *sistema* functions, that it is determined which faction will have access and which will not, and that changes in policy and direction (in a regime where elections count for little) are determined.

For those with money and the right access, thus, the Portuguese sistema works efficiently and well; for those with neither it is enormously time consuming, frustrating, and ultimately defeating. The Portuguese sistema, and especially the vast web of corporative legislation, decrees, and regulations that are an integral part of it, is hence class based and class prejudiced, favoring the elites and, in a nation where the total social product remained for a long time relatively fixed, at the expense of the lower classes. Our analysis has shown that the original corporative sistema was not purposely or necessarily designed that way and that such class prejudice is not necessarily inherent within the corporative structure and ideas, but that is certainly the way the sistema had evolved in Portugal from about the mid-1930s on and how it had come to work in actual practice.

There is in fact a vast hierarchy of channels, actions, connections, and the proper deference that came to operate in the Portuguese system. Indeed, one measure of "making it" in Portugal is to leave off having to surmount personally all those bureaucratic and legalistic restrictions and to get to a position where access and connections (a *cunha,* literally a "wedge" in the Portuguese, roughly equivalent to the Brazilian *jeito*) serve to overcome such barriers. To achieve a position where *you* will call *them,* instead of going hat in hand as a petitioner and being constantly thwarted and rebuffed, is a mark of having bridged that almost insurmountable barrier that separates the directing classes from the rest in Portugal, the line that separates those who work with their hands or do menial chores from those who do not. In this sense, Portugal remained an essentially two-class society under Salazar rather than a multiclass or genuinely pluralist one, and the lines dividing the classes were both reinforced and perpetuated by Salazar's authoritarian rule and the way the corporative system was implemented. The sistema took care of its own, while at the same time keeping others out and in their "proper" place.

It is around the administrative state apparatus, centering in the person and office of the prime minister, that the sistema revolves. Portugal is an administrative or bureaucratic state par excellence.[11] Moreover, it has long been a bureaucratic state whether the external forms have been called absolute monarchy, constitutional monarchy, republic, or Estado Novo. Under Salazar, once the administration had been rationalized and "purified" from the excess of corruption and party influence under the Republic, the size and role of the state bureaucracy were greatly expanded. By ruling out party politics and interest group competition, the making and implementation of public policy became almost exclusively the monopoly of the bureaucracy and its dominant leader. The labels used were corporative and great attention was devoted to reorganizing social groups and political institutions in accord with corporatist principles, but the internal policy process, as Graham emphasizes, the decisions in economics, politics, and social policy which gave the Salazar regime its special character, were all the product of a civil-military bureaucracy that continued to function in a manner not altogether different from most Portuguese regimes in the past. Then, as today, Portugal remained an administrative state, hierarchical, elitist, and *corporatist,* in that broader historical and political-cultural sense to which we referred in chapter 1.

Graham's analysis emphasizes that there has been a marked continuity over the centuries in the role of the bureaucracy and the services provided. Historically, the bureaucracy has served as an agency of spoils and patronage, guaranteeing access to certain privileged groups and excluding others. Politics has revolved not so much around abstract ideologies (liberalism, corporatism, socialism) as around the question of which elite faction would control the central administration and hence all the benefits and spoils that accrue from it. In the maintenance and persistence of this essentially traditional Portuguese society and its periodic adjustments to changed circumstances (the events of 1820, 1910, 1926, and 1974 are examples of such readjustments, or "regenerations," as the Portuguese call them), the bureaucracy and apparatus of the administrative state have served both to help accommodate to the new conditions and to do so without breaking with the norms, values, and societal hierarchies that have so long dominated the country.

The Portuguese regime under Salazar and Caetano operated in the context of an authoritarian regime characterized by limited participation in its political life. Change came generally from the top down—administratively, by decree-law—rather than representing much grass-roots participation from below. Salazar embarked on a policy, Graham emphasizes, of establishing strict controls over the behavior and activities of government civil servants by imposing severe austerity and holding them personally accountable to him for their actions and loyalty. All administrative activity from 1928 on was subject to the "fiscalization" and control of Salazar's Finance Ministry, so that even before becoming prime minister four years later Salazar had already brought, through his manipulation of budget allocations, the major portion of the civil bureaucracy under his personal authority. As prime minister, with unrivaled control over the instruments of state power, he laid the groundwork for the establishment in the 1930s of his corporate state and consolidated his authority in the economic, political, and military spheres. What had emerged eventually by 1945, however, was on one level a corporate state but on another a centralized, stable, authoritarian, bureaucratic regime which, as Graham shows, increasingly accentuated the role and responsibilities assigned to the various administrative institutions.

In this system Salazar (later Caetano) remained supreme and ministerial operations and decision making generally were highly centralized and personalized. The Salazarista system differed little in fact from those historic forms established under royal absolutism, by Pombal and the nineteenth-century constitutional monarchs: it was a system of personalism, of pribends, and of favors granted in return for the loyalty and service (or fealty) of the top bureaucrats. It implied the "corporatization" and regulation of competing interests and social groups, and the concentration of bureaucratic power as a means to maintain control over subordinate authorities. If the prime minister himself and his office are accepted as part of the whole administrative structure, then Portugal may be seen as a political system where the public bureaucracy dominates and virtually monopolizes the policy-making process. Portugal modernized under the Estado Novo, but it did so under the auspices of an authoritarian-corporative-administrative state apparatus with little real change in the overall structure of class relations or in its fundamental and historic state-bureaucratic arrangements.[12]

The chief policy-making agencies and instruments of the Portuguese state, once again following Graham, are all a part of this bureaucratic-administrative apparatus. At the top, of course, under the 1933 Constitution, was the prime minister (technically, the president of the Council of Ministers), the position held by Salazar and then Caetano. It was here that decision-making power was focused. The prime minister heads a supraministerial organization called the Presidency of the Council, to which a technical advisory office was eventually added. The Council of Ministers (similar to a cabinet) varied in number somewhat but included the usual administrative and ministerial divisions: Defense, Finance, Economy, Public Works, Communications, Corporations and Social Security, Public Health and Welfare, Interior, Overseas, Foreign Affairs, Navy, Justice, Education. Members of the council were chosen both for their political loyalty and their administrative skills, and while the position of minister proved both prestigious and important in terms of the patronage linkages, most important decisions were made by the prime minister, with the obligation to carry them out given to the council.

In addition to the ministries, the policy-making core of government in Portugal consisted of twelve secretaries of state (Labor and Social Security, Army, Air Force, Commerce, Industry, Agriculture, Treasury, Budget, Information and Tourism, Public Works, Communications and Transportation, and Health and Welfare) and eight undersecretaries (such as Overseas Development, Overseas Administration, School Administration, Youth and Sports, Economic Planning). A secretary of state in the Portuguese bureaucratic system was defined as the head of a major public sector; the secretariats and subsecretariats consisted of the principal subunits within the existing ministries. Some of these had the status of separate mini-ministries (such as the Army, Air Force, and perhaps, in its early days, the old Subsecretariat of Corporations), while others had such important functions that they were almost equivalent in power to the ministries which administered them (such as the Subsecretariat of Labor and Social Security in the Ministry of Corporations). Depending on the times and circumstances, the nation's president could also be considered a part of this core decision-making team. For even though his formal powers were limited (with the exception of his power to dismiss the prime minister), General Carmona was widely thought to be a restraining influence on Salazar, and Admiral Thomaz was a perpetual thorn in the side of, and almost constant threat to, Caetano.[13]

There are no real constitutional checks and balances or formal separation of powers built into the Portuguese system. Diffuse and hence limited governmental authority was not the intention of the system's designers; in fact, in their plan, Portugal required strong government and *concentrated* authority. The other branches of government were hence conceived not as separate and coequal but as subordinate to the dominant, centralized state apparatus, whose hub was the prime minister's office. One important agency of this broader administrative network was the National Assembly. Not really an independent legislative body, as we have seen, its members constituted a collection of notables and men with administrative experience, preselected by the government on the basis of service and loyalty to the regime, whose chief function was to ratify decisions already arrived at by the government. The Corporative Chamber was similarly a part of the central state and executive-centered apparatus, another collection of notables supposed to represent the socioeconomic and other groups tied into the regime through the corporative structure. Then, there were such consultative organs as the Overseas Council, the Conference of Governors, and so on, also a part of the bureaucratic structure. At the local level, in the parishes and provinces, the juntas and local officials are merely the administrative representatives of the national government responsible for carrying out its decrees. There is no independent initiative or real participation and no means by which the villagers can make the government respond or even pay much attention. As Riegelhaupt concluded, "the parishes are merely monuments to autarchy." [14]

One important part of this administrative apparatus—and one of the primary props of the Salazar regime—was the extensive security and secret police network. The PIDE, or International and State Defense Police (later changed to the DGS, or Department of National Security, by Caetano), was the agency for enforcing the government's will on the population, quashing and silencing the opposition, and eliminating those who got out of line. The PIDE was efficient and notorious, with some of its techniques learned from Nazi teachers and the Italian Fascist secret police. In every village and in all political and economic groups, in all government agencies including the Army, there was someone who worked unofficially, as an informer, for the PIDE. Special courts were established to try political cases, while the secret police themselves were all but immune from arrest. The Civil Police, the National Republican Guard, the Legião, and other paramilitary groups were also tied into the secret police apparatus. The PIDE had the power to arrest anyone and imprison him without charge for up to six months, and hundreds of political prisoners were kept in prison in mainland Portugal and in the notorious concentration camps on Cape Verde and Timor. Systematic torture was widely practiced with and without the regime's approval; terror, surveillance, imprisonment, even murder became among the prime instruments of the regime's control.[15]

No professional person could obtain a job or a license to teach without the approval of the PIDE. Nor could any government bureaucrat hold his position without a security check. The PIDE in the postwar years was given power to ban meetings, close public performances, exercise censorship of foreign and domestic publications, search private residences, and close places used as headquarters for "subversive activity."[16] Its mandate was wide, its powers virtually unlimited, and the government's control over its activities often tenuous. Though a part of the regime and of its security apparatus, the secret police, in some respects like the Army, functioned as almost a separate government within the government. It was one of the most important pillars of Portuguese authoritarian rule; yet its position within the system was almost autonomous. Frequently the secret police rode roughshod not only over all human rights but over all human decency as well, and the government's capacity to control these events (such as the murder of General Delgado, whom the PIDE apparently beat so badly across the border in Spain that he died, when the government's intention was "merely" to kidnap him and bring him to Lisbon for a "show" trial) was often limited. A part of the regime, yet apart from it, the secret police under both Salazar and Caetano was widely hated, and it is no wonder that when the revolution came in April 1974 the PIDE's officials, agents, and informers were jailed, beaten, often set upon in the streets, and forced to flee the country.[17]

Another important pillar of the regime, again inseparable from the central governmental administration, was the União Nacional (Aliança Nacional Popular under Caetano). The UN, or ANP, was more a bureaucratic appendage of the regime than a political party in the Anglo-American sense. Described by Salazar as "an organization of the elite rather than of the mass membership," the original UN never had a membership of more than 100,000, mostly government bureaucrats who were obligated to join and pay dues as a condition of their employment. Among the least important of its functions was to present candidates for elections and draft a party platform. Indeed, the UN had been founded in 1931 as an antithesis to the party spirit that had reigned during the Republic. It was seen as a movement rather than a party, a civic action association, an agency of nationalism and national unity whose chief purposes were to fortify the executive power, help consolidate the state, provide for social coordination among diverse groups, and promote social and economic progress. Rather than being separate from the state, the UN was intimately in league with the state and inseparable from the administrative apparatus.

Salazar served as the UN president and chief guiding force, and virtually all civilian cabinet and subcabinet members were also officials of the UN and rose through its ranks. Civil governors and local officials were ordinarily also chairmen of the "party" organization at the provincial and parish levels; wherever one was located in the hierarchy, governmental and party programs—and personnel—overlapped or were one and the same. The party and its functionaries operated as a transmission belt for conveying (weakly) local needs to the top and for transmitting governmental decisions back down again and helping to implement them. It was also a charity agency; it served as the eyes and ears of the regime at the local level; it screened candidates for governmental positions; it provided indoctrination and sometimes served as a center for corporative studies and training. Perhaps above all the organization was a gigantic national patronage agency, a means for dispensing goods, favors, jobs, and government positions and for rewarding loyalty and faithful service. Hardly an independent body, occasionally giving advice and consultation, serving to ratify the government's policies rather than questioning them or initiating any of its own, functioning as an agency of national unity and of civic virtue and patriotism, this aggregation, like the National Assembly, was part of the *cortes gerais* of the regime.[18]

The UN bolstered and supported the regime, helped round up support for it, served as a channel by which new elites and governmental leaders were often recruited, and functioned as something of a mirror of the balance of forces in the regime and as an instrument for changing that balance.[19] It was used by both Salazar and Caetano as a way to reward and give important positions to those who had long served the regime, as well as to bring younger men along. The elections Portugal held periodically did not imply real choices but served as plebiscitary ratifications of the regime in power (and perhaps also as a rough gauge of opposition strength), but the balance *within* the UN or ANP *was* an indicator of both the nature of the regime and the direction it was taking.

By the 1960s the UN had become, like the government itself, old and tired. In 1965 Salazar announced the need for an overhaul and the recruitment of new young leaders. Beginning in 1968 and then with the 1969 elections, Caetano also attempted an overhaul, rebaptized the party, brought in his own followers, and sought to use the ANP as a way of increasing his popular support and consolidating his base of power. But in this Caetano was only partially successful, and throughout his tenure the ANP continued as a rough reflection of the major forces in the country: Caetano's own men, a powerful contingent of old Salazaristas, and many local politicians and government officials waiting to see which way the wind was blowing. It is in this sense that the elections held by Caetano in 1969 and 1973 were important, for they were a part of his continuing effort to gain a stronger grip on the ANP and on the nation as a whole.

The UN-ANP was probably comparable to the secret police and security apparatus as an important instrument of authoritarian state-bureaucratic rule. It was not like a party in the Anglo-American sense, for it could not be separated from the state, and the running of elections was only one, perhaps incidental, among its functions. Nevertheless, as a patronage agency in all its ramifications between elections and as a reflection and instrument for changing somewhat the balance of forces within the country, its role and position were often critical.[20]

As was the case with the "party" phenomenon, when one begins to talk of "interest groups" in Portugal, one is also employing a misnomer, or at least a term that requires qualification. Of course, there are *grupos* and *interesses* in Portugal, but these should not be thought of as more or less autonomous interest associations, again as in the Anglo-American conception. Rather, in such agencies as the Army, the Church, the gremios, and the sindicatos, we are looking at bureaucratic, essentially corporate components of the administrative state, which are, like the party or the security apparatus, inseparable from it. Of course, within the state, as within each of these agencies, there are rivalries, factions, and competitions; but this competition represents not so much rivalries between distinct, autonomous interest groups as factional struggles *within* the prevailing bureaucratic system, cutting across interest-group lines. That is, one faction of the Army (let us say, those who favored a continued Portuguese presence in Africa) may be aligned with a similar faction in the Church, some sindicato leaders, certain economic elites, and a number of *políticos* and government officials; while another faction, cutting across all these same groups, may be opposed to such policy. But in the absence of competitive party politics and open, free-wheeling, interest-group competition, such rivalries generally take place *within* the regime and within its various bureaucratic components. They are between numerous informal groups, personalities, cliques, and factions whose struggles for influence take place within the arena of the established administrative state structure rather than between formal groupings (the military officer corps, the Catholic hierarchy, the political and economic elites), whose views, in any case, are seldom unified on any policy issue.

Just as we referred to the "party" as the *cortes gerais* of the regime, we can thus refer to factional politics in Portugal as "court intrigue." Portugal is not a system of free associability and democratic, laissez-faire, interest-group pluralism; rather, we are looking at a closed system of more limited pluralism where the right to organize is carefully restricted by the state and where the interests that do exist are not outside the government but an integral, bureaucratic part of it. The traditional pillars of the ancient regime (Army, Church, nobility) have been expanded and new pillars have been added (secret police, gremios, sindicatos), reflecting the greater differentiation and complexity of social and political forces in the twentieth century. But the system itself is still remarkably similar to the ancient structure of corporate estates, organized vertically, all a part of the central administration of the patrimonialist state apparatus. Politics, then, tends to take place in two key arenas: (1) the struggles between the several factions, crosscutting the formal interest-group structure, to gain control of the all-important central state apparatus, and (2) the tension and virtually perpetual conflicts that arise as those who control the government seek to extend their hegemony over the nation's component corporate groups while the latter, in turn, seek to preserve their autonomy and time-honored "rights" or *foros*.

The armed forces provide one of the clearest examples. Consisting of the Army (by far the most important), Navy, Air Force, Guarda Nacional Republicana, Legião, perhaps the PIDE and other paramilitary units, the military officer corps constituted one of the prime pillars of the Estado Novo, a part of the bureaucratic state and at the same time the ultimate arbiter of national political affairs. It took Salazar almost a full decade to establish his control over the military, but it still retained a separate identity and continued to constitute both the main prop and the prime threat to the continuation of the corporative regime. Salazar was clever in manipulating the armed forces, relatively lavish in his expenditures on them, and careful to cultivate them and give them what they wanted. He promoted officers loyal to him, honored the armed forces, gave them modern weapons, and played on their patriotism. Thinking of itself as a unified force whose duty was to defend the nation and its own institutional integrity, the military remained nonetheless divided by factional struggles as to how best to achieve these goals. Several of these factions showed their disagreement (or the power-seeking ambitions of their leaders) by launching revolts of various seriousness against the regime, of which the Spínola-led rebellion in 1974 was only the most recent.

Up until that time, however, despite the occasional restiveness, the military had been relatively cohesive on the major national issues (the need for order and stability, defense of Portugal's position and the wars in Africa, and opposition to all forms of socialism and communism) and strongly concerned to maintain its autonomy as an institution. Indeed, the wars in Africa provided one means of retaining this autonomy and cohesiveness and, not coincidentally, of keeping the military busy, giving it promotions, and preventing its meddling in domestic politics. But by the 1970s this had begun to change. The military had become deeply divided between its conservative "ultras," whose spokesman was President (and ex-Admiral) Thomaz and who consisted of both older active officers and those active in such powerful veterans' groups as the Liga de Ex-combatentes; the "developmentalists," who wanted the Army to involve itself more in civic action programs; the Caetanistas who, like many of their civilian counterparts in the ANP, owed their positions and loyalty to Caetano; and the "reformers," who saw potentially disastrous consequences in the African wars, both for the Army and for Portugal itself. In addition, there was a sharp split along age and generational lines between the more conservative and traditional senior officers and the junior officers, who not only disagreed with their superiors politically but were also chafing at the barriers to advancement and promotions placed in their way by such an aged, top-heavy military hierarchy.

These military factions, of course, overlapped with factions in the Church, the government, and elsewhere; and as it became more politicized again in the 1970s the military's autonomy necessarily was sacrificed. The military remained, as it had been since the nineteenth century, the final voice in national political affairs; but to say that is not to say that voice was or is necessarily unified. Of necessity the ultimate base of support for any government that comes to power, a part of the state yet with a certain continuing independence from it, divided by the same factions that divide the civilian population but at the same time thinking of itself as above mere partisan politics, the armed forces are bound up closely with the administrative regime, are part and parcel of the whole sistema, and cannot be strictly segregated, as implied in the hyphenated term "civil-military relations," from the rest of bureaucratic politics and in-fighting. Both the struggle over the place and position of the military in society and the rivalries between the various military factions (crosscutting those of various civilian factions) will undoubtedly go on.[21]

Many of the same issues and comments pertain to the Church. Portugal has, historically, been considered a Catholic country, and Catholicism is intimately associated with the nation's political culture and the form of its institutions. Like the Army, the Church is bound up closely with the state structure and, except for a brief interlude during the Republic, has always been one of the chief institutional pillars of the regime. It is, again like the Army, more than a pressure group; it constitutes the backbone of the entire national system. Salazar, himself a former seminarian, steadfast Catholic, and founder of the CADC, grew up intellectually precisely during that chaotic Republican period when the Church was disassociated from the state, and he reacted strongly against this. In addition, it hardly needs repeating that the corporate state itself was based explicitly on Church doctrine and the papal encyclicals. The Salazar regime in the 1930s was looked on with favor by the Church; more than that, it was considered a "model state" for other Catholic nations to emulate. And the state, in turn, showered numerous benefits on the Church. These relations were cemented in 1940 in the concordat signed between Portugal and the Vatican which, though it did not establish Catholicism as the official state religion, provided special access and privileges to the Church in return for the legitimization which it provided the government. Church and state were hence inseparable and mutually reinforcing institutions. The stability, order, and hierarchy of the Salazar regime, in the words of Thomas C. Bruneau, provided "an ideal environment for the Church of the First Vatican Council (1870)," which was based on the same or similar concepts.[22]

In this context, Bruneau continues, neither Church nor state was called upon to defend itself from strong attack or to innovate. The Portuguese system largely guaranteed the status quo, and after a time both the regime and the Church became petrified. Both Church and state accepted the Catholic-corporate ethic articulated in the late nineteenth century, a largely static ethic that continued to assume the obligation of each man to accept his station in life. The official position of the Church was steadily augmented after 1940, and it continued to serve as a buttress of the regime. Despite this (or perhaps because of it), the Church was subsequently characterized by a lack of innovation, a general absence of activity, an isolation from the changes taking place elsewhere in the Catholic world. With regard to the Concordat, the educational system, the Church's special role in the Mocidade and other institutions, Bruneau has concluded, the Church was part and parcel of the state system. It was afforded representation in the Corporative Chamber, was privileged in terms of the influence it could exert, took part in all civic activities, and was promoted by the regime as a kind of civic religion which was also strongly present in the state concept. Although the relations between Salazar and Cardinal Cerejeira were never so close as is sometimes imagined and though the term "clerico-fascist regime" is undoubtedly a considerable exaggeration, there can be no doubt that Church and state were closely tied together, that the Church, like the corporative system and indeed the entire Salazar regime, served as an agent of social control rather than of social change, and that little questioning of this role was allowed. The stability, order, and control of the political regime guarded and preserved the Church's traditional approach to influence, and thus there was little or no incentive to change. By the same token, the freezing and petrification of the Church also removed another incentive for the state system to change. Bruneau's research shows clearly how the "dinosauric" nature of the Salazar government was repeated in the "dinosauric" character of the Church (and maybe of the Army and of the whole state system), with the two outdated structures mutually reinforcing and supporting each other.[23]

By the 1960s, with Pope John and Vatican II, some cracks became visible in the monolith. Both the Church and the state sought to adjust themselves to the new Catholic realities, but Bruneau shows how weak and unsuccessful these efforts were in both institutions. By the 1970s, however, under Caetano's more open rule, the cracks had widened, more open debate was taking place, and both Church and state were seeking to renovate themselves, to adjust to the new realities. There were Christian-democratic groups, Catholic liberals, a new prelate to replace Cerejeira, even some Catholic socialists and revolutionaries. The Church had begun to disassociate itself from allegiance to the corporative-Salazarista elements and to come out in favor of some of the newer currents. It sought to reestablish a greater degree of institutional autonomy and to get on the side of change now that it was beginning to occur. But the splits within its ranks had weakened the Church, and in any case the changes occurring were piecemeal. Nor, with vocations down, attendance down, and the Church generally discredited for its stand-patism and closeness to Salazarism, should its political strength be overemphasized. Certainly the Church remained one of the major bastions of the state and its system, but its role was never so great as that of the Army and, in the increasingly secular and materialistic Portugal of the 1960s and 1970s, one doubts whether its force could match that of the civil bureaucracy or of a number of powerful economic elites.

The civil bureaucracy, by definition a part of the state system, is another important interest, or corporate pillar, to be considered in understanding how the Portuguese system works. The government is by far the country's largest employer, and the sheer size of the bureaucracy plus its strategic importance in this state-centered and almost wholly regulated system make it immensely influential. The administration is, of course, headed by the prime minister and the other ministers, who together make up what Graham called the "governing team." [24] The "team" usually reflects the preponderance of power in the country at a given time, and a prudent prime minister will be careful to balance his team by including representatives from the various forces and factions making up his coalition. Thus, when Caetano first came to power in 1968 he kept the entire team inherited from Salazar; by 1970 he had sufficiently consolidated his hold to begin bringing in some members more closely identified with his own policies. But the role and power of these Caetanistas remained limited, and the prime minister was always careful (some would say too careful) to balance his team with representatives identified with the policies of the former regime. In the party, the Army, the secret police, and the civil bureaucracy, the Salazaristas remained rather consistently strong.

The major avenue to recruitment as part of the governing team lies through the civil bureaucracy. Loyalty to the regime and long and faithful execution of its policies are the two major requirements of anyone with aspirations for a top post. Of course, some "team" members come directly out of the Army, the universities, or private business, but these institutions too are hardly separable from the broader administrative state. Each member of the governing team will ordinarily have charge of a single ministry (sometimes two). The ministries themselves, Graham notes, are almost like separate holding companies, each operating more or less autonomously within its own policy area and jealously guarding its programs and prerogatives against interference from other agencies. (Recall Pereira's difficulties in the 1930s in extending the corporative system to agencies and ministries other than his own.) Among the ministerial subunits there is a similar fragmentation, with each agency or bureau involved in its own affairs and little concerned with general policy. These agencies and bureaus, usually headed by career bureaucrats over whom the minister may have but limited control, are often extremely important since it is largely at this level that programs and policies are fashioned and carried out. It is often at this level also that private economic interests plug directly into the decision-making process.[25]

The Portuguese civil service functions much like the civil services in other Latin countries and those with legal-administrative structures based upon the Napoleonic Code.[26] Formalism and legalism are wide-spread. At the same time personalism and the proper connections are critical for getting anything done. Elaborate patronage patterns and systems of access and connections have evolved and been worked out over the years; for those falling outside these networks, the bureaucracy is not at all responsive. Face-to-face contacts are avoided with those who do not belong; the "administrative system" can then be enormously frustrating and time-consuming, and if one is poor and has no connections, it is avoided as much as possible. For those who do have the proper connections or belong to known families or groups, the system can be responsive—and enormously profitable. As in the older patrimonial pattern, the line between the public domain and the private one is indistinct, and enormous private profit can be made out of the public weal. In the Portuguese system it is not at all unusual for a minister or bureau head to go back and forth between public service and a private company involved in the business of that bureau—or to hold both high government position and chairs on the boards of several major corporations dependent on the regime for contracts at one and the same time! Thus, not only is the civil service, quite naturally, a part of the broader apparatus of the administrative state, but so is what passes for private enterprise.

If Portugal has been called an administrative state, a corporative state, a dictatorship, or an autarchy, it has also been called a capitalistic state. That is true only in a restricted sense, however, since Portugal wholly lacks some of the prime ingredients of capitalist systems: free competition, individual initiative and entrepreneurship, and a laissez-faire market economy. In Portugal it is once more *the state* that initiates virtually all economic enterprises, that helps raise capital, that grants charters or monopolies to prospective business establishments, and that continues to regulate the economy on all levels. It was the state that served as the great impetus to Portuguese industrial development beginning in the 1930s, that fashioned the comprehensive development plans beginning in 1953, and that protected and shielded Portuguese enterprise both by its restrictive import policies and by its granting of monopolies internally. At best then, we can say the Portuguese economy is one of state capitalism rather than free-enterprise capitalism; the author's own interpretation of the Portuguese economic system is that it functions more on the basis of the historic structure of imperial mercantilism and may not be capitalistic at all.[27]

The Portuguese economy under Salazar and Caetano was dominated by a handful of large *grupos, sociedades,* and oligarchs closely tied in with and, again, inseparable from the state. These included the hundred-year-old CUF (Companhia União Fabril) with more than 100 integrated companies in all sectors of the Portuguese economy (including large holdings and concessions in Africa) and over 10 percent of all capital of the incorporated enterprises in continental Portugal; the Grupo Espírito Santo, heavily involved in banking, insurance, paper, tires, Africa, communications; the Grupo Champalimaud with large holdings in cement (a virtual monopoly), steel (ditto), banking, insurance, paper; the Grupo Português do Atlântico, which owned or controlled three banks, an insurance company, and various investment societies; the Grupo Borges e Irmão, also in banks, insurance, textiles, pharmaceuticals, chemical products, construction materials, fishing, travel, hotels, newspapers; the Grupo BNU (Banco Nacional Ultramarino), a huge financial trust with major interests also in insurance, mining, transport, tourism; the Grupo Fonsecas e Burnay—banks, railroad concessions, overseas exploration, and other interests; the Grupo BIP (Banco Intercontinental Português), or of Jorge de Brito—road construction, banks, insurance, maritime transport; the Grupo SACOR, the state oil monopoly, with sixteen linked companies and itself owned in part by the Grupo Espírito Santo and the Grupo Português do Atlântico; and perhaps one or two other major concerns.[28]

These constituted the major economic groups and *interesses* in Portugal. It is interesting to note how banking formed the cornerstone of each. They were all giant conglomerates, heavily tied in with U.S. and other foreign capital. Also interesting is the diversity of holdings of each, so that if one enterprise turned out to be a loser, the grupo would still do well on the strength of the other companies. Almost all had major interests and concessions in Portugal's African colonies (especially Angola) as well as on the mainland, holdings which gave them a vital interest in the final solution of "the African question." Almost all had newspapers and radio stations, which provided them ample opportunities to publicize their own activities as well as to promote their own political viewpoints. And all were closely tied in with and dependent on state concessions, a system which helped guarantee both their profits and their privacy.

The way the Portuguese system works is through the granting by charter of a concession to a well-connected grupo. These charters, like the charters of the ancient trading companies in colonial times, convey a monopoly to a certain firm for a given, usually extended, period of time. The entire Portuguese economy is organized on this state-subsidized, protected, monopolistic (or at best oligopolistic) basis, which serves to promote both enormous profit and incredible inefficiency. Thus, if one wishes to travel from Lisbon to Southampton by boat, there is only one travel company to handle the arrangements; if one wants to purchase a Land Rover, only one company. The tobacco monopoly in Angola was given over to one grupo, sugar to another, textiles to a third, imports and exports to another, and so on. Everything works on a concession basis where government and private business are inseparable. In those areas where the state has by law made something compulsory—for example, auto insurance—each grupo may have an insurance company. What is critical, of course, is the original concession—and that is where the politics enter in. All the grupos are so well connected in so many economic areas as well as with so many different political factions and in so many government agencies that they will likely be protected and their profits assured no matter which political faction might come to power. Each grupo has dozens of ex- and current government officials on its payroll, usually including those in charge of the ministry or agencies from which their concessions emanate. The companies also serve as a prime ground for the recruitment of government officials in areas of concern to the companies. Many of them are partners with the government in various economic ventures crucial to the functioning of the national economy; they also loan the government money, lend it technical skills, and help keep the economy afloat. In this as in other respects the grupos, or holding companies, and their extended web of connections and retainers are so closely involved in government and the functioning of the entire system that they are inseparable from it.[29]

Although these are *groups* of influence (and might be called interest groups), typically influence works through individual personal contacts rather than the impersonal group. On economic and political-economic questions one of the Espirito Santos, Jorge de Brito, or Champalimaud, or one of their numerous lieutenants, simply gets on the phone to a cousin, nephew, godchild, or friend who owes him a favor and who works in the agency from which a particular paper or permit must be extracted. Most often an arrangement can be worked out quickly on that basis. Or, if the decision is required from a higher level, the friend, nephew, or whomever can be counted on to carry the case directly to the appropriate minister or to the prime minister himself. Neither Salazar nor Caetano was directly beholden to these groups, although ordinarily each man went along with the particular policies recommended because, particularly at the beginning of his rule, his own political position was shaky and he also saw the entire economy sliding downhill if he failed to give the major economic interests what they wanted.

These are the major economic interests in Portugal, closely bound up with the government and often having a virtual monopoly on decision making in their respective spheres. It is no accident that there are so many government officials on the boards of these banks and major concerns, or that so many go into these concerns after leaving government.[30] Most often the groups themselves are also interrelated and interconnected by family, personal, and political ties. This oligarchy is held together like a vast web; its interests are coordinated and its business policies planned and carried out through a bureaucratic system that probably functions more closely in tune with the planned, closed, and centralized systems of Eastern Europe than with the open, freer systems of the West. Some estimates have put the combined influence of these *grupos* on economic policy at 90 percent or higher.

There are also some individual landowners, wine growers, cork growers, and so on, who have, by these estimates, maybe a 5 percent influence. In addition, there are other commercial groups and associations of small businessmen who have some modest influence on government economic policy. The *sindicatos* also have an influence, though under Salazar's corporate system an extremely limited one, as we have seen, and they too are closely tied into the governmental-bureaucratic apparatus. Finally, there are the *técnicos,* economists, and planners in the São Bento Palace and the various ministries who can sometimes be influential because they have some degree of access to the prime minister. They have influence largely via their reports and recommendations, which are sent to a minister or even the prime minister for action. Their influence, on obviously a rough and impressionistic index, may amount to perhaps 2 percent. These are the major economic interests and, at least prior to the 1974 turnover, their relative degrees of importance.[31]

During the period of the Estado Novo the Army had relatively little influence on economic policy; that was left to the civilian government establishment and the major economic groups tied up with it. But the Army did have a great deal to say concerning its view of the destiny of the nation. In its "moderating" role and as guardian of the Constitution, the Army always acted *close to* the surface of power, if not, as in 1926 and 1974, *at* the surface of power. It had direct access to the prime minister's office, and an influential general like António de Spínola would frequently go directly to Caetano to get what he wanted rather than through the cumbersome defense bureaucracy. Jealous of its prerogatives, concerned for its status and place in society, preoccupied with unity and national security, the military in Portugal is highly politicized, but not necessarily any less professional for also being political.[32] Caetano gave the armed forces virtually everything they wanted to keep them contented and loyal. But in the end he miscalculated the balance of forces within the military and he fell.

Then there were a number of *persons* in Portugal influential during the Salazar-Caetano era more as individuals than as members of any very clearly identifiable groups. In the emphasis given to corporate groups and broader social forces, this personal influence should not be neglected. Occasionally an oppositionist like Humberto Delgado or Mario Soares might achieve this distinction; more often, old cabinet and government officials associated with the former regime or men of especially great wealth or prestige continued to play important roles as elder statesmen with considerable influence on policy making. Before his death in November 1972, Teotonio Pereira was such a figure,[33] Costa Leite another. The major bankers and grupo leaders (Jorge de Brito, Champalimaud) were also extremely influential individuals. On the Right politically, such figures as Franco Nogueira, Veiga de Macedo, and Silva Cunha continued to be important, also as individuals. Their influence was considerable, their ideas and speeches usually made people sit up and take notice, and Franco Nogueira was so influential he would most likely have been prime minister if the Right had come to power in the wake of Salazar.[34] Caetano was fearful of such strong and decisive individuals—and usually with good reason since they remained ever-present in the wings ready to take over should he falter.

Finally, one must take account of the opposition itself. On the Right were the old Salazaristas—not wanting change, afraid of reform, fearful that Caetano would allow independence to Angola and Mozambique, and perhaps most of all eager to return to those high government posts and sinecures from which they had been excluded since 1970. The Right was concentrated in the Assembly, the ANP, the Army, the DGS organization, and the Ministry of Interior. The Right also published the daily newspaper *Epoca* and the reviews *Política* and *Opinião*. The Right proved powerful and adept at giving "signals" that would force Caetano and his *técnicos* back in their place: the armed forces promised that it would remain "vigilant" during election campaigns, Franco Nogueira forced Caetano to revert to a strong public position in favor of holding onto Portugal's African territories, the Liga de Ex-combatentes obligated the regime to hew to that same line. These were often elaborate scenarios, unfolding with careful orchestration, careful planning, and complex strategies. Despite the absence of independent, institutionalized interest groups or opposition political parties, the Right thus remained a major influence, particularly as it intertwined with influential economic forces and military and secret police factions. That would be a coalition to look out for and was indeed Caetano's main preoccupation. Most observers of Portuguese politics were agreed that the Right was far stronger than the Left and that it was from the Right that the main threat to the Caetano government came.[35]

In the late 1960s and early 1970s the Left opposition had also been growing in influence. Its ranks included Communists, Socialists, liberal democrats, and the Catholic Left—students, labor leaders, young professionals, intellectuals, newspaper writers and editors, and virtually the entire educated younger generation. Increasingly, through such journals as *Expresso, Seara nova, Vida mundial,* and *Republica,* as well as through some of the major unions and the universities and an occasional rally or public demonstration, the Left was able to make its voice heard. With the ban on political parties, the Left opposition formed "associations," "societies," or "study groups," such as the influential SEDES (the Society for Economic and Social Development), and began to rally support—all activities that were more or less tolerated by the regime but were anathema to the Right and the traditionalists.

Few of these groups had any direct access to decision making, but increasingly they were able to make the government respond to their arguments. When Caetano went on television and talked about educational reform and how the regime was following the newer social doctrines of the Church, he was speaking in response to public statements made earlier by reform-minded prelates, the students, and a number of young people and some government officials involved in a demonstration at a church in the Rato. When he pushed through a series of collective contracts involving major wage increases, he was responding directly to the protests, slowdowns, and work "stoppages" of the big unions. And when he went ahead with certain social reforms even though the Right objected, he was responding to the widespread discontent he felt in the nation, to the longing for a better life, and perhaps even to the bombs and threats of bombs that rocked Portugal from the 1960s on. For an "administrative state," there was a considerable amount of politics going on in the Portugal of Marcello Caetano and, increasingly, some genuine political competitiveness, bargaining, grass-roots activities, and even government responsiveness.[36]

That is also how change more generally occurred and went forward in the Portuguese system—not through revolutionary transformations (until 1974) but through a small adjustment here, a change in emphasis there, a cabinet shuffle and reshuffle, a new initiative or slight shift in direction, a nudge here and a nudge there. Change in Portugal occurred gradually, incrementally, and in an evolutionary fashion—that is, when change occurred at all. One of Salazar's problems, we have seen, perhaps the major problem, was that he froze the system, closed off openings, refused to innovate, and cast Portuguese society and polity in a stagnant, impermeable, almost nineteenth-century mold. To use the familiar metaphor, the regime went to sleep, it became petrified and dinosauric. Salazar never tampered with the basic structures of Portuguese society and special privilege; but, perhaps worse than that, by freezing the elite and indeed the entire system he closed off the access routes and channels by which others might also rise to privileged status. His miserly economic policies, particularly in the postwar period, served to retard economic growth and to perpetuate poverty, stagnation, and backwardness. At the same time, increasingly impervious, centralized, one-man rule deprived the newer generation of both training in government and the chance to advance economically through the holding of public positions. With few exceptions, the ruling elites were largely frozen until the 1960s when a modest acceleration of economic growth helped stimulate new possibilities and bring in some new faces. It was thus not so much that Salazar was a corporatist or that his regime was authoritarian and paternalistic (traits which have been characteristic of probably all Portuguese regimes) but that he failed to make room for and accommodate the newer social forces, open up opportunities, and provide for expanded change, however controlled and regulated that change might be.[37]

Caetano, in contrast, while preserving all the old structures, opened up a number of new opportunities, sought to expand the elite, generated new possibilities for enrichment, and made operational many of the corporate and other structures Salazar had allowed to rust. Still within the framework inherited from the preceding regime, Caetano's rule was characterized by far more consultation with the nation's various interests, a far more open society, and far more activity and dynamism in government policy making. Caetano brought Portugal and her economy toward a closer interdependence with Europe, opened up the country to foreign capital and business, stimulated exports, and relaxed some of the controls on emigration. Politically, he also opened up the system somewhat, provided new opportunities, brought in more new faces. In contrast to Salazar, but still within the confines of the structure the two had been instrumental in designing, Caetano helped create new channels of access and wealth, began to accommodate the newer social groups (middle and labor sectors), and provided for considerable change. Indeed, it was because these changes were going forward, were genuine and thorough, that the Right reacted so strongly and the Left was stirred to greater action. It was not a wholly stagnant regime, as under Salazar, that was overthrown in April 1974; rather, it was a regime that, "while remaining faithful to the corporative ideal," was also moving away from the older corporatism and gradually but progressively and incrementally moving toward a more open and socially just society.

If one asks, therefore, how the Portuguese system works (or at least used to work before the April 1974 coup—and perhaps still does work in many important respects), the answer is ambiguous. To begin with, there were times, as during Salazar's last years, when it hardly *worked* or functioned at all; at other times (let us say, the 1930s and early 1970s), it worked perhaps about as well as any Portuguese regime may be expected to work. If one asks at what level or levels it worked, and what one could call it, the answer is again complex. At one level Portugal could be called a corporative system, but as we have seen, the corporatist functions and activities were increasingly confined to two major activities (labor relations and social security) and could hardly be said to characterize the entire system.

At another level, Portugal functioned as an extremely personalist and autocratic regime, characterized (especially under Salazar) by absolutist one-man rule and dominated by the power and personality of its ruler. In its rural landholding and agricultural patterns, in its traditional attitudes and institutions, and in its overriding emphasis upon status, hierarchy, rank, and position, Portugal remained positively feudal, or at best nineteenth century, in character. Then we must consider the dictatorship, the police state, the state within a state, used by Salazar and Caetano as an instrument of control but frequently going in its own autonomous directions. It is also useful, as Graham's research makes clear, to look at Portugal as an administrative state, a modern-day extension of imperial patrimonialist rule, an authoritarian-bureaucratic regime with all the *interesses creados* integrated into the structure of the state apparatus. Within this scheme the backbone of the regime was clearly the Army, on which the regime depended for everyday survival and which served as the ultimate arbiter of all national politics. With the industrialization and economic growth fostered over the past forty years, a number of powerful economic interests, or grupos, also emerged, all closely intertwined with the state, with the result that Portugal came eventually to be characterized as a capitalistic system, or at least one of state capitalism, and as a system which favored the wealthy oligarchic classes at the expense of others. Finally, there is the increasingly consultative, pluralistic, genuine (although limited) political bargaining system that had begun to develop under

Caetano, and which in turn was replaced by a regime of reformist, even revolutionary tendencies in April 1974, but reformist and/or revolutionary as carried out under military-authoritarian auspices.

How then does the Portuguese system work? It works in various ways and at various levels. No one, nice 'n' neat label ("fascist" or "clerico-fascist" or "capitalist") is sufficient to characterize it adequately. Perhaps most accurately the Portuguese system represents a frequently confused, overlapping, jumbled, crazy-quilt pattern of *all* the characteristics described above (and doubtless others as well), with the relative weight and importance of each varying over time and according to circumstances. The Portuguese "system" is thus really several systems, all requiring distinct models and modes of interpretation, and yet all interrelated. The complex nature of the several patterns and overlaps is related to the growing complexity of the Portuguese system as a whole and to the fact that over a period of forty years new features and characteristics of the system were constantly being added on, in layerlike fashion, with none of the old features ever being discarded, submerged, or cast aside. If these are some of the dominant characteristics of the Portuguese system, they are also remarkably similar to the broader model of Iberian and Latin American politics, and the change process, as fashioned by Anderson, Chalmers, Silvert, and others.[38]

XI

Conclusion and Implications

On April 25, 1974, a successful coup was carried out by a faction of the Portuguese military, led by António de Spínola and a nucleus of younger officers calling themselves the "Armed Forces Movement." Meticulously planned, the coup succeeded almost without bloodshed. Caetano, President Thomaz, and the entire government quickly fell, Caetano and Thomaz were sent into exile, and almost literally overnight the entire control apparatus of the regime—secret police, party, Legião, censorship, National Republican Guard, and so on—collapsed. Within days the political system existent since 1933, including much of the formal corporative structure, had also been largely swept aside.

The foreign press accounts portrayed these events as a great national liberal and liberating movement—and in a sense they were. Surely the new freedom which the Portuguese enjoyed, the end of press censorship, the joy in the streets, the smiling faces and camaraderie—symbolized by the red carnations which sprouted everywhere—marked a welcome change from the dour, usually gray regime that had gone before. The 1974 revolution was far more complex than the press portrayed it, however;[1] the euphoria occasioned by the new liberation was really only one aspect—and a relatively surface one at that—of what was a far more subtle, long-term transformation whose subsurface currents are only now beginning to be sorted out. In the first part of this chapter we shall seek to analyze some of the complex causes leading to the coup, the coup itself, and the immediate political aftermath; in the second and third parts we shall seek to assess the entire Portuguese corporative experience from 1933 to the present and explore some of the implications of that experience—for Portugal, for other nations in the Iberic-Latin culture area, and perhaps for ourselves.

The Portuguese Coup d'Etat of April 25, 1974: Some Background and a Preliminary Assessment[2]

The Portugal of Marcello Caetano in 1973/74 was a far cry from that of his predecessor—or even from that of the early Caetano years. Many of the older control mechanisms had been retained, but the Caetano regime had become far more open, dynamic, change-oriented, nascently pluralist, almost a bargaining-type political system, especially as compared with the monolith of the Salazar regime. Caetano, of course, remained within the corporative-authoritarian mold, but the adjustments he had made, the new accommodations, the incremental changes were beginning to add up in cumulative fashion to a more profound structural alteration.

By 1973/74 the pressures were also beginning to multiply. Caetano's mandate was still tentative, his power base still insecure. The greater freedom and new opportunities he had encouraged also served, ironically, to stimulate political dissent and to encourage those on both the Left and the Right who were working for his overthrow. In addition, Portugal in 1973/74 was a far more complex, diversified, modernized nation and society than had been the case at any time previously, with all the growing divisions and potential for conflict that that implies. At the same time the disruptive and frequently disastrous consequences of the long guerrilla campaigns in Africa, galloping inflation (spurred by Caetano's more expansive economic policies and social programs), the question of Portugal's entry into the European community and its consequences for Portuguese businesses, foreign pressures both as regards Portuguese policy in Africa and internally, various military rumblings of discontent, the demands of liberals and the Left that the government go further, the demands of the Right that the reforms (and the reformers) be reined in, the ambitions of the old bureaucrats ousted in the 1970 cabinet shuffle and of rival claimants to Caetano's throne (a rightist coup attempt had been launched—and quashed—in late 1973, but Franco Nogueira, Adriano Moreira, and other Caetano rivals stood ready to step in), and the shifting quicksands of Portuguese politics—all these lent an air of dynamism, activity, and potential for change to the Caetano regime that had been lacking under the dinosauric Salazar. But it also made Caetano's rule extremely precarious and tenuous.

It is in this context of both accelerated change *and* profound political uncertainty regarding the future that General Spínola's book appeared.[3] The book was a bombshell. It is difficult for those in open societies to conceive how important a book of this sort can be in a more or less closed regime where political debate was usually handled elliptically and behind the scenes. In pointing out the futility of Portugal's African campaigns, the need for self-determination in the colonies and, hopefully, a kind of federation arrangement, the Spínola essay caused a tremendous stir. But much more than that, it also launched

General Spínola as a major force in Portuguese politics, a man of ideas (necessary in Portugal's *catedrátocracia*) who had a definite program for the future (in contrast with Caetano's seeming indecision). The book caused a major upheaval within the government, with the Right forcing Caetano to pension off Spínola and retire the officers agreeing with him. My own interpretation based on the field work in Portugal during this period was that the book had to do chiefly with domestic Portuguese politics and with Spínola's private political ambitions and was only secondarily concerned with Africa. The image we have from the press accounts of a general (with previous experience with the Franco forces in the civil war and the Nazi Blue Division in World War II) who suddenly saw the light, rallied the liberal and reform-oriented forces, and staged his liberating movement is far too superficial.[4]

The fact is that what Spínola said in his book was very close to what was the official (though unstated) Caetano policy. Caetano too had a timetable for withdrawal from Africa (by the 1980s, by which time he believed the African colonies could be largely self-governing and Portuguese industry would be able to compete in the unprotected European marketplace), with a hoped-for federated or commonwealth arrangement (or some "special understanding" in a broader "Lusitanian" framework a la Brazil). But Caetano could not state this publicly or proceed too fast in implementing it for fear of provoking the Right and perhaps his own overthrow. His agreement to maintain the Portuguese position in Africa, after all, had been one of the conditions of his being allowed to take office in 1968 and of his continuation as prime minister.[5] Caetano, we know, personally waived the censorship so that Spínola could publish his book (it could not otherwise have come out at all), hoping to use it as a trial balloon for his own ideas. Caetano was also known to consider Spínola his protégé in the military, a potential successor to Thomaz, whom Caetano wished to get rid of. The question then becomes: Who was using whom? Was Caetano using Spínola (he certainly thought so)? Or (as now seems most likely) did Spínola have ambitions of his own, seeing himself as a viable alternative to *both* Thomaz and Caetano, using his book to embarrass Caetano, staking out an independent claim to authority and influence, and beginning the maneuvering that led to the coup? By publishing his book, Spínola clearly upset (by accelerating) the government's own timetable for African policy. And by saying what he did publicly in a system where this just was not done, he also embarrassed the government and gave the Right an opportunity to force a clamp-down and maybe even get rid of Caetano, which the Right had been seeking to do all along. Instead of ridding themselves of Caetano, however, the rightist maneuvering ironically resulted in bringing the regime down on their own heads.[6]

The revolt of April 1974 had at least as much to do with Spínola's personal ambitions as with his self-professed idealism. Further, many of the younger officers who supported him were hardly flaming liberals or necessarily sympathetic to the cause of African liberation. Their concerns were as much personal and professional as they were political, ideological, or idealistic: pay, promotions, prestige, opportunities for social status and advancement, the disruption in their lives and careers caused by five-year stints in Africa, and increasingly, as the guerrillas began to receive more sophisticated weapons from China and the Soviet Union in the aftermath of the U.S. Vietnam withdrawal, the possibility of being shot or of humiliating defeat, in which case they and the Army would likely be the scapegoats. That is what had happened to the officers after Portugal's humiliation by the Indian army in Goa, and it was a lesson the present officers did not forget. These young officers, hence, tied their political and professional fortunes to Spínola, who promised pay raises, promotions, and relief from the African imbroglio.

One of Spínola's sins (in the hard-liners' eyes) was to accept in his book much of the Left opposition's (especially SEDES) arguments of the disastrous effects of the African wars on the Portuguese economy, society, and international position. Accepting the opposition's argument gave it legitimacy, and that was unforgivable to the "ultras." President Thomaz, as their spokesman, demanded that Spínola and the officers aligned with him be arrested. Caetano, however, walking a middle path, offered Spínola a pension and placed his residence under observation.

Once Spínola's book had appeared, therefore, the Right and the old Salazaristas used it as a means of embarrassing Caetano, putting him on the spot, and perhaps replacing him altogether. Via Thomaz the message was telegraphed clearly: the opening of the political system, the Caetano reforms, must not be permitted to proceed too far too fast. It was time to rein in the progressives in the cabinet like Veiga Simão (Education) and Silva Pinto (Labor) and put them in their place. The Right exerted strong pressure to tighten things up, silence or dismiss the upstarts, and narrow the bounds of permissible political debate.

The tense situation (a premature and unsuccessful coup had been launched in March 1974 by the young rebels and pro-Spínola officers) also provided an opportunity for Caetano's old rivals and the government officials ousted in the 1968–70 period to attempt to make a comeback. In the weeks preceding the April coup, men like Nogueira, Moreira, and Veiga de Macedo, to say nothing of Spínola, were very active politically. Similarly, the cabinet and subcabinet officials out of office for several years were maneuvering. This too had little to do with ideology or with Africa; rather, it had to do with money, status, patronage, power, and the opportunities for advancement and enrichment that go with high government positions and from which these elements had, from their own perspective, been excluded too long.

Finally, these events helped the resurgence of President Thomaz as an important force in Portuguese political affairs, particularly as a spokesman for traditionalist, rightist, anti-Caetano military and civilian elements. He brought the pressure to bear on Caetano, forcing him to tighten up. Thomaz also saw the threat to his position posed by the Spínola challenge and continued to insist on his arrest. Caetano resisted, since he still preferred almost any other president to Thomaz. In March and early April he and Caetano were locked in a life-and-death struggle for political survival. They were not at all together on African or virtually any other policy. The post-coup press accounts, however, seeing that they were both part of the same regime and were exiled together, assumed they must have been together on the policy front. Nothing could be farther from the truth; indeed, the glossing over of their differences served to disguise the severe political infighting going on before the coup and the subtleties of Portuguese politics. Meanwhile, Spínola and the Armed Forces Movement, taking advantage of these rivalries, were secretly plotting another scenario whose seriousness was disguised by the attention given the argument between Caetano and the Right. That other scenario climaxed in the revolt of April 25, which resulted in the overthrow of the regime and the exile of *both* Caetano *and* Thomaz. That tactic clearly served Spínola's private political ambitions more than it indicated that Caetano and Thomaz were of one and the same mind.

The events leading up to the April coup seem in many ways a classic illustration of how the Portuguese system works.[7] It shows how diverse views and interests are expressed in a closed society, how political messages are telegraphed elliptically and indirectly, how personal ambitions are developed and served, how personal and factional power plays are, as in all governmental systems, glossed over with the language of great national issues (in this case, the debate over Africa and the Portuguese future). The Spínola affair, act 1, while not devoid of a certain degree of idealism, was perhaps more a rather melodramatic opening, a tentative feeling of the terrain by a number of politically ambitious men, an exploration by rival elites of the balance of political forces, an example almost of "politics as usual" as practiced in Portugal rather than some sharp and abrupt break with the past.

During this series of inconclusive skirmishes in the month before the coup, some adjustments were made (for example, Spínola was pensioned off and retired but not arrested), some new accommodations were reached (Caetano and the Right), several score persons were dismissed in the Army while a number of civilian ministers were also reined in, and a number of new alignments were in the process of being formed. Various forces and energies were set in motion—in Africa, but particularly in Portuguese domestic politics. Various political "jugglers" (Caetano, Thomaz, Spínola, others) launched a number of balls into the air. As act I was being played out, Portuguese observers and politicians alike were waiting to see who would catch most of them (the betting was on Caetano), which balls would be dropped, or on whose head one might fall. In this arena it appears that Caetano miscalculated and failed to see the strength and gathering momentum of the Spínola-AFM coalition. Both Caetano and Thomas were so busy looking out for each other that they lost sight of some of the other balls still up in the air. Caetano especially was so concerned with the threat from the Right (with good reason) that he neglected any other; at this late date he was probably also convinced that Spínola remained his "boy" and that the earlier plot had been ferreted out with the dismissal of the conspiring officers. Thus, it turned out to be *both* Thomaz's *and* Caetano's heads on whom the balls dropped. When that occurred, it became Spínola's turn to serve temporarily as the new "juggler," although under quite new ground rules than had been the case before. For unlike the classic "circulation of elites" implying new faces, modest readjustments but no fundamental transformations, the Spínola coup and succeeding events ushered in something of a revolution, a basic realignment of political forces.

The coup of April 25 caught everyone by surprise: Right, Left, Caetano, the American embassy, everyone. But more than that, it occurred, in its initial stages, not as the result of any great mass rebellion and uprising or as the culmination of a long history of revolutionary activity. Rather, the coup was a result of a series of intraelite rivalries and maneuverings whose dynamics, in part by accident, in part by plan, helped produce a genuinely social-revolutionary situation. Although the Portuguese, and especially the small 5–10 percent who were politically active, had numerous reasons to complain, and although the coup itself served as a trigger to release all these long-pent-up frustrations, the fact is that many Portuguese had never had it so good. Although still badly off by European standards, which was the gauge used by the educated, the opposition, and many emigrant workers, middle- and many working-class Portuguese were better off economically, socially, and to some extent politically than their parents or even they themselves had been only a few years before. GNP was rising rapidly and so was the standard

of living. The IPOPE surveys had recently shown that the vast majority
of Portuguese were prospering both relatively and absolutely, their standard of living was considerably higher than it had been five or ten years
earlier, and they shared a widespread sense of optimism as regards both
their own future and that of their children.[8] As we noted in chapter 9,
the 1974 revolt occurred when conditions were not so bad but in fact
getting better, although probably not fast enough to satisfy the new expectations and probably not proceeding in the directions the growing
number of Portuguese in the Left and Center wished to go. The coup
galvanized these forces into action, served to release the varied popular
discontents that had been simmering over the years, and paved the way
for the subsequent radicalization of the revolution.

The initial response to the military take-over was one of shock and
disbelief. For a day the population stood by, stunned. Then, as the
institutions of the old regime began crumbling all around (it remains a
mystery how the Right, which everyone assumed to be so powerful,
seemed so rapidly to melt away, and how such a tightly knit, authoritarian, even "fascist" regime as we assumed the Portuguese to be, with
all its web of controls, could collapse in a matter of a few hours), the
disbelief gave way to euphoria. The Portuguese emptied into the streets
in an outpouring of joy and freedom they had not experienced in nearly
half a century. All the social controls and political restraints in effect
for so long went at once, and what had been a gloomy, morose, inward-
drawn population exploded with happiness and spontaneity. As the
euphoria slowly gave way in the next few days to more realistic assessments of the nation's possibilities and prospects, the far more difficult
task of reconstructing the nation on the ruins of the crumbled old one
began.

The last week of April and the first days of May 1974 (which, of
course, included May Day) amounted to a near two-week-long national
holiday in Portugal. An exuberant, joyful people marched happily, yet
peacefully, along Portugal's main thoroughfares. It was a national celebration, a time of liberation, of great hope for better days. Soon after,
however, the public euphoria that had followed the overthrow of the old
regime began to give way to an atmosphere of uncertainty and political
tension.

The big coup of April 25 had been followed by a series of mini-
coups all over Portugal. Students began getting rid of faculty members
associated with the former regime, faculties and students joined to overturn their administrations, workers in the major industries began challenging employers, employees of the rich and prestigious Gulbenkian
Foundation had a showdown with its secretary-general, civil service em-

ployees demanded the ouster of higher level managers and administrators, whole ministries were sacked and purged. These changes implied not the usual circulation of elites but the beginning of a genuine class transformation. Militant leaders from the Socialist and Communist parties took over from the old government-controlled sindicatos and began demanding large wage increases and renegotiation of all collective contracts—demands that were soon enforced through the government's naming for a time of a Communist trade union leader as head of a reorganized Labor Ministry and the appointment of Communist Secretary-General Alvaro Cunhal as minister without portfolio, from which position he too began directing the Communist take-over of numerous trade unions. As the purges spread, a wave of crippling strikes also broke out, and the confrontations multiplied.

Few would deny that many Portuguese institutions needed a thorough overhaul (or *regeneração*), that many employers and administrators ought to have been confronted or purged, that the old sindicato leadership was often corrupt and ineffective, and that the workers had the right to strike and to get higher wages. This message was carried in fact by General Spínola, by the military junta that had staged the coup, and by the civilian cabinet appointed to help run the country, to employers and industrialists—most of whom were scrambling to realign themselves at least publicly with the new regime. The questions remained, however, of whether a purge of all the officials associated with the former regime (of necessity, including virtually all educated persons) would not leave the country bereft of all leadership and administrative skills, whether turning the Labor Ministry and the unions over to the Communists was wise, whether the social assistance and social security programs, limited though they were, would not collapse with disastrous consequences as the network of corporative agencies and institutions disintegrated, whether the rash of strikes, conflicts, and demonstrations would not force economic and political breakdown, and whether Portugal's struggling economy could afford the mammoth wage increases being given out. Would the new freedoms not lead to anarchy, could a people unschooled and inexperienced in democracy adapt to a democratic give and take, might not the Portuguese lower classes be worse off as a result of the new uncertainty and chaos than they had been under the former regime? These are difficult and troubling questions, and they have by no means yet been answered. As Tom Wicker remarked in a *New York Times* feature, the wage increases achieved literally overnight and the new minimum wage decreed by the regime were undoubtedly long overdue and just, but they would be inflationary justice if production did not increase, too.[9]

As the restraints of the corporative regime gave way, the strikes spread, and the time consumed by endless rounds of meetings and by workers' participation in the running of unions and firms increased, industrial production fell off sharply. So did the remittances sent home by Portuguese emigrant workers, while tourism all but stopped and the flight of Portuguese capital began. GNP dropped precipitously. An atmosphere of uneasiness began setting in as the social agitation reached chronic proportions. The sudden erasure of the old repressive apparatus was spawning such ferment and disruption that sheer chaos and national disintegration seemed a strong possibility. The resignation of General Spínola in October 1974 at once demonstrated the divisive, chaotic currents within the regime and removed the one man who might have been capable of holding the country together. In a pattern familiar in the patrimonialist tradition, once the apex or pinnacle of the authoritarian-autocratic pyramid was removed, the disparate elements that make up political society began to fragment and fall apart.

The Communists followed a double-edged strategy. Under Cunhal's direction they had moved quickly, surely, but cautiously and with restraint into the trade union movement so as not to lose the favor of the military and the privileged, preponderant position in labor affairs they had already achieved. At the same time, they followed a second, clandestine strategy of underground activities and infiltration, frequently employing strong-arm tactics, directed at the take-over of local government agencies and other key institutions. Meanwhile, other extreme Left groups, Maoists and others, sought to instigate as much disruption as possible. And at the other end of the spectrum, Portugal's wealthy industrialists and the "100 families" or *grupos* who dominated the economy were desperately maneuvering behind the scenes and using their connections to keep the junta from making too many concessions to the restive workers. In the time-honored way they sought to make the case that unless restraints were applied the entire economy would disintegrate. Other conservative and rightist forces, both civilian and military, also began maneuvering for a countercoup, planning to wait a bit until the euphoria with the new "freedom" had passed and the demand for order had been renewed. Only a few months old, Portugal's experiment in "democracy" was already endangered. The result was a feeling that none of the problems of the old regime had been solved and some had been aggravated. Meanwhile, the currents of polarization and fragmentation continued to multiply and the country drifted toward collapse, confrontation, and possible civil war.[10]

The corporative institutions existing since 1933 were all but completely swept away. The Corporative Chamber (along with the National

Assembly) was dissolved. The Corporations Ministry became the focus of a strong "anti-fascist" attack. It was redivided into a Ministry of Labor (given initially to the Communists) and a Ministry of Social Assistance and Welfare, which tried to maintain the essential social services but was also torn by disruption, upheaval, and uncertainty regarding the future, and by such administrative confusion as to result in a diminishing of the already woefully inadequate social services provided the Portuguese people. Most of the legislation and institutions governing labor relations (the Labor Statute, the labor courts, the arbitration commissions, the collective contracts, and so on) were overturned by the plethora of strikes and the rush of events, before any new labor laws and agencies were created to replace them. Labor relations, the restructuring of the sindicatos, the rewriting of the labor laws were placed in new, inexperienced, often Communist hands. Those in the most favored unions (largely Communist-dominated, since Caetano's time) were able to get anywhere from 100 to 300 percent wage increases; "restraint" was urged on the rest. In an effort to preserve continuity, responsibility for administering social services and assistance was turned over initially to F. Cid Proença, a long-time member of the corporative administrative hierarchy, but within that establishment a strong critic of its misdirected or misapplied functions as well.[11] His tenure was short-lived, however, and disorganization and indiscipline spread further. It had proven relatively easy to abolish the corporative name, label, and institutions, but it was clearly a far more difficult matter to create other institutions to carry out the positive and useful services and functions the corporative system had been carrying out. In the absence of either the corporative agencies or those of a more liberal or social-democratic sort, the result was chaos and breakdown. Some of the formal structure of the administrative state system remained in place, of course, but it lacked direction and coherence and was torn by the same uncertainties and tendencies toward fragmentation and paralysis as the society at large.

The corporations themselves, whose functions had always been limited, were also dissolved. The corporative agencies in the Ministry of the Economy responsible for the "disciplining" and regulation of prices, wages, and production were similarly declared "extinct." The ordens of lawyers, doctors, engineers, and agronomists announced that they had thrown out their "fascist" leadership. There was recognition that the casas do povo and casas dos pescadores, once reorganized, could serve some useful functions. Many gremios were changed into class associations for business, industrial, and landowning interests; that implied chiefly a name change, for their functions had always been chiefly to represent the viewpoints of the major economic interests to the government and to serve as instruments for the government to enforce its economic regulations. Later, some stronger measures were enacted to regulate and control business activity, to restrict the wealth and influence of the Portuguese plutocracy, and to nationalize various industries. The sindicatos were perhaps the major focus of activity, as they too were now organized as frankly class associations rather than, as in the old system, instruments for class solidarity. Socialists, Communists, and others began racing to organize the new sindicatos in factories, shops, offices, and the *freguesias,* or to gain control of the structures left over from the old regime. Signs began appearing on office buildings announcing "free" unions, as the memberships succeeded in ousting the governing bodies largely imposed by the government under the old system. In this race to organize the new workers' groups and to dominate the newly created national labor confederation, the Communists were generally conceded to have had the upper hand, a development that was causing increasing alarm in both civilian and military circles.[12]

Portugal's problems were formidable. It remained a poor country in terms of its resources and economic potential, a fact which no change of regimes could alter. The government was meanwhile faced by widespread strikes by rebellious workers, bringing to a halt large numbers of public services and industrial concerns and seemingly determined to overthrow all authority at once. The young colonels and majors who had helped organize the April 1974 coup sounded like the young nationalist and developmentalist officers who launched a revolution in Peru in 1968, but unfortunately the Portuguese officers had neither the training in their service academies nor the administrative, managerial, developmentalist skills and background that their Peruvian counterparts had. And despite the official expressions of confidence and assurances of continuity, many business leaders were frightened, unused to the new assertiveness of the workers (backed by the government and the Labor Ministry), fearing their wealth and holdings might be taken over by their employees or nationalized, and particularly vulnerable because of their close association with the former regime. The middle class grew similarly restive; many began emigrating. Meanwhile the purges continued and chaos and disorder (political, economic, administrative) multiplied. The fabric of Portuguese society began to unravel and political discord, institutional decay, and disintegration spread.

Inevitably, the crackdown began. The military-civilian junta that had been set up with General Spínola at its head was, after all, an essentially conservative group. It wanted change and was content to let the "thousand flowers" bloom temporarily, but it wanted change within certain bounds and certainly not under Communist-Socialist domination. The junta allowed a definite turn to the Left, but it stood itself to the Right. Soon it began warning against anarchy and calling for a halt to the purges. It broke up a number of demonstrations. It warned public employees to stop seeking to remove their superiors. It jailed a few people. Then it took over full control of the state-run radio network and imposed new curbs on the news media. It urged a halt to the disruptive strikes, warned against provocateurs, and promised that the military would intervene where necessary to preserve order and discipline. It issued a series of decrees imposing new restrictions on political party and labor union activity and returned to some of the carefully regulative methods of managing change of the older Portuguese tradition. These moves in turn stimulated considerable strain within the government and between the new regime and its earlier supporters. Spínola resigned, power shifted to the younger and more leftist officers, the Right intensified its plotting, and a major confrontation loomed. As the general discontent spread, the divisions multiplied, the fragmentation of national political life accelerated, and the danger of national breakdown increased, the parallels with the last months of the earlier Portuguese Republic, 1910–26, were inevitably drawn. Then, a powerful rightist military-civilian movement had finally stepped in to stem the chaos, reestablished discipline and order with a vengeance, and paved the way for the establishment of Salazar's forty-year Estado Novo.

It is not our purpose here to bring the Portuguese chronology exactly up to date or to trace all the ups and downs of the succession of Portuguese governments since April 1974, the waxing and waning of the revolution, the leftist challenges and the rightist countermoves. Rather, our purpose has been to outline the more enduring aspects of the Portuguese political system, as well as to analyze how change within the system occurs. For in the wake of April 1974, Portugal will never be the same again. At this juncture, given the deep and profound transformations that have occurred, socially, politically, and economically, it would seem impossible for any regime totally to reharness all the energies set loose or not to ratify the major changes that have occurred. At the same time, it would be wrong to emphasize the changes since the revolution without paying attention to the continuities. The coup clearly represented a major shift and realignment of political forces, a significant thrust and opening to the Left, but it should not be forgotten it was carried out under military, authoritarian auspices. The coup represented an accommodation to new political realities and class changes and a restructuring of some key institutions and political processes; it was in this sense a "critical coup" or a "transforming coup" rather than the usual barracks revolt. Yet it remains to be seen how much of a fundamental class shift the coup ushered in and whether any of the major power contenders (elites, Army, bourgeoisie, Church, and so on) will be eliminated or merely eclipsed temporarily. Obviously the power of the older elites has been reduced and that of the newer ones enhanced, but whether that will be a total or a more limited process lies still at the heart of Portuguese political dispute. The events of April 1974 and thereafter represent a regeneration in Portuguese social and political life, an important reordering and restucturing. Whether this "regeneration" also implies a full-scale revolution, or only a partial one, in terms of a fundamental transformation in the class bases of power still is uncertain.[13]

The regime—any regime that comes to power in Portugal—will almost certainly continue to play a powerful tutelary role. It will opt for controlled and regulated change, almost certainly under statist-authoritarian direction, and it will likely seek to prevent change from getting out of hand. In government and the economy the faces will change, some new or aspiring elites will be brought in, new openings and opportunities for advancement will appear. The corporate label will no longer be used, and the formal institutions associated with the old regime will be transformed. These are not modest accomplishments; they mark several long steps from the previous system. Still, the differences between old and new should not be exaggerated. A regime that was carrying out orderly change in a gradual way (perhaps *too* orderly and gradual) has been replaced by one that precipitously accelerated these modernizing trends—but did so at the cost of enormous disruption of the economy and political life. After two years, however, it may be that the chaotic, disruptive phase of this regenerating revolution has come to an end and a new consolidating phase begun. The succession of governments that followed the original 1974 coup, after all, were all military-dominated regimes whose popular support was probably just as transitory as the one that went before. Whether the Portuguese government will hence remain locked in the authoritarian-patrimonialist mold, whether it will actually transcend authoritarianism and corporatism, or whether it will evolve toward a newer, more modernized, more complex corporative form, such as syndicalism or a variant of socialism, remains a critical albeit as yet unanswered question.

It should be remembered that both the Salazar-Caetano regime and its successor were paternalistic, organicist, directed from the top. Both were middle class. Both involved movements and changes initiated not by the people or the lower classes but by intellectuals and civilian and military elites presuming to act on the people's behalf. Although both paid lip service to popular democratic rule, neither went very far toward implementing these goals. After an initial period of allowing the "thousand flowers" to bloom, both sought to limit and control grass-roots activity and to provide a system of structured participation under the hegemony of a strong state. The new government has certainly instigated some strongly nationalistic and *potentially* revolutionary programs (with emphasis more on the potential than the revolutionary), but these too will likely continue to emanate from the top. Finally, although the new regime expressly repudiated the corporatist label, one is nonetheless struck by the persistence of corporative forms: the organicist and etatist conception, the continuing pattern of functionalist representation, the segmented, vertical structure of interest group organization and articulation, the deprecation of popular opinion as expressed in the elections, the continuation of hierarchical, authoritarian, and elitist decision making, and the special place in the system accorded such primary corporate groups as, especially, the Army, which moved in its pact with the political parties and the new Portuguese constitution to ensure that it would remain the ultimate arbiter of national politics.

It is in this context of change *and* continuity that we should examine the Portuguese revolution. While much has changed, much also remains the same. A major shift and restructuring took place beginning in April 1974, but in the long run the Portuguese regime, and the broader national system, will probably continue to conform to many of its more enduring features. It seems unlikely that Portugal can suddenly and irrevocably cast off or escape from some seven centuries of history. Hence, no matter the name or label the newer system goes by, it will likely remain strongly elitist, hierarchical, patrimonialist, authoritarian, statist, bureaucratic, and, yes, even corporatist, to its core. It will be corporatist no longer in the 1930s, *Rerum Novarum,* Salazarista sense of that term but in that more general historical and political-cultural sense of the "corporative model" or the "corporative tradition" outlined in chapter 1. Reflecting the social changes that have occurred in Portugal in the last thirty years, the relations between and power of the several corporate elements that make up Portuguese society may be altered, the scheme and balance of functional representation may be changed, and a newer form of populist-, socialist-, or syndicalist-corporatist rule may ensue, like that of the Peruvian corporatist-revolutionary regime or perhaps patterned on some other model or blends. But whatever the final outcome, it will certainly be a Portuguese solution; and that almost necessarily implies one or another form of corporatist structure and organization.

The Portuguese Corporative System:
An Assessment

This book began as an examination of an existent, on-going corporative system, a system that liked to think of itself and was often thought of by outsiders as "the third way," an alternative to liberalism, on the one hand, and socialism, on the other. It ends almost as an epitaph to the Salazar and post-Salazar regimes, since the revolution of April 1974 brought an end both to an era in Portuguese politics and to the particular corporative experiment we set out to examine. An assessment now is thus both timely and opportune not only for purposes of evaluating the successes and failures of the now-completed Portuguese experiment with corporatism but also because the broader corporative tradition lives on in Portugal, it is present in so many other regimes and polities of Iberia and Latin America, and it may even have implications as regards recent sociopolitical developments in the United States and other modern nations.[14]

The themes treated are important. It can be said that the world of labor relations, of employer-employee relations, of freedom and associability, of class interaction between workers and owners, of the "social question," constitutes the anvil on which much of the modern and certainly the twentieth-century world and present-day social structure were forged. Among the various "isms" and ideologies for dealing with the issues and forces that industrialization and its accompanying social changes raised from the middle of the last century to the present, corporatism was for a time one of the most influential. It had an enormous impact in Europe and elsewhere during the period between World Wars I and II and was particularly important in shaping the polities and social programs of the Iberic and Latin nations. More recently, corporatist forms, ideology, and modes of organization and interpretation have enjoyed a powerful resurgence in nations as diverse as Argentina, Brazil, Chile, Mexico, and Peru. In the case under discussion here, corporatism was also closely intertwined with Portuguese industrialization and the emergence of a new, more modern social and political structure, although the precise nature of these relationships deserves very close scrutiny. The issues are thus critical; they merit serious attention.

Any evaluation of the Portuguese corporative regime must begin by recognizing both its successes and its failures. From start to finish it was an exceedingly mixed bag. Further it was a complex, changing system which was not always what it seemed and often seemed to be what it was not. Corporatism's stated goals were one thing, its actual aims often another. Hence, any examination of it must look both at what its leaders said and at what they actually did, as well as appraising the gaps between the two. Deceptive, opaque, far subtler than is usually supposed, the Portuguese corporative system was neither the great success its admirers (usually knowing little about it) have proclaimed nor merely the "confidence trick" of its detractors.

One can probably make a fairly solid case for the Portuguese corporative regime in the 1930s and perhaps during the war years. Particularly coming on the heels of a century-long, often ruinous experiment with British-style parliamentarism capped by sixteen years of chaotic, disintegrative republicanism, corporatism seemed to offer a return to order and stability, a period of needed peace, a restoration of a historic nationalist and *Portuguese* tradition and set of institutions after more than a hundred years of trying out what was probably an inappropriate foreign model. The military regime that took power in 1926 succeeded in restoring order and stability and gave the country a new measure of national dignity and self-respect. Salazar brought a new honesty and responsibility to the management of financial and administrative affairs. Indeed, the reestablishment of a stable, functioning regime and the strengthening of the Portuguese economy over a two-decade period from 1926 to 1945 were among the more notable accomplishments of Salazar's rule. This strengthening was related to the creation of a host of corporative and semicorporative agencies and bureaus to help coordinate, regulate, and administer an expanding, industrializing economy. The corporative "revolution" of 1933, the Constitution, the Labor Statute, and the other corporative legislation were thus important ingredients in the policy to restore economic and political stability. Via the corporative system, the regime had sought to organize and coordinate the various groups "loose" in a disorganized civil society and to subordinate them to the state. Corporatism also provided Portugal with a new national mythos, badly needed after the failure of republicanism, with a new sense of national purpose and destiny, and with a set of institutions to fill what had been an almost total void in previous Portuguese associational life.[15] Young, dynamic, enjoying considerable popularity at home and abroad, filled with idealism to stimulate development and provide for social justice, corporatism in the 1930s seemed to offer Portugal new hope, new promise, a way out of its national malaise and out of the country's unhappy position as Europe's laughingstock, the butt of many cruel jokes.

A historical perspective is also useful. These factors do not necessarily explain corporatism in Portugal or the particular direction it took, but they do help put it in perspective. First, there is the presence of the Portuguese historical tradition, of religion, hierarchy, gremios, ordens, authority, community, family, paternalism, patrimonialism, and "natural" corporatism, a tradition which the young corporatist intellectuals of the 1920s and 1930s sought to recapture and update. This was not just a return to medievalism or an attempt to turn the clock back, as some of the popular commentaries have alleged, but a way to meet the challenge of the modern world (industrialization, capitalism, rapid urbanization, the rise of mass society) without sacrificing in their entirety the amenities and useful social institutions of the past. Portugal sought to adapt to modernity but in ways that would enable the country to preserve that which was worthwhile in her own history and traditions, to resurrect in renovated form the institutions and traditions of her earlier "golden age." These traditions included authoritarian leadership, orderly and controlled paternalistic rule, a hierarchy of orders and social classes, functional representation, an organic-unified view of the state and society, and, as indicated, a pattern of powerful corporatist-patrimonialist structures and behavior. The corporatist revival of the interwar period in Portugal was thus a strongly nationalistic one, aimed at resurrecting what was viable and distinctly Portuguese in her own historical institutions and of ridding the country of disastrous, dysfunctional, foreign-based constitutional and political practices.

Second, there is the Pombal phenomenon. In the eighteenth century, too, the country had turned to dictatorship as the only remedy for a crisis deemed incurable. The earthquake of 1755 had given Pombal his chance, enabling him—at considerable costs—to free Portugal (if only for a time) from the disaster and incoherence that threatened national life. Thereafter, throughout the nineteenth century and until the establishment of the corporative state, varying degrees of chaos had again held back national progress. Repeated civil wars, fratricidal strife among contending factions of the royal family, selfish and narrowly based partisan politics, *pronunciamentos* and coups d'état, foreign domination, poverty, and an almost endemic incapacity to govern or to be governed combined to keep Portugal the poorest and most retrogressive of European nations. Now it was the chaos of the Republic, the national humiliation in World War I and the early 1920s, the widespread corruption, the depression, and then the gathering storm in Europe that ushered in the military and Salazar. Personally, Salazar had little in common with the mercurial Pombal, but he did share with him a genius for organization and political maneuver. Hence, when it became plain that democratic institutions had failed and held little appeal in the

Portuguese political culture, when renewed crises seemed to threaten the very existence of the nation, it was to a new Pombal, a new autocrat and "savior," that the nation turned.[16]

Third, the particular form that corporatism took in Portugal was also related to the kind of society Portugal was in the 1930s—and to some degree still is. The Portuguese corporative state was a reflection of a society that remained predominantly rural, Catholic, agricultural, paternalistic, static, and backward. We have already remarked on how closely it reflected also the small-town, petit bourgeois attitudes of Salazar's own background. To the extent that Portugal remains rural, Catholic, and small town, corporatism in the 1930s sense is still probably appropriate. It was in the more dynamic, urban, secular, industrializing, modernizing areas like Lisbon, Porto, and Setúbal in the post-World War II period, however, that the corporative scheme became increasingly inappropriate and the opposition to it the strongest. The usefulness and appropriateness of the Portuguese corporative system, in other words, were directly related to the historical epoch and kind of society in which it was founded and took shape. Clearly in the period after 1945, as we shall see in a moment, that particular form was no longer appropriate.[17]

This is not to say, however, that the corporative system was entirely unyielding, rigid, and inflexible. The pragmatic adaptations undertaken in the 1930s, the uses of the corporative agencies during World War II, the revival of the 1950s, the social assistance orientation of the 1960s, and Caetano's rejuvenation and his concept of the Estado Social all demonstrate a considerable degree of flexibility. Whether it was sufficiently adaptable for the changed circumstances and society of the 1960s and 1970s, or whether it had been rendered irrelevant by the growth of other instruments of dictatorship and repression, are, of course, questions to which we must address ourselves.

The corporative regime, in its time, performed numerous useful and positive functions. To some extent at least, it *was* a viable, functioning system that undertook numerous services and activities for the regime. Through the casas dos pescadores, sindicatos, and gremios (and to a more limited extent the ordens and casas do povo), it provided Portugal with a level of institutionalization it had never had before, a nascent system of grass-roots organizations, a means for tapping (to some extent) public opinion, and a set of agencies for implementing and enforcing government policies. It helped establish and administer the numerous regulatory agencies, boards, and commissions necessary in any modern state. Although implemented at best unevenly, the 1933 Labor Statute and subsequent legislation gave Portuguese workers a recognition and legitimacy they had never achieved before. The corporative scheme provided for a system of representation (however limited in its authority) by which the major functional interests could make their voices heard (however weakly). Though prejudicial against worker interests for a long period, the system also provided for an elaborate network of labor courts, arbitration commissions, collective contract mechanisms, and so on. Through the Corporations Subsecretariat and, later, Ministry, the structure for a modern, nationwide system of social security, assistance, and labor protection was laid out. Vast volumes of labor legislation, social security law, and corporative organizational reforms were put on the books; the system of labor relations, assistance, and associational life became highly rationalized, elaborate, bureaucratic, and complex. Of course, for long periods much of this structure went unused and was often perverted in directions not intended by its original founders, but under Caetano especially the system began to function more justly and equitably than before and the gap between theory and practice narrowed.

Portugal was never, however, a fully corporative system. This was due, on the one hand, to the country's historic, continuing poverty, which made it impossible for such a complete restructuring of the national life as the corporatists envisioned to be actually carried out. The lack of resources both human (in the form of trained leaders and organizers) and material (in terms of budgetary support) was a constant lament of those charged with implementing corporative programs. Second, based on Pereira's memoirs and particularly the interviewing, my research turned up much evidence to support the contention that, despite the constitutional statements proclaiming Portugal a corporative state and despite the political theory pointing to the corporaive base of the entire national system, Salazar *never* intended to give any real political authority to the corporative agencies. Some social and economic functions, yes; but political power, no. Whether this had to do with pressures from the Army or his own predisposition to rule absolutely (probably both at first; later it also had to do with the capture of the corporative apparatus by business and economic elites), it seems clear that right from the beginning in 1933 Salazar had no intention of sharing any real decision-making authority with the corporative agencies. This helps explain why for twenty-three years Portugal was a "corporative state without corporations" and why, when they were finally adopted in 1956, they acquired little real power.

From the start, then, Portugal was a corporative regime in *some* respects and in *some* areas of national life, but by no means in all. Moreover, as time went on the areas where corporatism was influential became more and more circumscribed. These included labor relations, the administration of social security, and to some limited degree interest articulation, aggregation, and representation. The rest of the national structure—military, Church, politics, bureaucracy, machinery of dictatorship—remained almost wholly outside the corporate system. The economy was never completely corporatized, except unevenly and in a way that favored some groups at the expense of others. Even in the area of labor relations or social security, further, all major decisions were made by Salazar himself on grounds that usually had little to do with corporative principles. By the postwar period, we have seen, corporatism was even less at the heart of the system than it had been in the 1930s. Caetano gave the corporative system a shot in the arm by providing it with a new thrust and direction, but even under Caetano the narrowing of the range of manifestly corporative activities continued until they were confined to only one floor of twenty-six in the Corporations Ministry. Although it continued to be called "corporative" largely for historical and sentimental reasons (and there was *some* degree of pride in this unique Portuguese institution), in fact the Corporations Ministry could just as easily have been called the Ministry of Labor and Social Assistance. This title would have more accurately portrayed its more recent functions, and probably only a handful of old 1930s ideologues would have lamented the change.

By the 1960s and 1970s, thus, the real concerns in the Portuguese system had become management, administration, economic development, getting ahead, European integration, and relations with Africa. Corporatism was no longer *the* foundation of the system; rather, it became only one institutional pillar among many. Although the corporative agencies continued to perform a variety of useful and necessary functions, though new casas do povo and other agencies continued to be founded, though new refinements were always being introduced, and though Salazar and Caetano continued to voice their adherence to the hallowed corporative principles, it was clear that corporative ideology was no longer a concern of major importance. It was wholly unattractive to the younger generation, and even the middle-aged planners and technicians in São Bento and the ministries formulated their proposals without any consideration of remaining true to some vague, dated corporative ideology. Some of the old guard were still promoting corporatism (although even such rightist papers as *Epoca* and *Novidades* often had little idea what corporatism was all about), and, of course, on the other side the Socialists and Communists were employing the familiar ideological labels. By the 1960s and 1970s, however, after *two* generations had grown up who hardly remembered and knew even less of the ideological quarrels of their fathers, most of the old arguments from the pre-World War II period fell on deaf ears. They were forgotten, irrelevant. Portugal, like the rest of the West, had experienced a certain decline of ideology since the 1930s. This is obviously not to say that Portugal was yet a wholly technocratic state or that ideology had died or disappeared; the revolution in 1974 demonstrated that it had not. But clearly the issues had changed, and many of the ideological arguments from that earlier era could no longer move or inspire large numbers of Portuguese of whatever class. Even within the corporative system this decline was evident. The administration of social security was handled in a pragmatic fashion that had almost nothing to do with corporatism; the Corporations Ministry was similarly concerned with labor relations, not corporatism. Even the last corporations minister, Rebelo de Sousa, began talking of the unfortunate connotations of the term and of the possibility of abandoning the corporative label. Corporatism as a body of ideas was no longer significant. It could even be said that the "corporatist" regime of Caetano was overthrown when "corporatism" per se had ceased to be an issue of major importance.

But if corporatism as a manifest ideology had declined and was no longer of critical importance, the broader political-cultural tradition of corporatism remained very much alive. Portugal may have been in the process of abandoning or sloughing off its 1930s doctrines, but it could not so easily dispense with habits and traditions built up over centuries. It seems likely that even before the revolution, if Portugal had formally abandoned "corporatism" in favor of another label like the "Estado Social" or "liberalism" (Caetano had begun talking in these terms toward the end), the Portuguese *system* would have likely remained authoritarian, hierarchical, bureaucratic, patrimonialist, *and* corporatist in that more general historical sense. Even if the 1930s concept had been dropped, the more permanent, *naturally* corporative features of the system would have remained. Portugal would still have represented a closed and controlled system, probably with some adjustments made to reflect more recent changes, but nevertheless a system whose major features still conformed closely to that broader political-cultural tradition we have called the "corporative model." That indeed, as we have seen, is one of the more likely outcomes of the "revolution" of 1974.

The question may thus be raised as to whether Portugal was ever a corporative system. The answer, with the qualifications discussed above, is yes, but then it must additionally be said that Portugal was also a great number of other things: a dictatorship, a police state, an autarchy, an administrative state, a system of authoritarianism and of state capitalism. Any assessments of corporatism's successes or failures in Portugal must be qualified by the fact that a full-fledged corporatism was never really tried, that Portugal was only a partial or "mixed" (in the Manoïlesco sense) form of corporatism *and* these other features, that corporatism was one of the regime's props—but only one among several and perhaps not the most important.

Was corporatism a dependent or an independent variable? Here also the going gets tricky, for again the answer depends on how one uses the term. I would say that certainly in the broad political-cultural sense implying the accumulated habits and behavior patterns of the Portuguese nation, corporatism was an independent variable, probably as important as class structure in determining political outcomes and maybe more so. As regards the manifestly corporative experiments specifically of Salazar's Estado Novo, the answer is ambiguous. The case could probably be made either way. Was it really corporatism that Salazar was trying to implement in the early 1930s, or was it autocratic or authoritarian rule, of which corporatism was only one instrument? And after the mid-1930s, by which time Pereira was out and the point of view of the business elites often prevailed at the expense of further corporative implementation, which was the dependent and which the independent variable? An unrefined Marxist would have no trouble with this question, but his response would of necessity have to be based more on ideological preconceptions than on direct, hard evidence. The truth is we do not know precisely what the relationship between all these variables was. In fact, all were operating at the same time, usually with considerable autonomy, and with the relative importance varying depending on the period, the circumstances, and the particular issue at stake. My own research leads me to conclude that in the early 1930s (and perhaps for a time under Caetano) corporatist implementation was an independent variable, although it may have not been first among the regime's list of priorities; as the 1930s passed and particularly under Salazar in the postwar period, corporatism was probably a dependent variable, used chiefly to keep the labor class and the people in general controlled and in their place. But there are on this issue no final and absolutely certain answers.

The next question to be raised, hence, is: Do systems matter at all? That is, if Portugal has always been corporatist in the broad political-cultural sense used here, does it matter if it is called liberalism, socialism, or corporatism? The answer is yes, of course it matters, but probably not to as great a degree as we ordinarily think. The natural resources available to Portugal are limited, and for this reason it will never "catch up" with the rest of Europe no matter what "ism" is employed. There are no magic formulas by which one *system* or another can achieve rapid development for Portugal. Surely the pattern of distribution can be altered (and has been since the 1974 revolution), and there are probably some things a new regime, or system, could do to expand production and enlarge social programs. These gains would likely be marginal, however, and in the long run Portugal remains and will remain among the less developed countries of Europe—as it was under its monarchs, during the era of republicanism and liberalism, under the corporatist regime, and in the new, post-1974 era, whatever it may be called. Its place among the nations, ranked by GNP, per capital income, or whatever, remains relatively constant—and relatively low—no matter the name or label of the particular "system" that happens to be in existence.

Because Portugal was, besides being a corporative state, an administrative state, a capitalist state, a dictatorship, and doubtless other things, models of interpretation that focus on these other aspects are as critical as the corporative one employed here for viewing and interpreting the entire national system. Our analysis has focused on the corporative aspects of the regime and the relations of the corporative structure to the entire national system because these areas are both critical and long neglected. But no presumption is made that this is the only or the most important way of approaching and understanding the Portuguese system. Clearly other frameworks must be employed to get at those aspects and relationships that this analysis has left out or touched on only briefly. The corporative focus is a useful one and tells us much about the workings (or lack thereof) of the Portuguese system, but obviously other approaches need to be made to investigate facets parallel or complementary to the ones examined here.

We have said that corporatism in the *Rerum Novarum* and *Quadragesimo Anno* pattern may have been appropriate and served the nation well in the 1930s. But it was clearly no longer appropriate by the 1960s and 1970s. This is related to the discrediting of all such corporative schemes by the Nazi and Fascist experiences, but there is more to it than that. For rather than a positive and even progressive force for equality and social justice, as corporatism often was in the early period, it became in the postwar period a negative force holding the country back. Salazar used the corporative system as one means of applying the brakes to economic growth and social and political modernization. Instead of promoting change, Portugal's corporative structure served to retard it. Rather than being neutral in the clash between capital and labor, the corporative system was increasingly used to hold labor in check while favoring the interests of large capital. No less important than the political police, the censorship, or other authoritarian controls, the corporative system became a way of assuring state and capitalistic dominance over the working class by means of a subtle and complex scheme of professional and economic associations controlled and manipulated by the regime.[18]

Of course, even in 1935 the first biases within the system in favor of the business-commercial interests were already evident, but this had been disguised by the righteous corporative fervor of Pereira and then by the rapid increase in state power (at the expense of both labor *and* business) during the period of the Spanish civil war and World War II. By the end of the war, however, the position of the industrial, banking, and other moneyed interests had been enhanced and their close association with the state cemented. The workers were now called upon to bear the costs of the industrialization in the form of woefully low wages and inadequate social security. Salazar remained wedded to the corporative system as a control mechanism even though the vast social changes occurring after 1945 made corporatism in its 1930s form less and less appropriate. His dogmatism and absolutism in hanging onto an outmoded scheme meant that Portugal was forced farther and farther behind the rest of Europe. Portugal missed out on, among other things, a period comparable to the earlier Spanish decades of development in the 1950s and 1960s, and the general European prosperity of the postwar era. As a result, the entire Portuguese system had become hidebound and dated. Given the increasingly urbanized and middle-class nature of Portuguese society by the 1960s, the corporative structure became more and more an anachronism, unloved and unwanted by the general population, a vestige of an earlier era, no longer very useful or functional. The corporative system under Salazar's direction had locked Portugal into a 1930s (or perhaps pre-World War I) social order that no longer applied by the later date.

We may speculate as to some of the reasons that the Portuguese adopted the corporative form and then hung onto it so tenaciously beyond its period of usefulness. One explanation lies in the long-time sense of national inferiority the Portuguese harbor and to their tradition of importing whole solutions from outside. In the nineteenth and early twentieth centuries the *moda* was British parliamentarism and liberalism; in the 1920s it became corporatism a la Action Française, the Carta del Lavoro, and the papal encyclicals; following the 1974 revolution, it became, for a time, "socialism." Had the Portuguese been more selective, they might have absorbed the most useful ideas and institutions of corporatism (as France, Spain, and other nations did) while rejecting the rest or blending corporatism with other currents (for clearly by 1926 both the corporative *and* the liberal currents were prominent in Portugal). Instead, the Portuguese corporative ideologues took over the corporative idea in its entirety as *the* solution to the national ills and in their zeal were forced to suppress the liberal elements. Absolutist and unbending, the Portuguese regime was saddled with a particular and intransigent brand of corporatism in the postwar period at a time when other blends or mixtures (a la Brazil after 1945) were called for. The Portuguese, of course, tried to tie this form of corporatism to their own traditions and preached theirs as a nationalist solution. If their own institutions had been stronger to begin with, however, and if they had not been burdened with such a pervasive sense of inferiority, they would not have copied so closely the Italian labor code, Manoïlesco, Maurras, or other foreign inspirations. A republic like that of 1910–26 was probably inappropriate and unworkable, given the Portuguese background and tradition, but after that experience with liberalism and the social changes from the 1930s on, corporatism a la Tour du Pin, the Freiburg Theses, and the earlier encyclicals was no longer relevant either. There should and could have been a more judicious blend of what was useful from the corporative model as well as from other models of society and polity that also fitted the Portuguese system in varying degrees. Such a blend was precisely what Caetano was trying to achieve when he was overthrown.[19]

There were other reasons for adopting and rigidly perpetuating the corporative system. One relates to Salazar's own background and character. He was an absolutist and a dogmatist who had found his final vision of the truth and was loathe to alter it or give it up in the post-1945 period, even though circumstances by then probably called for a scrapping of the system or its complete overhaul. Contrast this with the more pragmatic policies pursued by Franco, Vargas, or Perón, for example, whose regimes were also born during this epoch but who seldom let abstract ideology get in the way of pragmatic decision making. Another reason lies in Salazar's attitudes toward change. He wanted economic growth for Portugal and industrialization, but he would permit none of the social and political concomitants (greater pluralism and participation in society and polity) that normally accompany the modernization process. The corporative scheme thus provided a way to stimulate economic expansion through state initiative while holding in check any rising lower-class demands.

Third, there is the nature of the Portuguese economic take-off itself and the emerging structure of power in postwar Portugal. In the 1930s and during the war period Salazar was able to extend the state's control over the nation's fledgling business and economic interests and to place them, as with the sindicatos, under the supervision of the regime. By the postwar period, however, the major grupos had grown into conglomerates of great size and influence, they had learned to manipulate the corporative regulatory agencies and the corporations to their advantage (they often controlled and sometimes monopolized them), and they had maneuvered into a position where virtually all the government's ambitious development programs, in Africa as well as at home, were dependent on them. Portugal was too "sleepy" and too backward to be a full-fledged capitalistic system before the war; but afterward, it certainly was, with the state and the major economic elites joined together in mutually supporting roles. Hence, the increasing use of the corporative system to keep the sindicatos weak and fragmented, to hold the workers and indeed the entire society in place rather than stimulating genuinely *national* development or, as in the original conception, providing for social justice.

It is this last, postwar, and essentially negative function of the corporative system on which Philippe C. Schmitter has concentrated.[20] He argues that the corporative system was important not so much for what it accomplished positively as for what it prevented from happening—chiefly, the denial of any equal bargaining rights or higher wages and benefits for workers, so that Portuguese capitalism could go forward unhindered by strikes or disruptive labor demands. In this way the corporative system became an instrument of class domination. Schmitter is correct, in my view, in emphasizing these negative or "negating" functions of the corporative system, but not at the expense of wholly ignoring the other, more positive accomplishments or the subtler relations between corporatism and Portuguese political culture and society. My research and the analysis presented here indicate that both sets of functions, positive and negative, were important, perhaps about in equal proportions, and that the entire system needs to be explained not by resort to a single cause (class analysis, for example) but by examining a multiplicity of causes and explanations. For the fact is that the regime itself was frequently confused and divided as to what paths to pursue, it faced often in two or more directions at once, it followed contradictory, often ambiguous and multisided policies, and these policies were sometimes positive and sometimes negative. In some areas the regime and the corporative system were more successful than in others, and one's assessment of the successes or failures depends in part on which features one studies, the time period under consideration, and especially on whether one studies the system as a whole or only some particular aspects of it. One thing seems clear, however, and that is that the mix and balance between "positive" and "negative" evaluations must be derived from an objective examination of the dynamics of the Portuguese system itself and the interplay of political forces and influences within it, and not from some preconceived notions regarding corporatism or its alleged class determinants.

In Schmitter's analysis (and we do need to emphasize here the system's negative functions) corporatism was seen aimed at disarming the groups (namely, labor) which might have prevented the more rapid accumulation of national capital for investment, at rendering them dependent on state paternalism, and at enabling a rising bourgeoisie to capture and control the centers of political decision making. Toward these ends, in Schmitter's view, Portuguese corporatism performed four essentially negating functions: (1) it was *preemptive* in its organization of structures of associability from above rather than allowing the formation of genuinely grass-roots, independent class associations from below; (2) it was *preventive* in that it served to occupy a certain organizational space, meanwhile ruling out all possibly conflicting organizations; (3) it was *defensive* in encouraging the corporative agencies to defend certain "rights" granted by the regime rather than aggressively bargaining for more positive programs; and (4) it was *compartmental* in that it confined potential conflicts to a certain narrow arena and prevented them from becoming broader general or "class" issues that might pose a threat to the regime. The existence of corporatism in Portugal, Schmitter concludes, was thus closely related to the requirements of capital accumulation and production undertaken by an authoritarian-capitalistic state apparatus.

Was Portuguese corporatism a progressive movement, as some have implied, or was it wholly reactionary in accord with the "negating" functions listed above? Closely related to this is the question of whether it was a middle-class movement or an elitist and traditionalist one. We have already rejected the notion that corporatism was an elitist and wholly traditionalist undertaking: neither the class background of those who made up the various governments under Salazar and Caetano nor the policies they pursued will support that contention. The fact is there were few members of the nobility or old oligarchy in power all during this nearly fifty-year period going back to 1926, neither Salazar nor Caetano was of the elite and both were often hostile to it, and the programs initiated by the government were frequently directed against the old ruling class. But the regime was thoroughly bourgeois and middle-class in its makeup and policies, and that fact does help explain the direction Portuguese corporatism took and sheds some light on the progressive *vs.* reactionary issue. Moreover, there can be little doubt that the Salazar-Caetano regime was manipulated by the new men of wealth, and sometimes also the old elites, and that the government recognized that continued economic prosperity and even the survival of the regime was dependent on these same elements. These comments help us get at some of the differences of interpretation regarding corporatism and its place in the broader Portuguese system that have surfaced throughout this book.

As a middle-sector movement in the 1920s and 1930s, the corporatists sought to wrest control both from the old nineteenth-century oligarchic and ruling elites, still powerful in Portugal, and from other middle-sector groups that had risen to prominence during the Republic. To secure their movement's success the corporatists had to appeal to Catholic, Center, nationalist, and middle-class opinion *and* assume a strongly reformist and social justice orientation to gain the adherence of the rising laboring class. This helps explain the more-or-less progressive nature of the corporatist movement up through 1935, its labor legislation, and its programs of welfare and social security.

But by the 1950s and 1960s the old oligarchic and traditionalist elements were no longer a threat, and the middle class, as well as an emerging "new rich," had largely consolidated its hold over virtually all the nation's institutions: Army, Church, government, political party, bureaucracy, and the like. No longer threatened, the bourgeoisie had little need for the labor support it had earlier cultivated; it conveniently forgot the terms of the alliance made initially with the popular classes; and it turned increasingly reactionary. The situation was similar to the arguments about the Latin American middle classes and whether they are progressive or reactionary. The answer, of course, is that it depends: in the interwar period, trying to gain control of their countries from the older ruling elites and vying among themselves, the Latin American middle sectors often turned to the new urban labor groups for support and hence followed some progressive (up to a point) and "populist" policies; later, when they had consolidated their position, they turned reactionary, imitating upper-class ways and protecting their place in society against the newer challenges.[21] In seeking to demonstrate the class-based and "elitist" nature of the Portuguese corporative system, some scholars have concentrated on this later and admittedly reactionary period almost exclusively; my own viewpoint is that a longer perspective and a more balanced consideration of both the progressive and the reactionary strategies is necessary to understand the evolution of the Portuguese corporative scheme.

Another perspective on the progressive *vs.* reactionary dispute, and a way of helping resolve the class *vs.* culturalist explanations of Portuguese corporatism, are provided by Kenneth Sharpe.[22] The question is:

if the Portuguese corporatists, in the early days, were genuinely concerned with establishing a regime of social justice, how could the system then be so perverted as to favor the privileged classes at the expense of the rest? The evidence accumulated here seems to demonstrate that the corporatists were sincere in their concern for social justice. But Sharpe shows that it is precisely the Catholic-corporatist emphasis on fashioning better men as a solution to that problem that blinds the corporatist to the realities of existing power structures and who controls them. If one accepts the Catholic-corporatist assumption that men may be *educated* to their proper Christian obligations, such as assisting the poor through charity, then there is no need to tamper with existing institutions or social structure. All that is necessary is to educate men to their responsibilities. Catholic-corporatist ideology, defined as the search for the "common good" and as a way of correcting the evil in men, hence acts as a set of blinders masking existing power relations and obscuring the way existing institutions and class structure *do* determine outcomes.

No doubt Salazar, Caetano, Pereira and other early founders really believed they could carry out their reforms through the new corporative system by educating both workers and employers to their obligations to Christian brotherhood and communalism. But it was this very way of thinking, Sharpe argues, that kept them from seeing the powerful impact of money, land, class structure, and elemental self-interest. These same blinders prevented them from seeing that the old institutions would inevitably lead to dominance by the old elites and the newer men-on-the-make, and to the frustration of the corporatist regime's reform efforts. Of course in retrospect these outcomes are clearer, and doubtless some also saw them at the time—that is, that Salazar and the young corporatists could be manipulated by those with wealth and power and that the corporative system could be used as a means chiefly of controlling labor. But in the early 1930s that outcome was not seen as inevitable, and certainly the corporatist intellectuals of that time believed they would succeed in their social justice goals. It was the very corporatist framework in which Salazar operated that thus hindered an adequate understanding of why the system failed to achieve its desired aims. Meanwhile, the successive crises of the 1930s and the war years, the requirements of the regime maintaining itself in power and preserving economic solvency, and doubtless the machinations of the elites themselves had already dictated the main directions the corporative system would take and helped postpone indefinitely the intended reforms. Indeed, the corporatist system actually served to reinforce the social and economic disparities existent by creating a set of institutions which allowed the rising entrepreneurial and capitalist elements to regulate and control the lower classes more effectively.

Corporatism as a manifest philosophy and set of institutions probably reached its heyday in the 1920s and 1930s. By the end of World War II that era had passed, in Portugal as elsewhere in Europe. It was not just that its ideas were old-fashioned and discredited but that the entire class and social configuration on which corporatism in the *Rerum Novarum-Quadragesimo Anno* sense, based on upper- and especially middle-class paternalism, had also passed. Students, trade unions, even large portions of the middle class itself, no longer accepted it. Moreover, the "proud tower" of pre-World War I society was now more rapidly being undermined. The old agricultural class was disappearing into the cities (or abroad), and between the new industrial proletariat replacing it and the new middle-class and bourgeois owners of capital, we have seen, there was neither much love nor even common interest, as the corporatist conception assumed. An emergent working class was putting pressure on the regime and was no longer content with the old paternalism. But the bourgeois and middle-class ruling elites (including Salazar) still believed they could speak *for* the laboring classes; they favored benevolence as long as it did not upset the established order they now dominated. They wished genuinely to ameliorate the legitimate grievances of the working elements, but they would not condone any tampering with the basic pillars of society, and when it came to specific actions to aid labor they often backed away. They continued to think of the workers as they did of their meek, unassuming household servants, or the peasants who doffed their hats along rural roadways.[23]

But paternalism was no longer enough, and by the postwar period it was increasingly maintained with force and secret police. For the fact was that neither Salazar nor the men around him knew anything of the urban proletariat, of mill hands and metallurgists, of ship builders or even clerks; their vision, especially Salazar's, was still that of the sleepy rural agricultural villages of their childhood. Even in the area of economics, Salazar's forte, it was generally agreed that the restrictive, austere, penny-pinching budget and financial policies begun in 1928 and never really abandoned had been prolonged too long.[24] Salazar's effort to maintain a vision and structure of society that no longer existed was often what forced the regime to seek and use still more repressive tactics.[25]

The Portuguese regime and the corporative system in the 1960s were really in trouble. The whole national mythos was under challenge and in decline. There was not a single group (Church, Army, students, labor, business) that really supported corporatism, and the regime itself had increasingly shunted it aside. The corporative order taken from Vatican I made little provision for social change, while Portugal had changed greatly since the war. The particular form of Portuguese corporatism served to lock people into their station in life in accord with an older and more stable social order. It made no provision by which one might go up the social scale from a casa do povo to a sindicato or from a sindicato to a gremio. There were no formal prohibitions, of course, but the informal barriers were everywhere present, reinforced by the immutability of Salazar-style corporatism. The corporatist system came increasingly to be used as a means of maintaining the existing social structure. Class conflict was smothered. But that meant mainly controls on those at the bottom while providing no accountability for those on top. More and more the negative and preventive functions as described by Schmitter had taken precedence over positive social justice programs. The result was a stalemated, frozen, stagnant society and economy, made even worse by the prolonged African conflicts. What was needed was a new development ethic and some major structural changes reflecting the changed nature of Portuguese society. But such changes Salazar would or could not make, and hence the regime continued to drift indecisively, trying to adjust somewhat to the new circumstances in Africa and Europe and seeking to achieve limited modernization within a framework of backwardness and immobilism. Refusing or unable to make the changes required within and without the corporative system, Salazar's Portugal remained largely in place. It did not fall much further behind, but it certainly did not do much catching up, while the restiveness of the population grew. The inflexibility of the latter-day Salazar system in the 1960s and its incapacity to adapt itself led to arteriosclerosis and eventually to the overthrow of the system itself.

Portuguese corporatism was an abstract, reified, intellectuals' scheme, a system that by the 1960s had little to do with Portuguese realities or the way the system actually functioned. The principle of class harmony and coequal representation had given way to the reality of dominance by a single class. The principles of self-regulation and corporatism of free association had given way to an incredibly centralized and bureaucratic regime, increasingly obliged to use totalitarian-like controls to maintain the system intact. A regime founded on a pluralist conception (in the Catholic-corporatist sense) had become both monolithic politically and monopolistic economically. Instead of strengthening local government and grass-roots participation, the corporative system had taken power entirely out of the hands of such organizations. A system founded upon a conception of a limited state became one of the most dictatorial of regimes, and a free and open *corporatisme d'association* became a closed, centralized *corporatisme d'état*. Anticapitalist (as well as antisocialist) at the beginning, the regime was converted into one of the strongest of state capitalist systems whose complex of bureaucratic controls could be matched only (and ironically) in the Communist nations. Portraying itself a la Manoïlesco ("The Century of Corporatism") as the wave of the future, the regime became isolated internationally, desperate for support and understanding, and willing to grasp at any favorable straw in the international winds. Some of these incongruities are hinted at in a passage by Manuel Lucena:

> Portuguese corporatism gives one the impression of an astonishing mixture of untruths and political vision. Always contradictory, its institutions are often founded "in order not to exist," then exist "in order not to function," finally one discovers that they have become consistent, but are not what they are said to be. Looking even closer, one suspects that this is more-or-less the way they were intended in the first place and that, therefore, the scheme is strong and at the same time ridiculous.[26]

The anomalies multiply. Founded upon a principle of freedom, the Portuguese system became one of the more repressive of police states. Organized to do away with class conflict, it became a system where one class dominated and another was exploited. Begun on the corporative idea of harmony between employers and employees, it became a system where both elements hated and despised each other *and* the corporative system, about in equal degrees. Supposed to preserve what was useful and worthwhile in the Portuguese tradition, to balance traditional and modern, in fact the regime broke down all sense of community and solidarity. It failed to achieve the desired balance and thus ended up both backward and undeveloped *and* without the amenities and traditional values it sought to preserve. In terms of such esteemed human values as honesty, trustworthiness, strong interpersonal relations, and sense of community, the Portuguese system was woefully lacking. Supposed to foster unselfish motives under the corporative regime, Portugal and especially its rapacious, aspiring, new-rich economic elites, became instead as crass, grasping, and materialistic as the rest of us. And rather than preserving that which was valuable in the past, the Portuguese regime gave rise to some of the worst features of modern life: widespread juvenile delinquency, immense corruption, indiscriminate and mindless violence and terrorism, bitterness, alienation. As *Expresso* once editorialized in summing up the negative aspects of the regime, "our form of corporatism has its days counted." [27]

Right from the beginning came the conflict between the desire for implementing corporative reforms and the need to control those who opposed such changes by means of repressive instruments. Although the regime never became a full-fledged and systematic dictatorship until the growth of the postwar opposition made that necessary, a number of revolts had to be put down in the late 1920s and 1930s, the CGT and the old Republican parties were suppressed, and censorship and bureaucratic loyalty checks were imposed. All this came at the same time the corporative system was being created and implanted. Indeed, all through the Salazar era there was a constant debate concerning the need to ensure public order as a first-order priority, economic stability as a second, and corporative implementation as a distant third. And what of Salazar's own desire for power? Although he constantly said he did not desire power and would readily give it up, in fact Salazar was extremely jealous of his place and position, a subtle manipulator of power, and a man constantly seeking to consolidate and expand his power while closely guarding against its usurpation by others. This was, of course, always identified with the best interests of the nation—and probably in the 1930s and through the war years it was. But not beyond! The intense guarding of his power beyond the time he could use it effectively, Salazar's conception of himself as the indispensable man, implied more and more that he would use the corporative system as a holding force, a means to slow down and control the processes of change that potentially threatened him and his regime. In this power struggle Portugal itself, and her people, were the certain losers.

Even in its least authoritarian periods—and with the whole gamut of corporative agencies established—the regime hence never functioned in the truly representative, participatory way that was the original vision. Decisions were always made at the top, almost always by Salazar himself, with practically no participation at the grass roots. Decisions were announced, without opportunity for real discussion, dissent, or give and take. Occasionally the regime consulted with the representatives of the corporative agencies and adhered to the technical advice of the corporations or Corporative Chamber, but the corporative leaders were all well-established figures and no more in tune with the grass roots than the government. Certainly the casas and sindicatos were in no sense involved in decision making. Corporatism in Portugal did not enable the workers to make their voices heard, or, if it did to a limited extent, their voices were not listened to anyway. And although the gremios helped the directing classes to speak with an organized voice, they provided little more than a formal institutional structure to sectors whose informal ties and contacts had already made their voices heard and heeded. Government became government by decree-law, emanating from the top, without popular participation, independent of the corporative system, and increasingly divorced from the realities of people, work, life, activity at lower levels. Decisions made affecting any one sector were usually abstract and theoretical, done in that professorial, didactic, paternalistic way that Salazar had. Even under Caetano, despite the slightly more pluralist nature of his rule, that was still how government was run. Decisions came from the top, and there was precious little popular involvement. Officials of the government were "canceled" by decree, programs were promulgated in the same heavy-handed way, without a hearing or any public airing of the issue. The entire system remained authoritarian to its core.

Portugal in the 1960s was facing a severe, multifacted crisis. Internally its economy and society were stagnant, ossified, disequilibrated; externally it was isolated and alone. Rather than narrowing, the economic gaps between Portugal and the rest of Europe widened and the sense of relative deprivation grew even faster. The Portuguese system was strained by social, demographic, and economic transformations it could no longer control. Portugal's economy, society, and polity resembled those of the less-developed nations—at a time of rapidly rising popular expectations. First-time visitors to the country were consistently appalled at the poverty, misery, malnutrition, poor housing, inadequate social services, and miserable living standards. One "expects" to find such poverty in Africa or Latin America, but in Western Europe it was shocking. The ideology and nature of the Portuguese regime had been repudiated by both the outside world and, by now, its own people. It was unable to cope with the value and secularizing changes that came to a head in the 1960s. The country needed but wholly lacked a new national belief system and ideology to replace the discredited old ones; more than that the system required *renovação,* a full-scale overhaul of its societal and governmental institutions. Meanwhile, the pressures were building up, stemming from both the internal and external environments. Salazar, in the face of all these difficulties, remained impervious; he did not, in Douglas L. Wheeler's words, turn back the clock as much as he tried to hold its hands still. His successor proved unable to do so.[28]

The corporative system thus never functioned as intended, or at least as its ideology proclaimed. Even under Caetano, when much of this rusting structure and the attendant legislation were finally put into operation, the real political action and bargaining (when that took place at all) was between the gremios and the government or the sindicatos and the government, and only occasionally directly between the gremios and the sindicatos. In the first case, although they too were subservient to the government and not always consulted by it on policy decisions, the gremios could exercise considerable influence in such areas as day-to-day economic policy implementation. In the second, the sindicatos eventually gained a degree of influence under Caetano in the setting of higher wage rates and benefits. And finally, on the common everyday matters of lesser importance, the sindicatos and gremios could bargain directly, although most often with the government again heavily involved. On none of these fronts were the corporations themselves involved, and the other corporative agencies were always and consistently subordinate to the heavy presence of the state. The corporative complex was thus largely bypassed even on those decisions directly within its already limited domain and purview.

Was corporatism in Portugal, therefore, as similarly alleged for Italy, a mere "confidence trick"? Was corporatism a hoax and a fraud in that its institutions were sustained largely by a system of political repression and perpetuated socioeconomic class relationships in sharp contrast to its stated aims? [29] The answer is both yes and no. Certainly the historical record suggests distressingly large gaps between theory and practice. More and more the corporative system, contrary to its stated goals, functioned as an administrative appendage to the authoritarian regime to control social and economic life. The system helped contain and control modernization so as to permit the stronger and wealthier elements of society to accommodate to modernizing changes and profit from them, without any fundamental alterations of society's basic structures. There is no doubt also that the strong, original social justice motive of corporatism was, even under Caetano, really a system of largesse and paternalistic charity, prompted by considerations of political expediency by those in power, without giving any say to the recipients. The formal political institutions of Portuguese corporatism, such as the corporations, were either very late in being created or quickly fell into disuse. They were not so much effective agencies as a means of providing still more bureaucratic sinecures. Power was given not to the corporative agencies but to the juntas, boards, and commissions that carried out government decree-laws. In practice a nonautonomous and frequently trivial role was assigned to the corporative agencies. Believed to be viable alternatives to mass society and alienation, they became in time cynical devices of control at the service of the Portuguese dictatorship and the elites that undergirded it. In these ways the corporative system could be said to represent a "confidence trick." [30]

There is truth in the allegations that the system was a facade, even a hoax. But that is not the whole truth. For clearly much of the foregoing criticism was aimed not at the entire corporative system but only at one part of it: the corporations. They *were* weak and powerless, a kind of ineffectual confidence trick. I am not sure the same could be said for the Corporations Ministry, however, or for the Organizations of Economic Coordination, the gremios, or even the sindicatos, especially under Caetano. These agencies often did play a strong and influential role. Second, this critique ignores the many functions the corporative system did perform, both positively and negatively. For there *were* many positive accomplishments of Portuguese corporatism in the areas of labor relations, social security, and the like that went far beyond mere confidence tricks. One cannot dismiss these forward strides so quickly. And surely the use of the corporative agencies as control mechanisms for the government to assist it and large entrepreneurs in the accumulation of capital for investment was more than a "facade"; it was a careful and conscious policy aimed at steering the country in certain directions—directions with which we may quarrel but which we cannot dismiss. Nor does the "confidence trick" syndrome come to grips adequately with the historic pattern of corporatist-patrimonialist organization, with the fact that virtually all Portuguese regimes have been so constituted. For to say that the *formal* corporative institutions of the 1930s seldom functioned adequately or as intended has little to do with the *natural* corporatism, in the political-cultural sense, that was virtually everywhere present in the Portuguese regime, in its hierarchy, its organicism, its authority, patrimonialism, and the like. The "corporative model" thus still holds even though the institutions of corporatism as fashioned in the 1930s were weak and slow to come into existence.[31]

If the question of whether corporatism was a confidence trick must be answered ambiguously, so must the question of whether it was "fascistic." "Fascism" has become more a label for regimes of which we disapprove than a precise term of analysis. If by fascism we mean racial persecution and mass murder, then clearly the term does not apply to Portugal. Nor was the full gamut of totalitarian-fascist controls ever applied in Portugal as it was in Nazi Germany or Mussolini's Italy. Nor am I convinced by some of the trappings and superficial resemblances: the youth organizations, the paramilitary Legião, the Mocidade, the salutes, the uniforms, even the occasional homage to the German regime or the admiration for Mussolini and his system. These were largely the familiar Portuguese efforts of seeking to show, rather pathetically oftentimes, that they were "up to" their neighbors, that they too were part of the "wave of the future." If in the previous century Portuguese institutions were *para inglês ver,* in the 1930s they were for the French, the Italians, the Austrians, the Belgians, the Germans, seemingly everyone at the time to see. None of these purportedly fascist agencies or institutions was ever at the core of Portuguese corporatism or authoritarianism.

If, however, one accepts A. F. K. Organski's definition that fascism is a model of development based on a partnership between agricultural and industrial interests to carry out industrialization but to impose its costs primarily on the industrial working class,[32] then Portugal comes closer to qualifying. There *was* in the corporative system an effort to disarm and depoliticize the workers, to rule out a system of genuine pluralism and class bargaining, to concentrate governing power in the hands of a bourgeois ruling group, to carry out capital investment and economic development policies based on austerity and low wages, and to use the corporative system as a negative or "negating" influence in Schmitter's terms. In this sense, Portugal probably can be labeled "fascistic." But then, that would also be true of virtually every other regime in Latin America—and perhaps of every nation that has ever achieved industrialization.

Was Portuguese corporatism a success or a failure? That too depends, obviously, on what one means by "success" or "failure," on one's personal social and political values, and on what period is being discussed. In my mind at least, it seems clear that the failures came after a while to outweigh the successes. Corporatism could be said to have been successful in the 1930s in pulling a fragmented, ruined economy and nation back together, putting it on its feet again, renewing its elite, and providing a new sense of drive and national purpose, as well as a host of new agencies, programs, and bureaucratic structures. It provided a framework for later national development, even if its own implementation of the new legislation regarding labor, social security, and so on, was often spotty. It was probably a failure in the postwar period, however, especially under Salazar, serving more to retard and frustrate Portugal's national growth and modernization than to stimulate it. The later Caetano regime was a mix of both successes and failures.

But perhaps "success" or "failure" is the wrong way to answer the questions. Perhaps we should simply take Portugal on its own terms and in its own context. In that sense the regime neither succeeded nor failed; it was rather a product of a historical period whose time had simply passed. The 1920s and 1930s were both the high point of corporatism in the global context *and* an era when the earlier corporative forms fitted fairly well the structure of Portuguese society. By the postwar period this was no longer the case. Portugal had changed, and so had the international context. What was required was no longer a corporatism of control, demobilization, and selective repression, but a corporatism of change and movement. Corporatism in the Portuguese form (based on the conceptions of Tour du Pin and the papal encyclicals) was hence an idea and mode of organization whose epoch had been superseded. It belonged to another, prewar era that no longer existed. Time had passed the Portuguese regime by, while Salazar continued to cling to and enforce a system that had become outdated and anachronistic—even on its own corporative terms!

Here, then, lies the real difficulty with the Portuguese regime. It was not that it refused to go toward liberalism or socialism (both probably inappropriate, or at least not wholly appropriate, in the Portuguese context) but that it failed to modernize even the corporative structures that it did have. In the postwar period and especially the 1960s, the evidence is clear, the regime went to sleep, stagnated, became moribund and dinosauric. While other Iberic-Latin countries similarly cast in a corporative mold—Spain, Chile, Mexico, Argentina, Brazil, eventually Peru—were abandoning the 1930s concept and stepping off in newer and more dynamic corporative-developmentalist directions, Portugal remained locked in the older conception. Its corporative character was still cast in the *Rerum Novarum* mold, in the conservative bourgeois ideal of that earlier time, of an ordered, hierarchical, undemocratic, paternalistic state and society. That conception was largely Salazar's conception and also his legacy, for it is on his shoulders that the responsibility largely rests for keeping the country tied so rigidly and absolutely to that outmoded ideal. Elsewhere in the Iberic-Latin political-cultural world, however, the corporative structures fashioned in the interwar period were ignored or jettisoned in favor generally of more open, pluralist, more broadly participatory forms, or of a mixture of corporatism and liberalism and/or socialism. Portugal experienced none of this—at least until Caetano, by which time it was already too late. Portugal's chief problem thus was that it failed to modernize and update its ideas, programs, and institutions even within the corporative framework it had set for itself.

By the same token it was not so much corporatism per se, in its broader political-cultural sense, that was increasingly rejected by the Portuguese population in the postwar period and in the revolution of 1974 but the particular direction it took under Salazar. If Salazar had proved more flexible, if he had modernized the nation, its economy and its polity, if he had not run Portugal as a dictatorship, and if he had recognized the changing nature of Portuguese society and the just demands of the middle and lower classes (all big *ifs* obviously, but *ifs* that had come to pass in the warp and woof of postwar political change in other nations), the corporative system might well have lasted. It became instead a symbol of dictatorship and backwardness, a thing to be despised. The 1930s (or 1890s?) corporative conception was eventually repudiated, as it deserved to be. Had that conception and its accompanying institutional arrangements proved more flexible, adaptable, and accommodative, however, there seems little doubt Portugal would still be a corporative state—not in that old-fashioned, discredited 1930s sense but in a newer, more modern sense providing for the development of the Portuguese nation and its people. That is how development has gone forward elsewhere in the Iberic-Latin world; unfortunately, it did not take place in Portugal.

Final Considerations

The "corporative model" has proved useful in looking at the development process in the nations of the Iberic-Latin culture area. In chapter 1 of this volume and in other writings,[33] I have argued that the classic liberal or Marxian models are often of limited usefulness in looking at these nations and are so closely tied to particular North American-North European developmental experiences that they frequently cloud and distort our understanding of the southern European and Latin American experiences. I have been concerned with identifying, tracing, exploring, and analyzing the political theory, political sociology, political economy, and structural organization and policies of a distinctively southern European, particularly Iberic and Latin American model of development, and seeking to show how it has sought to deal with the great issues and social forces of the twentieth century: industrialization, accelerated social change, mass society and alienation, rising popular demands for goods and services, and the like. I have labeled this distinct tradition and political-cultural framework the "corporative model," since corporatism in one form or another seems to be one of its particular, lasting, almost inherent features.

In using that term, however, a confusion has sometimes arisen, since corporatism has often been used in two different ways: one to refer to a broad corporatist historical tradition of authority, hierarchy, organicism, and patrimonialism; and the other to refer to the narrower, manifestly "corporatist" structures and ideology of the 1920s and 1930s. The confusion is compounded by the fact that Portugal has not only a strong *natural* corporatist tradition, to use Newton's term, but was also, at least in the formal-legal sense, one of the most complete of corporative regimes in the 1920s–1930s meaning. Our concern in this study has been not only to trace the broader Portuguese political-cultural tradition of corporatism but also to show how Salazar's Estado Novo was a logical extension of it. The New State represented an attempt to resurrect and fuse the older corporative tradition with a newer, explicitly "corporative" ideology and organization, to update the historical forms with then-modern thinking and concepts. It represented an attempt, albeit a not very successful one in the final analysis, to deal with the new realities, to accommodate, incorporate, and fuse some new corporate pillars and the social groups that had recently grown up with Portuguese economic development (business groups, the bourgeoisie, labor, eventually the peasantry) onto an ancient, hierarchical, vertical, authoritarian, segmented, patrimonialist, and organicist structure that had always been corporative in nature.

If this emphasis on the importance of a historic corporative tradition periodically updated with newer corporative pillars is correct, then we might continue to look for evidence of corporative tendencies in the new regime that came to power in 1974. The evidence is considerable, despite the "liberal," "liberating," and "socialist" labels, that the historic tradition has reasserted itself, that decisions are still handled in an authoritarian and nonparticipatory way, that various control and regulatory mechanisms are being resurrected, that organicist and monistic structures and ideas remain, that vertical-segmented, corporative-syndicalist mentalities and forms of organization and representation persist, and that change is still being carried out paternalistically, by decree-law, from above. Despite the chaos, the uncertainty, and the rapid change-overs most recently of programs and personnel, many of the structures and institutions of the older Portuguese *sistema* continue to function and the machinery of the administrative state is still in place. There are new organic laws governing political parties, labor, the press, and so on, which reflect and ratify the changes that have recently taken place in Portugal, but the new laws are also restrictive in character, organicist and "integralist" in underlying philosophy, and frequently closer still to a corporatist, albeit perhaps now an updated "syndicalist," tradition than to a liberal and pluralist one. The fact is that Portugal is authoritarian and corporativist, in this broader political-cultural sense, not just on the surface, by imposition, and at the top but thoroughly and all the way down the social structure. The Salazar and Caetano regimes were not just apparitions or accidents but reflected and represented an authoritarian tradition that, if anything, was even stronger in Portugal than in Spain or Latin America.

Many aspects of the Portuguese political culture in this sense remain fundamentally aliberal and even antiliberal. Portugal is still in many ways a closed, hierarchical, and stratified society where the processes of change, of opening up, of growing pluralization are certain to be long and painful, and may perhaps never come at all. Authoritarianism and corporatism in Portugal encompass more than just governmental relations, the relations of the state to its people, or the usual *patrão-cliente* relations; they characterize virtually all aspects of national life: religion, schools, family, interpersonal relations, political associability. In offices, stores, conversations, business transactions—all involve first the establishment of one's superiority over the other party; sale, profit, efficiency are secondary. Bus drivers, entrepreneurs, conductors, *porteiros,* teachers, parents, clerks, as well as government officials are preoccupied with the status and authority issue. Personal dealings are hence marked often by an unwillingness to bend and compromise and by that all-pervasive sense of hierarchy and class so omnipresent in pre-World War I society. The assumption remains of a natural inequality among men, of a hierarchy of orders and classes, of rule by elites and of a subject political culture rather than a fully participatory one. The Portuguese would seem to have few of those traits identified by Almond and Verba as part of the "civic" political community and which constitute the indispensable environmental base for liberal democracy.[34] The number of Portuguese of a genuinely social-democratic persuasion is small and they often tend to be as authoritarian ("Socialists also beat their maids," the Portuguese say, only one-fourth in jest), as class conscious, as concerned with appearance and social status, as the rest of society. Liberalism and egalitarianism can hardly be expected to grow quickly or naturally in this context.

As a result of the April 1974 revolt, hence, a new elite has taken power which proclaims itself liberal, democratic, and socialist; but it remains an elite nonetheless, and a Portuguese and a military elite. It is still cast in the authoritarian mold. It believes in hierarchy, discipline, and order more than liberty and the free expression of countervailing opinion or the open and democratic clash of opposed interests. These comments imply that Portugal may not have executed such a complete about-face as the numerous popular, and often surface, accounts have emphasized. All this, of course, is not to deny that some profound, even revolutionary changes, have occurred, that the system has opened up immeasurably, or that structural transformations have taken place. But they have occurred still within an organicist-patrimonialist framework and not necessarily a liberal one. No doubt the final outcome of this renovative, regenerative process will also be in accord with that earlier and very Portuguese tradition, updated and modernized, to be sure, with new access routes opened up and room made in the system for those groups (especially labor and the middle classes) denied opportunities for so long. A newer revolutionary and even socialist or syndicalist form may come into existence, and Portugal may overcome or transcend its earlier corporatist forms. But one should not be surprised if these newer institutions, whatever their precise names or dimensions, were also in accord with that older and broader corporative political-cultural tradition.[35]

Although the corporative model employed here has proved a useful one in coming to grips with and understanding the Portuguese system, it bears reiterating that this is not the only way to view Portuguese society and politics. By itself, this essentially political-cultural approach cannot explain all of the workings of the Portuguese system. Particularly in chapter 10, "How the Portuguese System Really Works," we saw that models of autocracy, of the administrative state, of class rule, and others are also useful. Moreover, as Portugal has developed, still other frameworks and interpretations have additionally proved useful: a model of state capitalism, a model of the modern authoritarian state, and particularly under Caetano and his successors, some newer, as yet nascent, but evolving models of broader citizen participation, pluralist bargaining, perhaps even liberalism or an organic form of socialism or military "Nasserism" and syndicalism. None of these models can be used any more to the exclusion of all others; all have something to contribute. No one of them can be employed alone to present a true and complete picture of the Portuguese system.

We need, therefore, to be eclectic in our approach, using different models to get at different aspects of the system. Only then will the operations of the whole become clear. The corporative model, for instance, while useful in some ways, cannot explain all of Portuguese or Iberic-Latin political phenomena since all these nations are at best only incompletely corporatized, since the real centers of power and influence often lie outside the formal corporative institutions, since new frameworks (liberal, socialist, participatory) have arisen to challenge the corporative one, and since even in the corporative context recourse to revolutionary action (a la Portugal in 1974) beyond the confines of the formal constitutional and corporatist order is always possible. Indeed, it would seem that some of the most exciting areas for research lie precisely in that murky area where our models overlap, where corporatist attitudes and forms of organization are jumbled together (as in Portugal in the 1970s) with liberal and/or socialist ones, where the traditional groups and institutions are seeking to modernize while the modernizing ones

continue to use the traditional techniques of patronage, spoils, paternalism, authority, and decree-law.

At the same time we must recognize that the relative importance of
one model as opposed to another is itself related to the development
process, that what may be a useful approach in one country or in one
historical epoch may not be the same in another. What makes the corporative model especially useful, however, is that it helps us bridge the
gaps between historical eras by focusing on the continuities as well as
the changes, the constants as well as the innovations. It argues that even
the changes, despite the usual outward appearances of "liberalism" or
"revolution," may take place within a deeper corporative context. For
corporatism can take many different forms, both in time and space.
Corporatist theory and institutions may range from Left to Right on the
political spectrum, from traditional, backward-looking regimes such as
the Portuguese in the postwar period to such diversely modernizing ones
as those of Spain, Mexico, Brazil, and Peru. It is hoped that the new,
postrevolutionary Portuguese regime may be one of the forward-
looking, modernizing types rather than one of the other kind. But of the
fact it will be corporatist in broad outlines there can be little doubt.[36]

Corporatism thus is not merely or necessarily a throwback to an earlier and more conservative form of society (although in Portugal that
plainly became the situation) or an attempt to turn the clock back to
some vague status quo ante. The equation with fascism, except in the
limited sense outlined here, and hence a blanket condemnation of corporatism, is not very useful either. Rather, what we are looking at in
the corporatist model is a complex and varied form which may take
several different directions, which is yet distinct from both liberalism
and totalitarianism, which has a long tradition of its own (particularly
but not exclusively in the Latin nations) and a great body of political
thought and sociology with which, because we have ignored it or condemned it out of hand, we are almost wholly unfamiliar. Moreover,
corporatism is not necessarily reactionary and counterrevolutionary; it
can be and has been a progressive, dynamic, and modernizing force,
whether in the form of modern Christian-democracy, centralized
bureaucratic-authoritarianism (as in Peru), or one or another of the
types of guild socialism or syndicalism. Overall, given our deep-rooted
prejudices regarding corporatism, what needs emphasis are the distinc-
tiveness and viability of the several corporative routes to development,
the diversity and complexity of its forms, and the fact that what we
are dealing with here is literally a fourth "world of development" in the
Iberic-Latin tradition, one of the twentieth century's major (now all but

forgotten) great "isms," which requires analysis and understanding on its own terms and in its own context, not through some frame of reference derived from another tradition and inapplicable to the Iberic-Latin one.

One last set of considerations involves the applicability of the corporative model to other systems and its relevance to our own time, place, and society. Clearly, much of what we have said regarding corporatism and patrimonialism in the Iberic-Latin tradition applies in varying degrees in other societies as well. One thinks of Yugoslavia or the Soviet Union, for example, India and perhaps Japan, Tanzania, and maybe Ghana. The Catholic-Roman-Latin form is no doubt distinctive and there are some unique historical roots in Iberia and Latin America, but corporatism and patrimonialism are obviously not the private preserve of these nations alone. In recent years the importance and persistence of corporatist-patrimonialist forms, as contrasted with the argument for their supposed "withering away" in much of the earlier development literature, have been increasingly recognized.[37] We need to sort out these diverse threads and currents, the common corporative ingredients as well as the national and political-cultural variations.

Then, there is the convergence idea. Portugal had long argued that its governmental structures, other than the labels used, were not really so different from those of the rest of Europe, that the Portuguese regime (particularly under Caetano) was far more liberal than it was given credit for, while the other European nations were practicing a kind of disguised corporatism. Surely in Portugal the evidence presented here points to the decline of the corporative ideology over a long period of time, the rise of an increasingly technocratic-administrative state, the performance of numerous functions by the corporative agencies which had to be carried out in any modern state and could just as easily have been called by other names. The gremios and sindicatos, for example, had largely abandoned corporatist principles and were functioning in effect as class-based interest groups, the Corporations Ministry was really a Ministry of Labor and Social Assistance, the Organizations of Economic Coordination were really modern regulatory agencies, the Corporative Chamber and the corporations served to institutionalize limited interest group representation inside the system, and so forth. At the same time, one need only look at the growth of similar regulatory agencies and councils of state in the other European nations, the absorption of the trade unions and other class and professional associations as bureaucratic appendages of the modern state, the existence of both de facto and de jure functional representation, the doing away as much as possible with costly strikes and lockouts and the instigation of mandatory collective bargaining, the emergence of various forms of state capitalism, to see that there is something to the convergence idea.[38] The lines are not all that sharp and the differences are more of degrees than of absolutes. If Portugal was unfairly pilloried for its corporative forms, surely the other European nations have been, to a degree, unfairly lauded for their supposed liberal and democratic forms. The truth lies somewhere in between.

And finally, what of our own society? Surely as the tendencies toward bureaucratization and government control of prices and wages continue (through such agencies as Nixon's Cost of Living Council and the Wage and Price Board as well as a myriad of regulatory agencies and administrative directives), as ours becomes more a system of state-supported capitalism (Lockheed, Boeing, the Penn Central) than of genuine laissez-faire, as administration increasingly replaces politics and genuine citizen participation, as functional representation (quotas and other such devices) replaces individual merit as the means for determining who shall have a voice, as rules and *papelada* proliferate and the regulative state continues to grow, as the major interest groups become integrated into and a regular part of the agencies designed to regulate them, as centralization and governmental paternalism increase, as the abuse of domestic security agencies is translated into surveillance of the opposition and an abrogation of civil liberties, as the judicial system is perverted to help protect the friends of those in power and annihilate their enemies, and as official corruption and governmental sinecures mushroom, we must guard against too hasty an attitude of superiority toward systems like the Portuguese. The "Latin Americanization of the United States" has been occurring for some time, not just in terms of the surface aspects of student protests, a helicopter shooting its guns landing on the White House lawn, and a corrupt vice-president and president being forced from office by means not altogether different from the classic coup d'état, but more importantly in terms of those deeper—and often disturbing—trends toward statism, bureaucratic-authoritarianism, and top-down corporatism discussed in this book. Countries like Portugal, Spain, and those of Latin America have had far more experience than we with the costs and implications of corporative-authoritarian rule. How ironic it would be if, instead of the United States and its interest-group liberalism constituting the model for nations such as those of Iberia and Latin America to emulate, they instead provided the corporative and bureaucratic-authoritarian vision of our future! It is a possibility we must now ponder.[39]

Appendixes

A Membership in the Corporative Chamber as Originally Conceived

1st Section: Cereals and Cattle Raising (6 members)
1 representative of the wheat producers (National Federation of Wheat Producers)
1 representative of the other cereal producers
1 representative of the millers (National Federation of Millers)
1 representative of the bread industry
1 representative of farm labor (selected from the *casas do povo* in the cereal region)
1 representative of industrial labor (selected from the National Bakery Syndicates)

2d Section: Wines (5 members)
1 representative of the (liquorous) wineries (Federation of Vintners of the Douro Region [*Casa do Douro*], Carcavelos Wine Union, Setúbal [Moscatel] Wine Union)
1 representative of the common wineries and their products (National Federation of Vintners of South and Central Portugal, Vintners Federation of Dão, Regional Vintners of Colares, Bucelas Wine Union)
1 representative of (liquorous) wine exporters (Wine Exporters Guild of Porto, of Carcavelos, and of Setúbal)
1 representative of the exporters of common wines (Commercial Wine Exporters Guild and Exporters Guild of Bucelas)
1 representative of vineyard labor (selected from the *casas do povo* in the vineyard regions)

3d Section: Forestry (3 members)
2 representatives of the producers of cork, lumber, and resinous products
1 representative of the exporters of cork, lumber, and resinous products

4th Section: General Agricultural Production (2 members)
1 representative of agricultural producers (fruits and horticulture)
1 representative of commerce and exportation (Exporters of Fruit and Horticultural Products Guild of Algarve and Fruit Exportation and Commerce Guild)

5th Section: Fish and Preserves (4 members)
1 representative of the fishing industry
1 representative of the canning and preserves industry (Union of the Industrialists and Exporters of Preserved Fish)
1 representative of industrial labor (selected from the national syndicates of the preserve industry)
1 representative of fishing labor (selected from the *casas dos pescadores*)

6th Section: Mines, Mineral Waters, Quarries, and Chemical Products (3 members)
1 representative of the mining and quarrying interests
2 representatives of the chemical industries, including tanneries

7th Section: Textiles (4 members)
1 representative of the cotton (elaboration) industry
1 representative of the wool (elaboration) industry
1 representative of the cotton and wool trading industry
1 representative of industrial labor (selected from the National Syndicates of the Textile Industries)

8th Section: Electricity (2 members)
1 representative of the electricity generating plants
1 representative of the electricity distributors

9th Section: Building and Building Materials (4 members)
2 representatives of the building materials industries
1 representative of the building contractors
1 representative of the National Syndicates of Builders

10th Section: Transportation (5 members)
1 representative of the navigation firms
1 representative of the railroads
1 representative of the trucking industry
1 representative of maritime labor (selected from the National Maritime Syndicates)
1 representative of railroad labor (selected from the National Railroad Syndicates)

11th Section: Graphic Arts and Printing (4 members)
1 representative of the Graphic Arts Industry
1 representative of the newspaper publishers
1 representative of the National Newspaper Syndicates
1 representative of the pressmen (selected from the National Pressmen Syndicates)

12th Section: Credit and Insurance (3 members)
1 representative of the credit establishments
1 representative of the insurance agencies (Insurance Guild)
1 representative of labor (selected from the National Syndicates of Bankers and Insurance Employees)

13th Section: General Commercial Activities (3 members)
2 representatives of the warehousemen and retailers
1 representative of labor (selected from the National Syndicates of Merchandise)

14th Section: Tourism (2 members)
1 representative of the hotels
1 representative of the other interests connected with tourism

15th Section: Spiritual and Moral Interests (4 members)
1 representative of the Catholic Church
1 representative of the missionary institutes
1 representative of the houses of charity
1 representative of the other private welfare agencies

16th Section: Science, Letters, and Arts (5 members)
1 representative of the Academies and Institutes of Higher Scientific and Literary Culture
1 representative of the universities
1 representative of the academies and societies of liberal arts
1 representative of the National Syndicates of Architects
1 representative of the National Syndicates of Musicians

17th Section: Physical Education and Sports (3 members)
1 representative of the Portuguese Olympic Commission
1 representative of the Sports Federations
1 physician specializing in physical education

18th Section: Policy and Public Administration (3 members)

19th Section: National Defense (2 members)

20th Section: Justice (2 members)

21st Section: Public Works and Communications (2 members)

22d Section: Economic and Colonial Policy (3 members)

23d Section: Local Administration (8 members)
1 representative of the Municipality of Lisbon
1 representative of the Municipality of Porto
1 representative of the rest of the continental urban municipalities
1 representative of the rural municipalities beyond the Douro
1 representative of the rural municipalities between Douro and Tagus
1 representative of the rural municipalities south of Tagus
1 representative of the municipalities of the Islands of Madeira and Porto Santo
1 representative of the municipalities of the Azores

24th Section: Finance (2 members)

Note: This organization is provided for in decree-law no. 24,683, published in the *Diário do governo,* series 1, no. 279 (November 27, 1934); and decree-law no. 24,834, in *Suplemento ao diário do governo,* series 1, no. 1 (January 2, 1935).

Art. 4, decree law no. 24,683, provides the following membership for the professions in the Corporative Chamber:

Order of Lawyers—members of the 20th section, Justice

Order of Physicians—members of the 15th section, Spiritual and Moral Interests; and of the 18th section, Policy and Public Administration, when public health problems are being considered

Order of Engineers—members of the 8th section, Electricity; of the 9th section, Building and Building Materials; of the 10th section, Transportation; and of the 21st section, Public Works and Communication

Order of Agronomists, Veterinarians, and Silviculturists—1st section, Cereals and Cattle Raising; 2d Section, Wines; 3d section, Forestry; and 4th section, General Agricultural Production

B   Numerical Growth of the Corporative Agencies, 1933–1972

Corporative Agencies	1935	1940	1945	1950	1955	1960	1965	1970	1972
Sindicatos	191	276	308	312	313	323	324	326	326
Casas do povo	141	319	506	498	512	568	625	677	736
Casas dos pescadores	0	16	25	27	27	28	28	28	28
Gremios						530		572	576

Source: Instituto Nacional de Estatística, *Estatísticas da Organização Corporativa e Previdência* (yearly). Unfortunately, the statistics on employer gremios were not included in the early volumes.

C A Note on Methodology

Three principal methods were used in the preparation of this book: (1) an exploration of the written sources available, (2) participant observation, and (3) interviewing.

The written record is rich and formed an indispensable base for the study; the materials used are included in the notes and the bibliography. Portugal, of course, has an abundance of libraries and archives for historians; for social scientists interested in contemporary affairs, however, the holdings are spottier. My own research was undertaken mainly in the university libraries of Coimbra and Lisbon, the Instituto Superior de Economia e Finanças, the Instituto Superior de Ciencias Sociais e Política Ultramarina, the National Library, the library of the Ministry of Corporations and Social Assistance, and the libraries and archives of a number of gremios, corporations, and political associations. Professors J. Pires Cardoso, J. Pereira Neto, and João Pinto da Costa Leite provided materials from their private collections.

As "participant observers" in Portugal during 1972/73, we sought to sample as much as we could of Portuguese culture, society, and politics. We lived in a Portuguese neighborhood rather than one of the foreign enclaves; we stayed away from the U.S. embassy and avoided the "American community"; we bought a car and toured the country extensively from the Algarve in the south to Trás os Montes in the north; we opened a Portuguese bank account; we shopped at the *mercados* and stores catering to Portuguese clientele; in short, we tried to get close to the Portuguese as much as we could and to live as much as possible as the Portuguese lived. So as to understand better the broader context of Portuguese politics, we visited numerous government offices and talked at length with many officials whose responsibilities covered areas not specifically the subject of this research. We attended scholarly colloquiums, went to opposition gatherings, met with press and publishing officials, attended government and official party meetings, established contacts with university students and professors, visited banks, *sindicatos,* and industrial firms, and attended cultural events. Sometimes we simply sat and observed: at the Café Suiça, in Edward VII Park, along the Avenida da Liberdade or in the Chiado, in restaurants and *pastelarias*. We talked and exchanged impressions with hundreds, probably thousands, of Portuguese in the course of going about our—and their—business. Through these means we sought to get a "feel" for Portugal and its people, a sense of its culture and society that cannot be obtained from archival sources. Unsystematic though these activities often were, they enabled us to build up a storehouse of lore and understanding of Portuguese social and political behavior and how the Portuguese system works.

The library and archival research dealing with the theory and practice of Portuguese corporatism was supplemented by interviewing. Interviewing in Portugal was a difficult and complex undertaking. This was so not only because the authoritarian nature of the Portuguese regime made most government officials wary of speaking openly and freely, particularly to an outsider who for all they knew might be an *agent provocateur,* but for other reasons as well: the closed nature of Portuguese society, the absence of any tradition of social science and survey research, a certain lack of respect for New World academic degrees and institutions, and the formality, legalisms, rigidities, and exaggerated sense of social distance built into the Portuguese system more generally. It should perhaps be said that I am used to operating within the context of Latin societies, with the emphasis on social class, personalism, and the proper connections; but I still found Portugal the toughest nut to crack, in the interviewing sense, of any country in which I have worked. Fortunately, the written materials were so rich that I was able to use the interviews chiefly as supplements, as a means of probing under and behind the written word. Had the research been based on interviewing alone, it is doubtful the project could have been carried through successfully.[1]

Altogether, sixty-seven formal, in-depth, elite interviews were conducted, in addition to numerous other shorter sessions or brief encounters. The interviewees were chiefly present or former corporative and government officials and included representatives from the Ministry of Corporations, the Ministry of Health and Assistance, the Ministry of the Economy, the Planning Office, the cabinet, the Assembly, the Corporative Chamber, the Presidency of the Council of Ministers, the Secretariats of State for Commerce, Industry, and Labor and Welfare, as well as from the sindicatos, gremios, casas do povo, casas dos pescadores, and corporations. Although some of those interviewed consented to allow their names to be used and are referred to in the notes, others insisted as a condition of the interview that their names not be cited. The authoritarian nature of the Portuguese regime and the sensitive nature of the issues being probed frequently made it necessary to provide such preinterview assurances of complete anonymity, and I have felt obligated to honor these commitments.

Each interview was conducted personally by the author. Although there were a number of common questions, each interview was planned on an individual basis, depending on the position or past experience of the interviewee, and the main questions written out beforehand. The questionnaire was only semistructured, however, and some of the most valuable information came from probes and responses and general discussion not included in my formal list of questions. Notes were taken during the course of the interview, and the interviews were typed up fully as soon afterward as possible.

These interviews were by no means a random sample or a scientific survey; those techniques would not have usefully served the purposes of my research. Rather these were elite, in-depth interviews, and their use in this study is subject to the qualifications that all such interviewing implies. Mainly, the interviews served to get at some of the below-the-surface issues and conflicts in the operation of the corporative system, to show how it worked and how it did not work and for what reasons. When used in conjunction with data generated by more traditional research methods, archival research and participant observation, these interviews provide a major source of information unavailable from any other source and shed a great deal of light on the nature of the authoritarian-corporatist system that emerged in Portugal.

Notes

Chapter I

1. Unlike the Department of State, the foundations, and many academic institutions, which segregate the world into rather rigid geographic divisions, the author here employs a culture-area approach that sees Spain, Portugal, and the nations of Latin America as sharing many important characteristics. The differences between and among them are of course also important, but for now it is the common features that command our attention.

2. Among the more important early works in this tradition are Gabriel A. Almond and James S. Coleman, eds., *The Politics of the Developing Areas*; W. W. Rostow, *The Stages of Economic Growth*; Karl W. Deutsch, "The Growth of Nations: Some Recurrent Patterns of Political and Social Integration"; and Seymour M. Lipset, "Some Social Requisites of Democracy: Economic Development and Political Legitimacy." These and other studies set the tone and ideological direction for an entire genre of literature dealing with national development written during the 1960s. The value assumptions inherent in this model are discussed in, among other places, Arthur Mitzman, *The Iron Cage: An Historical Interpretation of Max Weber* (New York: Knopf, 1970); Robert A. Nisbet, *Social Change and History: Aspects of the Western Theory of Development* (New York: Oxford University Press, 1969); and Howard J. Wiarda, *Dictatorship, Development, and Disintegration: Politics and Social Change in the Dominican Republic,* chap. I.

3. Samuel P. Huntington, *Political Order in Changing Societies,* chap. 2.

4. See Richard M. Morse, "The Strange Career of Latin American Studies," p. 11.

5. A good discussion of some of these prejudices is Ellery Sedgwick, "Something New in Dictators: Salazar of Portugal."

6. See Howard J. Wiarda, *The Corporative Origins of the Iberian and Latin American Labor Relations Systems.*

7. Useful as starters are Matthew Elbow, *French Corporative Theory, 1789–1948: A Chapter in the History of Ideas*; and Joaquín Azpiazu, *The Corporative State.* See also the useful bibliography compiled by

Philippe C. Schmitter at the end of his "Still the Century of Corporatism?" pp. 128–31.

8. Thomas Stritch, introduction to *The New Corporatism: Social-Political Structures in the Iberian World,* ed. Fredrick B. Pike and Thomas Stritch.

9. Corporatism is of course not confined to the southern European and Latin nations. In addition to the other European polities already noted, corporatist influences may be found in nations as diverse as Japan, India, Vietnam, Yugoslavia, Tanzania, and the Soviet Union. If corporatism is indeed so ubiquitous, present in so many culture areas, then its usefulness as a term of analysis becomes more limited. In this book we shall be concerned primarily with the particularly Roman, Catholic, and Iberic-Latin tradition of corporatism; but on this whole issue see David B. H. Denoon, "The Corporate Model: How Relevant and for Which Countries?"

10. See especially Charles W. Anderson, *The Political Economy of Modern Spain,* chaps. 1–3 and 9; Jacques Ploncard d'Assac, *Salazar,* p. 244; H. R. Trevor-Roper, "The Phenomenon of Fascism," in S. J. Woolf, ed., *European Fascism,* pp. 18–38; and João Manuel Cortez Pinto, *A corporação: Subsidio para o seu estudo.* An interesting statement by Catholic writer Marie R. Madden appears in the *New York Times,* August 7, 1941, p. 16; see also the special reports in the *Times* (London), May 22, 1959, p. 13, and November 16, 1961, p. 13.

11. The best collection dealing with these themes is James Malloy, ed., *Authoritarianism and Corporatism in Latin America.*

12. Mihail Manoïlesco, *Le siècle du corporatisme.*

13. Brazil, for example, is less manifestly corporatist than Portugal in terms of its operating ideology, but it, Mexico, Argentina, Peru, and others are probably just as corporatist in their actual functioning. The comments offered here are not meant to imply that Portugal is in any sense the model for these others (although it was to a considerable degree in the 1930s) but that the whole framework of corporative theory and institutions, which was articulated more completely, institutionalized more fully and explicitly, and lasted longer in Portugal than in these other nations, still remains probably the dominant one throughout the Iberic-Latin world. For a paper developed independently but which is concerned with some themes parallel to those explored in this study, see Philippe C. Schmitter, "Corporatist Interest Representation and Public Policy-Making in Portugal."

14. The definition here used is derived from Elbow, *French Corporative Theory,* pp. 11–12; Schmitter, "Corporatist Interest Representation," pp. 3–4; and Marcello Caetano, *Principios e definições,* pp. 41–51. (The European literature is rich but almost completely unknown in this country; in English, see Azpiazu, *Corporative State,* and Elbow, *French Corporative Theory.*)

15. Howard J. Wiarda, "Toward a Framework for the Study of Political Change in the Iberic-Latin Tradition: The Corporative Model."

16. See the special issue of the *Review of Politics*, vol. 36 (January 1974), dealing with corporatism in the Iberic-Latin world. A useful study that makes the link between corporatism in Iberia and in Latin America is Frederick B. Pike, *Hispanismo, 1898–1936: Spanish Conservatives and Liberals and Their Relations with Spanish America.*

17. Perhaps the best statement of this view is Glen Dealy, *The Public Man: A Cultural Interpretation of Latin America and other Catholic Countries.*

18. De Gaulle remained a corporatist in many ways. See also Samuel H. Beer, *British Politics in the Collectivist Age*; and Stein Rokkan, "Norway: Numerical Democracy and Corporate Pluralism," in R. Dahl, ed., *Political Oppositions in Western Democracies*, pp. 70–115.

19. Daniel Bell, *The End of Ideology* (New York: Free Press, 1959). This is, of course, a controversial subject area on which there is by now a great deal of literature; further comment on this theme is reserved for later in the study.

20. This is another running debate about which we shall have more to say later; a recent—and inconclusive—discussion was the panel on "Mediterranean Politics" of the 1973 American Political Science Association, New Orleans, September 4–8. Illustrative of the problems and issues in this debate are two of the papers presented at that panel: Samuel H. Barnes and Giacomo Sani, "Mediterranean Political Culture and Italian Politics: An Interpretation"; and Alan Zuckerman, "On the Institutionalization of Political Clienteles: Party Factions and Cabinet Coalitions in Italy."

21. For some parallel arguments see A. James Gregor, *The Ideology of Fascism*, introduction.

22. The intellectuals-in-power issue stems from, among other places, William Buckley's famous crack to the effect that he would rather be governed by the first 200 names in the Boston phone directory than by the whole of the Harvard faculty. In Portugal it was the Coimbra and University of Lisbon faculties (especially lawyers and economists) who played such a prominent role. On the corporatist-patrimonialist tradition in Brazil and its adaptations, see Philippe C. Schmitter, *Interest Conflict and Political Change in Brazil*; and Riordan Roett, *Brazil: Politics in a Patrimonial Society.*

23. Arpad von Lazar, "Latin America and the Politics of Post-Authoritarianism." See also John H. Herz, "The Problem of Successorship in Dictatorial Regimes: A Study in Comparative Law and Institutions"; and Keith Botsford, "Succession and Ideology in Spain and Portugal."

24. William F. Connolly, ed., *The Bias of Pluralism*; and Theodore Lowi, *The End of Liberalism*. See also the recent critiques of Lockean liberalism, as well as the upcoming books dealing with Nixon, Watergate, and

the like. A useful collection of these critiques from diverse perspectives is Jerome M. Mileur, *The Liberal Tradition in Crisis* (Lexington, Mass.: Heath, 1974).

25. Howard J. Wiarda, "The Latin Americanization of the United States."

26. Some of the materials in this section were published previously in Wiarda, "Toward a Framework." For fuller elaborations see the author's "Corporatism and Development in the Iberic-Latin World"; "Law and Political Development in Latin America: Toward a Framework for Analysis"; "The Latin American Development Process and the New Developmental Alternatives: Military 'Nasserism' and 'Dictatorship with Popular Support' "; and "Elites in Crisis: The Decline of the Old Order and the Fragmentation of the New in Latin America." For efforts at applying the model, see also the author's "The Catholic Labor Movement in Brazil: Corporatism, Populism, Paternalism, and Change," in William H. Tyler and H. Jon Rosenbaum, eds., *Contemporary Brazil,* pp. 323–47; and *Dictatorship, Development, and Disintegration.*

27. For an argument parallel to this one, that Latin America should be regarded "as something of a Fourth World, with characteristics of its own which entitle it to be studied in its own right and not forced to conform to whatever generalizations can be made about the Third," see J. D. B. Miller, *The Politics of the Third World.* See also John Martz, "The Place of Latin America in the Study of Comparative Politics."

28. Alfred Stepan, "Political Development: The Latin American Experience"; Milton Vanger, "Politics and Class in Twentieth Century Latin America"; Juan Marsal, *Cambio social en América Latina: Crítica de algunas interpretaciones dominantes en las ciencias sociales;* and Wiarda, "Elites in Crisis."

29. Rafael Altamira, *A History of Spain,* trans. Muna Lee; and Ronald Glassman, *A History of Latin America* (New York: Funk & Wagnalls, 1969).

30. Irving A. Leonard, "Science, Technology, and Hispanic America: The Basis of Regional Characteristics." It should be noted that these descriptive classifications represent simplified "ideal types" in the Weberian sense, rather than precise mirrors of reality.

31. See Louis Hartz et al., *The Founding of New Societies,* especially the essay, "The Heritage of Latin America," by Richard M. Morse, pp. 123–77.

32. Ibid.

33. See Mariano Picón-Salas, *A Cultural History of Spanish America,* pp. 39–40; and Richard M. Morse, "Recent Research on Latin American Urbanization: A Selective Survey with Commentary," p. 41.

34. Picón-Salas, *Cultural History;* also Dealy, *Public Man.*

35. Bernice Hamilton, *Political Thought in Sixteenth-Century Spain;* and Guenter Lewy, *Constitutionalism and Statecraft during the Golden*

Age of Spain: A Study of the Political Philosophy of Juan de Mariana, S.J.

36. L. N. McAlister, "Social Structure and Social Change in New Spain"; and Magali Sarfatti, *Spanish Bureaucratic-Patrimonialism in America.* For the Portuguese-Brazilian tradition, see Raymundo Faoro, *Os donos do poder: Formação do patronato politico brasileiro.*

37. Glen Dealy, "Prolegomena on the Spanish American Political Tradition"; and Charles A. Hale, *Mexican Liberalism in the Age of Mora, 1821–1853.*

38. See Warren Dean, *The Industrialization of São Paulo, 1880–1945;* Jane-Lee Woolridge Yare, "Middle Sector Political Behavior in Latin America;" and Kenneth P. Erickson, *The Brazilian Corporative State and Working Class Politics.*

39. Morse, "Recent Research," p. 41; and Economic Commission for Latin America (ECLA), *Social Development of Latin America in the Post-War Period,* introduction.

40. Lewy, *Constitutionalism and Statecraft;* and Ronald C. Newton, "On 'Functional Groups,' 'Fragmentation,' and 'Pluralism' in Spanish American Political Society."

41. Claudio Veliz, "Centralism and Nationalism in Latin America"; and John D. Powell, "Peasant Society and Clientelist Politics."

42. The discussion here draws heavily from James Petras, *Political and Social Forces in Chilean Development;* and the introduction by the editor in John J. Johnson, ed., *Continuity and Change in Latin America* (Stanford: Stanford University Press, 1964).

43. Michel Crozier, *The Bureaucratic Phenomenon.*

44. An illustrative case study of this process is Roett, *Brazil.*

45. The concepts derive from the Italian sociologists Mosca and Pareto. For an application see Orlando Fals Borda, "Marginality and Revolution in Latin America, 1809–1969."

46. See James L. Payne, *Labor and Politics in Peru.*

47. For the countries mentioned, see Frank Bonilla, *The Failure of Elites,* vol. 2, and José A. Silva Michelena, *The Illusion of Democracy in Dependent Nations,* vol. 3, of *The Politics of Change in Venezuela;* James L. Payne, *Patterns of Conflict in Colombia;* Susan Kaufman Purcell, "Decision-Making in an Authoritarian Regime: Mexico"; and Charles F. Denton, *Patterns of Costa Rican Politics.*

48. Petras, *Political and Social Forces.*

49. Erickson, *The Brazilian Corporative State*; Lawrence S. Graham, *Civil Service Reform in Brazil: Principles versus Practice*; and Robert E. Scott, "The Government Bureaucrats and Political Change in Latin America."

50. Erickson, *The Brazilian Corporative State;* and Faoro, *Os donos do poder.*

51. The argument here is derived from Morse, "Heritage"; ECLA, *Social*

Development; and especially Charles W. Anderson, "Toward a Theory of Latin American Politics" (Occasional Paper No. 2, Graduate Center for Latin American Studies, Vanderbilt University, February 1964), incorporated as chap. 4 in his *Politics and Economic Change in Latin America* (Princeton, N.J.: Van Nostrand, 1967).

52. "Toward a Theory of Latin American Politics."

53. Anderson, *Political Economy*.

54. Richard N. Adams, *The Second Sowing: Power and Secondary Development in Latin America*.

55. Anderson, *Political Economy*.

56. This is the special merit of the Erickson case study and of Schmitter, *Interest Conflict*.

57. See especially *The Conflict Society* and *Man's Power*.

58. Roett, *Brazil*, conclusion.

59. Juan Linz, "An Authoritarian Regime: Spain," in Erik Allardt and Yrjö Littunen, eds., *Cleavages, Ideologies, and Party Systems,* 10: 291–342.

60. A collection of essays that emphasizes this point and also brings together some of the leading sources cited here is Howard J. Wiarda, ed., *Politics and Social Change in Latin America: The Distinct Tradition.*

Chapter II

1. A good example of this tendency is vol. 10 of Will Durant's epochal *The Story of Civilization,* entitled *Rousseau and the Revolution,* chap. 10; also, Marcus Chique, *Dictator of Portugal: A Life of the Marques of Pombal;* C. J. H. Hayes, *History of Europe to 1870*; and Arnold J. Toynbee, *A Study of History.*

2. Useful surveys in English include William C. Atkinson, *A History of Spain and Portugal;* W. J. Barnes, *Portugal: Gateway to Greatness;* H. V. Livermore, *A New History of Portugal*; A. H. de Oliveira Marques, *History of Portugal*; Charles E. Nowell, *A History of Portugal*; and Stanley Payne, *A History of Spain and Portugal.*

3. Roman rule in Iberia is summarized in Rafael Altamira, *A History of Spain,* chap. 3. For the corporative link see Marcello Caetano, *O sistema corporativo.*

4. Atkinson, *History.*

5. Patrimonialism, of course, was one of Weber's forms of traditional authority. See the discussion in Reinhard Bendix, *Max Weber: An Intellectual Portrait,* pp. 329–81. For an application to Latin America see Richard Morse, in Louis Hartz et al., *The Founding of New Societies,* published also in Howard J. Wiarda, ed., *Politics and Social Change in Latin America.*

6. The discussion here is derived chiefly from Manuel Paulo Merêa, *O poder real e as cortes;* Raymundo Faoro, *Os donos do poder*; and

Henrique de Gama Barros, *Historia da administração pública em Portugal nos séculos XII–XV*.

7. Faoro, *Os donos do poder*, pp. 3–8. For a contemporary extension, see Lawrence S. Graham, "Portugal: The Bureaucracy of Empire."

8. Guenter Lewy, *Constitutionalism and Statecraft during the Golden Age of Spain*. The critical importance of Catholicism and the Church in Portuguese history and political culture is stressed by Thomas C. Bruneau, "The Politics of Religion in an Authoritarian Regime: The Case of Portugual."

9. Martins, "Portugal," in Archer and Giner, eds., *Contemporary Europe: Class, Status, and Power*.

10. The concept of the administrative state is elaborated in Graham, "Portugal." See also Magali Sarfatti, *Spanish Bureaucratic-Patrimonialism in America;* and Faoro, *Os donos do poder*.

11. See Arnold Strickon and Sidney M. Greenfield, eds., *Structure and Process in Latin America: Patronage, Clientage, and Power Systems*.

12. Later corporatist theorists, in harking back to the order, stability, and unity of this era, would largely ignore its violence, terror, conflict, and misery. In fact, the medieval era and the guild system, which the corporatists so romanticized, were not always very efficient, happy, or pleasant. See Barros, *Historia*, 4: 113–72.

13. Faoro, *Os donos do poder*; Merêa, *O poder real*.

14. Merêa, *O poder real*, p. 9.

15. Ibid. See also Morse, in Hartz, *Founding of New Societies*, pp. 123–77.

16. Merêa, *O poder real*.

17. Ibid.

18. Ibid.

19. Barros, *Historia*, 3: 104 and 129ff; also Vitorino Magalhães Godinho, *A estrutura na antiga sociedade portuguesa*.

20. Merêa, *O poder real*.

21. The importance of Dom Pedro in articulating the model of a national patronage system has been stressed by Sidney Greenfield, "The Patrimonial State and Patron-Client Systems in the Fifteenth Century Writings of the Infante D. Pedro of Portugal." For the importance of Suárez, see Morse, in Hartz, *Founding of New Societies*, and Ronald C. Newton, "On 'Functional Groups,' 'Fragmentation,' and 'Pluralism' in Spanish American Political Society." Both the Morse and Newton essays are reprinted in Wiarda, *Politics and Social Change*.

22. Stuart Schwartz, *Sovereignty and Society of Colonial Brazil* (Berkeley: University of California Press, 1973). See also Graham, "Portugal."

23. Bernice Hamilton, *Political Thought in Sixteenth-Century Spain*.

24. Faoro, *Os donos do poder;* and Schwartz, *Sovereignty and Society*.

25. Ibid.; and José Calvet de Magalhães, *Historia do pensamento económico em Portugal: Da idade média ao mercantilismo*.

26. An excellent discussion is Francisco Sarsfield Cabral, *Uma perspectiva sobre Portugal*.

27. This interpretation derives from the preliminary research findings of two University of Massachusetts colleagues, Susan Schneider and Robert White.
28. Sarsfield Cabral, *Uma perspectiva sobre Portugal.*
29. Merêa, *O poder real.*
30. Nowell, *History,* p. 209.
31. See Joel Serrão, " 'Decadence' and 'Regeneration' in Contemporary Portugal."
32. Marques, *History of Portugal,* vol. 2: *From Empire to Corporate State.*
33. An interesting historical interpretation of how Portuguese elites have been broadened without this implying much fundamental change in the nature of elitist rule is Henry Keith, "Point, Counterpoint in Reforming Portuguese Education, 1750–1973"; see also Godinho, *A estrutura.*
34. Marques, *History of Portugal,* 2: 48.
35. A balanced treatment is Douglas L. Wheeler, "The Portuguese Revolution of 1910."
36. Douglas L. Wheeler is writing a book on this period; my own interpretation relies on his thorough historical investigations.
37. See the entertaining account by Murray Teigh Bloom, *The Man Who Stole Portugal.*
38. See the three-volume study by Carlos Ferrão, *O integralismo e a República.*
39. This comes out clearly in the memoirs of Salazar's first secretary and military aide, Assis Gonçalves, *Intimidades de Salazar: O homem e a sua epoca.*
40. See A. H. de Oliveira Marques, "The Portuguese 1920s: A General Survey."
41. Richard A. H. Robinson, "The Religious Question and the Catholic Revival in Portugal, circa 1900–1930."
42. Based on Wheeler's oral account to the author of some of his research findings.
43. Marques, *History of Portugal,* 2: 139–40; and H. Martins, "Portugal," in S. J. Woolf, ed., *European Fascism,* pp. 312ff.
44. The material in this section is based upon the statistical materials available, as well as my own investigations, interviewing, and participant observation. Among the useful descriptive works are Charles E. Nowell, *Portugal,* chap. 1.
45. This division is the classic one in the geography books. For a study that discusses the distinct social patterns implied in these regional differences, see Martins, "Portugal."
46. Massimo Livi Bacci, *A Century of Portuguese Fertility.*
47. An interesting historical interpretation is Cabral, *Uma perspectiva sobre Portugal;* the best sociological discussion is that of Martins, "Portugal."
48. João Baptista Nunes Pereira Neto, "Social Evolution in Portugal since 1945," in Raymond S. Sayers, ed., *Portugal and Brazil in Transition,* pp. 212–27.

49. Portugal in many respects still reminds one of Barbara Tuchman's description of Europe on the eve of the twentieth century; see *The Proud Tower*. See also Godinho, *A estrutura*.

50. A useful survey compiled by the Bureau of International Commerce of the U.S. Department of Commerce is "Basic Data on the Economy of Portugal," *Overseas Business Reports,* October 1971; official Portuguese data are summarized in the *Sinopse de dados estatísticos*.

51. See the excellent work by José Cutileiro, *A Portuguese Rural Society*.

52. Cabral, *Uma perspectiva sobre Portugal;* Magalhães, *Historia do pensamento económico;* and Martins, "Portugal." For a general discussion, see also Andrew Shonfield, *Modern Capitalism: The Changing Balance of Public and Private Power*.

53. Graham, "Portugal."

54. Sergio Ribeiro, *O mercado comun*; and Francisco Pereira da Moura, *Por onde vai a economia portuguesa?*

55. See, for example, the useful books by Hugh Kay, *Salazar and Modern Portugal,* and Peter Fryer and Patricia McGowan-Pinheiro, *Oldest Ally: A Portrait of Salazar's Portugal.* It is significant that it is not just conservatives who point to the seemingly inherently conservative character of Portugal but liberals and men of the Left as well.

56. The reference is to the significant book by Gabriel Almond and Sidney Verba, *The Civic Culture.* The most thorough comparable study of Portuguese political and social attitudes is Instituto Português de Opinião Publica e da Estudos de Mercado (IPOPE), *Os Portugueses e a política —1973.*

Chapter III

1. The argument is presented in Philippe C. Schmitter, "Corporatist Interest Representation and Public Policy-Making in Portugal"; also Ronald C. Newton, "The Corporate Idea and the Authoritarian Tradition in Spain and Spanish America: Some Critical Observations."

2. Howard J. Wiarda, "Toward a Framework for the Study of Political Change in the Iberic-Latin Tradition: The Corporative Model," and "Corporatism and Development in the Iberic-Latin World: Persistent Strains and New Variations."

3. For the comparison see Stanley Payne, *Falange*.

4. See Charles W. Anderson, *The Political Economy of Modern Spain*.

5. Fernando Campos, *O principio da organização corporativa através da historia;* and Emile Lousse, *Organização e representação corporativa*.

6. Manoïlesco, "Le génie latin dans le nouveau régime portugais," in *VI Congresso do Mundo Português: Publicações,* 8: 621–39. A contemporary exposition of these same currents of thought is Glen Dealy, "The Tradition of Monistic Democracy in Latin America," in Wiarda, *Politics and Social Change in Latin America*.

7. Manoïlesco, "Le génie latin"; also Francisco Elias de Tejeda Spínola, *Las doctrinas políticas em Portugal (edad media)*.

8. The analysis here follows that of Matthew Elbow, *French Corporative Theory*, pp. 14–16.

9. In the course of one of many trips to the Prado Museum in Madrid, the author was particularly struck by two paintings of Denis Van Sloot, a 17th-century Flemish master, which portrayed the corporate bases of society, politics, and economics in the Brussels of 1615. In the paintings (located in a hallway near the cafeteria) all the corporate bodies—clerics, burghers, and guilds, municipal officials, university faculty, military orders, various artisan associations, merchants, traders, etc.—are present, each with distinct uniforms, each with its established place in the line, each with its own flag, saint, medals, and symbols, each group itself internally organized by hierarchy and rank, all carefully arranged. One cannot help but be impressed by the parallels between the life and social order depicted in these paintings and the structure of society in mid-twentieth-century corporate Portugal, perhaps most notably the way in which each rank order still has its distinctive uniform and accompanying accouterments depicting the wearer's particular place in the social hierarchy.

10. Elbow, *French Corporative Theory*, p. 15; also, Amado de Aguilar, *Donde veio e para onde vai o corporativismo português*.

11. Elbow, *French Corporative Theory*, pp. 15–16.

12. "Recent Research on Latin American Urbanization: A Selective Survey with Commentary," p. 41.

13. Mariano Picón-Salas, *A Cultural History of Spanish America*, pp. 39–40; the argument here is derived also from Wiarda, "Toward a Framework," pp. 209–17.

14. Bernice Hamilton, *Political Thought in Sixteenth-Century Spain.*

15. Lewy, *Constitutionalism and Statecraft during the Golden Age of Spain*, pp. 49–50.

16. Ibid.; and Hamilton, *Political Thought*, introduction and conclusion.

17. Fernando Campos, *O pensamento contra-revolucionario em Portugal (Século XIX).*

18. Elbow, *French Corporative Theory*, pp. 51–52.

19. "The Strange Career of Latin-American Studies," p. 11.

20. Michael P. Fogarty, *Christian Democracy in Western Europe, 1820–1953*, chaps. 11–12.

21. Elbow, *French Corporative Theory*, chap. 2.

22. Ibid.; also J. Pires Cardoso, *O corporativismo e a igreja* (Lisbon: Graf. Lisbonense, 1949).

23. Cardoso, *O corporativismo.*

24. See Fogarty, *Christian Democracy:* also Emile Lousse, *Corporativismo antigo e moderno.*

25. Fogarty, *Christian Democracy*, chaps. 15–16.

26. Miguel Jorrin and John Martz, *Latin American Political Thought and Ideology,* pp. 406–9.
27. See A. James Gregor, *The Ideology of Fascism,* chap. 2.
28. See Charles W. Anderson, "Toward a Theory of Latin American Politics," in Wiarda, ed., *Politics and Social Change,* pp. 249–65.
29. Ibid.; also Joseph N. Moody, ed., *Church and Society: Catholic Social and Political Thought and Movements, 1789–1950.*
30. "Corporatist Interest Representation," p. 4.
31. For this tradition in English, consult Elbow, *French Corporative Theory;* Fogarty, *Christian Democracy;* and Joaquín Azpiazu, *The Corporative State.*
32. Manoïlesco, *Le siècle du corporatisme.*
33. For Durkheim's argument, see his "The Solidarity of Occupational Groups," in Talcott Parsons et al., eds., *Theories of Society,* pp. 356–63.
34. For example, G. D. H. Cole, *Guild Socialism.*
35. See the discussion in Wiarda, "Corporatism and Development."
36. The discussion here follows the excellent analysis of Richard A. H. Robinson, "The Religious Question and the Catholic Revival in Portugal, circa 1900–1930."
37. Ibid., p. 3.
38. Ibid.; see also Abranches Martins, "O renascimento católico em Portugal."
39. Robinson, "Religious Question"; based also upon an examination of *Estudos sociais.*
40. Based upon an examination of such Catholic periodicals of these times as *A Epoca, Ordem nova, Novidades,* and *Política.* The liberal, social-democratic response was most strongly articulated in the periodical *Seara Nova.* This response was weak, came terribly late, and seemed curiously out of touch with Portuguese realities.
41. Based upon H. Martins, "Portugal," in S. J. Woolf, ed., *European Fascism,* pp. 302–3.
42. Ibid., pp. 303–12.
43. Based upon an examination of *Ordem nova* during this period.
44. See especially Sardinha's voluminous writings on these themes; also Caetano, "A nossa 'adesão.' "
45. Especially Fernando Campos, *A genealogia do pensamento nacional* (Lisbon: José Fernandes Junior, 1931).
46. *Política* I (1929).
47. Pereira, "O pesadelo de Gonçalo Ramires."
48. Thomas Bruneau, "The Politics of Religion in an Authoritarian Regime: The Case of Portugal," pp. 15–16.
49. Martins, "Portugal"; and Carlos Ferrão, *O integralismo e a República.* Ferrão's interpretation stresses the conspiratorial tactics of the Integralists in undermining the Republic.
50. Martins, "Portugal"; based also on interviews with some of the surviving Integralists.

51. On the several factions of the Integralist movement, see Martins, "Portugal," pp. 310–12.
52. See the discussion in Robinson, "Religious Question"; also Salazar, *Centro Católico Português: Principios e organização.* Salazar's writings in such Catholic journals as *Novidades* during this same period are also crucial for an understanding of the dominant currents in his thought.
53. This theme runs through various perceptive analyses: W. C. Atkinson, "The Political Structure of the Portuguese 'New State'"; Francis E. McMahon, "Thirty Years of Salazar"; Robinson, "Religious Question"; and Martins, "Portugal."
54. See Hugh Kay, *Salazar and Modern Portugal,* the best work in English on the subject.
55. Among the principal Portuguese works, see João de Almeida, *O estado novo;* João Ameal, *Construção de novo estado;* Campos, *O principio;* J. M. P. da Costa, *Ensaios doutrinarios: Capitalismo, socialismo, e corporatismo;* Luis da Cunha Gonçalves, *Causas e efeitos do corporativismo português;* João Pinto da Costa Leite, *A doutrina corporativa em Portugal;* Rui C. de Manchete, *Os principios e classificações fundamentais do corporatismo;* Henrique Marques, *Essencia do corporativismo em Portugal;* Antonio C. de Almeida e Oliveira, *Principios fundamentais do estado novo corporativo;* João Manuel Cortez Pinto, *A Corporação: Subsidio para o seu estudo;* Augusto de Morais Sarmento, *O corporativismo português e os postulados da sociologia católica* (Braga: Liv. Cruz, 1964).

Salazar's thought at this time is summarized in vol. I (1928–34) of his *Discursos;* the best secondary account is J. Silva Saraiva, *O pensamento político de Salazar.* For Caetano, see *O sistema corporativo.*

Useful accounts of Portuguese corporative theory in English include Atkinson, "Political Structure"; Michael Derrick, "Portugal and Dr. Salazar"; Derrick, *The Portugal of Salazar;* Eugene Bagger, "Portugal: Anti-Totalitarian Outpost"; and S. George West, *The New Corporative State of Portugal.*
56. These ideas are contained in Salazar's writings.
57. Ibid.; and John McAdams, "Corporate State in Portugal," Chap. 3.
58. This concept lies behind the American theory of countervailing interest groups; it is also inherent in the prevailing Eastonian model of "the political system." See on this David Easton, *A Systems Analysis of Political Life.*
59. Costa Leite, *Doutrina corporativa.*
60. This crucial distinction is made by Juan Linz, "An Authoritarian Regime: Spain," in E. Allardt and Y. Littunen, eds., *Cleavages, Ideologies, and Party Systems,* pp. 291–341. In contrast to the model of totalitarianism familiar in the literature, Linz defines authoritarian regimes as those with limited but not responsible pluralism, low popular mobilization, lack of an articulated ideology but prevalence of a typical mentality, and

the often arbitrary but usually predictable exercise of power by a leader or a small group.

61. Bagger, "Portugal."
62. Costa, *Ensaios doutrinarios*; and Atkinson, "Political Structure."
63. José C. de Magalhães, *Historia do pensamento económico em Portugal: Da idade média ao mercantilismo*; and William Glade, *The Latin American Economies*.
64. Cunha Gonçalves, *Causas e efeitos*.
65. By the same token, when the state violated, abused, or ran roughshod over the corporate group rights of its citizens, it sacrificed its own right to expect continued loyalty and service. Its people could then invoke a hallowed right of resistance. As we shall see, as the Salazar regime increasingly abused the rights of the Portuguese people, became more dictatorial, and was divorced from Portuguese realities in the late 1940s, 1950s, and 1960s, resistance and opposition grew culminating eventually in the regime's overthrow in 1974. This pattern and the doctrine of the right to resist an "unjust prince" also have their roots deep in Catholic thought and the Portuguese tradition. The right of resistance to tyranny is the opposite side of the obligation-to-obedience coin.
66. Costa Leite, *Doutrina corporativa*.
67. Caetano, *O sistema corporativo*.
68. Bagger, "Portugal."
69. This theme comes through clearly in all the literature; see especially the writings of Salazar, Caetano, Costa Leite, Cortez Pinto, and others, loc. cit., n. 55.

Chapter IV

1. "General Carmona and the New Portugal," p. 481. See also João Pinto da Costa Leite, *A doutrina corporativa em Portugal*.
2. *A batalha do futuro: Organização corporativa*.
3. *Posição actual do corporativismo português*.
4. A. H. de Oliveira Marques, *History of Portugal,* vol. 2, *From Empire to Corporate State,* pp. 139–40.
5. Carmona's role has been underplayed in most accounts of the Portuguese regime. He was, of course, later overshadowed by Salazar, but under the Portuguese Constitution the president enjoyed wide authority, including the power to dismiss the prime minister (Salazar) if he wished. In fact, Carmona exercised his authority with restraint. Most Portuguese observers agree, however, that his presence, his widespread prestige as a leader of the 1926 revolution, his popularity, his position as a military commander, and his constitutional power ultimately to replace the prime minister all served as restraints on certain of Salazar's excesses.
6. These are the main themes of the influential book by Fernando Pessoa, *Defesa e justificacão da ditadura militar em Portugal*.

7. The analysis here and in the succeeding paragraphs follows that of Herminio Martins, "Portugal," in S. J. Woolf, ed., *European Fascism,* pp. 312f.

8. "Os problemas nacionais e a ordem da sua solução," in *Discursos,* vol. *I, 1928–1934.*

9. Some of the laudatory biographies cover these accomplishments in great detail. See especially Michael Derrick, *The Portugal of Salazar;* and F. C. C. Egerton, *Salazar: Rebuilder of Portugal.*

10. Martins, "Portugal," p. 314.

11. Several research projects have recently been undertaken on this period.

12. This is the contention of Professor Douglas L. Wheeler, whose research on the Republican period and the coup of 1926 leads him to this conclusion (oral communication to the author). This theme is present also in the first volume of Teotonio Pereira's *Memorias.* Pereira had close connections with many of these young officers.

13. Vol. I of his *Discursos.*

14. See his speech at the First Conference of the União Nacional, held in Lisbon in 1946; excerpts reprinted in Caetano, *Princípios e definições,* p. 46.

15. See on this Caetano de Melo Beirão, "O sistema corporativo perante o estado."

16. On the Italian influence, see Caetano, *Lições de direito corporativo.*

17. On the influence of *Quadragesimo Anno,* see Douglas Stacey, "An Exemplar."

18. "Política de verdade, política de sacrificio, política nacional," in *Discursos.*

19. "Principios fundamentais da revolução política," in *Discursos.*

20. These developments may be followed in *Cadernos corporativos.* Led by Integralist Augusto da Costa, this group represented the manifestly pro-Fascist element within the country.

21. "Salazar and the New State of Portugal," *Studies* 25 (March 1936): 131–44.

22. *Memorias,* p. 22.

23. The best account is Francisco I. Pereira dos Santos, *Un état corporatif: La constitution sociale et politique portugaise;* also Marcello Caetano, *A constituição de 1933: Estudo de direito político* (Coimbra: Coimbra Ed., 1956).

24. Caetano, *Manual de direito administrativo português.*

25. Vitor Vera Lopes, "A constituição portuguesa de 1933." The comparison may not be so ludicrous: de Gaulle was not only an exceptionally strong figure; he had also been a corporatist in the 1930s.

26. A. H. de Oliveira Marques, *A primeira legislatura do estado novo* (1935–1938).

27. Marcello Caetano, *Manual de ciencia política e direito constitucional,* 5th ed.; also, *Expresso,* February 3, 1973, p. 12.

28. The entire structure is detailed in the *Código administrativo.*

29. Caetano admitted this candidly when he wrote: "Even in the autonomous administration of the municipality and in the exercise . . . of specifically municipal powers, the law admits the intervention of the government for the purpose of coordinating the action of the municipalities, maintaining its administration within legal bounds, and correcting illegal acts undertaken by its organs or to remedy deficiencies demonstrated in the exercise of autonomy granted them." See his *Manual de direito administrativo*, p. 216.

30. Based on information supplied by Professor Norman Blume of the Department of Political Science, University of Toledo, who in 1972/73 carried out an extensive survey of Portuguese local government activities; see his "The Portuguese Freguesia." But see also Joyce Riegelhaupt, "Peasants and Politics in Portugal: The Corporative State and Village 'Non-Politics.' "

31. Marcello Caetano, *O sistema corporativo*, p. 69.

32. See both the text of this "political constitution" and the learned constitutional-legal commentaries on it: Santos, *Un état corporatif*; Caetano, *A constituição*; Augusto da Costa, *Factos e principios corporativos*.

33. Fernando Andrade Pires de Lima and João de Matos Atunes Varela, *Código civil português* (Coimbra: Coimbra Ed., 1948).

34. The statute was promulgated as decree-law 23,048 of September 23, 1933, and was the first and foremost of a series of six extraordinary decrees promulgated that same day.

35. Augusto da Costa, *A nação corporativa*; and Manuel Guimarães, "Corporativismo."

36. See the discussion in Howard J. Wiarda, "The Portuguese Corporative System: Basic Structures and Current Functions."

37. The charter of the institute was published as decree-law 23,053, also dated September 23, 1933. For the secretariat, see its *Boletim*, where all this legislation was republished.

38. Pereira, *Memorias*, p. 103.

39. Caetano, *O sistema*.

40. J. Pires Cardoso, *Questões corporativas: Doutrina e factos*. Based also on interviews with a number of those involved in these disputes.

41. Much of the following analysis is taken directly from the decree-laws. See also da Costa, *A nação*; Santos, *Un état corporatif*; Adelina Costa, *Organização política e administrativa da nação*; Ministerio das Corporações, "Organização corporativa portuguesa"; and Emilio A. Ferreira, *Corporativismo português: Doutrina e aplicação*. A useful pamphlet summarizing this structure and put out in English by the Office of the Secretary of State of Information and Tourism is *Occupational Organization*.

42. One of the few solid social science studies to have been written on Portugal describes these features admirably; see José Cutileiro, *A Portuguese Rural Society*, pts. 3 and 4.

43. Da Costa, *A nação*, p. 95.

44. See decree-law 29,494.
45. Based on interviews with Portuguese government and corporative officials, 1972/73.
46. See decree-law 1953 of March 11, 1937; also Jeronimo de Melo Osorio de Castro, "Acción social de las casas de pescadores." Based also on interviews with officials of the *casas dos pescadores*.
47. Adelina Costa, *Organização*; and Ministerio das Corporações, *Organização*.
48. A useful theoretical justification is found in Cardoso, *Questões corporativas*. Again, the classic work is Manoïlesco, *Le siècle du corporatisme*.
49. Caetano was the leading advocate of allowing the corporations to grow from below rather than being imposed from above.
50. See Article 1 of the decree-law of July 8, 1936, published in the *Diario do governo*. A number of these agencies had actually begun functioning prior to 1936. Manoïlesco's book, published just before, may have provided the rationale for the creation of these agencies and for the increasingly statist system.
51. A useful study of these agencies and their links with the economic and social system is Freppel Cotta, *Economic Planning in Corporative Portugal*, preface by Marcello Caetano.
52. Pires Cardoso was one of these intellectuals; for a discussion of his role, see chap. 7.
53. For a discussion of this bureaucratic state apparatus, see Lawrence S. Graham, "Portugal: The Bureaucracy of Empire."
54. See the *Estatutos da União Nacional* as promulgated in decree-law 21,603 of August 20, 1932.
55. See the numerous statements and speeches of Salazar to this effect, as in Antonio Ferro, *Salazar: Portugal and Her Leader*.
56. The best discussion is Mihail Manoïlesco, *La parti unique: Institution politique des régimes nouveaux*, pp. 216–26.
57. See *Legislação sobre a Mocidade portuguesa*.
58. Secretariado da Propaganda Nacional, *A revolução continua: União Nacional, Mocidade, Legião*.
59. Based on interviews with former Mocidade leaders.
60. Martins, "Portugal," pp. 324–25; also *Keesing's Contemporary Archives*, vol. 1 (September 16, 1936).
61. SPN, *A revolução continua*.
62. Martins, "Portugal."
63. Ibid.; based also on the field work in Portugal, 1972/73.
64. Pires Cardoso, *Questões corporativas*; also his writings in *Revista do Gabinete de Estudos Corporativos*.
65. See the discussions in Manoïlesco and other corporative theorists.
66. The Army and its role remain wholly unstudied; for some enlightened comments, see Hugh Kay, *Salazar and Modern Portugal*.
67. Again the general discussion of Manoïlesco and other theorists is useful.
68. See *Vida mundial* 35 (April 17, 1973): 21–23.

69. See J. Pires Cardoso, *O corporativismo e a igreja*; and by the same author, *Corporações morais e culturais*.
70. Caetano and student leaders had numerous exchanges on this point; and see J. Pires Cardoso, *A universidade: Instituição corporativa*.
71. See especially Graham's general comments on the bureaucratic-administrative structure of the entire Portuguese system, in "Portugal."
72. Wiarda, "The Portuguese Corporative System."
73. Antonio Julio de Castro Fernandes, *Temas corporativos*. Castro Fernandes was subsecretary of corporations at the time.
74. Oliveira Marques, *History of Portugal*, vol. 2, esp. pp. 183, 209.
75. Salazar, *Doctrine and Action*, p. 192.
76. This is the conclusion reached by John McAdams, "The Corporate State in Portugal," pp. 154–56.

Chapter V

1. The priorities were listed in this order in a personal communication to the author by historian Douglas L. Wheeler, who has researched this period thoroughly. My own research into the literature of the period confirms this assessment.
2. Caetano, *O sistema corporativo*; and Pereira, *Memorias*.
3. The fact that Salazar and others in power were exceedingly cautious in implementing corporative reforms and saw other concerns as having higher priority comes through clearly in Pereira's memoirs. Pereira, as the first subsecretary of corporations, was in a position close enough to Salazar to see policy unfolding; his memoirs, though disappointingly vague in some regards, are a rich source for corporative developments during the 1930s. Although Pereira died only three weeks prior to the beginning of the author's field research in Portugal, the written legacy he left is vast; these materials have been supplemented through interviews: João Pinto da Costa Leite, Pereira's successor in the Corporations Subsecretariat and a long-time, high-level government servant in a variety of important posts; Antonio Julio de Castro Fernandes, wartime corporations subsecretary; Antonio da Silva Leal and J. Pires Cardoso, corporative scholars and intellectuals who know the 1930s period intimately.
4. Pereira, *Memorias,* p. 103.
5. Based on an examination of the newspapers and news magazines of the period.
6. Published in his book, *A batalha do futuro: Organização corporativa*.
7. This legislation is published in the *Boletim do Instituto Nacional do Trabalho e Previdência,* hereafter referred to as the *Boletim do INTP*.
8. The growth of the sindicatos and other corporative agencies may be traced in the *Estatísticas da organização corporativa*.
9. Pereira, *Memorias,* chap. 12; and Augusto da Costa, *Factos e principios corporativos*.

10. See his comments in "Corporatist Interest Representation and Public Policy-Making in Portugal." It should be said that despite an occasional factual mistake or interpretive lapse, this paper remains one of the most stimulating and provocative interpretations of Portuguese policy making and corporative development. In a later paper, Prof. Schmitter offers a more open and multicausal explanation of Portuguese corporatism; see his "The Social Origins, Economic Bases, and Political Imperatives of Authoritarian Rule in Portugal."

11. Harry M. Makler, "The Portuguese Industrial Elite and Its Corporative Relations."

12. *Memorias,* pp. 152–57; also the *Boletim do INTP* during this period. *The Boletim do INTP* is a particularly rich source containing the texts of all Pereira's speeches and those of Salazar related to corporative development, the names of all the Corporations Subsecretariat's staff and its organizational structure, the complete texts of all the new social legislation, the lists of officially recognized sindicatos, gremios, etc. A critical assessment of the social assistance programs of this period is in *Expresso,* September 7, 1974, p. 18.

13. See his *Lições de direito corporativo.*

14. For information on this agency and its evolution, see *Vida mundial* 35 (August 17, 1973): 21–23; also *Expresso,* June 16, 1973, p. 4.

15. Pereira, *Memorias.*

16. Ibid.; da Costa, *Factos e principios corporativos*; and the *Boletim do INTP* for this period.

17. *Boletim do INTP,* vol. 1 (November 1934); and Schmitter, "Corporatist Interest Representation," pp. 18–21.

18. For the structure, see Freppel Cotta, *Economic Planning in Corporative Portugal*; the class bias is stressed by Schmitter, "Corporatist Interest Representation." It should be reemphasized that the class bias emerged from the dynamics of the Portuguese system, not from any inherent characteristics of corporatism per se.

19. *Boletim do INTP, vols. 1–4* (1933–37).

20. "Corporatist Interest Representation," p. 9.

21. The chapter subheading here used is parallel to my colleague William E. Connolly's *The Bias of Pluralism.* As we shall see, some of the biases in "pluralism" and some of the biases in "corporatism" turned out to be remarkably similar.

22. Numerous regime figures—Pereira, Caetano, Salazar—referred continuously to the absence of "corporative consciousness" among all classes of the population.

23. The strike is reported in the *New York Times,* January 20, 1934; for the intrigues of the period, see Assis Gonçalves, *Intimidades de Salazar.*

24. Although repression was frequently used during this period, its occurrence was far less pronounced than is pictured in most of the exile literature. Sheer self-interest on the part of the labor leaders and workers generally, a recognition of the realities of the situation, and a tradition

of working out accommodations with whatever government happened to be in power, no matter its political coloration, were far more important than repression in determining labor's acquiescence to corporative rule.

25. The opposition of various professionals to the corporative restructuring is mentioned in *Boletim do INTP*; Pereira, *Memorias*; see also Candido da Cruz, "Ordem dos Medicos," *Republica social 2* (May 5, 1933): 69–74.

26. Pereira, *Batalha*. This book, published as Pereira stepped down as corporations subsecretary, is frequently more revealing than his later *Memorias*. Read in conjunction, these two books by the corporative system's chief administrator in its early years tell us a great deal about how it functioned and the difficulties encountered.

27. Fernando Campos, *A solução corporativa*. Campos was subsecretary of corporations at the time; this slim pamphlet is the text of the speech he gave as the Associação Comercial de Lojistas [shopkeepers] de Lisboa was about to be reorganized as the União de Gremios de Lojistas de Lisboa. Although this finally brought the bulk of middle-sized shopkeepers under government control, the life of the shopkeepers changed little. In his speech Campos appealed to the commercial class to assist in the corporatization of the nation; in fact, little help was forthcoming and, apart from the regulations they had to follow and licenses they had to buy, the daily activities of the merchant class remained little affected by corporatization.

28. See *Boletim do INTP* 1 (January 1934): 16.

29. Pereira, *Batalha* and *Memorias*. Pereira was called upon to respond to the objections raised to this grant of special treatment to business interests. For other considerations of these episodes, see João Pinto da Costa Leite, *A doutrina corporativa em Portugal*; and da Costa, *Factos e principios corporativos*, pp. 199ff. A critique is in John McAdams, "The Corporative State in Portugal," p. 127.

30. The entire interview was reprinted in *Boletim do INTP* (August 15, 1934): 2–4.

31. These developments may be traced in the *Boletim do INTP* for this period.

32. A good treatment of some of the early operations of the system is in the *New York Times*, September 23, 1934, p. 2.

33. For Lowi's critique, see *The End of Liberalism*. Based also upon the author's field work and interviews among high Portuguese government officials.

34. "Corporatist Interest Representation," p. 11. The *parecer* of the Corporative Chamber setting forth the rationale for creating the gremios da lavoura was published in *Boletim do INTP* 4 (March 1937): 204–14. For details on landholder domination and the tradition of peasant deference, see José Cutileiro, *A Portuguese Rural Society*.

35. By 1972, which is the only year for which I have seen exact figures, the

volume of *papelada* had multiplied several times over. During that year the Ministry of Corporations recorded 23,000 documents referring to hours of work, had registered more than 11,000 exceptions, had processed over 7,000 documents dealing with special cases, dealt with 24,000 applications requiring approval, processed 15,500 professional licences, approved 1,100 constitutions or alterations of corporative commissions, passed on 4,500 authorizations for work abroad, ratified 115 of the corporative commissions' decisions regarding wage disputes, helped prepare 256 *pareceres* (reports) dealing with labor legislation, and recorded more than 18,000 "other documents." Based on data supplied by the Corporations Ministry to *A capital,* February 24, 1973, p. 2.

36. Based on interviews with officials of the corporative agencies.
37. *Boletim do INTP* 4 (December 31, 1936): 47–50.
38. Pereira, *Memorias*; and Costa Leite, *Doutrina corporativa.* That Salazar was aware of these biases in the system comes out clearly in Antonio Ferro, *Salazar: Portugal and Her Leader,* p. 18.
39. Pereira, *Memorias,* is particularly revealing in this regard.
40. *Discursos, vol. 1, Problemas da organização corporativa* pp. 287–302.
41. See his *Lições* and his *O estado corporativo.*
42. Pereira, *Batalha.*
43. Ibid.; and Alexandre Herculano da Cal, *Legislação corporativa: gremios e sindicatos.*
44. Pereira and Costa Leite offered the strongest defenses.
45. Pereira, *Batalha,* pp. 16–17.
46. See the *Boletim do INTP* for this period.
47. The full texts of the laws are in *Boletim do INTP,* vol. 5 (November 15, 1938).
48. *Boletim do INTP,* vols. 6 (March 15, 1939) and 7 (July 31, 1939).
49. "Corporatist Interest Representation," p. 14.
50. Paraphrased from ibid.
51. Especially his *L'organisation politique portugaise.*

Chapter VI

1. See the generally laudatory comments in the books of Derrick, Ferro, Atkinson, Ploncard, d'Assac, Cotta, and other pro-Salazar authors. An interesting disclaimer using comparative figures for Portugal, Ireland, and Greece is Philippe C. Schmitter, "Corporatist Interest Representation and Public Policy-Making in Portugal." Unfortunately, most of Schmitter's data are for the post-World War II period, when Portugal not only lagged behind but also lagged *farther* behind. The 1930s accomplishments, thus, remain impressive.
2. "Portugal," in S. J. Woolf, ed., *European Fascism,* pp. 326–27.
3. The figures may be traced in the yearly publication of the Instituto Nacional de Estatística, *Estatística da organização corporativa e previdência.*

4. *Memorias,* chaps. 19–22. Salazar apparently both favored the bright, able young men in his regime and feared them. A case in point was Pereira, whom Salazar admired for his talents and upper-class connections and feared as a possible rival. There was, in 1935/36, a series of fallings-out between Salazar and Pereira, and the latter's assignment to Spain was also a way of banishing him. Pereira had his own ambitions, however, and apparently was using both the corporative agencies and the Mocidade to build up his own political support. He had arranged a Mocidade demonstration in his favor at every stop along the train ride to Spain, but an "obstruction" on the tracks forced his train to take another route and the demonstrations never took place. With his exit, the corporative system went into a long decline from which it never fully recovered. Pereira had picked up the corporate ball and run with it, too far and too fast to suit Salazar and perhaps in a way that Salazar saw as a potential challenge to his own rule. Could it be that the decline of the corporative system after 1936 had more to do with these personalistic and private political rivalries than with any great ideological transformations or crises or class biases in the system?

5. "Portugal," p. 327.

6. A. H. de Oliveira Marques, *History of Portugal,* vol. 2, *From Empire to Corporate State,* p. 215.

7. A number of "horror stories" as to what happened to these funds came out publicly following the 1974 coup; see *Vida mundial* 35 (June 14, 1974): 1off.

8. "Revolução corporativa," in *Discursos,* vol. 3, *1938–1943.*

9. Caetano, *Problemas da revolução corporativa.*

10. This trend was recognized by Frank C. Hanighen as early as 1937; see his article, "Portugal's Plight," p. 49.

11. "Corporatist Interest Representation," p. 14.

12. This paragraph is based heavily on the assessment in ibid., confirmed or modified somewhat by my own research findings.

13. Based on interviews with Ministry of Corporations and other officials.

14. See the *Boletim do INTP* for this period. After 1939 the *Boletim* records few instances of corporative expansion or innovations, except for the creation of more and more regulatory commissions. See also Antonio Jorge da Mota Veiga, *A economia corporativa e o problema dos preços.*

15. *Boletim do INTP,* vol. 7 (June 15, June 29, August 15–31, 1940).

16. Ibid., November 30, 1940.

17. Salazar, "Address at the Special Sitting of the National Assembly," Beira, 1940.

18. See especially the "Conclusion: Unpleasant Remarks," in Salazar, *The Principles and Work of the Revolution, in Their Internal and International Aspects.*

19. The best account is Hugh Kay, *Salazar and Modern Portugal,* chaps. 7–8. Kay's account is a sympathetic one, aimed principally at justifying

Portuguese neutrality to a British audience, but the treatment is balanced and fair.

20. See his "Address at the Special Sitting."
21. One of the best accounts is the long feature, "War-Time Portugal," *Times* (London), September 8, 1943, p. 5.
22. Based on the *Boletim do INTP* for this period.
23. Costa Leite, personal interview, Lisbon, May 21, 1973.
24. The only source, to my knowledge, for these events is the *Times* (London), especially the dispatches of July 23 and July 25, 1942. The Portuguese press carried some heavily censored accounts.
25. Ibid., July 25, 1942, p. 3.
26. Ibid., February 18, 1943, p. 3; also *Boletim do INTP,* vol. 10 (March 31, 1943).
27. *Times* (London), July 30, 1943, p. 3.
28. The liberal reviews carried some interesting articles on Portugal at this time: J. R. Migueis, "Salazar of Portugal"; J. L. Teller, "Salazar Is Next"; and J. Alvarez del Vayo, "Salazar: Franco's Junior Partner."
29. The anguish of the corporative system was described in detail in the report of a Parliamentary Commission for the Investigation of the Elements of the Corporative Organization; see also Antonio Julio de Castro Fernandes, *Enfrentando o destino das casas do povo.* As subsecretary of corporations during this period, Castro Fernandes made use of the investigatory commission's findings.
30. "O destino do corporatismo," p. 51.
31. "Corporatismo subordinado, corporatismo integral, corporatismo em marcha," *Diario da manhã,* April 9, 1944.
32. *Principios fundamentais da organização corporativa portuguesa.* See also his more enthusiastic *Temas corporativos,* written after he was in his new post.
33. Given the frequently capricious and dictatorial nature of the Portuguese regime, the degree of internal criticism it tolerated was rather consistently remarkable. Except for the period of the Spanish civil war, in-house criticism of a vigorous sort, such as that produced by Teixeira Ribeiro and Castro Fernandes and later by Caetano, Sedas Nunes, and others, was condoned and often welcomed. It was only those who rejected the system in its entirety who found themselves in trouble.
34. "A revolução nacional," in *Discursos,* vol. 4, *1943–1950.*
35. *Times* (London), May 19, 1945, p. 1.
36. "Corporatist Interest Representation," p. 15.
37. Caetano, "Problemas actuales de la administración pública portuguesa," pp. 260–61; quoted in Schmitter, n. 48.
38. Based on interviews with Corporations Ministry officials.
39. Based on interviews with João Pinto da Costa Leite, cabinet minister and close Salazar collaborator during this period, Lisbon, May 21, 1973.
40. Kay, *Salazar and Modern Portugal,* p. 432.
41. These events, treated briefly here, are most fairly discussed in ibid.

42. Based chiefly on the extensive documentation in the *Boletim do INTP*.

43. *Keesing's Contemporary Archives,* January 5–12, 1946, p. 7646; William Atkinson, "What Next in Portugal?"; Kay, *Salazar and Modern Portugal,* chap. 11.

44. These criticisms are present in any number of social-democratic opposition statements in the postwar period.

45. The most balanced account is again Kay, *Salazar and Modern Portugal.* Other accounts of the dictatorship, ranging from violent opposition to more neutral analysis, include: Oliveira Marques, *History of Portugal,* chap. 13; Mario Soares, *Le Portugal baillonné: Un témoignage; 43 anos de fascismo em Portugal,* special issue of *Paz e terra;* Martins, "Portugal"; Peter Fryer and Patricia McGowan-Pinheiro, *Oldest Ally: A Portrait of Salazar's Portugal,* chap. 9–10; Humberto Delgado, *The Memoirs of General Delgado;* Antonio de Figueiredo, *Portugal and Its Empire: The Truth;* Henrique Galvão, *The Santa Maria: My Crusade for Portugal;* Atkinson, "What Next in Portugal?"; Christian Rudel, *Le Portugal et Salazar;* Andrew Marshall, "Portugal: A Determined Empire"; Christine Garnier, *Salazar: An Intimate Portrait;* P. W., "Portugal," *New Republic* 120 (February 21, 1949): 10–11; James Duffy, *Portugal in Africa,* pt. 3; J. A. Page, "Portugal," pp. 42ff.; Ronald H. Chilcote, *Portuguese Africa;* Mario Mendez Fonseca, *42 anos de Estado Novo;* Toni Howard, "The World's Most Durable Dictator"; Armando Cortesão, "Democracy and Fascism in Portugal." For additional references, see below. n. 49.

46. Bowen, *German Theories of the Corporative State,* pp. 2–3; Olive Holmes, "Spain and Portugal: A Dilemma for the West"; and Council of Europe, Consultative Assembly, *"Introductory Report on Human Rights in Portugal"* p. 20.

47. Some of the comments in this paragraph were derived from interviews with Salazar cabinet officials of this period and officials of the Corporations Subsecretariat. In thinking about the renewal of corporatism in Portugal at a time when its global popularity was obviously on the wane, one cannot help but think of the contrast with next-door Franco's Spain. Franco was never so committed to the Falangist ideology as Salazar was to corporatism, and he thus found it easy after the war to relegate the Falange and its ideas to a distinctly secondary place. Although obviously other variables are also involved, such pragmatism on the part of Franco enabled the Spanish regime to pursue new policy directions in the postwar period that led to an era of unprecedented economic growth and prosperity; in Portugal, in contrast, the ideological commitment was far stronger, the regime hence remained locked into its outdated 1930s structure, few new policy directions were taken, and the economy also stagnated. See Stanley Payne, *Falange: A History of Spanish Fascism.*

48. On the freezing of Portuguese society, see Henry H. Keith, "Point, Counterpoint in Reforming Portuguese Education, 1750–1973," p. 9.

For the societal changes meanwhile occurring, see João Baptista Nunes Pereira Neto, "Social Evolution in Portugal since 1945," in Raymond S. Sayers, ed., *Portugal and Brazil in Transition*, pp. 212–27.

49. Among the more useful accounts are Kay, *Salazar and Modern Portugal*, chaps. 11–13; Fryer and McGowan-Pinheiro, *Oldest Ally*; C. L. Sulzberger, "Salazar Controls Portugal by Limited Dictatorship," *New York Times*, November 23, 1948; Tad Szulc, "Austere Dictator," *New York Times*, November 6, 1965, p. 10; "Portugal and Its Dictator," *Current History* 50 (August 1939): 46; Martins, "Portugal"; Atkinson, "What Next in Portugal?"; Howard, "World's Most Durable Dictator."

Chapter VII

1. Some of the comments contained in these introductory remarks derive from interviews with government officials and officials of the corporative agencies during this period.
2. See the *Boletim do INTP* for this period, 1945–47.
3. The text of this wide-ranging interview was published in *Diario de noticias*, November 14 and 15, 1945.
4. Comissão Parlamentar do Inquérito aos Elementos da Organização Corporativa, "Relatorio," published in the *Diario das sessões* of the National Assembly. Based also on interviews with corporative officials involved in the investigation and its aftermath.
5. Antonio Julio de Castro Fernandes, *Enfrentando o destino das casas do povo.*
6. Carlos Hermenegildo de Sousa, "O panorama da organização corporativa em Portugal."
7. Pintado, "Necessidade de meios de acção especificamente corporativos."
8. Pires Cardoso was the editor of the new *Revista do Gabinete de Estudos Corporativos* (hereafter referred to as *RGEC*); he and the *RGEC*, as we shall see, played key roles in the corporative revival of the 1950s.
9. Graça, "O corporativismo na agricultura."
10. Proença, "Para a explicação de uma crise de ambiente."
11. Ferreira, *Corporativismo português: Doutrina e aplicação.*
12. Barros, "Subsidio para a revisão do corporativismo português."
13. Proença, "Sobre algumas deficiencias de espírito corporativo."
14. Vital, "Desvios do corporativismo português."
15. Caetano, *Posição actual do corporativismo português.*
16. Caetano was shortly named minister of the presidency and was perhaps second in power only to Salazar.
17. Sedas Nunes, *Situação e problemas de corporativismo: Principios corporativos e realidades sociais.*
18. Ironically, Manoïlesco, the inspiration of so much Portuguese corporatist thought, had hinted at much the same thing twenty years earlier in his classic *Le siècle du corporatisme*. On the relations between corpo-

ratism and capitalism, see Philippe C. Schmitter, "Still the Century of Corporatism?"; and Andrew Schoenfield, *Modern Capitalism*.

19. Vol. 1, no. 1, of the *RGEC* appeared in early 1950; between that time and 1961, when it ceased publication, forty-eight issues were published of this important journal.

20. Based on interviews; the critiques in the *RGEC*; and the documents and papers contained in I Coloquio Nacional do Trabalho, da Organização Corporativa e da Previdência Social, *Comunicações*, vol. 3. This volume, based upon a colloquium organized by the Ministry of Corporations, contains 569 pages of tough, biting criticism.

21. Based on the report of the Parliamentary Investigatory Commission as well as the *relatorios* of the Corporative Chamber prepared during this period.

22. Salazar, *Mais um passo na definição e consolidação do regime*, based on a speech to the National Union, and *Discursos*, vol. 5, *1951–1958*, pp. 141–42.

23. Schmitter, "Corporatist Interest Representation and Public Policy-Making in Portugal," p. 15.

24. Salazar, *Revolução corporativa*, esp. the chapter, "Estatuto das corporações," pp. 53–74.

25. See esp. the series of articles by Alves Dinis in *Seara nova*, vol. 28 (1949), dealing with the economic crisis and its relation to the postponement of corporative reforms.

26. Salazar, *Mais um passo*.

27. See his speech reprinted, among other places, in *Boletim do INTP*, vol. 20 (July 15, 1953). In this important speech, Salazar also pointed to the novelty of the corporative experiment which, he said, helped explain some early errors. He also said that the regime had had to stop its growth for a time in order to plan new revisions, take care of certain administrative problems, and make required adjustments. He said the government was aware of the problems of the system and again pointed to the disruptive effects of the war. But, he said, it was necessary to retain the corporative system in order to preserve continuity and to avoid class conflict. Corporatism, he said, was still "at the base" of the system, and now, unless the Portuguese wished to retrogress, it was necessary to complete its construction.

28. Based on interviews with ex-Gabinete officials, Lisbon, 1972/73.

29. *RGEC*, vol. 1 (January-March 1950).

30. In my private library I have the complete collection of the *Revista do Gabinete de Estudos Corporativos*, 1950–61.

31. The creation of a separate Corporations Ministry was attacked both by liberals, who still clung to the hope the whole corporatist structure would wither away, and by corporatist purists like Caetano, who felt the entire national system should be corporatized and that there was hence no need to create a separate Corporations Ministry (indeed, that that

was self-defeating). The discussion of the issue was most intense within the National Assembly; see both the reports of its debates and the final *Relatorio*. The *RGEC* contained several editorials, and the final decree was published in the *Boletim do INTP 17* (September 15, 1950): 413–15.

32. Based on the *Boletim do INTP* for this period.

33. Ibid.; and interviews with Corporations Ministry officials, Lisbon, April 1974.

34. João Manuel Cortez Pinto, *Estrutura e funções da corporação*. After publishing this book, as was the case with so many Portuguese scholars who wrote learnedly on great national themes, Cortez Pinto was soon given a high government position to put his ideas into operation.

35. *Boletim do INTP*, vol. 22 (July 15, 1955). What the editorial writer had in mind by these "bad suggestions" is not specified, though presumably they included the recommendation made by a handful of politicians during this period to abolish entirely the corporative system.

36. The *parecer* was republished as a separate volume by the Ministry of Corporations under the title of *Corporações*, vol. 2 of a 3-vol. series. Vol. 1 of the series contains the full text of the legal statute of the corporations; vol. 3 contains much of the debate as expressed in the National Assembly.

37. See the reports in the press of the discussion in the Assembly for this period, especially "A grande batalha corporativa," *Diario de noticias*, April 4, 1956; based also on interviews with Pires Cardoso and his collaborators, Lisbon, Spring 1973.

38. This argument was presented in great detail in his *parecer*; based also on materials supplied the author by Pires Cardoso.

39. Pires Cardoso, "O problema actual da corporação portuguesa," *Questões corporativas: Doutrina e factos*; Caetano, *Problemas politicos e sociais da actualidade portuguesa*, and *O sistema corporativo*, p. 96. Based also on interviews.

40. Ministerio das Corporações e Previdência Social, *Corporações: Proposta da lei* (Lisbon: Imp. Nacional, 1956).

41. The decree-laws creating the corporations and the respective organic laws were published in the *Boletim do INTP*.

42. See the discussion in Schmitter, "Corporatist Interest Representation," pp. 15–16.

43. The text of the press conference was carried in the Portuguese newspapers of the time; brief excerpts appeared in the *New York Times*, March 18, 1956, p. 2, and in *Keesing's Contemporary Archives* (1956), p. 14,779.

44. Ministerio das Corporações e Previdência Social, *Plano de formação social e corporativa: Proposta da lei* (Lisbon: Imp. Nacional, 1956). More details can be gleaned from Pires Cardoso's *parecer* and from the discussion in the National Assembly.

45. The speeches are reprinted in the *Boletim do INTP*; see esp. 1955–57.

46. The innovations were all recorded in the *Boletim do INTP*.
47. Based on a series of in-house criticisms of the time published later by the Ministry of Corporations (see above, n. 20), as well as on a reading of press accounts and even official statements published in the *Boletim do INTP*; also on opposition documents issued in great numbers during this period.
48. Based on the *Boletim do INTP* for this period.
49. The new journal was called *Análise social*; it came to be Portugal's leading social science journal.
50. I Colóquio Nacional do Trabalho, da Organização Corporativa e da Previdência Social, *Comunicações*. This volume criticized the corporative system from all directions: its philosophical bases, its organization, functions, lack of implementation, etc. One wonders again how such a devastating critique was permitted unless, as seems increasingly clear, the purpose was not as stated, to strengthen the system, but in fact to undermine it.
51. See the critiques of Humberto Delgado, *The Memoirs of General Delgado*; Henrique Galvão, *The Santa Maria: My Crusade for Portugal*; and Antonio de Figueiredo, *Portugal and Its Empire: The Truth*. This was also the assessment of less biased accounts: Oliveira Marques, *History of Portugal*, vol. 2, chap. 13; Kay, *Salazar and Modern Portugal*, chaps. 11–13; and Peter Fryer and Patricia McGowan-Pinheiro, *Oldest Ally*, chaps. 9–10.

Chapter VIII

1. On the economic development, see Francisco Pereira da Moura, "The Development of the Portuguese Economy, 1945–1973." The social changes are outlined in João Baptista Nunes Pereira Neto, "Social Evolution in Portugal since 1945" in Raymond S. Sayers, ed., *Portugal and Brazil in Transition*.
2. See in general Hugh Kay, *Salazar and Modern Portugal*, chap. 12; and Elizabeth Morris, "Portugal's Politics Remain Unaltered." A useful monthly survey of Portuguese events during this period is the *Hispanic American Report*.
3. Morris, "Portugal's Politics," p. 21.
4. Based on interviews with Corporations Ministry officials.
5. It is perhaps appropriate to note at this point the importance of the corporations complex as a political base for a young and ambitious politician. Teotonio Pereira, Marcello Caetano, Trigo de Negreiros, Veiga de Macedo, Gonçalves Proença, and more recently Rebelo de Andrade and Silva Pinto all came out of this context. The reason for this is that work in the corporative system provided one of the few opportunities for a Portuguese politician to get out and see the country, make speeches, establish contacts, and make himself known. As the Corporations Ministry became more a social assistance agency in the 1960s, it

also served an aspiring politician as an almost bottomless bank for funds, favors, assistance, and patronage—a new housing project here, a health facility there, a pension elsewhere, money for a widow here, medical assistance there, a new school, a job, and so on—all of which would eventually have its political payoff in terms of a returned favor from a local politician or support from those served by the ministry.

6. See the *Boletim do INTP* for this period, which contains many of Gonçalves Proença's speeches. See also his *Diálogo corporativo,* and especially his *Corporativismo e política social,* in which the social service orientation is most clearly spelled out.

7. The establishment of the new agencies may be traced in the *Boletim do INTP* as well as in the new scholarly and theoretical journal of the Corporations Ministry, *Estudos sociais e corporativos.*

8. All these activities may be followed in ibid.

9. Reprinted in *Boletim do INTP,* February 28, 1963.

10. Ibid., December 15, 1963.

11. Based on the *Boletim do INTP* for this entire period.

12. *New York Times,* January 20, 1964, p. 4; and May 27, 1966, p. 19.

13. The Center and the Instituto de Estudos Sociais, the latter inaugurated on December 6, 1963, were to be agencies for the study of social problems, in keeping with the new functions of the Corporations Ministry.

14. This and the following information based on an exploration of all issues, from 1962 to present, of *Estudos sociais e corporativos* hereafter referred to as *ESeC.*

15. The reforms of John XXIII, Vatican Council, and the papal encyclicals *Mater et Magistra* and *Pacem in Terris* provided great difficulties for the Portuguese corporatists. For a movement begun in large part on the basis of the corporatist philosophy set forth in *Rerum Novarum* and *Quadragesimo Anno* and which had remained locked in that kind of nineteenth-century Catholic thinking, the strongly reformist and social-democratic pronouncements of the newer encyclicals was little short of revolutionary. The Portuguese corporatists sought, not very successfully, to reconcile the two conceptions, but their national system remained truer to the older than to the newer Catholic ideas. In brief, the Catholic Church had updated itself more rapidly than had the Portuguese system, and for an old-fashioned Catholic-corporatist regime the new orientation of the Church was difficult to accommodate. The failure of the Portuguese regime to adjust and modernize itself, even within the Catholic-corporatist mold, is a theme we return to in the conclusion.

16. See, for example, the editorial in the edition of December 1967; Fernanda Paula Moreira de Freitas Nunes Agria, "O problema da liberdade sindical: Principios e realidades"; José Antonio Moreira, "Corporações: Uma hipótese de integração."

17. Based on interviews with Corporations Ministry officials and especially those of the Centro de Estudos Sociais e Corporativos, the Junta da Acção Social, and the Instituto de Estudos Sociais.

18. The corruption extended upward, apparently to the minister of corporations himself. The minister in question had apparently transferred large sums from the caixas into his personal accounts; when questioned, he said that the money earned higher interest in his own account than in the caixas and that he was merely "protecting" the money for the workers and securing for them a higher interest rate. This kind of embezzlement had become widespread in Portugal by the 1960s. In addition, the government regularly tapped the caixa funds to purchase military hardware for its African wars. Thus not only did Portugal have the lowest by far ratio of funds for social security to GNP in all of Western Europe, but even the small funds it did have were systematically siphoned off.

19. Paraphrased from Philippe C. Schmitter, "Corporatist Interest Representation and Public Policy-Making in Portugal," p. 16.

20. Ibid.

21. The conclusion here also echoes that of Schmitter, ibid., p. 17.

22. It should be noted that we lack solid monographic studies of almost all these agencies; the analysis that follows is based on the materials currently available.

23. "O problema dos fundamentos do corporativismo," in I Coloquio Nacional do Trabalho, da Organização Corporativa e da Previdência Social, *Comunicações,* vol. 3.

24. *ESeC,* vol. 1 (April-June 1962).

25. *ESeC,* vol. 6 (December 1967), editorial.

26. Based on interviews with Junta da Acção Social and Instituto de Estudos Sociais officials, who were the leading contributors to *Estudos sociais e corporativos.*

27. See his writings as mentioned in n. 6 above, as well as the evolution of his ideas in the speeches printed in the *Boletim do INTP.*

28. This theme is dealt with in more detail below; see Harry Makler, "Political Men among the Portuguese Industrial Elite."

29. Based on field work and interviews in Portugal, 1972/73.

30. Decree-law 40,324 of October 6, 1955.

31. Kay, *Salazar and Modern Portugal,* p. 329. See also the volumes of *pareceres* issued annually by the Chamber from 1935 on; and also J. Pires Cardoso, *Questões corporativas,* pp. 140–50. Pires Cardoso was also a member of the Corporative Chamber .

32. "Corporatist Interest Representation," pp. 18–21.

33. His data are presented in a series of charts interspersed through pp. 18–21. It is worth noting that sometimes the cooptation function failed to work; General Delgado, for example, who presented the regime with a serious political challenge in 1958, got his start in politics in the early 1950s as a representative of the armed forces in the Corporative Chamber. See his *Memoirs,* p. 87.

34. Schmitter, "Corporatist Interest Representation," p. 21; based also on interviews with former Chamber representatives.

35. A useful summary is "The Corporate State: An Incomplete Experiment in Portugal," *Times-Supplement,* October 25, 1955.

36. Based on interviews with Portuguese government and Corporations Ministry officials, and with officers of the corporations, Lisbon, 1972/73 and March/April 1974.

37. See especially Jerónimo de Melo Osorio de Castro and Maria Adelaide Wanderley de Sousa Martins, *A actividade da Corporação da Pesca e Conservas.*

38. Silva Pinto, *Corporações já instituidas: Análise da sua estrutura e funcionamento.*

39. *República,* June 26, 1973, p. 7.

40. Osorio de Castro and Sousa Martins, *A actividade da Corporação;* and Corporação do Comercio, *As corporações na economia nacional.* The latter study is one of the most thorough made of the corporations. Based also on interviews with corporations officials and on participant observation within the corporations.

41. Ibid.

42. Schmitter, "Corporatist Interest Representation"; Manuel Alberto Andrade e Sousa (president of the Corporation of Commerce), *O corporativismo português;* I Coloquio Nacional do Comércio, *Resume e conclusões dos Temas apresentados;* and Makler, "Political Men." Makler's study points especially to the exchange and interrelations between the business elites and the corporative agencies, the fact that many of the industrial elite simultaneously held positions in the corporative complex, and the fact that there was a constant and reciprocal "coming and going" between the business and industrial elites (especially its younger elements) and the offices and directing councils of the gremios and corporative bodies.

43. J. Pires Cardoso, *Corporações morais e culturais;* and Jorge Sampaio and Jorge Santos, "Em torno da universidade." Based also on interviews with Corporations Ministry officials.

44. João Manuel Cortez Pinto, *As corporações no espaço português.* Given Cortez Pinto's position within the corporative establishment and his role as the spokesman for the new (limited) conception of corporatism, his statement may be considered as the official, although perhaps inadvertently spoken, view. The creation of corporative entities designed purposely not to function is a theme that also runs through Manuel Lucena's *L'evolution du système corporatif portugais à travers les lois (1933–1971).*

45. Freeman, *The Political Process: Executive Bureau-Legislative Committee Relations.*

46. These functions are given in detail in Corporação do Comercio, *As corporações;* and in Osorio de Castro and Sousa Martins, *A actividade da corporação.*

47. A useful general description is Edmund Stevens, "Portugal under Dr. Salazar."

48. Budget figures provided in the government's *Anuario estatístico* (Lisbon: Instituto Nacional de Estatística).
49. Paraphrased from Stevens, "Portugal," p. 65; see also Freppel Cotta, *Economic Planning in Corporative Portugal.*
50. A recent study is Francisco Pereira da Moura, *Por onde vai a economia portuguesa?*; also Alvaro Cunhal, *A questão agraria em Portugal.*
51. Many of these horror stories regarding corruption at high levels came out in the uncensored press following the April 1974 coup.
52. See the *Boletim do INTP* for this period.
53. Based on interviews with Corporations Ministry officials.
54. There is as yet no adequate study of the Corporations Ministry itself; Laurence S. Graham included this ministry among the four he studied as a part of his research on the Portuguese "Bureaucracy of Empire," but the results of his research are not yet available.
55. Based on interviewing and participant observation, 1972/73.
56. See the discussion in Howard J. Wiarda, "The Portuguese Corporative System: Basic Structures and Current Functions"; also José Antonio Barreiros, "Comissões Corporativas," a series of articles published in *Republica,* March/April 1974.
57. Ibid.; based also on interviews with Corporations Ministry officials, most of whom were quite frank and open about the biases built into the system. See also Ernesto Coutinho, "Negociações colectivas e abuso do direito de despedimento." Coutinho wrote a series of sensitive articles on labor affairs for *Expresso.*
58. See the discussion in Chap. 4.
59. Peter Fryer and Patricia McGowan-Pinheiro, *Oldest Ally,* p. 124.
60. The positions are stated in Mario Morais de Oliveira, *Aspectos actuais do corporativismo perante a vida económica,* and in his *O regime corporativo e os Organismos de Coordenação Económica.* Oliveira was a deputy in the National Assembly, in whose proceedings this debate can be followed in detail.
61. This conclusion echoes Schmitter's in "Corporatist Interest Representations," p. 18.
62. *Oldest Ally,* p. 124.
63. Mário Pinto and Carlos Moura, "Estruturas sindicais portuguesas: Contributo para o seu estudo." See also A. Ramos, "Industry in Portugal."
64. Of course, if one counts the "contributing members," the figure goes up slightly, but that would imply counting employers in with workers, hardly a fair measure of the extent of working-class organization. The figures used in the Pinto and Moura study are contained in *Estatísticas da organização corporativa* (1969), published yearly by the Instituto Nacional de Estatística.
65. "La CISL internazionale per la libertà sindicale in Portogallo."
66. The exile literature, however biased, is the best source for analyses of the inequities and abuses of the system; see, for instance, Luiza Almeida, "Some Aspects of Labour Organisation under Salazar's Fascist

Regime"; and Mario Soares, *Le Portugal bailloné: Un témoignage.*

67. Barbara Tuchman's portrait of pre-World War I society in the more developed European nations provides an interesting parallel to Portugal in the 1960s; see *The Proud Tower,* pp. 50–51, 367–68.

68. Makler, "Political Men."

69. The discussion here follows Schmitter, "Corporatist Interest Representation," pp. 11–14.

70. Alvaro Henriques de Almeida, "Os gremios obrigatorios e as suas funções de intervenção económica."

71. Schmitter, "Corporatist Interest Representation," pp. 11–14.

72. Based on interviews with corporations and gremio officials.

73. Ibid.

74. Makler, "Political Men," pp. 6, 11; refer also to n. 4, above.

75. For the ideas and conclusions in this paragraph the author has relied upon the careful analysis of Harry M. Makler "The Portuguese Industrial Elite and Its Corporative Relations: A Study of Compartmentalization in an Authoritarian Regime."

76. Information on the ordens is extremely spotty; I have relied upon episodic information, some interviews, and occasional published reports in such periodicals as *Expresso, Republica,* and *Vida mundial.* The lack of information is probably related to the ordens' limited importance. Some individual members were influential, especially those in the Ordem dos Advogados, if they also held important government posititions; but their professional associations were not very influential and usually functioned as still another bureaucratic control mechanism of the regime.

77. See the useful pamphlet put out by the office of the Secretary of State of Information and Tourism, *Occupational Organization,* in the "Portugal Today" series.

78. Based on interviews with corporations and casa do povo officials; also on participant observation within these agencies; as well as on data supplied in the *Boletim do INTP,* the *RGEC, ESeC,* and the monthly *Mensario das casas do povo,* a small, twenty-page magazine begun in 1946, full of practical advice aimed at casa do povo members but containing also a wealth of information about the casas.

79. *Actualidades,* January 14, 1973, pp. 1ff.

80. Castro Fernandes, *Enfrentando o destino das casas do povo.*

81. F. Cid Proença, "Problemas actuais da organização corporativa do meio rural," in I Coloquio Nacional do Trabalho, da Organização Corporativa e da Previdência Social, *Comunicações,* 3: 313–32.

82. Fryer and McGowan-Pinheiro, *Oldest Ally,* p. 124.

83. Comissão de Política Social Rural, INTP, *Inquérito sobre organização corporativa rural (casas do povo).* As noted, this was one of the regime's few attempts to find out what the *casas* themselves wanted, but even this effort did not really reach very far down: only *casa do povo* leaders were sampled, and they were obligated to respond collectively, as a casa delegation, not individually.

84. Ministerio das Corporações e da Previdência Social, *A reorganização das casas do povo e a previdência social*; H. Veiga de Macedo, *Casas do povo e previdência rural*; and Junta Central das Casas do Povo, *Protecção aos trabalhadores rurais atraves a solução corporativa.*
85. "Peasants and Politics in Portugal: The Corporate State and Village 'Non-Politics.' "
86. *A Portuguese Rural Society,* chaps. 14–15.
87. Based on a perusal of the relevant parts of the theses written under Pereira Neto's direction, and on data supplied by Pereira Neto.
88. Cutileiro, *Portuguese Rural Society*; also *New York Times,* April 15, 1955, p. 4.
89. Branca do Amaral, "A organização corporativa da lavoura e a crise da agricultura portuguesa"; and by the same author, "Política agricola e gremios da lavoura."
90. See especially Jerónimo de Melo Osorio de Castro, "Acción social de las casas de pescadores"; and de Castro and Francisco Roseiro e Maia, "Reestruturação das casas dos pescadores," in 11 Coloquio Nacional do Trabalho, da Organização Corporativa e da Previdência Social, *Comunicações,* pp. 185–91. Based also on interviews with corporations and casa officials and on participant observation.
91. Christine Garnier, *Salazar: An Intimate Portrait,* p. 196.
92. Pereira Neto, "Social Evolution," p. 212.
93. *Programa para a democratização da republica* (Porto: Tip. J. R. Gonçalves, 1961).
94. F. Cid Proença, "Autenticidade e eficacia em organização corporativa." Among other things Proença asked whether the corporative agencies' functions were not such that they could be performed by other agencies.
95. José Cardosa Pires' *Dinossauro excelentissimo,* a thinly disguised parody of the Salazar regime, achieved instant best-seller status by concentrating on this theme.

Chapter IX

1. For some general comments on the succession problem in authoritarian systems, see J. D. Hertzler, "The Typical Life Style of Dictatorships"; John H. Herz, "The Problem of Successorship in Dictatorial Regimes: A Study in Comparative Law and Institutions"; Lewis J. Edinger, "Post-Totalitarian Leadership Elites in the German Federal Republic"; Arpad von Lazar, "Latin America and the Politics of Post-Authoritarianism"; and Keith Botsford, "Succession and Ideology in Spain and Portugal."
2. The chronology follows that given in *Keesing's Contemporary Archives,* October 5–12, 1968, p. 22,959.
3. Salazar lingered on in a fitful state for nearly two more years; he died on July 27, 1970, apparently without knowing he had been removed as prime minister. He was denied access to newspapers, radio, and television on the grounds they might tire him; aides and ministers kept up

the charade of talking with him as though he were still head of state, and he continued to live in the São Bento Palace, the premier's official residence. But he no longer made decisions and, except as his ghost and influence remained even after death, had no impact on the policies of the new government.

4. See his *Lições de direito corporativo* (1935), *A constituição de 1933* (1956), *Manual do direito administrativo* (1947), *Problemas políticos e sociais da actualidade portuguesa* (1956), *Manual de ciencia política e direito constitucional* (numerous eds.), *O sistema corporativo* (1938), *Problemas da revolução corporativa* (1941), *Tradições, principios, e metodos da colonização portuguesa* (1951), and numerous others.

5. See the dispatch from Lisbon of Richard Eder in the *New York Times,* September 21, 1968, p. 13.

6. Quoted in ibid. For Caetano's own statement of his aims, as well as the conditions on which he was allowed to take office, see his *Depoimento.*

7. A good interpretation is Henry H. Keith, "Point, Counterpoint in Reforming Portuguese Education, 1750–1973."

8. One cannot resist remarking that, after viewing so many of the plastic Nixon PR efforts on television, the Caetano appearances were a welcome change. Appearing sans makeup and without a formal text, Caetano, perhaps Portugal's leading political scientist and constitutional lawyer, would explain the government's actions and rationale like a superb scholar informally spinning off and developing ideas in a classroom—in Caetano's case, complete with televised footnotes!

9. On the "forms" and "appearances," see Loren Jenkins, "New Style of Tyranny"; the quote is from *New York Times,* May 25, 1969.

10. An account sensitive to the real political issues involved is that of Richard Eder in *New York Times,* October 26, 1969, p. 18.

11. See especially the account of Marvine Howe in *New York Times,* August 20, 1972, p. 16.

12. "Point, Counterpoint," pp. 1, 2, 9, 10.

13. The discussion here follows the useful background provided by Marvine Howe in *New York Times,* April 5, 1971, p. 20. Another useful account is Bonnie Potter, "Election Time in Portugal: A Time for Reflection." For the decrees, see *Boletim do INTP;* based also on interviews and field work in Portugal, 1972/73.

14. The changes are summarized in Henrique Nascimento Rodrigues, *Regime juridico das relações colectivas de trabalho.*

15. One of the claims made by the Communists after the 1974 coup was that during the preceding years they had *secretly* been able to infiltrate a number of key unions and thus build a base of support. The fact is the Caetano government largely knew who the Communists were and what unions (clerks, bank workers, metallurgists) they had infiltrated; for its own political purposes, the government had acquiesced in and even encouraged to a degree the Communist activities. The secret Communist activity took place chiefly in the clandestine factory "unity committees."

16. A thoughtful, subtle discussion of the Caetano changes is Douglas L. Wheeler, "Thaw in Portugal." Caetano's turn back to the Right had already begun by the time Wheeler's essay with its emphasis on the "thaw" appeared.

17. It may be, in other words, if the third interpretation is correct, that Caetano was neither "liberal" nor so authoritarian as Salazar but mainly weak and indecisive, that we must look for explanations of Salazar's long-lived rule—and the subsequent collapse of the Estado Novo—not so much in terms of its authoritarian structures as in its autocratic nature. Salazar's Portugal may have been, in other words, more the rule of one man than of "a system." This helps explain Caetano's failure, for he simply lacked the personal strength and power that his predecessor wielded, as well as the ability by sheer force of personality and strong will to hold the nation together. An explanation that focuses on the autocratic aspects of Salazar's rule may also help explain why an "authoritarian" system thought to be so impregnable collapsed so quickly and completely in the wake of the April 1974 coup. What was thought to be a *system* of authoritarian state controls may in fact have been the power of one man; and when he gave way, they too collapsed. Without Salazar's guidance and strong direction, without the *chefe* and iron-willed ruler who had guided the country for almost forty years, the system began to come apart. And under his less strong-willed successor, who held the reins more loosely but, because of that, began increasingly to lose control, the political system began to fragment further, culminating in the 1974 revolt, which in turn resulted in the unleashing of additional disintegrative tendencies.

18. Some useful summaries of the Caetano regime are Council of Europe, "Introductory Report on Human Rights in Portugal"; R. C., "Portugal: A Political and Economic Survey"; and *New York Times,* May 10, 1969, p. 10; April 18, 1971, p. 1; and August 20, 1972, p. 16.

19. In making this statement Caetano was seeking to dispel the suspicion that the government was *not* planning to be faithful to the corporative ideals; in fact, in the aftermath of Salazar's incapacity, there was talk, not widespread and quickly quashed by Caetano's speeches and action, of doing away with the corporative system. The Caetano speech of October 10, 1968, was published in the *Boletim do INTP,* vol. 35 (October 15, 1968), and also as an independent pamphlet by the National Information Service. See also the article, "A fidelidade de Marcello Caetano" ["The fidelity or loyalty of Marcello Caetano"] in the right-wing Salazarista journal, *Opinião,* no. 15 (2d fortnight of October 1972).

20. Published in *Boletim do INTP,* vol. 25 (November 15, 1968), and again as a separate pamphlet by the SNI under the title, "Corporative Revolution, Permanent Revolution." It was significant that Caetano stressed the *promise* of corporatism rather than its accomplishments—a backhanded slap at Salazar.

21. These changes may be followed in the *Boletim do INTP* as well as in the *Diario de noticias,* which regularly published the full text of government decrees and pronouncements.
22. See Caetano's statement in *Boletim do INTP,* vol. 37 (January 31, 1970), and Rebelo's in *Diario de noticias,* January 16, 1973, p. 7.
23. *A reorganização das casas do povo e a previdência rural.*
24. *Diario de noticias,* February 25, 1973, p. 7; *Boletim do INTP,* May 31, 1969, pp. 512f; *ESeC* (June 1969): 5–18; *Jornal do comércio,* October 10, 1972, p. 2.
25. João F. de Almeida Policarpo, "Conflitos colectivos de trabalho e sistema corporativo," *ESeC,* VIII (September 1969), 17–34; see also the editorial in this issue.
26. At the end of 1972 there were six institutes, three juntas, and two commissions still functioning, a total of eleven Organizations of Economic Coordination. They were the Institute of Olive Oil and Oil Products, the Institute of Cereals, the Institute of Forestry Products, the Institute of Textiles, the Institute of Port Wine, the Portuguese Institute of Fish Products, the National Junta of Fruits, the National Junta of Meat Products, the National Junta of Wine, the Regulatory Commission for the Cod Trade, and the Regulatory Commission of Chemical and Pharmaceutical Products.
27. Brinton, *Anatomy of Revolution*; and Ted Robert Gurr, *Why Men Rebel.* For basic data on the Portuguese economy, see the annual OECD economic surveys, *Portugal* (Paris: Organization for Economic Cooperation and Development, 1971, 1972, 1973).
28. This list was elaborated in a major summary of corporative accomplishments by the secretary of state of labor and social assistance, Joaquim Dias da Silva Pinto in *Boletim do INTP* 40 (October 8, 1973): 3247–60. See also his summary presented at the I Congress of the ANP, published in *Diario de noticias,* July 5, 1973, esp. articles 40–59.
29. The new programs are elaborated in the *Boletim do INTP* for this period. See also the pamphlet issued by the SNI, *Present Trends in Portuguese Social Policy.* The philosophy of the *Estado Social* was best explained in the collected volumes of Caetano's speeches, especially his *Estado social,* as well as in two immense volumes by Labor and Social Assistance Secretary of State Silva Pinto, *Política do trabalho: Factor de desenvolvimento* (1972) and *Desenvolvimento social: Objectivo prioritário* (1974), both published under the auspices of the Junta da Acção Social. See also Caetano's later summing up in his *Depoimento,* chap. 4.
30. These programs, although confined often to the labor elites of Luanda and Lourenço Marques, were significant nonetheless; see the journal *Trabalho* (Bulletin of the Institute of Labor, Assistance, and Social Action of Angola), of which I have a complete collection, nos. 1–40, in my personal library.

31. See especially the position papers dealing with labor and corporative affairs presented at the III Congresso da Oposição Demácratica, Aveiro, April 4–8, 1973.
32. Taken from *Programa para a democratização da Republica*. This opposition statement served as the base for the dismantling and reorganization of the corporative system in the wake of the 1974 revolution.
33. On labor relations, see especially the columns of Ernesto Coutinho; for the theme of the superfluousness of corporatism, see Soares Martinez, "A evolução para o estado pos-corporativo."
34. Based on interviews with Portuguese labor leaders, 1972/73.
35. Based on interviews with officials of the corporative system; for an official statement taking cognizance of the system's problems, see the remarks of Silva Pinto in *Boletim do INTP* 40 (March 8, 1973): 370–78.
36. Based on interviews with Caetano government officials and officials of the corporative system, Lisbon, 1972/73, and March/April 1974.
37. The best source is the *Boletim do INTP*. For additional documentation, see the *Diario de noticias* for this period. Based also on interviews and participant observation in Portugal during this period.
38. On this theme, see the intriguing essay by Philippe C. Schmitter, "Still the Century of Corporatism?" Schmitter's point is that the twentieth century *has* turned out to be the century of de facto corporatism, in accord with Manoïlesco's famous book, although the labels used are not necessarily the corporatist ones.

Chapter X

1. For Portugal, these questions are raised also by Philippe C. Schmitter in his "Corporatist Interest Representation and Public Policy-Making in Portugal"; and Manuel Lucena, *L'evolution du système portugais à travers les lois (1933–1971)*. The issue of the actual functions and role of corporatism is raised more generally by Ronald C. Newton, "The Corporate Idea and the Authoritarian Tradition in Spain and Spanish America: Some Critical Observations"; and Ralph Bowen, *German Theories of the Corporate State*.
2. The Bonapartist model is presented in Karl Marx, *The Eighteenth Brumaire of Louis Bonaparte;* and in Philippe C. Schmitter, "The 'Portugalization' of Brazil," in Alfred Stepan, ed., *Authoritarian Brazil*, pp. 179–232. On *cacique* rule, see Robert Kern, ed., *The Caciques*, especially the essay by William Brisk on "The New *Caciquismo*." The concept of the moderating role of the monarchy stems from much nineteenth-century Portuguese *and* Brazilian literature; it is worth noting that when long-time President Carmona died in 1951 Salazar seriously considered a restoration of much the same kind of limited, constitutional monarchical rule, but with Salazar himself continuing to make the major decisions. The continuing and central role of Salazar in the Portuguese

system during this entire period is stressed by Christine Garnier, *Salazar: An Intimate Portrait*; Christian Rudel, *Le Portugal et Salazar*; and Hugh Kay, *Salazar and Modern Portugal*.

3. Galvão, *The Santa Maria: My Crusade for Portugal*.

4. H. R. Trevor-Roper, "The Phenomenon of Fascism," in S. J. Woolf, ed., *European Fascism*.

5. The analysis here follows closely and in part paraphrases that of Peter Fryer and Patricia McGowan-Pinheiro, *Oldest Ally: A Portrait of Salazar's Portugal*, pp. 136–70. A fascinating parallel is Spain; see Stanley Payne, *Falange: A History of Spanish Fascism*.

6. *Oldest Ally*.

7. Ibid.; also Schmitter, "Corporatist Interest Representation," conclusion.

8. See his "Corporatist Interest Representation," pp. 16–17. This paragraph and the next two draw heavily on that account; see also Garnier, *Salazar*.

9. See again Barbara Tuchman, *The Proud Tower*.

10. Based on the field work, interviews, and personal observations in Portugal, 1972/73; see also sociologist A. Sedas Nunes' treatment of "dualistic society" in Portugal (*Sociologia e ideologia do desenvolvimento*), a work which parallels similar studies done for Brazil and other Latin American countries.

11. The analysis here and in the following paragraphs follows closely that of Laurence S. Graham, "Portugal: The Bureaucracy of Empire."

12. Ibid., pp. 3–8, 42–44. See also Marcello Caetano, *Manual de direito administrativo português*; and also his "Problemas actuales de la administración pública portuguesa," pp. 260–63.

13. Graham, "Portugal," pp. 14–18.

14. Joyce Riegelhaupt, "Peasants and Politics in Portugal: The Corporate State and Village 'Non-Politics,'" p. 23. See also Norman Blume, "The Portuguese Freguesia."

15. A useful summary is in Fryer and McGowan-Pinheiro, *Oldest Ally*, pp. 193–98.

16. See especially decree-law 35,042 published in the *Diario do governo*, October 20, 1945; also decree-law 37,447, likewise published in the *Diario*.

17. Almost everyone who traveled to Portugal encountered the secret police in one capacity or another, and those who lived there for a time usually had one or another horror story to relate. My own encounters were rather limited: the DGS, which in addition to its other functions also handled passports and immigration permits, double-checked our visas and raised a question concerning whether our papers were in order on two occasions when we entered Portugal; reports concerning the materials I had used were submitted to the DGS by several agencies and libraries where I had carried out research; after a bomb went off on the third floor of the Corporations Ministry, my briefcase and person were searched by DGS agents on several subsequent occasions

when I entered the building to conduct interviews or to use the ministry's library; almost certainly not my own, but the phones of others (U.S. embassy officials, fellow scholars, Portuguese politicians) with whom I talked were tapped.

18. Fernando Antunes, "As cortes gerais do regime." Other useful summaries may be found in *Expresso,* May 5, 1973, p. 12; March 30, 1974, p. 17; and April 13, 1974, p. 17.

19. For these uses of the party, which are far more subtle than those implied in the term "single-party regime," see *Vida mundial,* January 5, 1973, pp. 9-16ff; May 16, 1973, pp. 16ff; and November 2, 1973, pp. 3ff.

20. It should be noted here that the corporative system was also tied into the party in various ways: the party had its own corporative studies center; it helped diffuse the corporative ideology; corporative leaders (Salazar, Caetano, Castro Fernandes, Silva Pinto) often occupied simultaneously high posts within the party; the corporative agencies and personnel at the local level often overlapped with governmental and party agencies and personnel; the Corporations Ministry's health and assistance programs often served as the patronage local party officials dispensed; the *jornadas* and other meetings organized by the Corporations Ministry were often ways of mobilizing support for the government and its political machine; etc.

21. These comments regarding the role of the military in Portuguese politics were formulated with the Salazar-Caetano regime in mind, but, with the appropriate refinements and qualifications, they may have continuing relevance for the period since the 1974 revolution—for a detailed treatment, see Howard J. Wiarda "The Portuguese Revolution: Towards Explaining the Political Behavior of the Armed Forces Movement."

22. Bruneau, "The Politics of Religion in an Authoritarian Regime: The Case of Portugal," p. 20; see also Joaquim Maria Lourenço, *Situação jurídica da igreja em Portugal.*

23. "Politics of Religion," pp. 20, 22, 25, 31, and 43; an interesting interpretation is Silas Cerqueira, "L'eglise et la dictature portugaise."

24. See especially Graham, "Portugal," pp. 34–39.

25. Ibid.

26. An especially good discussion is Laurence S. Graham, "Latin America: Illusion or Reality? A Case for a New Analytic Framework for the Region," in Wiarda, ed., *Politics and Social Change in Latin America,* pp. 231–48.

27. Andrew Shonfield, *Modern Capitalism;* for the Iberic-Latin tradition, see William P. Glade, *The Latin American Economies: A Study of Their Institutional Evolution,* esp. pt. 2. The theme of the "mercantilist" nature of the Portuguese economic system merits a more detailed treatment.

28. The best source on these groups and their holdings is Maria Belmira Martins, *Sociedades e grupos em Portugal.* The tracing of these hold-

ings, their interconnections, the channels of influence, etc., would be an extremely important contribution to our understanding of how the Portuguese system worked. Many of these holdings were nationalized following the 1974 revolution, a step that was not quite so radical as it might sound given the fact, as the present discussion emphasizes, that they were inseparable from the state system to begin with.

29. Based on interviews with representatives of these groups, with Portuguese government officials, and with U.S. embassy personnel in the political and commercial sections. My own experience with the workings of these grupos comes from (1) trying to function in Portugal at levels other than that of a tourist—opening and operating a bank account, renting an apartment, purchasing a car and auto insurance, etc.; and (2) trying to complete my interview schedule. In seeking to locate and arrange appointments with present or former officials of the corporative agencies, I invariably found myself chasing them down in the plush, thickly carpeted, limousine world of SACOR, the banks, the big holding companies. Simply viewing the opulence of these enterprises from the inside is an experience that every student of Portuguese society and politics, regardless of his specific research interests, should have.

30. For the patterns see Harry Makler, "Political Men among the Portuguese Industrial Elite."

31. This and the following paragraphs are based on widespread interviewing of representatives of all the groups mentioned, Portuguese government officials, and informed foreign observers.

32. For an essay on the Brazilian military which analyzes both its rising professionalism and its rising politicization, see Alfred Stepan, "The New Professionalism of Internal Warfare and Military Role Expansion," in Stepan, ed., *Authoritarian Brazil,* pp. 47–65.

33. A statue of Teotonio Pereira was scheduled to be placed in the Praça de Londres in front of the Corporations Ministry which he had helped originate, but those plans were canceled after the 1974 coup.

34. For some of Franco Nogueira's ideas, see his *As crises e os homens.*

35. Based on the interviews and on participant observation.

36. Ibid.; see also the newspaper accounts for the period 1972–74. A useful survey of the "political currents' in Portugal during this period is *Expresso,* June 16, 1973. A sensitive account of the opposition and its strategies is Herminio Martins, "Opposition in Portugal."

37. The distinction between a rejection of the system per se and a rejection of the particular form it took under Salazar was made in numerous interviews, especially by government officials. On the freezing of the elite, see especially Henry H. Keith, "Point, Counterpoint in Reforming Portuguese Education, 1750–1973"; also Armando Castro, *Desenvolvimento económico ou estagnação?*

38. Charles W. Anderson, "Toward a Theory of Latin American Politics"; Douglas Chalmers, "Crisis and Change in Latin America"; and Kalman

Silvert, "The Politics of Social and Economic Change in Latin America." Both the Anderson and the Silvert essays are included in Wiarda, ed., *Politics and Social Change*.

Chapter XI

1. At the time of the coup there was not (to my knowledge) a single U.S. reporter in Portugal or one stationed there on a permanent and regular basis. The press accounts almost inevitably, therefore, focused on the surface aspects without much comprehension of the subtler undercurrents of Portuguese politics or the immediate and long-range events leading up to the overthrow.

2. This account is based on renewed field work in Portugal during March/April 1974 and May/June, 1975. The author's assessment of the coup and the revolution that followed are contained in the following reports and essays: "The Portuguese Coup of April, 1974: Background and Preliminary Assessment"; "Prospects for Portugal"; *Transcending Corporatism? The Portuguese Corporative System and the Revolution of 1974*; "Can We Learn to Live with a Socialist World? Foreign Policy Implications Stemming from the Portuguese Revolution and Other 'New Forces' "; "The Portuguese Revolution: Towards Explaining the Political Behavior of the Armed Forces Movement"; and "Portugal: The Two Revolutions."

3. *Portugal e o futuro* (Arcadia, 1974). Arcadia is a publishing house that is part of Portugal's largest conglomerate, the Grupo CUF. The reasons for the book's publication by a CUF subsidiary are interesting to ponder.

4. The book is hardly a major work of political philosophy; it is really a political tract, a manifesto, vague but uplifting, and clearly designed to appeal to the widest range of political opinion. See the discussion in Neil Bruce, *Portugal: The Last Empire*.

5. See Caetano's *Depoimento,* published after his ouster.

6. See Kenneth Maxwell, "Portugal: A Neat Revolution"; based also on interviews in the prime minister's office, March/April 1974.

7. For two articles whose treatments, although from varied political perspectives, parallel this one, see Maxwell, "Portugal"; and Peter Witonski, "Portugal: The Spirit of Regeneration." See also Steven Ussach, seven articles following the Portuguese revolution of April, 1974, in the *New Bedford Standard Times,* May/June 1974.

8. *Os Portugueses e a política: 1973*; for the economic figures, see Philippe C. Schmitter, "Liberation by Golpe: Retrospective Thoughts on the Demise of Authoritarian Rule in Portugal."

9. *New York Times,* June 11, 1974. Wicker's point is precisely the one Salazar and Caetano used to make in arguing for wage restraint in a country without the wealth to afford more.

10. *New York Times,* June 18, 1974, October 5, 1974, and October 6, 1974. The dispatch by Henry Giniger on October 5 is an especially insightful interpretation.

11. *Vida mundial* 35 (May 10, 1974): 3. In its post-coup issues *Vida mundial* carried a useful day-by-day chronology of the revolution's major events.

12. A useful summary of the changes in and prospects for the corporative system appeared in *Expresso,* May 4, 1974, p. 19; also September 7, 1974, p. 13. The decrees dissolving or reorganizing the corporative system are found in the *Boletim do INTP* for this period. These and other research materials were collected by the author in May/June, 1975, during field work for a study of the dismantling of the corporative system.

13. Witonski, "Portugal"; and Wiarda, "Portugal: The Two Revolutions."

14. Recall the arguments presented in chapter 1 as well as in Wiarda, "Toward a Framework for the Study of Political Change in the Iberic-Latin Tradition: The Corporative Model"; and "Corporatism and Development in the Iberic-Latin World: Persistent Strains and New Variations." Consult also the essay by Philippe C. Schmitter, "Still the Century of Corporatism?" the latter two articles published in book form and with two new essays added, under the editorship of Frederick B. Pike and Thomas Stritch, *The New Corporatism: Social and Political Structures in the Iberian World.*

15. In attempting to portray the earlier "liberal" era in a favorable light and to make the succeeding "corporatist" one look worse, Schmitter has probably exaggerated the level of Portuguese "associability" prior to 1926. See his "Corporatist Interest Representation and Public Policy-Making in Portugal," esp. pp. 6–8.

16. See the feature essay in the *Times* (London), May 21, 1959, p. 11.

17. In Schmitter's essay, "Corporatist Interest Representation," there are some interesting statistics comparing Portugal, Greece, and Ireland in terms of public policy output in the postwar period. Although the record is mixed, Portugal comes out slightly lower than the others. Purporting to compare *system* performance, these statistics are a bit misleading chiefly in terms of the time period covered. No one quarrels with the conclusion that Portugal's public policy output declined relatively in the postwar period, but if comparable figures were available for the prewar decade the picture would likely be different. Further, the medio-cre Portuguese performance in the postwar period may have been due not so much to the corporative system as a "system" but to Salazar's stubbornness and eventual senility, or to other variables. In this regard, it is interesting to speculate regarding recent comparative data generated for a longer period, going back to 1900, which show that most nations have remained largely "in place," in terms of the rank order of economi-cally developed countries, neither shooting ahead nor falling far behind

—despite changes of regime, various "isms," and experimentation with several "systems." Germany is perhaps a case in point; so probably, at the other end of the spectrum, is Portugal.

18. *Expresso,* June 22, 1974, p. 10.

19. It should be emphasized that a number of the comments here made are speculative rather than following conclusively from the evidence presented in the text. Given the absence of much research on Portugal, such speculation is justified, I believe, as hopefully stimulating further research into these questions.

20. "Corporatist Interest Representation," esp. p. 11 and conclusion.

21. For the debate, see the initial statement by John J. Johnson, *Political Change in Latin America: The Emergence of the Middle Sectors,* which focuses on this earlier period and argues for the "progressive" nature of the middle class; the "reactionary" view is presented by James Petras, "The Latin American Middle Class"; perspectives emphasizing both viewpoints include Charles Wagley, *The Latin American Tradition,* chap. 7; and Luis Ratinoff, "The New Urban Groups: The Middle Classes," in Lipset and Solari, eds., *Elites in Latin America,* pp. 61–93.

22. Sharpe, "In-Corporation through Agrarian Reform: The Consequences of Catholic *Acción Social,*" in James M. Malloy, ed., *Authoritarianism and Corporatism in Latin America.*

23. The parallel with pre-World War I Europe is again remarkable; see Barbara Tuchman, *The Proud Tower,* esp. pp. 50–51 and 367–68.

24. See the comments of Jacques Rueff, a French economist and inspirer of Salazar's financial policies going back to 1928, in *Expresso,* June 2, 1973.

25. There are some significant developmental parallels here with the regime of Rafael Trujillo in the Dominican Republic, which spanned roughly the same historical epochs; see Howard J. Wiarda, *Dictatorship and Development: The Methods of Control in Trujillo's Dominican Republic,* conclusion.

26. *L'evolution du système corporatif portugais à travers les lois (1933–1971),* quoted in Schmitter, "Corporatist Interest Representation," p. 1 of conclusion.

27. October 20, 1973.

28. Wheeler, "Thaw in Portugal"; also Peter McDonough, "Structural Factors in the Decline and Fall of Portuguese Corporatism."

29. The question is raised in Ronald C. Newton, "The Corporate Idea and the Authoritarian Tradition in Spain and Spanish America: Some Critical Observations."

30. The discussion here follows that of ibid., pp. 1–8; and Ralph Bowen, *German Theories of the Corporate State.*

31. In the essay cited above, Newton had objected to the use of the term *corporatism* to describe this tradition, but in a more recent essay he expressly repudiates these objections and uses the term *natural cor-*

poratism in much the same way this study has referred to a distinctly "corporative tradition" or "corporative model." See Ronald C. Newton, "Natural Corporatism and the Passing of Populism in Spanish America."

32. Organski, *The Stages of Political Development* (New York: Knopf, 1965), esp. chap. 5; see also his "Fascism and Modernization," in S. J. Woolf, ed., *The Nature of Fascism*; and Gino Germani's essay, "Fascism and Class," in the same volume.

33. Wiarda, "Toward a Framework for the Study of Political Change in the Iberic-Latin Tradition," "Corporatism and Development in the Iberic-Latin World," and *Politics and Social Change in Latin America.*

34. Gabriel A. Almond and Sidney Verba, *The Civic Culture: Policy Attitudes and Democracy in Five Nations.*

35. Witonski, "Portugal"; and Wiarda, *Transcending Corporatism?*

36. The possibility should also be borne in mind that Salazar may have so thoroughly discredited corporatism that no new government will be able to build upon that heritage. Portugal may thus remain ineffective and inefficient, chaotic, fragmented, and disintegrated, subject to recurrent breakdowns, a kind of crippled nation unable to establish *any* functioning system, be it an updated form of corporate pluralism or a newer variant of Marxian syndicalism, to replace the older corporative form that the new regime has dismantled.

37. See, for example, Ronald Rogowski and Lois Wasserspring, *Does Political Development Exist? Corporatism in Old and New Societies*; S. N. Eisenstadt, *Traditional Patrimonialism and Modern Neopatrimonialism,* "Post-Traditional Societies and the Continuity and Reconstruction of Tradition," and "Tradition, Change, and Modernity: Modern Society and Sociological Theory." For the application of corporatism to other systems, see David B. H. Denoon, "The Corporate Model: How Relevant and for Which Countries?"; and Philip B. Coulter, *Social Mobilization and Political Democracy: A Macro-Quantitative Analysis of Global and Regional Models,* esp. the conclusion.

38. Schmitter hints at these themes in the conclusion of his "Corporatist Interest Representation" and develops it more fully in his "Still the Century of Corporatism?"

39. These preliminary formulations have been given more concrete expression in Howard J. Wiarda, "The Latin Americanization of the United States."

Appendix C

1. For some parallel comments, see Laurence S. Graham, "Portugal: The Bureaucracy of Empire," appendix.

A Selected Bibliography

The bibliography is divided into five sections: (1) items pertaining to the Portuguese background—society, history, political culture—that the author found particularly useful; (2) studies and essays dealing more specifically with Portuguese politics, the Estado Novo, and the Salazar and Caetano eras; (3) general studies dealing with political theory and comparative politics and directed especially at contributing to our understanding of corporatism and development in the Iberic-Latin tradition; (4) an extensive listing of the books and articles dealing, again more specifically, with the theory and practice of *Portuguese* corporatism; and (5) the periodicals used in the preparation for this study. Comments on the most useful and relevant of these items are included in the notes.

Portuguese names present some difficulty for purposes of listing in alphabetical order. It needs to be said first that, unlike the Spanish where the father's family name is usually placed before the mother's family name and forms the "last name" of their offspring (Rafael *López* Mendez), in Portuguese the mother's name comes first and the father's last (Antonio de Oliveira *Salazar*). But the situation is considerably complicated by the fact that frequently one name is dropped, another (or several) may be added (especially if it is prestigious), the spelling may change, individuals may use different forms of their name in different writings, and so on. One needs almost to know personally the individual and family history of each person in the bibliography (as Portuguese of stature and influence often do) to render a completely accurate alphabetical listing. Barring that, I have tried to stick as much as possible to the general rule (and official library usage) that the final name is the father's (family) name.

The Portuguese Background: Society, History, and Political Culture

Altamira, Rafael. *A History of Spain.* Translated by Muna Lee. New York: Van Nostrand, 1949.

Araquistain, L. "Dictatorship in Portugal." *Foreign Affairs* 7 (October 1928): 41–53.

Atkinson, William C. *A History of Spain and Portugal.* Middlesex and Baltimore: Penguin, 1960.

Bacci, Massimo Livi. *A Century of Portuguese Fertility.* Princeton: Princeton University Press, 1971.

Barnes, W. J. *Portugal: Gateway to Greatness.* London: Stanford, 1950.

Barros, Henrique de Gama. *Historia da administração pública em Portugal nos Séculos XII–XV.* Lisbon: Liv. Sa da Costa, 1945.

"Basic Data on the Economy of Portugal." *Overseas Business Reports.* U.S. Department of Commerce, Bureau of International Commerce, October 1971.

"Between Africa and Europe: A Survey of Portugal." *Economist* 242 (February 26, 1972): 1–28.

Blanshard, Paul. *Freedom and Catholic Power in Spain and Portugal (An American Interpretation).* Boston: Beacon, 1962.

Bloom, Murray Teigh. *The Man Who Stole Portugal.* London: Secker and Warburg, 1966.

Cabral, Francisco Sarsfield. *Uma Perspectiva sobre Portugal.* Lisbon: Moraes, 1973.

Caetano, Marcello. *Historia breve das constituições portuguesas.* Lisbon: Verbo, 1971.

————. *Manual de ciencia política e direito constitucional.* Coimbra: Coimbra Ed., numerous eds.

————. "A nossa 'Adesão'." *Ordem nova* 1 (June/July 1926): 147–51.

Campos, Fernando. *A genealogia do pensamento nacional.* Lisbon: José Fernandes Junior, 1931.

————. *O pensamento contra-revolucionario em Portugal (Século XIX).* 2 vols. Lisbon: Ed. de José Fernandes Junior, 1931.

Castro, Armando. *Desenvolvimento económico ou estagnação?* Lisbon: Dom Quixote, 1970.

————. *A evolução económica de Portugal dos Séculos XII a XV.* Lisbon: Portugalia, 1966.

Chique, Marcus. *Dictator of Portugal: A Life of the Marques of Pombal.* London: Sedwig and Jacobson, 1938.

Cortesão, Jaime. *Historia do regimen republicano em Portugal.* Lisbon, 1930.

Costa, Junior. *Historia breve do movimento operario português.* Lisbon: Verbo, 1964.

Cunhal, Alvaro. *A questão agraria em Portugal.* Rio de Janeiro: Civilização Brasileira, 1958.

Cutileiro, José. *A Portuguese Rural Society.* Oxford: Clarendon, 1971.

O desenvolvimento em Portugal: Aspectos sociais e institucionais. Lisbon: special ed. of *Análise social,* 1969.

Durant, Will. *Rousseau and the Revolution.* New York: Simon and Schuster, 1967.

Ferrão, Carlos. *O integralismo e a Republica.* 3 vols. Lisbon: vols. 1 and 2, Inquérito.; vol. 3, O Século, 1964/65.

Godinho, Vitorino Magalhães. *A estrutura na antiga sociedade portuguesa.* Lisbon: Ed. Arcadia, 1971.

Graham, Lawrence S. "Portugal: The Bureaucracy of Empire." Paper presented at the Workshop on Modern Portugal, University of New Hampshire, Durham, October 10–14, 1973.

Greenfield, Sidney M. "The Patrimonial State and Patron-Client Systems in the Fifteenth Century Writings of the Infante D. Pedro of Portugal." Occasional Papers Series, Program in Latin American Studies, University of Massachusetts, 1976.

Heathcote, Dudley. "General Carmona and the New Portugal." *Fortnightly* 127 (April 1, 1927): 481–88.

Keith, Henry H. "Point, Counterpoint in Reforming Portuguese Education: 1750–1973." Paper presented at the Workshop on Modern Portugal, University of New Hampshire, Durham, October 10–14, 1973.

Langhans, Franz-Paul. *A Casa dos Vinte e Quatro de Lisboa.* Lisbon, 1948.

Livermore, H. V. *A New History of Portugal.* Cambridge: Cambridge University Press, 1969.

Lourenço, Joaquim Maria Conego. *Situação jurídica da Igreja em Portugal: Análise histórico-jurídico e critica das relações da Igreja católica com o Estado Portugues.* 2d ed. Coimbra: Coimbra Ed., 1946.

Magalhães, José Calvet de. *Historia do pensamento económico em Portugal.* Coimbra: Coimbra Ed., 1967.

Makler, Harry Marks. *A "Elite" industrial portuguesa.* Lisbon: Gulbenkian Foundation, 1969.

———. "Political Men among the Portuguese Industrial Elite." Paper presented at the Workshop on Modern Portugal, University of New Hampshire, Durham, October 10–14, 1973.

Marques, A. H. de Oliveira. *History of Portugal.* 2 vols. New York: Columbia University Press, 1972.

———. "The Portuguese 1920s: A General Survey." *Iberian Studies* 2 (Spring 1973): 32–40.

———. "Revolution and Counterrevolution in Portugal: Problems of Portuguese History, 1900–1930." In *Studien uber de Revolution,* pp. 403–18. Berlin: Akademie-Verlag, 1969.

———. *A sociedad medieval portuguesa.* Lisbon: Sa da Costa, 1964.

Martins, Abranches. "O renascimento católico em Portugal." *Estudos políticos* 3 (June 1924): 81–90, and (July/August 1924): 204–15.

Martins, Herminio. "Portugal." In *Contemporary Europe: Class Status, and Power.* Edited by Archer and Giner. London: Weidenfeld and Nicolson, 1971.

Martins, Maria Belmira. *Sociedades e grupos em Portugal.* Lisbon: Ed. Estampa, 1973.

Merêa, Manuel Paulo. *O poder real e as cortes.* Coimbra: Coimbra Ed., 1923.

Ministerio das Obras Públicas, Comercio e Industria. *Organização das associações de classe aprovada por decreto de 9 de Maio de 1891.* Lisbon: Imp. Nacional, 1891.

Moses, Gerald M. "The Campaign of *Seara Nova* and Its Impact on Portuguese Literature, 1921–61." *Luso Brazilian Review* 2 (June 1965): 15–42.

Moura, Francisco Pereira da. "The Development of the Portuguese Economy, 1945–1973." Paper presented at the Workshop on Modern Portugal, University of New Hampshire, Durham, October 10–14, 1973.

Namorado, Rui. *Movimento estudantil e política educacional.* Lisbon: Tip. Agueda, 1972.

Nowell, Charles E. *A History of Portugal.* Princeton, N.J.: Van Nostrand, 1952.

———. *Portugal.* Englewood Cliffs, N.J.: Prentice-Hall, 1973.

Nunes, A. Sedas. "Portugal: Sociedade dualista em evolução." *Análise social,* 7–8 (1964).

———. *A situação universitaria portuguesa.* Lisbon: Liv. Horizante, n.d.

———. *Sociologia e ideologia do desenvolvimento.* Lisbon, 1968.

Pattee, Richard. *Portugal and the Portuguese World.* Milwaukee: Bruce, 1957.

Payne, Stanley. *A History of Spain and Portugal.* 2 vols. Madison: University of Wisconsin Press, 1973.

Pereira, Pedro Teotonio. "O pesadelo de Gonçalo Ramires." *Ordem nova* 1 (April 1926): 41–46.

Pereira Neto, João Baptista Nunes. "Social Evolution in Portugal since 1945." In *Portugal and Brazil in Transition.* Edited by Raymond S. Sayers. Minneapolis: University of Minnesota Press, 1968.

Pessoa, Fernando. *Defesa e justificação da ditadura militar em Portugal.* Lisbon: Nucleo de Acção Nacional, 1928.

Pintado, V. Xavier. *Structure and Growth of the Portuguese Economy.* Geneva: EFTA, 1964.

Portugal. Paris: Organization for Economic Cooperation and Development, yearly.

Proença, Raul. *Acerca do integralismo lusitano.* Lisbon: Seara Nova, 1964.

Robinson, Richard A. H. "The Religious Question and the Catholic Revival in Portugal, circa 1900–1930." Paper presented at the Workshop on Modern Portugal, University of New Hampshire, Durham, October 10–14, 1973.

Salazar, Antonio de Oliveira. *Centro Católico Português: Principios e organização.* Coimbra: Coimbra Ed., 1922.

Serrão, Joel. " 'Decadence' and 'Regeneration' in Contemporary Portugal." Paper presented at the Workshop on Modern Portugal, University of New Hampshire, Durham, October 10–14, 1973.

Sinopse de dados estatísticos. Lisbon: Instituto Nacional de Estatística, 1971.

Sousa, Manuel Joaquim de. *O sindicalismo em Portugal.* Oporto: Movimento Operario Português, 1931, 1972.

Spínola, Francisco Elias de Tejeda. *Las doctrinas políticas em Portugal (edad media).* Madrid: Escelicer, 1943.

Trend, J. B. *Portugal.* London: Ernest Benn, 1957.

Tuchman, Barbara. *The Proud Tower.* New York: Macmillan, 1962.

Villier, Franz. *Portugal.* London: Vista, 1963.

Wallich, Henry C. *The Financial System of Portugal.* Lisbon: Economic Cooperation Administration, Special Mission to Portugal, 1951.

Wheeler, Douglas L. "The Portuguese Revolution of 1910." *Journal of Modern History* 44 (June 1972): 172–94.

Portuguese Politics: The Estado Novo
and the Salazar and Caetano Eras

Abel, Deryck. "Portuguese Challenge." *Contemporary Review* 196 (October 1959): 161–64.

Alvarez del Vayo, J. "Salazar: Franco's Junior Partner." *The Nation* 163 (July 27, 1946): 91–93.

Antunes, Fernando. "As cortes gerais do regime." *Vida mundial* 34 (May 11, 1973): 3–8.

Assac, Jacques Ploncard d'. *Salazar.* Paris: La Table Ronde, 1967.

Atkinson, W. C. "The Political Structure of the Portuguese 'New State.' " *19th Century* 122 (September 1937): 346–54.

Bagger, Eugene. "Portugal: Anti-Totalitarian Outpost." *Catholic World* 164 (December 1946): 203–11.

Ballard, Eric A. C. "Salazar of Portugal." *Contemporary Review* 158 (September 1940): 320–24.

Belgrano, Mario Carlos. *El Nuevo Estado del Portugal.* Buenos Aires: Ed. Depalma, 1943.

Bender, Gerald. "Portugal and Her Colonies Join the Twentieth Century: Causes and Initial Implications of the Military Coup." *Ufahamu* 4 (Winter 1974): 121–62.

Blume, Norman. "The Portuguese Freguesia." Paper, University of Toledo, Dept. of Political Science, 1974.

Bruce, Neil. *Portugal: The Last Empire.* New York: Halsted-Wiley, 1975.

Bruneau, Thomas. "The Politics of Religion in an Authoritarian Regime: The Case of Portugal." Ms., McGill University, Dept. of Political Science, April 1974.

Caetano, Marcello. *Manual de ciencia política e direito constitucional.* 5th ed. Coimbra: Coimbra Ed., 1967.

———. *Manual de direito administrativo Português.* Lisbon: Ed. Coimbra, 1968.

———. *L'organisation politique portugaise.* Lisbon: Serviço Nacional de Informação, n.d.

———. "Problemas actuales de la administración pública portuguesa." *Documentación administrativa* (Madrid), 100 (April 1966).

Carneiro, Sa. *Revisão da constituição política: Discursos dos deputados subscritores do projeto.* Porto: Figueirinhas, 1971.

Caymon, A. E. "Portuguese Republic since the War." *Current History* 32 (July 1930): 686–88.

Cerqueira, Silas. "L'eglise et la dictature portugaise." *Revue française de science politique* 23 (June 1973): 473–513.

Chilcote, Ronald H. *Portuguese Africa.* Englewood Cliffs, N.J.: Prentice-Hall, 1967.

————. "Salazar's Portugal: Anniversary on Thin Ice." *The Nation* 202 (May 30, 1966): 638–41.

3º Congresso da Oposição Democrática. *Relatorios e Conclusões.* Aveiro, April 1973.

Cortesão, Armando. "Democracy and Fascism in Portugal." *Political Quarterly* 16 (1945): 329–41.

Council of Europe. "Introductory Report on Human Rights in Portugal." Brussels, April 8, 1970.

DaSilva, Milton. "Authoritarian Dictators in the Iberian Peninsula: Franco and Salazar." Master's thesis, University of Massachusetts, Dept. of Political Science, 1967.

Delgado, Humberto. *The Memoirs of General Delgado.* London: Cassell, 1964.

Derrick, Michael. "Portugal and Dr. Salazar." *Dublin Review* 201 (October 1937): 271–85.

————. *The Portugal of Salazar.* London: Paladin, 1938.

Duffy, James. *Portugal in Africa.* Baltimore: Penguin, 1962.

Egerton, F. C. C. *Salazar: Rebuilder of Portugal.* London: Hodder and Stoughton, 1943.

Ferro, Antonio. *Salazar: Portugal and Her Leader.* London: Faber and Faber, 1939.

Figueiredo, Antonio de. *Portugal and Its Empire: The Truth.* London: Gollancz, 1961.

Fonseca, Mario Mendez. *42 anos de Estado Novo.* Caracas: Tip. Remar, 1970.

Fryer, Peter, and McGowan-Pinheiro, Patricia. *Oldest Ally: A Portrait of Salazar's Portugal.* London: Dobson, 1961.

Galvão, Henrique. "Salazar: Man and Mask." *The Nation* 190 (January 9, 1960): 24–26.

————. *The Santa Maria: My Crusade for Portugal.* London: Weidenfeld and Nicolson, 1961.

Garnier, Christine. *Salazar: An Intimate Portrait.* New York: Farrar, Strauss and Young, 1954.

Gersh, Gabriel. "The Land That Lives in the Past." *Progressive,* March 1962, pp. 30–33.

————. "Portugal in Transition." *America* 105 (April 1, 1961): 20–21.

Gonçalves, Assis. *Intimidades de Salazar: O homem e a sua epoca.* Lisbon: Liv. Bertrand, 1972.

Hanighen, F. C. "Portugal's Plight." *Current History* 45 (March 1937): 47–51.

Hirsch, F. E. "In Defense of Portugal." *Current History* 12 (June 1947): 565–72.

————. "Post-War Portugal." *Current History* 18 (April 1950): 197–200.

Holmes, Olive. "Portugal: Free Nation's Partner." *Foreign Policy Reports* 25 (May 1, 1949): 48–52.

————. "Spain and Portugal: A Dilemma for the West." *Foreign Policy Reports* 25 (May 1, 1949): 42–52.

Howard, Toni. "The World's Most Durable Dictator." *Saturday Evening Post* 232 (April 9, 1960): 34ff.

Hyde, D. A. "Salazar's Portugal." *Catholic World* 174 (March 1952): 436–52.

IPOPE. *Os Portugueses e a política: 1973.* Lisbon: Moraes, 1973.

Jenkins, Loren. "New Style of Tyranny." *The Nation* 209 (November 17, 1969): 532–34.

Kay, Hugh. *Salazar and Modern Portugal.* London: Eyrie and Spottiswoode, 1970.

Kramer, Jane. "Letter from Lisbon." *New Yorker,* September 23, 1974, pp. 101ff.

————. "The Portuguese Revolution." *New Yorker,* December 15, 1975, pp. 92ff.

Lefevre, F. "Hour with Oliveira Salazar." *Living Age* 394 (November 1935): 224–31.

Legislação sobre a Mocidade portuguesa. Lisbon: Imp. Nacional, 1937.

Lewinsohn, R. "Portugal's Teacher-Dictator." *Current History* 41 (January 1935): 429–33.

Lins, Alvaro. *Missão em Portugal.* Rio de Janeiro: Ed. Civilização Brasileira, 1960.

Lourenço, Joaquim Maria. *Situação jurídica da igreja em Portugal.* Coimbra: Coimbra Ed., 1943.

Marshall, Andrew. "Portugal: A Determined Empire." *World Today* 17 (March 1961): 95–101.

Martins, Herminio. "Opposition in Portugal." *Government and Opposition* 4 (Spring 1969): 250–63.

————. "Portugal." In *European Fascism.* Edited by S. J. Woolf. London: Weidenfeld and Nicolson, 1968.

Maxwell, Kenneth. "The Hidden Revolution in Portugal." *New York Review of Books* (April 17, 1975): 29ff.

————. "Portugal: A Neat Revolution." *New York Review of Books* 21 (June 13, 1974): 16–21.

McMahon, Francis E. "Thirty Years of Salazar." *Commonweal* 68 (May 30, 1958): 223–25.

Migueis, J. R. "Salazar of Portugal: Forgotten Fascist." *The Nation* 159 (December 9, 1944): 715–16.

Morris, Elizabeth. "Portugal's Politics Remain Unaltered." *World Today* 20 (January 1964): 18–25.

Moura, Francisco Pereira da. *Por onde vai a economia portuguesa?* Lisbon: Dom Quixote, 1970.

Nogueira, Franco. *As crises e os homens.* Lisbon: Atica, 1971.

———. *Debate Singular.* Lisbon: Atica, 1970.

O'Donnell, Thomas J. "Salazar and the New State of Portugal." *Studies* 25 (March 1936): 131–44.

Page, Joseph A. "Portugal." *Atlantic* 222 (October 1958): 42ff.

Pires, José Cardoso. *Dinossauro excelentissimo.* Lisbon: Ed. Arcadia, 1972.

"Portugal's Clerical Fascism." *Weekly People,* January 27, 1962, p. 304.

Potter, Bonnie. "Election Time in Portugal: A Time for Reflection." *Ms.,* New York, 1973.

Programa para a democratização da República. Porto: Tip. J. R. Gonçalves, 1961.

R. C. "Portugal: A Political and Economic Survey." *Bolsa Review* 5 (August 1971): 460–70.

Rudel, Christian. *Le Portugal et Salazar.* Paris: Ed. Economie et Humanisme, Ed. Ouvrières, 1968.

———. *Salazar.* Paris: Mercure de France, 1969.

Salazar, Antonio de Oliveira. *The Development Plan: Principles and Presuppositions.* Lisbon: Casa Portuguesa, 1953.

———. *Doctrine and Action.* London: Faber and Faber, 1939.

———. "Realities and Trends of Portugal's Policies." *International Affairs* 34 (April 1963): 169–83.

Sanders, Paul R. "Europe's Mildest Dictator." *Scribner's Commentator* 2 (November 1941): 31–36.

Schmitter, Philippe C. "Liberation by *Golpe:* Retrospective Thoughts on the Demise of Authoritarian Rule in Portugal." *Armed Forces and Society* 2 (November 1975): 5–33.

Secretariado da Propaganda Nacional. *A revolução continua: União Nacional, Mocidade, Legião.* (Lisbon: SPN, 1943).

Sedgwick, Ellery. "Something New in Dictators: Salazar of Portugal." *Atlantic* 193 (January 1954): 40–45.

Sevilla Andres, Diego. *El Portugal de Oliveira Salazar.* Madrid: Ed. del Movimiento, 1957.

Smyser, W. L. "General Carmona: Dictatorship without a Dictator in Portugal." *Contemporary Review* 138 (September 1930): 328–33.

Soares, Mario. "Oliveira Martins e a questão de regime." *Tempo e o modo* 1 (January 1963): 25–34.

———. *Le Portugal baillonné: Un témoignage.* Paris: Calmann-Lévy, 1972.

Spínola, António de. *Portugal e o futuro.* Lisbon: Arcadia, 1974.

Stacey, Douglas. "An Exemplar." *Catholic World* 155 (May 1947): 232–33.

Sterling, Claire. "Crumbling Castle of Dr. Salazar." *Reporter* 127 (July 19, 1962): 40–43.

Teller, J. L. "Salazar Is Next." *The Nation* 162 (March 23, 1946): 339–40.

Ussach, Steven. Seven articles following the Portuguese revolution of April 1974. *New Bedford Standard Times,* May/June 1974.

Vasconcelos, José C. de. *Liberdade de prensa: Lei de imprensa.* Lisbon: Prelo, 1972.

Visson, A. "Portugal's Salazar." *U.N. World* 6 (April 1952): 24–26.

Wakeham, Eric. "Portugal Today." *19th Century* 124 (September 1938): 257–69.

West, S. George. "The Present Situation in Portugal." *International Affairs* 17 (March 1938): 211–32.

Wheeler, Douglas L. "Thaw in Portugal." *Foreign Affairs* 48 (July 1970): 769–81.

Wiarda, Howard J. "Background and Preliminary Assessment: The Portuguese Coup d'Etat of April 25, 1974." Memorandum prepared for the Conference on Portugal and Africa, Dept. of State, Washington, D.C., May 6, 1974.

————. "Can We Learn to Live with a Socialist World? Foreign Policy Implications Stemming from the Portuguese Revolution and Other 'New Forces.'" Paper presented at the Conference on "Spain and Portugal: The Politics of Economics and Defense," Institute for the Study of Conflict, London, May 29–31, 1975.

————. "Portugal: The Two Revolutions." Paper presented at the 17th Annual Meeting of the International Studies Association, Toronto, February 1976.

————. "The Portuguese Revolution: Toward Explaining the Political Behavior of the Armed Forces Movement." *Iberian Studies* IV, Autumn 1975, pp. 53–61.

————. "Prospects for Portugal." Paper prepared for the Office of External Research, Dept. of State, October 16, 1974.

Witonski, Peter. "Portugal: The Spirit of Regeneration." *National Review,* May 24, 1974, pp. 583–84.

The General Framework:
Comparative, Theoretical, Corporative

Adams, Richard N. *The Second Sowing: Power and Secondary Development in Latin America.* San Francisco: Chandler, 1967.

Almond, Gabriel, and Verba, Sidney. *The Civic Culture: Policy Attitudes and Democracy in Five Nations.* Boston: Little, Brown, 1963.

Almond, Gabriel A., and Coleman, James S., eds. *The Politics of the Developing Areas.* Princeton: Princeton University Press, 1960.

Anderson, Charles W. *The Political Economy of Modern Spain: Policy-Making in an Authoritarian System.* Madison: University of Wisconsin Press, 1970.

————. *Politics and Economic Change in Latin America.* Princeton, N.J.: Van Nostrand, 1967.

————. "Toward a Theory of Latin American Politics." In *Politics and Social Change in Latin America.* Edited by Howard J. Wiarda. Amherst: University of Massachusetts Press, 1974.

Azpiazu, José Joaquín. *The Corporative State*. St. Louis: Herder, 1951.

Bailey, John J. "Pluralist and Corporatist Dimensions of Interest Representation in Colombia." Paper presented at the Conference on Corporatism and the Corporate State, University of Pittsburgh, April 4–6, 1974.

Barnes, Samuel H., and Sani, Giacomo. "Mediterranean Political Culture and Italian Politics: An Interpretation." Paper presented at the Annual Meeting of the American Political Science Association, New Orleans, September 4–8, 1973.

Baudin, Louis. *Le corporatisme: Italie, Portugal, Allemagne*. Paris: Librairie Générale de Droit et de Jurisprudence, 1942.

Beer, Samuel H. *British Politics in the Collectivist Age*. New York: Knopf, 1965.

Bendix, Reinhard. *Max Weber: An Intellectual Portrait*. Garden City, N.Y.: Anchor-Doubleday, 1960.

Bonilla, Frank. *The Failure of Elites*. Vol. 2 of *The Politics of Change in Venezuela*. Cambridge: MIT Press, 1970.

Botsford, Keith. "Succession and Ideology in Spain and Portugal." *Journal of International Affairs* 18 (1964): 76–85.

Bowen, Ralph. *German Theories of the Corporate State*. New York: Whittlesey House, McGraw-Hill, 1947.

Burke, Melvin, and Malloy, James M. "Del populismo nacional al corporativismo nacional: El caso de Bolivia, 1952–70." *Aportes* 26 (October 1972): 66–96.

Camp, Richard L. *The Papal Ideology of Social Reform*. Leiden, 1969.

Campos, Fernando. *O principio da organização corporativa através da historia*. Lisbon: Nação Portuguesa, 1936.

Cardoso, J. Pires. *O corporativismo como ideologia para o Occidente*. Lisbon, 1961.

Chalmers, Douglas. "Crisis and Change in Latin America." *Journal of International Affairs* 23 (1969): 76–88.

Chicca, Guiseppe. *Tradição romanista e sentido corporativo*. Braga: Liv. Cruz, 1959.

Cole, G. D. H. *Guild Socialism*. New York: Stokes, 1921.

Cole, Taylor. "Corporative Organization of the Third Reich." *Review of Politics* 2 (1940): 461–62.

Collier, David, and Collier, Ruth. "Cross-National Research on Regime Characteristics in Latin America: The Neglect of Corporatism." Paper presented at the Conference on Corporatism and the Corporate State, University of Pittsburgh, April 4–6, 1974.

Connolly, William E., ed. *The Bias of Pluralism*. New York: Atherton, 1971.

Cotler, Julio. "Bases del corporativismo en el Peru." *Sociedad y politica* 1 (October 1972): 3–11.

Coulter, Philip B. *Social Mobilization and Political Democracy: A Macro-*

Quantitative Analysis of Global and Regional Models. Lexington, Mass.: Lexington, 1975.

Crozier, Michael. *The Bureaucratic Phenomenon.* Chicago: University of Chicago Press, 1964.

Dealy, Glen. "Latin America: Pluralist, Corporatist, or Monist?" Paper presented at the Latin American Studies Association National Meeting, Atlanta, March 1976.

————. "Prolegomena on the Spanish American Political Tradition." *Hispanic American Historical Review,* vol. 48 (February 1968).

————. *The Public Man: A Cultural Interpretation of Latin America and Other Catholic Countries.* Amherst, University of Massachusetts Press, forthcoming.

————. "The Tradition of Monistic Democracy in Latin America." In *Politics and Social Change in Latin America.* Edited by Howard J. Wiarda. Amherst: University of Massachusetts Press, 1974.

Dean, Warren. *The Industrialization of São Paulo, 1880–1945.* Austin: University of Texas Press, 1969.

Delzell, Charles F. *Mediterranean Fascism, 1919–1945.* New York: Harper and Row, 1970.

Denoon, David B. H. "The Corporate Model: How Relevant and for Which Countries?" Paper, MIT, Dept. of Political Science, 1973.

Denton, Charles F. *Patterns of Costa Rican Politics.* Boston: Allyn and Bacon, 1971.

Deutsch, Karl W. "The Growth of Nations: Some Recurrent Patterns of Political and Social Integration." *World Politics* 5 (January 1953): 168–95.

Durkheim, Emile. "The Solidarity of Occupational Groups." In *Theories of Society.* Edited by Talcott Parsons et al. New York: Free Press, 1965.

Easton, David. *A Systems Analysis of Political Life.* New York: Wiley, 1965.

Economic Commission for Latin America (ECLA). *Social Development of Latin America in the Post-War Period.* New York: UNESCO, 1964.

Eisenstadt, S. N. "Post-Traditional Societies and the Continuity and Reconstruction of Tradition." *Daedalus* 102 (Winter 1973): 1–27.

————. "Tradition, Change, and Modernity: Modern Society and Sociological Theory." Ms., n.d.

————. *Traditional Patrimonialism and Modern Neopatrimonialism.* Beverly Hills: Sage, 1973.

Elbow, Matthew H. *French Corporative Theory, 1789–1948: A Chapter in the History of Ideas.* New York: Columbia University Press, 1953.

Erickson, Kenneth P. *The Brazilian Corporative State and Working Class Politics.* Berkeley: University of California Press, 1977.

Fals Borda, Orlando. "Marginality and Revolution in Latin America, 1809–1969." *Studies in Comparative International Development* 6 (1970/71): 63–89.

Faoro, Raymundo. *Os donos do poder: Formação do patronato político brasileiro.* Pôrto Alegre: Ed Globo, 1958.

Field, G. Lowell. *The Syndical and Corporative Institutions of Italian Fascism.* New York: Columbia University Press, 1938.

Finer, Herman. *Representative Government and a Parliament of Industry.* Westminster: 1923.

Fogarty, Michael P. *Christian Democracy in Western Europe, 1820–1953.* London: Routledge and Kegan Paul, 1957.

Freeman, J. Leiper. *The Political Process: Executive Bureau-Legislative Committee Relations.* New York: Random, 1965.

Freemantle, Anne, ed. *The Papal Encyclicals.* New York, 1956.

Germani, Gino. "Fascism and Class." In *The Nature of Fascism.* Edited by S. J. Woolf. New York: Vantage, 1969.

Glade, William P. *The Latin American Economies: A Study of Their Institutional Evolution.* New York: American, 1969.

————. "Economic Policy-Making and the Structures of Corporatism in Latin America." Paper presented at the Latin American Studies Association, National Meeting, Atlanta, March 1976.

Goad, Harold E. *The Making of the Corporative State: A Study of Fascist Development.* London, 1932.

Graham, Lawrence S. *Civil Service Reform in Brazil: Principles versus Practice.* Austin: University of Texas Press, 1968.

Gregor, A. James. *The Ideology of Fascism.* New York: Free Press, 1969.

Haider, Carmen. *Capital and Labor under Fascism.* New York, 1930.

Hale, Charles A. *Mexican Liberalism in the Age of Mora, 1821–1953.* New Haven: Yale University Press, 1968.

Hamilton, Bernice. *Political Thought in Sixteenth-Century Spain.* Oxford: Oxford University Press, 1963.

Hartz, Louis, et al. *The Founding of New Societies.* New York: Harcourt, Brace, 1964.

Hayward, J. E. S. *Private Interest and Public Policy: The Experience of the French Economic and Social Council.* London, 1966.

Herz, John H. "The Problem of Successorship in Dictatorial Regimes: A Study in Comparative Law and Institutions." *Journal of Politics* 14 (February 1952): 19–40.

Huntington, Samuel P. *Political Order in Changing Societies.* New Haven: Yale University Press, 1968.

Jaquette, Jane. "Revolution by Fiat: The Context of Policy-Making in Peru." *Western Political Quarterly,* December 1972, pp. 648–66.

Johnson, John J. *Political Change in Latin America: The Emergence of the Middle Sectors.* Stanford: Stanford University Press, 1958.

Kaufman, Robert R. "Transitions to Stable Authoritarian-Corporate Regimes: The Chilean Case?" Paper presented to the Inter-University Seminar on the Armed Forces and Society at the 1974 Annual Meeting of the American Political Science Association, Chicago, August 29–September 2, 1974.

Kern, Robert, ed. *The Caciques*. Albuquerque: University of New Mexico Press, 1973.

Leonard, Irving A. "Science, Technology, and Hispanic America: The Basis of Regional Characteristics." *Michigan Quarterly Review* 2 (October 1963): 237–45.

Lewy, Guenter. *Constitutionalism and Statecraft during the Golden Age of Spain: A Study of the Political Philosophy of Juan de Mariana, S.J.* Geneva: E. Droz, 1960.

Linz, Juan. "An Authoritarian Regime: Spain." In *Cleavages, Ideologies, and Party Systems*. Edited by E. Allardt and Y. Littunen. Helsinki: Transactions of the Westermarck Society, 1964.

Lipset, Seymour M. "Some Social Requisites of Democracy: Economic Development and Political Legitimacy." *American Political Science Review* 53 (March 1959): 69–105.

Loewenstein, Karl. "Occupational Representation and the Idea of an Economic Parliament." *Social Science* 12 (1937): 420–31, 529.

Lousse, Emile. *Corporativismo antigo e moderno*. Lisbon: Liv. Cruz, 1959.

———. *Organização e representação corporativa*. Lisbon: Junta da Acção Social, n.d.

Lowi, Theodore. *The End of Liberalism*. New York: Norton, 1969.

Maeztu, Ramiro. *Un ideal sindicalista*. Madrid, 1953.

Malloy, James M. "Authoritarianism, Corporatism, and Mobilization in Peru." *Review of Politics* 36 (January 1974): 52–84.

———, ed. *Authoritarianism and Corporatism in Latin America*. Pittsburgh: University of Pittsburgh Press, 1976.

Manoïlesco, Mihail. *Le parti unique: Institution politique des régimes nouveaux*. Paris: Les Oeuvres Françaises, 1936.

———. *Le siècle du corporatisme*. Paris: Felix Alcan, 1934.

Marsal, Juan. *Cambio social en América Latina: Crítica de algunas interpretaciones dominantes en las ciencias sociales*. Buenos Aires: Solar Hachette, 1967.

Martz, John. "The Place of Latin America in the Study of Comparative Politics." *Journal of Politics* 28 (February 1966): 57–80.

Marx, Karl. *The Eighteenth Brumaire of Louis Bonaparte*. New York: International Publishers, 1963.

McAlister, L. N. "Social Structure and Social Change in New Spain." *Hispanic American Historical Review* 43 (August 1963): 349–70.

Michelis, Guiseppe di. *World Reorganization on Corporative Lines*. London, 1935.

Miller, J. D. B. *The Politics of the Third World*. London: Oxford University Press, 1967.

Moody, Joseph N., ed. *Church and Society: Catholic Social and Political Thought and Movements, 1789–1950*. New York: Arts, 1953.

Morse, Richard M. "Recent Research on Latin American Urbanization: A Selective Survey with Commentary." *Latin American Research Review* 1 (Fall 1965).

————. "The Strange Career of Latin American Studies." *Annals of the American Academy of Political and Social Studies,* vol. 356 (November 1964).

Newton, Ronald C. "The Corporate Idea and the Authoritarian Tradition in Spain and Spanish America: Some Critical Observations." Paper presented at the 4th Meeting of the Latin American Studies Association, Madison, Wisconsin, May 1973.

————. "Natural Corporatism and the Passing of Populism in Spanish America." *Review of Politics* 36 (January 1974): 34–51.

————. "On 'Functional Groups,' 'Fragmentation,' and 'Pluralism' in Spanish American Political Society," *Hispanic American Historical Review* 50 (February 1970): 1–27.

Nolte, Ernst. *Three Faces of Fascism: Action Française, Italian Fascism, National Socialism.* New York: Holt, Rinehart and Winston, 1966.

Organski, A. F. K. "Fascism and Modernization." In *The Nature of Fascism.* Edited by S. J. Woolf. New York: Vintage, 1969.

Palmer, David Scott, and Middlebrook, Kevin Jay. "Corporatist Participation under Military Rule in Peru." Paper, Harvard University, Center for International Affairs, n.d.

Payne, James L. *Labor and Politics in Peru.* New Haven: Yale University Press, 1965.

————. *Patterns of Conflict in Colombia.* New Haven: Yale University Press, 1968.

Payne, Stanley. *Falange: A History of Spanish Fascism.* Stanford: Stanford University Press, 1961.

Petras, James. "The Latin American Middle Class." *New Politics* 4 (Winter 1965): 74–85.

————. *Political and Social Forces in Chilean Development.* Stanford: Stanford University Press, 1969.

Picon-Salas, Mariano. *A Cultural History of Spanish America.* Berkeley: University of California Press, 1968.

Pike, Fredrick B. "Corporatism and Latin American-United States Relations." *Review of Politics* 36 (January 1974): 132–70.

————. *Hispanismo, 1898–1936: Spanish Conservatives and Liberals and Their Relations with Spanish America.* Notre Dame, Ind.: University of Notre Dame Press, 1971.

————, and Stritch, Thomas, eds. *The New Corporatism: Social-Political Structures in the Iberian World.* Notre Dame, Ind.: Notre Dame University Press, 1974.

Pitigliami, Fausto. *The Italian Corporative State.* London: King, 1933.

Powell, John D. "Peasant Society and Clientelist Politics." *American Political Science Review* 64 (June 1970): 411–25.

Purcell, Susan Kaufman. "Decision-Making in an Authoritarian Regime: Mexico." Paper presented at the Annual Meeting of American Political Science Association, Chicago, September 7–11, 1971.

Ratinoff, Luis. "The New Urban Groups: The Middle Classes." In *Elites in Latin America.* Edited by Lipset and Solari. New York: Oxford University Press, 1967.

Roett, Riordan. *Brazil: Politics in a Patrimonial Society.* Boston: Allyn and Bacon, 1972.

Rogowski, Ronald, and Wasserspring, Lois. *Does Political Development Exist? Corporatism in Old and New Societies.* Beverly Hills: Sage, 1971.

Rokkan, Stein. "Norway: Numerical Democracy and Corporate Pluralism." In *Political Oppositions in Western Democracies.* Edited by R. Dahl. New Haven: Yale University Press, 1966.

Rostow, W. W. *The Stages of Economic Growth.* Cambridge: Cambridge University Press, 1960.

Sarfatti, Magali. *Spanish Bureaucratic-Patrimonialism in America.* Berkeley: Institute of International Studies, University of California, 1966.

Sarti, Roland. "Fascist Modernization in Italy: Traditional or Revolutionary?" *American Historical Review* 75 (April 1970):1,029–45.

Schmidt, Carl. *The Corporate State in Action.* New York: Oxford University Press, 1939.

Schmitter, Philippe C. *Interest Conflict and Political Change in Brazil.* Stanford: Stanford University Press, 1971.

———. "Paths to Political Development in Latin America." In *Changing Latin America.* Edited by Douglas A. Chalmers. New York: Columbia University, Academy of Political Science, 1972.

———. "The 'Portugalization' of Brazil." In *Authoritarian Brazil.* Edited by Alfred Stepan. New Haven: Yale University Press, 1973.

———. "Still the Century of Corporatism?" *Review of Politics* 36 (January 1974): 85–131.

Scott, Robert E. "The Government Bureaucrats and Political Change in Latin America." *Journal of International Affairs* 20 (1966): 289–308.

Shonfield, Andrew. *Modern Capitalism: The Changing Balance of Public and Private Power.* London: Oxford University Press, 1965.

Silva Michelena, José A. *The Illusion of Democracy in Dependent Nations.* Vol. 3 of *The Politics of Change in Venezuela.* Cambridge: MIT Press, 1971.

Silvert, Kalman H. *The Conflict Society.* New York: American Universities Field Staff, 1966.

———. *Man's Power.* New York: Viking, 1970.

———. "The Politics of Social and Economic Change in Latin America." In *Politics and Social Change in Latin America.* Edited by Howard J. Wiarda. Amherst: University of Massachusetts Press, 1974.

Spann, Othmar. *Types of Economic Theory.* London, 1930.

Spirito, Ugo. *Capitalismo e corporativismo.* Florence: Sansoni, 1933.

———. *Il corporativismo nazionalsocialista.* Florence: Sansoni, 1934.

Stepan, Alfred. "Political Development: The Latin American Experience." *Journal of International Affairs* 20 (1966): 223–34.

Stevens, Evelyn P. "Mexico's P.R.I.: The Institutionalization of Corporatism." Paper presented at the Annual Meeting of the American Political Science Association, Chicago, August 29–September 2, 1974.

Strickon, Arnold, and Greenfield, Sidney M., eds. *Structure and Process in Latin America: Patronage, Clientage, and Power Systems.* Albuquerque: University of New Mexico Press, 1972.

Tour du Pin, M. de la. *Vers un ordre social chretien.* Paris, 1942.

Trevor-Roper, H. R. "The Phenomenon of Fascism." In *European Fascism.* Edited by S. J. Woolf. New York: Vintage, 1969.

Vanger, Milton. "Politics and Class in Twentieth Century Latin America." *Hispanic American Historical Review* 49 (February 1969): 80–93.

Veliz, Claudio. "Centralism and Nationalism in Latin America." *Foreign Affairs,* 47 (October 1968): 68–83.

von Lazar, Arpad. "Latin America and the Politics of Post-Authoritarianism." *Comparative Political Studies,* vol. 1. (October 1968).

Wagley, Charles. *The Latin American Tradition.* New York: Columbia University Press, 1968.

Weber, Max. *Economy and Society.* 3 vols. New York, 1968.

Wiarda, Howard J. "The Catholic Labor Movement in Brazil: Corporatism, Populism, Paternalism, and Change." In *Contemporary Brazil.* Edited by William H. Tyler and H. Jon Rosenbaum. New York: Praeger, 1972.

———. "Corporatism and Development in the Iberic-Latin World: Persistent Strains and New Variations." *Review of Politics* 36 (January 1974): 3–33.

———. *The Corporative Origins of the Iberian and Latin American Labor Relations System.* Amherst: Labor Relations and Research Center, University of Massachusetts, 1976.

———. *Dictatorship and Development: The Methods of Control in Trujillo's Dominican Republic.* Gainesville: University of Florida Press, 1968, 1970.

———. *Dictatorship, Development, and Disintegration: Politics and Social Change in the Dominican Republic.* Ann Arbor, Mich.: Xerox University Microfilms Monograph Series. Sponsored by the Program in Latin American Studies of the University of Massachusetts, 1975.

———. "Elites in Crisis: The Decline of the Old Order and the Fragmentation of the New in Latin America." University of Massachusetts, Dept. of Political Science, 1972.

———. "The Latin Americanization of the United States." Paper, University of Massachusetts, Dept. of Political Science, October 1974.

———. "The Latin American Development Process and the New Developmental Alternatives: Military 'Nasserism' and 'Dictatorship with Popular Support.'" *Western Political Quarterly* 25 (September 1972): 464–90.

———. "Law and Political Development in Latin America: Toward a

Framework for Analysis." *American Journal of Comparative Law* 19 (Summer 1971): 434–63.

———, ed. *Politics and Social Change in Latin America: The Distinct Tradition.* Amherst: University of Massachusetts Press, 1974.

———. "Toward a Framework for the Study of Political Change in the Iberic-Latin Tradition: The Corporative Model." *World Politics* 25 (January 1973): 206–35.

Williams, Edward J. *Latin American Christian Democratic Parties.* Knoxville: University of Tennessee Press, 1967.

Yare, Jane-Lee Woolridge. "Middle Sector Political Behavior in Latin America." Paper, University of Massachusetts, Dept of Political Science, 1971.

Zuckerman, Alan. "On the Institutionalization of Political Clienteles: Party Factions and Cabinet Coalitions in Italy." Paper presented at the Annual Meeting of the American Political Science Association, New Orleans, September 4–8, 1973.

The Theory and Practice of Portuguese Corporatism

"Acerca da previdência social portuguesa." *Elo* 26 (October 1969): 3–8.

Aguilar, Amado de. *Donde veio e para onde vai o corporativismo português.* Lisbon: Liv. Portugalia, n.d.

Almeida, Alvaro Henriques de. "Os gremios obrigatorios e as suas funções de intervenção económica." *Revista do Gabinete de Estudos Corporativos* 11 (January-March 1960): 20–25.

Almeida, João de. *O estado novo.* Lisbon: Parceira Ant. Maria Pereira, 1932.

———. *Nacionalismo e estado novo.* Lisbon: Ed. Bertrand, 1932.

Almeida, Luiza. "Some Aspects of Labour Organisation under Salazar's Fascist Regime." *Portuguese and Colonial Bulletin,* June/July 1963, pp. 138–39.

Almeida e Oliveira, Antonio C. de. *Principios fundamentais do estado novo corporativo.* Coimbra: Ed. Tipografia Gráfica, 1937.

Amaral, Branca do. "A organização corporativa da lavoura e a crise da agricultura portuguesa." *Estudos sociais e corporativos* 7 (December 1968): 45–89.

———. "Política agricola e gremios da lavoura." *Estudos sociais e corporativos* 7 (June 1969): 88–120.

Ameal, João. *Construção do novo estado.* Lisbon: Liv. Tavares Martins, 1938.

Andrade e Sousa, Manuel Alberto. *O corporativismo português.* Lisbon: Ed. Nacional, 1966.

Araujo, Cesar. *Colectanea de leis corporativas.* Lisbon: Tip. Sado, 1972.

Araujo, Correia. *Directrizes económicas do estado novo.* Lisbon, 1935.

Baião, Rodrigo José. "O ultramar e a organização corporativa." *Trabalho* 11 (1965): 53–67.

Baptista, José da Silva. *Reorganização industrial e ordem corporativa.* Lisbon, 1957.

Barros, José Augusto Correa de. "Subsidio para a revisão do corporativismo português." *Revista do Gabinete de Estudos Corporativos* 2 (October-December 1951): 5–25.

Bastos, João Pereira. *O estado corporativo.* Salvador, Baía: Ed. Progresso, 1958.

Beirão, Caetano de Melo. "O sistema corporativo perante o estado." *Tempo presente,* vol. 3 (1961): 21–33.

Beja, Mons. Fino. *A igreja, o operario e o corporativismo.* Lisbon: Liv. Popular de Francisco Franco, 1941.

Borkenau, Franz. "Portugal's Corporate State." *Christian Science Monitor Weekly Section,* February 9, 1938, pp. 1–2.

Braga, João. *Corporativismo agrícola em Portugal.* 1939.

Branco, Carlos. "Fundamentos filosóficos do corporativismo." In I Coloquio Nacional do Trabalho, da Organização Corporativa e da Previdência Social, *Comunicações.* Vol. 3. Lisbon: Junta da Acção Social, 1961.

Brito, Antonio José de. "O problema dos fundamentos do corporativismo." In I Coloquio Nacional do Trabalho, da Organização Corporativa e da Previdência Social, *Comunicações.* Vol. 3. Lisbon: Junta da Acção Social, 1961.

Caetano, Marcello. *Aspectos institucionais do fomento regional: A função dos municipios.* Lisbon: Ed. Coimbra, 1967.

———. *Codificação administrativa em Portugal.* Lisbon: Emp. Nacional, 1935.

———. *A constituição de 1933: Estudo de direito político.* Coimbra: Coimbra Ed., 1956.

———. *Corporative Revolution, Permanent Revolution.* Lisbon: SNI, 1969.

———. *Depoimento.* Rio de Janeiro: Record, 1974.

———. *Ensaios pouco políticos.* Lisbon: Ed. Verbo, 1970.

———. *El estado social.* Lisbon: SNI, 1970.

———. *Uma experiencia política bem sucedida: O estado novo portugues.* In Congresso da União Nacional, IV. Lisbon, 1956. May/June, Sessões Plenarias, pp. 165–83.

———. *Lições de direito corporativo.* Lisbon: Oliveira, 1935.

———. *A missão dos dirigentes: Reflexões e directivas sobre a Mocidade portuguesa.* Lisbon: Tip. E. M., 1952.

———. *Portuguese Political Organization.* Lisbon: Emp. Nacional, n.d.

———. *Posição actual do corporativismo portugues.* Lisbon: Gabinete de Estudos Corporativos do Centro Universitario de Lisboa da Mocidade Portuguesa, 1950.

———. *Princípios e definições.* Lisbon: Ed. Panorama, 1969.

———. *Problemas da revolução corporativa.* Lisbon: Ed. Acção, 1941.

———. *Problemas políticos e sociais da actualidade portuguesa.* Lisbon: SNI, 1956.

———. *Renovação na continuidade.* Lisbon: Verbo, 1971.

————. *O sistema corporativo.* Lisbon: Oficinas Gráficas de O Jornal do Comercio e das Colonias, 1938.

Cal, Alexandre Herculano da. *Legislação corporativa: Gremios e sindicatos.* Porto: Ed. do Autor, 1955.

"A Cámara Corporativa como 'Orgão Constitucional' e como 'Organismo Corporativo Supreme.' " *Revista do Gabinete de Estudos Corporativos* 4 (October-December 1953): 297–308.

Campos, Fernando. *Páginas corporativas.* Lisbon: Oficinas Graficas, 1941.

————. *A solução corporativa.* Lisbon: Ed. Imperio, 1939.

Cardoso, J. Pires. "Corporações e Orgãos de Coordenação Económica." *Revista do Gabinete de Estudos Corporativos* 10 (January-March 1959): 1–10.

————. *Corporações morais e culturais.* Lisbon: Centro de Estudos de Estatística Economica, 1962.

————. *O corporativismo e a igreja.* Lisbon: Graf. Lisbonense, 1949.

————. *Para uma corporação auténtica.* Coimbra: Coimbra Ed., 1961.

————. *O problema actual da corporação portuguesa.* Lisbon: Gabinete de Estudos Corporativos, 1955.

————. "O problema da intervenção em sistema corporativo." *Revista do Gabinete de Estudos Corporativos* 1 (January–March 1950): 22–30.

————. *Questões corporativas: Doutrina e fatos.* Lisbon: Gabinete de Estudos Corporativos do Centro Universitario da Mocidade Portuguesa, 1958.

————. "Resolução dos conflitos colectivos de trabalho." *Revista do Gabinete de Estudos Corporativos* 9 (January-March 1958): 1–6.

————. *Sentido social da revolução: O sistema corporativo.* Lisbon: Ed. Panorama, 1966.

————. *A universidade: Instituição corporativa.* Lisbon: Ed. Império, 1952.

Carvalho, Carlos Afonso de. "Organização corporativa e serviço social." *Revista do Gabinete de Estudos Corporativos* 1 (October-December 1950): 5–13.

Carvalho, Rivera Martins de. *O pensamento integralista perante o estado novo.* Lisbon: São José, 1971.

"La CISL internazionale per la liberta sindicale in Portogallo." *Politica sindicale* (Rome) 4 (June 1961): 263–66.

I Coloquio Nacional do Comercio. *Resume e conclusões dos temas apresentados.* Lisbon: Graf. Boa Hora, 1965.

I Coloquio Nacional do Trabalho, da Organização Corporativa e da Previdência Social. *Comunicações.* 5 vols. Lisbon: Junta da Acção Social, 1961.

II Coloquio Nacional do Trabalho, da Organização Corporativa e da Previdência Social. *Comunicações.* Lisbon: Ramos, Afonso e Moita, 1963.

III Coloquio Nacional do Trabalho, da Organização Corporativa e da Previdência Social. *Comunicações e conclusões.* Lisbon: Ministerio das Corporações e Previdência Social, 1965.

IV Coloquio Nacional do Trabalho, da Organização Corporativa e da Segurança Social. *Corporações: Sua extensão ao ultramar.* Luanda, 1966.

Comissão de Política Social Rural, INTP. *Inquérito sobre organização corporativa rural (casas do povo).* Lisbon: Comissão de Política Social, 1967.

―――. *Previdência social e organização corporativa do trabalho rural.* Lisbon: Comissão de Política Social, 1966.

Corporação do Comercio. *As corporações na economia nacional.* Lisbon: Nacional Ed., 1971.

"The Corporate State: An Incomplete Experiment in Portugal." *Times-Supplement,* October 25, 1955.

Costa, Adelina. *Organização política e administrativa da nação.* Lisbon: Liv. Popular, 1945.

Costa, Augusto da. *Aspectos sociais da constituição do estado novo.* Lisbon: Ed. Império, 1942.

―――. *Código do trabalho.* Lisbon: Liv. Rodrigues, 1937.

―――. *Factos e principios corporativos.* Lisbon: Liv. Rodrigues, 1934.

―――. *A nação corporativa.* Lisbon: Imp. Nacional, 1933.

―――. *O valor universal do corporativismo.* Oporto: Ed. Portugalense, 1944.

Costa, J. M. P. da. *Ensaios doutrinarios: Capitalismo, socialismo, e corporatismo.* Lisbon: Fundação Nacional para a Alegria no Trabalho, 1958.

Costa Leite, João Pinto da. *A doutrina corporativa em Portugal.* Lisbon: Liv. Classica, 1936.

Cotta, Freppel. *Economic Planning in Corporative Portugal.* Westminster: King and Staples, 1937.

Coutinho, Ernesto. "Negociações colectivas e abuso do direito de despedimento." *Expresso,* April 21, 1973, p. 8.

"A crise do corporativismo." *Expresso,* Oct. 20, 1973.

Cruz, Moises Silva da. "Uma nova era social: O neo corporativismo." *Itinerarium* 2, no. 12: 591–608.

Dias, Arnaldo Joaquim. "O magisterio da igreja e o corporativismo." *Itinerarium* 4 (January-March 1960): 42–76.

Estatísticas da organização corporativa. Lisbon: Instituto Nacional de Estatística, yearly.

Fernandes, Antonio J. de Castro. "Corporações e Organizações Corporativas Patronais." *Revista do Gabinete de Estudos Corporativos* 1 (July-Sept. 1950): 7–25.

―――. *Corporativismo de Associação.* Lisbon: author's ed., 1942.

―――. *Enfrentando o destino das casas do povo.* Lisbon: Casa Portuguesa, 1947.

―――. *Páginas corporativas.* Lisbon, 1941.

―――. *Principios fundamentais da organização corporativa portuguesa.* Lisbon: Ed. Imperio, 1944.

―――. "A revolução social portuguesa." *Boletim do INTP* 12 (August 15, 1945): 27–29.

―――. *A solução corporativa.* Lisbon, 1942.

―――. *Temas corporativos.* Lisbon: SPN, 1944.

Fereira, Emilio A. *Corporativismo português: Doutrina e aplicação.* Coimbra: Coimbra Ed, 1951.

Ferreira, Cesar Araujo Silva, and Gonçalves, Teotonio. *Colecção de legislação corporativa do Trabalho e Previdência Social.* Vol. 1, *Legislação corporativa.* Lisbon: Graf. Santelmo, 1969.

43 anos de facismo em Portugal. Rio de Janeiro: Paz e Terra, 1969.

Franco, Eduardo Maia. *Corporativismo português.* Recife: União Gráfica, 1954.

Gonçalves, Caetano. *O estado corporativo e a política do imperio no direito constitucional português.* Lisbon, 1935.

Gonçalves, Luis da Cunha. *Causas e efeitos do corporativismo português.* Lisbon: Inst. Superior de Ciencias Económicas e Financeiras, 1936.

―――. *Principios de direito corporativo.* Lisbon: Oficinas Gráficas, 1935.

Graça, Luis Quartin. "O corporativismo na agricultura." *Revista do Gabinete de Estudos Corporativos 1* (April-June 1950): 12–15.

"A grande batalha corporativa." *Diario de noticias,* April 4, 1956.

Guimarães, Manuel. "Corporativismo." Lisbon: mimeographed, n.d.

Gutierrez, Diez O'Neil. *Portugal corporativo.* Madrid: Ed. Aldecoa, 1940.

Junta Central das Casas do Povo. *Protecção aos trabalhadores rurais atraves a solução corporativa.* Lisbon: Junta Central das Casas do Povo, 1959.

Kenny, Michel. "Model Republic Reviewed by Its Modeler: Portugal's Democratic Corporative System." *Catholic World* 147 (April 1938): 44–51.

Lopes, Vitor Vera. "A constituição portuguesa de 1933." *Broteria* 5 (May 1966): 615–23.

Lucena, Manuel. *L'evolution du systeme corporatif portugais à travers les lois (1933–1971).* Paris: Institut des Sciences Sociales du Travail, 1971.

―――. "Sur le passé et l'avenir du corporatisme au Portugal." Paper presented at the conference on "Crisis in Portugal," University of Toronto, April 15–17, 1976.

Luiz, Armando. "Trabalho e previdência." *Observador* 3 (July 6–12, 1973): 45–52.

"Lusitano" (Marcello Caetano?). "Corporatismo subordinado, corporatismo integral, corporatismo em marcha." *Diario da manhã,* April 9, 1944.

Macedo, Henrique Veiga de. *Casas do povo e previdência rural.* Lisbon: Rios e Irmão, 1971.

―――. *Coloquio de direito corporativo e do trabalho: Discurso do Ministro das Corporações e da Previdência Social.* Braga: Liv. Cruz, 1959.

Machete, Rui C. de. *Os principios e classificações fundamentais do corporativismo.* Braga: Liv. Cruz, 1969.

Makler, Harry M. "The Portuguese Industrial Elite and Its Corporative Relations: A Study of Compartmentalization in an Authoritarian Regime." Paper presented at the Mini-Conference on Modern Portugal, New Haven, Yale University, March 28/29, 1975.

Manoïlesco, Mihail. "La génie latin dans le nouveau régime portuguais." In *VI Congresso do Mundo Portugues: Publicações.* Vol. 8. Lisbon: Comissão Executiva dos Centenarios, Congresso de Historia Moderna e Contemporánea de Portugal, 1940.

Marques, A. H. de Oliveira. *A Primeira Legislatura do Estado Novo (1935–1938)* Lisbon: Pub. Europa-América, 1973.

Marques, Henrique. *Essencia do corporativismo em Portugal.* Braga: Liv. Cruz, 1952.

————. "A fisionomia da corporação portuguesa." *Revista do Gabinete de Estudos Corporativos* 5 (July-Sept. 1954): 217–25.

Martinez, Pedro Soares. *Curso do direito corporativo.* Vol. 1. Lisbon, 1962.

————. "A evolução para o estado pos-corporativo." *Expresso,* November 12, 1973, p. 12.

Martins, Mario Pinto dos Santos. *Organização corporativa: Gremios da industria e do comercio, organizações de coorderação económica, corporações—legislação actualizada, despachos, e notas.* Lisbon: Ed. Império, n.d.

Matoso, Antonio G., and Henriques, Antonio. *Formação corporativa.* Lisbon: Sa da Costa, 1964.

Mattos, J. Rodrigues de. *Corporativismo em Portugal.* Lisbon: Liv. Moraes, 1937.

McAdams, John. "The Corporate State in Portugal." Ph.D. diss., Fordham University, Dept. of Political Philosophy, 1952.

McDonough, Peter. "Structural Factors in the Decline and Fall of Portuguese Corporatism." Paper presented at the Mini-Conference on Modern Portugal, New Haven, Yale University, March 28/29, 1975.

Mendes, Afonso. *O trabalhador assalariado em Angola.* Lisbon: Inst. Superior de Ciencias Sociais e Política Ultramar, 1966.

Mexia, João. "Corporativismo universitario." *Estudos* 35 (May 1957): 278–89.

Ministerio das Corporações e Previdência Social. *Alguns principios da política social e corporativa portuguesa.* Lisbon: Junta da Acção Social, 1958.

————. *Corporações: Estatuto juridico das corporações.* Lisbon: Junta da Acção Social, 1958.

————. *Corporações: Parecer da Cámara Corporativa.* Lisbon: Junta da Acção Social, 1958.

————. *Formação social e organização corporativa.* Lisbon: Junta da Acção Social, n.d.

————. "Organização corporativa portuguesa." Lisbon: mimeographed, n.d.

————. *Plano de formação social e corporativa.* Lisbon: Junta da Acção Social, 1958.

————. *A reorganização das casas do povo e a previdência social.* Lisbon: Junta da Accão Social, 1969.

Morais e Castro, Armando Fernandes de. *As corporações e o custo de produção.* Coimbra: Centro de Estudos Económicos-Corporativos, 1945.

Moreira, José Antonio. "Corporações: Uma Hipótese de integração." *Estudos sociais e corporativos* 5 (April-June 1966): 40–59.

Murteira, Mario. "Poder económico e grupos de pressão." *Revista do Gabinete de Estudos Corporativos* 9 (July-December 1958): 305–26.

Neto, A. B. Cotrim. *Doutrina e formação do corporativismo.* Rio de Janeiro: Ed. Coelho Branco, 1938.

Nunes, A. Sedas. *Situação e Problemas do Corporativismo: Principios Corporativos e Realidades Sociais.* Lisbon: Gabinete de Estudos Corporativos do Centro Universitario da Mocidade Portuguesa, 1954.

———. "Teoria e problemas do corporativismo." *Revista do Gabinete dos Estudos Corporativos,* vol. 4 (October-December 1953), and vol. 5 (January-March 1954).

Nunes Agria, Fernanda Paula Moreira de Freitas. "O problema da liberdade sindical: Principios e realidades." *Estudos sociais e corporativos* 5 (December 1965): 11–35.

Oliveira, Mario Morais de. *Aspectos actuais do corporativismo perante a vida económica.* Lisbon: Graf. Santelmo, 1958.

———. "O corporativismo e a unidade política." *Revista do Gabinete de Estudos Corporativos,* vol. 2 (April-June 1951).

———. *O regime corporativo e os Organismos de Coordenação Economica.* Lisbon: Imp. Nacional, 1959.

Oliveira e Sousa, João de Saldanha. *O Corporativismo Portugues.* Lisbon: Tip. Inglesa, 1937.

Osorio de Castro, Jerónimo de Melo. "Acción social de las casas de pescadores." *Seguridad social* (Mexico) 15 (Sept./Oct. 1966): 35–40.

———, and Sousa Martins, Maria Adelaide Wanderley de. *A actividade da Corporação da Pesca e Convervas.* Lisbon: Corporação da Pesca e Conservas, 1966.

Pereira, Pedro Teotonio. *A batalha do futuro: Organização corporativa.* Lisbon: Liv. Classica, 1937.

———. *As entidades patronais na organização corporativa.* Lisbon: Ed. do Sec. de Estado das Corporações e Previdência Social, 1934.

———. *Memorias.* Lisbon: Verbo, 1972.

———. *O principio da organização corporativa atraves da historia.* Lisbon: Emisora Nacional, 1938.

Pintado, Xavier. "Exigencies de reformas de base: Para um corporativismo auténtico—o corporativismo comunitario." *Revista do Gabinete de Estudos Corporativos* 2 (October-December 1951): 26–36.

———. "Integração corporativa da agricultura." *Revista do Gabinete de Estudos Corporativos* 4 (1953): 29–41.

———. "Necessidade de meios de acção especificamente corporativos." *Revista do Gabinete de Estudos Corporativos* 1 (January-March 1950): 16–21.

Pinto, J. M. Cortez. *A actual situação económica e social portuguesa.* Coimbra: Atlántido, 1956.

————. "Algumas considerações sobre formação corporativa." *Revista do Gabinete de Estudos Corporativos* 8 (October-December 1957): 346–54.

————. *A corporação: Subsidio para o seu estudo.* Coimbra: Coimbra Ed., 1955.

————. "As corporações e os orgãos consultivos dos ministros." *Revista do Gabinete de Estudos Corporativos* 10 (April-June 1959): 114–20.

————. *As corporações no espaço português.* Lisbon: Nacional Ed., 1966.

————. *Estrutura e funções da corporação.* Coimbra: Coimbra Ed., 1956.

————. *Principios corporativos.* Lisbon: Fundação Nacional para a Alegria no Trabalho, 1966.

Pinto, Joaquim Silva. *Corporações ja instituidas: Análise da sua estrutura e funcionamento.* Lisbon: Corporação da Industria, 1961.

————. *Desenvolvimento social: Objectivo prioritario.* Lisbon: Junta da Acção Social, 1974.

————. *Política do trabalho: Factor de desenvolvimento.* Lisbon: Junta da Acção Social, 1972.

Pinto, Luiz Supico. "Organização económica corporativa." *Boletim do INTP* 12 (October 31, 1945): 539–42.

Pinto, Mário. "Reestruturação sindical: Tópicos para um questão." *Análise social* 8 (1971): 716–20.

————, and Moura, Carlos. "Estruturas sindicais portuguesas: Contributo para o seu estudo." *Análise social* 9 (1972-1⁰): 140–90.

Policarpo, João F. de Almeida. "Conflitos colectivos de trabalho e sistema corporativo." *Estudos sociais e corporativos* 8 (September 1969): 17–34.

Present Trends in Portuguese Social Policy. Lisbon: SNI, 1972.

Proença, F. Cid. "Autenticidade e eficacia em organização corporativa." *Estudos sociais e corporativos* 4 (March 1965): 13–35.

————. "Para a explicação de uma crise de ambiente." *Revista do Gabinete de Estudos Corporativos* 1 (April-June 1950): 16–22.

————. "Sobre algumas deficiencas de espírito corporativo." *Revista do Gabinete de Estudos Corporativos* 5 (April-June 1954): 138–48.

Proença, José Gonçalves. *Corporativismo e política social.* Lisbon: Junta da Acção Social, 1963.

————. *Diálogo corporativo.* Lisbon: Junta da Acção Social, 1969.

Quay, Stucky de. "O corporatismo sera uma solução?" *Jornal por economia e finanças,* 66 (January 1956): 11–13.

Queiro, Afonso Rodrigues. "O futuro da Cámara Corporativa." *Revista do Gabinete de Estudos Corporativos* 5 (October-December 1954): 319–22.

Ramos, A. "Industry in Portugal." *Portuguese and Colonial Bulletin,* August/ September 1963 and December 1963/January 1964.

Rato, Antonio. *Administração local e corporativismo.* Coimbra: Coimbra Ed., 1962.

Regimento da Corporação do Comercio. Lisbon: Tip. Mario Contreras, 1961.

"Renascimento da idea corporativa." *Boletim do INTP* 12 (March 31, 1945): 155–57.

Ribeiro, A. M. *Organização politica e administrativa de Portugal.* Oporto, 1949.

Ribeiro, José Joaquim Teixeira. "O destino do corporativismo." *Revista de Direito e Estudos Sociais* (Coimbra), vol. 1 (April 1945).

———. *Legislação corporativa.* Coimbra, 1946.

———. *Lições do direito corporativo.* Coimbra: Coimbra Ed., 1938.

Ribeiro, Luis de Abreu. *Regulamentação do trabalho.* Lisbon: Platano Ed., 1972.

Riegelhaupt, Joyce. "Peasants and Politics in Portugal: The Corporative State and Village 'Non-Politics.' " Paper presented at the Workshop on Modern Portugal, University of New Hampshire, Durham, October 10–14, 1973.

Rodrigues, Henrique Nascimento. *Regime jurídico das relações colectivas de trabalho.* Coimbra: Atlantida, 1971.

Rosendo, Joaquim. *A unidade corporativa da nação.* Lisbon: Jornal de Fereira, 1964.

Salazar, Antonio de Oliveira. *Discursos.* 5 vols. Coimbra: Coimbra Ed., 1961.

———. *Government and Politics.* Lisbon: Sec. Nac. de Informação, 1956.

———. *Mais um passo na definição e consolidação do regime.* Lisbon: SNI, 1949.

———. *The Principles and Work of the Revolution, in Their Internal and International Aspects.* Lisbon: Ed. Império, 1943.

———. *Revolução corporativa.* Oporto: Diario do norte, 1960.

———. *The Road for the Future.* Lisbon: SNI, 1963.

Sampaio, Jorge, and Santos, Jorge. "Em torno da universidade." *O tempo e o modo* 1 (January 1973): 12–14.

Samson, Odette. *Le corporatisme au Portugal.* Paris: Lib. Technique et Economique, 1938.

Santos, Francisco I. Pereira dos. *Un état corporatif: La constitution sociale et politique portugaise.* 2d ed. Paris: Lib. du Recueil Sirey, 1940.

Saraiva, J. Silva. *O pensamento político de Salazar.* Coimbra: Coimbra Ed., 1953.

Sarmento, Augusto de Morais. *O corporativismo português e o pensamento social católico.* Coimbra: Graf. de Coimbra, 1960.

Seabra, Fernando Maria Alberta. *O corporativismo e o problema do salario.* Coimbra: Centro de Estudos Economicos-Corporativos, 1943.

Schmitter, Philippe C. "Corporatist Interest Representation and Public Policy-Making in Portugal." Paper presented at the Annual Meeting of the American Political Science Association, Washington, D.C., September 5–7, 1972.

―――. "The Social Origins, Economic Bases and Political Imperatives of Authoritarian Rule in Portugal." Paper presented at the Conference on "Crisis in Portugal," University of Toronto, April 15–17, 1976.

Secretary of State of Information and Tourism. *Occupational Organization*. Portugal Today series, n.d.

Silva, Con. Francisco Maria da. *Acção católica e acção corporativa*. Lisbon, 1940.

"Os sindicatos e a previdência." *Vida mundial* 35 (August 17, 1973): 38–43.

Soares, Henrique. *Corporativismo: Antecedentes e princípios*. Lisbon: E. Ultramar, 1946.

Soares, Pedro Mario Martinez. *Curso de direito corporativo*. Lisbon: Pacheco, 1962.

Soares, Vicente Henrique Varella. *Os fundamentos tradicionais do corporativismo português*. Luanda: Tip. Mondego, 1941.

Sousa, Carlos Hermenegildo de. "O panorama da organização corporativa em Portugal." *Broteria* 45 (November 1947): 477–90.

Sousa, José Pedro Galvão de. *Direito corporativo e sociologia jurídica*. Braga: Liv. Cruz, 1958.

Sousa, Manuel Alberto Andrade. *O corporativismo: Sua historia, evolução, e reflexos no comercio atraves do tempos*. Vila Nova de Famalicão: Centro Gráfica, 1971.

―――. *Principios gerais da organização corporativa e integração nela do comercio retalhista dos produtos alimentares*. Lisbon: Corporação do Comercio, 1969.

Sousa, R. Soeiro de. "A previdência social portuguesa: Dados e comentarios." *Análise social* 4 (3rd Trimester of 1966): 377–410.

Texeira, Luiz. *Principios e fins do sistema corporativo portugues*. Coimbra: Ed., 1939.

O trabalho e as corporações no pensamento de Salazar. Lisbon: Junta da Acção Social, 1960.

"Universidade—corporação de mestres e estudantes." *Revista do Gabinete de Estudos Corporativos* 4 (January-March 1953).

Valente, Antunes, "Aspectos da evolução sindical em Angola." *Trabalho* 20 (1967): 79–96.

―――. "Contribuição para o estudo da classificação profissional em Angola." *Trabalho* 13 (1966): 91–162.

Vasconcelos, Manuel de Almeida de Azevedo. *Vivencia do corporativismo*. Lisbon: Ed. Nacional, 1969.

Veiga, Antonio Jorge da Mota. *A economia corporativa e o problema dos preços*. Lisbon: author's ed., 1941.

―――. "Finanças corporativas." *Revista do Gabinete de Estudos Corporativos* 5 (October-December 1954): 313–18.

Vieira, Lopes. "Organização corporativa patronal de Angola." *Trabalho* 17 (1967): 101–54.

Vital, Fezas. "Desvios do corporativismo portugues." *Revista do Gabinete de Estudos Corporativos* 1 (January-March 1950): 4–8.

West, S. George. *The New Corporative State of Portugal.* London: New Temple Press, 1937.

Wiarda, Howard J. "The Portuguese Corporative System: Basic Structures and Current Functions." *Iberian Studies* 2 (Autumn 1973): 73–80.

———. *Transcending Corporatism? The Portuguese Corporative System and the Revolution of 1974.* Columbia: Institute of International Studies, University of South Carolina, 1976.

Periodicals

Actualidades, 1972–73.

Análise social, 1963–74.

Boletim do Instituto Nacional do Trabalho e Previdência, 1933-present.

Broteria, intermittently.

Cadernos corporativos, 1933.

Diario de noticias, 1972–73.

Diario popular, intermittently.

Epoca, 1972–73.

Estudos do Centro Académico Democracia Cristã de Coimbra, intermittently.

Estudos sociais e corporativos, 1962–74.

Expresso, 1973-present.

Hispanic American Report, 1948–63.

Itinerarium, intermittently.

Luso-Brazilian Review, 1964-present.

Mensario das casas do povo, intermittently.

Nação portuguesa, intermittently in 1920s.

New York Times, 1925-present.

Novidades, intermittently in 1920s and 1970s.

Observador, 1972–73.

Opinião, 1972–73.

Ordem nova, intermittently in 1920s.

Politica, 1920 and 1972–73.

Portuguese and Colonial Bulletin, intermittently.

República, 1972–73.

Revista do Gabinete de Estudos Corporativos, 1950–61.

Seara nova, 1922–74.

O tempo e o modo, intermittently.

Tempo presente, intermittently.

Times (London), 1925-present.

Trabalho, 1963–74.

Vida mundial, 1972-present.

Index

Republicanism, 44; failures of, 326; impact of, 19; inappropriateness of, for Portugal, 335; in Portugal, 90, 93
Rerum Novarum, 67, 68, 69, 70, 72, 87, 97, 324, 333, 340
Resistance, Right of, 375 n.65
Res publica, 34, 41
Revista do Gabinete de Estudos Corporativos, 192, 193, 195, 196
Revolt of 1936, 159
Revolutionary change, challenge of, 24
Revolution of 1974, xi, 14, 274, 281, 310, 311 ff., 351; aftermath of, 317 ff.; continuities in, 322, 325; effect of, on economy, 319; impact of, 54; politics of, 313 ff.; pressures of, 312; response to, 317
Ribeiro, Teixeira, 171
Riegelhaupt, Joyce, 248, 293
Right: strength of, 265, 266, 267, 274, 278, 306, 312, 313; fading of, 317
Rivera, Primo de, 77, 96
Robinson, Richard A. H., 72, 80
Rome: corporatism in, 57; impact of, on Iberia, 14, 15–16; law of, 35; rule of, 30
Rostovian "stages," 15
Rousseau, 62, 64
Royal authority, 35. *See also* Crown; King; Monarchy
Royal Councils, 39
Russian revolution, 3

Saint-Simon, 63, 71
Salazar, Antonio de Oliveira, 38, 39; accomplishments of, 156, 326; as autocrat, 282, 297 n.17; and base of support, 80; Catholic background of, 283, 299; in CCP, 79; character of, 335; and conception of society, 348; as corporatist, 115, 147, 163, 175, 179, 193, 195, 221, 229, 334, 348, 353, 355, 379 n.3, 385 n.47, 387 n.27; dictatorship of, 91; as economics minister, 283; government career of, 94; ideology of, 78 ff., 339–40; incapacitation of, 253, 395 n.3; inflexibility of, 341; isolation of, 217; as leader, 119, 128, 142, 194, 207, 210, 282 ff.; manipulation of, 339; as middle class, 284; paralleled with Trujillo, 405

n.25; personality of, 95–96, 283 ff.; as politician, 80–81; power of, 161; as power seeker, 283, 343, 382 n.4; and Pombal, 327; as prime minister, 99, 100, 291, 292; program of, 48; regime of, xi, 308
Salazaristas, 257, 265, 266, 301, 306
Salazarista system, 291
Salgueiro, João, 260
Sanches, Rui, 260
Santa Comba Dão, 285
Santos, Ribeiro dos, 43
São Bento Palace, 305
Saraiva, Antonio Ribeiro, 62
Sardinha, Antonio, 74, 78, 92
Schmitter, Philippe C., 8, 55, 70, 131–33, 137, 145, 154, 163, 164, 174, 218, 219, 223, 286, 336 ff., 379 n.10
Scholasticism, 60
Seara Nova, 278, 307
Secret police, 160, 181, 293, 311, 340, 400 n.17
Secretaries of state, 292
SEDES, 307, 314
Self-government, 43
Seneca, 17
Separation of powers, 61, 293
Serviço de Acção Social, 132
Setúbal, 263, 328
Sharpe, Kenneth, 338
Shopkeepers, 381 n.27
Silva, Jacinto da, 72
Silvert, Kalman, 26, 310
Simão, Veiga, 260, 314
Sindicatos, 86, 111, 166, 170, 205, 206, 237–41, 328, 354; as corporative agency, 61; development of, 130, 214, 359; disillusionment of, with corporatism, 192; impotency of, 206, 237; influence of, 305; as interest, 296; organization of, 237; power of, 343, 345, 346; pressure of, 264; strength of, 263; reorganization of, 272, 275, 320; revolutionized, 318
Sindicato system, 211
"Sistema," 285–86, 289, 351
Soares, Mario, 258, 261, 306
Socialism, 334; as ideology, 12; as inappropriate for Portugal, 348; as rejected by corporatists, 81
Socialist movement, 2

Library of Congress Cataloging in Publication Data
Wiarda, Howard J   1939–
Corporatism and development.
Bibliography: p.
Includes index.
1. Corporate state—Portugal—History. 2. Portugal
—Politics and government—20th century. I. Title.
JN8501.W52   321.9   76–8761
ISBN 0–87023–221–5